The National Security Law of Hong Kong

The National Security Law of Hong Kong

Restoration and Transformation

Edited by Hualing Fu and Michael Hor

HKU PRESS
香港大學出版社

Hong Kong University Press
The University of Hong Kong
Pokfulam Road
Hong Kong
https://hkupress.hku.hk

ISBN 978-988-8754-19-9 (*Hardback*)

British Library Cataloguing-in-Publication Data
A catalogue record for this book is available from the British Library.

Digitally printed

Contents

1. Introduction: Re-balancing Freedom and Security in Post-NSL Hong Kong 1
   Hualing Fu and Michael Hor
2. The National Security Law of the HKSAR: A Contextual and Legal Study 20
   Albert H. Y. Chen
3. The Hong Kong National Security Law: The Shifted Grundnorm of Hong Kong's Legal Order and Its Implications 49
   Han Zhu
4. Theories of Sovereignty in the Origins and Implementation of Hong Kong's National Security Law 72
   Ryan Mitchell
5. Hong Kong's Constitutional Order after the National Security Law 94
   Jie Cheng
6. National Security and Judicial Independence: A Clash of Fundamental Values 119
   Johannes Chan
7. Judging Hong Kong's National Security Law 149
   Po Jen Yap
8. Police Powers under the National Security Law: A Commentary 167
   Simon N. M. Young
9. The Return of High Policing in Hong Kong 187
   Hualing Fu and Xiaobo Zhai
10. State Secrets in the Hong Kong National Security Law 211
    Zheng Tang and Xu Huang
11. Extraterritorial Application of the Hong Kong National Security Law: A Legal Appraisal 231
    Bing Ling

12. Academic Freedom in the Shadow of Hong Kong's National Security Law 255
Kelley Loper and Carole J. Petersen

13. The Business of National Security in Hong Kong: Do Human Rights Matter? 279
Surya Deva

14. Echoes Enhanced to a Cacophony: Hong Kong's Security Law Compared to Illiberal Elements of the Security Laws of Liberal Democracies 306
Kent Roach

15. Media Freedom and Censorship under Post-Orwellian Authoritarianism 335
Cherian George

16. The New National Security Law: Exploring a Meaningful Comparison with Singapore 358
Michael Hor

List of Abbreviations 377

List of Contributors 379

Index 381

1

Introduction

Re-balancing Freedom and Security in Post-NSL Hong Kong

Hualing Fu and Michael Hor

Introduction

This book offers a dialogic study of the Law of the People's Republic of China on Safeguarding National Security Law (NSL) in the Hong Kong Special Administrative Region (HKSAR). It examines the text and the context of the NSL, what caused it and what it has caused, and highlights the changes—real, potential, or merely imagined—that the NSL has brought and is likely to bring to Hong Kong. Constitutional development is not brought about by isolated events but by a series of connected episodes that have taken place over a long duration with each act done in response to an earlier one and, in turn, generating future dialectical reactions in multiple fields, some contemplated and others unforeseen, or, perhaps, still unforeseeable. It is a complicated process and emotions may run high, but there is always a logic to be discovered and explained to make sense of what, at first sight, appear to be chaotic, random occurrences. This book studies the political and constitutional roots of the NSL as well as its practical operation in Hong Kong. The book also attempts to view the NSL in the larger Chinese, and comparative law, perspectives.

This introductory chapter first situates the enactment of the NSL in the context of Hong Kong's own constitutional context and, in particular, the failed attempt to enact Hong Kong national security law in 2003 as required by the Basic Law (BL), and the tortuous path of democratic pursuit that Hong Kong had trodden. The chapter then explores the constitutional and political roots of the NSL in the Chinese constitutional order. Part three addresses several key issues on the impact of the NSL on the legal system, academic freedom, business, and media among others. Finally, part four assesses the future prospects of Hong Kong's one country two systems doctrine (OCTS) and Hong Kong's freedoms under rule of law in the post-NSL era, assessed from a comparative perspective by referencing the development in national security law in mainland China, Singapore, and liberal democracies.

Balancing Article 23 and Article 45 of the Basic Law

The constitutional contention in Hong Kong over the past three decades has been centred on the tension between the imperative to protect national security and interest as demanded by the Central Authorities[1] and the imperative to safeguard autonomy in order to preserve and enhance democratic governance in Hong Kong. At the heart of the contention are two articles in the Basic Law and their implementation (or, more precisely, the lack of it): Article 23 which requires Hong Kong to enact laws "on its own" to protect China's national security and to prevent Hong Kong from turning into a separatist and subversive base against the motherland, and Article 45 which, on the other hand, aspires to achieve ultimate democratisation in Hong Kong through a cautious and incremental process befitting Hong Kong's unique circumstances. "One country two systems" is conditioned on and sustained by this unique bargain and trade-off between security and freedom. There are structural constraints, but human agency also matters in overcoming those constraints. Handled well, there are opportunities to achieve a win-win equilibrium between freedom and security. Misjudged and mismanaged, all parties lose.

While BL adjudication may have offered effective legal remedies for the basic rights and freedom of its residents, it is unable to resolve the fundamental contradiction between Article 23 and Article 45. These articles are framed in open-ended terms and crafted in aspirational language to allow maximum discretion in interpretation and provide opportunities for avoidance and manipulation. There is no authoritative and neutral organ in the BL structure to settle disputes within the OCTS framework. The BL is a well-designed constitutional document to facilitate reunification. It also embodies systematic tensions that were not sorted out politically but written into the document, thus temporarily putting aside and suppressing these unresolved issues. Not unexpectedly, they surfaced gradually but significantly soon after the implementation of OCTS.

As it turned out, neither constitutional imperative has been fulfilled since the enactment of the BL. Both sides, championing one or the other imperative, have been drifting further apart, leading to a near collapse in 2019 of the bargain that sustained the constitutional design. The "on its own" clause has empowered Hong Kong to decide when to legislate to protect China's security, if at all; and "incremental" democratisation suitable for Hong Kong's actual circumstances has been interpreted in ways that have been perceived to narrow and stall a genuine democratic process. The distrust between the two systems has run too deep to make an acceptable or, at least, tolerable trade-off between freedom and security. As the contention escalated, neither side found the other trustworthy and, as suspicion turned to hostility, each side decided to take the extreme position of denying each other's

1. Central Authorities is a shorthand to decision-makers in the State Council, the National People's Congress (NPC) or its Standing Committee (NPCSC), and above all the Communist Party.

legitimate requests, leading to a vicious cycle of two self-fulfilling prophecies: in 2019, Hong Kong, in the eyes of the Central Authorities and many others, turned out to be a subversive base against China after all, as Li Ho famously warned in the aftermath of 1989;[2] and the political logic of the Party State made OCTS inherently unstable, if not impossible, as cynical commentators may have prophesied to be the case.[3] At a fundamental level, the BL has created two incompatible systems which have been forced to co-exist, aggravated by mismanagement at critical moments, making a trade-off envisaged by the BL impossible within the BL framework.

This contradiction within the OCTS made meaningful dialogue difficult. Constitutional dialogue takes place between institutions in stable democracies and rarely crosses the authoritarianism and democracy divide, although in countries experiencing democratic backsliding, the contention between a populist executive and a defiant court has introduced a new dimension to theories of constitutional dialogue.[4] A constitutional dialogue is more likely to take place if there is a clear understanding of each other's original beliefs. If beliefs inform and guide political action then a false or biased belief would misinform and misguide political action, rendering a dialogue meaningless and indeed impossible. There must be common ground and a shared foundation for dialogue to be sustained and productive.[5] This is the crucial element missing in the OCTS context. The foundation for dialogue was new and fragile; channels for dialogue were often informal, with a low level of institutionalisation; the level of trust between the parties was low. The informality of the process caused the parties in the dialogue to be uncertain, with proxies invariably participating on behalf of their invisible principals.[6] OCTS is a grand political bargain that was struck between two fundamentally different political systems guided by opposing ideologies. Hong Kong is an excellent case for comparative study of an attempt at authoritarian and liberal dialogue.

Having created the Special Administrative Region (SAR) according to the OCTS design, China demanded a national security legislation. In 2003, the Hong Kong government proceeded to draft such a law to comply with Article 23, but the initiative was met with a passionate and well-organised resistance. Led by the Bar,

---

2. *See* Hualing Fu and Richard Cullen, "National Security Law in Hong Kong: Quo Vadis: A study of Article 23 of the Basic Law of Hong Kong" (2002) 19 *UCLA Pacific Basin Law Journal* 185–230.
3. *See* Benny Tai, "Pursuing Democracy in an Authoritarian State: Protest and the Rule of Law in Hong Kong" (2019) 29(1) *Social & Legal Studies* 107–145.
4. *See* Kim Lane Scheppele, "Autocratic Legalism" (2018) 85(2) *The University of Chicago Law Review* 85–545; *see also* Martin Belov (ed), *Populist Constitutionalism and Illegal Democracies* (Cambridge: Intersentia, 2021).
5. Geoffrey Sigalet, Gregoire Webber, and Rosalind Dixon (eds), *Constitutional Dialogue: Rights, Democracy, Institutions* (Cambridge: Cambridge University Press, 2019); for an Asian perspective, *see* Po Jen Yap, *Constitutional Dialogue in Common Law Asia* (Oxford: Oxford University Press, 2015).
6. *See* Eric C. Ip, *Hybrid Constitutionalism: The Politics of Constitutional Review in the Chinese Special Administrative Regions* (Cambridge: Cambridge University Press, 2019); *see also* Cora Chan, "Thirty Years from Tiananmen: China, Hong Kong, and The Ongoing Experiment to Preserve Liberal Values in An Authoritarian State" (2019) 17(2) *International Journal of Constitutional Law* 439–452.

the entire society was mobilised to push back what was perceived to be a major political encroachment of the mainland system into Hong Kong. While the proposed law may be considered to have complied with international human rights requirements, and to have been tightly drafted and rights-friendly, it was nevertheless not regarded as politically acceptable by those who opposed it. Half a million people took to the streets to express their discontent towards the proposed law, sending a strong signal which was perceived by the Central Authorities that the people of Hong Kong did not consider China's national security a significant matter. Faced with the massive and well-orchestrated protest and the collapse of a pro-government coalition, the government was forced to withdraw the National Security (Legislative Provisions) Bill (Bill). There are multiple explanations, with different degrees of persuasiveness, as to why fresh legislation was not thought to be urgent or necessary.[7] Nonetheless, in the eyes of the Central Authorities, the reluctance or unwillingness of Hong Kong to enact such a law was regarded as a colossal failure to fulfil Hong Kong's constitutional duty and received with hostility.

The defeat of the Bill triggered the formation of a pan-democratic force in Hong Kong and created momentum for a fresh democratic reform impetus that the BL had promised. The success of the anti-Article 23 law effort popularised opposition political leaders, energised political society, and emboldened the people in Hong Kong, and their political leaders alike, to press forward for political reform. Having denied China a national security law, Hong Kong started to organise and strategise for democratisation.

Hong Kong celebrated the victory of the opposition and, riding on the tide of its success, shifted the battlefield from anti-security legislation to democracy promotion. The Central Authorities were delivered a wake-up call and started to reflect on its Hong Kong policy failure. It immediately took pre-emptive measures to fend off potential democratic reform initiated from Hong Kong. Four months after Hong Kong denied China a national security law, the Standing Committee of the National People's Congress (NPC) made a landmark interpretation of the Basic Law on the election of the Chief Executive and members of the Legislative Council. In that aggressive and carefully drafted interpretation, the Central Authorities took away the agenda-setting power of initiating constitutional reform from Hong Kong.[8] The 2004 Interpretation formed the basis for other subsequent decisions that further shaped the direction of Hong Kong's democratic direction, marking the beginning

7. For the intellectual background of the debate and articulation of different perspectives, *see* Fu and Cullen n 2 above; Hualing Fu, Carole J. Petersen, and Simon Young, *National Security and Fundamental Freedoms: Hong Kong's Article 23 under Scrutiny* (Hong Kong: Hong Kong University Press, 2005); Cora Chan and Fiona de Londras (eds), *China's National Security: Endangering Hong Kong's Rule of Law?* (Oxford: Hart Publishing, 2020).

8. *See* Ip, n 6 above.

of a constitutional escalation leading to the Occupy Central Movement,[9] subsequent waves of disqualification of opposition lawmakers, and ultimately the 2020 NSL.

The reckless promotion of the Extradition Bill in 2019 became a rallying point for anti-government forces. The successful mobilisation of local and international forces to support the protest created a perfect storm that pushed the OCTS constitutional design to a breaking point. Shockingly, localism, which had started as a movement to advocate Hong Kong identity, radicalised into a secessionist movement, often through violence and mass destruction of property, fundamentally uncharacteristic of Hong Kong yet with not insubstantial, wide local buy-in and international support.[10] The democratic pursuit, in the eyes of the Central Authorities, was intrinsically subversive and secessionist, a Trojan horse for a colour revolution, as Li Hou had warned, and with which the Central Authorities have always been concerned.[11]

Hong Kong's alternative system has always presented a governance challenge to China. Governing a free society with rule of law and an independent judiciary, with the potential to fully democratise, is an alien, and indeed intimidating, concept to the Central Authorities. Engaging Hong Kong on Hong Kong's terms proved to be a frustrating process in which China faced a steep learning curve. Hong Kong is the only entity that fell outside the socialist system and was not under direct Party rule. When the Central Authorities conversed with Hong Kong, the Party had to check its authoritarian tendencies, put aside familiar governance tools, and step out of its comfort zone. The 2019 crisis was an open invitation to the Central Authorities to intervene directly, and the NSL is the game changer that allowed the Central Authorities to govern Hong Kong on its own terms. In that sense, the NSL is the second BL that facilitates the second reunification.[12]

The Sovereign Root of the NSL

Several chapters in the book present a focused analysis on the political-constitutional foundation of the NSL, repositioning Hong Kong's constitutional status in the NSL era from the perspective of the sovereign power of the Chinese state. The

9. *See* Brian Christopher Jones (ed), *Law and Politics of the Taiwan Sunflower and Hong Kong Umbrella Movements* (New York: Routledge, 2017); Francis L. F. Lee and Joseph M. Chan, *Media and Protest Logic in the Digital Era: The Umbrella Movement in Hong Kong* (Oxford: Oxford University Press, 2018); Ching Kwan Lee and Ming Sing (eds), *Take Back Our Future: An Eventful Sociology of the Hong Kong Umbrella Movement* (Ithaca, NY: ILR Press, an imprint of Cornell University Press, 2019); Ngok Ma and Edmund W. Cheng (eds), *The Umbrella Movement: Civil Resistance and Contentious Space in Hong Kong* (Amsterdam: Amsterdam University Press, 2020).
10. *See* Albert H. Y. Chen, "Constitutional Controversies in the Aftermath of the Anti-Extradition Movement of 2019" (2020) 50(2) *Hong Kong Law Journal* 609–632.
11. Fu and Cullen, n 2 above.
12. *See* Anthony Bingliang Cheung, *Erci Guodu—Xianggang 2020 Zhengju Fansi: Weiji Yu Qiantu* [Second transition—reflections on Hong Kong's political situation in 2020: Crisis and the way forward] (Hong Kong: Chung Hwa Book Company, 2021).

immediate legal question concerns the NSL's compatibility with the BL: if Article 23 pre-empts the Central Authorities' intervention because Hong Kong is to act "on its own", how can the NSL be justified, it being an instance where the Central Authorities have legislated in a domain reserved for the SAR? The new understanding, as discussed in several of the chapters in this volume and elsewhere, might be rationalised as an exercise of concurrent jurisdiction or the doctrine of delegation. Concurrent jurisdiction means that matters of national security, notwithstanding Article 23, cannot be the exclusive jurisdiction of an SAR, and the sovereign necessarily has an inherent power of self-defence.[13]

The delegation theory stands on a narrower legal ground according to which the SAR was delegated the power to legislate on national security, but when the SAR fails to fulfil the duty in pre-empting and removing a national security risk exposing China to an imminent security crisis, the Central Authorities can withdraw the delegated power and act on its own. Zhu's chapter elaborates this principle and how its operation has been deliberated in the mainland scholarship. The combined effect of the two principles seems to have supported the legislative initiative.[14] While the NPC and the National People's Congress Standing Committee (NPCSC) can pass stop-gap legislation, Hong Kong continues to be obliged to enact what remains of the requirements of Article 23 of the BL.

The theories of concurrent jurisdiction and delegated authority are both anchored in the Chinese Constitution, the application of which in Hong Kong has always been a contentious issue since the establishment of the SAR. The conventional view is that the BL is self-contained and that the Constitution does not apply directly in Hong Kong.[15] Rather it is embodied in the BL *via* its Article 31. Although it was a view that dominated the field in the first decade of BL research and held dear by many, it needs to be revised. Since 2014 when the State Council released a White Paper on Hong Kong, the constitutional foundation, or the *grundnorm*, has been shifting decisively from the BL in and of itself to a joint enterprise of the Constitution and the BL. As it is stated in the White Paper, which has effectively become the new orthodoxy, the Constitution and the Basic Law jointly constitute the constitutional foundation for the governance of Hong Kong SAR.[16] This is of

13. *See* Po Jen Yap, "Judging Hong Kong's National Security Law", Chapter 7 of this volume. *See also* Chen, n 10 above.
14. *See* Han Zhu, "The Hong Kong National Security Law: The Shifted *Grundnorm* of Hong Kong's Legal Order and Its Implications", Chapter 3 of this volume.
15. Yash Ghai, "Litigating the Basic Law", in Johannes Chan, Hualing Fu, and Yash Ghai (eds), *Constitutional Debate on the Right of Abode: Conflict on the Approach to Interpretation* (Hong Kong: Hong Kong University Press, 2000), p 46.
16. *See* Wenye Zha and Bo Zhao, "Xianfa He Xianggang Jiben Fa Gongtong Goucheng Xianggang Tebie Xingzhengqu de Xianzhi Jichu" [The Constitution and The Hong Kong Basic Law together form the constitutional basis of the Hong Kong Special Administrative Region], *Xinhua News Agency*, 10 June 2014, available at http://www.gov.cn/xinwen/2014-06/10/content_2697910.htm.

course not a rhetorical statement. It has real consequences and the NSL is an exhibit of that profound impact.

The NPC triggered the legislative process for the NSL through a Decision to authorise its Standing Committee to enact the NSL. In doing so, the NPC Decision relied directly on Art 62(2, 12, and 14) of the Constitution. Art 62 of the Constitution sets out the functions and powers of the NPC, and Art 62(2) gives the NPC the plenary power to supervise the implementation of the Constitution. The NPC Decision on the NSL is revolutionary and presents the most significant development in the history of OCTS jurisprudence. Constitutionally speaking, the NPC now has the power to enact a wide range of laws of national interest for Hong Kong as circumstances demand, leaving the door wide open for future legislative intervention from the Central Authorities.[17] Once we accept the premise that sovereign power is the originating power in legislative competence over national security in the OCTS context, the BL is no longer controlling. The post-NSL world is Chinese Constitution-centric. As Chan[18] points out, the question would no longer be whether the Central Authorities can make a national security law, but what kind of national security law they can make. We move to the next level of the substance of the legislation and the process of its implementation.

Fundamentally, we need to reconceptualise Hong Kong's legal status in China's constitutional order. Mitchell's chapter offers a clear map for that thought process. For him, the NSL extends far beyond policing and criminal law power per se and touches on security matters. It is about sovereign power in a moment of existential risk facing the state. It is indeed misconceived to examine the origin and implementation of the NSL principally from an Anglo-American public law stance that prioritises individual freedom and rights because the fulcrum has shifted to the sovereignty of the state and the fundamental structure of the polity beyond the constitutional text. The starting point of our analysis then shifts from the BL text to the political context of the Constitution. China relies on the theories of state and law derived from late nineteenth- to early twentieth-century conservative German ideas in building a twenty-first-century socialist rule of law state.

This is a view that Cheng confirms through her distinction between a normative view that is based on liberal values, as the Hong Kong court has traditionally

17. *See* Hualing Fu, "National Security", in Johannes Chan and C. L. Lim (eds), *Law of The Hong Kong Constitution* (Pyrmont, New South Wales: Thomson Reuters Corporation Pte, 2021); commentaries on the NSL, *see* Carole J. Petersen, "The Disappearing Firewall: International Consequences of Beijing's Decision to Impose a National Security Law and Operate National Security Institutions in Hong Kong" (2020) 50(2) *Hong Kong Law Journal* 633; *see also* Cora Chan, "Can Hong Kong Remain a Liberal Enclave within China? Analysis of the Hong Kong National Security Law" (2021) *Public Law* 271–292; Simon N. M. Young, "Introductory Note to the Law of the People's Republic of China on Safeguarding National Security in the Hong Kong Special Administrative Region" (2021) 60 *International Legal Materials* 1.

18. *See* Johannes Chan, "National Security and Judicial Independence: A Clash of Fundamental Values", Chapter 6 of this volume.

based its jurisprudence on, and a positivist conception that the legal text of the NSL should not be underpinned by (liberal) normative values. For Cheng, the NSL represents authoritarian legalism of sorts in a bare, positive form, stripped of all trappings of values, convictions, or commitments based on normative theories. It is mainly, if not merely, about "facts and effects" on the narrow ground of the NSL. In that sense, what the NSL introduces to Hong Kong is still law-based but firmly anchored in the strong statist tradition of the Chinese Constitution with a thin, if any, commitment to liberalism. Under this positivist approach, the NSL realigns the Central-SAR relations, redesigns the SAR power relations, and places new restrictions on rights under the BL. She puts it directly: "But one thing is for sure: the NSL has put new restrictions on the human rights in Hong Kong and the courts could do little to negate these restrictions."

The Impact of the NSL

The NSL has introduced transformative changes to Hong Kong's legal system at multiple levels. First of all, new legal norms are created. They include new criminal offences which are far more restrictive of rights and freedom than what was proposed in the Bill which was withdrawn by the government in 2003 under much public pressure. Some of the offences, such as secession and foreign collusion, are more broadly defined than China's own criminal law. Chen's chapter offers a succinct discussion of the offences, showing similarities between the NSL offences and those in Chinese criminal law.[19] The NSL, through Article 38, creates a broad extraterritorial jurisdiction aiming at all Hong Kong residents or companies and any other persons. It sends, and perhaps intends to, a global chilling effect. Ling's chapter offers a careful analysis of the political and legal hurdles in the way of exercising such a far-reaching jurisdiction.[20]

Second, procedural rules are tightened to limit rights of the suspects or defendants in the criminal process. The changed rules on bail offer an excellent example. Hong Kong's liberal bail regime, effective as it was in managing ordinary offences, was considered to be ill-equipped to cope with a determined, well-organised, and often violent protest of 2019. The police-detain-judge-release revolving door was much lamented by the pro-government press. The NSL has effectively addressed this concern by restricting successful bail applications. The courts, through a series of cases, seem to be adapting, though painfully, to the new legislative and political environment by developing a jurisprudence that rests on a presumption against bail without slipping into a presumption of guilt, thus complying with the NSL

19. *See* Albert Chen, "The National Security Law of the HKSAR: A Contextual and Legal Study", Chapter 2 of this volume; Jie Cheng, "Hong Kong's Constitutional Order after the National Security Law", Chapter 5 of this volume.
20. Bing Ling, "Extraterritorial Application of the Hong Kong National Security Law: A Legal Appraisal", Chapter 11 of this volume.

requirement without endangering the integrity of the criminal process in Hong Kong.[21]

Correspondingly, the NSL empowers the police to investigate national security offences and weakens the traditional accountability mechanisms, and especially judicial oversight, in relation to police powers of search, seizure, or interception of communication. As Young's chapter clearly points out, the national security police enjoy all the powers currently available to deal with the most serious crimes, including powers to freeze and forfeit property, seize travel documents, and compel answers from persons on pain of penalty. They have also been given new powers to allow for the regulation of online content, the supply of information by foreign agents of their activities with foreign governments or foreign political organisations, and the interception of private communication and other kinds of surveillance. In expanding police powers and weakening accountability, Young echoes views expressed in other chapters that the NSL signals a new shift in the equilibrium of relations between the police and residents in the context of law enforcement in Hong Kong.

Indeed, judicial power, a core feature in any liberal legal system, is in general retreat in these national security cases. Several chapters in the book highlight the challenges that the judiciary faces and its vulnerability. Chan's chapter points out that the NSL has effectively created an exceptional zone in the criminal process for national security offences in which the regular criminal justice rules, and in particular the role of judicial oversight, no longer apply. Chan tracks the contraction of judicial power in adjudicating national security cases and offers a sharp comparison between the normal state of affairs of the criminal process and the departures mandated by the NSL. Similarly, Cheng highlights a number of pre-emptive or ousting provisions which keep the courts out of NSL decisions.

The institutional change is equally drastic. In designing the NSL regime, the Central Authorities focused on the enforcement mechanism. It sought not only to create new offences endangering national security but also to design a mechanism to ensure effective enforcement of the new law. As a result, a key aspect of the NSL, and the most contentious one, is the creation of a range of interlocking national security organs that are powerful, detached from the pre-existing institutions, and accountable to the Central Authorities, either directly or indirectly. The disbanded colonial Special Branch of the police[22] has in fact returned with a vengeance. A special prosecution unit is to be set up for the prosecution of national security offences, and national security judges are specially appointed to hear national security cases. The NSL has created a seamless national security grid in Hong Kong that embeds the Central Authorities in the SAR decision-making process and has the

21. *See* Johannes Chan, "Judicial Responses to the National Security Law: HKSAR v Lai Chee Ying" (2021) 51(1) *Hong Kong Law Journal* 1–14.

22. *See* Hualing Fu and Richard Cullen, "Political Policing in Hong Kong" (2003) 33 *Hong Kong Law Journal* 199–230.

potential to unify the entire criminal process from investigation to final adjudication in the implementation of the NSL, making Hong Kong a perfectly securitised society, a point that Fu and Zhai and other authors raise.

The NSL also creates a "nuclear option"—a national jurisdiction in Hong Kong over three types of scenarios under Article 55. Under those three circumstances, which are open-ended, the Central Authorities are empowered to take jurisdiction and remove a case from Hong Kong. The presence of the national security office in Hong Kong, reinforced by wide surveillance and investigation power, and the power to trigger the national jurisdiction represent the most transformative change that raises a series of very thorny questions, ranging from the application of other national laws, such as the Chinese Criminal Procedure Law, to technical operations of the national jurisdiction, and to the overall accountability under Hong Kong law and national law. Several chapters highlight different aspects of the features of the national jurisdiction and address related concerns.

What impact has the NSL and its enforcement had in its first year?[23] There are two types of emergency powers: one is restorative and the other transformative. A restorative emergency power aims to return to and save the pre-existing legal order. The transformative one modifies and even destroys the old system and replaces it with a new one.[24] The NSL clearly has both a restorative and transformative dimension, as would be expected with any emergency law. The restorative imperative demands immediate corrective measures, manifesting in gap-filling legislation to restore law and order, enhanced enforcement of law, and criminal prosecution.

But an emergency law is not necessarily limited to temporary measures to address the symptoms of a security crisis, to be withdrawn once risk factors that triggered an emergency are removed. Indeed, most of the emergency laws passed in history have stayed on in their respective statute books, accumulating into a dense national security legal universe. More likely than not, emergency laws are intended not only to address the symptoms of risks, but they also aim to cure the underlining root causes of those risks. In the case of the NSL, the enforcement has gone far beyond the corrective measure of prosecution of individual leaders and key participants in the 2019 mobilisation, ranging from veteran politicians to young students. While each arrest generates its own uncertainties and creates its own deterrent effect, the direct application of the NSL remains limited, targeting the organisers and key participants of the 2019 protest and those who may be perceived as acting in defiance of the NSL after it came into force. While the rule of

23. *See* Lydia Wong and Thomas E. Kellogg, *Hong Kong's National Security Law: A Human Rights and Rule of Law Analysis* (Center for Asian Law Georgetown Law, 2021), available at https://www.law.georgetown.edu/law-asia/wp-content/uploads/sites/31/2021/02/GT-HK-Report-Accessible.pdf.

24. *See* Schmitt's distinction between "commissary dictatorship" and "sovereign dictatorship" relevant to the discussion. *See also* Carl Schmitt, *Dictatorship: From the Origin of the Modern Concept of Sovereignty to the Proletarian Class Struggle*, translated by Michael Hoelzl and Graham Ward (Cambridge: Polity Press, 2014).

non-retrospectivity continues to hold the line for NSL offences and there seems to be a degree of constraint,[25] the NSL seems to have prompted the resuscitation of the existing offence of sedition in the Crimes Ordinance, thereby diluting, in effect, the principle of non-retrospectivity. The direct application of the NSL remains volatile and continues to evolve, an issue this volume can only begin to grapple with.

If the restorative imperative addresses the symptoms of the problems which surfaced in Hong Kong in 2019, the transformative imperative aims to tackle the root causes and introduces correctives to the real or perceived structural flaws.[26] Beyond individuals who have been prosecuted are civil society organisations whose vibrancy and activism used to define Hong Kong. The protests of 2019 had the support of many of them. They have been forced to dissolve for what they may have done, real or perceived. *Apple Daily*, Hong Kong Professional Teachers' Union, Hong Kong Confederation of Trade Union, and, of course, Hong Kong Alliance in Support of Patriotic Democratic Movements of China, among several others, have ended their operations, fallen under the weight of the NSL. Others, such as the Bar, RTHK (Radio Television Hong Kong), and Hong Kong Journalists Association, had been placed under pressure and, although they still survive, have been duly warned to behave. To use a medical metaphor, those who are deemed to be primary "cancers" of Hong Kong are surgically removed, and lesser tumours are put under notice and subject to radiation therapy.

Beyond the strictly legal and political, the NSL has the potential to affect the broader culture and social ecosystem of Hong Kong society. Loper and Petersen analyse the impact of the NSL on educational autonomy and academic freedom in tertiary education. Their chapter offers a conceptual framework of academic freedom, examines the controversies and vulnerabilities of higher education in Hong Kong prior, and subsequent, to the NSL, and provides a balanced discussion of the impact of further inhibitions, real or potential, on academic freedom. They suggest some useful recommendations in response to these challenges. George focuses on the NSL's impact on media and the freedom of the press, an area that attracted the most political attention in the initial month of its operation. The media is a key pillar in China's understanding of political power and, as George points out, the action against *Apple Daily* and Jimmy Lai exemplified China's resolve to remove any anti-Beijing elements in the media sector. In contrast to the massive show of force and swift police action, the quieter purge of the RTHK and stern warnings sent to other media outlets have naturally maximised the NSL's deterrent and the chilling

---

25. *See* Greg Torode, "Court Rulings Free Hong Kong Police to Probe Older Offences Under Security Law", *Reuters*, 19 October 2021, available at https://www.reuters.com/article/us-hongkong-security-legal-idAFKBN2H903C.
26. *See* Simon Young, "Political System Transformation in Hong Kong", *Verfassungsblog*, 13 April 2021, available at https://verfassungsblog.de/political-system-transformation-in-hong-kong/; *see also* Richard Cullen, "HK's New Political Realities after 2019 Watershed Year", *China Daily*, 13 March 2021, available at https://www.chinadaily.com.cn/a/202103/13/WS604c76cda31024ad0baaefd5.html.

effect. George also raises questions on how far-reaching the persecution and purge would extend to the media sector and the extent of the detrimental impact that the NSL may create on the media in Hong Kong and the political culture in general.

Deva assesses the NSL's impact on business enterprises in Hong Kong in relation to their human rights obligations or responsibilities under relevant domestic and international norms. The chapter focuses on three types of legal and regulatory conflicts that international business enterprises have had to face: between the NSL and the long-arm legislation of foreign countries, in particular the conflicting demands of different legal authorities in the context of foreign sanctions against officials in Hong Kong; between the NSL and other laws of Hong Kong; and between the NSL and international human rights standards of business. While there is nothing new about the interface between global business transactions and national security concerns, the NSL poses a unique challenge for Hong Kong because of its traditional status as an international financial centre with its new role in geopolitical competition.[27]

The Resilience of the OCTS

What remains of OCTS, which the Central Authorities in the post-NSL era insist on maintaining, though with a "correct understanding"? The exceptional measures in the NSL have been institutionalised and become permanent features of Hong Kong's political and legal systems. In that sense, the NSL has effectively routinised the exceptional. There is no doubt the NSL has had and will continue to have a significant impact on the political and legal systems, and it is for good reason it is sometimes referred to as the second Basic Law to bring about a second reunification of Hong Kong. The NSL clarifies the priority and significance of certain articles of the BL.[28] It supplements the BL where the latter is silent and modifies it to the degree necessary to safeguard China's national security and interest. But, except for a few radical voices, no one holds the view that, at this moment in time, OCTS, even in the era of NSL enforcement, has ceased to exist or is likely to end in the near future.

This is not to deny that the NSL has adjusted the course of Hong Kong's political development. Yet the OCTS doctrine, after these revisions and recalibrations, as discussed above, may continue to survive in terms of setting Hong Kong firmly apart from the Mainland even in the most sensitive area of the NSL. There divergence remains the rule, and convergence—especially in the circumstances of Article 55 to be enforced by the national office—will be exceptional. There are sound political, legal, and sociological reasons that national security rules and practices in the

27. Surya Deva, "The Business of National Security in Hong Kong: Do Human Rights Matter", Chapter 13 of this volume.
28. In a novel manner, Article 2 of the NSL states that Articles 1 and 12 are "fundamental" provisions and the exercise of rights is subject to such provisions.

Mainland will not come across the border and be replicated in Hong Kong through the NSL in the foreseeable future, as chapters in this volume illustrate.

The political message from the Central Authorities focuses on the restorative imperative of the NSL, although the transformative effect is clearly evident. By enacting the NSL, the Central Authorities are merely asserting a constitutional authority they already had under the Chinese Constitution. The way in which the NSL was enacted and implemented in Hong Kong demonstrates a level of deference to the BL and the OCTS principle it enshrines, even in addressing the most challenging issues. It complies with the essential aspects of legality which Chinese law requires. Lawmakers in Beijing also reiterate that the NSL was enacted to stop the violence and lawlessness that Hong Kong tragically suffered from in 2019, and to restore law and order within the framework of OCTS.[29]

The inclusion of the human rights provisions in the NSL and especially the reference to the International Covenant on Civil and Political Rights (ICCPR) and other international rights regimes are significant in signalling a commitment to maintaining OCTS. This should not be regarded as a mere window dressing exercise not meant to have any constraints over enforcement. The rights provisions in the NSL also anchor the NSL in the common law and connect an otherwise harsh legislation to the pre-existing rules and standards of Hong Kong. Significantly, while the NSL carves out a national jurisdiction and in various respects restricts the jurisdiction of Hong Kong courts, the application of the NSL is largely, if not entirely, in the hands of the Hong Kong courts, which follow a sound common law tradition.

For Loper and Petersen, with the inclusion of the ICCPR and the International Covenant on Economic, Social, and Cultural Rights, any policies adopted by Hong Kong's educational institutions should comply with both treaties, and cases litigated should use the ICCPR as a guide to interpret provisions in the NSL. The inclusion of the two Covenants invites the relevant UN monitoring bodies to offer guidance on matters relating to education and academic freedom and to support academic freedom and university autonomy.[30] George similarly notes the essentiality of media freedom which the ICCPR, an integral component of the NSL, recognises. As George notes, the jury is out on whether critical journalism can continue to exist in Hong Kong in post-NSL Hong Kong. Meaningful journalism is possible in diverse political environments, but Hong Kong journalists cannot now take liberalism for granted and will need to learn to thrive in a "navigable, though certainly dangerous, minefield."[31]

29. Chen, n 19 above; Cheng, n 19 above; and Han Zhu, "The Hong Kong National Security Law: The Shifted *Grundnorm* of Hong Kong's Legal Order and Its Implications", Chapter 3 of this volume.
30. Kelley Loper and Carole J. Petersen, "Academic Freedom in the Shadow of Hong Kong's National Security Law", Chapter 12 of this volume.
31. Cherian George, "Media Freedom and Censorship under Post-Orwellian Authoritarianism", Chapter 15 of this volume.

On judicial power, Yap points out there is still room for the court to provide "remedial" interpretations of the NSL so that it will operate within the broader BL framework. As he states, "while the [NSL] is a done deal, its *interpretation* is not." Thus, interpretation should be taken seriously. Facing the dilemma of maintaining its worthy tradition of judicial autonomy and common law methodology, on the one hand, and addressing the Central Authorities' political concerns over political stability, on the other, courts in Hong Kong have to be politically astute and strategic, as they have always been in BL interpretation.[32] The NSL defines at least some offences with relative clarity. For the others, there are opportunities and, indeed, a duty to read criminal law offences strictly according to the common law tradition. The audience is not only in Hong Kong and the Mainland, but the world will be watching and evaluating the situation.

Fu and Zhai point out that OCTS, even in the area of national security, will continue in spite of the NSL. The enforcement of national security law needs more than legal provisions and institutions. Mainland-style enforcement requires a particular political structure and social milieu and, in particular, a series of authoritarian features, such as censorship of the press, restrictions on NGOs, cultivation of informants, other measures of early and proactive interventions, and above all, pervasive self-censorship. Hong Kong, on the other hand, has an intrinsically liberal political, institutional, and social background. This creates room for Hong Kong to manoeuvre to adapt to the NSL without becoming more authoritarian than is necessary.[33]

A significant concern over the implementation of the NSL is the relevance of national criminal law and the degree to which mainland law punishing national security offences may be referred to as authority. It is true that the interpretative power of the NSL belongs to the NPCSC, consistent with the Chinese legislative tradition,[34] but it is also significant to note that Article 41 provides that, as a general principle, Hong Kong law continues to apply to procedural matters with respect to offences endangering national security. The NSL need not be a serious challenge to Hong Kong's common law system. It is unlikely, judging by the BL interpretative practices of the NPCSC, that the NPCSC will intrude frequently into the interpretative space of the NSL. It lacks the will and capacity to make extensive and repeated interpretations to micromanage Hong Kong and its courts. It will intervene and give interpretations on what it perceives to be crucial issues at critical junctures, but it has to rely on the courts of Hong Kong to give much of the meaning to the NSL. Thus, Article 65 should be read as referring to the "ultimate or final interpretation"

32. *See* Po Jen Yap, "Judging Hong Kong's National Security Law", Chapter 7 of this volume and his "Constitutional Review under the Basic Law: The Rise, Retreat and Resurgence of Judicial Power in Hong Kong" (2007) 37 *Hong Kong Law Journal* 449.
33. Hualing Fu and Xiaobo Zhai, "The Return of High Policing in Hong Kong", Chapter 9 of this volume.
34. *See* Art 65, NSL.

of the NSL, modelled, in essence, on the interpretative structure of Article 158 of the BL.[35]

It is certainly of academic interest to refer to Chinese criminal law and practices in relation to offences endangering state security, as Chen does in offering examples of subversion, secession, and terrorism prosecutions under Chinese criminal law,[36] as Fu and Zhai do in comparing national security enforcement in Hong Kong and mainland China, and as Tang and Huang do in offering insights on the state secrets law regime in the Mainland, rarely available in the English literature.[37] However, Hong Kong courts have so far refrained from considering cases decided by mainland courts. They have avoided doing this, though without straying from fidelity to the Chinese constitutional order and legal rules applying to Hong Kong. Chinese law on national security offences, given that it aims to protect the socialist system under one System, is not expected, and thus unlikely, to shed light on the meaning of the NSL, which was enacted explicitly to protect the national security in the capitalist system under the other System. Undoubtedly, the NSL relied extensively on the wording of Chinese national security laws. This should not be a surprise as it is a law drafted by mainland lawyers. Nonetheless, the lawmakers were at pains to differentiate the NSL from national laws, which they did by providing more detailed and clearer definitions for the offences created, and by laying down express provisions on the protection of rights and freedoms. The judicial decisions to date tend to show that Hong Kong remains deeply embedded in the common law universe in terms of authorities, methodology, and temperament despite all the challenges it faces.

The NSL reflects particularistic Chinese sensitivities concerning sovereignty and political order, and offences like secession and subversion, as defined in the NSL and enforced by the National Security Department, reflect specific historical and political concerns. It is precisely at this historical junction, when the socialist system encounters the liberal order, that the courts in Hong Kong have to step out and step up, to serve not only as the guardians of Hong Kong's legal order as it existed before the NSL, but also to make decisions that reflect national sentiment and transcend narrow political divisions, as they continue to develop Hong Kong's common law system in the post-NSL era.

---

35. For a critical comparison between common law interpretation and the NPCSC legislative interpretation, *see* Johannes Chan, "Reconciliation of the NPCSC's Power of Interpretation of the Basic Law within the Common Law in the HKSAR" (2020) 50(3) *Hong Kong Law Journal* 657.
36. Chen, n 19 above.
37. Zheng Tang and Xu Huang, "State Secrets in the Hong Kong National Security Law", Chapter 10 of this volume.

The NSL from Comparative Perspectives

The realm of political freedom, including political advocacy and political speech as practised prior to July 2020 and especially during 2019, has been and will be curtailed, and courts will be operating in a context of diminished political pluralism and enhanced political correctness, but Hong Kong is not the only jurisdiction that has been placed under a stress test, as Roach's chapter well illustrates. Many states have made secession illegal and criminal; defined national security offences broadly and vaguely; punished speech, such as provoking hatred or advocating terrorism, as a crime; extended their criminal laws extraterritorially; and conferred special powers to the police and prosecutors. These measures are among a long list of issues that show some, at least formalistic, similarities between the NSL and its counterparts in liberal democracies. Democracies should reflect on their own domestic practices while criticising the NSL.[38]

Of course, the NSL is not an invitation to a tea party. Rather, it is a weapon to end what is perceived to be a revolt to turn Hong Kong into a site of struggle against the Central Authorities. Its purposes are to reset Hong Kong's political direction, transform the political structure, and move forward according to a "correct" understanding of OCTS. Yet, the harsh law is to be implemented in a society with a liberal tradition, supported by a mature common law system, an independent legal profession, and a still active civil society, including the media and the religious sector. As authors in several chapters reiterate, the jury is still out in assessing the structural impact on Hong Kong's governance. In that sense, the courts, with the support of remnants of the liberal institutions, can still offer some meaningful corrective to some of the potential political excesses—the authoritarian enhancement, distortion, and the cacophony that Roach points out.[39]

Will Singapore be our future? In a fundamental sense, the two cities are not compatible because of the simple fact that Hong Kong is a part of a much larger political entity, and Singapore, a city-state, is what it is. While recognising the incompatibility at the foundational level, the mechanism to safeguard national security and exert political control in Singapore can shed some light on the path that Hong Kong may tread. Hor's chapter first identifies an anomaly: an analysis of the letter of the law—the NSL and Singapore's Internal Security Act (ISA)—reveals a potentially far more authoritarian administrative detention without trial in Singapore for national security offences, compared with the criminal law approach embodied in the NSL. So the anxieties that some people may have and the willingness to relocate to Singapore to escape from a national security legislation illustrate forcefully that the issue is not the text of the law but its political context and the

---

38. Kent Roach, "Echoes Enhanced to a Cacophony: Hong Kong's Security Law Compared to Illiberal Elements of the Security Laws of Liberal Democracies", Chapter 14 of this volume.
39. *Ibid.*

resulting perception in Hong Kong and internationally.[40] What are the lessons that Hong Kong may draw from Singapore and what should be the best response from Hong Kong?

One answer is a depressing and brutal one: it takes time for people to get used to it and sooner or later people will get used to it. Nothing could be more general and vague and generate more uncertainty than the ISA test of "prejudicial to the security of Singapore", but there is a "novelty effect" as Hor calls it. As Hor puts it, "Whatever is going on in Singapore has been going on for decades—more than enough time for the expected desensitization." That Singapore is "like that" is no longer news. Hong Kong's changes are fresh, barely a year old. Hong Kong is not supposed to be "like this". That can change as time goes by.

More importantly, after the NSL has removed the real or perceived enemies and adversaries from the political landscape, the political context may stabilise, reducing the level of legal volatility in application of the NSL. As Singapore demonstrates, the stability in the political order and confidence of the ruling Party to govern effectively would necessarily lead to a more circumspect and cautious use of the ISA. The predominant perception in Singapore is that the limited use of ISA—essentially targeting religiously motivated terrorists—"is, if not justified, not unreasonable". As the overall political atmosphere improves, Hong Kong judges may well regain their confidence to uphold the liberal standard and, by that time, they would have gained more experience and confidence in dealing with NSL cases and be ready to curtail some of the NSL excesses. The general lesson is that when societies encounter "scares", the government responds expediently and repressively. But the repressive moment will pass when a more relaxed political context arrives.

While Hor sees some possibility of a convergence between Hong Kong and Singapore in the application of the respective national security law, George sees divergence in the management of the media sector in the two cities. George makes a convincing argument that scrutinising the legal text or its selective application can only reveal so much about the state of affairs of Hong Kong's media freedom. Lawyers, law professors included, may dutifully imagine the worst-case scenarios, but the societal reactions may differ. The difference matters a lot in setting Hong Kong apart from Singapore when close examination is given to Hong Kong and Singapore in terms of the broader political control of media and the potential pushbacks by professionals and media organisations, which, of course, exist with a particular political background, with different resources and resilience, and in which journalists make their political judgments. George concludes that "the kind of hegemonic domination that the Singapore regime achieved over mainstream media—where resistance is conspicuous in its absence—may be harder to replicate.

40. Michael Hor, "The New National Security Law: Exploring a Meaningful Comparison with Singapore", Chapter 16 of this volume.

This chapter explains why a Singapore-style equilibrium will elude Hong Kong's grasp."

There are answers from both the "supply" side and the "demand" side which showcase the differences between Hong Kong and Singapore. Similar to Hor's "novelty effect" argument, George points out the obvious difference that the effective censorship in Singapore was achieved through a decades-long direct and coercive censorship, begun with "a scorched earth strategy to remove once and for all any oppositional media in the 1960s and 70s." The enforcement of the NSL and the media ecosystem it is creating has not yet produced its Sword of Damocles as it did in Singapore. On the demand side, Singapore's censorship was designed at a particular historical moment. "Singaporeans were probably more easily persuaded in the 1970s and 1980s to exchange their civil liberties for economic rewards, than Hongkongers would be today." Given Hong Kong's political environment in the post-NSL era, legal repression is unlikely to be sustainable and to be used frequently against media outlets. A more likely scenario is the use of administrative and economic means to incentivise calibrated censorship and self-censorship to achieve compliance, although the distinct Singaporean style of media manipulation and control may not be replicated in Hong Kong.[41]

Conclusion

It is an understatement to say that 2019 was a difficult year for Hong Kong. Depending on one's political stance, it was a year of hope, a year of desperation, a year of chaos, or a year of crisis. Putting aside our normative positions, 2019 presented an emergency to the Central Authorities and a crisis that Hong Kong was ill-equipped to manage. This necessitated a constitutional intervention. What happened in Hong Kong in 2019, as it was presented to the Central Authorities in China, was so dramatic and extreme that the enactment of the NSL appeared to them a natural response. It also became a highly politicised matter internationally due to the geopolitical concerns that made Hong Kong a focal point.

The 2019 protest and the enactment of the NSL should be examined in the larger context of the contention between Articles 23 and 45 of the BL, and a dismal failure of constitutional dialogue between the Central Authorities and the SAR, resulting in a lose-lose situation on both freedom and security. The 2003 anti-national security movement, whether seen as a success or a failure, catalysed a sea change in China's Hong Kong policy. It resulted in, or at least contributed significantly to, the NPCSC Decision of 2014, which, arising from the decisive political changes in China in the Xi era, significantly limited the democratic reform of the election of the Chief Executive in 2017. The 2014 Decision in turn triggered a prolonged civil

41. Cherian George, "Media Freedom and Censorship under Post-Orwellian Authoritarianism", Chapter 15 of this volume.

disobedience that rocked Hong Kong. An escalation of confrontational political protest in Hong Kong led to the debut of violent confrontation between protesters and the police, and the beginnings of a potentially secessionist movement. The violent clashes and open advocacy of Hong Kong independence in 2019, though initially triggered by the ill-conceived Extradition Bill, should be seen as an eruption of all the pressures that had been building up in Hong Kong. The subsequent enactment of the NSL, in response to the violence and secessionist mobilisation, is part of that political continuum.

What is the future then? The historical success in the past relied on the establishment of stable political order and good governance.[42] If security is undermined, then inevitably freedom diminishes and governance deteriorates. With a stable political order, rights can be respected and society can prosper. Freedom and the rule of law are enduring concerns for Hong Kong. The rule of law, as it was introduced to and then evolved in Hong Kong in its short 180-year history from a colonised territory to an SAR, has experienced periodic stress tests. External shocks and internal turmoil, in difficult historical times, have put the rule of law with its corresponding rights and freedom into a state of suspended animation. The year 2019 proved to be yet another challenging one, likely to catalyse significant political changes in Hong Kong, and perhaps the rest of China.

Many wondered in the aftermath of the NSL, as they probably did before, whether the system that was built is collapsing, whether the foundation for it is eroding, and whether the freedom and security that Hong Kong treasures dearly is to be lost. The NSL has restored law, order, and security to Hong Kong, but it has also created uncertainties, anxieties, and vulnerabilities. This book offers an exploratory study of the law and its impact on the legal system and the principle of the rule of law in Hong Kong. Hong Kong is a pragmatic place that always manages to create synergies between the larger political order and individual rights and freedom, thereby developing a symbiotic relationship between this highly autonomous city and core national interests, including security. Freedom under the rule of law with political stability is a universal human pursuit, and national security is the condition and foundation for freedom to nurture and the rule of law to flourish. This holds within it the possibility of a new equilibrium in Hong Kong in the age of the NSL.

42. *See* Yash Ghai, *Hong Kong's New Constitutional Order: The Resumption of Chinese Sovereignty and the Basic Law* (Hong Kong: Hong Kong University Press, 1997); *see also* Steve Tsang, *A Modern History of Hong Kong* (Hong Kong: Hong Kong University Press, 2006). *See also* Francis Fukuyama, *Political Order and Political Decay: From the Industrial Revolution to the Globalization of Democracy* (London: Profile Books, 2014).

2

The National Security Law of the HKSAR

A Contextual and Legal Study

Albert H. Y. Chen

Introduction

The adoption by the National People's Congress (NPC) in May 2020 of a Decision on Safeguarding National Security in the Hong Kong Special Administrative Region (HKSAR) and the enactment shortly thereafter by the Standing Committee of the National People's Congress (NPCSC) of the HKSAR National Security Law (NSL) were momentous events in the history of the HKSAR, marking a new era in the implementation of the "One Country, Two Systems" (OCTS) policy. Critics have suggested that these acts by the government of the People's Republic of China (PRC) portend the end of OCTS. On the other hand, defenders of the Chinese action argue that, given the riots and turmoil Hong Kong had experienced in 2019, the imposition of the NSL was necessary and was designed to and likely to ensure the continued operation of OCTS.

This chapter attempts to understand the nature, significance, and implications of the NSL. Part I situates the Chinese action within the relevant constitutional, legal, political, and historical contexts. Part II examines the NSL in the light of Chinese law relating to matters of national security. Part III considers the impact of the NSL on Hong Kong's existing law. Part IV concludes by reflecting on the significance and implications of the NSL in the context of the evolution of the OCTS policy and changing circumstances in Hong Kong.

I. The Legal and Political Context of the NSL

In this part of the chapter, we seek to understand why the Chinese Central Authorities intervened to legislate on national security in the HKSAR in mid-2020. There are two related questions: Why did the intervention occur at this point in time? And why did the intervention take the form it did, i.e. the "two-step approach" of an

NPC Decision followed by a law enacted by the NPCSC and applied to the HKSAR under Article 18 of the Basic Law (BL)? We shall begin by looking into the legislative history of the BL. This will be followed by a brief review of relevant developments since the BL began to be implemented in 1997.

Although this issue was not dealt with in the Sino-British Joint Declaration (1984), it was soon recognised during the process of BL drafting (in 1985–1990) that there was a need for certain Chinese laws to be applied to the HKSAR, and a need for laws in the HKSAR to protect China's national security. Provisions corresponding to what were eventually enacted as Articles 18 and 23 of the BL first appeared in the draft of Chapter 2 of the BL (on the Central-SAR relationship) presented to the fourth plenary session of the Basic Law Drafting Committee (BLDC) in April 1987.[1] Article 5 of this draft chapter contained two alternative models for the application to the HKSAR of "laws enacted by the NPC and the NPCSC" (without indicating the subject matters which such laws may deal with).[2] Article 12 provided that "the HKSAR shall make laws to prohibit any activity that splits the nation or subverts the Central People's Government".

In the revised draft of Chapter 2 presented to the fifth plenary session of the BLDC in August 1987, the revised Article 7 (on the application of Chinese laws in the HKSAR) limited the Chinese laws that could be applied to the HKSAR to those that related to foreign affairs or defence, or those that gave effect to national unity and territorial integrity and were outside the high degree of autonomy of the HKSAR. Article 12 required the HKSAR to legislate to prohibit any activity that "damages national unity or subverts the Central People's Government".

At the seventh plenary session of the BLDC held in April 1988, the first draft of the BL was finalised and published for the first round of public consultation.[3] In Article 17 of this draft, the scope of the subject matters dealt with by laws enacted by the NPC or NPCSC that could be applied to the HKSAR was the same as that formulated at the fifth plenary session. Article 22 followed the wording of draft Article 12 as formulated at the fifth plenary session.

1. *See* Basic Law Drafting Committee (BLDC) Secretariat, *Zhonghua renmin gongheguo Xianggang tebie xingzhengqu jibenfa qicao weiyuanhui quanti huiyi wenjian huibian* [Collection of documents of plenary sessions of the HKSAR Basic Law Drafting Committee of the PRC 1985–1990], available at https://sunzi.lib.hku.hk/bldho/home.action (Basic Law Drafting History Online); https://library.legco.gov.hk (LegCo Library).
2. In the papers for the fourth plenary session (*ibid.*), there was a footnote stating that some members of the BLDC suggested that such laws should be confined to those relating to defence and foreign affairs. During the discussion at the fourth plenary session, one suggestion was that such laws should relate to defence, foreign affairs, or matters that were not within the high degree of autonomy of the HKSAR and that should be managed by the Central Authorities: *see* Han Dayuan, "The Process of Formation of Article 18 of the Basic Law of the HKSAR and Its Normative Content" (2020) 1 *Faxue Pinglun* [Law Review] 14.
3. *The Draft Basic Law of the Hong Kong Special Administrative Region of the People's Republic of China (for Solicitation of Opinions)* (Secretariat of the Basic Law Consultative Committee, April 1988).

Upon completion of the consultation exercise, the draft was fairly extensively revised; the second draft was adopted by the eighth plenary session of the BLDC in January 1989 and then published for a second round of consultation.[4] Article 18 of the second draft introduced a new mechanism of listing applicable "national laws" in Annex III to the BL. Such national laws were limited to those relating to defence, foreign affairs, and other matters not within the autonomy of the HKSAR. The revised Article 23 required the HKSAR to legislate to prohibit treason, secession, sedition, and theft of state secrets.

In the final version of Article 18 of the BL adopted by the NPC in April 1990, the scope of subject matters dealt with by national laws applicable to the HKSAR remains the same as that defined in the second draft. In the final version of Article 23 (BL23), acts to be prohibited include not only treason, secession, sedition, and theft of state secrets but also subversion (a word that had appeared before in the first draft of the BL), foreign political organisations' activities in the HKSAR, and ties between local and foreign political organisations.

It may therefore be seen that two policies relevant to our present study were developed in the course of the drafting of the BL. First, one of the sources of HKSAR law should be national laws (or "laws made by the NPC or NPCSC"—an expression used in an earlier draft of Article 18) that concern defence, foreign affairs, and other matters outside the autonomy of the HKSAR (which probably include "national unity and territorial integrity"—an expression used in an earlier draft of Article 18). Secondly, the HKSAR should discharge a constitutional duty to legislate to protect national unity and security and to prevent subversion of the regime in the Mainland. In a footnote to an earlier draft of BL23,[5] it was pointed out that the existing Crimes Ordinance (Cap 200) contained provisions on matters such as treason against Britain, but these provisions would not be applicable after 1997; hence the need to have new laws on national unity and security in the HKSAR. It is also noteworthy that at the time the BL was drafted, the mainland law on matters of national security took the form of the criminal law on "counter-revolutionary offences".[6] "Offences against national security" did not exist then; the concept of such offences was only introduced in 1997 when a new Criminal Code of the People's Republic of China was enacted. It was obvious that the concept of counter-revolutionary offences, which was a uniquely socialist legal concept, was not appropriate for the

---

4. *The Basic Law of the Hong Kong Special Administrative Region of the People's Republic of China (Draft)* (Secretariat of the Consultative Committee for the Basic Law, February 1989).
5. *Documents of the Fourth Plenary Sessions of the HKSAR Basic Law Drafting Committee of the PRC* (n 1 above), note to draft Article 12 of Chapter 2 (relationship between the Central Authorities and the HKSAR) of the Basic Law.
6. *See* Chapter 1 (counter-revolutionary crimes) (Art 90–104) of the PRC Criminal Code enacted in 1979. In the new Criminal Code enacted in 1997, this chapter was replaced by a new chapter on "crimes endangering national security"; the concept of counter-revolutionary crimes was thus removed from the Criminal Code.

HKSAR. Hence, there was no question of applying existing mainland Chinese law on this matter to the HKSAR.

We now turn to post-1997 developments. The failed attempt to legislate to implement BL23 in 2002–2003 was well known. Although it is widely believed that the resignation of Chief Executive (CE) Tung Cheehwa in early 2005 was largely a result of the BL23 episode, his successor, Donald Tsang, elected in 2005 for the remainder of Tung's term and re-elected in 2007 to serve a full five-year term, did not make any attempt to reintroduce a BL23 Bill. Instead, he prioritised the project of political reform towards the goals of universal suffrage for the election of the CE and the whole of the Legislative Council (LegCo). It is noteworthy that during the Tsang era the Central Authorities were willing to let the HKSAR move forward in the domain of political reform and democratisation without requiring or insisting that it should first fulfil its constitutional duty to implement BL23.

If no BL23 Bill was put forward during the Tsang era because of a lack of will, the lack of progress in this regard when Leung Chun-ying was the CE (2012–2017) was due to sociopolitical circumstances beyond the CE's control. Soon after Leung took office as CE, he was confronted by a social movement against the proposed "national education" curriculum in schools, which ultimately led to the curriculum reform being abandoned. As the timetable (set by the NPCSC in 2007)[7] for universal suffrage in the election of the CE stipulated 2017 as the target date, the "Occupy Central" movement unfolded in 2013 to press for "genuine universal suffrage", culminating in the actual occupation of Admiralty and other districts in autumn 2014. What opposition politicians condemned as a "fake universal suffrage" proposal was vetoed by LegCo in 2015.[8] The LegCo election of 2016 saw the rise of "localist" political forces. As a result of court proceedings and the NPCSC's interpretation of Article 104 of the BL issued in late 2016, six legislators in the "localist" and "pan-democrat" camps were disqualified for failing to comply with the oath-taking requirement in the BL.[9] With all these dramatic developments occurring, Leung was not able to devote much attention to the issue of BL23 during his term as CE.

When Carrie Lam campaigned for election as CE in 2017, her platform emphasised issues of economy and people's livelihood; she admitted that BL23 was not a priority for her. For many years, the HKSAR government's official stance was that the HKSAR had the constitutional duty to implement BL23, but the government

7. *Decision of the NPCSC on Issues Relating to the Methods for Selecting the Chief Executive of the HKSAR and for Forming the Legislative Council of the HKSAR in the Year 2012 and on Issues Relating to Universal Suffrage*, available at https://www.legco.gov.hk/yr07-08/english/panels/ca/papers/ca0121-ppr071229-e.pdf.
8. *See* Albert Chen, "The Law and Politics of the Struggle for Universal Suffrage in Hong Kong, 2013–15" (2016) 3 *Asian Journal of Law and Society* 189.
9. *See* Johannes Chan, "A Storm of Unprecedented Ferocity" (2018) 16(2) *International Journal of Constitutional Law* 373.

did not have any timetable yet on this matter. This position was reiterated by Carrie Lam in her speech at the "National Security Day" seminar on 15 April 2019.[10] Instead of addressing the issue of Article 23 legislation, Lam's attention was diverted to the issue of extradition law by the Chan Tong-kai incident.[11]

In 2019, a political storm in Hong Kong was generated by resistance to the creation of an institutional channel of extradition of Hongkongers to the Mainland. The anti-extradition movement resulted in the most severe and prolonged civil unrest in the history of the HKSAR,[12] unparalleled in the history of Hong Kong itself except possibly the riots of 1967. The intensity and scale of both peaceful and violent protests and their persistence for months, despite Lam's decision to shelve the Extradition Bill and subsequently to withdraw the Bill, revealed the depth and breadth of discontent in Hong Kong society with not only the Carrie Lam administration and the police action in quelling the riots but also the political and constitutional arrangement of OCTS itself. The anti-government and anti-China sentiments expressed by protesters and the violence they resorted to, as well as the social movement to enlist foreign governments to put pressure on the Hong Kong and Chinese governments to accede to the protesters' "five principal demands", apparently convinced the Chinese authorities that decisive actions were required to quell the unrest and to fundamentally reverse these political trends in Hong Kong.

When it was announced in May 2020—to the surprise of the Hong Kong and international community—that the NPC was going to make a decision on national security in Hong Kong, it was disclosed that the Chinese authorities had already decided at the fourth plenary session of the Nineteenth Central Committee of the Chinese Community Party (CCP) in November 2019 to take direct actions to safeguard national security in the HKSAR.[13] It was subsequently also disclosed that the Chinese authorities had considered several alternative courses of action for the purpose of achieving this objective.[14] It was eventually decided to adopt the "two-stage approach" of the NPC decision followed by the NPCSC's enactment of a national security law for Hong Kong.

---

10. For the full Chinese text of the speech, *see* "Hong Kong Should Have the Obligation to Protect National Security—Full Script of Hong Kong Chief Executive Carrie Lam's Speech on 2019 National Security Day in Hong Kong Seminar", *Wen Wei Po*, 16 April 2019, p A12 (in Chinese).
11. *See* Albert Chen, "A Perfect Storm: Hong Kong-Mainland Rendition of Fugitive Offenders" (2019) 49 *Hong Kong Law Journal* 419.
12. *See* generally Z. Ibrahim and J. Lam (eds), *Rebel City: Hong Kong's Year of Water and Fire* (Singapore: World Scientific, 2020); Sonny Lo, Steven Hung, and Jeff Loo, *The Dynamics of Peaceful and Violent Protests in Hong Kong: The Anti-extradition Movement* (London: Palgrave Macmillan, 2021).
13. "*Wangchen Zuo Guanyu 'Quanguo Remin Daibiao Dahui Guanyu Jianli Jianquan Xianggang Tebiexingzhengqu Weihu Guojia Anquan de Falu Zhidu he Zhixing Jizhi de Jueding (Caoan)' de Shuoming*" [Wang Chen explains the bill for decision on establishing and improving the legal system and enforcement mechanisms for the HKSAR to safeguard national security], *Xinhua News*, 22 May 2020, available at www.xinhuanet.com/politics/2020-05/22/c_1126019468.htm.
14. *Ibid.*

Although there was no official explanation of why this two-stage approach was chosen in preference to the other options, we may seek to understand the rationale or considerations behind this approach as follows. The original design of the BL was such that the HKSAR should enact laws to protect national security under BL23. However, the reality was that 23 years after the handover the HKSAR had not yet discharged this constitutional duty. The circumstances revealed by the anti-extradition movement were such that there was now an urgent need to plug this legislative loophole and to put in place a set of laws on matters of national security such as secession and subversion.

Yet the sociopolitical situation in Hong Kong was such that it was now practically and politically impossible to get a BL23 Bill through LegCo. The resistance to any such legislative exercise would not be less than, but would probably even be stronger than, the widespread and violent resistance to the Extradition Bill. Indeed, when the proposed decision of the NPC on national security in the HKSAR was announced in May 2020, Carrie Lam publicly admitted that the HKSAR was not in a position to enact a BL23 law in the present circumstances.

The situation was therefore as follows. The Central Authorities had not instructed previous CEs to resurrect the BL23 exercise, probably because it was not perceived that there was an urgent need for a BL23 law to be enacted. The Central Authorities were willing to leave the timing of the BL23 exercise to the discretion of the CE. Apparently, this was still the case at the time when Carrie Lam assumed office. But then the situation changed drastically during the anti-extradition movement. From the perspective of the Central Authorities, there was now an urgent need to put in place a set of national security laws and an effective enforcement machinery for them. However, and ironically, the very circumstances that necessitated the national security laws had made it difficult for such laws to be pushed through LegCo in the midst of anticipated opposition in society. This explains why the Central Authorities considered that their direct intervention was the only viable option.

As I have explained elsewhere, the power to make national security laws applicable to the HKSAR is a concurrent power of the Central Authorities and the HKSAR rather than an exclusive power of the HKSAR.[15] It may not, strictly speaking, be necessary for the Central Authorities to adopt the two-stage approach. A single step of the application by the NPCSC of a national security law to the HKSAR under BL18 would suffice.[16] The two-stage approach involves the making of a decision by the NPC that sets out some basic principles and then authorises the NPCSC to make a national security law for the HKSAR. The adoption of this approach may perhaps be understood as follows. The NPC is the supreme organ of state power in the PRC.

---

15. Albert Chen, "Constitutional Controversies in the Aftermath of the Anti-extradition Movement of 2019" (2020) 50 *Hong Kong Law Journal* 609.
16. *Ibid.*, pp 625–627.

It has the highest political and legal standing and speaks in a more authoritative voice than the NPCSC. The NPC has never acted with regard to the HKSAR since April 1990 when the NPC enacted the BL. The making of a decision on matters of national security in the HKSAR by the NPC itself is a solemn declaration that the content of the decision is of the highest possible legal and political authority within the PRC system. It removes any possible doubt from a legal or political standpoint regarding the constitutional and legal basis of a national security law made by the NPCSC and applied to the HKSAR under BL18.

The preamble of the NPC Decision refers to both Articles 31 and 62 of the PRC Constitution. Article 31 is the article that provides for the existence of SARs and enables the NPC to decide on the systems to be practised in an SAR. The NPC Decision may therefore be regarded as an act by the NPC to supplement the BL previously made by the NPC itself in response to the changing circumstances of Hong Kong. For example, the Decision expressly provides for the possibility of the establishment in the HKSAR by the Central Authorities of an organ specialising in national security protection in Hong Kong. This provides a firmer legal basis for such an organ and its activities than if the organ were established merely by a law made by the NPCSC without direct authorisation by the NPC itself.

II. The NSL and Chinese Law

The PRC Criminal Code promulgated in 1997 contains a chapter—actually the first chapter among many chapters on substantive offences—on crimes against national security. In the Xi Jinping era, a very broad conception of national security and national security laws has been developed.[17] In theory, the Central Authorities could have chosen to apply some of these laws directly to the HKSAR under BL18. Fortunately—from the perspective of Hong Kong—the Central Authorities have not done so but have chosen to introduce a national security law tailor-made for Hong Kong that is of limited scope or coverage. The drafting of the NSL drew mainly on the relevant mainland law rather than Hong Kong law or the common law. The NSL is significantly different from both the BL23 Bill in 2003 and the National Security Law enacted by Macau's legislature in 2009. In this part of this chapter, we will demonstrate how the NSL can be understood as a product of the mainland legal system but also contains some provisions specially tailored for the HKSAR and its

17. The concept of national security embraces not only the security of the regime, national unity, and territorial integrity but also matters of economy, technology, information, society, culture, and the environment. Laws on national security include not only the National Security Law but also other laws, such as the Anti-Espionage Law, National Intelligence Law, Anti-Terrorism Law, National Defence Law, Anti-Secession Law, Law on Martial Law, Internet Security Law, Biological Security Law, etc. *See* generally Qiao Xiaoyang (ed), *Zhonghua Renmin Gongheguo Guojia Anquan Fa Shiyi* [Commentary on the PRC National Security Law] (Beijing: Law Press, 2016); Zheng Shuna (ed), *Zhonghua Renmin Gongheguo Guojia Anquan Fa Jiedu* [Understanding the PRC National Security Law] (Beijing: China Legal System Press, 2016).

circumstances, particularly those that emerged during the anti-extradition movement of 2019.

The scope of the offences to be covered by the NSL was specified in the NPC Decision. There were to be four categories of offences: secession, subversion against the regime, terrorism, and foreign interference with HKSAR affairs. These four categories overlap with but do not directly correspond to the seven kinds of acts to be prohibited under BL23. The NPC Decision expressly provides that the HKSAR should as soon as possible complete the task of legislating to protect national security as required by the BL. Official comments have confirmed that the HKSAR still has to legislate to fulfil the requirements of BL23 despite the enactment of the NSL.[18]

The relationship between BL23 and the NSL may perhaps be understood as follows. The NPC Decision authorised and required the NPCSC to legislate on four types of matters pertaining to national security that needed to be more urgently dealt with given the circumstances prevailing in Hong Kong. As for matters in BL23 that have not been covered by the NSL, the HKSAR still has the constitutional duty to legislate on them.

As regards the four categories of offences covered by the NSL, only two—secession and subversion—correspond to subjects covered by BL23. As far as subversion is concerned, the NSL deals with subversion against the regime, which is broader than subversion against the Central People's Government under BL23. As indicated by Article 22 of the NSL, subversion against the regime includes subversion of the local SAR government.

As regards terrorism, this is not covered by BL23 at all. This subject was included in the NSL probably because some of the activities that occurred during the anti-extradition movement could be considered terrorist attacks in the sense that they were violent acts designed to intimidate the government and members of the public and to force the government to accede to the protesters' demands.

As regards foreign interference in Hong Kong affairs, this overlaps with but is broader than the provision in BL23 prohibiting foreign political organisations from engaging in political activities in the HKSAR and prohibiting ties between Hong Kong and foreign political organisations. The inclusion in the NPC Decision of the prohibition of foreign interference in Hong Kong affairs can probably be explained by the fact that the anti-extradition movement was perceived by the Central Authorities as having the flavour of a "colour revolution" (aimed at subversion of the regime) that was supported by foreign political forces.[19] However, in the NSL that

18. "*Guowuyuan Xinwenban Jiu Xianggang Tebie Xingzhengqu Weihu Guojia Anquan Fa Youguan Qingkuang Juxing Fabuhui*" [State Council Information Office holds press conference on the law of the PRC on safeguarding national security in the HKSAR], 1 July 2020, available at http://www.gov.cn/xinwen/2020-07/01/content_5523217.htm.

19. "*Gangaoban Jiu Xianggang Jushi Da Jizhe Wen*" [Hong Kong and Macau Affairs Office speaks to press on Hong Kong situation], *Chinese Review News*, 3 September 2019, available at http://hk.crntt.com/doc/1055/3/1/0/105531031.html?coluid=93&kindid=10095&docid=105531031.

was eventually enacted, the concept of foreign interference in Hong Kong affairs was replaced by that of collusion with foreign forces to endanger national security, which is probably a narrower concept.

(a) Secession (NSL, Articles 20 and 21)

In the Chinese Criminal Code (CCC), "secession" and "incitement of secession" are both dealt with in Article 103, which is the second article of Chapter 1 (offences against national security) of Part II ("special provisions", as distinguished from the "general provisions" in Part I) of the Code. The first article of Chapter 1—Article 102—concerns collusion with foreign states or foreigners to endanger the sovereignty, territorial integrity, and security of the PRC (the offence in Article 102 may be translated as treason).[20]

In the NSL, Part 1 of Chapter 3 (offences and penalties) consists of two articles: Article 20 (secession) and Article 21 (incitement of secession, assisting in, abetting secession, etc). On the basis of a textual comparison of Article 103 of the CCC and Articles 20 and 21 of the NSL, and taking into account published commentaries on Article 103, the following observations may be made.

The core concepts and terms used in Articles 20 and 21 can be traced back to Article 103. Generally speaking, the two NSL Articles are expressed in more detailed language than Article 103. Also, part of the content of Article 20 is not covered by Article 103; Article 20 of the NSL may therefore be said to have a broader coverage (in terms of acts prohibited and punishable by the law) than Article 103 of the CCC.

Article 20 refers to "organising, planning, implementing [committing] or participating in implementing" activities that "split the nation" or "damage national unity". These words, with the exception of "participating in implementing", can also be found in Article 103. However, Article 20 is more detailed than Article 103 in that it elaborates the meaning of secession by specifying three kinds of circumstances: (1) separating the HKSAR or any other part of the PRC from the PRC; (2) altering by unlawful means the legal status of the HKSAR or any other part of the PRC; and (3) surrendering the HKSAR or any other part of the PRC to a foreign country. It seems that (1) and (3) are implicit in Article 103, while (2) is a new formulation that probably goes beyond what is already in Article 103 of the CCC.

Whereas (1) and (3) refer to the withdrawal of a piece of geographical territory from the PRC, (2) does not refer to territorial secession but to a change in the legal status of the HKSAR or any other part of China. Thus, an attempt to alter by "unlawful means" the status of the HKSAR as a SAR and give it a different constitutional status—even if still as a region within the PRC—may be covered by Article 20.

---

20. *See* Wang Aili (ed), *Zhonghua renmin gongheguo xingfa jiedu* [Understanding the PRC Criminal Law] (Beijing: China Legal System Press, 5th edn, 2018), p 159.

It is noteworthy that the penalty provision (which prescribes three penalty ranges depending on the circumstances) in the last paragraph of Article 20 is identical to that in Article 103. The terms used to express the penalty are those applicable in the PRC legal system rather than those used in Hong Kong. There is another provision in the NSL—Article 64—that provides for how these mainland-style penalties are to be "converted" into modes of punishment under Hong Kong's legal system.

Article 103(2) of the CCC provides for the offence of incitement of secession, while Article 21 of the NSL deals with incitement as well as "assisting in, abetting or providing pecuniary or other financial assistance or property for the commission by other persons of" an Article 20 offence. The latter activities, though not expressly covered by Article 103(2), would also be punishable under the CCC as Chinese criminal law (like Hong Kong or English law) also provides for jointly committed offences and accomplice liability.[21] As far as financial assistance is concerned, this is covered by Article 107 of the CCC.

As Articles 20 and 21 of the NSL were partly derived from and modelled on Article 103 of the CCC, published commentaries and case law on Article 103 may be relevant to our understanding of these NSL Articles.[22] Commentaries have pointed out that whereas incitement to secession under Article 103(2) may be committed by a lone person (inciting one or more other persons), secession under Article 103(1) is usually committed by a group of persons led by persons in some positions of importance or influence or by ethnic nationalists.[23] "Organising" means recruiting people and organising them into a group with a common purpose. "Planning" means developing plans of actions for the purpose of achieving the objective. "Implementing" refers to actually carrying out acts that have been planned. Thus, the three words refer to different stages in the execution of the criminal activities concerned.[24] It has also been pointed out that offences under Article 103 may be committed even if the harmful consequence concerned has not materialised.[25] Thus, secession can be committed even if there is no actual splitting up of the nation; incitement to secession can be committed even if the persons incited are not persuaded to believe in the content of the incitement or do not commit the act incited.

---

21. *See* PRC Criminal Code (1997), Art 25–29.
22. For commentaries, *see* Wang, n 20 above, pp 161–163; Lang Sheng (ed), *Zhonghua Renmin Gongheguo Xingfa Shiyi* [Commentary on the PRC Criminal Law] (Beijing: Law Press, 6th edn, 2015), pp 116–117; Zhang Jun (ed), *Xingfa (fenze) JI Peitao Guiding Xinshi Xinjie (shang)* [Criminal Law (Specific Provisions) and Related Provisions (Part I)] (Beijing: People's Court Press, 2nd edn, 2011), pp 21–24.
23. Wang, n 20 above, p 162; Lang, n 22 above, p 116; Zhang, n 22 above, pp 21–23.
24. Wang, n 20 above, p 162; Lang, n 22 above, p 117; Zhang, n 22 above, p 21.
25. Zhang, n 22 above, pp 21–22.

There are some reported cases in mainland courts of convictions under Article 103, mainly for incitement and sometimes for secession itself.[26] One of the most publicised cases is that of 伊力哈木・土赫提 (Ilham Tohti), lecturer at the Central Minzu University in Beijing and organiser of the "Uyghur Online" website, who was convicted of secession in 2014 and sentenced to life imprisonment.[27] Seven students at this university were also convicted for participating in secessionist activities and sentenced to three to eight years' imprisonment.[28] Most of the other reported cases were in the context of alleged separatists in Xinjiang and Tibet. Mere private communications of materials considered "sensitive" in such a context may amount to incitement to secession. The mainland case law is unlikely to be of much reference value in Hong Kong, since the provisions in the NSL on secession are more detailed in defining the elements of the offence, and Hong Kong courts may take into account human rights standards (as set out in the International Covenant on Civil and Political Rights) in interpreting the nature and scope of the offence.[29]

In particular, the offence under Article 21 of the NSL is more precisely defined and is probably narrower than the corresponding offence under Article 103(2) of the CCC. Whereas the latter refers generally to "inciting secession and damage to national unity", Article 21 refers to "inciting the commission of an offense under Article 20"; Article 20 refers to "organizing, planning, implementing or participating in implementing" the relevant activities with the requisite intention.[30]

(b) Subversion (NSL, Articles 22 and 23)

The internal structures of Articles 22 and 23 of the NSL are similar to those of Articles 20 and 21 respectively. And the relationship between Articles 22 and 23 of the NSL and Article 105 of the CCC is similar to that between Articles 20 and 21 of the NSL and Article 103 of the CCC. The basic concepts and terms used in Articles 22 and 23 are derived from Article 105, but Articles 22 and 23 contain more detailed

---

26. I am grateful to Adrienne Lam, PhD student at the Faculty of Law, University of Hong Kong, for sharing with me relevant materials on secession cases in the PRC which will form part of her doctoral dissertation on issues of secession in Hong Kong.
27. In 2019, the EU Parliament awarded the Sakharov Prize to Tohti. *See* "Sakharov Prize: Jailed Uighur Academic Ilham Tohti Wins Award", *BBC*, 24 October 2019, available at https://www.bbc.com/news/world-asia-china-50166713.
28. *See* generally information on the Ilham Tohti case at www.pkulaw.com.
29. Art 4 and 5 of the NSL expressly give recognition to principles of human rights protection and Rule of Law. The Court of Final Appeal in *HKSAR v Lai Chee Ying* [2021] 1 HKC 344, para 41 held as follows: "NSL 4 and NSL 5 . . . which emphasi[z]e protection and respect for human rights and adherence to rule of law values while safeguarding national security, are also centrally important to the interpretation of the NSL generally."
30. It is noteworthy in this regard that in *HKSAR v Tong Ying Kit* [2021] HKCFI 2200—the first NSL case that has been tried and decided by the court, the Court of First Instance expansively interpreted the incitement provision in Article 21; such interpretation renders it not significantly different from Article 103(2) of the CCC. See also n 72 below.

language and have a broader coverage than Article 105, except with regard to one element which makes the relevant NSL offences narrower than those under Article 105. As in the case of penalties for secession, the relevant penalty provisions for subversion in the NSL and the CCC are also the same.

Article 105(1) provides for the offence of "organizing, planning, and implementing subversion of the State's regime or the overthrow of the socialist system". The related offence of incitement to subversion is provided for in Article 105(2), which refers to inciting subversion of the regime or the overthrow of the socialist system "by spreading rumours, defamation or other means".

These provisions may be compared with Articles 22 and 23. Like Article 105, Article 22 also refers to "organising, planning, implementing" particular activities (and adds "participating in implementing" the activities), but is narrower than Article 105 insofar as it provides that the relevant activities must involve the use of "force, threat of force or other unlawful means". The relevant activities must be intended to subvert the regime by one of four means: (1) overthrowing or undermining the basic system of the PRC established by its Constitution; (2) overthrowing an organ of the regime of the Central Authorities or an organ of the HKSAR political system; (3) interfering with, obstructing or undermining the discharge of functions and duties in accordance with law by an organ of the regime of the Central Authorities or an organ of the HKSAR political system; or (4) attacking or damaging the premises and facilities of an organ of the HKSAR political system so as to render it incapable of discharging its normal functions and duties.

Among these four elements, elements one and two are probably implicit in Article 105. Insofar as elements three and four are probably not covered by Article 105, the subversion offence under Article 22 has a broader coverage than Article 105. However, unlike Article 105, the offence under Article 22 is limited to circumstances involving the use of "force, threat of force or other unlawful means". This requirement does not exist in Article 105.[31] Therefore, Article 22 is narrower than Article 105 as regards situations covered by elements one and two above.

This narrower scope of Article 105 is highly significant and reveals a legislative intent that the criteria for the criminalisation of subversion in the HKSAR under OCTS need not be as strict (and entail as broad a coverage) as those applicable in the Mainland. In mainland China, the offence of subversion and the related offence of incitement of subversion (both provided for in Article 105) have been used to prosecute critics of the regime,[32] advocates of political reform, and democratisation

31. Published commentaries on Art 105 point out that where the subversion involves an armed rebellion or armed riot, it will be dealt with under Art 104 (on organising, planning, or implementing an armed rebellion or armed riot). *See* Wang, n 20 above, p 166. It would appear that the offences under both Art 104 and 105 of the CCC are in the case of Hong Kong covered by Art 22 of the NSL.

32. It has been pointed out that Art 105 involves "crimes of expression" or "speech crimes". *See* Eva Pils, *Human Rights in China* (Cambridge: Polity Press, 2018), pp 82–83. Teng Biao, a legal scholar and human rights advocate, wrote that those "convicted of crimes of 'subverting state power' are 'political

by peaceful means[33] as well as *weiquan*—rights-defence—lawyers (also known as human rights lawyers) who mobilised public criticism and protests against alleged abuse of power by the police,[34] NGO activists who fought for the rights of the underprivileged,[35] and "underground church" leaders.[36]

It is noteworthy that the limitation of relevant proscribed activities in Article 22 of the NSL to those involving "force, threat of force or other unlawful means" does not exist in Article 20 with regard to the secession offence. This shows that the legislative intent behind the NSL was to cast a wider criminalising net with regard to secession than subversion. As far as the latter is concerned, "organising, planning, implementing or participating in implementing" potentially subversive activities is not criminalised so long as the activities concerned do not involve "force, threat of

prisoners—prisoners of conscience"". *See* Teng Biao, "The Political Meaning of the Crime of Subverting State Power", in Jean-Philippe Beja, Fu Hualing, and Eva Pils (eds), *Liu Xiaobo, Charter 08 and the Challenges of Political Reform in China* (Hong Kong: Hong Kong University Press, 2012), p 271 at p 278. Another scholar pointed out that "[i]n order to understand the nature of these prohibitions against subversion, one must recognize their roots in earlier laws covering 'counter-revolutionary' crime." *See* Joshua Rosenzweig, "The Sky Is Falling: Inciting Subversion and the Defense of Liu Xiaobo", in Jean-Philippe Beja, Fu Hualing, and Eva Pils (eds), *Liu Xiaobo, Charter 08 and the Challenges of Political Reform in China* (Hong Kong: Hong Kong University Press, 2012), p 31 at p 32. "Any word or act opposing the Communist Party or the government, opposing the official ideology, or opposing individual leaders' words or acts could all lead to a person being branded a 'counter-revolutionary'". *See* Teng Biao, "The Political Meaning of the Crime of Subverting State Power", in Jean-Philippe Beja, Fu Hualing, and Eva Pils (eds), *Liu Xiaobo, Charter 08 and the Challenges of Political Reform in China* (Hong Kong: Hong Kong University Press, 2012), p 271 at p 273.

33. E.g. Liu Xiaobo (convicted for incitement of subversion in 2009 and sentenced to eleven years' imprisonment; he was awarded a Nobel Peace Prize in 2010 and died in prison in 2017); Tan Zuoren (who advocated, among other causes, commemoration of the June 4th events; convicted for incitement of subversion in 2009 and sentenced to five years' imprisonment); Lee Mingcheh (a philosophy scholar in Taiwan arrested while visiting the Mainland; convicted of subversion in 2017 and sentenced to five years' imprisonment).

34. E.g. lawyers arrested during the "709 Crackdown" on 9 July 2015 and subsequently convicted of subversion (Zhou Shifeng, Hu Shigen, Zhai Yanmin, and Guo Hongguo were all convicted in 2016. Zhou and Hu were sentenced to seven years' imprisonment, whereas Zhai and Guo were given suspended sentences; Wu Gan was convicted in 2017 and sentenced to eight years' imprisonment; Wang Quanzhang was convicted in 2018 and sentenced to four-and-a-half years' imprisonment) or incitement of subversion (Jiang Tianyong was convicted in 2017 and sentenced to two years' imprisonment; Xie Yang was convicted in 2017 and exempted from punishment). Other well-known cases of human rights lawyers being convicted of incitement to subversion include Gao Zhisheng (sentenced to three years' imprisonment in 2011), Tang Jingling (convicted in 2016 and sentenced to five years' imprisonment), and most recently Yu Wensheng (convicted in 2020 and sentenced to four years' imprisonment). See report of China Human Rights Lawyers Concern Group, available at business-humanrights.org/en/.

35. E.g. the case of the NGO known as "Changsha Funeng" (長沙富能) in which Cheng Yuan, Liu Dazhi, and Wu Gejianxiong were convicted for subversion and sentenced to imprisonment in 2021. I am grateful to my colleague Dr Zhu Han for drawing my attention to this case. *See* Han Zhu and Lu Jun, "The Crackdown on Rights-Advocacy NGOs in Xi's China", *Journal of Contemporary China* (forthcoming).

36. E.g. Wang Yi, founder and leader of the Qiuyu church in Chengdu, was convicted of incitement of subversion in 2019 and sentenced to nine years' imprisonment.

force or other unlawful means". The extent to which this expression limits the scope of Article 22 would depend crucially on whether "other unlawful means" is to be narrowly or broadly interpreted.[37]

Elements three and four mentioned above, which make the offence under Article 22 broader than the subversion offence under Article 105, were obviously included in Article 22 with a view to deterring acts like those that occurred in Hong Kong during the anti-extradition movement, such as protesters breaking into LegCo on 1 July 2019 and destroying many of its facilities, or large crowds of people on different dates during 2019 besieging the LegCo building, buildings which house offices of the HKSAR government, police stations, and even the building of the Liaison Office of the Central People's Government in the HKSAR. Whether Article 22(3) may be used to convict opposition politicians who organised or ran as candidates in the unofficial "primary election" in July 2019 to select candidates for the September 2019 election is more arguable.[38] As they had threatened to veto the government's budget proposal in LegCo (so as to force the CE to dissolve LegCo and eventually to resign) if the government did not accede to the "five principal demands" of the anti-extradition movement, they were charged with conspiracy to commit an offence under Article 22(3).[39] Whether any prosecution against them would succeed depends crucially on what evidence as to "unlawful means" is produced at trial, and how "unlawful means" is to be interpreted by the court.[40]

37. *See* the discussion in the next paragraph of the case of the "primary election" in July 2019.

38. Fifty-three persons were arrested on 6 January 2021 on the ground of suspected violation of Art 22 of the NSL in organising the "primary election". *See* Brian Wong, "All 53 Hong Kong Opposition Figures Arrested under National Security Law Released, Except Former Lawmaker Who Failed to Surrender BN(O) Passport", *South China Morning Post*, 8 January 2021, available at https://www.scmp.com/news/hong-kong/law-and-crime/article/3116892/former-hong-kong-lawmaker-returned-jail-after-failing; Lilian Cheng and Tony Cheung, "Hong Kong National Security Law: Four Big Questions Raised by Mass Arrests of 53 Opposition Figures", *South China Morning Post*, 9 January 2021, available at https://www.scmp.com/news/hong-kong/politics/article/3117010/hong-kong-national-security-law-four-big-questions-raised. Among the 53 persons, 47 were eventually charged with conspiracy to commit an offence under Art 22 (case number WKCC813/21); Natalie Wong, "Opposition Hit with Subversion Charges", *South China Morning Post*, 1 March 2021; Chris Lau and Brian Wong, "Hundreds Gather at Court as Bail Hearing Commences", *South China Morning Post*, 2 March 2021. As of mid-August 2021, 13 of the defendants had been granted bail pending trial. For the bail judgments, *see* www.judiciary.hk, cases nos. HCCP 110/21, 111/21, 112/21, . . . , 118/21, 119/21, 120/21, 126/21, 134/21, 135/21, 136/21, 137/21, 141/21, 294/21, 417/21. The trial is expected to take place in the High Court.

39. For the official position of the HKSAR government, *see* its press releases: HKSAR government, "HKSAR Government Will Not Tolerate any Offense of Subversion", 6 January 2021, available at www.info.gov.hk/gia/general/202101/06/P2021010600675.htm; HKSAR government, "S for S Speaks on Police Arrest of People on Suspicion of Subversion", 6 January 2021, available at www.info.gov.hk/gia/general/202101/06/P2021010600580.htm. The persons arrested were suspected of attempting to implement the "10-step plan for mutual destruction" (攬炒 *landchao*) proposed by former legal academic Benny Tai in an article published in *Apple Daily* on 28 April 2020: "*Zhen Lanchao Shibu, Zheshi Xianggang Xiuming*" ["真攬炒十步，這是香港宿命"] [Ten steps for the true mutual destruction, this is the fate of Hong Kong], *Apple Daily*, 28 April 2020, p A12.

40. In the absence of evidence of any criminal offence and any act attracting civil liability, the government is likely to argue that voting down the budget in LegCo irrespective of its content and with

As regards Article 23, the wording is similar to that of Article 21. Like Article 21, Article 23 is more broadly worded than its mainland counterpart in Article 105(2) as Article 23 applies not only to incitement but also to "assisting in, abetting or providing pecuniary or other financial assistance or property for" subversion.[41] However, as far as incitement is concerned, the offence under Article 23 is more precisely defined and has a narrower coverage than Article 105(2). Whereas Article 105(2) criminalises "incitement of subversion of the regime or the overthrow of the socialist system by spreading [rumors], defamation or other means", Article 23 applies only to incitement of the commission of an offence under Article 22, which requires an element of force, threat of force, or other unlawful means. Thus, if there is no incitement of the use of force, threat of force, or other unlawful means to achieve the subversive end, the offence under Article 23 cannot be established. This means that whereas in the Mainland, strong criticisms of its political system might amount to an offence under Article 105(2),[42] the same criticisms might not constitute an offence under Article 23 so long as the speech or writing concerned does not incite the commission of any offence as defined in Article 22.

As mentioned above, much depends on how "unlawful means" in Article 22 is to be interpreted. If the acts incited are to be committed in Hong Kong, there is little doubt that Hong Kong law should be used in determining what is unlawful. (It is arguable whether only the criminal law of Hong Kong is relevant in this regard, or whether a tort or other act which results in civil liability may also be considered an unlawful act for the purpose of Article 22. In the above-mentioned case of the "primary election", an issue may be whether an alleged abuse of power by legislators is an unlawful act for the purpose of Article 22.)[43] If it is intended that the acts incited are to be committed in the Mainland (even though the incitement takes place in Hong Kong), it is arguable that mainland law should be used for the purpose of determining whether an "unlawful means" is involved for the purpose of Article 23.

---

the sole purpose to bring down the government is an abuse of power akin to "misconduct in public office" and thus an "unlawful means" for the purpose of Art 22. For relevant legal discussion, *see* Tony Kwok, "NSL Arrests in the SAR Fully Supported by Law, Evidence", *China Daily (Hong Kong Edition)*, 8 January 2021, available at https://www.chinadailyasia.com/article/154353 (arguing that the proposed veto of the budget in LegCo would constitute the common law offence of "misconduct in public office"); Grenville Cross, "National Security Arrests: Criminal Justice Dominant throughout Entire Process", *DotDotNews*, 10 January 2021, available at https://english.dotdotnews.com/a/202101/10/AP5ffa7023e4b00123a56464cb.html; Henry Litton, "Mass Arrests: The Sinister Aspect of Democrats' '35-Plus' Primaries Strategy for the Legco Elections", *South China Morning Post*, 26 January 2021, available at https://www.scmp.com/comment/opinion/article/3119167/mass-arrests-sinister-aspect-democrats-35-plus-primaries-strategy. *See also* Richard Cullen, "'35-Plus' Violates the Spirit of HK Basic Law", *China Daily Global*, 23 July 2020, available at http://global.chinadaily.com.cn/a/202007/23/WS5f18e119a31083481725b78b.html .

41. In the CCC, financial assistance for secession and subversion is criminalised by Art 107.
42. *See* n 32 above and the accompanying text.
43. *See* n 40 above and the accompanying text.

(c) Terrorism (NSL, Articles 24–28)

The next few articles in the NSL deal with offences relating to terrorism. Before investigating into these articles, the mainland law relating to terrorism may first be summarised. In the CCC, offences relating to terrorism are provided for in Chapter 2 (offences against public order) of Part II of the Code, which should be read together with the Anti-Terrorism Law.

The relevant CCC provisions underwent a process of development until they took their present form in 2015. When first enacted in 1997, the CCC already contained Article 120, which criminalises the organising of, leadership of, and participation in "terrorist organizations" (which were not defined in the CCC itself). In 2001, under the third amendment to the CCC, this Article was revised to increase the penalty concerned. At the same time, Article 120(1) was introduced which criminalises financial assistance to terrorist organisations or individuals engaged in terrorist activities.

Then, in August 2015, the ninth amendment to the CCC introduced additional articles relating to terrorism or "extremism". Finally, in December 2015, the Anti-Terrorism Law (ATL) was enacted by the NPCSC. The predecessor of this law was the Decision of the NPCSC on Several Questions relating to the Strengthening of Anti-Terrorism Work promulgated in 2011.

The ATL provides definitions of terrorism, terrorist activities, terrorist organisations, terrorist personnel, and terrorist incidents. The ATL establishes a "state organ for leadership of anti-terrorism work" (SOAT).[44] The public security department (police), the national security department, and the foreign affairs department of the State Council, as well as provincial organs for leadership of anti-terrorism work, may apply to SOAT for the designation of particular groups and individuals as terrorist organisations and terrorist personnel. In the course of the trial of a criminal case, the court may make such designations.

We now turn to the provisions on terrorism in the NSL. On the basis of a textual comparison with the relevant mainland law, the following observations may be made. Article 24 of the NSL in effect creates an offence of terrorism or committing a terrorist act. It does not have a direct counterpart in mainland law. (In mainland law, terrorist acts, such as killing, bombing, arson, etc., are criminalised by laws that directly criminalise such acts rather than by anti-terrorism provisions.) However, the concepts of terrorism and terrorist used in Article 24 are based on the ATL. As regards Articles 25–27, there do exist counterparts in mainland law. Article 25 and

---

44. This is the State Council's organ entitled the 國家反恐部工作領導小組 *Guojia Fankong Bu Gongzuo Lingdao Xiaozu* [Leading group on the state's anti-terrorism work], information available at https://baike.baidu.com/item/%E5%9B%BD%E5%AE%B6%E5%8F%8D%E6%81%90%E6%80%96%E5%B7%A5%E4%BD%9C%E9%A2%86%E5%AF%BC%E5%B0%8F%E7%BB%84/13979388?fr=aladdin. There is also the Central National Security Committee established by the Third Plenum of the eighteenth CCP Central Committee in November 2013.

Article 120 of the CCC have similar coverage. So do Article 26 and Articles 120(1) and (2) of the CCC, and Article 27 and Article 120(3) of the CCC. The penalty provisions are also similar.[45]

An offence under Article 24 is committed by "organi[z]ing, planning, implementing, participating in implementing or threatening to implement" a "terrorist act" that "causes or is intended to cause grave social harm", "for the purpose of reali[z]ing one's political objectives by coercing the central or HKSAR government or an international organi[z]ation or intimidating members of the public". A "terrorist act" is one that falls within any of five specified categories.

The concept of terrorism in Article 24 is similar to, though not identical to, that in Article 3 of the ATL. Article 3(2) defines "terrorist activities" as any of five specified types of activities that are terrorist in nature. What is terrorist in nature has to be understood in light of Article 3(1), which stipulates that terrorism consists of "opinions and actions that seek to reali[z]e one's political or ideological objective by means of violence, sabotage or intimidation, causing panic in society, endangering public security, violating persons or property, or coercing state organs or international organi[z]ations".

Article 24 is mainly based on the first of the five specified types of activities in the definition of terrorist activities in Article 3(2), together with the definition of terrorism in Article 3(1). As regards the other elements of the definition of terrorist activities in Article 3(2), they are dealt with in Articles 25–27 of the NSL. The description of the concrete ingredients of different types of terrorist activities in Article 24—particularly the five limbs of terrorist activities—is more detailed than in Article 3(2). As in Article 3(1), Article 24 refers to the element of intimidation and coercion of the government or international organisations for the purpose of realising one's political objective. However, realisation of one's "ideological objective" (as distinguished from "political objectives") is mentioned only in Article 3(1) but not in Article 24. Article 3(2)(1) includes a reference to "serious damage to property", but this is not explicitly mentioned in Article 24.

As discussed in the next part of this chapter, committing a terrorist act is not in itself an offence under Hong Kong's existing law, but the act would be punishable under other laws, such as those on homicide, arson, wounding, or inflicting grievous bodily harm, etc. The position is similar under mainland law where there is also no specific offence of committing a terrorist act. By contrast, in some other jurisdictions, anti-terrorism law has included the creation of an offence of committing a terrorist act.[46]

45. Except that the most severe penalty range under Art 26 and 27 is five to ten years' imprisonment, while that under Art 120(1), (2), and (3) is imprisonment for five years or more (without any upper limit).

46. *See* e.g. s 6A of New Zealand's Terrorism Suppression Act 2002, providing as follows: "(1) A person commits an offence who engages in a terrorist act. (2) A person who commits a terrorist act is liable on conviction to imprisonment for life or a lesser term."

It may be questioned why the Central Authorities in drafting the NSL decided to go beyond the existing approach in Chinese law and to create a new offence of committing a terrorist act. This was probably due to the need to deter acts of violence like those which took place during the anti-extradition movement for the purpose of putting pressure on the government to accede to the protesters' demands. The creation of an offence of committing a terrorist act sends a clear signal to society that the kind of violence that occurred during the anti-extradition movement designed to intimidate the government and members of the public would not be tolerated in the future and would be subject to particularly heavy punishment. This, then, is probably the intended deterrent effect of Article 24. It is noteworthy that Article 24 provides that persons convicted under it will be sentenced to at least three years' imprisonment, even if no serious bodily injury, death, or significant loss of property has been caused by the terrorist act.

Article 25 criminalises the "organi[z]ing or exercising leadership of a terrorist organi[z]ation" and defines terrorist organisations as organisations that commit or intend to commit the offences specified in Article 24 or participate in or assist the commission of such offences. This definition of terrorist organisations is similar to but slightly more elaborated than that under the ATL, which defines a terrorist organisation as a group formed by three or more persons for the purpose of committing terrorist activities. However, unlike the ATL, there is no mechanism under the NSL for designation of a group of persons as a terrorist organisation by any administrative authority.

(d) Collusion with Foreign Forces to Endanger National Security (NSL, Articles 29 and 30)

In terms of drafting, Article 29 is probably the most complicated provision in the NSL. Understanding Article 29 is made difficult by its complex structure and absence of numbered subsections and paragraphs. To facilitate discussion of this Article, we can insert numbering or designations (in square brackets below; the numbers in round brackets are in the original text of Article 29) for subsections or paragraphs:

> **Article 29**
>
> [A] A person who steals, spies, obtains with payment, or unlawfully provides State secrets or intelligence concerning national security for a foreign country... shall be guilty of an offence;
>
> [B] a person who
>
> [a] requests a foreign country or an institution, . . . , or
>
> [b] conspires with a foreign country or an institution, . . . , or

[c] directly or indirectly receives instructions, control, funding or other kinds of support from a foreign country or an institution, . . . ,

to commit any of the following acts shall be guilty of an offence:

(1) waging a war against the PRC, or using or threatening to use force to seriously undermine the sovereignty, unification and territorial integrity of the PRC;

(2) seriously disrupting the formulation and implementation of laws or policies by the Government of the HKSAR or by the Central People's Government, which is likely to cause serious consequences;

(3) rigging or undermining an election in the HKSAR, which is likely to cause serious consequences;

(4) imposing sanctions or blockade, or engaging in other hostile activities against the HKSAR or the PRC; or

(5) provoking by unlawful means hatred among Hong Kong residents towards the Central People's Government or the Government of the Region, which is likely to cause serious consequences.

It may be observed that Article 29 actually creates two independent offences. The first is created by Article 29[A] and is concerned with leakage of official secrets to foreigners. The second is that covered by Article 29[B]; this offence is committed where the existence of any of [a], [b], or [c] is combined with any of (1), (2), (3), (4), or (5). In theory, this can give rise to 3x5=15 possible scenarios. In practice, as this author has written elsewhere,[47] given the language used in various limbs of Article 29[B] and considering what are natural or logical connections (between any of [a], [b], and [c] and any of (1), (2), (3), (4), and (5)), some combinations are impossible or unlikely. For example, as far as (4) (imposing a sanction, etc. on the HKSAR or the PRC) is concerned, its natural and logical combination is with [a] (requesting) or [b] (conspiring) rather than with [c] (receiving funding from or acting under the direction or control of foreigners); the criminalisation of [a]+(4) (requesting a foreign government to impose a sanction on the HKSAR or PRC—such requesting being actually committed by some Hong Kong politicians and activists during the anti-extradition movement) is the mischief that Article 29[B](4) was designed to address. The corollary is that banks that are required by foreign law (e.g. United States law) to comply with certain rules that form part of a sanction imposed by the foreign state on the HKSAR or the PRC should not incur criminal liability under Article 29[B].[48]

We now turn to study Article 29 from the perspective of Chinese law. As in the case of the previous articles, we can discern a close connection between Article 29

47. Albert Chen and Simon Young, "Liability for Imposing Sanctions under Hong Kong's National Security Law" (2020) 50 *Hong Kong Law Journal* 353.

48. *Ibid.* It may also be argued that banks in such circumstances do not have the relevant *mens rea* for the purpose of the offence.

and the existing law in the PRC. However, some of the provisions in Article 29 were apparently designed to address Hong Kong circumstances and do not have counterparts in mainland law. In particular, Article 29[A] and Article 29[B](1) correspond to existing provisions in Chinese law, while Article 29[B](2), (3), (4), and (5) are specially tailored for the HKSAR. The concept of "collusion", which is referred to in the title of Article 29 and is implicit in Article 29[B](a), (b), and (c), is a concept in Chinese law. These points will be elaborated below.

Article 29[A]: this provision creates an offence of leakage of state secrets or intelligence to foreigners. It is almost identical in wording to Article 111 of the CCC, which criminalises the supply of state secrets or intelligence to foreigners. The only main difference between the two provisions is that in Article 29[A], the reference to "state secrets or intelligence" is limited to those that "concern national security". What are "state secrets or intelligence concerning national security" are not defined in the NSL, although Article 47 provides that where an issue arises in a court case regarding whether particular materials are state secrets, the court should obtain a certificate from the CE on the issue.

What are state secrets for the purpose of Article 29[A] should probably be understood in the context of Chinese law. The main Chinese law on state secrets is the Law on Safeguarding State Secrets enacted by the NPCSC in 1988 and amended by it in 2010.[49] Other relevant legal sources include the Interpretation of the Supreme People's Court in 2000 on Several Questions regarding the Concrete Application of the Law in the Adjudication of Cases concerning Theft, Spying, and Purchase of and Unlawfully Providing State Secrets and Intelligence for Foreigners,[50] and the Implementing Rules enacted in 2014 for the Law on Safeguarding State Secrets.

Article 29[B]: Article 29 is entitled "collusion with a foreign country or with external elements to endanger national security", but the word "collusion" does not appear in the text of Article 29 itself. However, as explained below, the concept of "collusion" in Chinese law is reflected in the language of Article 29[B][b] and [c]. The word 勾結 *goujie*—collusion—is used in Article 102—the first article in Chapter 1 (offences against national security) of Part II of the CCC.

---

49. Art 9 of this Law provides a definition of state secrets consisting of seven categories. Art 10 provides for a three-tier classification of state secrets. Art 17 provides for the stamping of signs on documents to show that they are state secrets. *See* generally Fu Hualing, "The Secrets about State Secrets: The Burden of Over-Classification" (2019) 14(2) *Journal of Comparative Law* 249.

50. The Chinese title of this Interpretation is 最高人民法院關於審理為境外竊取、刺探、收買、非法提供國家秘密、情報案件具體應用法律若干問題的解釋. Art 1 of this Interpretation defines the terms "state secrets" and "intelligence" that appear in Art 111 of the CCC. Art 5 provides that where the defendant knows or ought to know that a particular piece of information which is not stamped a state secret concerns national security and interest, and steals, spies on, or purchases it and/or unlawfully provides it to foreigners, Art 111 of the CCC is applicable. Art 7 provides that in the trial of a case concerning leakage of state secrets to foreigners, if a question arises as to whether a particular piece of information is a state secret or as to the degree of secrecy classification applicable to it, the matter will be determined by the relevant state organ for the work of safeguarding state secrets.

Article 102 creates the offence of collusion with a foreign state or foreign organisations or individuals to endanger the sovereignty, territorial integrity, and security of the PRC. Chinese scholars refer to this as the offence of treason.[51] The meaning of "collusion"' is not elaborated in the CCC itself but was defined in Article 7 of the Implementing Rules (enacted in 1994) of the PRC National Security Law (enacted in 1993). Article 4 of this Law provided that acts that endangered national security included specified acts committed by foreign organisations or individuals, or by persons under the direction of or receiving funding from foreign organisations or individuals, or by local organisations or individuals in collusion with foreign organisations or individuals. Article 7 of the Implementing Rules provided that such collusion refers to any of three specified situations.

In 2014, a new Anti-Espionage Law was enacted and the National Security Law (1993) was repealed, although a new National Security Law was enacted in 2015. The Implementing Rules for the old National Security Law (1993) have now been replaced by the Implementing Rules (enacted in 2017) for the new Anti-Espionage Law, but the definition of "collusion" has remained unchanged and can be found in Article 7 of the new Implementing Rules.

Article 29[B][c] of the NSL contains the wording of "acting under the direction or control of, or receiving funding or other forms of support from, foreign organi[z]ations and personnel". Such wording can be traced back to the definition of collusion in the Implementing Rules mentioned above. Article 29[B][b] refers to conspiracy between a person and a foreign state, organisation, or individual. The meaning of "conspiracy" is similar to elements of the definition of collusion in the Implementing Rules, such as "planning together and jointly committing" an act against national security. It may therefore be said that Article 29[B][b] and [c] are both based on the concept of collusion in mainland law.

When Article 29[B][b] or [c] is combined with paragraph (1) (waging war, etc.), the offence produced is akin to that of treason under Article 102 of the CCC as discussed above. This NSL offence is narrower than Article 102, as the latter refers to collusion with foreign states and forces to "endanger the sovereignty, territorial integrity and security of the PRC", while the NSL offence only covers collusion with foreigners to "wage war against the PRC", or to "use force or threat of force to seriously undermine the sovereignty, unity and territorial integrity of the PRC".

The more original provisions in Article 29 that do not have counterparts in mainland law and were probably specially drafted to deal with Hong Kong's circumstances are Article 29[B][a] (requesting) and Article 29[B](2) (serious obstruction of the enactment or enforcement of law by the HKSAR government or the Central Government), (3) (manipulating or undermining an election), (4) (imposing sanctions on the HKSAR or PRC), and (5) (using unlawful means to provoke hatred against the Central Government or the HKSAR government). The term and

51. *See* n 20 above.

concept of "requesting" is arguably a natural extension of the concept of "collusion" as discussed above. The "requesting" limb in Article 29[B][a] refers to requesting a foreign state or institution to commit one of the specified acts against China's national security. Thus, among the acts specified in Article 29[B](1), (2), (3), (4), and (5), "requesting" would be more relevant to (1) (requesting foreign invasion of the PRC) and (4) (requesting a foreign state to impose sanctions on the PRC or the HKSAR). The legislative intent behind adding the "requesting" limb to the concept of collusion is probably the intent to penalise Hongkongers who request or lobby foreign states to impose sanctions against the PRC or HKSAR. Such requests or lobbying did occur during the anti-extradition movement. The NSL is not retroactive and cannot be used to prosecute those who committed such acts in the past, but it will have a deterrent effect in the future.

Paragraphs (2) and (5) were probably also framed with what happened during the anti-extradition movement in mind. During the movement, riots and unlawful assemblies took place that were aimed at the obstruction of legislative and other government activities in Hong Kong. The mass media and social media were flooded with news (in many cases considered by the authorities to be fake news) promoting hatred against the Hong Kong and mainland authorities. The Beijing authorities considered that foreign forces were at work in supporting or promoting such political opposition against the HKSAR government.[52] As the objective of this part of the NSL was, in the words of the NPC Decision of May 2020, to deter and prohibit foreign interference with Hong Kong affairs, these NSL provisions were introduced to address these situations.

Foreign interference with Hong Kong politics may also take the form of giving support to local opposition forces participating in elections in Hong Kong. Article 29[B](3) was probably designed to forestall such foreign intervention in electoral politics in Hong Kong. The term and concept of "manipulating (alternatively translated as 'rigging') or undermining an election" is rather vague and how it may be interpreted remains to be seen. When the "pro-democracy" camp held its own "primary election" in July 2020 to choose candidates whom it would nominate to compete in the September 2020 LegCo election, one of the accusations was that this would amount to "manipulating or undermining" the election.[53] However, in the

---

52. Hong Kong and Macau Affairs Office speaks to press on Hong Kong situation, n 19 above.

53. *See* the press statement of the Hong Kong and Macau Affairs Office of the State Council: Hong Kong and Macau Affairs Office of the State Council, "*Juebu Rongxu Caokong Xianggang Lifahui Xuanju*" [Manipulation of Hong Kong LegCo election should not be allowed], 14 July 2020, available at www.locpg.gov.cn/jsdt/2020-07/14/c_1210702247.htm. The statement on this matter issued by the Liaison Office of the Central Government in Hong Kong on 13 July 2020 warned that the "primary election" could be manipulation of election as well as subversion under Art 22 of the NSL: Liaison Office of the Central Government, "*Yanli Qianze Fanduipai Cedong Feifa Chuxuan Pohuai Lifahui Xuanju Gongping, Juebu Rongxu Waibu Shili Caokong Xianggang de Zhengzhi Shiwu*" [We strongly condemn the opposition's organising an unlawful "primary election" that undermines a fair LegCo election; external forces must not be allowed to manipulate Hong Kong political affairs], available at www.locpg.

absence of evidence of "collusion" with foreign forces, mere "manipulation" of an election would not of itself amount to an offence under Article 29[B](5).

III. Impact on the Existing Law and Implications for the Future

The approach adopted by the NSL may be compared and contrasted with that of the BL23 Bill of 2003. The latter Bill dealt with five (treason, secession, subversion, sedition, and theft of state secrets) of the seven matters mentioned in BL23 by proposing amendments to the existing Crimes Ordinance (Cap 200) (which in colonial times already contained provisions on treason and sedition), the Societies Ordinance (Cap 151) (the proposed amendment introduced a new scheme for proscribing a local organisation that endangers national security, including one that is subordinate to an organisation in the Mainland that has been proscribed on the ground of national security), and the Official Secrets Ordinance (Cap 521). The two remaining matters (regarding foreign political organisations and their ties with local political organisations in Hong Kong) in BL23 were not dealt with in the legislative exercise in 2003, because the revised version of the Societies Ordinance introduced in 1997 already contained provisions prohibiting connections between local and foreign political organisations and empowering the government to ban a society on the ground of national security.[54]

Although the NSL overrides any existing local law in Hong Kong that is inconsistent with it,[55] it has not expressly amended any existing legislation of the HKSAR. In this respect, it is very different from the 2003 Bill. The approach of the NSL is to create a new set of legal rules that exist side by side with Hong Kong's existing law. Among the four types of offences created by it, secession, subversion, and collusion with foreign forces to endanger national security are entirely new offences grafted onto Hong Kong's legal system. As regards the anti-terrorism law in Articles 24–28 of the NSL, it has been superimposed on Hong Kong's existing anti-terrorism law.

Such law is mainly contained in the United Nations (Anti-Terrorism Measures) Ordinance (Cap 575) (UNATMO) enacted in 2002, which is supplemented by the Anti-Money Laundering and Counter-Terrorist Financing Ordinance (Cap 615) enacted in 2011. The UNATMO was introduced mainly for the purpose of implementing the United Nations Security Council's decision on 28 September 2001 regarding measures for the prevention of terrorist acts. The UNATMO provides definitions of "terrorist act", "terrorist", "terrorist associate" (which means an entity owned or controlled by a terrorist), and "terrorist property". It introduces

---

gov.cn/jsdt/2020-07/13/c_1210700891.htm. In March 2021, the organisers of and candidates for the "primary election" were charged under Art 22 (rather than Art 29) of the NSL: *see* n 38 above and the accompanying text.

54. Societies Ordinance (Cap 151), ss 2, 5A, 5D, and 8; Companies (Winding Up and Miscellaneous Provisions) Ordinance (Cap 32), ss 360B and 360C.

55. NSL, Art 62.

two "specification" mechanisms with regard to terrorists, terrorist associates, and terrorist property. It also provides for criminal prohibitions against supplying funds or weapons to, or making funds or financial services available to, terrorists and terrorist associates. The government is authorised to freeze funds suspected to be terrorist property. However, the Ordinance has not created any offence of committing a terrorist act itself.

The new NSL offence of committing a terrorist act does not overlap with the existing Hong Kong law (which does not provide for such an offence); this offence-creating provision in Article 24 can operate independently of the existing anti-terrorism law. The definition of terrorist act in the NSL overlaps with but is not identical to the definition of terrorist act in the UNATMO.[56] For example, the latter definition includes a terrorist act for the purpose of "advancing a religious cause" (in addition to "political or ideological cause"), but "religious cause" is not mentioned in the NSL. The definition in the UNATMO includes an express reference to "causing serious damage to property", but this limb is not expressly mentioned in the NSL. On the other hand, the definition in the UNATMO expressly excludes, in the context of three specified circumstances (that would otherwise amount to terrorism),[57] "the use or threat of action in the course of any advocacy, protest, dissent or industrial action", but this exclusion does not appear in the NSL.

In practice, the differing definitions of a terrorist act in the NSL and in the UNATMO are unlikely to cause problems. The NSL definition will be used in dealing with cases under Articles 24–27 of the NSL. As regards offences relating to terrorist organisations in Articles 25–26, since there is no scheme of "specifications" in the NSL that is similar to that in the UNATMO, the court will directly apply the definition of terrorist organisations in Article 25(2) of the NSL. On the other hand, any prosecutions or government actions under the UNATMO will of course be based on the relevant definitions, specifications, and provisions in that Ordinance.

Although the offence-creating provisions of the NSL form a legal regime that can operate independently of the law on other criminal offences under Hong Kong's existing law, this does not mean that the NSL will not have any significant impact on the operation of Hong Kong's existing law as regards non-NSL offences. This is because the NSL has made it clear that it is not the only law relating to national security in the HKSAR, and some of its provisions are applicable to other national security-related laws in Hong Kong.[58]

---

56. UNATMO, s 2.
57. The specified circumstances involve "serious risk to the health or safety of the public" and "seriously interfering with or seriously disrupting an electronic system" or "an essential service, facility or system".
58. The following articles in the NSL are relevant in this regard. Art 3 requires the executive, legislative, and judicial organs of the HKSAR to effectively prevent, stop, and punish acts and activities endangering national security in accordance with the NSL and other relevant laws. Art 6(2) requires organisations and individuals in Hong Kong to comply with the NSL and other Hong Kong laws concerning national security. Under Art 7, the HKSAR should as soon as practicable complete the legislative work on national security (this probably refers to BL Art 23 laws). Art 8 provides that law enforcement and

There is, however, no definition of "national security" in the NSL. As regards what are the other Hong Kong laws relating to national security, Zhang Xiaoming, Deputy Director of the Hong Kong and Macau Affairs Office of the State Council, speaking at a press conference held on 1 July 2020 immediately after the NSL was passed, mentioned the Crimes Ordinance (Cap 200), Societies Ordinance (Cap 151), Public Order Ordinance (Cap 245), and Official Secrets Ordinance (Cap 521).[59] He probably meant that some, though not all, provisions of these laws are relevant to national security.

The Court of Final Appeal (CFA) in the *Lai Chee Ying* case[60] "construe[d] 'acts endangering national security' in the context of the NSL 42(2) requirement as referring to acts of that nature capable of constituting an offence under the NSL *or the laws of the HKSAR safeguarding national security*".[61] The CFA judgment provides examples of national security offences outside the NSL: "the offences of treason, incitement to disaffection or sedition under Parts I and II of the Crimes Ordinance".[62] This means that the statutory provisions on these offences form part of HKSAR laws relating to national security.

The question of whether a particular law or legal provision concerns national security is practically significant because there are several NSL articles which are applicable to legal proceedings in cases concerning offences endangering national security. A prosecution under a legal provision relating to national security, irrespective of whether the provision is in the NSL or in another law, would trigger the operation of the NSL articles concerning trial by "designated judges",[63]

---

judicial organs should effectively enforce the NSL and Hong Kong's existing law on the prevention and punishment of acts and activities endangering national security.

59. State Council Information Office holds press conference on the Law of the PRC on Safeguarding National Security in the HKSAR, n 18 above.
60. *See* n 29 above.
61. *See* para 53(c)(ii) of the judgment; emphasis supplied.
62. In footnote 40 of the judgment. Footnote 74 of the judgment pointed out that the Court of First Instance in *Tong Ying Kit v HKSAR* [2020] 4 HKLRD 382 at para 37 "erroneously limits 'acts endangering national security' to offences under the NSL". In *HKSAR v Ng Hau Yi Sidney* [2021] HKCFA 42, DCCC 854/2021, FAMC 32/2021, the CFA held that article 42(2) (regarding the "threshold" for the grant of bail) is applicable to the sedition offence under the Crimes Ordinance.
63. In *HKSAR v Tam Tak Chi*, DCCC 927, 928, 930/2020; [2020] HKDC 1153; [2020] HKCU 4184; [2022] HKDC 208, 343, Tam, vice-chairman of the political group People Power, was charged with several non-NSL offences, including "uttering seditious words" under s 10 of the Crimes Ordinance (Cap 200). The prosecution argued that because sedition was an offence against national security, Tam should be tried before a "designated judge" under the NSL. The District Court, without deciding whether the sedition offence must be tried before a "designated judge" as a matter of law, arranged for Tam's case to be heard by a "designated judge". *See* the judgment at [2020] HKDC 1153; Jasmine Siu, "Hong Kong Judge to Decide if Cases Facing People Power Activist Warrant National Security Law Appointee", *South China Morning Post*, 2 December 2020, available at https://www.scmp.com/news/hong-kong/law-and-crime/article/3112301/hong-kong-judge-decide-if-cases-facing-people-power; Kelly Ho, "National Security Judge Assigned to Hong Kong Pro-Democracy Activist Tam Tak-chi's Sedition Case", *Hong Kong Free Press*, 3 December 2020, available at https://hongkongfp.com/2020/12/03/national-security-judge-assigned-to-hong-kong-pro-democracy-activist-tam-tak-chis-sedition-case/. Subsequently, the

bail,[64] the possibility of dispensing with a jury,[65] and the possibility of a non-public trial. Where there is doubt about whether the case concerns national security, Article 47 of the NSL enables the court to obtain a certificate from the CE regarding whether a relevant act in that case concerns national security.

It is also noteworthy that some of the enforcement powers under the NSL extend beyond circumstances in which there is suspicion that an offence against national security has been committed or there is a need to prevent an offence against national security. In particular, interception of communications and covert surveillance may be practised not only for the purpose of "preventing or detecting offences endangering national security" but also for the purpose of "protecting national security" where "there is reasonable suspicion that any person has been, is, or is likely to be, involved in. . . any activity which constitutes or would constitute the relevant threat to national security".[66]

District Court decided that it had jurisdiction to hear this sedition case and refused to grant a stay of proceedings. The defendant's lawyer indicated that he would challenge the constitutionality of the sedition offence. *See* Jasmine Siu, "District Court Has Jurisdiction on Sedition Cases", *South China Morning Post*, 10 Apr 2021; Jasmine Siu, "Court Rejects Bid to Quash Colonial-Era Sedition Charges", *South China Morning Post*, 27 Apr 2021. On 2 March 2022, the District Court ([2022] HKDC 208) found Tam guilty of several offences, including sedition. Before this time, 3 other sedition cases have also been decided by the courts: *HKSAR v Hui Pui Yee*, DCCC 177/2020, [2021] HKDC 504; *HKSAR v Cho Suet Sum*, DCCC 767/2021, [2022] HKDC 119; and *HKSAR v Chiang Chung Sang* (see Brian Wong, "Hong Kong Man, Woman Jailed on Sedition Charges for Insulting Judges, Advocating Independence", *South China Morning Post*, 31 Jan 2022). See also *HKSAR v Lai Man-ling* [2022] HKDC 355.

64. In *HKSAR v Wan Yiu Sing Edmund*, WKCC534/2021, 4076/2020; HCCP 143/2021, DCCC 615/2021. Wan (also known as "Giggs"), radio host at the online radio channel "D100", was charged with several counts of sedition under s 10 of the Crimes Ordinance (Cap 200) but not any NSL offence. On 10 February 2021, Chief Magistrate Victor So Wai-tak—a "designated judge" under the NSL—rejected Wan's bail application after hearing the prosecution's argument that the test of deciding whether to grant bail should be that prescribed by Art 42(2) of the NSL as interpreted by the CFA in the *Lai Chee Ying* case (n 29 above). *See* Jasmine Siu, "Radio Host Remanded in Custody on Sedition Charges", *South China Morning Post*, 11 February 2021. The High Court (HCCP 143/2021) also rejected Wan's bail application without deciding whether Art 42(2) of the NSL was applicable. However, subsequently the CFA in the *Ng Hau Yi* case (n 62 above) authoritatively decided that Art 42(2) is applicable to the sedition offence.
65. In *HKSAR v Tong Ying Kit (No 1)* [2020] 4 HKLRD 382; [2020] 6 HKC 110 and *HKSAR v Tong Ying Kit (No 2)* [2020] 4 HKLRD 416; [2020] 6 HKC 141; HCCC 280/2020—the first case of prosecution under the NSL, the Secretary for Justice for the first time invoked her power under Art 46 of the NSL to direct a trial in Court of First Instance without a jury but before a three-judge bench. Judicial review proceedings (HCAL 473/2021) brought to challenge the procedural aspects of the decision not to have a jury trial were unsuccessful: *Tong Ying Kit v Secretary for Justice* [2021] HKCFI 1397, [2021] HKCA 912.
66. Rules on Application for Authorisation to Conduct Interception and Covert Surveillance, Implementation Rules for Article 23 of the NSL, Instrument A406A, Sch 6, s 2.

IV. Concluding Reflections

This chapter was written one and a half years after the enactment of the NSL. We are still in the early stage of its enforcement. As of 25 January 2022, 162 persons had been arrested under the NSL, and among them more than 100 had been charged (including the 47 defendants in the "primary election" case mentioned above).[67] Since June 2021, highly publicised national security (NSL and sedition) cases include (a) the prosecution under Article 29 of the NSL of four more members of the senior management of *Apple Daily*,[68] (b) the prosecution for sedition of five leading members of the General Union of Hong Kong Speech Therapists, who published three picture books for children alleged to be seditious,[69] (c) the prosecution under Article 27 of the NSL for advocating terrorism of four leading members of the HKU (Hong Kong University) Students' Union involved in passing a motion to "thank" a suspected terrorist who attacked a policeman and then committed suicide on 1 July 2021,[70] and (d) the prosecution for sedition of two members of the senior management of *Stand News*, an online news portal.[71] As of mid-February 2022, there were only three cases[72] in which the court has rendered a verdict as to the defendant's guilt.[73] We do not yet have a full picture of how the NSL will be enforced by the authorities and interpreted and applied by the courts.

---

67. Christy Leung, "Press Freedom Not an Absolute Right, Police Chief Warns", SCMP, 28 Jan 2022. See also Xia Baolun, "*Quanmian shenru shishi Xianggang guoanfa*" [The full implementation of the Hong Kong National Security Law] (speech on 16 July 2021 at conference on the first anniversary of the promulgation of the NSL), *Bauhinia Magazine* (Zijing zazhi), August 2021, p 4. *See also* Lydia Wong and Thomas E. Kellogg, *Hong Kong's National Security Law: A Human Rights and Rule of Law Analysis* (Georgetown Center for Asian Law, February 2021), available at https://www.law.georgetown.edu/law-asia/wp-content/uploads/sites/31/2021/02/GT-HK-Report-Accessible.pdf; Thomas Kellogg, "New Data Show Hong Kong's National Security Arrests Follow a Pattern", *China File*, 3 May 3021, available at https://www.chinafile.com/reporting-opinion/features/new-data-show-hong-kongs-national-security-arrests-follow-pattern; "Bearing Witness: National Security Law Arrests in Hong Kong", available at http://hk.usconsulate.gov/bearing-witness/.
68. Clifford Lo and Jeffie Lam, "4 Ex-Apple Daily Staff Expected to Be Charged", *South China Morning Post* (*SCMP*), 22 July 2021; Chris Lau, "Four Former Apple Daily Employees Denied Bail", *SCMP*, 23 July 2021.
69. Clifford Lo and Tony Cheung, "5 Held over 'Seditious Books' for Children", *SCMP*, 23 July 2021; Brian Wong and Lilian Cheng, "No Bail for Publishers Accused of Sedition", *SCMP*, 24 July 2021; Brian Wong and Clifford Lo, "Sedition Charge for 3 over Children's Books", *SCMP*, 31 August 2021.
70. Lilian Cheng and Clifford Lo, "HKU Students Arrested over Motion on Police Attacker", *SCMP*, 19 August 2021; Chris Lau and Clifford Lo, "Bail for Student in Security Law Case", *SCMP*, 20 August 2021.
71. Chris Lau, Natalie Wong and Brian Wong, "Stand News Pair Denied Bail as Lam Slams Critics", *SCMP*, 31 Dec 2021.
72. They are the *Tong Ying Kit* case (n 30 above); *HKSAR v Ma Chun Man*, DCCC 122/2021, [2021] HKDC 1325, [2021] HKDC 1406; and *HKSAR v Chung Hon Lam*, DCCC 27/2021, [2021] HKDC 1484.
73. There was another NSL case (regarding Art 29) in which the defendants (Li Yu-hin Andy and Chan Tsz-wah) pleaded guilty, but the case has not yet been concluded: Brian Wong, "Lai Key Player in Sanctions Plot, High Court Told", *SCMP*, 20 August 2021.

The better scenario is that the NSL achieves a deterrent effect, very few prosecutions need to be brought, the prosecutions that are brought concern cases of relatively clear violations of the NSL, and the National Security Office established by the Central Authorities in Hong Kong never needs to resort to its power under Article 55.[74] The worse scenario is that numerous prosecutions are brought, and they include high-profile cases in which it is controversial—as a matter of law and evidence—whether the defendants are guilty. Judges who want to apply liberal values in the Basic Law and in the International Covenant on Civil and Political Rights[75] may then be put into a difficult position. There will also be increasing risks of conflict between the courts' interpretation and application of the NSL and the expectations of the Central Authorities, which may result in interpretations issued by the NPCSC or even the National Security Office exercising its jurisdiction.

It has been said that the HKSAR's political system is characterised by a kind of hybrid constitutionalism[76] or liberal authoritarianism[77] in which both liberal and authoritarian elements co-exist. The enactment of the NSL together with the electoral reform of 2021 introduced by the NPC;[78] rigorous law enforcement actions taken against opposition politicians and other activists who participated in the anti-extradition movement; and political pressures leading to the closure of *Apple Daily* and the dissolution of the Hong Kong Professional Teachers' Union, the Civil Human Rights Front, and the Hong Kong Alliance in Support of Patriotic Democratic Movements of China have increased the authoritarian elements and reduced the liberal elements in Hong Kong's political and legal system, and shifted the balance of OCTS towards the "One Country" principle.[79] What remains to be seen is what will be the degree of increase of authoritarian elements or "rule by law" in the future, or what will be the magnitude of the shift towards the "One Country"

74. Art 55 provides for three kinds of special or exceptional circumstances in which the National Security Office may directly investigate an NSL case, arrest and detain suspects, and arrange for defendants to be prosecuted and tried in the mainland.
75. *See* NSL, Art 4.
76. Eric C. Ip, *Hybrid Constitutionalism: The Politics of Constitutional Review in the Chinese Special Administrative Regions* (Cambridge: Cambridge University Press, 2019).
77. Lau Siu-kai, *Huigui hou Xianggang de dute zhengzhi xingtai* [The unique political form in post-handover Hong Kong] (Hong Kong: Commercial Press, 2017); Lau Siu-kai, *The Practice of "One Country, Two Systems" Policy in Hong Kong* (Hong Kong: Commercial Press, 2017).
78. For relevant materials, *see* https://www.cmab.gov.hk/improvement/en/home/index.html.
79. Zhang Xiaoming, Deputy Director of the Hong Kong and Macau Affairs Office, said at the press conference on the NSL on 1 July 2020 (in translation): "Hong Kong has seen phenomena deviating from the correct path of OCTS, some even challenged the bottom line of OCTS. This Law in a sense rectifies the situation, or, to put it figuratively, it pushes Hong Kong a little in the direction of 'One Country.' Ultimately, this is done in order to insist upon and improve OCTS, and not to change OCTS." *See* State Council Information Office holds press conference on the Law of the PRC on Safeguarding National Security in the HKSAR, n 18 above.

principle. It is impossible to predict at this stage how the increasingly challenging practice of OCTS will develop. In the final analysis, future developments depend on Beijing's Hong Kong policy and the internal dynamics of Hong Kong society, as well as the mutual interaction between Hong Kong and the Central Authorities.

3

The Hong Kong National Security Law

The Shifted Grundnorm of Hong Kong's Legal Order and Its Implications

Han Zhu*

Introduction

Since the 1997 handover, the Grundnorm of Hong Kong's legal system has undergone a fundamental shift, transitioning from presupposing the validity of the constitutional order of the United Kingdom to that of the Constitution of the People's Republic of China (PRC).[1] Although the Hong Kong Special Administrative Region (HKSAR) has been absorbed into the PRC legal order, its legal system has remained largely unchanged as deliberately designed by the Hong Kong Basic Law (Basic Law). The new socialist Grundnorm and the old common law system creates the inherent paradox in Hong Kong's legal order, foreshadowing the challenges of the implementation of "One Country, Two Systems" (OCTS).[2] Before the handover, it had already been foreseen that the Grundnorm transition would fundamentally influence Hong Kong's legal system,[3] but such impacts have not been widely felt until recent years, particularly since the 2014 Occupy Central Movement (OCM). In order to assert central authority in Hong Kong, Beijing has developed new constitutional and Basic Law narratives that stress the state and sovereignty to counteract the autonomy orthodoxies.[4] These discourses aim to break through the self-contained common law system and bridge the gap between the PRC Constitution—the

* I am indebted to Hualing Fu for his substantive inputs on this chapter and would also like to thank Po Jen Yap for his constructive comments on an earlier draft.

1. *See* Albert H. Y. Chen, "The Provisional Legislative Council of the SAR" (1997) 27(1) *Hong Kong Law Journal* 9, 9–10.
2. *See* Raymond Wacks, "One Country, Two Grundnormen? The Basic Law and the Basic Norm", in Raymond Wacks (ed), *Hong Kong, China and 1997: Essays in Legal Theory* (Hong Kong: Hong Kong University Press, 1993).
3. *See* Chen, n 1 above, p 10.
4. *See* Han Zhu, "Beijing's 'Rule of Law' Strategy for Covering Hong Kong Legalisation without Democratisation" (2019) 1 *China Perspectives* 23, 26–27.

embodiment of the new Grundnorm—and Hong Kong's legal system. As a response to the 2019 governance crisis, the promulgation of the 2020 Law of the PRC on Safeguarding National Security in the Hong Kong Special Administrative Region (NSL) is a direct manifestation of Central Authorities' efforts to fully complete the journey of the Grundnorm shift, which has exerted sweeping influences over Hong Kong's common law system.

This chapter aims to examine the theoretical advancement underlying the NSL legislation and the Chinese law implications of the NSL for Hong Kong's legal system. The first part introduces the key constitutional and Basic Law narratives advocated by mainland officials and scholars to justify the legality of the NSL legislation. Those constitutional narratives attempt to extend the validity of the PRC Constitution to Hong Kong and explain away the legal autonomy guaranteed by Article 18 of the Basic Law and Article 31 of the PRC Constitution. Now in the NSL era, Hong Kong is embracing a PRC Constitution–based legal order in place of the one based on the Basic Law. Along with the theoretical advancement, national norms and central institutions have been channelled into the HKSAR through the implementation of the NSL. The second part of this chapter explores the implications of such normative and institutional changes for Hong Kong law and Basic Law practices. It focuses on five areas: the application of mainland laws in Hong Kong, the interpretation of the NSL, cross-border criminal jurisdiction, national security institutional infrastructure, and the legal language. To some extent, the enactment of the NSL is like a silent constitutional reform that has reshaped, and will continue to reshape, a wide range of aspects of Hong Kong law as well as the Basic Law. Because of the dualistic nature of the NSL as a national law applying to both the Mainland and Hong Kong, the NSL has also expanded and deepened the interaction and conflict between legal systems in the two regions, highlighting the inherent tension of maintaining the unity of a heterogeneous legal order under OCTS.

I. Chinese Constitutional Narratives and Justification of the NSL Legislation

The NSL legislation has been widely criticised for contravening the Basic Law and intruding on the high degree of autonomy enjoyed by the HKSAR.[5] To justify the legality of the NSL, Chinese constitutional narratives that emphasise the sovereignty and supremacy of the PRC Constitution[6] have been deployed to circumvent the constraints of the Basic Law. The key constitutional theories underlying the

5. E.g., *see* Johannes Chan, "Five Reasons to Question the Legality of a National Security Law for Hong Kong", *Verfassungsblog*, 1 June 2020, available at https://verfassungsblog.de/five-reasons-to-question-the-legality-of-a-national-security-law-for-hong-kong/.
6. For a detailed introduction of the theories of sovereignty and norms in the context of Chinese law, *see* Ryan Mitchell, "Theories of Sovereignty in the Origins and Implementation of Hong Kong's National Security Law", Chapter 4 of this volume.

justification for the NSL legislation are the "theory of authorization" and the theory of the "validity of the Constitution in Hong Kong", supplemented by other Basic Law discourses such as "co-governance on national security matters", "supreme status of the National People's Congress (NPC) in China's constitutional order", and "the plenary power to govern Hong Kong". Those constitutional theories are not newly developed but have emerged in the past decade to facilitate the expanse of Central Authorities' power over Hong Kong. The enactment of the NSL marks the peak of the influence of these constitutional theories, which ultimately reconstrue Article 18 of the Basic Law and Article 31 of the PRC Constitution to legalise the imposition of the NSL and allow for continuous legal intervention in Hong Kong.

a. The Theory of Authorisation and Co-governance on National Security

The theory of authorisation was first developed during the drafting of the Basic Law and has become the officially adopted theory in the Mainland, as opposed to the idea of the Basic Law as a kind of political compact between Beijing and the HKSAR or as a mini-constitution in Hong Kong.[7] In contrast to the opinion that the Basic Law also imposes constraints on the exercise of central power, the authorisation theory emphasises that the Basic Law is simply "an authorisation of power" from the NPC. The authorisation theory derives from the orthodox socialist legal theory that regards the PRC Constitution as the "mother law", which is the source of all the other laws within a legal order. Accordingly, the PRC Constitution and the Basic Law are also viewed as a "mother law" and a subordinate law, and the concept of a "mini-constitution" is criticised for contradicting the unitary principle which characterises the PRC constitutional order.[8]

Following this line of reasoning, the power to enact national security laws prescribed by Article 23 of the Basic Law is also considered as a power delegated by the Central Government rather than a power exclusively enjoyed by the HKSAR, despite the article's stipulation that the HKSAR "shall enact laws on its own".[9] According to the authorisation theory, it is not only the Basic Law but also the PRC Constitution that constitute the legal basis of the Central Government's power over national security matters in Hong Kong, and Article 23 is only a delegation clause through which the Central Government authorises the HKSAR to enact a national security legislation. The wording that the HKSAR "shall" (*ying*) enact the law also indicates that the HKSAR has the constitutional duty to enact a national security

7. *See* Qiao Xiaoyang, "On the Relationship between the Constitution and Basic Law" (2020) 32(1) *Zhongwai Faxue* [Peking University Law Journal] 5.
8. *See* Zhang Youyu, "The Reasons for and Basic Principles in Formulating the Hong Kong Special Administrative Region Basic Law, and Its Essential Contents and Mode of Expression" (1988) 2 *Journal of Chinese Law* 5, 7–8.
9. Chan, n 5 above; Bing Ling, "*Renda Guoan Lifa, Fu Jibenfa Di 159 Tiao fou?*" [Is the NSL legislation consistent with Article 159 of the Basic Law?], *Mingpao*, 26 May 2020, p B09.

law. Thus, the Central Government retains the power to enact the law for Hong Kong when the SAR fails to fulfil this obligation.[10] Another piece of evidence presented by pro-NSL theorists is that Article 23 is situated in Chapter II entitled "Relationship between the Central Authorities and the HKSAR", implying that national security legislative power does not fall within the autonomy of the HKSAR.[11] In the *Lai Chee Ying* bail case, the Court of Final Appeal (CFA) followed the same line of reasoning by quoting the NPC decision on the NSL legislation (NPC decision)[12] and the NPCSC's (National People's Congress Standing Committee) official explanation on the draft of the NSL to confirm the constitutionality of the NSL.[13]

The authorisation theory implies that a delegated power could be taken back if it were not exercised constitutionally, whereas the Basic Law does not specify how the Central Government should follow certain legal procedures to grant or revoke powers so as to avoid arbitrary exercise of the authorisation power. To overcome the deficiency, a concept of co-governance on national security has been proposed to supplement the authorisation theory. The co-governance theory, or the so-called "dual-track legislation" theory,[14] claims that Beijing could enact the NSL for Hong Kong regardless of whether the HKSAR has fulfilled its constitutional duty, because if Article 23 means that the HKSAR exclusively enjoys national security legislative power, it may indefinitely postpone the making of the law and the Central Authorities have no power to intervene despite their interests in protecting sovereignty.[15] The co-governance theory further relieves Central Authorities of the constraints imposed by the Basic Law. There are two Basic Law grounds for the co-governance argument: First, Article 18(4) of the Basic Law states that in a state of emergency the Central Government may apply relevant national laws in Hong

10. Zhang Yong, "*Guojia Anquan Lifa: Xianzhuang Yu Zhanwang*" [National security legislation: Present circumstances and prospects], Keynote Address at the Seminar to Celebrate the 30th Anniversary of the Basic Law, 8 June 2020, available at https://www.hkcd.com/content/2020-06/08/content_1196633.html. Without referring to the theory of authorisation, Andrew Li Kwok Nang, former Chief Justice of the Court of Final Appeal, agreed that the HKSAR has a constitutional duty to enact national security legislation under Article 23, and thus it is "understandable and justifiable" that the NPC enacted the NSL for Hong Kong since the SAR failed to do so; *see* Andrew Li, "China-Enacted National Security Law Must Be Consistent with Hong Kong Legal Principle", *South China Morning Post*, 2 June 2020, available at https://www.scmp.com/comment/opinion/article/3086946/china-enacted-national-security-law-must-be-consistent-hong-kong.
11. "*Tam Wai-Chu: Rong Gang Shenan Wushi Dangran; Leong Kah-Kit: Gujiaguwei ZiziWaili*" [Tam Wai-Chu: Do not take HK's jurisdiction over national security cases for granted; Leong Kah-Kit: Bullying and misleading comments], *Mingpao*, 6 July 2020, p A03.
12. The full name of the decision is the "Decision on Establishing and Improving the Legal System and Enforcement Mechanisms for the Hong Kong Special Administrative Region to Safeguard National Security" (Adopted at the Third Session of the Thirteenth National People's Congress on 28 May 2020).
13. *HKSAR and Lai Chee Ying* [2021] HKCFA 3, paras 8–14.
14. Jiang Shigong, "'*Shuanggui Lifa' Yu Zhidu Wanshan*" ['Dual-Track Legislation' and improve the system—a legal analysis of the NSL], *Mingpao*, 11 June 2020, B12.
15. Albert H. Y. Chen, "Constitutional Controversies of the Anti-extradition Movement" (2020) 50(2) *Hong Kong Law Journal* 609, 625.

Kong, which implies the Central Authorities' power to maintain national security in the Region.[16] Second, national security falls under the "defence" umbrella, which is the Central Government's responsibility as prescribed by Article 14(1) of the Basic Law.[17] Although "defense" usually entails external military action while national security is non-military and involves only internal maintenance of peace, NSL supporters argued that national defence and national security are inseparable and that the offences set out in Article 23 of the Basic Law are also covered by national defence laws in many countries, such as the National Defence Act of Canada.[18] The scope of "national law" prescribed by Article 18 of the Basic Law has thus been expanded. Article 18 allows the NPCSC to enact national laws in Hong Kong through Annex III, but these laws shall be confined to those relating to defence, foreign affairs, or matters outside the limits of HKSAR's autonomy (Annex III national laws). Since national security is interpreted as part of "defense" and also the responsibility of the Central Government, the high degree of legal autonomy guaranteed by Articles 23 and 18 of the Basic Law has now been eroded.

It is worth noting that the term "national laws" exists only in the Hong Kong Basic Law and Macau Basic Law and does not appear in any other Chinese law. In the past, there had been some discussion about the definition of a "national law",[19] but these debates did not attract much attention until the promulgation of the NSL. It is disputable whether "national laws" should only refer to laws that are applicable to the entire nation or include those that are specifically designed for Hong Kong.[20] Those who regarded the NSL as a national law argued that whether a law is national or local depends on its law-making authority instead of its content; thus any law enacted by the national legislature is a national law,[21] and the NSL is applicable not only to Hong Kong but also the entire nation since all people in China must comply with the law.[22] The concern is that the NSL, compared to the Garrison Law, directly affects Hong Kong residents' rights,[23] and the broader understanding of the term "national law" would blur the line between a national law and a Hong Kong local

16. For a detailed analysis of Art 18(4) and emergency power, *see* Hualing Fu and Xiaobo Zhai, "Two Paradigms of Emergency Power: Hong Kong's Liberal Order Meeting the Authoritarian State" (2020) 50(2) *Hong Kong Law Journal* 489.
17. Art 14(1) of the Basic Law provides that "the central people's government shall be responsible for the defence of the HKSAR".
18. E.g., section 82 ("advocating governmental change by force" offence) of the National Defence Act of Canada; *see also* Simon Hoey Lee, "*Reda Jueding Wei Tequ Li Guoanfa De Fali Yiju*" [Legal basis of the NPC decision on enacting the NSL], *Mingpao*, 12 June 2020, p B12.
19. *See* Wang Yu, "An Analysis of Article 19 of the Hong Kong Basic Law" (2016) 2 *Journal of One Country Two System Studies* 20.
20. Chan, n 9 above.
21. Wang Shuwen, "The Basic Law Is a National Law that Embodies the 'One Country, Two Systems' Policy" (1990) 2 *Faxue Yanjiu* [Chinese Journal of Law] 1.
22. Lee, n 18 above.
23. For a more detailed discussion of the term "national law", *see* Po Jen Yap, "Judging Hong Kong's National Security Law", Chapter 7 of this volume.

law and would thereby become a convenient tool for the Central Authorities to promulgate laws specifically designed for Hong Kong.

Both the theories of authorisation and co-governance on national security have created legal uncertainties concerning whether and to what extent the NPC and its Standing Committee will continue to enact national security laws or even other laws for Hong Kong under Article 31 of the PRC Constitution, which provides that the "system to be instituted in SARs shall be prescribed by law enacted by the NPC". Deng Zhonghua, the Deputy Director of the Hong Kong and Macau Affairs Office of the State Council, emphasised that the authorisation the NPC granted to its Standing Committee to enact the NSL is not a one-off power, which implies that the NPCSC may enact more relevant laws depending on the actual situation in Hong Kong.[24] Similar concerns have also emerged in the co-location case in which the NPCSC approved the co-location arrangement at the West Kowloon Station so as to allow national laws not listed in Annex III (non–Annex III national laws) to apply in the terminus leased to mainland authorities.[25] The implementation of the NSL further aggravated the concern over the abuse of power by the NPCSC.

b. Constitutional Basis of the NSL and Implicit Amendment of the Basic Law

Another key controversial issue regarding the legality of the NSL legislation is whether the PRC Constitution constitutes the legal basis of the law. The underlying theoretical question is the validity and application of the PRC Constitution in Hong Kong. In the early stage following the handover, mainstream mainland scholars generally equated the implementation of the Basic Law with the implementation of the PRC Constitution in Hong Kong, thus excluding the direct application of the PRC Constitution and dissolving the tension between the two laws. However, in responding to the changing political dynamics, constitutional narratives have shifted to emphasise the PRC Constitution as a separate legal source of law in Hong Kong.[26] Such narratives are also reflected in the NPC decision, which explicitly states that the decision is based on Articles 31 and 62 (2)(14)(16) of the PRC Constitution, whereas no reference is made to any specific Basic Law article.[27] Article 31 and Article 62(14) authorise the NPC to decide on the systems of the SAR, and Article 62(2)(16) empowers the NPC to supervise the implementation of the PRC Constitution and to exercise other powers as the highest organ of state

24. Gang Wen, "Top Legislature 'Can Make More Laws' on National Security for HK", *China Daily*, 4 July 2020, available at https://www.chinadaily.com.cn/a/202007/04/WS5f007860a3108348172573ab.html.
25. Generally *see* Jiang Hui, "A Non-Legislative Reading of the Co-location Decision and the NPCSC's Constitutional Review Power under the Basic Law" (2019) 49(1) *Hong Kong Law Journal* 547.
26. *See* Zhu, n 4 above.
27. *See* Decision of the National People's Congress on Establishing and Improving the Legal System and Enforcement Mechanisms for the HKSAR to Safeguard National Security.

power should exercise. In addition, some mainland scholars asserted that Chinese citizens' constitutional obligation to maintain territorial integrity and state interests should also apply to Hong Kong, aiming to further enhance the legitimacy of the NSL.[28] This line of reasoning was later formally adopted by the NPCSC decision on the qualification of members of the Legislative Council (LegCo) of the HKSAR four months after the promulgation of the NSL,[29] resulting in disqualification of four pan-democratic LegCo members.[30]

As Fu points out, relying on the PRC Constitution as a basis of the NSL legislation is a significant development in the Basic Law jurisprudence and will have long-term consequences.[31] It gives rise to many serious concerns, such as the implicit amendment of the Basic Law, the relationship between the PRC Constitution and the Basic Law, and the compatibility between the Basic Law and the NSL—or any other national law promulgated for Hong Kong outside the Basic Law framework. The NSL critics insist that the exercise of Central Authorities' power should be constrained by the Basic Law based on the doctrine "*lex specialis derogate legi generali*"—a law governing a specific subject matter overrides a law governing only general matters; thus the NSL is unconstitutional for violating Article 159(4) of the Basic Law, which provides that no amendment of the Basic Law shall contravene the "established basic policies" of the PRC regarding Hong Kong.[32] The thorny problem here, however, is not whether the NPC should comply with the Basic Law (as Beijing has always claimed that the Central Authorities maintain and respect the Basic Law) but how to define the "established basic policies of the PRC regarding Hong Kong". Different political persuasions have different interpretations of the "One Country" and "Two Systems", with some prioritising the former while others prioritise the latter, which leads to contrasting views on whether NSL legislation is compatible with the Basic Law.

If the NSL legislation is considered inconsistent with Article 159(4), and/or Article 23, of the Basic Law, it has de facto amended the Basic Law without following

28. Such constitutional provisions include Art 51 (in exercising their freedoms and rights, citizens shall not undermine the interests of the state, society and other citizens), Art 52 (citizens shall have the obligation to safeguard the unification of the country), and Art 54 (citizens must not commit acts detrimental to the security of the motherland). Wang Lei, "*Quanguo Renda De Jueding Ju Chongfen Xianzhi Yiju*" [The NPC decision is constitutional], *Mingpao*, 26 May 2020, p B08; "*Xu Jinglin Jiaoshou, Li Jianyong Jioashou Canyu 'Guanyu Quanguo Renda Shegang Guoan Lifa Youguan Jueding' Zhuanti Yantaohui*" [Prof Xu Jinglin and Prof Li Jianyong attended the seminar "NPC Decision on National Security Legislation in Hong Kong"], *Shanghai Daxue Xinwen Wang* [Shanghai University News Network], 29 May 2020, available at https://news.shu.edu.cn/info/1012/56815.htm.
29. The Decision of the NPCSC on Issues Relating to the Qualification of the Members of the Legislative Council of the HKSAR, 11 November 2020.
30. Announcement Pursuant to the Decision of the NPCSC on Issues Relating to the Qualification of the Members of the Legislative Council of the HKSAR, 11 November 2020, available at https://www.elegislation.gov.hk/hk/A217A.
31. Fu Hualing, "National Security Law" in Johannes Chan & C. L. Lim (eds), *Law of Hong Kong Constitution* (Sweet & Maxwell, 2021), p 201.
32. Ling, n 9 above.

the procedures for amending the Basic Law as prescribed by Article 159.[33] NSL legislation defenders countered that the NPC's decision is not based on the mechanism of "interpretation" or "amendment" prescribed by the Basic Law but the mechanism of "decision" under Article 62(14) of the PRC Constitution, which authorises the NPC to decide on the systems of SARs, and, in practice, the NPC had issued several decisions on significant legal issues in Hong Kong.[34] Their arguments are based on the PRC Constitution outside of the Basic Law framework because the latter does not specify the decision-making power of the NPC and its Standing Committee, which has given rise to continuous disputes on the efficacy of the NPC's decisions in Hong Kong. In recent years, the line between the power to issue decisions and the power to interpret, or even de facto amend, the Basic Law has become increasingly blurred as highlighted in the 2018 co-location case[35] and the 2020 NPCSC decision on the qualification of LegCo members. The enactment of the NSL has certainly further complicated the issue.

All in all, the enactment of the NSL can be understood as a new "constitutional moment"[36] in the evolution of Hong Kong's legal order, as it ushered in a transition from a Basic Law–based legal order to a PRC Constitution–based legal order in Hong Kong. In the past, the Basic Law was the sole supreme legal authority in Hong Kong, but now its controlling effect is slipping away. Article 31 of the PRC Constitution and Article 18 of the Basic Law which were supposed to establish a firewall between the mainland Chinese law and Hong Kong common law have instead been reconstructed by Beijing to legalise the imposition of the NSL and probably continuous legal intervention. The only good news might be that Beijing still nominally interprets and applies Article 31 of the PRC Constitution within the Basic Law framework rather than explicitly overriding it. Consequently, the function of the Basic Law might be transformed from a shield to fend off national laws into a filter to screen certain mainland norms and institutions while keeping out those that radically and apparently contradict the Basic Law. The question is to what extent the PRC Constitution and mainland laws would be relevant to Hong Kong law under the new constitutional order.

---

33. *Ibid.*
34. *See* Lam Chi Yan, "*Gangban Guoanfa, Yiguo Liangzhi Shishi Yilai De Zuida Bianju*" [The NSL: The unprecedented change since the implementation of one country two systems], *Initium Media*, 25 May 2020, available at https://theinitium.com/article/20200225-opinion-national-security-law-in-hk-problem/.
35. For a detailed analysis, *see* Lin Feng, "Constitutionality of the Co-location Arrangement at the West Kowloon High-Speed Rail Terminus" (2017) 47(3) *Hong Kong Law Journal* 699.
36. Tian Feilong, "*Aiguozhe Zhigang: Xianggang Minzhu de Xinsheng*" [Patriots govern Hong Kong: Rebirth of Hong Kong's democracy], *Mingpao*, 3 March 2020, p B07; for an introduction of the "constitutional moment" theory and its application in the Chinese context, *see* Albert H. Y. Chen, "The Discourse of Political Constitutionalism in Contemporary China: Gao Quanxi's Studies on China's Political Constitution" (2014) 14(2) *The China Review* 183.

II. The NSL and Its Chinese Law Implications for Hong Kong's Legal System

While the Basic Law tried to freeze Hong Kong's political and legal systems[37] despite a changed constitutional foundation, the NSL attempts to readjust legal norms and institutions in Hong Kong to render the "convergence, compatibility and complementarity" between Hong Kong laws and national laws[38] in national security and other broader areas such as elections. Due to the dualistic nature of the NSL, it channels many Chinese law theories and elements into Hong Kong's legal system, expands the presence of Central Authorities in the SAR, and deepens the intersection as well as conflict between mainland law and Hong Kong common law, thus imposing unprecedented challenges to the rule of law in Hong Kong. This section focuses on the five major areas of legal interface that have been impacted by the NSL: a) the application of mainland laws in Hong Kong; b) the interpretation of the NSL; c) the cross-border criminal jurisdiction; d) the national security institutional infrastructure; and e) legal language.

a. Application of Mainland Laws in Hong Kong

Prior to the promulgation of the NSL, there were two ways in which mainland laws might be applied or recognised in Hong Kong. The first one is the implementation of Annex III national laws under Article 18 of the Basic Law, as discussed above. Among the fourteen Annex III national laws, nine are applied in Hong Kong by way of local legislation and four by promulgation.[39] Although the NSL is not the first national law to be applied by promulgation, it is regarded as the first one that directly concerns the rights and freedom of Hong Kong residents.[40] The second is the implicit application of non-Annex III national laws in Hong Kong. The 1997 *Ma Wai Kwan David* case and the right abode cases have both involved the issue of whether the validity of mainland laws that are implicated in the enforcement of Hong Kong laws should be recognised in Hong Kong. The most extreme scenario is the express rail co-location arrangement at the West Kowloon rail terminus. Under the arrangement, the HKSAR transferred territorial jurisdiction of a small piece

37. Wacks, n 2 above, p 169.
38. *See* "Explanation on the Draft Law of the NSL", Addressed to the Nineteenth Session of the Thirteenth Standing Committee of the NPC by the Director of the Legislative Affairs Commission of the NPCSC, 18 June 2020, available at http://www.npc.gov.cn/wxzlhgb/gb2020/202009/0901662705854983838478105e41f42b/files/c117a0386e174e01a5acd4bd00be906b.pdf.
39. The HKSAR government intends to implement the "Law of the PRC on Judicial Immunity from Compulsory Measures Concerning the Property of Foreign Central Banks" but has not yet taken action. *See* Government of the HKSAR, "National Law on Immunity of Property of Foreign Central Banks to be Applied in Hong Kong", 27 October 2005, available at https://www.info.gov.hk/gia/general/200510/27/P200510270271.htm.
40. Chan, n 9 above.

of land in Hong Kong to mainland authorities in which they could enforce non–Annex III laws. The co-location scheme has been criticised for contravening Article 18 of the Basic Law[41] and the case is still pending as of this writing.

The application of mainland laws has caused two major questions: (1) whether a national law, listed in Annex III or not, shall prevail if it contravenes the Basic Law and Hong Kong laws, and (2) whether the Hong Kong judiciary has the power to review the NPCSC's legislative act. In general, Hong Kong judges have averted a direct challenge to the authority of the Chinese legislature in Hong Kong,[42] leaving these issues unsettled. The implementation of the NSL brings the thorny issue back and compels the court to face it directly. Although the NPCSC has tried to avoid the issue by affirming the precedence of the NSL over Hong Kong laws (Article 62), challenges have still been brought to courts. For instance, the NSL's bail provision has been challenged for contravening the Basic Law in the *Tong Ying Kit habeas corpus* case (*habeas corpus* case)[43] and the *Lai Chee Ying* bail case.[44] In *Lai Chee Ying*, the CFA attempted to construe the NSL in tandem with constitutional rights guaranteed by Hong Kong laws[45] and confirmed the constitutionality of the NSL, thus circumventing the question of whether the court could hold any provision of the NSL unconstitutional.

In addition to the two scenarios, the NSL creates a new way to bring national law to Hong Kong: non–Annex III national laws may be directly applied to Hong Kong through Annex III national laws in a non-emergency period. According to Article 18(4) of the Basic Law, non–Annex III national laws could only be applied to Hong Kong when the NPCSC declares a state of war or emergency and issues an order applying the relevant national laws in Hong Kong. Articles 55 to 57 of the NSL de facto expand the scope of circumstances when non-Annex laws could be directly applied to Hong Kong. Article 55 authorises the Office for Safeguarding National Security of the Central People's Government in the HKSAR (National Security Office) to exercise jurisdiction over certain national security cases (Article 55 cases). Articles 56 and 57 further specify that the PRC Criminal Procedure Law and "other related national laws" shall apply to all the procedural matters in cases handled by the National Security Office, which contravenes Article 18(2) that stipulates only Annex III national laws could be applied in Hong Kong. Asserting that Article 55 of the NSL can pre-empt political turmoil, the Central Authorities apparently aimed

41. *See* Lin, n 35 above.
42. *See* Yash Ghai, "The Intersection of Chinese Law and the Common Law in the Hong Kong Special Administrative Region: Question of Technique or Politics?" (2007) 37(2) *Hong Kong Law Journal* 363, 376–377; *see also* Yap, n 23, p 13; Cora Chan, "Reconceptualising the Relationship between the Mainland Chinese Legal System and the Hong Kong Legal System" (2011) 6(1) *Asian Journal of Comparative Law* 1, 14–15.
43. *Tong Ying Kit and HKSAR* [2020] HKCFI 2133; [2020] 4 HKLRD 382; [2020] 6 HKC 110.
44. *Lai Chee Ying and HKSAR* [2020] HKCFI 3161; [2021] 1 HKC 331.
45. *See Lai Chee Ying*, n 13 above, para 29.

to bypass the limits imposed by Article 18 of the Basic Law that ties their hands in handling significant Hong Kong affairs, such as the Anti–Extradition Bill crisis.

In addition to the direct application of non–Annex III national laws in Hong Kong through the NSL, many Chinese law theories and elements embedded in the NSL would also apply to Hong Kong implicitly. First, as Chen has analysed in detail in his chapter, the NSL incorporates many Chinese criminal law provisions on offences and penalties that are alien to Hong Kong common law.

Second, Hong Kong's administrative organs, law enforcement, and courts might need to refer to relevant mainland laws and even commentaries or cases to clarify certain key concepts in the NSL or enforce the law. The most salient ones are the concepts of "state secrets" and "national security"—the two essential constitutive elements of the crime "collusion with foreign forces" (Article 29). Articles 41(4) and 46 also stipulate criminal procedures regarding cases involving "state secrets".[46] The law, however, does not define the two key concepts. It is unclear whether the courts would refer to Chinese law sources to clarify the two terms. However, in the *Lai Chee Ying* case, the CFA relied heavily on the NPC decision and the official explanation of the NSL draft to confirm the constitutional basis of the NSL,[47] which might provide some clues as to the courts' attitude toward implicated mainland laws. Moreover, it is highly likely that the chief executive (CE) would refer to the mainland law to define "national security" when issuing a certificate to certify a national security act under Article 47, which is immune from judicial review. There are other important concepts that might also need to be understood in the context of Chinese law, such as the definition of "unlawful means" (Article 22), "terrorism organizations" (Article 25), "collusion" (Article 29), and "conspiracy" (Article 29).[48] The implicated Chinese laws include the Chinese Criminal Law (CCL), the PRC National Security Law and its Implementation Rules, the PRC State Secrets Law, the Law on Guarding State Secrets of the PRC (PRC State Secrets Law), and the PRC Anti-Terrorism Law, etc.[49]

Third, Chinese constitutional and administrative laws regarding state organs are also implicated in the NSL. One key legal question concerning the legal status and scope of the National Security Office's power is whether it is an office set up by departments of the Central Government as prescribed by Article 22 of the Basic Law and, thus, should abide by Hong Kong laws. Chinese authorities and some mainland scholars have posited that the Office, like the Liaison Office of the Central People's Government in the HKSAR (Liaison Office), is an institution directly dispatched by the Central Government rather than an office set up by departments

46. *See also* Zheng Tang and Xu Huang, "State Secrets in the Hong Kong National Security Law", Chapter 10 of this volume.
47. *Lai Chee Ying*, n 13 above.
48. For a detailed analysis, *see* Albert Chen, "The National Security Law of the HKSAR: A Contextual and Legal Study", Chapter 2 of this volume.
49. *Ibid.*

of the Central Government. Thus, the Office is neither established nor bound by Article 22.[50] Chinese constitutional and administrative laws, including the PRC Legislation Law, the PRC Organic Law of the State Council, and the Regulations on Administration of the Establishment and Staffing of the Administrative Agencies of the State Council, constitute the legal basis for the legal status of the National Security Office and the Liaison Office.[51] Another administrative law related to the NSL is the PRC Supervision Law. Under the NSL, the performance of duty by the National Security Office staff is not subject to Hong Kong judiciary, while Article 50(3) provides a channel that might be used by Hong Kong residents to address their grievances. It stipulates that the National Security Office shall be subject to the supervision of the national supervisory authorities "in accordance with the law". The provision, however, does not specify which law should apply here, which level of supervisory authorities would supervise the Office, and what specific procedures should be followed. It is unclear whether a supervisory authority would be set up in Hong Kong or whether Hong Kong residents could go to a supervisory authority in mainland China to submit complaints under the PRC Supervision Law. In either case, it would imply the application of the Supervision Law in Hong Kong.

b. Conflicts of Laws and the Interpretation of the NSL

The interpretation of the NSL faces the same two disputed issues surrounding the interpretation of the Basic Law, i.e. who has the power and which approach should be adopted to interpret the law. The power of interpreting the Basic Law is divided between Beijing and Hong Kong judiciary under the Basic Law, but the NPCSC's plenary power in this matter has been recognised in practice, despite controversies. In contrast to the Basic Law, the NSL authorises only the NPCSC to interpret the law without mentioning Hong Kong courts (Article 65). Although there is a general consensus among the legal community that the Hong Kong court must have the power to interpret the NSL when adjudicating cases while the NPCSC shall retain the final say, some issues remain unresolved, e.g. the NSL does not provide any specific procedures regarding the interpretation of the law so that it is unclear to which extent the NPCSC would intervene in the enforcement of the NSL.

As to the question of interpretative techniques, it has been long debated whether Hong Kong courts should adopt common law or Chinese law approaches to interpret the Basic Law, NPCSC interpretations and decisions, and other

50. Zhang Xiaoming remarks at the Press Conference on the NSL hosted by the State Council Information Office, 1 July 2020. Full transcript of the press conference is available at https://news.sina.cn/gn/2020-07-01/detail-iircuyvk1390644.d.html.

51. *See* Simon Hoey Lee, "*Lijie Zhongguo Xingzheng Jiagou Liangban Fei 'Bumen'*" [Understanding administrative structure in China; liaison offices are not departments of the central government], *Mingpao*, 22 April 2020, available at https://news.mingpao.com/ins/文摘/article/20200422/s00022/1587460828226/理解中國行政架構-兩辦非「部門」(文-李浩然).

implicated mainland laws.[52] In the *habeas corpus* case, similar questions were raised as to whether the court should use common law techniques exclusively to construe the NSL given the law is a national law enacted under the civil law system.[53] Although the CFI (Court of First Instance) emphasised that the court would adhere to common law approaches to interpret the NSL,[54] the CFA in *Lai Chee Ying* relied largely on Chinese legal and official sources to uphold the constitutionality of the NSL.[55] It remains to be seen whether judges will also refer to relevant mainland laws and legal theories to understand and interpret other disputed terms and issues.

Compared to the interpretation of the Basic Law, the interpretation of the NSL has become even more complicated due to the multiple levels of norm conflicts as the NSL incorporates both Chinese and Hong Kong law elements. The implementation of the NSL may cause the following three layers of legal conflicts, which pose unprecedented challenges to Hong Kong courts.

(1) *The hierarchy and conflict between the NSL and the Basic Law.* Conflicts between the two laws have already surfaced, including oath-taking provisions,[56] bail requirements,[57] judge appointments,[58] and human rights protection. Theoretically, as the NPCSC has the power to interpret both the NSL and the Basic Law, the NPCSC could simply proclaim that the NSL is consistent with the Basic Law to exclude Hong Kong courts' power in reviewing the consistency of the two laws. Nevertheless, in practice, the inconsistency between the two laws was still challenged in both the *Tong Ying Kit* and *Lai Chee Ying* bail cases. In the *Tong Ying Kit habeas corpus* case, in addition to the contentious bail provision, the constitutionality of several other provisions of the NSL, including Articles 20, 21 and 24 (the offence and penalty provisions that impose mandatory minimum sentences), and Article 44 (the appointment of NSL judges by the CE) have also been challenged for undermining judicial independence guaranteed by the Basic Law. However, the court did not address the question of how to solve the consistency between the two laws[59] but ruled that none of the impugned provisions undermines judicial independence. Both the CFI and CFA in the bail cases circumvented this thorny issue by simply holding the constitutionality of the NSL and emphasising that the Basic Law and the NSL should be construed as a coherent whole.[60]

52. Such as the PRC Legislation Law in oath-taking cases, *see* Han Zhu and Albert H. Y. Chen, "The Oath-Taking Cases and the NPCSC Interpretation of 2016: Interface of Common Law and Chinese Law" (2019) 49(1) *Hong Kong Law Journal* 381.
53. *Tong Ying Kit*, n 43 above, paras 48–49.
54. *Ibid.*
55. *Lai Chee Ying*, n 13 above, paras 9–37.
56. Art 6 of the NSL and Art 104 of the Basic Law.
57. Art 42(2) of the NSL and Art 87 of the Basic Law (presumption of innocence principle).
58. Art 44 of the NSL and Arts 92 and 85 of the Basic Law.
59. *Tong Ying Kit*, n 43 above, para 26.
60. *HKSAR and Tong Ying Kit* [2020] HKCFI 2196, para 7; *Lai Chee Ying*, n 13 above, paras 43–44.

(2) *The conflict between the NSL and Hong Kong local laws*. As analysed above, the incompatibility between the bail provisions of the NSL and Hong Kong laws, particularly the Criminal Procedure Ordinance (Cap 221), are the focal point at present. There is also worrying inconsistency between the NSL and the Hong Kong Bill of Rights Ordinance (Cap 383) in a wide range of fields.[61] The CFA decision in *Lai Chee Ying* held that the NSL shall prevail over local ordinances as prescribed by Article 62 of the NSL and explicitly admitted the specific exception carved out by the NSL from the existing bail regime in Hong Kong. To some extent, the NSL, along with its subordinate rules, might become a more direct legal authority than the Basic Law in reshaping certain areas of Hong Kong law.

For instance, the Implementation Rules for Article 43 of the NSL (IR43) made under Article 43 of the NSL have incurred criticism for significantly expanding the existing police power and contravening relevant local ordinances.[62] The legal status of the IR43 within Hong Kong's legal system is unsettled from the outset. It was passed by the Committee for Safeguarding National Security of the HKSAR (National Security Committee), an administrative branch in nature, instead of going through normal legislative procedures, i.e. to be approved and promulgated by the LegCo in the form of a by-law. The hierarchy between the IR43, the Basic Law, and relevant Hong Kong laws is equivocal given the ambiguous nature of the IR43 as a legal document. Despite inconsistencies between the IR43 and other laws, it is claimed to be immune from judicial review based on Article 14 of the NSL, which exempts the National Security Committee and its decision from judicial review. If the IR43, like the NSL, prevails over Hong Kong local laws, it implies that the National Security Committee could exercise the power of legislation and operate above the LegCo as well as the judiciary when it comes to national security and other related matters. Consequently, the NSL and its subordinate rules would comprise an independent legal regime parallel to the existing legal system in Hong Kong.

(3) *The internal conflict among NSL provisions, particularly the potential conflict between Article 4 on guaranteeing human rights under the International Covenant on Civil and Political Rights (ICCPR) and International Covenant on Economic, Social, and Cultural Rights, and provisions related to offence and penalty, police powers, and criminal procedures*. One of the focal issues at present is the incompatibility of "bail

61. *See* "Mandates of the Special Rapporteur on the Promotion and Protection of Human Rights and Fundamental Freedoms while Countering Terrorism", an Open Letter by Special Rapporteurs of the United National Human Rights Council to the Chinese Government, 1 September 2020, available at https://spcommreports.ohchr.org/TMResultsBase/DownLoadPublicCommunicationFile?gId=25487; *see also* Kelley Loper and Carole J. Petersen, "Academic Freedom in the Shadow of Hong Kong's National Security Law", Chapter 12 of this volume.

62. *See* Human Rights in China, "Too Soon to Concede the Future: The Implementation of the National Security Law for Hong Kong", 16 October 2020, available at https://www.hrichina.org/en/press-work/press-release/too-soon-concede-future-implementation-national-security-law-hong-kong-hric; *see also* Fu, n 31 above, pp 210.

requirements" in Article 42(2) with the "presumption of innocence" principle in Articles 4 and 5. Both the CFI in the *habeas corpus* case and the CFA in *Lai Chee Ying* attempted to reconcile such inconsistencies but used different approaches. The CFI construed Article 42(2) narrowly by adopting the traditional method that gives a generous interpretation to the constitutional guarantee of rights and a narrow interpretation to provisions which restrict fundamental rights.[63] In contrast, the CFA admitted "a considerably more stringent threshold requirement"[64] imposed by the NSL. To justify the necessity of importing a higher threshold, the CFA emphasised the special nature of national security affairs and the purpose of the NSL to suppress activities endangering national security. The CFA also confirmed the compatibility of Article 42(2) with other rights provisions of the NSL and legal practices in other jurisdictions.[65] The current NSL decisions on bail cases show that courts are generally inclined to avoid identifying any inconsistency among different norms and laws, but underlying their different approaches to legal reasoning are different priorities given to the two values, i.e. maintaining national security and protecting human rights.

c. Increased Presence of Mainland Authorities in Hong Kong

The Basic Law has been criticised for failing to establish an effective institutional infrastructure to facilitate intergovernmental interaction and the settlement of legal disputes. The main institutions that bridge the two legal systems designed by the Basic Law are the Basic Law Committee and the National People's Congress deputies from Hong Kong, the roles of which, however, have been largely marginalised.[66] The primary forum for legal interaction is the mechanism of interpreting the Basic Law, which divides the interpretation power between the NPCSC and Hong Kong courts. Dispute settlement and cross-regional co-ordination in legal and broader areas have met obstacles over the past decades due to legal obstacles imposed by the Basic Law; while on the other hand, the Liaison Office and other Central Authorities in charge of Hong Kong affairs have been constantly criticised for interfering in Hong Kong affairs through informal channels.

The unprecedented governance crisis resulting from the 2019 anti-extradition protest forcefully exposed the institutional vacuum and ultimately prompted Beijing to tackle the design flaw. The NSL is certainly one of the most important measures to carry out the strategy to reshape the institutional landscape to address the immediate need to restore order and the long-term need to rebalance OCTS. One uncertainty, as mentioned earlier, relates to the relationship between the Basic

63. *Tong Ying Kit*, n 43 above, para 41.
64. *Lai Chee Ying*, n 13 above, para 53(b).
65. *Ibid.*, para 69.
66. *See* Fu Hualing and Richard Cullen, "But Hong Kong Should Seek a Better Way . . . " (2006) 2 *Hong Kong Journal*, available at https://carnegieendowment.org/hkjournal/PDF/2006_spring/fu.pdf.

Law and the NSL and potentially any other future national laws. That is whether the Basic Law measures, explicitly or implicitly provided, should be exhausted before establishing new or strengthening existing institutional mechanisms to increase the presence of Central Authorities in Hong Kong.

As Jie Cheng elaborates in her chapter, a set of new institutions and mechanisms that did not exist under the Basic Law has been established under the NSL. Although its main responsibilities are limited to national security issues, the new institutional arrangement to a great extent reshapes both the internal governance structure in Hong Kong and the relationship between Central Authorities and the HKSAR government. The set of dual-track institutions created by the NSL consists of the National Security Office and the National Security Committee.[67] The former could, as mentioned above, directly enforce mainland laws and execute the will of the Central Authorities in Hong Kong, while the latter plays a crucial role in bridging Central Authorities and the HKSAR government in not only national security matters but other broader areas. The Committee serves as a formal channel for Beijing to expand its influence in all branches of the HKSAR government through the following four ways.

First, Beijing exerts substantive controlling power over the Committee which consists of the CE and other senior executive officials of the HKSAR government. According to Article 12 of the NSL, the Committee is under the supervision of and accountable to the Central Government, and Beijing also holds plenary power to appoint the Secretary-General of the Committee, who is presumably responsible for the daily work of the Committee (Article 13).

Second, the National Security Advisor who sits on the Committee serves as a connecting point between the Central Authorities and the HKSAR government. The NSL legalises the interaction between the HKSAR government and the Liaison Office, and it is also the first time that the Central Authorities legitimately have direct access to the daily policy-making process within the Hong Kong government.[68] It certainly raises concerns that the Advisor's influence would go beyond national security matters but become the shadow source of power in Hong Kong's political system.[69]

Third, the Committee, along with the National Security Office, deepens Central Authorities' reach into the bureaucracy in Hong Kong by influencing personnel appointments.[70] According to the NSL, both the heads of the Department for Safeguarding National Security of the Hong Kong Police Force (DSNS) and the Specialised National Security Crimes Prosecution Division of the Department of

67. Donald Clarke, "Hong Kong's National Security Law: An Assessment", 13 July 2020, available at https://www.prcleader.org/clarke.

68. Fu, n 31 above, p 208.

69. For a detailed analysis, *see* Jie Cheng, "Hong Kong's Constitutional Order after the National Security Law", Chapter 5 of this volume.

70. Clarke, n 67 above.

Justice (SPD) must be appointed by the CE upon written consultation with the National Security Office,[71] and all the prosecutors in the SPD must be approved by the National Security Committee.[72] According to Article 17(2) of the NSL, the DSNS is required to perform tasks assigned by the National Security Committee, implying it answers not to the Hong Kong police force but to the Committee in handling national security matters.[73] The National Security Department enjoys a "unified intelligence, security and police power"[74] and has become a convenient tool for the central and Hong Kong authorities to handle national security matters. The newly established institutions, to some extent, disrupt the existing bureaucratic hierarchy and create a new structure of accountability paralleling the current one. In addition, the DSNS may recruit personnel from outside Hong Kong,[75] meaning that law enforcement officials from the Mainland could serve in Hong Kong's police force. During the Anti–Extradition Bill crisis, speculation circulated among the "yellow circle" that plainclothes mainland police officials were engaged in crackdowns on protests, leading to several high-profile attacks targeting mainlanders who seemed suspicious.[76] Ironically, the NSL, as a response to the crisis, ultimately legalised the engagement of mainland law enforcement with Hong Kong police.

The extended reach into the bureaucracy is also reflected in the NSL's provision on the new universal oath-taking requirement for public office holders (Article 6), indicating the Central Government's distrust in the bureaucracy in the aftermath of the Anti–Extradition Bill crisis and its agenda to ensure the loyalty of public servants. Even the Chinese government admitted that the scope of public servants who are required to take oaths under the NSL is incompatible with Article 104 of the Basic Law, as the latter only requires judges and high-level officials to take an oath when assuming office.[77]

Fourth, the establishment of the National Security Committee further orients the governance model of the HKSAR from the "separation of powers" favoured by the pro-liberal camp toward the "executive-led government" preferred by Beijing. As Jie Cheng elaborates in her chapter, the overarching and unchecked power of the Committee has a significant impact on the existing governance structure by enhancing the CE's power and Beijing's influences in the three branches of SAR government. Through the crackdown on the pan-democratic camp under the NSL[78]

71. NSL, Arts 16(2) and 18(1).
72. *Ibid.*, Art 18(2).
73. Human Rights in China, n 62 above; Fu, n 31 above, p 210.
74. Fu, n 31 above, p 208.
75. NSL, Art 16(3).
76. "Mainland Chinese Are Being Attacked in Hong Kong", *The Economist*, 9 November 2019, available at https://www.economist.com/china/2019/11/07/mainland-chinese-are-being-attacked-in-hong-kong.
77. Shen Chunyao, "The Hong Kong National Security Law Conference Hosted by the State Council Information Office (Full transcript)", *Sina*, 1 July 2020, available at https://news.sina.cn/gn/2020-07-01/detail-iircuyvk1390644.d.html.
78. Natalie Wong, "53 Arrested for 'Subversion'", *South China Morning Post*, 7 January 2021, p 1.

and the new round of electoral reform,[79] both the National Security Committee and the National Security Office are expected to play a role in influencing Hong Kong's election. They will probably provide assistance in screening electoral candidates and enhancing oath-taking requirements through the excuse of national security. Nevertheless, it remains to be seen whether such a new arrangement that brings the informal engagement between central and Hong Kong authorities out in the open would help restore order to Hong Kong's political process, which is something the city desperately needs.

d. Exceptions to Hong Kong's Criminal Jurisdiction[80]

The NSL creates two exceptions to Hong Kong's legal system in claiming criminal jurisdictions: the national jurisdiction and the extraterritorial jurisdiction, both of which have aroused widespread concerns.

The national jurisdiction prescribed by Articles 55 to 57 grants mainland authorities—including the National Security Office, procuratorates, and courts—to assert jurisdiction over Article 55 cases. The national jurisdiction provisions remove some legal obstacles for cross-border criminal co-operation and diminish the line between the two criminal legal systems in dealing with significant national security crimes. No Article 55 cases have yet arisen, while Beijing's mouthpiece had threatened that the Central Authority could take over the *Lai Chee Ying* case after his bail was granted by the CFI.[81] If Article 55 cases were to happen, the most challenging issue would be how to guarantee a suspect's ICCPR given that the jurisprudence of the ICCPR is explicitly recognised by the NSL but not yet by the Chinese legal system. It remains to be seen how mainland authorities would reconcile the NSL and Chinese criminal procedural laws in an Article 55 case.[82] In addition, many procedural difficulties might also arise due to cross-regional factors involved. Take the right to legal counsel as an example. According to Article 58, a suspect in an Article 55 case shall have the right to get access to a lawyer from the day the suspect first receives an inquiry made by the National Security Office. Since Chinese law applies to the whole proceeding of Article 55 cases (Article 57), it is unclear whether a suspect—if the person is inquired about or detained by the National Security Office in Hong Kong—could hire a Hong Kong registered lawyer who might not be familiar with the Chinese law or hire a mainland registered lawyer who is not allowed to practise in Hong Kong. If it is the former case, it implies that a lawyer

79. Decision of the NPC on Improving the Electoral System of the HKSAR (11 March 2021).
80. The author would like to thank Albert H. Y. Chen and Simon Young for their incisive comments on the cross-border jurisdiction part of this chapter.
81. "*Pizhun Li Zhiying Baoshi, Dui Xianggang Fazhi Shanghai Taishen*" [Bail granted to Lai Chee-ying severely hurt Hong Kong's rule of law], *People's Daily*, 26 December 2020, available at https://wap.peopleapp.com/article/6085777/5996965.
82. Fu, n 31 above, p 213.

who is not registered in the Mainland could practise mainland Chinese law in Hong Kong. Another related issue is whether a suspect should change his or her lawyer when being transferred from Hong Kong to the Mainland for further investigation or prosecution. The best choice for a suspect involved in Article 55 cases would be a criminal law lawyer who registers both in the Mainland and Hong Kong. Obviously, very few criminal law lawyers would be qualified. Such a dilemma certainly frustrates a suspect's right to legal counsel. The only feasible solution is to transfer the suspect immediately to Shenzhen upon the moment the first inquiry or a mandatory measure is taken.

The national jurisdiction enables mainland authorities to legally transfer a suspect from Hong Kong to the mainland in an Article 55 case. It de facto legalises the previously unlawful cross-border transferring of suspects involved in highly politically sensitive cases, such as the five booksellers[83] and the Chinese-born Canadian tycoon.[84] The powers that the National Security Office enjoys under the NSL also formalise the previous underground activities conducted by mainland law enforcement in Hong Kong. The NSL partly solves the rendition issue that the 2019 Extradition Bill targeted by directly imposing central jurisdiction on Hong Kong.

The other contentious exception is the extraterritorial jurisdiction prescribed by Article 38, which states that the NSL shall apply to non-permanent Hong Kong residents who commit an NSL offence outside the HKSAR. This differs from the relatively rigid territoriality principle of Hong Kong's common law system.[85] While significant attention has been paid to its long-arm effect over non-Chinese citizens who stay overseas,[86] its potential impact on cross-border jurisdiction has largely been ignored. Five scenarios might occur under the NSL that would give rise to concurrent jurisdiction and mutual legal assistance issues: (1) Hong Kong residents who violate the NSL in Hong Kong and are detained in the Mainland; (2) mainlanders who violate the NSL in Hong Kong and return to the Mainland; (3) mainlanders who violate the NSL in the Mainland and are detained in the Mainland; (4) mainlanders who violate the NSL in Mainland/Hong Kong and are detained in Hong Kong; and (5) an NSL crime that involves substantial cross-border elements. The concurrent jurisdiction issue is a result of the duality nature of the NSL as a national law applying to both regions and the uncertainty whether the HKSAR enjoys exclusive jurisdiction over NSL cases except Article 55 cases (ordinary NSL cases).[87]

83. *See* Carolyn Cartier, "Policing the Borders: Hong Kong Conundrums", in Jane Golley et al. (ed), *China Story Yearbook 2016* (Canberra: Australian National University Press, 2017), pp 245–249.

84. Sonny Shiu-Hing Lo et al., *The Dynamics of Peaceful and Violent Protest in Hong Kong: The Anti-extradition Movement* (Singapore: Palgrave Macmillan, 2021), pp 56–58.

85. Fu Hualing, "The Battle of Criminal Jurisdictions" (1998) 28(3) *Hong Kong Law Journal* 273, 277.

86. *See* Bing Ling, "Extraterritorial Application of the Hong Kong National Security Law: A Legal Appraisal", Chapter 11 of this volume.

87. Arts 40 and 41 of the NSL stipulate that the HKSAR "shall have jurisdiction over cases concerning offences under this Law" except in Article 55 cases, but the law does not explicitly exclude mainland authorities' jurisdiction.

The first scenario already occurred in the "12 Hongkongers" case, in which the 12 attempted to flee to Taiwan from Hong Kong but were intercepted by mainland law enforcement and charged with "illegal border crossing" under the Chinese law. One offender who had been charged under the NSL before fleeing will be returned to Hong Kong for prosecution after serving his sentence in the Mainland.[88] This case has invited some discussions about the cross-jurisdiction issue before the trial. The mainland authorities' decision indicates that they are unwilling to handle cases involving Hong Kong residents who commit NSL offences in Hong Kong, which is consistent with the previous practice of the separation of criminal jurisdictions between the two regions. Other scenarios, particularly (2) and (3), might be trickier and might involve a choice of law if an NSL suspect is tried in Mainland because of the overlap as well as nuanced differences between the NSL and the CCL (as elaborated in Chen's chapter of this volume).[89] Scenarios (2) and (3) might also have implications for the existing cases involving mainlanders who were arrested or prosecuted for supporting or participating in political movements in Hong Kong. In the past, most of those mainlanders were charged with "picking quarrels and provoking trouble", while only a handful were charged with "inciting subversion".[90] The former is apparently an ill-defined offence for charging online political speeches and mainlanders' activities in Hong Kong. Since the NSL, in some respects, expands the scope of national security offences under the CCL, it remains to be seen whether the charge for the same acts will be escalated to national security offences in the future, either under the NSL or the CCL, thus further increasing risks for mainlanders' engagement with political activities relating to Hong Kong. Such concerns have already been reflected in two national security cases involving mainland students who studied in Hong Kong and joined protests.[91] This chapter will not go into detail to analyse the five cross-jurisdictional scenarios one by one. It is simply worth pointing out that mainland authorities are not likely to recognise too strict of a separation of jurisdictions and responsibilities between central and regional administrations when it comes to national security. Both the national jurisdiction and the extraterritorial jurisdiction serve to break down the previous barriers that separate the criminal legal systems in the Mainland and Hong Kong in dealing with sensitive political crimes.

88. "10 Hongkongers Jailed for up to 3 Years in China after Trying to Flee City for Taiwan", *Hong Kong Free Press*, 30 December 2020, available at https://hongkongfp.com/2020/12/30/10-hongkongers-jailed-for-up-to-3-years-in-china-after-trying-to-flee-city-for-taiwan/.

89. *See also* Fu, n 31 above.

90. The list of cases is on file with the author; *see also* Human Rights in China, "*Yu Shengyuan Xianggang Kangyi Youguan de Juliu*" [Detention related to supporting Hong Kong's protests], 26 January 2015, available at https://www.hrichina.org/cht/yu-sheng-yuan-xiang-gang-kang-yi-you-guan-de-ju-liu-2014nian.

91. William Zheng, "China Reveals Foreigner Jailed for 11 Years, Mainland Students Arrested over Hong Kong Protests", *South China Morning Post*, 15 April 2021, https://www.scmp.com/news/china/politics/article/3129717/china-reveals-foreigner-jailed-11-years-mainland-students.

e. Legal Language

Before the 1997 handover, Basic Law scholars in Hong Kong raised concerns about the influence of the increased use of Chinese in Hong Kong common law practice, worrying whether a common law system could survive by incorporating the Chinese language since there is no such precedent in the English-dominated common law world.[92] In the past decades, despite the expanded use of Chinese in legal practice, its scale and influence remains limited. The NSL and the IR43 are probably the only laws that directly challenge the dominant position and priority of English in Hong Kong's legal system and raise serious concerns beyond the language itself. In a move that was widely criticised, the official English version of the NSL was not published by the Hong Kong Government Gazette along with its Chinese version on the day of promulgation. Hong Kong residents, judges, and professionals who were not proficient in Chinese were unable to fully understand the law. Before the official English version (for information only) was published, ten individuals had already been arrested for violating the law. In the *habeas corpus* case, the defendant submitted that the delayed publication and the absence of the English version of the law restricted a suspect's right to select lawyers. The court refuted this submission on the grounds that the junior counsels who can read Chinese in the suspect's legal defence team could provide sufficient assistance and that there is also a large pool of senior counsels who can read Chinese in Hong Kong who can represent the suspect.[93] This line of reasoning still implies the indispensable position of a Chinese-speaking counsel in defending an NSL suspect (particularly those who cannot read Chinese), which might increase the cost of legal representation. It also implies the advantageous position of a counsel who can read Chinese in the market for taking NSL cases. As a legal document closely related to citizens' basic rights, the IR43 has a similar problem. Article 4 of the rule states that only the Chinese version is authentic, whereas the English version of the rule is for reference only.

Another significant issue is the inconsistency between the Chinese and English versions of the NSL. The inconsistencies between the two versions of the NSL is largely caused by the ambiguous wording and the rushed passage of the law. Many parts of the English version have been criticised for their inaccuracy.[94] Since the NSL is largely based on Chinese law principles and is in Chinese legal language only, a deep understanding of the Chinese law is a prerequisite for an accurate translation. Re-translations of the law by academics and NGOs have shown the failure of the official English version to capture the nuanced but crucial differences between

---

92. Edward J. Epstein, "China and Hong Kong: Law, Ideology, and the Future Interaction of the Legal Systems", in Raymond Wacks (ed), *The Future of the Law in Hong Kong* (Oxford: Oxford University Press), p 74.
93. *Tong Ying Kit*, n 43 above, paras 69–77.
94. *See* Albert Chen and Simon Young, "Liability for Imposing Sanctions under Hong Kong's National Security Law" (2020) 50 *Hong Kong Law Journal* 353; *see also* Human Rights in China, n 64 above.

the ostensibly similar terms in the two criminal legal systems.[95] The question of whether a Hong Kong law should be promulgated in both languages and which version should prevail remains unsettled. Article 9 of the Basic Law stipulates that both Chinese and English are official languages in the HKSAR but does not clarify the hierarchy of the two. In 1990, the NPCSC issued a decision asserting that the Chinese version of the Basic Law shall prevail over the English one,[96] but the decision only applies to the Basic Law without referring to any other law applied in Hong Kong.

III. Conclusion

While the shift of Grundnorm in Hong Kong's legal order occurred in 1997, such a crucial transition did not attract too many concerns and disputes, except those over NPCSC's interpretations and decisions on Hong Kong affairs. It is mainly because the Basic Law had been able to play a controlling role in the implementation of OCTS and the interface between mainland law and Hong Kong law in the first two decades. The PRC Constitution, though remaining supreme in the OCTS framework, had largely hidden behind the scenes, and Article 31 of the PRC Constitution stayed dormant after fulfilling its historical role in imparting the legitimacy onto the Basic Law. Therefore, despite the shifted Grundnorm and Hong Kong's incorporation into the PRC legal order, there was optimism that Hong Kong's legal system could be largely insulated from the influence of Chinese law. Nevertheless, the contradiction between the socialist Grundnorm and the old self-contained legal system has become increasingly intensified since the OCM and ultimately culminated in the 2019 Anti–Extradition Bill crisis. In Beijing's view, the escalated disobediences and governance crisis in Hong Kong signify wide defiance of the Grundnorm, which significantly undermined the efficacy of Hong Kong's overall legal order as well as the Basic Law framework. The NSL legislation is Beijing's attempt to reassert general adherence to the Grundnorm and to establish the validity of the PRC Constitution in the HKSAR.

Henceforth, the PRC Constitution finally walks from behind the scenes to the front of stage, as Chinese Schmittian constitutional scholars would frame it. The Constitution, replacing the Basic Law, has become the supreme and separate legal source of law in Hong Kong. The NSL promulgated under this context is kind of like an undeclared legal reform that has, explicitly or implicitly, readjusted many key arrangements under the Basic Law and reshaped the existing legal regime of the SAR on a wide range of areas such as criminal law, criminal procedural law, police accountability, electoral law, and even financial regulations. Through the NSL, new national norms and central institutions have been brought into Hong Kong,

95. *Ibid.*
96. Decision of the NPCSC on the English Text of the Basic Law of the HKSAR of the PRC (28 June 1990).

governance structure has been reconstructed, Chinese law elements would further infiltrate into judicial interpretation, Chinese language has implicitly established its precedent status in the legal system, and the boundary between jurisdictions and criminal systems in the Mainland and Hong Kong are blurred in dealing with national security and political crimes. The NSL is a direct manifestation of the striking effects of the Grundnorm shift occurring in Hong Kong's legal order. Now a new round of constitutional transition in Hong Kong has begun, and the NSL is surely not the end but the beginning of the legal and political reconstruction process. The best hope is that the Basic Law could still serve as a filter to screen and control national norms and institutions into Hong Kong and the NSL would stay as a latent threat after accomplishing its historical mission of transforming the extraordinary politics in a "state of exception" into stabilised ordinary politics.

4

Theories of Sovereignty in the Origins and Implementation of Hong Kong's National Security Law

Ryan Mitchell

Introduction

The June 2020 National Security Law (NSL) was, in part, the product of a long-developing legal discourse regarding Hong Kong's territorial status within the People's Republic of China (PRC). The conceptual foundations of the NSL lie in specific propositions regarding the nature of the Central Government's role in the governance of Hong Kong as well as the hierarchy among relevant public law authorities, including constitutional texts and international agreements. It is important to understand these propositions, and the theoretical premises they reflect, in order to assess the NSL's role as a major element of Hong Kong's legal architecture extending far beyond policing and security matters per se.

Within the scope of Hong Kong's own common law legal system and in much Western commentary, such issues are usually discussed in relation to the Anglo-American public law tradition with its emphases on robust judicial review of state action and privileging of civil and political rights. However, this is not the case with respect to the central policies or justifications decided upon by the National People's Congress Standing Committee (NPCSC) and Hong Kong and Macau Affairs Office (HKMAO) of the PRC State Council, nor to much of the leading mainstream public law discourse in the PRC academic community. Both tend to draw ideas about state sovereignty, territorial status, courts' review of state action, individual rights, and the hierarchy of public law authorities, among other topics, from Chinese domestic legal thought as well as its key historical influences. More specifically, in recent years relevant PRC public law doctrine has come to increasingly embody a set of premises often drawn from late 19th to early 20th century conservative German

Staatsrechtslehre (theory of law and the State),[1] adapted in various respects to suit Beijing's 21st century "socialist rule of law State".

This chapter will examine how three key (related) premises have influenced the formulation and justification of the NSL. The first premise is the exclusive character of national sovereignty over state territory and the corresponding "strong dualist" view that international law may limit this authority only after explicit incorporation into domestic legislation. This position is in turn ultimately based on the illiberal constitutionalist premise of a centralised "state will" that subordinates contradictory legal obligations, such as those involved in treaties—a different rationale from the limitation of international law by reference to basic rights or democratic accountability grounds. The second premise is the Chinese doctrine that there is a fundamental structure of the polity (aka 國體 *guoti*—"State form"), beyond the text of the Constitution, that may overrule "lesser" norms that contradict that structure. The third premise, related to the previous two, is that unitary "state authority" (*Staatsgewalt*) as embodied primarily by the Executive has an autonomous legitimacy that includes the sovereign power of suspending legal norms in exceptional situations. This capacity, meanwhile, is inherently in tension with both the judicial and legislative organs of government: the NSL can thus be viewed alongside other significant public law developments as part of a progressive insulation of Hong Kong's Executive, alongside representatives of the Central Government, as holders of exceptional authority. The exact relation in practice of this exceptional authority to the judicial organs of "normal" legal interpretation and application, however, remains to be seen.

Each of the above three premises will be examined in connection with its manifestations in direct connection with positions taken by the central and Hong Kong governments on key aspects of the NSL and its relationship with Hong Kong's existing constitutional framework. Though rarely presented in a systematic fashion, some of the theories under consideration have recently received increasingly explicit focus in both academic and official contexts—as well as, in some cases, in venues bridging the academy and officialdom. For example, both of the first two annual "Constitution Day Seminars", held on 4 December 2019 and again in 2020 by the Constitutional and Mainland Affairs Bureau of the Hong Kong Government, were devoted to justifying the increasingly direct extension of Central Government power into Hong Kong. The constitutional scholars invited to present those lectures, Han Dayuan and Chen Duanhong—consultants for (respectively) the Hong Kong

1. For useful recent explorations in English of *Staatsrechtslehre* and the more capacious, older tradition of *Staatslehre* (i.e. State Theory), *see* Martin Loughlin, "In Defence of Staatslehre," *Der Staat* 48, no. 1 (2009): 1–28; Martin Loughlin, *Foundations of Public Law* (Oxford: Oxford University Press, 2010): 190–208; Michael Stolleis, *Public Law in Germany, 1800–1914* (New York and Oxford: Berghahn Books, 2001): 56–75 (explaining the basic presumptions of 19th century German legal/political scholarship on the structures of constitutional monarchy); cf. Stanley L. Paulson, "The Theory of Public Law in Germany 1914–1945" *Oxford Journal of Legal Studies* 25, no. 3 (2005): 525–545.

SAR (Special Administrative Region) Basic Law Committee and the Macau SAR Basic Law Committee of the National People's Congress Standing Committee—have presented there and in other relevant venues expositions of several of the theoretical presumptions informing the formulation and promulgation of the NSL. Along with those of other prominent PRC constitutional scholars, their views help to ascertain key aspects of the larger public law implications of the new security framework. However, the differences between their positions, and those of others writing on the same topics, are equally significant as their shared premises.

Indeed, this study concludes that, although the NSL will certainly play a significant transformative role in Hong Kong's local security state, there is reason to believe that pragmatic incentives and local input may ultimately serve to ameliorate the extent to which the legislation's innovations transform Hong Kong's overall public law environment. For each of the three theoretical premises under consideration proves, upon closer analysis, to leave considerable room for local courts and civil society actors to insist upon principled limits to the exercise of sovereign power—even without contesting the NSL's various a priori presumptions regarding central state authority.

I. "State Will": Territorial Sovereignty and International Norms

On 30 June 2017, the PRC Ministry of Foreign Affairs spokesperson Lu Kang stated that the 1984 Sino-British Joint Declaration (Joint Declaration) is a "historical document which no longer has any practical significance" (作為一個歷史文件，不具有任何現實意義).[2] The implications of this expired legal effect, Lu said, were that following the return of Hong Kong, the United Kingdom "does not have sovereignty, rights to administration, or rights to supervision" over Hong Kong.[3] The same or similar statements have been repeated on other occasions and emphasised with increasing regularity in the years since. Most recently, this position has also been applied by the PRC central authorities to British (and other states') criticisms over the NSL as a putative violation of the Joint Declaration.[4]

Despite denying "practical significance" for the Joint Declaration, the PRC side has not explicitly stated that it lacks any and all ongoing international obligations stemming from the agreement. However, it has rejected the argument that the Joint Declaration confers any rights of supervision or basis for protest by the

2. "2017 Nian 6 Yue 30 Ri Waijiaobu Fayanren Lu Kang Zhuchi Lixing Jizhe Hui [30 June 2017 Routine Press Conference of Ministry of Foreign Affairs Spokesman Lu Kang]," available at https://www.fmprc.gov.cn/web/fyrbt_673021/t1474476.shtml.
3. *Ibid.*
4. Office of the Commissioner of the Ministry of Foreign Affairs in the Hong Kong Special Administrative Region, "Spokesperson of Commissioner's Office Urges UK to Wake Up from Colonial Nostalgia and Stop Interfering in Hong Kong Affairs", 24 November 2020, available at http://www.fmcoprc.gov.hk/eng/gsxw/t1834883.htm.

United Kingdom with respect to events in Hong Kong, especially as to complaints that recent Basic Law interpretations by the NPCSC, and the passage of the NSL, violated the Joint Declaration's promises of "a high degree [of] autonomy, except in foreign and defence affairs which are the responsibility of the Central People's Government[,]" or that "[t]he laws currently in force in Hong Kong will remain basically unchanged[,]" etc.[5]

The PRC side's position that the Joint Declaration does not confer any ongoing rights upon the British side, which could form the basis of such complaints, is frequently connected with the view that establishment of the Hong Kong government under the Basic Law/"One Country Two Systems" (OCTS) framework was itself a fulfilment of the PRC's obligations under the Joint Declaration, which terminated upon transfer of sovereignty.[6] In this view, the Basic Law as a public law authority (along with relevant domestic sources of law) would displace all domestic legal effects of the Joint Declaration. Meanwhile, Hong Kong courts themselves have at times supported the "in-between" position that the Basic Law itself is not solely an international public law authority but rather "has at least three dimensions: international, domestic and constitutional".[7] Some role for "global constitutionalism"—the influence of legal norms at the transnational level—would thus be implied.[8]

PRC constitutional law scholars, however, have pointed to aspects of the national constitutional order to reinforce the view that sovereignty over Hong Kong and Macau per se confers plenary jurisdictional authority. This position was reflected in an important 2014 PRC State Council white paper on OCTS: "as the fundamental law of the state, the PRC Constitution is the supreme legal authority and has the highest legal efficacy throughout the territory of the People's Republic of China, including the Hong Kong Special Administrative Region".[9] In other words, any legal validity of the Joint Declaration and of the Basic Law of Hong Kong itself would be determined by the function of the PRC Constitution as a legal authority applicable in Hong Kong and Macau, despite not being fully in effect in those locations. Most mainland Chinese constitutional scholars who have commented on the Joint Declaration have adopted this view, thus regarding it as having at most "reference value" for interpretation of the Basic Law, as East China University of Politics

5. Joint Declaration, Art 3(2)–(3).
6. "Zhu Yingguo Dashi Liu Xiaoming: Suowei She Gang Guoan Lifa Weifan 'Zhong-Ying Lianhe Shengming' Chun Shu Wei Mingti [Ambassador to the United Kingdom Liu Xiaoming: The So-called Violation of the "Joint Declaration" by the Hong Kong National Security Law is a Fallacy]," *Jingji Ribao* [*Economic Press*], 29 May 2020, available at: http://www.ce.cn/xwzx/gnsz/gdxw/202005/29/t20200529_35002776.shtml.
7. *HKSAR v Ma Wai-kwan* [1997] 1 HKLRD 761.
8. For a discussion raising the question of Hong Kong's current and future role in global constitutionalism's "progress", *see* Jeffrey L. Dunoff, Antje Wiener, Mattias Kumm, Anthony F. Lang, and James Tully, "Hard Times: Progress Narratives, Historical Contingency and the Fate of Global Constitutionalism," *Global Constitutionalism* 4, no. 1 (2015): 1–17.
9. *The Practice of the "One Country, Two Systems" Policy in the Hong Kong Special Administrative Region* (2014 White Paper).

and Law's Wang Yong argued in 2020 shortly after the passage of the NSL in an essay that soon after received informal official endorsement.[10]

The lack of independent legal authority for the Joint Declaration is reflected in official texts and guidelines on China's legal system, including for example textbooks on constitutional law created as part of the "Marx Project" of updated, Party-approved educational materials.[11] The related doctrine that China has a "unitary" constitutional system in which state authority is ultimately unified in the Central Government, rather than being dispersed in a federal system, also forecloses the possibility of international treaties having quasi-constitutional status for specific regions of the state's territory, including special administrative regions.[12] One of China's leading constitutional law scholars Han Dayuan emphasised the unitary character of the PRC state system in his December 2019 Constitution Day Seminar, delivered at the invitation of the Hong Kong Government's Constitutional and Mainland Affairs Bureau. Han, also a research affiliate of the NPCSC's Hong Kong SAR Basic Law Committee, remarked before his audience of Hong Kong's leading government officials on how "all [legal] efficacy of the SAR originates in the PRC Constitution" and how "at any time, in any situation, the SAR cannot be separated from the unitary constitutional system of the State".[13] As to the legitimacy of the PRC Constitution itself, Han ties this both to that document's reflection of the "popular will" of the Chinese nation, including Hong Kong, as well as its embodiment of national history (principally, a shared history of turmoil and invasion)—indeed, it is for Han this function of the Constitution as a kind of "history textbook", rather than its democratic pedigree or evaluation in light of global constitutional norms, that generates its ability to unify the State and citizenry.[14]

While Han's 2019 address did not go into detail regarding either constitutional theory or its relationship with international legal norms such as those of the Joint Declaration, he explored these topics more concretely in a subsequent article that made especially clear the linkage of these positions with the *Staatslehre* intellectual framework. In his 2020 article on "The Normative Analysis of the Concept of State in the Hong Kong Basic Law", in particular, Han repeatedly invokes the concept of the "State will" (*guojia yizhi*) as the most important standard in determining the

10. "'Zhong-Ying Lianhe Shengming' Dui yu Zhongguo Zhili Xianggang Meiyou Falü Jushuli [The Sino-British Joint Declaration Has No Binding Legal Force with Respect to China's Governance of Hong Kong]", *Guangming Ribao* [*Guangming Daily*], 8 July 2020, available at https://epaper.gmw.cn/gmrb/html/2020-07/08/nw.D110000gmrb_20200708_3-12.htm; republished by authoritative Communist Party ideological journal *Qiu Shi*: http://www.qstheory.cn/llwx/2020-07/08/c_1126210603.htm.
11. *Xianfa Xue* Bianxie Xiaozu [*The Study of Constitutional Law* Editorial Team], *Xianfa Xue* (*Di Er Ban*) [*The Study of Constitutional Law* (Second Edition)] (Beijing: Gaodeng Jiaoyu Chubanshe, 2020): 291–317.
12. *Ibid.*
13. Han Dayuan, "Xianfa yu Guojia Fazhan [The Constitution and the Development of the State]," 2019 Constitution Day Seminar, 4 December 2019, available at https://www.cmab.gov.hk/doc/en/documents/basic_law/speech.pdf.
14. *Ibid.*

relationship of public law authorities in the context of Hong Kong's special status.[15] As he writes, "[i]nterpreted from the perspective of history, the State will was manifested continuously throughout the process of formulating the Basic Law."[16] Historical factors including the ostensibly universal desire to reunite the Chinese national polity as well as the process of negotiation that led to the Sino-British Joint Declaration and then the Basic Law, and the PRC government's process of formulating its policies on Hong Kong and Macau, all inform the content of this "State will". As a consequence, "[o]verall, the SAR system is a product of a political decision taken by the PRC as a political community, and fully embodies the State will [of the PRC] as a unified, unitary State [充分體現著作為一個統一的單一制國家的國家意志]".[17] Indeed, for Han, even the text of the Basic Law itself, with its many references to the (national) State, make it "extremely obvious that the Basic Law heavily emphasizes the State will and State consciousness" and, thus, "the interpretation and application of the Basic Law must take the concept of the State (*guojia guannian*) established in the PRC Constitution as its guide; it cannot separate itself from the will of the State (*guojia yizhi*), and all the more can it not challenge the State's political baselines (*dixian*)".[18]

Han's 2020 article invokes this notion of "State will" ten times and, indeed, makes it the single most central factor for the analysis of Hong Kong's Basic Law and its relationship with other public law texts, including the Joint Declaration. Moreover, he directly connects this position with the *Staatsrechtslehre* tradition, specifically citing the following quotation from Hegel's *Outlines of the Philosophy of Right*:

> Since states are related to one another as autonomous entities and so as particular wills (on which the very validity of treaties depends), and since the particular will of the whole is in content a will simply for its own interests and welfare (*Wohl*), it follows that those interests and welfare are the highest law governing relations between States.[19]

Han notes that it was a hallmark of "the classic theory of *Staatsräson/raison d'état* (*guojia lixing shuo*) that it . . . completely denied any general normativity and binding character of international law above and beyond the will of the sovereign State".[20] While the absolutist character of Hegel's version of sovereignty might have to

15. Han Dayuan, "Lun Xiang Gang Jibenfa Shang 'Guojia' de Guifan Neihan [The Normative Analysis of the Concept of the State in the Hong Kong Basic Law]," *Zhong Wai Faxue* [*Peking University Law Journal*] 32, no. 1 (2020): 19–40.
16. *Ibid.*
17. *Ibid.*
18. *Ibid.*
19. *Ibid.*, citing G. W. F. Hegel (translated by Fan Yang), *Fa Zhexue Yuanli* [*Principles of Legal Philosophy*] (Shanghai: Shangwu Yinshuguan, 2003): 349; slightly modified English translation here drawn from *Hegel's Philosophy of Right* (Oxford: Clarendon Press, 1952): 319, § 336.
20. Han, n 15 above.

be modified in the present era—if only for practical reasons having to do with international reputation and soft power concerns—Han nonetheless argues that in the particular context of Hong Kong "[t]he central government's exercise of jurisdiction in all of the areas of the Basic Law's implementation is beneficial for . . . embodying the will of the sovereign [in Hong Kong as in the rest of the national territory]."[21] A still stricter version of this doctrine is presented by Chen Duanhong, who argues (in terminology drawn from the thought of Carl Schmitt) that the respective Basic Laws of Hong Kong and Macau were "political decisions of the sovereign", while the 1984 Sino-British Joint Declaration and the 1987 Sino-Portuguese Joint Declaration were no more than "vehicles" (*zaiti*) for those political decisions.[22] In other words, the Joint Declarations should be regarded as lacking any legal content other than that provided by domestic sovereign authority.

The basic claim by PRC authorities and scholars that there is no independent domestic public law effect of international agreements such as the 1984 and 1987 Joint Declarations (i.e. of the sort that would preclude imposition of the NSL) is thus not entirely different from the similarly "dualist" positions on treaty applicability of other jurisdictions, including the United States and United Kingdom.[23] However, where some PRC constitutional scholars' position goes somewhat beyond contemporary dualist approaches globally—and instead more closely resembles the positions expressed by conservative *Staatsrechtslehre* theorists—is in attributing to the Joint Declarations a specific function as subordinate to other acts of the state (i.e. other expressions of "State will") and arguing that the international law texts *themselves* must be interpreted upon this basis. As Hans Kelsen analysed with respect to the thought of Heinrich Triepel, "if both domestic legislation and international treaties are expressions of state will, then they . . . cannot be treated as comprising separate legal orders. If they are instead part of the same legal order, then they must exist in some sort of hierarchical superior/inferior relationship."[24] Triepel, who was regarded as the leading dualist theorist of international law in the first decades of the 20th century, was a particularly vocal exponent of the position that "[o]nly the common will of some number of states flowing together towards unity of will,

21. *Ibid.*
22. Chen Duanhong, "Lun Gang Ao Jibenfa De Xianfa Xingzhi [On the Constitutional Character of the Hong Kong and Macau Basic Laws]," *Zhongwai Faxue* [*Peking University Law Journal*] 32, no. 1 (2020): 41, 58.
23. *See* e.g. Curtis A. Bradley, "Breard, Our Dualist Constitution, and the Internationalist Conception," *Stanford Law Review* 51, no. 3 (1999): 529–566; A. F. M. Maniruzzaman, "State Contracts in Contemporary International Law: Monist Versus Dualist Controversies," *European Journal of International Law* 12, no. 2 (2001): 309–328, 309.
24. Hans Kelsen, *Das Problem der Souveränität und die Theorie des Völkerrechts: Beitrag zu Einer Reinen Rechtslehre* [*The Problem of Sovereignty and the Theory of International Law: Contribution to a Pure Theory of Law*] (Tübingen: JCB Mohr, 2nd edn, 1928): 96, 134–135.

via unification of [their] wills, can be the source of international law."[25] That same State will, meanwhile, was doctrinally treated first and foremost as an emanation of domestic authority, which had precedence over any external source of law. Thus, as Carl Friedrich von Gerber wrote in 1865: "The power of the state to will, the ruling power [*Staatsgewalt*], *is* the law of the State."[26]

The *Staatsrechtslehre* approach to triangulating the relationship between national and international public law authorities differs from the majority of modern Anglo-American as well as Continental-style doctrines, including those of "dualist" states. In particular, it relies not on a determination of incompatibility between specific treaty provisions and rights enumerated under the domestic constitutional text as has, for example, been the basis for the modern German Constitutional Court's limits on treaty-based institutions.[27] Nor, as is often reiterated in Anglo-American common law contexts, are limits on the applicability of international treaty law in recent Chinese constitutional discourse premised on concerns over "self-determination, democracy, and accountability".[28] The doctrine of the State will, and even more so its Schmittian variant in Chen's presentation as "political decision", is a more extreme limit on treaty validity.

Correspondingly, while Anglo-American-style dualism would permit international treaties to be invoked by judges as (at minimum) persuasive authorities or for the purposes of reference in determining the interpretation of public law norms, this possibility is explicitly foreclosed with respect to the Sino-British Joint Declaration by a model of dualism whereby international law obligations are interpreted based on extrapolation from domestic public law. On the other hand, however, this same limitation would *not* prohibit binding obligations under the International Covenant on Civil and Political Rights (ICCPR) and International Covenant on Economic, Social, and Cultural Rights (ICESCR), the continued legal validity of which is specifically noted in both the Basic Law[29] and in the NSL itself.[30] Indeed, even

25. Heinrich Triepel, *Völkerrecht und Landesrecht* [*International Law and National Law*] (Aalen: Scientia Antiquariat, 1958) (original publication 1899): 32; Bardo Fassbender, "Heinrich Triepel und die Anfänge der dualistischen Sicht von 'Völkerrecht und Landesrecht' im späten 19. Jahrhundert [Heinrich Triepel and the Beginning of the Dualist Perspective on International Law and National Law in the Late 19th Century]", in Lukas Gschwend, Peter Hettich, Markus Müller-Chen, Benjamin Schindler, and Isabelle Wildhaber (eds), *Recht im digitalen Zeitalter: Festgabe Schweizerischer Juristentag 2015 in St. Gallen* [Law in the Digital Age: Publication of the 2015 Conference of Swiss Jurists in St. Gallen] (Zürich: Dike, 2015): 449.
26. Carl Friedrich von Gerber, 1823–1891, *Grundzüge eines Systems des deutschen Staatsrechts* [*The Core Features of a System of German Public Law*] (Leipzig: B. Tauchnitz, 1865), English translation drawn from Loughlin, n 1 above at 192 (emphasis added).
27. *See*, e.g. Dieter Grimm, Mattias Wendel, and Tobias Reinbacher, "European Constitutionalism and the German Basic Law", in *National Constitutions in European and Global Governance: Democracy, Rights, the Rule of Law* (The Hague: TMC Asser Press, 2019): 407–492.
28. David Feldman, "Monism, Dualism and Constitutional Legitimacy," *Australian Yearbook of International Law* 20 (1999): 105–126.
29. Hong Kong Basic Law (1997), Article 39.
30. National Security Law (2020), Article 4.

by the standards of the heightened version of dualism that is advocated by many PRC constitutional theorists, the provisions of these Covenants would have to be acknowledged as relevant manifestations of the State will and thus as a source of law that should inform interpretations of the law by the Hong Kong judiciary, especially where no contrary rule is specified in the NSL itself.

II. "State Form": Unwritten Constitutional Hierarchy

Given the fundamental character attributed by PRC constitutional theorists to the national Constitution vis-à-vis the Hong Kong Basic Law, the interpretation of the former is especially important for the purposes of determining the "true" relationship of the latter with respect to China's overall public law architecture. This is an "extremely necessary" task that Han describes as "accurately recognizing the normative content of the 'State' in the PRC Constitution and Hong Kong Basic Law, putting the State will, State perspective, and State consciousness in a commanding role, and creating a systematic order for 'One Country, Two Systems.'"[31] Though Han's approach to defining this "systematic order" is relatively conservative, declining to specify restrictions on the legal norms applicable in Hong Kong aside from those that challenge the State's vague "political baselines", Chen Duanhong has developed a more concrete and activist theory of the relationship of State and local authorities:

> Our [PRC] Constitution actually has two functions in terms of its constitutional efficacy. One is the function of serving as the "constitutional dome" (拱頂憲法的作用), and the other is the function of serving as the Constitution of [m]ainland China. It is beyond any doubt that the content serving as the "constitutional dome" is applicable to Hong Kong and Macau, while in the circumstances where the regulations of the Basic Laws [of the two regions] are different from those of the Constitution, the Constitution's relevant content is not applied. This is based on the principle "*lex specialis derogat legi generali*" [law governing a specific subject matter has priority over generally valid laws].[32]

The language of the "constitutional dome [or vault]" that Chen develops here ultimately draws on terminology associated with the Basic Law of the Federal Republic of Germany, itself referred to by Richard Thoma as the "dome of the *Rechtsstaat*".[33] Thoma's description referred to the function of the entire Basic Law as a structuring authority for the German (federal) polity—specifically, its extension of judiciable constitutional rights to all individuals. However, Chen's adaptation of

31. Han, n 15 above.
32. Chen, n 22 above.
33. Richard Thoma and Horst Dreier (ed), *Rechtsstaat-Demokratie-Grundrechte: Ausgewählte Abhandlungen aus fünf Jahrzehnten* [*Rule of Law State-Democracy-Basic Rights: Selections from Five Decades of Essays*] (Tübingen: Mohr Siebeck, 2009).

the "dome" or "vault" analogy is instead intended to illustrate how a constitution can establish a set of basic principles that unify different subsidiary jurisdictions with otherwise quite different public law frameworks. Viewed in this light, the Hong Kong and Macau Basic Laws are a variety of public law *lex specialis*—authoritative enough to locally replace any incompatible norms of the national constitution but having to be understood as emanations of and consistent with the basic principles of that same constitution.

Chen explicitly relates this interpretation of the Basic Law and its legal authority to Carl Schmitt's theory of the "absolute" versus the "relative" constitution.[34] Schmitt's view was that a specific core of norms or values either explicit or implicit in the state's constitutional order lay beyond the possibility of amendment. Thus, the true "absolute" constitutional order was that which reflected "inherent limits to the power of constitutional amendment".[35] This premise, which Chen shares with a number of other PRC constitutional scholars influenced by Schmitt's approach to public law questions,[36] suggests both a hierarchical relationship prioritising domestic public law over international agreements or other obligations and, in addition, a hierarchy among domestic public law authorities privileging, above all, the "unamendable" core norms of the highest domestic legal authority—in this case, the PRC Constitution.

For both Schmitt and Chen, the exact character of the "absolute constitution" is not a purely textual question but rather one relating to a hierarchical relationship among norms. Thus, for both, the preamble of a Constitution is key to interpretation of the overall document.[37] In the case of the Hong Kong and Macau Basic Laws, Chen identifies "three fundamental laws" (*san da genben fa*): (1) national unity and territorial integrity; (2) prosperity and stability; and (3) [maintaining] capitalism.[38] The first of these premises, "national unity and territorial integrity", is shared with the overall national PRC Constitution and, given the overall supremacy of the "absolute" dimension of the latter, must be interpreted in a manner consistent with it.

How, then, is the national Constitution to be interpreted, and what is the nature of its direct legal effect in Hong Kong? One possible approach to an answer is suggested by no less an authority than Xi Jinping himself. As various Communist Party and state media have recently declared, "Xi Jinping Thought on the Rule of Law is the

---

34. Chen, n 22 above, p 53, citing Carl Schmitt (translated by Liu Feng), *Xianfa Xueshuo* [*Constitutional Doctrine*] (Shanghai: Shanghai People's Press, 2016): 74.
35. *Ibid.*, p 152, citing Schmitt.
36. *See* Ryan Martinez Mitchell, "Chinese Receptions of Carl Schmitt Since 1929," *Penn State Journal of Law & International Affairs* 8, no. 1 (2020): 181–263; Sebastian Veg, "The Rise of China's Statist Intellectuals: Law, Sovereignty, and 'Repoliticization,'" *The China Journal* 82, no. 1 (2019): 23–45.
37. Chen, n 22 above, p 54.
38. *Ibid.*

latest achievement in the Sinicization of Marxism."[39] At an important 17 November 2020 meeting devoted to further detailing the content of this "Thought", Xi issued a call to "unwaveringly preserve the constitutionally determined 國體 *guoti* of the people's democratic dictatorship and the 政體 *zhengti* of the National People's Congress system".[40] Doing so, he invoked a public law doctrine that ultimately has its origins in *Staatsrechtslehre*, as adapted into Chinese public law doctrine.

The concept of *guoti*—literally "State form"—is used to refer to the most fundamental and notionally "unchangeable" characteristics of a state and is contrasted with *zhengti*—"form of governance"—which refers to specific administrative and policy institutions and structures.[41] Although both expressions had long traditional histories of usage in China's imperial history, their modern meanings (especially if taken as a binary pair) date only to the early 20th century and reflect the reinvention of the terms in the constitutional thought of the Japanese Empire, which combined them with notions drawn from German public law scholarship regarding the inherent "form of [each] State" (*Staatsform*), which could be democratic, oligarchic, monarchical, etc.[42] By the time of the 1949 establishment of the PRC, Chinese Communist Party leaders including Mao Zedong himself referred to the state's *guoti* as being that of "people's democratic dictatorship", in other words rule by the proletarian class over the other classes of society.[43] This claim has been periodically reinforced in official discourse ever since.

Xi's reaffirmation of the notion of *guoti* gives the concept more prominence as formal legal authority than has usually been the case in the Reform Era and also seemingly reflects recent scholarly discourse in which the term has received new emphasis. Xi's comments closely match earlier discussions of the concept like that of Xiao Jinming of Shandong University, who attributes to Communist Party leadership itself the character of *guoti*, while the NPC (National People's Congress) and its function as the supreme legislative organ of government is relegated to the lesser category of *zhengti*.[44] In this view, "legislative sovereignty" is indeed a feature of the

39. "Xi Jinping Fazhi Sixiang Shi Makesizhuyi Zhongguohua Zui Xin Chengguo [Xi Jinping Thought on the Rule of Law Is the Latest Achievement of the Sinicisation of Marxism]," *Renmin Ribao* [*People's Daily*], 30 December 2020, available at: http://politics.people.com.cn/n1/2020/1230/c1001-31983343.html.
40. *Ibid.*
41. On the conceptual origins of *guoti* and its modern constitutional significance, *see* Wang Hongbin, "'Zhengti' 'Guoti' Ciyi Zhi Shanbian Yu Jindai Shehui Sichao Zhi Bianqian [The Change of the Meaning of Regime and State System with the Evolution of Modern Social Thought]," *Anhui Shixue* [*Historical Study of Anhui*] 5 (2014): 49–60; Lin Laifan, "Guoti Gainian Shi: Kua Guo Yizhi Yu Yanbian [History of State Form as a Concept: Transnational Transplants and Evolution]," *Zhongguo Shehui Kexue* [*Social Science in China*] 3 (2013): 65–84.
42. *See* Lin, n 41 above.
43. *Ibid.*
44. Xiao Jinming, "Xin Zhongguo Xianfa Zhengzhi Fazhan De Huigu Yu Zhanwang [Retrospective and Prognosis for the Development of Constitutional Politics in New China]," *Faxue Luntan* [*Legal Forum*] 3, no. 33 (2018): 5–15.

form of government established under the PRC Constitution, but this cannot detract from the *State form* (i.e. *guoti*) of proletarian/Party leadership. Most recently, some constitutional scholars have explicitly characterised China's 2018 constitutional amendments as "deepening the public's understanding of China's *guoti*, and thus acting as a 'reconstruction' of China's *guoti*".[45]

Chen Duanhong has been a particularly important protagonist of this discourse, arguing that the Communist Party itself acts as the embodiment of the people's will and *pouvoir constituant*[46] but also shares this role with five other essential norms (or *genben fa*—fundamental laws) that together form China's true *guoti*: (1) "the leadership of the Communist Party"; (2) "socialism"; (3) "democratic centralism"; (4) "modernization"; and (5) "protection of basic rights".[47] As with Chen's "three fundamental laws" of the Hong Kong and Macau Basic Laws, his account of the "five fundamental laws" of the PRC *guoti* serves to create a hierarchy of public law norms. The order of these norms establishes a clear hierarchy: individual rights come after Party leadership, the commitment to socialist political economy, the authority of the "democratic" organs of NPC-led governance, and the basic programme of state-led modernisation. Any phenomenon that threatens the top norms of the *guoti*—such as a political insurgency, separatist movement, or even a political organisation or campaign that challenged "modernization" as a matter of basic policy—would thus be a problem that could be addressed directly at the central level and, if necessary, by circumventing lesser-ranked legal rules.

Chen's doctrine of the PRC *guoti* (as he defines it) fits with the "fundamental laws" at the core of the Hong Kong and Macau Basic Laws to justify the application of central legislation throughout China's state territory if needed to preserve the fundamental aspects of the polity. Though Chen has been one of the most focused expositors of China's *guoti*, other constitutional scholars that have engaged with issues related to Hong Kong and Macau have also invoked related concepts to justify a more interventionist role for Beijing in the SARs. Peking University's Jiang Shigong, for example, has been still more emphatic than Chen Duanhong in characterising the Party's "sovereign decisions" on political matters as embodying the

45. Fan Jinxue, "2018 Nian Xiuxian Yu Zhongguo Xin Xianfa Zhixu De Chonggou [The 2018 Constitutional Amendments and the Reconstruction of China's New Constitutional Order]," *Faxue Luntan* [*Legal Forum*] 3, no. 33 (2018): 16–26.
46. Chen Duanhong, "Xianfaxue De Zhishi Jiebei: Zhengzhi Xuezhe He Xianfa Xuezhe Guanyu Zhixianquan De Duihua [The Boundary Tablet Marking the Intellectual Province of Constitutional Law: A Dialogue about the Constituent Power between a Political Scientist and a Constitutional Legal Scholar]," *Kaifang Shidai* [*Open Times*] 3 (2010): 88–103 (noting that "Carl Schmitt tells us that the People continue to exist, without organization or shape, right alongside the Constitution").
47. Chen Duanhong, "Lun Xianfa Zuo Wei Guojia De Genben Fa Yu Gaoji Fa [On the Constitution as Fundamental Law and Superior Law]," *Zhongwai Faxue* [*Peking University Law Journal*] 4 (2008): 485–511.

Chinese people's will.[48] As a prominent voice opposing "judicialization" of political questions and issues, Jiang has argued that politically legitimate actors—specifically the Party—should be empowered to take action without extensive oversight by the courts.[49] Like Chen, Jiang has specifically argued that Hong Kong's relationship to the overall Chinese polity must be seen as an expression not only of public law texts but of political "sovereign decisions" taken by the Chinese polity, carried out via PRC acts of government and ultimately embodied in the policies of the Communist Party.

Jiang thus cites Deng Xiaoping's rejection of limited sovereignty in his negotiations with Margaret Thatcher as evidence of the full (at least potential) application of the PRC constitutional framework to Hong Kong.[50] Meanwhile, regarding the promise of a "high-level of autonomy" (*gaodu de zizhiquan*) contained in the Joint Declaration, Jiang again cites Deng in order to suggest that the latter had rejected that standard (despite its ultimate inclusion in the Joint Declaration) and that Deng instead preferred the formula "Hong Kong people governing Hong Kong" (*Gang ren zhi Gang*), which he, however, simultaneously qualified by saying that:

> There is a limit and standard for "Hong Kong people governing Hong Kong," which is that the main agent of governance in Hong Kong must be patriotic Hong Kong people. In the future, the main component of the Hong Kong government must be patriots . . . We don't require them to support China's socialist system, only that they must love the homeland and love Hong Kong.[51]

As to the standard for "patriotism", Deng remarked that this required "honestly and sincerely supporting the homeland in its restoration and exercise of sovereignty over Hong Kong, and not harming Hong Kong's prosperity or stability". Failure to meet this standard of "patriotism" could result in local leaders—even those elected by eventual universal suffrage—being subjected to administrative intervention

---

48. Jiang Shigong, "Chinese-Style Constitutionalism: On Backer's Chinese Party State Constitutionalism," *Modern China* 40, no. 2 (2014): 133; Jiang Shigong, "Weixian Shencha Zhidu De Di San Tiao Daolu: Zhongguo Xianzhi De Jiangou Yu Wanshan [The Third Road of Constitutional Review: The Construction and Improvement of China's Constitutional System]," *Wenhua Zongheng* [*Beijing Cultural Review*] 1 (2016): 40–49; Jiang Shigong, "Zhongguo Gongchandang yu Fazhi Jianshe de Guanxi [The Relationship Between the Chinese Communist Party and the Construction of the Rule of Law]," *Guanchazhe* [*Observer*], 21 October 2014, available at: https://www.guancha.cn/QiangShiGong/2014_10_21_278011.shtml.
49. Jiang Shigong, "Xianfa Sifahua De Bolun: Jian Lun Faxuejia Zai Tuidong Xianzheng Zhong De Kunjing [Paradoxes in the Discourse of Constitutional Adjudication: Discussed alongside the Predicament of Legal Scholars in Promoting Constitutional Government]," *Zhongguo Shehui Kexue* [*Social Science in China*] 2 (2003): 18–28.
50. Jiang Shigong, "Zhongyang Zhi Gang Fanzhen De Lishi Yuanyi Yu Guifan Yihan: Chong Wen Deng Xiaoping Guanyu "Yi Guo Liang Zhi" Fangzhen De Zhongyao Lunshu [The Historical Intention and Normative Meaning of the Central Government's Policy of Governing Hong Kong: A Review of Deng Xiaoping's Important Remarks on the 'One Country, Two Systems' Policy]," *Gang-Ao Yanjiu* [*Hong Kong and Macau Journal*] 2 (2020) [Hong Kong and Macau Journal] 3–22.
51. *Ibid.*

from Beijing.[52] Seeking to draw constitutional significance from Deng's various official remarks, Jiang argues that Deng's consistent emphasis upon the principle of "patriots governing Hong Kong" (*aiguozhe zhi Gang*) demonstrated "the central authority's possession of the authority to interpret and decide upon the concept of 'Hong Kong people governing Hong Kong,'" and also resulted in "'who is a patriot?' (*shei shi aiguozhe*?) having become a [relevant] theoretical or academic question".[53] Under Jiang's interpretation of the public law framework applicable to Hong Kong, then, the nature of and extent of local autonomy is subordinated to the principle of Communist Party leadership that he (and others) frequently treats as the essential feature of the PRC's *guoti*/State form.

A contrasting perspective is developed in commentary by Beihang University's Tian Feilong, who, like Chen, has also been influenced by Carl Schmitt's notion of the "absolute constitution" to delineate a definite set of fundamental norms such as territorial integrity.[54] In his recent writings on Hong Kong, Tian has suggested that it is a universally accepted principle around the world that Central Government authorities, even in federal states, have the "constitutional authority and constitutional responsibility" to enact domestic security legislation.[55] Like Jiang, Tian points to Deng Xiaoping's statements about "patriots governing Hong Kong" as indicating a relevant legal norm for the Beijing–Hong Kong relationship, though where Jiang focuses more on political decisions by the Communist Party leadership, Tian suggests instead that the patriotism requirement reflects "consciousness of rational boundaries to the degree of Hong Kong's autonomy", including those based on the preservation of overall national security. While Jiang's approach might then seem to justify a greater degree of interventionism—including via the innovation of new forms of centrally directed administration in Hong Kong affairs by means of the Office for Safeguarding National Security of the Central People's Government in the Hong Kong Special Administrative Region (HKSAR) (National Security Office)—Tian instead has suggested that national security enforcement should rely on "existing legal resources in Hong Kong . . . [and that t]he judiciary can develop the relevant case law system to safeguard national security".[56] Even if it is imported into Hong Kong public law, the *guoti* premise by itself does not necessarily imply that courts should lose judicial review powers, even in security contexts.

In its uses by Tian, Jiang, and Chen, however, the *guoti* concept does certainly justify expansion of the national security state and at least *potential* suspension

52. *Ibid.*
53. *Ibid.*, p 18.
54. Tian Feilong, "Shimite Dui Weima Xianzhi De Fansi Ji Qi Zhengzhi Xianfa Lilun De Jiangou [Schmitt's Reflections on the Weimar Constitutional System and Their Political-Constitutionalist Structure]," *Nanjing Daxue Falu Pinglun* [*Nanjing University Law Journal*] 2 (2014): 15–35.
55. Tian Feilong, "Weihu Guojia Anquan Shi Xianggang Tequ Xianzhi Gonggu De Guanjian [Safeguarding National Security Is the Key to Consolidating the Constitutional Order of Hong Kong SAR]," *Gang-Ao Yanjiu* [*Hong Kong and Macau Journal*] 2 (2020): 36–46.
56. *Ibid.*, pp 36, 46, and 94.

of valid legal norms. Chen's version of the doctrine is the most detailed, suggesting that lesser-ranked norms can be suspended whenever there is a threat to the "fundamental laws" of state unity and territorial integrity, prosperity and stability, and/or the capitalist system in Hong Kong, or to the national polity's core features of Party leadership, "socialism", and modernisation/development. The structural implications of carving out such zones of exception, and their implications for the separation of powers, remain to be explored.

III. "State Authority": Executive Autonomy and the State of Exception

In the previous two sections, we have examined the role of ideas of "State will" and "State form" in explaining and structuring approaches to the implementation of the NSL. However, as was noted, neither the NSL itself nor these accompanying principles override per se the role of Hong Kong courts as monitors of the new system's compliance with the requirements of the Basic Law. The question of the extent to which courts will indeed be able to continue fulfilling this role is linked with a broader range of issues connected with the allocation of sovereign authority and the structure of government in Hong Kong.

Indeed, one of the immediate consequences of the passage of the NSL was a public discussion in Hong Kong political and media circles about the very notion of a "separation of powers" and its applicability to the framework of local government, leading to a rejection of this concept and its deletion from government-approved teaching materials.[57] By endorsing "checks and balances" without a "separation of powers", the local government reprised a notion of Executive authority closely linked with the conservative *Staatsrechtslehre* tradition: that of the Executive as the main embodiment of a unitary *Staatsgewalt*, or joint power and authority of the State, whose division is based not on absolute constitutional rules but rather (as per one especially influential doctrine) on the Executive's own "self-limitation".[58] The question of how to reconcile an unelected and not merely symbolic monarchical Executive with a *Rechtsstaat*/rule of law State was, however, perhaps the key question of the entire *Staatslehre* tradition, and it generated different views of which "self-limitation" was one of the most logically consistent. A related but distinct presumption was that of the non-identity of the monarch and State; despite the former "embodying" the latter, and serving as "the highest will-institution *in* the state", the monarch's rights were still to be seen as "*of* the state", in other words, denoting the

57. *See*, e.g. "No Separation of Powers Mentioned in Basic Law: CE", *RTHK*, 1 September 2020, previously available at https://news.rthk.hk/rthk/en/component/k2/1547163-20200901.htm. This news report has since been deleted, along with a wide range of other RTHK articles. It remains available via the Internet Archive's Wayback Machine at the following link: https://web.archive.org/web/20200925174919/https://news.rthk.hk/rthk/en/component/k2/1547163-20200901.htm

58. *See* Loughlin, n 1 above at pp 217–218; 320.

view that "[t]he ruling power is not an absolute power of will[, but] ought only to serve the purpose[s] of the state[.]"[59]

Chen Duanhong's views on these subjects should be seen as especially relevant in part because he was an explicit proponent for the Central Government's passage of security legislation, well in advance of the actual decision to promulgate the NSL.[60] In various other contexts as well, including as a member of the NPCSC's Macau Basic Law Committee, Chen has been called upon to provide input on the proper orientation and approach of Beijing's policy towards the SARs. Moreover, the Hong Kong government, Liaison Office, and HKMAO signalled apparent enthusiasm for Chen's thought by inviting him to give the 4 December 2020 Constitution Day Seminar,[61] following Han's inaugural lecture the previous year. In contrast with the latter, Chen's address roughly five months after the passage of the NSL, and devoted to the topic of "The Constitution and National Security",[62] was far more specific as regards doctrine relating to Central Government interventions in Hong Kong as well as local governance.

Delving into the *raison d'état* tradition much more explicitly than Han had the previous year, Chen's address included references to the thought of Thomas Hobbes, the Italian political-legal historian, and philosopher Giorgio Agamben, and Carl Schmitt (whose thought is also the dominating influence in Agamben's work). The opening portion of the address discussed Hobbes's reasoning for the position that "the State is the only realistic mode of political existence" in order to escape the pre-state condition of the "war of all against all". Chen then related this to the federal government's insistence of preserving state unity during the American Civil War and the rejection of claims to independence by sub-national units of larger polities. The latter part of the talk then drew primarily on Agamben's writings connected with the constitutional value of oaths, the "sacred" character of government and constitutional order, and in particular Agamben's theory of "bare life", as developed in his writings since the 1995 book *Homo Sacer: Sovereign Power and Bare Life* and its 2003 follow-up *State of Exception*.[63]

The topic of "bare life" (*nuda vita* in Italian; ζοε in Ancient Greek) was developed by Agamben as a binary opposite to cultural or communal life (βιος in Ancient

59. *Ibid.*, p 223.
60. Chen Duanhong, "Lun 'Yi Guo Liang Zhi' Tiaojian Xia Tebie Xingzheng Qu Guojia Anquan Gainian De Teshu Xing [On the Unique Nature of the Concept of National Security in the Special Administrative Region under the Conditions of 'One Country, Two Systems']," zijing.org, 22 January 2018, available at http://hk.zijing.org/2018/0122/750657.shtml.
61. "2020 Constitution Day Seminar", *Constitutional and Mainland Affairs Bureau, Hong Kong*, available at https://www.cmab.gov.hk/en/issues/constitution_day.htm.
62. Chen Duanhong, "Keynote Lecture: National Security and the Constitution", 4 December 2020, available at https://www.cmab.gov.hk/en/issues/constitution_day.htm.
63. Giorgio Agamben, *Homo Sacer: Sovereign Power and Bare Life* (Palo Alto: Stanford University Press, 1998) (original publication 1995); Giorgio Agamben, *State of Exception* (Chicago: University of Chicago Press, 2005) (original publication 2003).

Greek).[64] This binary opposition serves as a framework to analyse the means by which sovereign power functions in political/legal communities, specifically by (he argues) the creation of exceptional spaces into which particular subjects are placed as objects of the legal system without any of the subjective rights conferred by that system. In other words, the subject of "bare life" is the person who is treated as the object of exceptional or emergency rule, having lost the status of a possessor of rights. This "outlaw" status is produced by the supreme holder of sovereign authority, who marks out the exceptional zones in which such rightless subjects are placed.[65]

Agamben's theory of bare life was originally constructed largely based on his adaptation of Carl Schmitt's theory of sovereignty and was formulated as a *critical* analysis of modern developments in Western public law.[66] For Chen and some other scholars in today's PRC, however, Agamben's thought is treated as a neutral description of supposedly universal aspects of modern statecraft and constitutional order.[67] Thus Chen argues that Hong Kong lawmakers, judges, or civil servants may be justifiably disqualified from their positions for disrespecting or violating their oaths to the PRC constitutional order, because in taking a political oath of this sort, "the oath-taker returns himself to the position of bare life" (起誓者把自己還原為赤裸的生命).[68] Any particular procedural rights that this individual might otherwise possess can be suspended for the purposes of enforcing the community defining oath—while any violation or misuse of the oath process is equivalent to "declaring war upon the sacred".[69] Tying his reading of Agamben to dominant themes in Schmitt's thought, Chen connected the issue of oaths and loyalty of government actors to the latter's "concept of the political", proclaiming that "the Friend/Enemy distinction is the true essence of loyalty to the State and to the Constitution".[70]

Though seemingly not directly connected with issues of the separation of powers or other such structural public law matters, Chen's focus on oaths reflects a key feature of the NSL system and a major factor in Hong Kong's recent public

64. Agamben, *Homo Sacer*, n 63 above, p 11 ("Bare life remains included in politics in the form of the exception, that is, as something that is included solely through an exclusion . . . Carl Schmitt's definition of sovereignty . . . became a commonplace even before there was any understanding that what was at issue in it was nothing less than the limit concept (*Grenzbegriff*) of the doctrine of law and the State").
65. *Ibid.*; *see also* Agamben, *State of Exception*, n 63 above, pp 3–5.
66. *Ibid.*
67. *See*, e.g. Wu Guanjun, "Shengming Zhengzhi: Zai Fu Ke Yu Aganben Zhi Jian [Biopolitics: Between Foucault and Agamben]," *Makesizhuyi yu Xianshi* [*Marxism and Reality*] 1 (2015): 93–99; Zhang Yibing, "Shengming Zhengzhi Gou Jing Zhong De Chiluo Shengming: Aganben De Zhengzhi Zhexue Huayu Zhi Yi [Bare Life in the Situating of Biopolitics: A Term in Agamben's Political Philosophy]," *Makesizhuyi yu Xianshi* [*Marxism and Reality*] 2 (2018): 94–102.
68. Chen, n 62 above. This discussion of oaths draws upon Agamben's recent work on this subject, which is in turn built on his earlier work on the state of exception. *See* Giorgio Agamben, *The Sacrament of Language: An Archaeology of the Oath* (Verlag: John Wiley & Sons, 2018), p 70.
69. *Ibid.*
70. Chen, n 62 above.

law history. Indeed, before the emergence of the extradition bill protest movement that was the immediate trigger for the formulation and imposition of the NSL, the "LegCo (Legislative Council) oath controversy" episode of 2016 had already raised many similar questions regarding the appropriate extent of central intervention into Hong Kong governance and the relationship between branches of government. With the NPCSC's 2016 interpretation of Basic Law Article 104 to require that "[n]o public office shall be assumed, no corresponding powers and functions shall be exercised, and no corresponding entitlements shall be enjoyed by anyone who fails to lawfully and validly take the [required] oath or who declines to take the oath[,]" the disqualification of all lawmakers who had not "solemnly and accurately" taken their oaths was decided as a matter of public law doctrine.[71] Those who in the future either fail to properly take their oaths to the national polity, or violate their oaths of allegiance (e.g. by advocating independence or, perhaps, questioning basic features of the national system), would by implication also be potentially subject to removal.

The NSL, indeed, also introduced relevant requirements now applicable to anyone "who stands for election or assumes public office".[72] Meanwhile, in November 2020, roughly a month before Chen's invited lecture, the National People's Congress passed a resolution permitting the disqualification of LegCo members found by the Hong Kong government to have engaged in any acts threatening or calling into question Beijing's sovereignty over the SAR, inviting foreign interference, challenging the Basic Law, or failing to demonstrate "allegiance" to the national polity.[73] The subsequent resignation of the last remaining opposition lawmakers in LegCo, in protest of this decision, has thrown the future of the legislature as an independent force in government or check on the Executive into question; the subsequent reforms introduced to the electoral system in 2021 have served to further intensify a shift towards Executive authority.[74] The use of the NSL to prosecute many of the participants in the July 2020 "pro-democracy primaries", construing an electoral

71. *See*, e.g. Han Zhu and Albert H. Y. Chen, "The Oath-Taking Cases and the NPCSC Interpretation of 2016: Interface of Common Law and Chinese Law," *Hong Kong Law Journal* 49 (2019): 381–415.
72. NSL, Art 6.
73. "Quanguo Renmin Dibiao Da Hui Changwu Weiyuanhui Guanyu Xiang Gang Tebie Xingzhengqu Lifa Hui Yiyuan Zige Wenti de Jueding [Decision of the National People's Congress Standing Committee Regarding the Qualifications for Members of the Legislative Council of the Hong Kong Special Administrative Region]." *Xinhua* [*New China News Agency*], 11 November 2020, available at http://www.xinhuanet.com/politics/2020-11/11/c_1126725802.htm.
74. *See* "NPC Hong Kong Electoral Reform Decision", *NPC Observer*, 11 May 2021, available at https://npcobserver.com/legislation/npc-hong-kong-electoral-reform-decision/; "Hong Kong Electoral Changes: Lawmakers Pass Landmark Bill to Drastically Reshape Political System", *South China Morning Post*, 27 May 2021, available at https://www.scmp.com/news/hong-kong/politics/article/3135008/hong-kong-elections-beijing-overhaul-will-bring-stability.

process as a fundamental threat to political order, marks the law's most important use so far to generally transform the overall political environment.[75]

Chen's seminar, coming in the midst of these changes to the balance of authorities within the Hong Kong government, seemed to imply an explicit Schmittian turn in Beijing's governance of Hong Kong, oriented towards the neutralisation of any and all "Enemies". Certainly, Schmitt's own approach to the state of exception was oriented towards the displacement of authority from the judiciary and legislature to the Executive during times of emergency or, as he argued in relation to the crisis-prone Weimar state, "in times of crisis or emergency sovereign power must be bestowed upon one individual and not derived from an abstract and depersonalized set of norms and rules".[76] The notion that the constitutional order of the State is not in itself absolute but rather is premised upon a certain factual state of affairs would mean that the authority of legislators (and judges) within that constitutional order is itself contingent and relative; it may be displaced by Executive authority where needed in order to end crises and restore normality. Thus, Schmitt writes, "the normal situation is the prerequisite for legal norms to be valid. Every norm presupposes a normal situation."[77]

Strikingly, just a few days after the 2020 Constitution Day seminar, Giorgio Agamben released a brief post on his infrequently updated personal website, which seemed almost calculated to respond to Chen's lecture.[78] Titled "Communist Capitalism", it detailed Agamben's denunciation of China's political and economic system as "capitalism in its communist variant, which unites an extremely rapid development of production with a totalitarian political regime".[79] Without touching on Hong Kong specifically, Agamben's comments harshly (if rather vaguely) criticised China's overall lack of the rule of law (*lo stato di diritto/Rechtsstaat*) and even suggested the likelihood of a dystopian future in which China's model might spread globally as a "new regime [that] will unite in itself the most inhuman aspect of capitalism with the most atrocious one of statist communism, combining the extreme alienation of relations between people with unprecedented social control".[80] Whether or not he had heard about his citation in Chen's lecture before the Hong Kong government, it is safe to say that Agamben would not have approved of how his thought was employed.

75. "Hong Kong Arrests 53 Activists under National Security Law", *Associated Press*, 6 January 2021, available at https://apnews.com/article/legislature-primary-elections-democracy-hong-kong-elections-25a66f7dd38e6606c9f8cce84106d916.
76. Carl Schmitt (translated by Michael Hoelzl and Graham Ward), *Dictatorship: From the Origin of the Modern Concept of Sovereignty to Proletarian Class Struggle* (Cambridge: Polity, 2014): xxiv.
77. Carl Schmitt (translated by Jeffrey Seitzer), *Legality and Legitimacy* (Durham and London: Duke University Press, 2004) (originally published 1934): 70.
78. Giorgio Agamben, "Capitalismo Comunista", *Quodlibet*, 15 December 2021, available at https://www.quodlibet.it/giorgio-agamben-capitalismo-comunista.
79. *Ibid.*
80. *Ibid.*

It is ironic, then, that Chen himself indeed points to "capitalism", along with national unity, territorial integrity, and "prosperity and stability" as the fundamental values which are supposed to be ensured in Hong Kong under OCTS—rather than, for example, judicial due process or democracy.[81] However, even the apparently vast empowerment of the Hong Kong Chief Executive and the Central Government suggested by Chen's approach has certain logical limits. Schmitt's own thought was premised not on the ever-increasing use of exceptional authority but rather its justification as a means of restoring the "normal situation" by dealing with moments of crisis. To use the security framework of the NSL to effect far-reaching changes in Hong Kong's electoral system or to regularly target opposition lawmakers for prosecution would exceed even the justifications for the suspension of legal norms entailed in Schmitt's theory. As a more pragmatic matter, this would also contradict the stated goals of "prosperity and stability", as an erratic and self-interested use of security powers by local authorities could further weaken international confidence in Hong Kong's rule of law and general business environment.[82] Given that Hong Kong's political opposition has now been effectively neutralised as a significant impediment to the implementation of central and local government policies, further political deployments of the NSL would seem to entail diminishing returns at a time when maintaining Hong Kong's status as a global financial centre is a more pressing concern. Even if formal separation of powers has been doctrinally rejected by the Hong Kong government, a "self-limitation" in the interests of capitalist imperatives may be its most rational course of action.

Of course, the German doctrine of "self-limitation" is inapposite to Hong Kong in one extremely important way: the Chief Executive is not the highest embodiment or wielder of the *Staatsgewalt*, which instead is deposited with the National People's Congress. Acting as an agent rather than a principal in the governance of Hong Kong, the local Executive cannot justify the self-interested usage of security powers except where these align with national-level objectives. Neither the elimination of any and all political opposition (outside of a broadly defined national security context involving China's overall territorial unity and Communist Party authority) nor extensive interference in the work of the judiciary would significantly advance such objectives. Rather, the presence of adversarial parliamentary debate within limits and the impartial administration of justice (albeit one compromised in highly politicised contexts) are widely recognised as forces for stability in general and elements of the economic success of similarly situated jurisdictions, such as Singapore.[83] The mandate for the present and future Chief Executives of Hong Kong

81. *See* Chen, n 22 above, p 54.
82. *See*, e.g. "Hong Kong Dumped from Economic Freedom List It Had Dominated", *Bloomberg*, 4 March 2021, available at https://www.bloomberg.com/news/articles/2021-03-04/hong-kong-dumped-from-economic-freedom-index-it-used-to-dominate.
83. Cf. Beng Huat Chua, *Liberalism Disavowed* (New York: Cornell University Press, 2017): 69–71 (discussing inter alia how "legal institutions are designed to 'play a policy implementing role in that they serve

would seem to entail maintaining such features in Hong Kong's public law framework to the greatest degree possible while quashing any and all political action or speech that calls Beijing's sovereignty or China's "State form" into question. The NSL may be viewed as a tool designed in the attempt to reconcile the inherent tensions between these aims.

IV. Conclusion

Public statements by PRC officials and departments of government have always consistently emphasised the state's exclusive sovereignty over Hong Kong. However, the detailed dimensions of how that sovereignty is interpreted and exercised, and its relationship to specific legal authorities at the domestic and international levels, has often been left ambiguous. The recent introduction of the NSL legislation for Hong Kong reflects not only a new institutional regime focused on enforcing national security policies but also a transition towards a more active assertion of state sovereignty in the form of direct local legislative and executive action. Although many specific dimensions of the NSL's future application remain unclear—such as the ultimate extent of involvement of or direction by mainland-appointed officials in the processes of investigation, detention, prosecution, trial, conviction, and sentencing—there are a set of clearer doctrinal implications for the structure of public law authorities, particularly the hierarchical relationship of domestic constitutional texts and their superiority over the 1984 Joint Declaration. In general, there has now been enunciated a clear shift to a public law theory focused on the central State's possession of potential interventionist powers derived from territorial sovereignty and the unitary character of State authority, a position that reflects premises closely resembling those of early 20th century *Staatsrechtslehre*.

At the same time, however, there still remain ambiguous elements and different possible ways of interpreting the specific nature of the relationship between the PRC Constitution and the Hong Kong Basic Law, as well as key aspects of Hong Kong's common law–based legal system such as the practice of judicial review. While the basic claim that the Central Government has a right to intervene to address exceptional situations and states of emergency can be endorsed based on various different public law theories, some justifications offered by PRC constitutional theorists may potentially establish more wide-ranging hierarchical powers

to enforce government objectives and policies'"); Jaclyn L. Neo (ed), *Constitutional Interpretation in Singapore: Theory and Practice* (London and New York: Routledge, 2016): 4, 8 (noting that "Singapore's political context, where only one political party has formed the government since independence, presumably shapes the judiciary's self-perception of its role within the constitutional system. This manifests itself in the acceptance that the government should be given the broadest benefit of the doubt, which is reflected in the doctrine of the presumption of constitutionality." However, arguing simultaneously that "[i]n the past decade, Singapore has witnessed a relatively significant expansion in political space for debate and opposition").

of continuous intervention. Comparing the outlook of several such theorists, it is evident that some advocate general rights of intervention based on the "leadership by the Communist Party" and the sovereign decision, while others suggest the continuation of a more removed relationship aimed at reconciling the unitary "State will" across different legal jurisdictions.

However, even the emphatically Schmittian approach of Chen Duanhong has its limits; despite arguing for powers of Central Government intervention based on a hierarchy of public law authorities with ultimate supremacy for the PRC Constitution, in practice, this signifies in his thought only the preservation of three supposedly "fundamental laws" at the core of Hong Kong's order: state unity and territorial integrity, prosperity and stability, and maintaining capitalism. If Hong Kong's "normal situation" in Schmitt's sense is indeed interpreted in line with those three linked values, then any exceptional interventions in the form of legislation or law enforcement aimed at preserving those values against potential threats would seemingly be permitted; but, on the other hand, erratic or self-interested use of security powers, or their deployment in a manner compromising the global economic status of Hong Kong, would not. As measures by which to assess the use of government power ostensibly in the public interest, global legal standards and institutions would retain a key role even for a Hong Kong public law framework largely embracing illiberal 19th century doctrines of State will, form, and authority.

The continued *legal validity* of the ICCPR and ICESCR, along with the precedents of the common law and the norms of the Basic Law, has not been challenged by the NSL; rather, going forward, it will be up to official actors to determine whether and how they can be reconciled. In doing so, they will be best advised to look not to the dramatic ethos of Carl Schmitt's "state of exception" and radical theory of sovereign power but rather to the more conservative model of *raison d'état* in which, as Hegel put it, "interests and welfare are the highest law governing the relations between States".[84] Repairing an international reputation damaged by fears over the possible abuse of security powers, and preserving a global economic role in part ensured by providing public goods associated with independent courts, fully promotes such interests.

84. Cf. Han, n 19 above.

5

Hong Kong's Constitutional Order after the National Security Law

Jie Cheng*

I. Introduction

The Law for Safeguarding National Security in Hong Kong (NSL) has triggered grave constitutional and legal concerns. Because the NSL has limited fundamental rights, many studies of the NSL have taken a normative approach. These reflections are indispensable for critical thinking. However, the normative approach has its limit: it presumes a higher normative ground and a higher court with constitutional jurisdiction. When these grounds are formally shifted, the normative analysis has to change course or else becomes political in nature. The result is partly reflected in the *Tong Ying Kit*[1] case and in the most recent *Lai Chee Ying*[2] case. In this chapter, I argue that in response to these concerns, we need both normative and positive perspectives. In particular, I hope to advance the discussion by investigating the NSL's impacts on the courts' constitutional jurisdiction and Hong Kong's (HK) constitutional order, including changing power dynamics within the Hong Kong Special Administrative Region (HKSAR) and between the HKSAR and China.

When speaking of normative and positive perspectives in legal studies, I take a relatively simplified understanding of the two terms: the positive legal approach is mainly about facts and effects, while the normative legal analysis is mainly about values and convictions.[3] Lawrence Solum provides a list of theories for each category which we can also use to illustrate the differences. For example, in the

* The author is grateful for the insightful comments of Po Jen Yap and Cora Chan, and the excellent research assistance provided by Cameron Fox, Crystal Szeto, and Sarah Wiley.

1. *HKSAR v Tong Ying Kit*, HCAL 1601/2020, [2020] HKCFI 2133. (Challenging the legitimacy of the NSL's limitations on bail and punishments).
2. *HKSAR v Lai Chee Ying*, FACC 1/2021, [2021] HKCFA 3. (Challenging the constitutionality of the NPCSC enacting the NSL).
3. *See* generally Adrian Vermeule, "Connecting Positive and Normative Legal Theory" (2014) 10 *U. Pa. J. Const. L.* 387.

category of positive legal theory, we have doctrinal theories, explanatory theories, and effect theories. By contrast, normative legal theories tend to be entwined with more general normative theories, such as deontology, utilitarianism, and virtue ethics—three of the most important general normative theories that have had an influence on the law.[4] The values of these two approaches have been well debated.[5] This chapter is not intended to join this debate between different approaches of legal studies; rather, it aims to describe and explain the impacts of the NSL on HK's constitutional order.

In an earlier chapter, Professor Fu highlights some of the key issues of concern. These issues have clear constitutional implications: for example, the questions about the NSL's legal status and its relationship with the Basic Law (BL) and the Constitution explore the nature of the NSL; the issue of the terms and construction of the national security offences, which tests the boundaries of criminalisation; the legitimacy of national security agencies; and the issue of interpretation of the NSL and its impacts on judicial independence. Some of the issues such as the National People's Congress Standing Committee's (NPCSC) interpretation power and decision-making power were discussed before the promulgation of the NSL and are still being debated.

There are no simple answers to these issues, and the legal discourse can easily turn into political debates. This chapter takes a positive approach to examining the NSL's impacts on HK's constitutional order for two reasons. First of all, discussions from the normative perspective have limits because the NSL is a national law applied in HK as part of the BL. The semi-constitutional nature of the NSL means that there is only a weak possibility of challenging its validity according to the BL. What's more, the NSL has expressly limited the constitutional jurisdiction of the HK judiciary, which adds complexity to the normative claim. Second, law in the books and law in action are not always the same. While most normative studies presume the universal understanding of law and uniform application of law, positivist studies help us to understand the law understood by judicial authorities in the social and political context. The latter is especially critical when there are competing constitutional authorities or when the constitutional authorities are still in formation. This is exactly the case in HK where both the NPCSC and the HK Court of Final Appeal (CFA) have the power to interpret the BL.

The rest of the chapter proceeds as follows: Part II gives an overview of the major constitutional issues under debate and explains the difficult situation of

4. Lawrence Solum, "Legal Theory Lexicon: Positive and Normative Legal Theory", *Legal Theory Blog*, 29 January 2012, available at https://lsolum.typepad.com/legaltheory/2012/01/legal-theory-lexicon-positive-and-normative-legal-theory.html.
5. For an interesting debate between Richard Epstein and Duncan Kennedy, see Richard Epstein, "Positive and Normative Elements in Legal Education" (1985) 8:2 *Harvard Journal of Law and Policy* 255 and Duncan Kennedy, "Positive and Normative Elements in Legal Education: A Response" (1985) 8(2) *Harvard Journal of Law & Public Policy* 263.

normative analysis with the illustration of the *Tong Ying Kit* case. Part III examines how the NSL limits the courts' constitutional jurisdiction in terms of interpretation and scope of judicial review. Part IV studies how the NSL will impact Hong Kong's political developments due to its limitations on elections and its empowerment of the executive branch. Part V examines the growing presence of the Central People's Government (CPG) in HK and its relationship with the Special Administrative Region (SAR). Part VI offers a conclusion.

II. The NSL and Constitutional Issues

The NSL has triggered both domestic and international concerns. Most critiques have emphasised the immediate and potential threat to freedom of expression, right to privacy, and freedom from search and seizure in Hong Kong.[6] The NSL has also prompted expressions of concern from the international community, including both the United States and the European Union.[7] The United States even imposed sanctions on individual government officials[8] and revoked HK's special trade status.[9] Many concerns are of a constitutional nature. Three of them are most relevant and have attracted many discussions:

> First, whether the NSL is ultra vires because it violates the principle of "One Country, Two Systems" (OCTS) as China has committed in the Sino-British Joint Declaration on HK and infringes HK's high degree of autonomy.

6. *See* generally Kent Roach, "Echoes That Build to a Cacophony: Hong Kong's New Security Law Compared to Illiberal Elements of the Security Laws of Liberal Democracies", Chapter 14 of this volume.
7. *See* Jan van der Made, "Hong Kong National Security Law Triggers Angry Reactions Against China", *Radio France International*, 23 May 2020. Available at rfi.fr/en/international/20200523-china-hong-kong-new-security-law-trigger-protests-pro-democracy-groups-umbrella-movement-carrie-lam-national-peoples-congress.
8. US President Donald Trump issued Executive Order (E.O.) 13936 on 14 July 2020, which provides for the imposition of sanctions on actors engaged in these malign activities. E.O. 13936 also builds on and implements provisions of the *Hong Kong Human Rights and Democracy Act* of 2019 and the *Hong Kong Autonomy Act* of 2020, available at federalregister.gov/documents/2020/07/17/2020-15646/the-presidents-executive-order-on-hong-kong-normalization. Subsequently, the US Treasury imposed sanctions on Carrie Lam, Chris Tang, Stephen Lo, John Lee Ka-chiu, Teresa Cheng, Erick Tsang, Xia Baolong, Zhang Xiaoming, Luo Huining, Zheng Yanxiong, and Eric Chan according to Executive Order (E.O.) 13936 on 7 August 2020, available at https://home.treasury.gov/news/press-releases/sm1088. As a result of the action, all property and interests in property of the individuals named above, and of any entities that are owned, directly or indirectly, 50 per cent or more by them, individually, or with other blocked persons, that are in the United States or in the possession or control of US persons, are blocked and must be reported to United States Office of Foreign Assets Control.
9. The US revoked Hong Kong's special trade status as separate from mainland China and passed the *Hong Kong Autonomy Act*, which became law on 14 July 2020, authorising the President to "impose sanctions on foreign individuals and entities that materially contribute to China's failure to preserve Hong Kong's autonomy". *See* "H.R.7440—Hong Kong Autonomy Act", available at congress.gov/bill/116thcongress/house-bill/7440.

Second, whether the enactment of the NSL fails to comply with the BL and/or the procedural requirements set by the Legislation Law.[10]

Third, whether the NSL violates China and HK's commitment to international human rights law.

It is not difficult to find that a normative approach to these issues tends to result in divided responses. In response to the first issue, many have questioned the constitutionality of the NSL for sidestepping the boundary of HK's autonomy with a national law. For example, Joshua Rosenzweig, the head of Amnesty International's China Team, stated that "from now on, China will have the power to impose its own laws on any criminal suspect it chooses".[11] But the NSL is not the first and only national law that applies in HK. Therefore, many others have found it understandable[12] or defendable because the enactment could end the controversy of Article 23 legislation and restore social order after a year-long period of social unrest and protest against the proposed extradition law in HK.[13] Regina Ip, a Legislative Council (LegCo) member and former government official, tried to explain "why Beijing's national security law for Hong Kong does not spell the end of 'one country two systems'" by affirming that "[o]nce [the NSL is] promulgated and applied in Hong Kong, the well-established common law safeguards of judicial review, habeas corpus, presumption of innocence and proof of guilt beyond reasonable doubt will kick in".[14]

In terms of procedural legitimacy, given the time and the manner in which it was promulgated, there are good reasons to have concerns regarding the legislation's adoption. In fact, there are several procedural hurdles that must be crossed in order for a law developed by the NPCSC to apply in HK—and some accused the NPCSC of failing to cross the hurdles in an appropriate manner. First, the NSL draft bill was

10. Adopted at the Third Session of the Ninth National People's Congress on 15 March 2000. The Law was recently revised in 2015.
11. Lily Kuo and Verna Yu, "China Passes Controversial Hong Kong National Security Law", *The Guardian*, 30 June 2020, available at theguardian.com/world/2020/jun/30/china-passes-controversial-hong-kong-national-security-law. *See also* Alex Lee and Davin Wong, "China's National Security Law: Is This the End of Hong Kong's Promised Autonomy?" (2020) Macdonald-Laurier Institute, available at macdonaldlaurier.ca/files/pdf/20200626_Davin_Wong_Alex_Lee_STRAIGHT_TALK_FWeb.pdf.
12. While calling Beijing's move understandable, Andrew Li argues that offences must be limited in scope, trials carried out openly, and defendants presumed innocent. *See* Andrew Li, "China-Enacted National Security Law Must Be Consistent with Hong Kong Legal Principles", *South China Morning Post*, 2 June 2020, available at scmp.com/comment/opinion/article/3086946/china-enacted-national-security-law-must-be-consistent-hong-kong?utm_source=copy_link&utm_medium=share_widget&utm_campaign=3086946.
13. Liping Gu, "Carrie Lam: Hong Kong National Security Law a 'Turning Point' to End Chaos", *China News*, 1 July 2020, available at http://www.ecns.cn/news/politics/2020-07-01/detail-ifzxrvxc0874286.shtml.
14. "Why Beijing's National Security Law for Hong Kong Does Not Spell the End of 'One Country, Two Systems'", *South China Morning Post*, 31 May 2020, available at https://www.scmp.com/comment/opinion/article/3086619/why-beijings-national-security-law-hong-kong-does-not-spell-end-one.

not published for public comments before its promulgation,[15] a step that is required by the Legislation Law.[16] Second, the legislation was passed with only one reading, which was also uncommon.[17] Last but not least, the legislation was added to the BL's Annex III without meaningful consultation with the BL Committee members. BL Article 18(3) states that the NPCSC "may add to or delete from the list of laws in Annex III after consulting its Committee for the Basic Law of the Hong Kong Special Administrative Region and the government of the Region. Laws listed in Annex III to this Law shall be confined to those relating to defence and foreign affairs as well as other matters outside the limits of the autonomy of the Region as specified by this Law." There were no signs that the Committee members from HK had access to the draft, because before the NSL was promulgated, all Committee members' comments were limited to the explanation of the earlier draft.[18] It was reported that the Basic Law Committee had been consulted in the afternoon of 30 June of 2020 after the NSL was passed on the same day. [19] But given the time limit,

15. "China Passes Draft of Highly Criticized National Security Bill for Hong Kong", *Global News*, 18 June 2020, available at globalnews.ca/news/7079527/china-draft-security-bill-hong-kong/.
16. Article 37 of the Legislation Law (as revised in 2015) states, "For bills that are on the agenda for a session of the Standing Committee, after the Standing Committee meeting, the draft law and an explanation of the drafting or revisions shall be released to the public for comments, except where the Council of Chairmen makes a decision to not release them. The period for release to the public for solicitation of comments is usually not to be less than thirty days. A report shall be made to the public on the solicitation of comments." *See* Legislation Law, n 10 above, Art 37.
17. Article 28 of the Legislation Law (as revised in 2015) provides that, as a rule, a legislative bill placed on the agenda of a meeting of the Standing Committee shall be put to vote after deliberations at three meetings of the Standing Committee. *See* Legislation Law, n 10 above.
18. For example, the interview of Committee Vice Director Maria Tam Wai-Chu on 28 June 2020 mentioned only the NPCSC's explanation of the draft. Nothing was mentioned about the draft itself. See *China News*, "Tan Huizhu: National Security Has Always Been the Responsibility of the Central Government, and Hong Kong Has Been Given Preferential Treatment" [譚惠珠：國家安全從來都是中央事權 香港已獲優待], 27 June 2020, video available at youtube.com/watch?v=KHNrebwobmE. For a summary of the interview, *see* "Tan Huizhu: Hong Kong's Draft Law on Safeguarding National Security Conveys Four Strong Signals from the Central Government" [譚惠珠：香港維護國家安全法草案說明傳遞中央四個強烈信號], *Sohu*, 28 June 2020, available at sohu.com/a/404482430_260616. Of course, this should not mean that no individual members were involved in the drafting. But it is noteworthy that the Committee as an institution did not play a significant role in the process.
19. According to Xinhua News Agency, the NPCSC consulted the Committee before it was added to Annex III: "The Standing Committee of the National People's Congress Passed the Law of the Hong Kong Special Administrative Region on Safeguarding National Security and Decided to Include its Annex III to the Basic Law of Hong Kong" [全國人大常委會通過香港特別行政區維護國家安全法並決定列入香港基本法附件三], *Xinhua News Agency*, 30 June 2020, available at xinhuanet.com/2020-06/30/c_1126178678.htm. However, given that the law was promulgated in the morning and the decision to add the NSL to Annex III was made in the afternoon, the consultation had to be minimal or symbolic to the utmost. For an interview of one of the Committee members, Huang Yushan, by *Ta Kung Pao*, a state-owned Chinese language newspaper from mainland China, *see* Lushan Shi, "Huang Yushan: The Basic Law Commission Supports the Inclusion of the 'Hong Kong National Security Law' in Annex III" [黃玉山：基本法委員會支持將"港區國安法"列入附件三], *Ta Kung Pao*, 30 June 2020, available at takungpao.com/hongkong/text/2020/0630/468882.html. The *Ta Kung Pao* article was dated "2020-06-30 15:45:01", after the consultation was completed.

the consultation was likely minimal or symbolic. Of course, some may argue that all these procedures are not compulsory and the consultation could take different forms. Therefore, it is not a matter of legality, but rather a matter of standards in interpreting the rules of the law.

In response to the issue of human rights, views are also divided. Although the NSL commits to protecting human rights according to the BL and the International Covenant on Civil and Political Rights (ICCPR) as applied to HK (Article 4), for many observers, this is merely an empty promise because the enactment will inevitably infringe freedom of expression and have chilling effects. *Voice of America* reported that on the fourth day of the legislation becoming law, the Hong Kong Public Library immediately took at least nine political books off its shelves, including the works of Chen Yun, a scholar, Joshua Wong, an activist, and Tanya Chan, a Legislative Council member.[20] Some prominent political organisations such as Demosisto, Studentlocalism, and Hong Kong National Front disbanded due to concerns related to the law.[21] But there are also reports and comments that support or defend the legislation. According to *Nature*, science researchers are divided on whether the law will affect research. Matthew Evans, dean of science at the University of Hong Kong, says he's seen no indication that publishing research on politically sensitive topics or participating in international projects and grants will be restricted under the law.[22]

The NSL's impacts on Hong Kong's human rights will depend on courts' application of the NSL. But one thing is for sure: the NSL has put new restrictions on human rights in HK and the courts can do little to negate these restrictions.[23] In the past, Annex III national laws have been localised and courts have thus exercised constitutional jurisdiction over the local ordinances according to the BL and the ICCPR.[24] In addition, Simon Young argues that courts do not have to limit themselves to the ICCPR standards. He found that courts in the past have reviewed restrictions of Basic Law rights according to international conventions if these rights overlap with

---

20. Stacey Hsui, "National Security Law Threatens Hong Kong's Publishers, Booksellers", *VOA News*, 31 August 2020, available at voanews.com/east-asia-pacific/voa-news-china/national-security-law-threatens-hong-kongs-publishers-booksellers.
21. "China: New Hong Kong Law a Roadmap for Repression", *Human Rights Watch*, 29 July 2020, available at hrw.org/news/2020/07/29/china-new-hong-kong-law-roadmap-repression.
22. Andrew Silver, "Hong Kong's Contentious National Security Law Concerns Some Academics", *Nature*, 12 June 2020, available at nature.com/articles/d41586-020-01693-y.
23. But *see* Po Jen Yap's chapter at page 11. (Noting that the CFA's decision of Ng Kong Siu is ostensibly dealing with the constitutionality of domestic legislation, but in reality was confronted with the local implementation of the PRC law. But he also admits that this approach may not be applicable to the NSL because the NSL is applied by promulgation and there is no local law passed to implement it).
24. Article 39 of the Basic Law says that "[t]he provisions of the International Covenant on Civil and Political Rights, the International Covenant on Economic, Social and Cultural Rights, and international labour conventions as applied to Hong Kong shall remain in force and shall be implemented *through the laws of the Hong Kong Special Administrative Region*. The rights and freedoms enjoyed by HK residents shall not be restricted *unless as prescribed by law. Such restrictions shall not contravene the provisions of the preceding paragraph of this Article*." *See* Basic Law, Art 39. Emphasis added.

the latter, or according to other principles if they are exclusive BL rights.[25] But the NSL makes a different case. For one thing, without a local ordinance, courts should hesitate to review the constitutionality of the NSL. What's more, the NSL shall be considered part of the BL and is not subordinate to the ICCPR. By contrast, the ICCPR shall be applied through the Bill of Rights Ordinance (BORO), which was recalibrated by the NPCSC's 1997 decision to comply with the BL.[26] In fact, if the national law listed in Annex III has expressly restricted certain rights, even if the national law is localised, the courts' review will be a weak review.[27]

The legitimacy concerns will continue. But given the divided views of these issues, it is hard to form meaningful political consensus and end the controversy. At the same time, it is clear that courts are not expected to decide broad constitutional issues. When it comes to the NSL, courts will play a more important role in adjudicating cases involved with technical issues such as the application of law and the measurement of liabilities under the NSL.[28] *Tong Ying Kit* illustrates the hard choices that courts have to make.

Tong Ying Kit is the first NSL case. The accused, Tong, was arrested and charged with offences contrary to Articles 20, 21, and 24 under the NSL. His application for bail was rejected by the magistrate for reasons including NSL Article 42.[29] Tong then applied for a writ of habeas corpus on the primary basis that the current detention under the Order is unlawful. Tong challenged the detention on four grounds: (i) NSL 42 violates the Applicant's presumptive right to bail based on the presumption of innocence; (ii) NSL 44 violates the principle of judicial independence for authorising the Chief Executive (CE) to appoint judges to handle NSL cases; (iii)

25. Young discusses the issue of restriction of rights in *Gurung Kesh Bahadur v Director of Immigration*, arguing that rights found in HK's constitution, the BL, are not subject to restrictions of the BORO. *See* Simon N. M. Young, "Restricting Basic Law Rights" (2004) 34 *Hong Kong Law Journal* 109, 116–130. (Identifying the CFA's approach to classify overlapping and exclusive BL rights in *Bahadur v Director of Immigration* but arguing for an autonomous and more generous approach).

26. Article 7 of Annex 2, *Decision of the Standing Committee of the National People's Congress on Treatment of the Laws Previously in Force in Hong Kong in Accordance with Article 160 of the Basic Law of the Hong Kong Special Administrative Region of the People's Republic of China* (Adopted at the Twenty-Fourth Session of the Standing Committee of the Eighth National People's Congress on 23 February 1997). According to the Decision, "provisions relating to the interpretation and application of the Ordinance in section 2(3), the effect on pre-existing legislation in section 3 and the interpretation of subsequent legislation in section 4 of the Hong Kong Bill of Rights Ordinance (Cap 383, Laws of Hong Kong) are not adopted as the laws of the Special Administrative Region for being 'in contravention of the Basic Law'".

27. This has been the case of the *National Flag Case*, or *HKSAR v Ng Kung Sui* [1999] HKCFA 10 (香港特別行政區訴吳恭劭及另一人) [1999] 3 HKLRD 907, (1999) 2 HKCFAR 442. The main issue of the case is whether the restriction on the freedom of expression by the criminalisation of desecration of the national and regional flags is constitutionally justifiable. The Court applied the principle of public order and used the test of necessity instead of proportionality.

28. *See* e.g. Albert H. Y. Chen and Simon N. M. Young, "Liability for Imposing Sanctions Against the PRC or Hong Kong under Hong Kong's National Security Law" (2020) 50 *Hong Kong L.J.* 353.

29. Case summary of the Department of Justice, available at https://www.doj.gov.hk/en/notable_judgments/pdf/HCAL_1601_2020e.pdf.

the creation of minimum terms of imprisonment in Articles 20, 21, and 24 of the NSL neutralises the HKSAR's exercise of independent judicial power; and (iv) the NSL has not been rendered into an official or authentic text in English so that the Applicant's right to choice of lawyers under BL 35 is frustrated.[30]

The High Court rejected all four grounds using technical standards. The first ground was rejected as being an "unreasonable reading of the article". The court held that "[i]t would be wholly illogical to read Article 42(2) as meaning that the person seeking bail is first required to admit his guilt . . . [the Defendant's] construction of Article 42(2) would be wholly inconsistent with the presumption of innocence, which is expressly recognized in Article 5". In terms of the appointment of the judges, the Court held that there is no proper or sufficient basis for contending that the Chief Executive or the Government is in the position to interfere with judicial independence according to international standards. The Court also found that the NPCSC as the legislature has the power to prescribe fixed punishment, to limit the discretion of judges, and to enact law in Chinese.[31]

This case is noteworthy because all four grounds are de facto constitutional challenges. If one of them is supported, the court will have to decide if the relevant NSL clauses shall be invalidated. The legitimacy question that is open in *Tong Ying Kit*[32] was again brought to the CFA in the *HKSAR v Lai Chee Ying* case.[33] Rather unsurprisingly, the CFA gives deference to the NPCSC. The immediate reason is that the NSL has expressly limited the court's constitutional jurisdiction of interpretation and scope of judicial review. What if the Court takes a different approach? Then it will probably trigger an NPCSC interpretation to override the CFA's interpretation. This will only intensify the controversy and cause a severe constitutional crisis similar to the 1999 right to abode case. Therefore, the deference choice will acknowledge the limit of the judicial power set by the NSL. But the other choice is self-destructive and was not taken even by the 1999 Court, which made the

30. *Tong Ying Kit*, n 1 above, para 12.
31. *Ibid.*, paras 27, 29 (rejecting Ground 1 allegation), paras 55 and 61 (rejecting Ground 2 allegation based on "The Bangalore Principles of Judicial Conduct" and the 1967 decision of the Privy Council in *Liyanage v The Queen*), para 66 (rejecting Ground 3 allegation with the 1977 Privy Council decision in *Hinds v The Queen*), and para 70 (rejecting Ground 4 allegation with BL 9).
32. *Ibid.*, para 26.
33. The High Court says that the Court of Final Appeal will determine "the ambit and effect of NSL Article 42(2) especially in the context of other NSL Articles, including Articles 1, 3–5, 41 and 42, and of provisions of the CPO as well as of the International Covenant on Civil and Political Rights as applied to HK by Hong Kong Bill of Rights Ordinance and provisions of the Basic Law". See *HKSAR v Lai Chee Ying* (黎智英), FAMP1/2020, [2020] HKCFA 45, paras 20 and 23. See also *HKSAR v Lai Chee Ying* (黎智英), n 2 above, para 37 (Holding that the legislative acts of the NPC and NPCSC leading to the promulgation of the NSL as a law of the HKSAR, done in accordance with the provisions of the Basic Law and the procedure therein, are not subject to review on the basis of any alleged incompatibility as between the NSL and the Basic Law or the ICCPR as applied to Hong Kong).

landmark decision of the *Ng Ka-Ling* case in the spirit of judicial activism.[34] Part III will explain how the NSL will restrict the courts' constitutional jurisdiction.

III. The NSL and Courts' Constitutional Jurisdiction

The NSL impacts on courts' constitutional jurisdiction both directly and indirectly. Before the NSL was passed, HK courts exercised constitutional judicial review over local legislation. Courts had also exercised certain judicial powers over national legislative acts and government decisions from other national government branches. But the NSL has set clear limitations on the courts' jurisdiction powers over NSL cases.

3.1 HK Courts' Constitutional Jurisdiction before the NSL

Courts in HK need to have constitutional and legal jurisdictions to deal with NSL issues, including those related to constitutional issues. In the 1997 *Ma Wai Kwan* case,[35] the first constitutional dispute right after 1 July 1997, the High Court took a conservative position by applying the British parliamentary sovereignty doctrine and the principle of constitutional hierarchy. According to the Court, when HK was under colonial rule, "Acts of Parliament and ministerial decisions were not subject to the Hong Kong Letters Patent".[36] Similarly, the Court concluded that "[t]his Court has no jurisdiction to entertain challenges to the legality of the Provisional Legislative Council, that being a body established by the sovereign."[37] This position was soon rejected by the CFA in *Ng Ka-ling*.[38] By contrast to the conservative approach, the CFA stated that:

> What has been controversial is the jurisdiction of the courts of the Region to examine whether any legislative acts of the National People's Congress or its Standing Committee (which we shall refer to simply as "acts") are consistent with the Basic Law and to declare them to be invalid if found to be inconsistent. In

34. Mr Justice Kemal Bokhary told the US consulate in 2007 that he and the other four judges of the CFA "seriously considered resignation" after the interpretation of the BL by the NPCSC in June 1999, which effectively overruled the ruling of the city's top court. Bokhary said they "decided not to do so because 'you can only do that once'", according to the confidential cable dated 28 August 2007, sent by then US Consul General James Cunningham to the State Department. *See* Gary Cheung, "All City's Top Judges 'Considered Quitting'", *South China Morning Post*, 8 September 2011, available at scmp.com/article/978391/all-citys-top-judges-considered-quitting. Professor Yap argues that the courts can read down the NSL without hollowing up the NPCSC's power. This presumes that the courts still have interpretation power over the NSL. But this seems to have ignored Article 65 of the NSL which precludes the interpretation power of the HK judiciary. *See* Yap, Chapter 7 in this volume, Part IV.
35. This was the first constitutional judicial review case after the handover: *HKSAR v Ma Wai Kwan David* [1997] HKLRD 761.
36. *Ibid.*, para 133.
37. *Ibid.*, para 159.
38. [1999] 1 HKLRD 577, FACV14/1998.

> our view, the courts of the Region do have this jurisdiction and indeed the duty to declare invalidity if inconsistency is found. It is right that we should take this opportunity of stating so unequivocally.[39]

What happened next was a series of controversial actions which almost led to a constitutional crisis: the HK Government requested that the CFA clarify the above statement. The CFA took an unprecedented action by issuing a statement which clarified that the CFA's judicial power, including the courts' jurisdiction to interpret the BL, "is derived from the Basic Law through the authorization of the NPCSC" and that "the Court's judgment on 29 January 1999 did not question the authority of the Standing Committee to make an interpretation under Article 158 which would have to be followed by the courts of the Region. The Court accepts that it cannot question that authority."[40] Subsequently, the NPCSC issued its first interpretation of the BL in 1999.[41]

The NPCSC proclaimed its interpretation power and literally struck down the interpretation of the CFA. But the NPCSC did not move on to deny the courts' jurisdiction of constitutional review, even though scholars such as Xiao Weiyun and Shao Tianren expressly objected in their statements regarding the constitutional review power of the judiciary.[42] This move represented a Chinese version of the "great compromise" between the NPCSC and the CFA. After this brief contention, there has been acquiescence to the courts' constitutional judicial review power from the CPG. At the same time, due to the NPCSC's overarching interpretation power, the courts' jurisdiction over national legislative acts is in a grey area. After *Ng Ka-ling*, the HK judiciary has carefully tested the borderline of the jurisdiction in cases such as *Chong Fung Yuen*[43] and *Democratic Republic of the Congo*[44] by ignoring documents issued by the NPCSC or the CPG. In *Chong Fung Yuen*, the Director argued that according to the statement of the Interpretation, the legislative intent of all other categories of Article 24(2) have been reflected in the *Preparatory Committee's Opinions on the Implementation of Article 24(2)*. This argument was rejected by the Court via a narrower definition of the NPCSC's interpretation, which excluded the Preparatory Committee's opinions.[45] In the *Democratic Republic*

39. *Ibid.*, para 61.
40. [1999] 1 HKLRD 577, para 6, (1999) 2 HKCFAR 141.
41. The NPCSC's interpretation of Articles 22(4) and 24(2)(3) of the BL of the HKSAR of the PRC (Adopted at the Tenth Session of the Standing Committee of the Ninth National People's Congress on 26 June 1999).
42. The statements were published as a press release by the Xinhua News Agency on 6 February 1999. For details, *see* "Why the Court of Final Appeal Was Wrong: Comments of the Mainland Scholars on the Judgment of the Court of Final Appeal", in Johannes M. M. Chan, *Hong Kong's Constitutional Debate: Conflict Over Interpretation* (Hong Kong: Hong Kong University Press, 2000), p 53.
43. *Director of Immigration v Chong Fung Yuen* [2001] HKCFA 48, [2001] 2 HKLRD 533.
44. *Democratic Republic of the Congo v FG Hemisphere Associates LLC* [2011] HKCFA 41, (2011) 14 HKCFAR 95 (first decision, rendered 8 June 2011).
45. *Chong Fung Yuen*, n 43 above, 8.3.

of the Congo case, the courts at three levels were asked to consider letters from the Office of the Commissioner of the Ministry of Foreign Affairs of China in HK as certificates prescribed by Article 19 of the BL.[46] All courts refused to consider the letters as certificates. It took the NPCSC another interpretation of the BL to clarify China's diplomatic policy as absolute state immunity and its application in HK as Article 13 issues.[47]

From the normative perspective that assumes parliamentary sovereignty, the courts' constitutional jurisdiction is still debatable. From the positive perspective, courts' constitutional jurisdiction is based on constitutional convention rather than the BL. Even though it is not written in the BL, it has become an indispensable part of HK's constitutional order. What's more, the overarching power of the NPCSC is also entrenched by the courts' subsequent judgments. Since then, the NPCSC's interpretation power has functioned like a Sword of Damocles, keeping the national legislation from any judicial review in HK. The NSL broke the silence for the first time with express limitations on the constitutional jurisdiction of the courts.

3.2 HK Courts' Constitutional Jurisdiction after the NSL

The NSL sets limits on the courts' constitutional jurisdiction as follows: Article 65 limits the judiciary's jurisdiction of statutory interpretation; Articles 14(2) and 47 limit courts' judicial review power; and Article 44 sets guidelines for which judges can adjudicate national security cases. These limitations were the grounds for challenges of the legitimacy of the NSL in *Tong Ying Kit*. As mentioned earlier, it is hypothetically possible for HK's judiciary to conduct constitutional judicial review of national legislation and national government decisions, yet unless the NSL is invalidated, the courts' jurisdiction over national security cases will be limited.

First of all, the NSL vests the power of interpretation exclusively with the NPCSC. Article 65 of the NSL provides that "[t]he power of interpretation of this Law shall be vested in the Standing Committee of the National People's Congress". Some argue that this will allow the NPCSC to interpret the laws with the terms in mainland Chinese laws.[48] If that is the purpose, it seems to be redundant, because

46. The first letter is dated 20 November 2008 and was meant for the High Court proceedings before Judge Reyes, while the second letter is dated 21 May 2009 and was meant for the appeal to the Court of Appeal. The third letter is dated 25 August 2010 and is meant for these appeals. The letters "[reiterate] the position of the CPG on state immunity and further [state] that the principled position of the State applies to [Hong Kong]". *See Democratic Republic of the Congo*, n 44 above, paras 43–47.

47. Interpretation of Paragraph 1, Article 13 and Article 19 of the Basic Law of the Hong Kong Special Administrative Region of the People's Republic of China by the Standing Committee of the National People's Congress (Adopted at the Twenty-Second Session of the Standing Committee of the Eleventh National People's Congress on 26 August 2011). This interpretation was accepted by the Court of Final Appeal in a judgement rendered on 8 September 2011, *Democratic Republic of the Congo v FG Hemisphere Associates LLC*, [2011] HKCFA 67; (2011) 14 HKCFAR 395.

48. *See* Kuo and Yu, n 11 above.

the NPCSC's interpretation is not limited by common law approaches. Rather, the purpose of the provision is to pre-empt future judicial action that is against the will of the NPCSC. Beijing understands that the NSL will be enforced in HK and the actual effects of the NSL will be dependent on the law enforcement agencies and the courts. Since 1999, the judiciary has been independent from any political appointment or financial control of Beijing, and the only legitimate influence Beijing could have on the judiciary is through statutory interpretation. As least this has been the case since 1999. In other words, by limiting the courts' power of statutory interpretation, the NPCSC aims to restrain the courts from judicial activism in NSL cases. Again, this seems to be the understanding of the *Tong Ying Kit* court as well. According to the court, Article 65 vests the ultimate or final power of interpretation in the NPCSC.[49]

Articles 14(2) and 47 of the NSL are also pre-emptive in nature. These provisions limit the courts' jurisdiction over two types of decisions: Article 14(2) precludes judicial review of decisions and the deliberations made by the National Security Committee (NSC); Article 47 precludes judicial review of the Chief Executive's national security and national secrets certificates. Article 14(2) states that "[n]o institution, organization or individual in the Region shall interfere with the work of the Committee. Information relating to the work of the Committee shall not be subject to disclosure. Decisions made by the Committee shall not be amenable to judicial review." Therefore, the Committee is not only secretive but also under no judicial control. The NSC, which bridges the CPG and HKSAR Government, is a new office created by the NSL. According to the NSL, the Committee "shall be under the supervision of and accountable to the Central People's Government" (Article 12); the Committee shall create a secretariat and the Secretary General of the Committee's secretariat "shall be appointed by the Central People's Government upon nomination by the Chief Executive" (Article 13); and the Committee shall have a National Security Adviser "who shall be designated by the Central People's Government and provide advice on matters relating to the duties and functions of the Committee. The National Security Adviser shall sit in on meetings of the Committee" (Article 15). Among other things, this is the first time that judicial review of government decision is expressly excluded.

According to Article 47, "The courts of the Hong Kong Special Administrative Region shall obtain a certificate from the Chief Executive to certify whether an act involves national security or whether the relevant evidence involves State secrets when such questions arise in the adjudication of a case. The certificate shall be binding on the courts." This provision creates an administrative privilege for the Chief Executive which is not reviewable by the courts. The certificate in the clause is

49. This is exactly what happened in *Tong Ying Kit*, in which the court interprets both the BL and the NSL. See *Tong Ying Kit*, n 1 above, at para 41 (Explaining that since there is no relevant interpretation of Article 42, it is not necessary to consider the effect of Article 65 in the present case).

an administrative decision in nature and certificates of this sort serve as documents of proof. Even in China, certificates from national secret agencies will be considered as evidence and courts will decide if they are admissible.[50] By prescribing that the certificate shall be binding on the courts, Article 47 limits courts' jurisdiction and makes national security certificates a sub-category of BL Article 19 "act of state" certificates.[51]

In addition, Article 44 authorises the Chief Executive to designate judges to adjudicate national security cases. As the judges in *Tong Ying Kit* noted, this designation will not affect specific cases, nor will it affect judges' exercise of their judicial independence. However, the appointment will block some individual judges from adjudicating national security cases. This will indirectly affect the courts' jurisdiction.

By pre-emptively excluding judicial interpretation and exempting judicial review of NSC decisions, Beijing wants to make sure that the NSL will be enforced according to its intent. This has inevitably limited the courts' jurisdiction. However, this does not necessarily mean that courts will not exercise these powers in practice.[52] At least from the positive perspective, these new limits only mean that the courts will have to deal with new requirements. Courts do have different options and different approaches to these restrictions. This at least partly explains why the Court in *Tong Ying Kit* did not address the question of whether or not HK courts have jurisdiction over national laws. But no matter what option the courts take, the courts cannot ignore their impacts on their constitutional jurisdiction.

Courts are not the only powers affected by the NSL. The other two government branches will also feel the weight of the NSL. Hong Kong's political development after 1997 has generally empowered the legislature and put more political restraints on the Chief Executive and the Government. But the political development in HK may change course due to the impacts of the NSL.

---

50. In mainland China, the National Secret Agency may provide certification for classified documents. Other government agencies that have power to classify national security information may also provide certification of national secrets. *See* State Council Regulations on Safeguarding National Secrets Law, Art 37 (government authorities qualified to certify classified information upon application). But these certificates are evidence according to evidence rules and by default are not legally binding.
51. According to BL Art 19(3), "The courts of the Hong Kong Special Administrative Region shall have no jurisdiction over acts of state such as defence and foreign affairs. The courts of the Region shall obtain a certificate from the Chief Executive on questions of fact concerning acts of state such as defence and foreign affairs whenever such questions arise in the adjudication of cases. This certificate shall be binding on the courts. Before issuing such a certificate, the Chief Executive shall obtain a certifying document from the Central People's Government." According to customary understanding, the scope of acts of state such as defence and foreign affairs is much narrower than for national security acts.
52. *See*, for example, Part IV of Yap, Chapter 7 in this volume at 13–20.

IV. The NSL and HK's Political Development

Constitutional judicial review and representative government are the two cornerstones of HK's new constitutional order. The NSL also sets limits on the election of the legislature and the Chief Executive, which may bring fundamental changes to the composition of the legislature and the power dynamics in the political system.

4.1 The Government System and Political Reform before the NSL

From 1843 to 1984, HK was under a British colonial constitution. The Letters Patent issued by the British Crown established a system of government which has been described as a "gubernatorial government" with a high degree of power concentrated in the hands of the Governor by London, who in turn appointed both the official and unofficial (non-government) members of the Executive and Legislative Councils. The Sino-British Joint Declaration of Hong Kong was signed in 1984. Between 1984 and 1997, when HK was in the transition from British colonial rule to the new constitutional order, its government system underwent fundamental political changes. The most salient change was the introduction of representative government during the transitional period. Albert Chen gives a concise account of the development of representative government in the later stage of the colonial government from a historical perspective.[53]

In 1990, the National People's Congress (NPC) promulgated HK's BL. The BL provides that both the Legislature and the Chief Executive shall be elected and that "the ultimate aim is the selection of the Chief Executive by universal suffrage upon nomination by a broadly representative nominating committee in accordance with democratic procedures" (Article 45(2)) and that "[t]he ultimate aim is the election of all the members of the Legislative Council by universal suffrage" (Article 68(2)). In addition, the Chief Executive is nominated and elected by the electoral committee instead of being appointed by the CPG.

After 1990, representative government reform was accelerated under the colonial government, partly as a response to the local concerns of Beijing's takeover after 1989.[54] However, this political background, as well as the lack of sufficient communication between the British Government and the Chinese Government, prompted China to suspect London's motives for electoral reform. As a result, Beijing rejected the reform and insisted on reappointing all of the LegCo members after 1997 before the first LegCo was elected in 1998. The study shows that between 1998 and 2004,

53. Albert Chen, "Development of Representative Government" (Chapter 8), in Johannes M. M. Chan and C. L. Lim, *Law of the Hong Kong Constitution* (Hong Kong: Thomson Reuters, 2015), pp 217–247.

54. *See* generally Sze Yuen Chung, *Hong Kong's Journey to Reunification: Memoirs of Sze-yuen Chung* (Chinese edition) (Hong Kong: Chinese University of Hong Kong Press, 2001) (鍾士元：《香港回歸歷程——鍾士元回憶錄》，香港中文大學出版社，2001).

the LegCo seats were composed roughly the same as in 1995's LegCo.[55] But, in spite of this similarity, the post-1997 electoral system failed to produce a "coalition government" that could "absorb politics".[56] Instead, the electoral system has become the core issue that has triggered endless disputes and political contentions within the SAR and against Beijing.

The major problem of this formula is that the combination of functional constituencies and direct election in practice guaranteed that pro-establishment interest groups could keep the majority of the seats. This created tensions between pro-establishment and pro-democracy groups. The latter has demanded further electoral reforms to change the formula while the former prefers moderate reforms. Both sides quote the same provisions of the BL while focusing on different aspects of the two clauses (Articles 45(2) and 68(2)). The pro-democrats emphasise that "the ultimate aim is universal suffrage" while the pro-establishments want to make piecemeal changes "with the principle of gradual and orderly progress".[57] The competition within the region soon developed into the rivalry between the pro-democrats and the alliance of the pro-establishment and the CPG. The battle-grounds used to be highly institutionalised: election campaigns, legal disputes, registered protests, and public opinion influences. While the pro-establishment camp has more formal and institutional resources, the pro-democracy camp is able to mobilise social movements with more appealing liberalism narratives.[58]

55. By 1995, there were no longer any appointed members. LegCo members were elected by geographical constituencies (20), functional constituencies (30), or the Election Committee (an electoral college which selects the Chief Executive) (10).

56. A. Y. C. King, "Administrative Absorption of Politics in Hong Kong: Emphasis on the Grassroots Level", in A. Y. C. King and R. P. L. Lee (eds), *Social Life and Development in Hong Kong* (Hong Kong: Chinese University Press, 1981), Ch 7.

57. The BL 45(2) provides: "The method for selecting the Chief Executive shall be specified in the light of the actual situation in the Hong Kong Special Administrative Region and in accordance with the principle of gradual and orderly progress. The ultimate aim is the selection of the Chief Executive by universal suffrage upon nomination by a broadly representative nominating committee in accordance with democratic procedures." The BL 68(2) provides: "The method for forming the Legislative Council shall be specified in the light of the actual situation in the Hong Kong Special Administrative Region and in accordance with the principle of gradual and orderly progress. The ultimate aim is the election of all the members of the Legislative Council by universal suffrage. The specific method for forming the Legislative Council and its procedures for voting on bills and motions are prescribed in Annex II: 'Method for the Formation of the Legislative Council of the Hong Kong Special Administrative Region and Its Voting Procedures.'" For an example of emphasis on the latter, *see* Henry Litton, "With Patriots in the Driving Seat, Upholding the Basic Law, Hong Kong is Pointing in the Right Direction." *South China Morning Post*, 12 February 2022, available at https://www.scmp.com/comment/opinion/article/3166516/patriots-driving-seat-upholding-basic-law-hong-kong-pointing-right.

58. Flowerdew examines the former HK Chief Executive's failed efforts to provide more appealing narratives to replace the legacy of former Governor Patten. *See* John Flowerdew, "Identity Politics and Hong Kong's Return to Chinese Sovereignty: Analysing the Discourse of Hong Kong's First Chief Executive" (2004) 36:9 *Journal of Pragmatics* 1551. Ch'eng explains the identity crisis behind the 2019 protests. *See* Henry Ch'eng, "How Shifting Identity Politics Are Shaping the Hong Kong Protests", *China Focus*, 8 October 2019, available at chinafocus.ucsd.edu/2019/10/08/how-shifting-identity-politics-are-shaping-the-hong-kong-protests/.

Prior to 2019, both sides constrained themselves in three areas. First, the contests presumed the legitimacy of the government, including the Beijing government. Second, the competitions were led by identifiable political parties. Third, the CPG was considered as the backdrop of the competition even though the pro-establishment camp is generally closer to the CPG and is nicknamed the pro-Beijing camp. In other words, before 2019, the competitions were kept within the reach of the Establishment. But the street movements after 2014 changed this dynamic. Not only the executive and police authority, but also the legislature and judiciary, were confronted and physically threatened.[59] Street movements were organised by loose organisations without identifiable, responsible leadership. In addition, the CPG became the direct target of some protesters instead of a backdrop. This full-frontal confrontation strategy polarised the political forces and provoked the CPG which used to stay behind the scenes. As if a spell had been lifted, the hostilities from both sides were released with little restraint. In this sense, the NSL is the CPG's response with the aim of suppressing social unrest. But sadly, it may ignite new contention.

4.2 Changing Power Dynamics after the NSL

The NSL aims to restore order and reclaim authority. But instead of rewinding the clock, it creates a new structure. This new structure changes the power dynamics by empowering the executive branch and screening out certain members from the LegCo and other government offices.

First, the NSL empowers the executive branch with new national security agencies, offices, and related authorisations. In Chapter 9, Fu and Zhao highlight that the NSL creates several national security agencies. The new institutions include: (a) a National Security Department within the police, which has been portrayed as a restoration of the colonial government's Special Branch, the political unit that was abolished immediately before reunification;[60] (b) the creation of a special prosecution unit within the Department of Justice; (c) the designation of specially selected national security judges to hear NSL-related cases; (d) an NSC within the HKSAR government; and most importantly, a National Security Office (NSO) that is dispatched by, and accountable to, the CPG. All of these agencies are administrative in nature and enjoy executive privileges that are immune from judicial review. Several UN human rights experts have expressed their concern for this lack of independent oversight.[61]

59. The CFA's anti-face covering judgment provides a list of vandalism and violence in 2019. See *Kwok Wing Hang v Chief Executive in Council*, FACV6/2020, FACV Nos 6, 7, 8, and 9 of 2020, [2020] HKCFA 42, paras 89–97.

60. Richard Cullen and H. L. Fu, "Political Policing in Hong Kong" (2003) 33 *Hong Kong Law Journal* 199.

61. For details of the letter, *see* UN Special Rapporteur on the Promotion and Protection of Human Rights and Fundamental Freedoms While Countering Terrorism, et al., "Comments on the Law of the People's Republic of China on Safeguarding National Security in the Hong Kong Special

Second, the NSL provides both direct and indirect limitations on the LegCo members' election. The NSL deprives convicted criminals of the right to take public office. Article 35 states that a person who is convicted of an offence endangering national security by a court shall be disqualified from standing *as a candidate* in the elections of the LegCo and district councils of the HKSAR, *holding any public office in the Region*, or *serving as a member* of the Election Committee for electing the Chief Executive.[62] The Article further provides that "If a person so convicted is a member of the LegCo, a government official, a public servant, a member of the Executive Council, a judge or a judicial officer, or a member of the district councils, who has taken an oath or made a declaration to uphold the BL of the HKSAR of the People's Republic of China (PRC) and swears allegiance to the HKSAR of the PRC, he or *she shall be removed from his or her office* upon conviction, and shall be disqualified from standing for the aforementioned elections or from holding any of the aforementioned posts".[63] On 11 November 2020, the NPCSC passed a resolution on the "legal requirements and preconditions" for holding a seat in HK's legislature. The decision listed four conditions that would disqualify someone from serving in the LegCo.[64] Following the NPCSC's interpretation of BL Article 104[65] and the subsequent oath-taking case,[66] all 15 opposition lawmakers resigned, leaving the LegCo with virtually no opposition presence.[67]

In addition to the direct limits, the NSL also has indirect impacts on the future elections due to its chilling effects. NSL Article 29 imposes sanctions on individuals and organisations that collaborate with "a foreign country or an institution,

---

Administrative Region", 1 September 2020, OL CHN 17/2020, p 11, available at spcommreports.ohchr.org/TMResultsBase/DownLoadPublicCommunicationFile?gId=25487. The missive was signed by six UN special rapporteurs and the vice-chair of the international body's working group on arbitrary detention. *See* Tony Cheung, "Beijing Slams Foreign 'Interference', 'Malicious Slander' after UN Rights Experts' Letter of Concern on Hong Kong National Security Law", *South China Morning Post*, 4 September 2020, available at scmp.com/news/hong-kong/politics/article/3100214/national-security-law-un-rights-experts-send-beijing-joint.

62. Article 35 of the NSL. Emphasis added.
63. *Ibid.*
64. "Decision of the Standing Committee of the National People's Congress on Issues Relating to the Qualification of the Members of the Legislative Council of the Hong Kong Special Administrative Region" (全國人民代表大會常務委員會關於香港特別行政區立法會議員資格問題的決定), *Xinhua News Agency*, 11 November 2020, available at xinhuanet.com/politics/2020-11/11/c_1126725802.htm.
65. *Interpretation of Article 104 of the Basic Law of the Hong Kong Special Administrative Region of the People's Republic of China by the Standing Committee of the National People's Congress* (Adopted by the Standing Committee of the Twelfth National People's Congress at its Twenty-Fourth Session on 7 November 2016). This Interpretation clarified the requirements of oath-taking to resume the position in the LegCo and disqualifying elected members who fail to comply with the requirements.
66. *Chief Executive of The Hong Kong Special Administrative Region v President of The Legislative Council*, CACV 224/2016, [2017] 1 HKLRD.
67. Lilian Cheng and Tony Cheung, "All Hong Kong Opposition Lawmakers Quit Following Camp's Vow to Resign En Masse over Beijing Resolution", *South China Morning Post*, 16 November 2020, available at scmp.com/news/hong-kong/politics/article/3109574/all-hong-kong-opposition-lawmakers-quit-following-camps-vow.

organisation or individual outside the mainland, HK and Macao of the PRC, or conspires with a foreign country or an institution, organisation or individual outside the mainland, HK and Macao of the PRC, or directly or indirectly receives instructions, control, funding or other kinds of support from a foreign country or an institution, organisation or individual outside the mainland, HK and Macao of the PRC, to commit any of the following acts shall be guilty of an offence: [. . .] rigging or undermining an election in the HKSAR, *which is likely to cause serious consequences*."[68] As mentioned earlier, the pro-democracy camp is able to mobilise social movements with more appealing liberalism narratives. These narratives have also helped the pro-democrats to gain support—including financial support—from other liberal democracies. With broad definitions such as "collaboration" and "likely to cause serious consequences", organisations receiving financial support, or other types of support, can be easy targets of the NSL. This will certainly have severe impacts on their future ability to raise funds and secure other types of support from abroad.

The chilling effects are immediate. As mentioned earlier, within days of the promulgation of the enactment, some prominent political organisations such as Demosisto, Studentlocalism, and Hong Kong National Front disbanded, due to concerns over the law.[69] Without sufficient funding, the electoral campaign will be affected, which will in turn weaken the competitiveness of the affected groups. A recent report predicted that as a result of the disqualification, the revival of Establishment control in the district councils is likely.[70] And it won't be a surprise if the NSL has similar effects on the LegCo. Since the reshuffling of the LegCo paralyses opposition parties, it will in turn weaken the checking power of the LegCo.

As a special region of China, HK's constitutional order is not independent from China's constitutional order. China is ready to tolerate a region with different political, legal, and economic systems. This is the core of the OCTS and the BL which creates an asymmetric structure between the CPG and the SAR for the purpose of OCTS. From the perspective of liberalism, the OCTS is to ensure local autonomy.

---

68. Article 29 of the NSL. Emphasis added.
69. *Human Rights Watch*, n 21 above. It is also reported that convicts will lose their right to elect the Chief Executive. *See* "Beijing Plans Further Moves to Alter Qualifications for the Chief Executive of Hong Kong" [北京擬在出手或廢除泛民選舉香港特首資格], *DW News*, 23 December 2020, available at dwnews.com/%E4%B8%AD%E5%9B%BD/60223532/%E5%8C%97%E4%BA%AC%E6%8B%9F%E5%86%8D%E5%87%BA%E6%89%8B%E6%88%96%E5%BA%9F%E9%99%A4%E6%B3%9B%E6%B0%91%E9%80%89%E4%B8%BE%E9%A6%99%E6%B8%AF%E7%89%B9%E9%A6%96%E8%B5%84%E6%A0%BC.
70. *See* Banshan Sha, "Analysis: Is it Possible for District Boards to Reshuffle the Pan Democracy-Led System or Revive it?" [區議會有可能大洗牌　泛民主導或變建制「復活」], *HK01*, 22 December 2020, available at https://www.hk01.com/%E6%94%BF%E6%83%85/565183/01%E5%88%86%E6%9E%90-%E5%8D%80%E8%AD%B0%E6%9C%83%E6%9C%89%E5%8F%AF%E8%83%BD%E5%A4%A7%E6%B4%97%E7%89%8C-%E6%B3%9B%E6%B0%91%E4%B8%BB%E5%B0%8E%E6%88%96%E8%AE%8A%E5%BB%BA%E5%88%B6-%E5%BE%A9%E6%B4%BB?utm_source=01appshare&utm_medium=referral.

For China, HK's special status is not based on liberalism. Instead, it is the consequence of regional disparity and social inclusion. In the history of China, other regions have been granted special status with self-governing powers. Therefore, China does not view the "high degree of autonomy" of HK as anything different from the practice in history. In other words, the structure between the CPG and HK is not based on the liberal imagination of a separation of powers. It is based on China's governing experience and the constitutional conventions between the CPG and the SAR. In Part V, we will examine how the relationship between the CPG and the SAR evolved before the NSL, and what changes the NSL will bring to this structure.

V. The Changing Power Structure between the CPG and the SAR

5.1 The Asymmetric Structure between the CPG and the SAR

The relationship between Beijing and HK is unique in the sense that it has an asymmetric structure. The asymmetry is created by the OCTS policy and the BL.[71] According to the BL, both the legislature and the executive are respectively accountable to the national branch. But the HK judiciary is independent from the oversight of Beijing's Supreme People's Court (SPC). Nonetheless, with the overarching interpretation power (Article 158 of the Basic Law), the NPCSC is not only the supervisor of the legislature of the HKSAR, but also has a checking power over the HK judiciary. The chart below shows the power structure and their relations. For the past 20 years, the NPCSC has been the major national authority that has a presence in HK through formal legislative decisions. Other agencies such as the State Council, HK and Macau Office, the Central People's Government Liaison Office, and the Ministry of Foreign Affairs Commission do not make decisions with direct legal effects in HK. According to Article 18 of the BL, the State Council can arguably "issue an order applying the relevant national laws in the Region" on behalf of the CPG. But even this power is limited by the power of the NPCSC to declare war and declare a state of emergency in the first place. In fact, the State Council, which does have legislative power according to Chinese law, has not made any legislative decisions for HK since 1997.[72]

71. *See* generally Jie Cheng, "Jurisprudential Basis for the New Constitutional Order of Hong Kong: Separation of Powers or Delegation of Powers" (2017) 5 *China Legal Science* 56, 75–80.

72. Before the co-location inspection arrangement was finalised, some proposed that the State Council should issue an order. But that proposal was rejected in the very early stage and the co-location arrangement was eventually approved by the NPCSC. *See* Co-operation Arrangement between the Mainland and the Hong Kong Special Administrative Region on the Establishment of the Port at the West Kowloon Station of the Guangzhou-Shenzhen-Hong Kong Express Rail Link for Implementing Co-location Arrangement [內地與香港特別行政區關於在廣深港高鐵西九龍站設立口岸實施"一地兩檢"的合作安排], signed on 18 November 2017, as approved by the NPCSC on 27 December 2017.

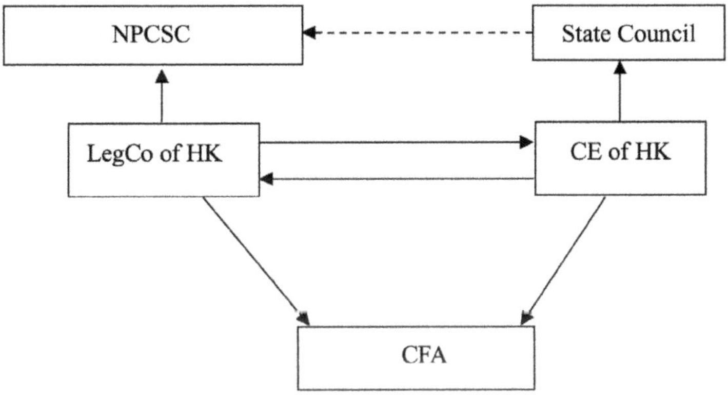

This structure has given HK and Macau more liberties and self-governing powers compared with other Chinese regions, but it has also created tension between the national government and the HKSAR.[73] There are two major criticisms of this structure. One criticism is focused on the unwanted influence of the national government in the asymmetric relationship.[74] Another criticism is less critical of the role of the NPCSC. Yet it also finds a case of weak judicial review in Hong Kong.[75] How should one deal with these tensions, and how can we evaluate the sustainability of the asymmetric structure? Before the NSL, the CPG has insisted that OCTS and HK's high degree of autonomy will be maintained "for a long time" while enthusiastically promoting the economic integration of the Greater Bay Area.[76] In other words, the previous approach has been characterised by the coexistence of political asymmetry and economic integration.

73. Jie Cheng, "Hong Kong's Judiciary under the Dual Track Politics: A Reflection from the Perspective of Constitutionalism" (2006) 5 *China Legal Science* 47 (程潔：《論雙軌政治下的香港司法權：憲政維度下的再思考》，《中國法學》2006年第5期).
74. Johannes Chan, "Asymmetry in the Face of Heavily Disproportionate Power Relations: Hong Kong", in M. Weller and K. Nobbs (eds), *Asymmetric Autonomy and the Settlement of Ethnic Conflicts* (Philadelphia: University of Pennsylvania Press 2010), pp 121–147.
75. Zhu and Kouroutakis argue that HK has weak judicial review due to the CFA's status and the catalytic role of the NPCSC. *See* Guobin Zhu and Antonios Kouroutakis, "The Hong Kong Subconstitutional Model of Separation of Powers: The Case of Weak Judicial Review" (2017) 47 *Hong Kong Law Journal* 221.
76. The Greater Bay Area's full name is the Guangdong–Hong Kong–Macau Greater Bay Area. On 1 July 2017, the "*Framework Agreement on Deepening Guangdong–Hong Kong–Macau Cooperation in the Development of the Bay Area*" was signed by the Hong Kong and Macau governments, Guangdong Province Government, and the National Development and Reform Commission in HK. The signing was witnessed by President Xi Jinping during his visit to HK.

5.2 Changing Power Dynamics after the NSL

The NSL will change the constitutional convention in place since 1997 and is likely to speed further integration of the two regions. First, the creation of the national security adviser legalises the interaction between the Liaison's Office and the HK Government. Second, the creation of the NSO adds yet another Central Government Office in addition to the Liaison's Office. The Office performs broad intelligence and policy functions and may also trigger national jurisdiction in investigating a narrow range of national security offences. Third, the CPG now has extraterritorial jurisdiction over HK. In addition to the NSC, NSL Article 55 grants the CPG authority to exercise jurisdiction over national security cases that are complex, serious, or pose a major and imminent threat, when requested by the HKSAR Government. Article 56 states that the SPC shall designate a court to adjudicate the case and Article 57 states that the Criminal Procedure Law of the PRC will be applied. If this procedure is invoked, HK courts' jurisdiction would be handed over to mainland Chinese courts.

This jurisdiction shifting has caused special concerns by the UN human rights experts.[77] Wang Chen, the Vice Chairman of the NPCSC, explained the rationale behind Article 55. He said that the NPCSC provided three reasons to justify the jurisdiction indicated in Article 55, which is to be exercised over "an extremely small number of criminal cases that endanger national security in specific circumstances". First, it is a manifestation of the comprehensive power to govern HK. It is the sovereign right of China to protect its core interest in a subsidiary entity. Second, the Article supports the HKSAR in its enforcement and application of the law to ensure the effective protection of national security, suggesting that the HKSAR has failed in the past and may fail again. Thirdly, Article 55 can pre-empt a political turmoil, as defined in BL Article 18(4), from taking effect; in other words, it aims to prevent a true emergency.[78] But all three reasons seem to make the NSL redundant exactly because of the assistance of Article 18(4) as well as the Article 14 Garrison Clause. In fact, the jurisdiction shifting shows that Beijing has intended to take back some of the powers devolved in the BL, such as the regulation of national security issues. Therefore, the NSL not only creates national crimes but also creates law enforcement agencies. Further, these agencies will be responsible to the CPG, which made them "as a putative successor to Special Branch which was abolished

77. *See* UN Special Rapporteur et al., n 61 above.

78. Chen Wang, "Explanations on the National Security Law of Hong Kong Administrative Region of the People's Republic of China" [法制工作委員會負責人向十三屆全國人大常委會第十九次會議作關於《中華人民共和國香港特別行政區維護國家安全法（草案）》的說明], *Xinhua News Agency*, 20 June 2020, available at xinhuanet.com/2020-06/20/c_1126139511.htm.

before the reunification".[79] Because of this intention, although it is possible for HK to make separate Article 23 legislation, there is no need to do so. Also because of this intention, the NSL has created new agencies that will inevitably change the existing constitutional order.

In the past, the NPCSC's interpretations, decisions, the LegCo's political activities, and the courts' judicial decisions have made constitutional changes without formally revising the BL. This time it is Annex III legislation that plays a similar role. As a result, HK's new constitutional order will look like the diagram below.

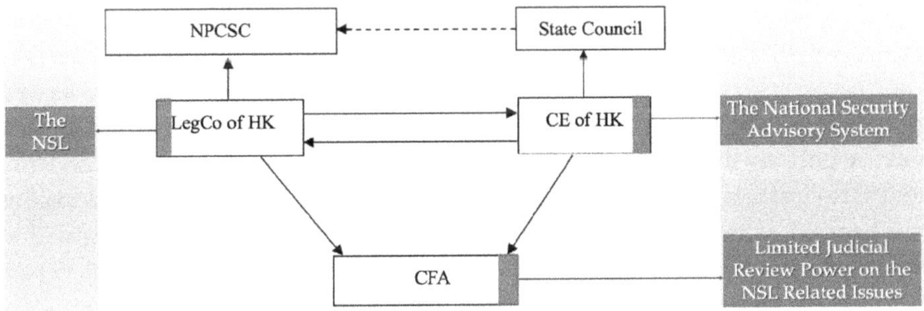

In the diagram, the shadows in the three government branches in HK represent new institutions from the CPG vested by the NSL. The NSL pre-empts the LegCo's national security legislation and other criminal law rules as demonstrated in *Tong Ying Kit* and *Lai Chee Ying*. The courts' constitutional jurisdiction and other jurisdictions are limited by the NSL. The CE and the Government will take more responsibilities and become more answerable to the CPG and its representatives, such as the National Security Adviser.

Will the NSL end the OCTS commitment? Most observers are still reluctant to make an early conclusion. I concur with Susan Shirk, a former State Department official now at the University of California, San Diego, who noted that the NSL is the "new law that integrates Hong Kong" into the Chinese security state.[80] In fact, HK's integration into China is expected according to the BL and that is the essence of reunification. It is also the general direction given the economic integration between HK and mainland China. But here lies the legitimacy issues of how, when,

79. Fu compares the National Security Department established within the institution of the Hong Kong Police Force as a putative successor to Special Branch during the British Colonial government. *See* Fu Hualing, "National Security Law", in Johannes M. M. Chan and C. L. Lim (eds), *Law of the Hong Kong Constitution* (Hong Kong: Thomson Reuters, 2015), Ch 6, 6.037. For more information of the Special Branch, *see* H. L. Fu and Richard Cullen, "Political Policing in Hong Kong" (2003) 33 *Hong Kong Law Journal* 199.

80. Edward Wong, "Hong Kong Has Lost Autonomy, Pompeo Says, Opening Door to U.S. Action", *The New York Times*, 27 May 2020, available at nytimes.com/2020/05/27/us/politics/china-hong-kong-pompeo-trade.html.

and under what conditions. The BL sets a 50-year time limit,[81] and there are various procedural requirements to change the BL.[82] But overall, the legitimacy of changes will not be a simple and easy legal choice.

The courts in HK can still play an important role in answering this question despite the overarching power of the CPG. According to NSL Article 1, the enactment was made "in accordance with" the BL. Therefore, courts can utilise their judicial review power to adjudicate NSL cases and supervise the enforcement of the NSL. But as discussed earlier in this chapter, the NSL has empowered the executive branch and the CPG. Unless the NSL's constitutionality is challenged, this will become the new norm in the future. In order for the courts to challenge the NSL, at least three conditions will have to be satisfied: first, HK courts need constitutional jurisdiction over the issues; second, judges adjudicating the cases will need to take a normative approach to the constitutional issues, which rely on principles derived from political liberalism and natural law theory instead of positive law; and third, it must be unlikely that an adjudication will be overturned by other authorities. Until now, HK courts have only challenged the legality of national legislative decisions in a handful of cases. None of these legislative decisions were formal legislation promulgated by the NPC or NPCSC. The closest one is the *Chong Fung Yuen case* in which the CFA refused to validate the *Preparatory Committee's Opinions on the Implementation of Article 24(2)* and therefore ostensibly parted from the NPCSC's *1999 Interpretation*. In fact, the NPCSC openly expressed its discontent with the CFA's construction of Article 24(2). However, the NPCSC did not take further action to override the court decision, probably for fear of an immediate constitutional crisis not long after the *Ng Ka-Ling case*. But things are quite different now. Immigration issues are also different from national security issues. It is unlikely that HK judges will challenge the constitutionality of any particular NSL clauses, never mind the law as a whole.

The constitutional jurisdiction of the courts is fundamentally and technically limited. Whether or not judges will challenge the legitimacy of the limitations is subject to the panel's choice of jurisprudence and its willingness to confront the NPCSC's authority. And even if the courts' judges decide to do so, they will need to have both legal and political wisdom to carefully balance the relationship with the NPCSC and other agencies of the CPG. Unless that is the case, courts will be more deferential to the HK Government and the CPG in the future. If that is the case, the question is no longer whether or not OCTS will exist after the NSL, because under "One Country", there are already many different forms of sub-national governments, such as special economic zones, ethnic autonomous regions, and most

81. Article 5 of the BL states that "the previous capitalist system and way of life shall remain unchanged for 50 years".
82. Article 159 prescribes powers and procedures to amend the BL. But as discussed in the earlier part, constitutional changes in HK have resulted from both legal and political practices as well.

recently, free trade zones. The question will then be what kind of system HK will have in the future.

VI. Conclusion

This chapter examines the NSL's direct and indirect impacts on HK's constitutional order. It looks into three aspects of institutional changes induced by the NSL and predicts impacts the NSL may have on HK's constitutional order: impacts on courts' constitutional jurisdiction, impacts on the SAR's political development, and impacts on the relationship between the CPG and the SAR.

The Basic Law laid the foundation for HK's new constitutional order.[83] After 1997, the new constitutional order evolved from an executive-led power structure to one that embodies checks and balances. There are two cornerstones of this new constitutional order: constitutional judicial review and representative government. Representative government is endorsed by the BL, but the current electoral system has become the source of contention for the pan-democrats. Constitutional judicial review is not expressly written in the BL. Instead, it has become the constitutional convention with the acquiescence of the CPG. But courts' jurisdiction over the national laws has been an open question since the first BL case. This constitutional order has been the shared consensus of various stakeholders, including the HK establishment, the general public in HK, and the CPG.

Post-2014 street protest movements challenged the existing political order and saw the rise of a populist social movement. The 2019 city-wide protests and the government's clumsy response exacerbated its relations with the opposition parties and led to further mutual distrust between the protesters and the government, as well as the CPG which stands behind the HK government. To restore social order and regain authority, the CPG responded with the NSL. But the NSL does not simply restore the previous power structure. The NSL also changes the power dynamics of the constitutional order of the SAR.

The NSL not only provides for national security crimes, it also creates new government agencies to enforce the law, which empowered the executive branch of the government. The NSL limits HK courts' constitutional jurisdiction to ensure that the government agencies can exercise their powers. The NSL also changes the power structure between the CPG and the SAR.

These changes are fundamental. For the past 20 years, the CFA has been an active constitutional court in human rights and some political issues. This cannot be simply attributed to HK's common law tradition, as argued by Johannes Chan.[84] In

83. The constitutional order of HK after 1997 is an issue from the normative perspective. For some, the constitutional order is based on the BL and Sino-British Joint Declaration. For others, the new constitutional order is based on the BL and the Constitution of the PRC. This chapter does not aim to dive into this question. For more discussion of the two sets of understanding, *see* Cheng, n 71 above.

84. Johannes Chan, Chapter 6 in this volume, pp 22–24.

fact, many common law courts do not have constitutional judicial review power[85] or have been troubled by political interferences. Political scientists believe that stakeholders tend to empower the courts when there is political fragmentation,[86] which has been the case in HK for the past 20 years. In other words, judicial independence is the result of consensus from all sides, including the pro-democracy, HK Establishment, and Beijing. Even so, both Chief Justice Andrew Li and Chief Justice Jeffery Ma have repeatedly expressed concerns with courts becoming involved in political issues. If the political fragmentation is replaced by a stable majority party due to the suppression of adversaries of the Establishment, it will be more challenging for Chief Justice Andrew Cheung Kui-Nung to take the baton of judicial activism. As a result, we can only expect that the HK judiciary will become more restrained and deferential in dealing with cases of a political nature. In that case, judges will have to be more creative and courageous to avoid an embarrassing result or other constitutional crisis if the political actors have expressed strong preferences. For example, judges can still navigate the issues through the legal procedures and application of law. But if judges step up and openly challenge the NSL, the NPCSC is likely to intervene. Some argue that "while the law is a done deal, its interpretation is not".[87] This is arguable because the NSL has expressly forestalled the courts from the interpretation of Article 65.

What are the other implications following from the enactment of the NSL? The most important one is probably the accelerating integration between the Mainland and the HKSAR. It is in China's interest to keep the OCTS and the rule of law in HK. Nevertheless, Beijing's policies are based on the imagination of HK being an apolitical port city driven by economic imperatives. This diverges from other imaginations offered by the local populist and pro-democracy narratives. The latter, although probably a political myth invented more recently, has provided a more attractive narrative about HK peoples' identity compared with the old one based on nationalism and paternalistic patriotism. Without being able to respond to the political outcry and build new consensus, the NSL will create political tensions in the future. This will in turn invite, from both sides, more doubts surrounding OCTS. The collective identity issue deserves at least another paper and I will not dwell on the subject here.

85. *See* Stephen Gardbaum, "The New Commonwealth Model of Constitutionalism" (2001) 49 *American Journal of Comparative Law* 707.
86. John Ferejohn, Frances Rosenbluth, and Charles R. Shipan, "Comparative Judicial Politics", in Carles Boix and Susan C. Stokes (eds), *The Oxford Handbook of Comparative Politics* (New York: Oxford University Press, 2009), pp 727–751.
87. Yap, Chapter X in this volume, at 21.

6

National Security and Judicial Independence

A Clash of Fundamental Values

Johannes Chan*

Drafted in Beijing without any meaningful local public consultation and promulgated only an hour before it came into force, the National Security Law (NSL) was imposed on the people of Hong Kong just before 1 July 2021. In less than a year, it has dramatically changed the civil and political scene in Hong Kong. One of the features of the NSL is the Central Government's distrust and determination to curb the power of the judiciary in Hong Kong. An independent judiciary is the hallmark of the rule of law, the only thing that still distinguishes the two systems between the Hong Kong Special Administrative Region (HKSAR) and the Mainland. Yet China has a very different conception of the judiciary, and an independent judiciary that could challenge the sovereign power is beyond tolerance. How this ideological difference led to the enactment of the NSL will be outlined in Part I of this chapter. Part II will examine the impact of the NSL on judicial independence. Judicial responses to the NSL will be discussed in Part III. Part IV explores the room for judicial creativity under the NSL in light of decided cases. It argues that the worst fear indeed comes from within. By adopting a deferential attitude towards any exercise of sovereign power, the judiciary will inevitably become compliant and there are already signs that the judiciary is losing public confidence in its independence. Sadly, while the judiciary at the moment is still robust and independent, there is little room for optimism for the future of judicial independence in the HKSAR.

* I am grateful to my colleagues Professor Yap Po Jen, Cora Chan, and Vivian Wong for their helpful comments on an earlier draft of this chapter. I would also like to acknowledge the support of the University Grants Committee's Prestigious Fellowship in Humanities and Social Sciences for the generous support of the research for this article.

I. An Ideological Conflict

An independent and impartial judiciary has been described as "an institution of the highest value in every society and an essential pillar of liberty and the rule of law".[1] The concept of judicial independence could be traced to the British Act of Settlement 1701, which provides, inter alia, that judges could only be removed by both Houses of Parliament for misbehaviour. It was soon spread to and took root in many other parts of the common law world and is now an internationally well-recognised concept.[2] It means that, in discharging its judicial functions and duties, the judiciary must be free from interference by both the legislative and the executive branches of government (institutional independence) as well as independent of its colleagues and superiors within the judiciary (internal independence). A judge shall adjudicate on the law and legal disputes fairly, impartially, and strictly in accordance with legal principle and the spirit of the law, without any restrictions, improper influences, inducements, pressures, threats or interferences, direct or indirect, from any quarter or for any reason.[3] Judicial independence serves as a foundation of the rule of law.[4] As all powers and authorities of the government must come from the law, an impartial interpretation and administration of the law by an independent judiciary will provide the best safeguards against arbitrary exercise of powers and the best guarantee for freedoms and liberties. At his farewell speech, Ma CJ emphasised that "the rule of law was about recognising and enforcing human rights and fundamental freedoms" and the concept of an independent judiciary is not related to politics.[5] In the institutional sense, judicial independence forms an essential part of the doctrine of separation of powers. However, the essence of

1. *Mount Scopus International Standards of Judicial Independence*, adopted by the International Association of Judicial Independence and World Peace in 2008 and consolidated in 2015, para 1.1, available at https://www.jiwp.org/mt-scopus-standards (visited 6 February 2022).
2. *See* International Covenant on Civil and Political Rights 1966; European Convention on Human Rights 1953; *Mount Scopus International Standards of Judicial Independence 2015*, which draws its inspirations from the *New Delhi Minimum Standards on Judicial Independence 1982, the Montreal Universal Declaration on the Independence of Justice 1983, the UN Basic Principles of Judicial Independence 1985*, and the long series of other international rules and standards relating to judicial independence and the right to a fair trial; *The Burgh House Principles of Judicial Independence in International Law* (for the international judiciary), the *Tokyo Law Asia Principles*; Council of Europe Statements on judicial independence, particularly the Recommendation of the Committee of Ministers to Member States on the independence, efficiency, and role of judges by the Council of Europe 1998, *The Bangalore Principles of Judicial Conduct 2002*, and the American Bar Association's revision of its ethical standards for judges.
3. UN Basic Principles on the Independence of the Judiciary 1985, para 2, available at https://www.ohchr.org/en/professionalinterest/pages/independencejudiciary.aspx (visited 6 January 2021) and the speech of Chief Justice Ma on his retirement: *see* n 5 below.
4. *See* The Bangalore Principles of Judicial Conduct 2002, value 1, available at https://www.unodc.org/pdf/crime/corruption/judicial_group/Bangalore_principles.pdf (visited 6 January 2021).
5. Ng Kang Chung, "Hong Kong's Departing Chief Justice Offering One Last Defense for Judicial Independence at Farewell Sitting", *South China Morning Post*, 6 January 2021, available at https://www.scmp.com/news/hong-kong/law-and-crime/article/3116685/hong-kongs-departing-chief-justice-offers-one-last (visited 7 January 2021).

judicial independence is that it provides checks and balances against excesses by the executive and the legislature and ensures that the other two branches exercise their powers within the confines of the law, and in this context it is justified by the rule of law and is not dependent on any particular notion of the doctrine of separation of powers, a political doctrine which may manifest in different forms of governance in different jurisdictions. Thus, notwithstanding the absence of a clear demarcation between the executive and the legislature, both in the United Kingdom and many British colonial systems including Hong Kong, judicial independence remains a constitutional principle, and the judiciary exists as an institution that is distinct and distanced from the other two branches of government.

The principle of judicial independence is expressly protected in the Sino-British Joint Declaration and entrenched in the Basic Law.[6] The importance of judicial independence has repeatedly been endorsed by successive Chief Justices.[7]

China does not share the same view of judicial independence. In a unitary system where power is concentrated in the hands of the executive government/ Communist Party, the Chinese Government is uncomfortable with an independent judiciary that wields wide powers to challenge the acts and decisions of the executive government. In the Chinese system, the role of the judiciary is to apply the law. While it is given a limited jurisdiction to correct abuses of powers by the administration in limited circumstances, the judiciary is expected to co-operate with other branches of the Government and shall support any major government policies and align its decisions accordingly. It shall not challenge the sovereign authority or create unnecessary hurdles in the implementation of state policies. The judiciary is internally supervised by a Judicial Committee within the court hierarchy to ensure that its decisions are politically correct and do not go beyond acceptable bounds, and externally supervised by the Procuratorate General and eventually by the Standing Committee of the National People's Congress (NPCSC). The power of interpretation of any law is vested in the NPCSC, a political body controlled by the Communist Party. Unlike the common law system where statutory interpretation is primarily a rational, objective process that is confined by the language of the text, the NPCSC is free to supplement or to fill a gap in existing law in order to pursue a political or policy goal.[8] Statutory interpretation in the Chinese legal system is a legislative/political process. There is no clear distinction between law and policy or between what is legally and politically expedient. In a unitary system, there is no room for a judiciary to reach a decision that is not aligned with or unacceptable to the governing regime. Pursuant to such ideological framework, the power of final

6. *See* Annex I, para 2 of the Sino-British Joint Declaration and Arts 19, 80–96 of the Basic Law.
7. *See*, for example, the speech of the Chief Justice at the Opening of the Legal Year 2020, available at https://www.info.gov.hk/gia/general/202001/13/P2020011300622.htm (visited 6 January 2021); *see also* n 5 above.
8. *See* Legislation Law of the PRC, Arts 45 and 50.

interpretation of the Basic Law must be vested in the NPCSC, which must also enjoy a power to "correct" any decision of the Court of Final Appeal of the HKSAR.

These differences were never properly addressed. Over time, the ideological conflict becomes more apparent and intense, which is attributable to (i) an unclear boundary of the jurisdiction of the HKSAR; (ii) the emergence of the Court of Final Appeal as a strong Constitutional Court; (iii) an increasing resort to the judiciary to resolve political disputes; (iv) judicial assertion of separation of powers in the Basic Law; (v) the polarisation of the community culminating in serious public disorder in 2019; and (vi) the increasing confidence and assertiveness of the Central Government when China became a global economic power.[9] These complex issues would have to be addressed elsewhere. A brief explanation is given here.

Firstly, the simplistic demarcation of jurisdiction between the two systems in the Basic Law soon proved highly inadequate. In the first place, the dividing line between internal affairs and external affairs is never clear. The distinction becomes more blurred when the subject matter may have an impact on the Mainland. A number of major cross-border infrastructure projects were challenged in court for failure to comply with certain legal or constitutional requirements, such as the challenges relating to the Hong Kong-Zhuhai-Macau Bridge[10] and the co-location of the High Speed Rail Terminal Project.[11]

The external/internal dichotomy becomes even more problematic in the context of democratic development. Direct election of both the Chief Executive and the Legislature is promised in the Basic Law. To many people in Hong Kong, the pace of democratic development is primarily a civil right that falls within domestic autonomy. The Chinese Government does not believe in full democracy, as it is perceived to mean a transfer of power and control from the government to the people. It adopted a suspicious attitude when the British Government introduced representative government in Hong Kong in the 1980s and insisted that no direct election should be introduced until after the Basic Law had been adopted.[12] Since the resumption of sovereignty, the NPCSC has tightly controlled the composition of the Legislative Council and the pace of democratisation in the HKSAR through a series of decisions to ensure that the pan-democratic faction could not obtain a

9. *See also* Cora Chan, "Can Hong Kong Remain a Liberal Enclave within China? Analysis of the Hong Kong National Security Law" (2021) *Public Law* 271, where she described the NSL as the culmination of decades of ideological tensions between China and Hong Kong. *See also* Cora Chan, "Thirty Years since Tiananmen: China, Hong Kong, and the Ongoing Experiment to Preserve Liberal Values in an Authoritarian State" (2019) 17(2) *International Journal of Constitutional Law* 439.

10. *Chu Yee Wah v Director of Environmental Protection* [2011] HKEC 555(CFI); [2011] 5 HKLRD 469 (CA).

11. *Leung Chung Hang Sixtus v President of Legislative Council and Secretary for Justice* [2018] HKCFI 2657; [2019] 1 HKLRD 292; [2019] 1 HKC 104; *Kwok Cheuk Kin v Secretary for Justice* [2021] 3 HKLRD 140 (CA).

12. Lo Siu Hing, "An Analysis of Sino-British Negotiations Over Hong Kong's Political Reform", *Contemporary Southeast Asia*, vol 16, No 2 (Sept 1994), 178–209.

majority in the Legislative Council. One of the consequences of democratic deficit is that the opposition is forced to go to the street or resort to the courts.

Secondly, Andrew Li, the first Chief Justice, was determined to establish one of the finest final appellate courts in the common law world. He successfully invited a panel of very distinguished judges from the common law world to serve as non-permanent judges on the Court of Final Appeal. In its first case, the Court of Final Appeal assumed the power of constitutional review, and soon established a liberal body of constitutional common law in Hong Kong.[13] The Court has completely revamped the refugee screening regime[14] and spearheaded a sea of change in the area of discrimination and equality, notably in relation to discrimination based on sexual preference.[15] Over the years, the courts have established a strong reputation of being the bastion of liberties and the rule of law and have consistently been rated by the public as the most trusted institution in the community. Some see the courts as an institution for social engineering when social reform could not get through the weak executive or the dysfunctional legislature. Some resort to the courts to champion their political causes or to resist restrictions imposed upon the opposition groups in the legislature. These challenges have been brought with a mixed record of success. Successive Chief Justices have repeatedly warned the public that the courts could only decide legal questions and not political or social issues. Nonetheless, the central authorities are increasingly alarmed by the expansive power of the courts under the jurisdiction of constitutional review.

Thirdly, the tension between the pan-democrats and the pro-establishment groups within the legislature has led to many legal challenges in courts. The courts were asked to address issues pertaining to the political system, such as the constitutionality of corporate voting in functional constituencies,[16] the power of the President to restrict a member from bringing an amendment to a bill on the ground that it had charging effect,[17] the power to cut short parliamentary debates,[18] the power to allow a newly elected legislator to retake the oath of office,[19] and whether

---

13. Eric Ip, "The Politics of Constitutional Common Law in Hong Kong under Chinese Sovereignty" (2016) 25 *Pacific Rim of Law and Policy Journal* 565; Johannes Chan, "A Shrinking Space: A Dynamic Relationship between the Judiciary in a Liberal Society of Hong Kong and a Socialist-Leninist Sovereign State" (2019) 72(1) *Current Legal Problems* 85.
14. Michael Ramsden, "Use of International Law in Hong Kong Courts: An Examination on Non-Refoulement Litigation" (2013) 42(4) *Common Law World Review* 354; Kelley Loper, "Toward Comprehensive Refugee Legislation in Hong Kong: Reflections on Reform of the 'Torture Screeding' Procedures" (2009) 39(2) *Hong Kong Law Journal* 253; Johannes Chan, "Nationality, Permanent Residents and Refugees", in Johannes Chan and C. L. Lim (eds), *Law of the Hong Kong Constitution* (Singapore: Sweet & Maxwell, 3rd edn, 2021), Ch 5.
15. Kelley Loper, "Right to Equality and Discrimination", in Chan and Lim, n 14 above, Ch 28.
16. *Chan Yu Nam v Secretary for Justice* [2012] 3 HKC 38.
17. *Leung Kwok Hung v President of the Legislative Council* [2007] 1 HKLRD 387.
18. *Leung Kwok Hung v President of the Legislative Council* (2014) 17 HKCFAR 689.
19. *Chief Executive of the HKSAR v President of the Legislative Council* [2016] 6 HKC 417 (CFI); [2017] 1 HKLRD 460 (CA); (2017) 20 HKCFAR 390.

the legislature could restrict the right of a resigned legislator to take part in a by-election generated by his resignation.[20] These cases inevitably touched on the relationship between the courts and the legislature. The courts have, on various occasions, held that the system enshrined in the Basic Law is one of separation of powers, whereas independence of the judiciary lies at its heart.[21] This is intended to be a neutral statement which could work both ways. On the one hand, it reaffirms the independent role of the judiciary in ensuring that the executive and the legislature operate within the confines of the law. On the other hand, it allows the judiciary to exercise restraints not to interfere with matters that fall within the exclusive competence of the other two branches.[22]

However, the assertion of separation of powers is perceived as an attempt to exert the dominance of the judiciary over the executive government. Hence, Chinese leaders keep reminding the people of Hong Kong that the HKSAR does not practise a system of separation of powers; instead, it is an executive-led system, and the judiciary has to be co-operative with the other branches of government. The scepticism over an independent judiciary was first expressed by Xi Jinping in 2008 when he was the Vice-President of China. During his visit to Hong Kong he expressed the view that the executive, the legislature, and the judiciary should mutually accommodate and support one another (互相理解，互相支持).[23] The principle of mutual support was reiterated again in the *White Paper on One Country, Two Systems*, which was issued in June 2014 shortly before the outbreak of the Occupy Central Movement.[24] The *White Paper* treated judges as part of the government administration and required judges, alongside other administrators of the HKSAR, to be patriotic.[25] It underlined the Central Government's dissatisfaction with the

20. *Kwok Cheuk Kin v Secretary for Constitutional and Mainland Affairs* [2014] 2 HKLRD 283.
21. For a summary of these cases, *see* P. Y. Lo and Albert Chen, "The Judicial Perspective of 'Separation of Powers' in the Hong Kong Special Administrative Region of the People's Republic of China" (2018) 5(2) *Journal of International and Comparative Law* 337; Danny Gittings, "Separation of Powers in Hong Kong: Inching towards a More Flexible Judicial Interpretation" (2019) 49 *Hong Kong Law Journal* 187.
22. E.g. *Leung Kwok Hung v President of the Legislative Council* (2014) 17 HKCFAR 689 (the filibuster case, where the court held that, while it is for the court to determine the existence of the power to cut short legislative debates, it is for the President of Legislative Council to decide how to exercise this power).
23. "習近平贈港府官員字箴言：'通情達理，團結高效'", *China Net*, 8 July 2008: https://wwws.chinanews.com.cn/ga/zqmd/news/2008/07-08/1305089.shtml (visited 10 Feb 2021); Xi's remarks had attracted strong responses from the community on the concern for judicial independence, see, for example, "聚焦香港：習近平訪港和香港的司法獨立", *New Century Net*, 14 July 2008 (visited 10 Feb 2021).
24. State Council, *White Paper on the Practice of "One Country, Two Systems" Policy in the Hong Kong Special Administrative Region*, 10 June 2014, available at http://english.www.gov.cn/archive/white_paper/2014/08/23/content_281474982986578.htm (visited 12 January 2021).
25. *Ibid.*, s V(3).

judiciary and foreshadowed the position that the doctrine of separation of powers was the synonym of dominance of the judiciary.[26]

Fourthly, while the peaceful movement of Occupy Central has achieved little in terms of democratic reform, it bred a young generation of political leaders and activists who are prepared to adopt more aggressive or confrontational means. Some even advocated for independence of Hong Kong, resulting in the government declaring Hong Kong National Party an unlawful society. A few young leaders were successfully returned to the Legislative Council in the 2016 election. When two of them expressed their support for Hong Kong independence when taking their oath of office, the Secretary for Justice decided to take out disqualification proceedings against them.[27] However, in a surprising move, the NPCSC decided, shortly before the court was to render judgment, to give an interpretation on the oath provision in the Basic Law. This interpretation effectively determined the issues before the court. In contrast to its approach in the *Congo* case,[28] which involved a far more substantial financial interest from China, the Central Government was not prepared to take any risk in the oath case and decided to intervene at an early stage to pre-empt the court from making any unacceptable decision. Four other legislators, who did not advocate independence of Hong Kong, were subsequently disqualified.[29]

The NPCSC interpretation further extended the oath taking requirement upon assumption of certain public offices to become an eligibility requirement for running these offices. It formed the basis for disqualification of many candidates for election to the legislature and district level councils in the following years. An attempt to challenge the constitutionality of the disqualification failed.[30] The oath requirement became a means to exclude the opposition.

These political events led to a highly polarised community and more incidents of confrontation in public assemblies. Increasingly, courts and even individual judges were criticised for decisions that were found not in accordance with one's political beliefs. The community was divided into the yellow camp ("pan-democrats")

26. The former Chief Justice sought to explain that judges owe only a duty to the law, and the requirement of patriotism would be satisfied by taking the judicial oath to faithfully and impartially apply the law: Peter So, "Judges Don't Need to Be Patriots, says former top judge Andrew Li", *South China Morning Post*, 15 August 2014, available at https://www.scmp.com/news/hong-kong/article/1573867/judges-dont-need-be-patriots-andrew-li (visited 6 February 2022).
27. *Chief Executive and Secretary for Justice v President of Legislative Council* [2016] 6 HKLRD 417 (CFI); [2017] 1 HKLRD 460 (CA); (2017) 20 HKCFAR 390 (CFA) (sub nom *Yau Wai Ching v Chief Executive of the HKSAR*). For a more detailed analysis, *see* Johannes Chan, "A Shrinking Space: A Dynamic Relationship between the Judiciary in a Liberal Society of Hong Kong and a Socialist-Leninist Sovereign State" (2019) 72(1) *Current Legal Problems* 85.
28. *Democratic Republic of the Congo v FG Hemisphere Associates LLC (No 1)* (2011) 14 HKCFAR 95. The Central Government participated as an intervenor via the Secretary for Justice and participated fully as party to the judicial process.
29. *Chief Executive and Secretary for Justice v President of Legislative Council* [2017] 1 HKLRD 115 (CFI); *Secretary for Justice v Leung Kwok Hung* [2019] HKCA 173; [2019] 2 HKC 244.
30. *Chan Ho Tin v Lo Ying Ki Alan* [2018] 2 HKLRD 7.

and the blue camp ("pro-establishment"), and judges were accordingly labelled and ridiculed depending on their decisions.

Fifthly, in 2019, the HKSAR government introduced the controversial Extradition Bill which, among other things, would have permitted extradition from Hong Kong to China.[31] It sparked the fear of many people in Hong Kong of a dismantling of the firewall between the two legal systems. When the government insisted on pushing the Bill through the legislative process despite a million people taking to the streets to oppose it, some protesters stormed the Legislative Council and successfully halted the legislative process. This marked a turning point in the recent history of Hong Kong. Many protesters considered that they had exhausted all peaceful means to no avail. They were prepared to resort to violence, and unlike the time of the Umbrella Movement, the community also tended to be more tolerant of violence. In response, the government relied on the police to clamp down on the protesters. There were numerous reports of the excessive use of force by the police. Both sides accused the other side of carrying out excessive violence and abuses. The political environment in Hong Kong changed dramatically after the storming of the Legislative Council in June 2019. The courts have to handle a large number of prosecutions under tremendous pressure and continuous attacks. Not surprisingly, the courts were vehemently criticised left, right, and centre, whatever be their decisions.

As the number of politically based complaints increased, Ma CJ considered it necessary to issue a twelve-page statement reminding the community of "certain basic, essential principles governing the administration of justice in Hong Kong" and that "the proper administration of justice is crucial to the existence of the rule of law".[32] This explanation did not stop the continuous attacks and attempts to put pressure on the courts.

In October 2019, the Chief Executive in Council invoked the emergency power to introduce the Prohibition of Facial Recognition Regulation (Cap 241K). Twenty-four legislators soon launched a challenge against both the Emergency Regulations Ordinance (Cap 241) and the Regulation. One of the arguments was that the Ordinance conferred on the Chief Executive in Council effectively plenary legislative power that was inconsistent with the design of the Basic Law, which is premised on a separation of powers. In response, the government argued that the system under the Basic Law has always been executive-led. These arguments brought the dispute on the doctrine of separation of powers to the forecourt. Without deciding whether the constitutional design under the Basic Law was based on the doctrine

---

31. For details, *see* Albert Chen, "A Perfect Storm: Hong Kong-China Rendition of Fugitive Offenders 2019" (2019) 49(2) *Hong Kong Law Journal* 419; Johannes Chan, "Ten Days That Shocked the World: The Rendition Proposal in Hong Kong" (2019) 49(2) *Hong Kong Law Journal* 431.
32. "Statement by the Hon Chief Justice Geoffrey Ma", *Hong Kong Court of Final Appeal*, 23 September 2020, available at https://www.hkcfa.hk/filemanager/common/pdf/Statement%20by%20CJ%20of%20CFA%20(23%20Sep%202020)%20Eng.pdf (visited 6 January 2021).

of separation of powers or meant to be executive-led, the Court of First Instance held that the Ordinance was too sweeping to effectively give the Chief Executive in Council a plenary power to legislate and was therefore inconsistent with the Basic Law. The Divisional Bench, comprising Anderson Chow and Godfrey Lam JJ, also struck down the main provisions of the Regulation for being inconsistent with the right to freedom of peaceful assemblies and right to freedom of expression under the Bill of Rights. The judgment, as well as the judges themselves, was unprecedentedly attacked by the China Liaison Office of the Central People's Government, the Hong Kong and Macau Affairs Office of the State Council, and the Legal Affairs Committee of the NPCSC, alongside numerous virulent attacks from the pro-China propaganda and media.[33] Among other things, they criticised the court for usurping a power of constitutional review that they did not have and regarding themselves above the other branches of government. In December 2020, the Court of Final Appeal reversed the judgment of the Divisional Bench.[34] It upheld the constitutionality of the Emergency Regulation Ordinance and the Regulation, including the prohibition of wearing masks in entirely peaceful and lawful assemblies.

On 1 September 2020, the Chief Executive declared that the constitutional system in Hong Kong was never one of separation of powers. She stated that the three institutions are all accountable to the Central Government under an executive-led system of governance and the three institutions should work together.[35] This was generally perceived to be targeted at the judiciary. Shortly thereafter, Zhang Xiaoming, Deputy Director of Hong Kong and Macau Affairs Office, commented without any details that it was an appropriate time to consider judicial reforms in Hong Kong.[36] This was the first time a senior Chinese government official called for judicial reform in Hong Kong. He further reiterated that patriotism is now a legal requirement and that HKSAR has never practised separation of powers. In January 2021, the Hon. Tam Yiu Chung, the only Hong Kong member on the NPCSC, stated

---

33. Alvin Cheung, "Hong Kong Judiciary and Beijing's Temper Tantrum", *Verfassungsblog*, 22 November 2019, available at https://verfassungsblog.de/the-hong-kong-judiciary-and-beijings-temper-tantrum/ (visited 12 January 2021); Jackson Neagli, "The New Battleground of Hong Kong's Independence: Beijing's Responses to the Mask Ban", *Rice University's Baker Institute for Public Policy*, 18 December 2019, available at https://www.bakerinstitute.org/media/files/files/3db31746/bi-report-121819-china-maskban.pdf (visited 12 January 2021).
34. [2020] HKCA 192; [2020] 2 HKLRD 771 (CA). The decision of the Court of Final Appeal is discussed below.
35. Jennifer Creery, "No Separation of Powers in Hong Kong Says Chief Exec. Carrie Lam, Despite Previous Comments from Top Judges", *Hong Kong Free Press*, 1 September 2020, available at https://hongkongfp.com/2020/09/01/no-separation-of-powers-in-hong-kong-says-chief-exec-carrie-lam-despite-previous-comments-from-top-judges/ (visited 6 January 2021).
36. Tony Cheung and Lilian Cheng, "Beijing Calls for Judicial Reform in Hong Kong, Declaring 'Patriotism' Is a Legal Requirement Now", *South China Morning Post*, 17 November 2020, available at https://www.scmp.com/news/hong-kong/politics/article/3110123/top-beijing-official-tells-hong-kong-legal-summit-time-has; "*Zhang Xiaoming Yinshu Liexianlun, Shi Shihou Jinxing Sifa Gaige*" [Zhang Xiaoming quoted Henry Litton—it's time for judicial revolution], *RTHK*, 17 November 2020, available at https://news.rthk.hk/rthk/ch/component/k2/1560388-20201117.htm (visited 6 January 2021).

that the court should pay greater respect to the power of the Central Government and the policy-making power of the Executive Government of the HKSAR. It should not arbitrarily create new law, adopt an elitist attitude in discharging its duties, and excessively inflate its power and its role.[37] The message is clear: the courts have overstepped the acceptable limits. Ma CJ replied that the fact that one did not like the court's decision was not a sufficient or acceptable ground for judicial reform. Nonetheless, the scene is set for the NSL.

II. The National Security Law and Judicial Independence

The theme of distrust of the judiciary is evident in the NSL. While the NSL is to be enforced by the Hong Kong judiciary,[38] it has imposed various restrictions on the judiciary. These restrictions can be grouped under three broad categories: (a) general directives; (b) restrictions removing judicial discretion; and (c) restrictions removing the jurisdiction of the courts altogether.

(a) Policy Directives

Article 3 of the NSL provides that the judiciary, alongside the executive authorities and the legislature, shall "effectively prevent, suppress and impose punishment for any act or activities endangering national security in accordance with this Law and other relevant laws". Article 8 further casts this directive as a constitutional duty of the judiciary to "fully enforce this Law and the laws in force in the Region concerning the prevention of, suppression of, and imposition of punishment for acts and activities endangering national security". Such kind of directives is rare in the common law system. To the extent that it requires the judiciary to enforce the law, it is stating the obvious. The duty of the judiciary is to impartially and fairly apply and enforce the law in accordance with evidence. The directive, in contrast, emphasises the duty to *prevent, suppress, and punish* acts and activities endangering national security, and under Article 3, this should be done "effectively". Such policy directive is fairly common in mainland legislation and serves as an overall policy guide to the interpretation of the law.[39] This directive, which reflects the Chinese approach that the judiciary should co-operate with other branches of government, could be seen to set the general tone for the interpretation of the NSL—to err on the strict side in

37. Tam Yiu Chung, "*Sifa Gaige Yingdang Yushi Jujin*" [Judicial reform should go with time], reproduced in *Ta Kung Pao*, 11 January 2021, available at https://www.tkww.hk/a/202101/11/AP5ffc17c5e4b060b720375253.html (visited 12 January 2021). For Ma CJ's reply, *see* n 5 above.

38. Art 45 of the NSL provides that the courts in Hong Kong shall handle proceedings in relation to the prosecution of offences endangering national security in accordance with the laws of the HKSAR, "unless otherwise provided by this Law".

39. A similar policy directive appears in the National Anthem Ordinance, which is to implement the PRC National Anthem Law.

the interpretation of the NSL. While it is unlikely that the judiciary would convict without sufficient evidence and the long-term impact of such directives remains to be seen, the case law so far suggests that the courts are ready to take an expansive interpretation of the national security offences at the expense of fundamental rights, as well as a greater readiness to impose a harsh sentence upon conviction of public order offences after the coming into force of the NSL.[40]

(b) Restrictions on Judicial Discretion

The second category of restrictions imposes restrictions on judicial discretion. Article 42 provides that "no bail shall be granted to a criminal suspect or defendant unless the judge has sufficient grounds for believing that the criminal suspect or defendant will not continue to commit acts endangering national security". It purports to restrict judicial discretion over the granting of bail. This article will be considered in more detail in the next section. Suffice to point out that up to the time of writing, only a handful of defendants charged with national security offences have been granted bail. A lengthy pretrial detention has a strong chilling effect, and the readiness to deny bail encourages police practice of arbitrary arrest and prosecution, as the police seem to have adopted an extremely wide meaning of national security in enforcing the NSL.

Article 46 provides that in criminal trials before the High Court, the Secretary for Justice may issue a certificate directing that the case shall be tried without a jury on the grounds of, among others, the protection of state secrets, involvement of foreign factors in the case, and the protection of personal safety of jurors and their family members. These are extremely broad grounds. A jury has been considered as "the bulwark of liberty" in the common law system and is regarded as particularly valuable in trials of offences of a political nature.[41] Despite the shortcomings of the jury system, it is particularly significant in political trials when the conviction has to rest on the conscience of the general public. Public abhorrence to oppressive prosecution or draconian law may serve as an ultimate safeguard for liberty.[42] While the Secretary for Justice already controls the availability of a jury trial by controlling the venue of trial, as there is no jury trial at the District Court, Article 46 gives the

40. For bail cases, *see* Section III (a) below. For public order offences, see *HKSAR v Wong Chi Fung* [2018] 2 HKLRD 657; *HKSAR v Wong, Chow and Lam* [2020] HKMagC 16 where the court adopted the sentencing guidelines for violent behaviour in public assembly and applied them to a public assembly with no violence; appeal by Chow Ting was dismissed; *see* "Agnes Chow's Jail Sentence Serves as 'Warning to Others', High Court Says", *The Standard*, 16 December 2020, available at https://www.thestandard.com.hk/breaking-news/section/4/161282/Agnes-Chow's-jail-sentence-serves-as-%22warning-to-others%22,-High-Court-says (visited 12 January 2021).
41. *See*, for example, the well-known *Ponting Case* and Patrick Delvin, *Trial by Jury* (London: Stevens and Sons, 1956), pp 160–161.
42. Although there are studies suggesting that Hong Kong juries tend to be more conviction-minded than a single judge, these studies are dated and do not cover politically sensitive prosecution.

Secretary for Justice a further power to remove a jury from High Court criminal trials. Once the Secretary for Justice has issued the certificate, the case shall be tried by a panel of three judges, thus depriving a defendant facing a political trial of the invaluable safeguard of an opportunity to be judged by his own peers on what is considered right and wrong in the eyes of the community.

Article 47 provides that the courts shall obtain a certificate from the Chief Executive to certify whether an act involves national security or whether the relevant evidence involves state secrets when such questions arise in the course of adjudication and the certificate is binding on the courts. Under Article 19 of the Basic Law, there is a similar requirement that the courts shall obtain a certificate from the Chief Executive on questions of facts concerning acts of state such as defence and foreign affairs whenever such questions arise in the adjudication of cases, and such a certificate is likewise binding on the courts. This is to a large extent an echo of the common law evidential principles of fact of state. Article 47 of the NSL goes far beyond Article 19 of the Basic Law or the common law principle in that, first, national security is a much wider concept than defence and foreign affairs; secondly, Article 47 is not confined to questions of evidence but also the legal definition of whether an act involves national security. It goes beyond the common law principle governing acts of state under which it is for the court to determine whether certain acts amount to an act of state, and the court will have no jurisdiction after it has determined that the issues before the court involve an act of state.[43] In contrast, Article 47 deprives the court of the power to determine, as a matter of law, whether any act involves national security. This is particularly worrying as some of the offences in the NSL are broadly worded to cover mere speeches without any action, and such certificates may pre-empt any determination of the causal relationship and effect between an act and national security, leaving the courts to decide only the narrow factual questions on whether the act has taken place and by whom. Such an interpretation will drastically reduce the scope of judicial determination in criminal proceedings. While a robust court could reject such an interpretation, as the determination of cause and effect must form part and parcel of judicial determination, the final power of interpretation of Article 47, and indeed the entire NSL, rests not with the courts, but with the NPCSC.[44]

The most glaring restriction on the judiciary lies in Article 44, which empowers the Chief Executive to designate judges to handle cases concerning offences endangering national security. The designation shall be for one year only, subject to renewal. It sends a worrying message that some judges are preferred by the government, and the Chief Justice is not to be trusted to assign the right judge

43. See *Mohammed v Ministry of Defence* [2017] 2 WLR 287. For a more detailed discussion on acts of state, *see* Johannes Chan, "Maintaining Institutional Strength: The Court, the Acts of State and the Rule of Law", in Fiona de Londras and Cora Chan (eds), *China's National Security and Hong Kong's Rule of Law* (Cambridge: Hart Publishing, 2020), pp 251–274.

44. NSL, Art 65.

to handle national security cases. Article 44 expressly states that no judge shall be designated, or if designated, a judge shall be removed from the designation list if he or she makes any statement or behaves in any manner endangering national security during the term of office. While it is certainly inappropriate for judges to express their personal views on a social event such that they may be perceived to be biased in discharging their judicial duties, these are matters that could be dealt with adequately by the judiciary. Article 44 is at best unnecessary as it is already a constitutional requirement for any judge to be impartial in discharging his or her judicial duties and is at worst an exercise of discipline by the executive government over the judiciary. Under Article 44, "statement or behavior endangering national security" is far broader than "giving an impression of being bias[ed]" and could easily be interpreted to mean a disapproval of the judge's decision in a particular case, such as a decision to acquit a defendant which the Central Government considers plainly guilty. While there are established mechanisms to address judicial bias within the judiciary, it is, under Article 44, for the Chief Executive to decide if the statement or behaviour of the judge concerned amounts to an act endangering national security, and the removal from the designation list could serve as a form of summary discipline on the judge.[45] In *HKSAR v Tong Ying Kit*, the court rejected a challenge against Article 44 as ludicrous,[46] suggesting that professional judges would not lose their independence or impartiality merely because they were designated to handle national security cases. While this is no doubt laudable, it does not explain why the Chief Executive should be given a power to designate judges in the first place. Judicial independence means not only actual independence of the judges but also public confidence in the independence of the judges. In this regard, public perception of independence is as important as actual independence in maintaining the rule of law. It is accepted that there is no reason to doubt the actual independence and impartiality of the designated judges, but the perceived risk that the executive government could tamper with judicial independence by removing a judge from the designation list is equally damaging to the maintenance of the rule of law. The public concern is even more justified in the case of magistrates who do not enjoy security of tenure.

The Chief Executive justified this requirement by suggesting that this is no different from designating judges for specialised types of cases, such as Admiralty or

---

45. A worse scenario is that the behaviour of the judge justifying a removal from the designation list could form the basis for a charge of a breach of judicial oath which, under Art 35, could result in the removal of a judge from his or her office. A judge under this article is treated in the same way as any other public officer. It is unclear how this article is to be reconciled with the procedures for protecting removal of judges under the Basic Law. The designated judge system was heavily criticised by the United Nations (UN) experts: Communique of 6 UN Special Rapporteurs and the Vice-Chairman of the Working Group Against Arbitrary Detention to China on NSL, OL CHN 17/2020, 1 September 2020, available at https://spcommreports.ohchr.org/TMResultsBase/DownLoadPublicCommunicationFile?gId=25487 (visited 12 January 2021).
46. [2020] 4 HKLRD 382, paras 54, 55, 58, 59, and 64.

Family Law, and denied that this would interfere with judicial independence as it is still for the Chief Justice to assign designated judges to take charge of national security cases. This is hardly convincing, as it does not explain why a designation system by the Chief Executive is needed in the first place. There is already a serious problem in listing criminal cases due to a shortage of judges and a large number of prosecutions arising from the confrontations in 2019.[47] The requirement would only aggravate the problem of delay, which is particularly serious given most defendants are denied bail. The designated judge system clearly restricts the discretion of the Chief Justice and allows the Chief Executive to pick judges with a similar predisposition. The discretion would be non-existent if only a small number of judges are designated as national security judges, which appears to be the case. Ironically, the government refused to disclose the number and the identity of designated judges on the ground of protecting the judges concerned. The refusal is absurd, but the more worrying concern is the cloak of secrecy that is to be imposed on judicial determination when open justice lies at the heart of fair administration of justice.

Article 63 of the NSL imposes on judges and lawyers a duty of confidentiality in handling national security cases. Article 41 allows trial behind closed doors when the trial involves state secrets or public order, a matter that could be certified by the Chief Executive. When these provisions are taken together, the system of designated judges could easily lead to the development of a non-transparent political court for national security cases. Examples are abundant in history that such kinds of courts are more conducive to achieving injustice than dispensing justice.

(c) Ousting the Jurisdiction of the Courts

The third kind of restrictions is to remove the jurisdiction of the courts altogether. Article 12 of the NSL requires the HKSAR to set up a Committee for Safeguarding National Security, which shall be responsible for affairs relating to and assuming primary responsibility for safeguarding national security in the Region. This high-power Committee is chaired by the Chief Executive.[48] Its membership includes the National Security Advisor, who shall be designated by the Central People's

47. Some of these defendants have their cases listed till 2023 and were denied bail. According to an internal survey of the Bar Association, it is not uncommon to have up to one-year pre-trial detention: Bar Circular 090/21 (22 June 2021). For concerns about lengthy pre-trial detention under the National Security Law, see Hong Kong Watch, "From bail bans to solitary confinement: Concerns about the treatment of detained lawmakers and protesters", 20 December 2021: https://www.hongkongwatch.org/all-posts/2021/12/20/pol-prisoners-bail-ban; (visited 10 February 2022).
48. Art 13. Its members include the Chief Secretary for Administration, the Financial Secretary, the Secretary for Justice, the Secretary for Security, the Commissioner of Police, the head of the department for safeguarding national security of the Hong Kong Police Force established under Art 16 of the NSL, the Director of Immigration, the Commissioner of Customs and Excise, and the Director of the Chief Executive's Office. The Secretary-General of the secretariat shall be appointed by the Central People's Government upon nomination by the Chief Executive. It shall also have a National Security Advisor under Art 15, who shall be designated by the Central People's Government.

Government; the head of the national security unit of the Hong Kong Police Force, who shall be appointed by the Chief Executive upon consultation of the Office for Safeguarding National Security of the Central People's Government in the HKSAR (National Security Office); and the Secretary-General of the secretariat, who shall be appointed by the Central People's Government upon nomination by the Chief Executive. Their presence ensures strong influence of if not also control by the Central Government. Its functions include formulating policies for safeguarding national security in the HKSAR, advancing the development of the legal system and enforcement mechanisms of the Region for safeguarding national security, and co-ordinating major work and significant operations for safeguarding national security in the HKSAR. These decisions may have major implications for the community and may have affected different walks of life in a significant manner. Under Article 14, information relating to the work of this Committee shall not be subject to disclosure, and its decisions shall not be amenable to judicial review.

Article 48 establishes the powerful National Security Office, which represents the Central People's Government in Hong Kong.[49] It is an intelligence gathering, an advisory, as well as an executive body with specific powers. Its mandate includes, among other things, collecting and analysing intelligence and information concerning national security; advising the HKSAR on major strategies and important policies for safeguarding national security; and overseeing, guiding, co-ordinating with, and providing support to the HKSAR in the performance of its duties for safeguarding national security. Its staff are under the direct supervision of the national authorities.[50] While the staff of this Office are required to abide by the laws of the HKSAR,[51] Article 60 ousts the jurisdiction of the court over the acts performed by the officers of this Office in the course of duty. It is almost unthinkable that a body with power to interfere with the liberty and privacy of the people could operate without being subject to the jurisdiction of the courts.

The most worrying power of the National Security Office is that it may, under three situations, exercise jurisdiction over a case concerning offences under the NSL.[52] These three situations include when: (1) the case is complex due to the involvement of a foreign country or external elements, thus making it difficult for the HKSAR to exercise jurisdiction over the case; (2) a serious situation occurs where the HKSAR government is unable to effectively enforce the NSL; or (3) a

49. This is the fourth official body of the Central People's Government in Hong Kong after the China Liaison Office, the Office of the Commissioner of the Foreign Affairs Ministry, and the Garrison. The relationship among them, and notably between the National Security Office and the China Liaison Office, is rather unclear: *see* Art 52 of the NSL.

50. The National Security Office set up its office in Hong Kong within days after the NSL was adopted by the NPCSC. It occupied an entire hotel in Causeway Bay overlooking Victoria Park, the venue for many major public demonstrations and the annual Candle Lights Vigil in commemoration of the 4 June event in Tiananmen Square in 1989.

51. NSL, Art 50.

52. *Ibid.*, Art 55.

major and imminent threat to national security has occurred. These situations are vaguely defined, and the only safeguard is a requirement to seek the approval of the Central People's Government. The request could be made by either the HKSAR or the National Security Office. There is nothing on the procedure or the standard of scrutiny of such requests. Nor is it likely that the procedure would be transparent. Once the National Security Office exercises jurisdiction, a defendant would be taken out of the jurisdiction of the Hong Kong courts. The National Security Office will initiate investigation into the case (with unspecified powers), and the defendant will be prosecuted and tried by the mainland authorities.[53] This power of the National Security Office poses a serious threat to the integrity of the criminal justice system in the HKSAR, as a defendant who has allegedly committed a crime in Hong Kong could be tried in another jurisdiction and lose all the protection that is afforded to him or her under the legal system in the HKSAR. Extradition of a fugitive offender from the HKSAR would at least have to go through a judicial process so that a judge is satisfied that a prima facie case has been made out and all the safeguards in an extradition arrangement have been complied with, whereas under Article 55, a person could be removed out of jurisdiction physically or legally without any transparent procedure or due process. The Hong Kong courts would have no role to play at all. The dividing line between the two legal systems becomes extremely fragile.

Finally, although the Hong Kong courts would have power to interpret the NSL, the power of final interpretation is vested in the NPCSC.[54] In the mainland legal system, the power of interpretation is a legislative process that can be invoked to fill a gap in existing legislation. It can also be exercised at any time. As in the oath case, the NPCSC can give an interpretation on the issues that the Hong Kong court is to decide in a pending case so as to effectively direct how the Hong Kong court should decide the case.[55] This power is to ensure that the Hong Kong courts could not interpret the NSL in a manner that is unacceptable to the central authorities.

While it is possible to rationalise some of these provisions, their cumulative effect is clearly to undermine the dominance of the judiciary and to keep it under close monitor. Central and comprehensive control is the key. Thus, while Article 4 provides that the rights and freedoms enshrined under the Basic Law and the International Bills of Rights as applied to Hong Kong shall be protected, it is highly doubtful if the Central Government would tolerate a decision of the HKSAR court to strike down any provision of the NSL for contravening the human rights provisions of the Basic Law or to read down any provision that is not acceptable to the

53. *Ibid.*, Arts 56–58.
54. *Ibid.*, Art 65.
55. For a comment of the NPCSC's exercise of the power of interpretation, *see* Johannes Chan, "Reconciliation of the NPCSC's Power of Interpretation of the Basic Law with the Common Law in the HKSAR" (2020) 50(2) *Hong Kong Law Journal* 14.

Central Government. There could still be an independent judiciary, but it would have little room to manoeuvre.

III. Judicial Responses to the NSL

(a) Loss of the Presumption of Bail

Since the coming into force of the NSL, the police have arrested and charged a large number of defendants with national security offences. In an overwhelming majority of these cases, bail was denied by the courts.

In *HKSAR v Tong Ying Kit*, the first NSL case,[56] the applicant applied for habeas corpus after he had been refused bail. The Division Bench held that Article 42 did not change the existing legal principles on bail. The court emphasised that it is under a duty to protect fundamental rights under the Basic Law and the Bill of Rights, and the provisions of the NSL shall be construed, as far as reasonably practical, to be consistent with the Basic Law and the International Covenant on Civil and Political Rights (ICCPR) as applied to Hong Kong.[57] The court further added that it should adopt the common law approach in construing the NSL.[58] Thus, construing Article 42(2) of the NSL in light of the presumption of innocence, the Divisional Bench held that Article 42(2) merely provided for a specific situation where bail should not be granted and did not impose absolute prohibition or even a presumption against bail.[59] In assessing whether a defendant is likely to continue to commit acts endangering national security, which is a relevant factor in any bail application, the court should resolve any reasonable doubt in favour of the accused person. Thus, the court concluded that, while there is a difference of emphasis between section 9G(1) of the Criminal Procedures Ordinance (Cap 221) and Article 42 of the NSL, the impact of Article 42 of the NSL is more apparent than real, as the practical application is unlikely to result in a different outcome in a bail application in the vast majority of cases.[60]

This is an enlightening judgment where the court tried to reconcile the NSL with protection of fundamental rights and read down the broad and sweeping provisions of the NSL. These general principles were reiterated in the subsequent bail review of this case. However, bail was eventually refused on consideration of the conventional factors of flight risk and risk of re-offending, although Alex Lee J held that Article 42 did contemplate that there would be cases where bail might be granted, if needed be with the imposition of tailor-made conditions.[61]

56. [2020] HKCFI 2133; [2020] 4 HKLRD 382; [2020] 6 HKC 110. For the hearing on jury trial and the substantive decision on trial, *see* Section III (b) below.
57. *Ibid.*, paras 38–42, 48.
58. *Ibid.*, para 49.
59. *Ibid.*, paras 36 and 48.
60. *Ibid.*, paras 38–45.
61. [2020] HKCFI 2196; [2020] 4 HKLRD 416; [2020] 6 HKC 141.

Lee J provided more details in refusing to grant bail in *HKSAR v Ma Chun Man*.[62] The defendant was also charged with the offence of incitement to secession contrary to Articles 21 and 22 of the NSL. The charge was based on nineteen incidents during which he chanted various slogans, including "Hong Kong Independence, the Only Way Out" and "Armed Revolt". The defendant argued, inter alia, that there was not a likelihood of conviction or a likelihood of lengthy sentence. On the first point, it was argued that Articles 21 and 22 did not criminalise "peaceful advocacy for secessionist ideas", even though the articles expressly state that the offence could be committed "whether or not by force or the threat of force". It was argued that the phrase "not by force" referred to "non-violent acts that are both unlawful and unacceptable such as terrorist acts or other serious unlawful acts".[63] The court rejected that argument as a matter of literal interpretation.[64] While it accepted that Articles 21 and 22 have to be interpreted purposely and, as far as reasonably possible, consistently with fundamental rights as protected by the Basic Law and the Bill of Rights, the court emphasised Articles 1 and 12 of the Basic Law, which provide that Hong Kong is an inalienable part of China and is only a special administrative region with a high degree of autonomy, as the foundation of the Basic Law. It also rejected the argument that the offence in Articles 21 and 22, taking into account the background of the enactment of the NSL, is indefensible in light of the guarantee of freedom of expression.[65] On the likelihood of a lengthy sentence, while the defendant's case is not the most serious of its type, the court indicated that, in light of what was before the court, a custodial sentence of not less than three months was to be expected. While these views are necessarily tentative and do not represent the final view of the court, they appear to be a retraction from the liberal sentiment as expressed in *Tong Ying Kit*. They are indicative that the court is not prepared to read down the offence in Articles 21 and 22 or accept that a peaceful advocacy for secession is protected by the right to freedom of expression. It also takes a serious view on a conviction of national security offence where a custodial sentence is to be expected. Indeed, Ma was eventually convicted and sentenced to imprisonment of 5 years and 9 months.[66]

Considering these cases, the decision of Lee J in *HKSAR v Lai Chee Ying* came as a surprise,[67] and as a result it attracted severe criticism from the pro-China quarter. The applicant, a media mogul and supporter of democratic movement in Hong Kong, was initially charged with an offence of fraud and was later charged with an offence of collusion with a foreign country or foreign elements to endanger national security. The fraud offence is nothing more than a breach of a condition

62. [2020] HKCFI 3132; [2021] 1 HKC 316.
63. *Ibid.*, paras 7 and 20.
64. *Ibid.*, paras 21–23.
65. *Ibid.*, paras 25–30.
66. *HKSAR v Ma Chun Man* [2021] HKDC 1325.
67. [2020] HKCFI 3161; [2021] 1 HKC 331.

of permitted use in a land lease by allowing a secretarial company to use about 50 sq. m. or 0.13 per cent of the land, which sounds like a civil matter inflating into a criminal charge. The court applied the general principles in bail application and focused on the weight and evidence of the prosecution case. On the fraud charge, the court found that the evidence on the element of deceit and dishonesty was in favour of the defendant. On the national security charge, the charge was primarily based on what the applicant said in some articles, in interviews with various overseas media, and in Twitter posts. The court found that these views on their face appeared to be comments and criticisms rather than requests. In light of the relatively weak prosecution case, the court was prepared to grant bail, albeit upon very stringent conditions. Apart from a very substantial cash bail (HK$10 million), the usual reporting obligations and surrender of all travel documents, the applicant was required to stay at his residence at all times (except going to court or to the police station for reporting) and not allowed to meet with any official of a foreign government, attend or host any interviews, or express any views in public, including any form of social media. Effectively he was put under house arrest.

The prosecution appealed to the Court of Final Appeal.[68] At issue was whether the court was right to apply the common law principles to grant bail and the relationship between Articles 21 and 22 of the NSL and the ICCPR as applied to Hong Kong, that is, whether *Tong Ying Kit* was rightly decided. This is a fair question of great public importance, and it is right that the Court of Final Appeal should grant leave. However, what is surprising is that the Court of Final Appeal then revoked the bail of the applicant on the ground that, since the principle that the bail judge has adopted is arguable, the Court would be seen to treat the bail judge's decision as correct by granting bail. This line of reasoning is hardly convincing. First, the reverse is equally true. By revoking bail the Court could be seen to treat the bail judge's decision as incorrect before the Court has a chance to consider the merits of his decision. Secondly, the issue is one of law. It is trite that until a court's decision is reversed by a higher court, the decision of the court on law remains the correct interpretation of the law. The mere fact that leave to appeal has been granted does not undermine the authority of the judgment under appeal regarding its interpretation of the law.[69] Thirdly, while it is possible to justify the decision of the Court to preserve the status quo before it has an opportunity to consider what the appropriate bail principles should be, there is no explanation why the very stringent bail conditions or further additional restrictions are insufficient to reduce the risk of absconding. The only consolation is that the Court ordered an expedited hearing of the appeal within a month, but that is not a sufficient reason to deprive someone of his or her liberty.

---

68. [2021] HKCFAR 45. The court held that it has no jurisdiction to entertain an appeal on bail, but it has jurisdiction to entertain an appeal on a question of law arising from the bail application.
69. *A v Director of Immigration* [2008] 4 HKLRD 752, para 8.

The decision of the Court of Final Appeal turned out to be rather disappointing.[70] While the Court held that Article 42 of the NSL must be given a meaning and effect compatible with the rights and freedoms and the rule of law under Articles 4 and 5 of the NSL, this appears to be nothing more than lip service. The Court readily accepted that the presumption of bail was reversed by Article 42 without explaining how the reversal of the presumption of bail would be consistent with the protection of personal liberty and the presumption of innocence under Articles 4 and 5 of the NSL. Instead, it introduced a two-stage test: first, the court has to determine whether, on all the evidence available, there is any reason to believe that the defendant would not commit any national security offence whilst on bail. This requires the establishment of a negative state of affairs. Bail shall be denied unless this negative state of affairs could be established. It is only when this negative state of affairs is established that the court would then consider other factors pertaining to normal bail applications, such as the strength of the prosecution case or the risk of the defendant absconding. The Court overruled *Tong Ying Kit* and acknowledged that the threshold that it imposed for granting bail was very high. Not surprisingly, very few defendants managed to get bail after this Court of Final Appeal's decision.

The Court of First Instance's approach in *Tong Ying Kit*, namely giving prominence to the factor of risk of committing national security offence but without excluding the consideration and balancing of this factor against other factors, is equally consistent with the language of Art 42 and is a better reflection of the right to be presumed innocent under Art 5 of the NSL. The purpose of bail is to ensure the appearance of a defendant to face the trial, and not to punish the defendant. There is no reason to exclude other factors in considering bail applications. Nor is there any justification to impose a requirement of satisfaction of a negative state of affairs to the exclusion of other factors pertaining to a bail application. The absurdity of the two-stage test is best reflected in the *Lai Chee Ying* case itself: bail was denied under this test even when the Court of First Instance initially found that the prosecution case was so weak that it was prepared to grant bail, albeit on very stringent conditions.[71] It would be absurd to deny bail when the prosecution case rests on a flimsy evidential basis. The Court of Final Appeal's approach encourages arbitrary arrest and prosecution of an NSL offence. This has created strong chilling effect, as an accused is likely to face a lengthy period of pretrial detention once an NSL charge is laid.

---

70. For a more detailed analysis, *see* Johannes Chan, "Judicial Responses to the National Security Law: *HKSAR v Lai Chee Ying*" (2021) 51(1) *Hong Kong Law Journal* 1.
71. The case was remitted to another judge for consideration. Just the day before the rehearing of the bail application, the prosecution preferred a further charge against Lai Chee Ying to ensure that he would not get bail. Bail was denied by Pang J (as she then was): [2021] HKCFI 448. In *HKSAR v Ng Hau Yi Sidney* [2021] HKCFA 42, the Appeal Committee of the Court of Final Appeal refused to grant leave to appeal to re-visit the correctness of the bail principles in *Lai Chee Ying*. It merely suggested proactive case management to avoid lengthy pre-trial detention (at [34]).

In *HKSAR v Tam Tak Chi*,[72] the defendant was charged with seditious libel under the Crimes Ordinance (Cap 200) for chanting slogans and distributing leaflets on the street. This charge was laid apparently after the police were advised that there was no case under the NSL.[73] Nonetheless, the prosecution asked for a designated judge to handle the case on the ground that the charge was in the nature of national security, and the court applied the same bail principle under the NSL to deny bail. It is difficult to see why a provision in the NSL could just be transported to a criminal offence under another ordinance without any clear statutory indication. The decision seems to be a clear violation of the principle of legality, and the court seems to be too ready to go along with the prosecution. Instead of adopting a strict approach to interpreting penal provisions, the Court of Final Appeal, in *HKSAR v Ng Hau Yi Sidney*,[74] adopted a purposive approach to interpreting the NSL and held that it supplemented other laws in Hong Kong and therefore the bail provision in Art 42 of the NSL applied to other offences endangering national security under HKSAR law.

Another noticeable case is the arrest of about 50 activists and former politicians for participation in a primary election in preparation of the election to the Legislative Council scheduled for September 2021, which was later postponed for a year. The organiser aimed at winning a majority in the Legislature and proposed, if elected, to veto major government bills and the budget to pressurise the government to speed up the democratic process. Participants in the primary election did not have to agree with that aim. Eventually 46 of them were charged with various offences of subversion and only a few were granted bail.[75] The arrest and prosecution were widely perceived to be a major crackdown on the opposition. At the time of writing, the defendants have been detained for over twelve months, and the trial is expected to take place not before 2023.

---

72. Mary Hui, "A Law That Once Outlawed Insulting the Queen Is Now Being Used to Stifle Speech in Hong Kong", *Quartz*, 9 September 2020, available at https://qz.com/1901125/hong-kong-uses-colonial-era-sedition-law-to-stifle-speech/ (visited 12 January 2021).
73. Helen Davidson, "Hong Kong Activist Denied Bail after Being Charged with Sedition", *The Guardian*, 17 September 2020, available at https://www.theguardian.com/world/2020/sep/17/hong-kong-activist-denied-bail-after-being-charge-with-sedition-tam-tak-chi; *see also* the news report by *Hong Kong International Business Channel* on Facebook, available at https://www.facebook.com/hkibcnews/posts/1267092566999784 (both visited 12 January 2021).
74. [2021] HKCFA 42.
75. One of the organisers, Benny Tai, was already in jail for organising Occupy Central in 2014. The accused included many well-known activists in the pan-democratic camp. Some were denied bail on the flimsiest basis. For example, Tam, a former legislator, was invited to meet with members of a foreign consulate. He did not reply and was prepared to undertake not to meet with any foreign government officials whilst on bail. The court held that the invitation meant that he would be able to commit an offence of collusion with foreign government, and bail was denied. The bail application of the 46 accused lasted for four days, during which most accused were exhausted without adequate rest.

(b) Loss of the Right to Jury

Back to the *Tong Ying Kit* case, the Secretary for Justice applied for a dispensation of the jury trial allegedly on the ground of protection of jurors and their family members under Article 46 of the NSL.[76] In an earlier case, given that jury trial is only available at the High Court and that it is for the Secretary for Justice to determine the venue of trials, the Court of Final Appeal held that there was no right to jury trial in Hong Kong.[77] In the *Tong* case, the defendant argued that once the Secretary for Justice had decided to proceed by way of indictment, there was a right to jury trial. This was rejected by the Court of First Instance on two grounds.[78] First, the defendant could not waive the right to jury trial, and there could not be a right that could not be waived. Secondly, the Court has a power to remit the case back to the District Court, where there is no jury. Hence, there could not be a right to jury trial if it could be defeated by transferring the case to the District Court. Neither ground is convincing. One may not waive the right to be killed or the right not to be tortured. It does not follow that one has no right to life or no right not to be tortured. Likewise, the mere fact that a right could be limited, especially when this is done by the court after hearing the parties, does not mean that the right does not exist. Most rights could be restricted. Nonetheless, the judgment was upheld on appeal.[79] Despite the wealth of common law authorities that described the immense value and unique features of jury trial, the Court of Appeal downgraded jury trial to merely a mode of criminal trial that is subject to prosecutorial discretion. What is more worrying is that the Court treated the NSL as a law of constitutional status and adopted a broad and purposive approach of construction. It is well established that this approach is most apt for construing constitutional rights. By a twist of logic, the Court of Appeal adopted this approach in interpreting, not rights, but restrictions of rights.

(c) A Verbal Offence to Commit Another Verbal Offence

The trial of *Tong Ying Kit* took place in June 2021 before a panel of three judges at the Court of First Instance.[80] The facts were largely not in dispute. On 1 July 2020, the defendant rode his motorcycle with a backpack from which a black flag containing a slogan of "Liberate Hong Kong; Revolution of Our Times" was hoisted upward and publicly displayed while he drove the motorcycle. He ignored police's attempts

76. Art 46 allows the Secretary for Justice to issue a certificate to direct a trial without jury on the ground of, inter alia, protection of national secrets, involvement of foreign factors, and protection of jurors and their family members.
77. *HKSAR v Chiang Lily* (2010) 13 HKCFAR 208.
78. [2021] HKCFI 1397.
79. [2021] HKCA 912 (22 June 2021).
80. [2021] HKCFI 2200 (27 July 2021).

to stop him and eventually injured three policemen. He was charged with two NSL offences of incitement of others with a view to committing secession and carrying out terrorist activities, with an alternative charge of causing grievous bodily harm by dangerous driving.

The argument focused on the meaning of the slogan "Liberate Hong Kong; Revolution of Our Times". Both sides adduced expert evidence. The prosecution expert, a history professor, testified from a historical perspective that the phrase carried a secessionist meaning. This interpretation was disputed by two experts on the defence side, a political scientist and a professor in journalism. Their evidence is that the slogan has to be interpreted in context and carried a multitude of meanings. Different persons may interpret and understand the slogan differently. Without resolving the dispute, the Court held that the slogan was at least capable of carrying a secessionist meaning, and that was sufficient for the offence of incitement to secession. It also held that the defendant, by choosing to carry out the act on a date of political significance, clearly intended to carry out the act to intimidate the public with a view to pursuing a political agenda. He was convicted of both NSL offences and was sentenced to nine years' imprisonment.

A surprising feature of the judgment is that it made no reference at all to the constitutional right to freedom of expression. It applied the common law of incitement and held that it was sufficient for the offence of incitement if the inciting act or word was capable of referring to a criminal offence. The court relied on a few English and New Zealand cases, which were related to the offence of murder, procuring unlawful sexual intercourse, and assaulting a police officer.[81] These were relatively well-defined offences in the common law system. In contrast, the offence of secession is ill-defined and unknown to the common law system. In the present case, the only evidence in support of the offence of secession is a slogan that could carry a variety of meanings, and the act of incitement was nothing more than displaying the slogan while he was driving in public. That is, the offence of incitement to secession is essentially a verbal offence leading to a verbal offence. Such kind of offence should call for the most stringent scrutiny of the court. There is a lot to be said that there has to be some specific act leading to the conclusion that secession is a possible consequence. Secession is breaking up a country, and how could a country be broken up by a mere display of a slogan? The court relied on a vague meaning of incitement. Yet it failed to consider how the proportionate requirement for restricting a constitutional right to freedom of expression could be satisfied by a standard of "capable of carrying a secessionist meaning". The audience of the incitement is the ordinary members of the public. If the meaning can only be ascertained by an expert, how could it incite anyone who is not an expert? And if the experts could not agree among themselves of the meaning, is there not a reasonable doubt that it

81. At paras 17–34. The cases were respectively *R v Most* (1881) 7 QBD 224; *R v M* [2014] EWCA Crim 2823; *Invicta Plastics Ltd v Claire* [2001] EWCA Crim 1684; and *Young v Cassells* (1914) 33 NZLR 852.

would be able to incite the public? And what is the public incited to do? The court has asked the wrong question. The right question is not just whether the slogan is capable of carrying a secessionist meaning, but also whether it can be proved beyond reasonable doubt that if an audience carries out the act as incited it will amount to an offence of secession. There are many different ways of receiving the meaning of the slogan, and even if the audience adopts the secessionist meaning, there are still many different ways of carrying it out; not every way will necessarily amount to a secession act. It can readily be seen that the Court has glossed over many important issues in coming to its conclusion.

The reasoning is equally weak in relation to the terrorist offence. There is no question that the act amounted to causing serious harm to others by dangerous driving, which the court found unnecessary to deal with. There was little evidence that the act was carried out to intimidate the public. The only evidence in this regard was a driver in a vehicle who witnessed the defendant's motorcycle crashed into some police officers. Any reasonable person would be frightened in such circumstances, but the fear has nothing to do with the political nature of the act. There was also little evidence that the act caused grave harm to society. The Court took the view that a serious challenge to the police would "instill a sense of fear amongst the law-abiding members of the society", that there would be a breakdown of law and order, and thereby "grave harm would certainly be caused to society".[82] This is a rather tenuous argument as any notorious crime or any attack on the police could be said to have this effect, but certainly not all such criminal offences could be regarded as a terrorist act. For a terrorist offence, the harm to society has to reach a certain degree of severity, and the act has to aim at causing harm to at least a considerable segment of society rather than an act of reckless driving causing serious harm to a few police officers. The Court also adopted a rather loose meaning of political agenda. Despite the ambiguous meaning of the slogan, the court held that a meaning to recover what was lost and the need for a fundamental change in Hong Kong could equally amount to a political agenda.[83] While such acts could be loosely regarded as political in nature, it is highly doubtful that they could be considered a political agenda for a terrorist offence that could carry a maximum sentence of life imprisonment. Such an offence certainly requires a much more precise and narrower definition, or otherwise any advocacy for reform could run the risk of being a terrorist act if it results in a confrontation with the police. Finally, what exactly is the political agenda, which has to be proved beyond reasonable doubt? Expert evidence was divided on the meaning of the slogan, and this weakness cannot be remedied by the political significance of the date or the fact that he drove to and fro a few times along the road with a view to displaying the slogan.

82. [2021] HKCA 2200, at [162].

83. *Ibid.*, at para 165.

IV. Judicial Independence and Judicial Deference

The NSL provides an inroad to many fundamental rights, and so far the record of the judiciary in protecting the fundamental rights is not impressive. What options do the courts have?

An obvious option is to challenge the constitutionality of the sweeping offences in the NSL. Detailed analysis of this question has to be done elsewhere.[84] Suffice to say that these offences, if challenged, would most likely be held to be constitutional. First, under Article 62 of the NSL, it prevails over any local law of the HKSAR, including the Bill of Rights. Second, while the reference to "local law" in Article 62 may not include the Basic Law, this is likely to be a moot point. Leaving aside whether the Basic Law would prevail over the NSL, any argument based on the Basic Law is unlikely to go beyond the argument of whether the NSL offences are consistent with Articles 4 and 5 of the NSL. The coexistence of these two articles and the NSL offences in the same law by itself precludes any argument that the sweeping national security offences would be inconsistent with the human rights provisions in the NSL. The constitutionality of the NSL is fait accompli.

Hence, the more realistic option is that the courts would read down the sweeping national security offences to ensure their consistency with Articles 4 and 5 of the NSL. In this regard, there is potentially plenty of room for Hong Kong judges to mitigate the draconian nature of the national security offences. The decision of the Divisional Bench in *Tong Ying Kit* is encouraging, as it exemplifies the attempt of the judiciary to bring the NSL provision on bail in line with the common law principles. It is also open to the court to adopt the common law principles to interpret the NSL. These principles may include a strict approach to interpreting penal provisions, the requirement of *mens rea* and a presumption against strict liability offences, the legality principle such that Parliament is not presumed to restrict liberty and freedoms without the clearest language,[85] and the well-known principle of proportionality. There is also room for judicial creativity on procedural or evidential matters. It is open to the court to require a certain degree of proximity or a causal link between an act and the object of substantive national security offences such as secession or subversion. In particular, the courts enjoy considerable latitude in finding of facts and inferences. The burden and the standard of proof in criminal trials would likely prove to be of particular significance, especially when the evidence is flimsy.

However, this approach suffers from a few constraints. First, an obvious constraint is the language of the text. The court could not adopt an interpretation that

84. *See* Po Jen Yap, "Judging Hong Kong's National Security Law", Chapter 7, and Simon Young, "Police Powers under the National Security Law: A Commentary", Chapter 8 in this volume.

85. *R v Secretary of State for the Home Department, ex parte Simms* [2000] 2 AC 115, 131; *A v Commissioner of ICAC* (2012) 15 HKCFAR 362, paras 68–69; *R (Unison) v Lord Chancellor* [2017] 3 WLR 409, paras 65 and 68.

the language could not bear.[86] Thus, the court in *HKSAR v Ma Chun Man* found it impossible to read down the clear words of "whether or not by force or threat of force". Second, in adopting a purposive approach, the court may be constrained by the purpose of the NSL, which was explained by the NPCSC in the broadest sense to suggest that mere advocacy for Hong Kong independence is sufficient to constitute a threat to national security.[87] The cautious and deferential approach to interpretation adopted in *HKSAR v Ma Chun Man*, including its ready acceptance of the broad purpose of the NSL, does not instill confidence that the court would adopt a highly imaginative or critical approach to interpretation of the NSL.

Thirdly, as argued before, the NSL is the result of decades of ideological conflicts between the two systems. The NSL represents a shift to a more interventionist Central Government and a determined attempt to curb the powers of the judiciary. It is unlikely that the Central Government would allow the Hong Kong courts a free rein to interpret or apply the NSL. An NPCSC interpretation to pre-empt or reverse a judgment of the court is not a remote possibility. Indeed, the purpose of Article 62 of the NSL is to ensure that the courts would not go beyond what is acceptable to the Central Government. The tide has changed.

In this regard, the courts are rather exposed.[88] It has been a convention in the common law system for the Secretary for Justice to defend the judiciary, as it is inappropriate for the judiciary to engage in any public debates. Yet in the last few years, the Secretary for Justice had to be reminded of her duties on a number of occasions. In November 2020, the NPCSC disqualified four opposition legislators. This led to the resignation in protest of all pan-democrat legislators. Thus, as from November 2020, the Legislative Council became essentially a compliant body with no opposition. Without the support and protection of both the Legislature and the Executive Government, the judiciary becomes particularly vulnerable.[89]

Fourthly, there are signs that the courts, and notably the Court of Final Appeal, have become increasingly deferential. Space constraint does not allow a

86. *Comilang Milagos Tescon v Director of Immigration* [2018] 2 HKLRD 534, paras 66–67; *Director of Immigration v Chong Fung Yuen* (2001) 4 HKCFAR 211 at 223–225.
87. "The [Third Session of the Thirteenth NPC] considered that the risks for national security in the Hong Kong Special Administrative Region (HKSAR) have become notable in recent years. Various unlawful activities such as advocacy for 'Hong Kong independence' as well as acts of secession, violence and terrorism, etc have seriously jeopardised national sovereignty, unity and territorial integrity. Certain foreign or external forces have flagrantly interfered in Hong Kong's affairs and utilised Hong Kong to carry out activities endangering national security. To safeguard national sovereignty, security and development interests, uphold and improve the 'one country, two systems' regime, safeguard the long-term prosperity and stability of Hong Kong, and safeguard the legitimate rights and interests of Hong Kong residents."
88. As Chief Justice Geoffrey Ma observed at his retirement speech, the judiciary has been subject to intense attacks and scurrilous abuses in recent years: *see* n 5 above.
89. Michael Davies, as quoted by Hui, n 72 above.

full exposition of this fascinating topic of deference.[90] In applying the NSL, the core question at the end of the day is how far inroads to fundamental rights and freedoms are to be tolerated for the protection of national security. This is a question of proportionality, which is ultimately a value judgment. Studies elsewhere have shown that since the adoption of the *Hysan* test, the courts have tended to be more deferential and are more ready to find the test of proportionality satisfied.[91] In the oath case, the Court of Appeal could have affirmed the decision of the lower court to disqualify the two legislators under local law without reliance on the controversial interpretation of the NPCSC, but it chose to embrace fully the NPCSC interpretation which was made after the event. This reasoning gave rise to an important issue of retrospective effect of the NPCSC interpretation and its impact on existing judicial proceedings, but the Court of Final Appeal refused to grant leave on the nebulous ground that retrospectivity of the NPCSC interpretation was well settled.[92] In the co-location case, the court readily accepted that an NPCSC decision could provide the legal basis for introducing wholesale the law of the Mainland to the HKSAR without compliance with the requirements of the Basic Law and accepted that any attempt to challenge the decision would be futile.[93] In December 2020, the Court of Final Appeal held that both the Emergency Regulation Ordinance and the Regulation were constitutional.[94] Regarding the former, the Court was prepared to uphold the almost unlimited legislative power of the Chief Executive in Council in the undefined circumstances of public danger, and was satisfied with the unrealistic safeguards that the decision to invoke this power is subject to judicial review.[95] Regarding the latter, the Court upheld the Regulation prohibiting the wearing of facial covering in peaceful public assemblies on the ground that preventive action was necessary to prevent these public assemblies from becoming violent. Its decision to uphold the prohibition of face masks when practically everyone in the community has been wearing health masks as a result of the pandemic for almost a year is so divorced from reality that it would hardly command public respect. The

90. *See*, for example, Cora Chan, "Rights, Proportionality and Deference: A Study of Post-Handover Judgments in Hong Kong" (2018) 48(1) *Hong Kong Law Journal* 51; Rehan Abeyratne, "More Structure, More Deference? Proportionality in Hong Kong", in Po Jen Yap (ed), *Proportionality in Asia* (Cambridge: Cambridge University Press, 2020), p 25; Johannes Chan, "Proportionality after Hysan: Fair Balance, Manifestly without Reasonable Foundation, and Wednesbury Unreasonableness" (2019) 49 *Hong Kong Law Journal* 265.

91. Abeyratne, *ibid.*; Alec Stone-Sweet, "The Necessity of Balancing: Hong Kong's Flawed Approach to Proportionality, and Why It Matters" (2020) 50(2) *Hong Kong Law Journal* 541; Johannes Chan, *ibid.*

92. *See* Chan, "A Shrinking Space: A Dynamic Relationship between the Judiciary in a Liberal Society of Hong Kong and a Socialist-Leninist Sovereign State", n 13 above.

93. *Leung Chung Hang Sixtus v President of Legislative Council and Secretary for Justice* [2018] HKCFI 2657; [2019] 1 HKLRD 292; [2019] 1 HKC 104.

94. *Kwok Wing Hang v Chief Executive in Council* [2020] HKCFA 42; (2020) 23 HKCFAR 518.

95. The Chief Executive in Council is under no duty to provide reasons for declaring an emergency, let alone the vague notion of public danger. An attempt to seek discovery of the discussion at the Executive Council will likely be strenuously resisted on the ground of public interest immunity. Nor is there any realistic ground to challenge the failure to bring an emergency to an end.

decisions of various courts to refuse bail in national security cases when the facts of those cases involved no more than peaceful advocacy could hardly inspire confidence. Within a year of the entry into force of the NSL, the courts have given up the presumption of bail, the right to jury trial, and adopted a low standard of scrutiny of verbal offences. The prosecution of Jimmy Lai is widely perceived to be political persecution, yet the Court of Final Appeal did not seem to demonstrate the sensitivity that is called for when personal liberty is at stake.

It is unfortunate that political pressure has continuously been asserted on the judiciary. When Chow J held that the police were in breach of the Bill of Rights by failing to show their identification whilst on duty,[96] *Ta Kung Pao* launched a virulent attack at the judge.[97] Attempts to put pressure on the Court of Final Appeal to revoke the bail of Jimmy Lai were both intense and blatant. *People's Daily* carried an article suggesting that if bail were to be granted by the Court of Final Appeal, it would have justified intervention under Article 55 of the NSL to take the matter out of the jurisdiction of the Hong Kong courts and urged the Court of Final Appeal to "make the correct decision". *Ta Kung Pao* also carried an editorial suggesting that the High Court's decision to grant bail to Mr Lai was not only contrary to the rule of law but had a shadow of foreign interference behind it. These statements, which were published shortly before the hearing before the Court of Final Appeal, could be perceived by the public as putting pressure on the judiciary in relation to extant legal proceedings and bordered on a contempt of court.[98] While it may be accepted that the Court of Final Appeal has not been affected by these comments, its unconvincing decision to revoke bail unfortunately reinforces the public perception that the court has succumbed to such political pressure. The readiness of the court to give up fundamental rights and to convict on tenuous grounds give no cause for comfort about judicial independence.

Of course, in all these cases, it is easy to put the blame on the draconian law and argue that there is no ground to believe that the court is not discharging its duties independently. The problem is that the court is too ready to give significant weight to national security or public order and too deferential to the authority in taking out even draconian measures. It may be thought that the adoption of a deferential approach could spare the attacks on the judiciary and, hence, allow judicial independence in other less sensitive areas. This is a self-defeating proposition, for independence carved is independence lost. While judicial independence and judicial deference are two different issues, the consequences may be the same. One is

96. *Hong Kong Journalists Association v Commissioner of Police* [2020] HKCFI 3101; [2021] 1 HKLRD 427.
97. Anita Yip, "Letter of the Hong Kong Bar Association to the Secretary for Justice," Hong Kong Bar Association, 28 December 2020, available at https://www.hkba.org/sites/default/files/Letter%20to%20Secretary%20for%20Justice%2028%20Dec%202020%20re%20Attack%20on%20Judges.pdf (visited 12 January 2021).
98. This led the Hong Kong Bar Association to appeal to the Secretary for Justice to take appropriate actions to uphold the rule of law: *see* Yip, *ibid*. No action has been taken by the Secretary for Justice.

about resistance to external pressure; the other is about internalisation of external pressure. The former is apparent and may be temporary; the latter is subtle and long lasting, and arguably more damaging in an authoritarian era, for it tends to provide intellectual rationalisation for a repressive regime and renders the court part of the repressive regime. The loss of public confidence in an independent judiciary is equally, if not more, damaging to the maintenance of judicial independence.

Finally, it is still in the early days of the NSL, and the conclusion here is necessarily tentative, but a few developments would be indicative of the future of judicial independence. First, the Judicial Officers Recommendation Commission is responsible for recommending judicial appointment. So far its recommendations have always been accepted, but the Chief Executive takes the view that she is free to reject the recommendations. The whole purpose of the establishment of the Commission is to shield judicial appointments from political interference. It would be a fatal blow to judicial independence if the Chief Executive decides to reject the recommendations of the Commission, especially if her decision is a result of interference by Beijing. A more subtle interference with judicial appointment is to tamper with the composition of the Commission, which comprises three lay members who are appointed by the Chief Executive. Two dissenting votes are sufficient to block a judicial appointment and promotion. The credibility of the lay persons to be appointed by the Chief Executive would be indicative of the extent the government is going to influence judicial appointments.[99] Secondly, a few overseas judges have expressed their uneasiness to serve or continue to serve on the Court of Final Appeal with the NSL in place. Those who agreed to serve adopted a wait and see attitude. Resignation of further overseas judges or their refusal to continue to serve on the Court would be fatal to the independence of the judicial system in Hong Kong. Thirdly, the decision of the Court of Final Appeal in the bail application of *HKSAR v Lai Chee Ying* has resulted in lengthy pretrial detention of a large number of political activists. The chilling effect is so strong that the community has effectively been silenced. While *HKSAR v Tong Ying Kit* would provide the next opportunity for the Court of Final Appeal to mitigate the full rigour of the NSL, the defendant has since decided not to appeal. There would be other opportunities for the Court of Final Appeal to consider these national security offences, and its approach would be of pivotal importance to maintaining the integrity and the public confidence in the independence of the judiciary.

99. Three senior judges have expressed concern that China would meddle with judicial appointments: *see* Greg Torode and James Pomfret, "Hong Kong Judges Battle Beijing over Rule of Law as Pandemic Chills Protests", *Reuters Investigates*, available at https://www.reuters.com/investigates/special-report/hongkong-politics-judiciary/ (visited 12 January 2021).

Epilogue

The NSL has brought to the forefront and deepened the long-existing ideological conflicts. In Hong Kong, judicial independence is about the rule of law. For the Mainland, judicial independence is about power and authority. What it wants is a compliant judiciary. Judicial independence may still be tolerated, but only to the extent that it does not interfere with what the Central Government regards as national interest. In a system of the rule of law, the function of law is to protect fundamental rights and freedoms of the governed. In a system of rule by law, law becomes predominantly an instrument to govern and to consolidate the power and position of the governing. So far, the NSL charges have resulted in wiping out the opposition, suppressing the dissenting views, and destruction of a civil society. They have turned what used to be peaceful and lawful exercise of fundamental rights into criminal offences, and the judiciary seems willing to condone such consequences. Politicians, journalists, social workers, academics, and students are rigorously pursued by the prosecution for what appears to be entirely peaceful acts and have been put under lengthy pretrial detention. Civic rights groups, political parties, media organisations, teachers' unions, students' unions, and professional bodies have either disbanded or simply collapsed one after another. When some of these national security cases come to trial, they may present not only a legal but also a stark moral challenge to the judiciary—a choice between being mechanical to the letter of the law or faithful to one's conscience; a choice to be deferential or to be principled. Judicial independence will be subject to the most strenuous challenge, and sadly, there is little cause for optimism.

7

Judging Hong Kong's National Security Law

Po Jen Yap*

Introduction

An hour before the twenty-third anniversary of the Hong Kong Special Administrative Region's (HKSAR) establishment, the Standing Committee of the National People's Congress (NPCSC) bequeathed a new National Security Law (NSL) to Hong Kong. Presented as a "birthday gift",[1] this offering was prepared behind closed doors—the details were not subject to any public consultation and the law was only unveiled before the awaiting population *after* it took effect. Surprise!

Secession, which includes independence advocacy;[2] subversion of state power, which includes the use of unlawful means to seriously undermine the operations of "the body of central power of the People's Republic of China or the body of power of [the HKSAR]";[3] and collusion with foreign governments, which includes the receipt of any funding or support from a foreign country to provoke by unlawful means hatred among Hong Kong residents towards the Central or Hong Kong Government[4] are all national security penal offences now. Terrorism has also been defined to include the sabotage of vehicular transport and traffic facilities for political ends.[5] For all four crimes, offenders face sentences of up to life imprisonment for grave violations. Even non–Hong Kong residents based outside the jurisdiction are liable for prosecution if they commit any of these penal offences against

* The author is grateful for the insightful comments of Cora Chan and Johannes Chan, and the excellent research assistance provided by Raphael Leung and Diana Siu.

1. Asia News, "Zhang Xiaoming: Security Law Beijing's 'Gift' to Hong Kong", 1 July 2020, available at https://www.asianews.it/news-en/Zhang-Xiaoming:-security-law-Beijing%E2%80%99s-'gift'-to-Hong-Kong-50480.html.
2. NSL, Art 20.
3. *Ibid.*, Art 22(3).
4. *Ibid.*, Art 29(5).
5. *Ibid.*, Art 24(3).

Hong Kong.[6] A national security agency established by Beijing to gather intelligence can now operate legally in Hong Kong but must abide by local laws,[7] though these mainland officials are not subject to local jurisdiction for acts performed in the course of duty.[8] The enforcement and prosecution decisions made under this NSL are entrusted to local officials[9] and Hong Kong courts are also empowered to adjudicate the vast majority of cases brought under this law.[10] Most local criminal law procedures and human rights safeguards continue to apply.[11] But jury trial in individual cases can be replaced with a panel of three judges,[12] and where state secrets are involved, all or part of the trial can be closed to the public, though the verdict must still be announced in open court.[13] In those rare serious cases where foreign governments are involved or the Hong Kong government is unable to enforce the law effectively, the Chinese procuratorate and courts are legally empowered to take over from local counterparts.[14] The law opens up the chilling possibility that for these exceptional cases, the offenders, if in Hong Kong, can be extradited to the Mainland to face trial. Finally, the power of interpreting this national security law lies with the NPCSC,[15] which expressly allows mainland officials to overrule the Hong Kong judiciary's interpretation of this NSL.

As to be expected, responses to this NSL have been sharply divided. Western media has largely portrayed the NSL as the "final nail in Hong Kong's coffin"[16] and mourned the city's death.[17] On the other hand, Beijing loyalists fete the law as a "new social contract"[18] that restores stability[19] and recovers Hong Kong's "original aspiration of 'One Country, Two Systems'".[20]

6. *Ibid.*, Art 38.
7. *Ibid.*, Art 50.
8. *Ibid.*, Art 60.
9. *Ibid.*, Arts 16 and 18.
10. *Ibid.*, Art 40.
11. *Ibid.*, Arts 4, 5, and 41. For example, the right to trial by jury can be suspended if the Secretary for Justice so decides in individual cases. See *ibid.*, Art 46.
12. *Ibid.*, Art 46.
13. *Ibid.*, Art 41.
14. *Ibid.*, Art 55.
15. *Ibid.*, Art 65.
16. Jake Hazelwood, "Beijing Has Lit Hong Kong's Funeral Pyre", *Foreign Policy*, 22 May 2020, available at https://foreignpolicy.com/2020/05/22/beijing-has-lit-hong-kongs-funeral-pyre/.
17. Keith B. Richburg, "The Hong Kong We Know Is Dead", *The Strategist*, 2 July 2020, available at https://www.aspistrategist.org.au/the-hong-kong-we-know-is-dead/.
18. The Standard, "National Security Law is like a 'new social contract'", 4 July 2020, available at https://www.thestandard.com.hk/breaking-news/section/4/150330/National-Security-Law-is-like-a-%22new-social-contract%22,-Albert-Chen-says.
19. Huaxia, "Interview: National Security Law to Help Effectively Restore Stability in Hong Kong: Former Justice Secretary", *Xinhuanet*, 4 July 2020, available at http://www.xinhuanet.com/english/2020-07/04/c_139188711.htm.
20. Huaxia, "Interview: National Security Law Helps HK Recover Original Aspiration of 'One Country, Two Systems': Basic Law Drafter", *Xinhuanet*, 11 July 2020, available at http://www.xinhuanet.com/english/2020-07/11/c_139205610.htm.

In this chapter, I do not intend to engage with the histrionics or propaganda. Neither do I seek to navel-gaze and portend the long-term impact—salubrious or deleterious—that the NSL would have on Hong Kong's economic and civic life. My aim is more modest: I shall examine whether the NSL is constitutional and explore the options Hong Kong judges have in assessing its legality and interpreting its operative scope.

In essence, my arguments are as follows. First, it is defensible—as Albert Chen has argued—that the HKSAR's constitutional duty to enact national security laws "on its own"[21] is subject to an implied requirement that this duty be fulfilled within a reasonable time, or the Central Government may intervene and legislate on the HKSAR's behalf.[22] But to be consistent, Beijing should also act unilaterally on another mothballed provision—Article 68 of the Basic Law (BL)—which guarantees the election of all members of the Legislative Council by universal suffrage. Second, the insertion of the NSL into Annex III BL is problematic as the BL only authorises the inclusion of 全國性法律[23]—People's Republic of China (PRC) laws that have nation-wide applications or effects. Notably, the NSL only applies to Hong Kong and not to the Mainland. Nevertheless, it will be a fool's errand for the Hong Kong courts to reject the NSL wholesale, or invalidate it in part, as Beijing can legally overrule the courts[24] and oust those judges from future national security disputes.[25] Instead, Hong Kong judges should engage in a remedial interpretation of the NSL, such that the law's operative scope is read down and additional safeguards are judicially inserted into the legislation.

I. Article 23 of the BL

I have no doubt that the NSL complies with PRC constitutional law.[26] The more interesting question is whether the NSL is consistent with Hong Kong's own charter—the BL.

21. BL, Art 23.
22. Albert Chen, "Constitutional Controversies in the Aftermath of the Anti-Extradition Movement of 2019" (2020) 50 *Hong Kong Law Journal* 609, 625.
23. BL, Art 18.
24. BL, Art 158.
25. NSL, Art 44.
26. Chen, n 22 above, 627.

Critics[27] have argued that Beijing's enactment of the NSL violates Article 23 BL's requirement that laws of this nature must be enacted by the HKSAR "on its own".[28]

The Secretary for Justice (SJ), on the other hand, has defended the NSL's compliance with Article 23 BL in the following terms:

> Under Article 23 of the Basic Law, the HKSAR is authorised to enact laws to prohibit specific acts relating to national security. Given the purpose and context of Article 23 as well as the ordinary meaning of the terms used, such authorisation clearly does not preclude the Central Authorities from introducing a national security legislation.[29]

One should note that the SJ's explanation simply omits the phrase "*on its own*" from Article 23 BL. It is not self-evident how the "ordinary meaning"[30] of the phrase "*on its own*" would authorise Beijing to enact a national security law on the HKSAR's behalf.

In contrast, Albert Chen has provided a more robust defence of Beijing's position. Even though Article 23 states that the HKSAR shall enact such laws "*on its own*", he argues that this constitutional duty must be discharged by the HKSAR *within a reasonable time*, or the Central Government may exercise its concurrent powers to legislate on the HKSAR's behalf.[31] Otherwise, Chen argues, Article 23 would be conferring on the HKSAR "the power to *postpone indefinitely* the making of laws"[32] of this nature and render a constitutional duty nugatory.

In essence, Chen is reading an implied "reasonable time" requirement into Article 23 BL, such that Beijing has an implied power to legislate after a reasonable time has elapsed. This is a *defensible* position to take. Other implied BL duties and powers have been recognised and applied in Hong Kong. One such implied duty pertains to the Hong Kong courts' power to invalidate local legislation deemed inconsistent with the BL.[33] The BL does not expressly state that the Hong Kong judiciary has this constitutional power. But the BL provides that "no law enacted by the

27. Johannes M. M. Chan, "Five Reasons to Question the Legality of a National Security Law for Hong Kong", *Verfassungsblog*, 1 June 2020, available at https://verfassungsblog.de/five-reasons-to-question-the-legality-of-a-national-security-law-for-hong-kong/; Hong Kong Bar Association, "Statement of Hong Kong Bar Association on Proposal of National People's Congress to Enact National Security Law in Hong Kong", 25 May 2020, available at https://www.hkba.org/sites/default/files/20200525%20-%20Proposal%20of%20National%20People%27s%20Congress%20to%20enact%20National%20Security%20Law%20in%20Hong%20Kong%20%28E%29.pdf.
28. BL, Art 23.
29. Teresa Cheng, "Correctly Understanding the National Security Legislation from the Perspective of the Constitutional Order", *Department of Justice*, 26 May 2020, available at https://www.doj.gov.hk/eng/public/blog/20200526_blog1.html (last accessed: 30 June 2021)
30. *Ibid.*
31. Chen, n 22 above, 625.
32. *Ibid.*
33. As the CFA held in *Ng Ka Ling v Director of Immigration* (1999) 2 HKCFAR 4, para 25, the exercise of this jurisdiction is "a matter of obligation, not of discretion".

legislature of the [HKSAR] shall contravene [the BL]"[34] and it also confers upon the Hong Kong judiciary the power to interpret the BL.[35] Therefore, in exercising this power of constitutional interpretation, the Hong Kong judiciary also possesses the implied duty and power to invalidate any local legislation that contravenes the BL.[36] Equally, the Hong Kong courts have recognised that they also have "the *implied* powers . . . to adopt a remedial interpretation of a legislative provision which will, so far as it is possible, make it [BL]-consistent".[37]

Therefore, it is reasonable to argue that Article 23 BL confers upon the HKSAR an implied constitutional duty to legislate national security legislation "on its own" within a reasonable time, or upon default, Beijing can intervene and exercise its implied power to legislate on the HKSAR's behalf. But to be consistent, this implied "reasonable time" requirement must also apply to other constitutional duties imposed on the HKSAR government. One such example is Article 68 BL, which requires the government to ultimately ensure the "election of all the members of the Legislative Council by universal suffrage". The BL has almost reached its halfway point, and we have seen little progress over this mothballed provision. Will Beijing—to be consistent—also legislate on the HKSAR's behalf and allow the election of all members of the Legislative Council by universal suffrage? Or is Beijing just cherry-picking the constitutional duties it wants fulfilled?

II. Article 18 of the BL

Even if Beijing's enactment of the NSL complies with Article 23 BL, it is a separate question whether this law is consistent with Article 18 BL. The NSL is listed within Annex III of the BL, but Article 18 BL only permits national laws to be listed there. Albert Chen has argued that "national laws" herein refer to any "law made by the NPC or NPCSC (as legislative organs of the central authorities), which has the force of law in the PRC".[38] But one must note that in the Chinese text of Article 18 BL, the Chinese term used for "national laws" is 全國性法律, which refers to laws that have nation-wide applications or effects. Notably, the NSL only applies to Hong Kong and not to the Mainland. And as we know, when there is a discrepancy between the Chinese text of the Basic Law and its English translation, the Chinese version prevails.[39]

34. BL, Art 11.
35. BL, Art 158.
36. *See also* Eric Ip, "The Logical Foundations of Judicial Review of Legislation in the Hong Kong Special Administrative Region" (2020) 50 *Hong Kong Law Journal* 19, 23 (where he argues that this obligation arises from the implicit assumption that the BL is justiciable and that judges have sworn to uphold the BL).
37. *HKSAR v Lam Kwong Wai* (2006) 9 HKCFAR 574, para 78.
38. Chen, n 22 above, 626.
39. Decision of the Standing Committee of the National People's Congress on the English Text of the Basic Law of the Hong Kong Special Administrative Region of the People's Republic of China (Adopted on 28 June 1990).

Pre-empting this objection, Albert Chen points to the Garrison Law of the HKSAR, another Annex III law that only applies to Hong Kong.[40] First, one must note that the Garrison Law is the only Annex III law, prior to the NSL, which applies exclusively to Hong Kong. All the other Annex III laws have nation-wide coverage: Law of the People's Republic of China on the National Flag; Regulations of the People's Republic of China concerning Consular Privileges and Immunities; Law of the People's Republic of China on the National Emblem; Law of the People's Republic of China on the Territorial Sea and the Contiguous Zone; Law of the People's Republic of China on the Exclusive Economic Zone and the Continental Shelf; Law of the People's Republic of China on Judicial Immunity from Compulsory Measures Concerning the Property of Foreign Central Banks; and Law of the People's Republic of China on the National Anthem. As the saying goes, one swallow does not a summer make. The Garrison Law may simply be listed wrongly in Annex III. One should also note that Annex III laws can be removed from the list without a BL amendment, unlike the actual language of the constitutional text.

Second, as Johannes Chan rightly points out:

> The target of the Garrison Law is the People's Liberation Army stationed in Hong Kong. It defines the duties and responsibilities of the Garrison, and does not concern or affect the rights of ordinary citizens in Hong Kong. In contrast, the national security law will infringe the rights and liberty of the people of Hong Kong which are protected by the Basic Law.[41]

I agree. Article 18 was enacted as a firewall to insulate Hong Kong residents from the application of PRC laws.[42] The Garrison Law does not affect Hong Kong residents in any tangible way as it only regulates members of the Hong Kong Garrison who are "not . . . treated as ordinarily resident in Hong Kong".[43] On the other hand, the NSL subjects everyone in Hong Kong to penal liability.

Although one may have reservations about whether the NSL is a national law for the purpose of Article 18 BL, it would be unwise for Hong Kong judges to invalidate the law on this basis. After all, our NSL is a *watered-down* version of the national security law that applies across the Mainland. If only national laws that have nation-wide applications can be listed under Annex III, one would simply be inviting Beijing to annex its own amped-up version to our Basic Law instead. The offence-creating provisions of the PRC's national security law are found in the Criminal Law of the People's Republic of China. In Hong Kong, the minimum sentence for colluding with foreign powers is three years.[44] In the Mainland, the

40. Chen, n 22 above, 626.
41. Chan, n 27 above.
42. Carole J. Petersen, "The Disappearing Firewall: International Consequences of Beijing's Decision to Impose a National Security Law and Operate National Security Institutions in Hong Kong" (2020) 50 *Hong Kong Law Journal* 633.
43. Immigration Ordinance (Cap 115), s 2(4)(a)(viii).
44. NSL, Art 29.

mandatory minimum is ten.[45] In the Mainland, one can be convicted of subverting of state power by merely "spreading rumours".[46] This is not a crime under Hong Kong's NSL. Private property can be confiscated and the death penalty imposed for national security violations in the Mainland,[47] but such sanctions are not permissible under our NSL.

III. Judicial Power to Invalidate NPC/NPCSC Legislative Acts

Even if it is unwise for Hong Kong judges to reject the NSL *wholesale* on the basis that it is an invalid Annex III law, it is a separate question whether our courts can assess the constitutionality of *piecemeal* provisions in the NSL. In other words, can individual provisions of the NSL be jettisoned à la carte?

Hualing Fu seems to suggest they can. As he argues:

> [T]he NSL is an ordinary piece of NPCSC legislation, subordinate in status and force to the Basic Law. It is self-evident the NSL, according to the NSL itself (Article 1), was made "in accordance with" the Basic Law. The Basic Law remains a superior law to the NSL and the supreme law in Hong Kong. This is so not merely because the Basic Law is a basic law enacted by the NPC—the NPC can make other basic laws. Rather it is due to the Basic Law's quasi-constitutional status. The Basic Law remains Hong Kong's constitution by its nature.[48]

If the BL is superior to the NSL, then by implication, the Hong Kong courts can rely on the BL to invalidate individual provisions of the NSL that conflict with it.

This position is also shared by the Court of Final Appeal (CFA). In the first constitutional decision handed down by the CFA, the unanimous court in *Ng Ka Ling v Director of Immigration*[49] emphatically asserted its power to engage in constitutional review, even after the PRC's resumption of sovereignty over the city.[50] On the facts, the CFA held that the Immigration Ordinance (Cap 115) was unconstitutional to the extent that it required permanent residents of the HKSAR residing in the Mainland to obtain a one-way permit—mainland authorities' permission to leave for Hong Kong—before these residents could enjoy the constitutional right of abode in Hong Kong. Moreover, in *Chan Kam Nga v Director of Immigration*,[51] a judgment issued on the same day as *Ng Ka Ling*, the CFA also invalidated a statutory

45. Criminal Law of the People's Republic of China, Art 102.
46. *Ibid.*, Art 105.
47. *Ibid.*, Art 113.
48. Hualing Fu, "Hualing Fu on the Relationship between Hong Kong's Basic Law and the National Security Law", *HKU Legal Scholarships Blog*, 12 August 2020, available at http://researchblog.law.hku.hk/2020/08/hualing-fu-on-relationship-between-hong.html. *See* Hualing Fu, "National Security Law: Challenges and Prospects", in Johannes Chan and C. L. Lim, (eds), *Law of the Hong Kong Constitution* (Hong Kong: Sweet & Maxwell, 3rd edn, 2021).
49. (1999) 2 HKCFAR 4.
50. *Ibid.*, at 25.
51. (1999) 2 HKCFAR 82.

bar that excluded children, who were born before their parents acquired the right of permanent residency, from claiming their right of abode by descent in Hong Kong. What is most controversial about *Ng Ka Ling* was that the CFA also declared the "duty to declare invalid"[52] any act of the NPC or NPCSC that is inconsistent with the BL. As the CFA explained, the BL was enacted to implement China's commitment—under the Joint Declaration with the British—to preserve its basic policies regarding Hong Kong for 50 years.[53] A fortiori, the courts' jurisdiction to interpret the BL "necessarily entails the jurisdiction stated above over acts of the National People's Congress and its Standing Committee to ensure their consistency with the Basic Law".[54]

Naturally, Beijing was infuriated as it perceived the CFA's provocative grab for power as a direct challenge to its sovereignty and interpretive mandate. The Hong Kong government swiftly proceeded with a request for the CFA to "clarify" its decision in *Ng Ka Ling*. The court acceded to this request. In a very terse judgment, the CFA accepted that NPCSC had the authority to issue a constitutional interpretation under Article 158 of the BL, and this interpretation would have to be followed by the courts of the HKSAR.[55] But more interestingly, the CFA followed this concession with a veiled reassertion of judicial power:

> [T]he Court accepts that it cannot question, the authority of the National People's Congress or the Standing Committee to do any act which is in accordance with the provisions of the Basic Law and the procedure therein.[56]

What the CFA left deliberately unspoken was the court's amenability to questioning acts of the NPC or the Standing Committee which it deemed *not* to be in accordance with the BL. Oddly, the subversive nuances in *Ng Ka Ling (No 2)* were lost on the Central Government and Beijing was sufficiently appeased by this clarification.[57] The Hong Kong government was, however, not placated. It was more concerned about the practical ramifications that would result from the massive influx of mainland Chinese immigrants into Hong Kong and the strain this would impose on the city's healthcare, housing, and social welfare system. Therefore, the HKSAR government returned to Beijing and requested for an NPCSC Interpretation to reverse *Ng Ka Ling/Chan Kam Nga* definitively.

Soon after, the NPCSC's first Interpretation[58] under the BL—issued within six months of *Ng Ka Ling*—stated unequivocally that mainland children born to Hong

52. See *Ng Ka Ling*, n 49 above, at 26.
53. *Ibid.*
54. *Ibid.*
55. (1999) 2 HKCFAR 141 at 142.
56. *Ibid.*
57. Albert H. Y. Chen and Anne S. Y. Cheung, "Debating the Rule of Law in Hong Kong", in Randall Peerenboom (ed), *Asian Discourses of Rule of Law* (London: Routledge, 2004), p 257.
58. The Interpretation by the Standing Committee of the National People's Congress of Articles 22(4) and 24(2)(3) of the Basic Law of the Hong Kong Special Administrative Region of the People's Republic

Kong permanent residents had to first obtain the requisite one-way permits before they could acquire the right of abode in Hong Kong. Furthermore, for this right to arise under Article 24(3), either parent of the child had to be a Hong Kong permanent resident at the time of the child's birth. The original parties in the *Ng Ka Ling / Chan Kam Nga* litigations were held not to be affected by this Interpretation, but the rights of all others would be determined by reference to the Interpretation. Thereafter, in *Lau Kong Yung v Director of Immigration*,[59] the CFA enforced the NPCSC Interpretation against persons who were not parties in the original litigation and affirmed the Director of Immigration's right to issue the removal orders against them. In that case, the CFA affirmed that the NPCSC's power of constitutional interpretation is "general and unqualified",[60] and its interpretation on any BL provision is "binding on the courts of the HKSAR".[61]

But while the CFA has accepted the supremacy of NPCSC Interpretations in Hong Kong,[62] the constitutional status of other NPC and NPCSC legislative acts remains unclear. Technically, in *Lau Kong Yung*, the CFA had not retracted its assertions in *Ng Ka Ling* and *Na Ka Ling (No 2)* that it could question or invalidate any legislative acts of the NPC or NPCSC, which the judges deemed not to be in accordance with the BL.

Hot on the heels of *Lau Kung Yung* was the politically charged decision of *Ng Kung Siu*.[63] In that case, the accused argued that the statutory sanctions against the desecration of the national and regional flags were unconstitutional violations of their right to free speech. Ostensibly, the CFA was dealing with the constitutionality of domestic legislation,[64] but in reality the Court was confronted with the local implementation of the PRC Law on the National Flag, which was listed in Annex III BL. Nevertheless, by treating the impugned laws as domestic legislation and upholding them as such, the Court adroitly avoided the dicey question of whether the Hong Kong judiciary could invalidate Annex III laws in the first place. Unfortunately, this legal fiction is unavailable vis-à-vis the NSL, because the NSL is applied by promulgation and there is no local law passed to implement it.

Unlike the CFA, the lower courts in Hong Kong have openly disavowed any judicial role in invalidating NPCSC legislative acts. In 2014, the NPCSC issued its

---

of China (Adopted at the Tenth Session of the Standing Committee of the Ninth National People's Congress on 26 June 1999).

59. *Lau Kong Yung v Director of Immigration* (1999) 2 HKCFAR 300.
60. *Ibid.*, at 323.
61. Ibid., at 324.
62. For a contrary view, Cora Chan has argued that the CFA can impose legal limits on the NPCSC's power of interpretation. *See* Cora Chan, "The Legal Limits on Beijing's Powers to Interpret Hong Kong's Basic Law", *HKU Legal Scholarship Blog*, 3 November 2016, available at http://researchblog.law.hku.hk/2016/11/cora-chan-on-legal-limits-of-beijings.html.
63. *HKSAR v Ng Kung Siu & Another* [1999] 3 HKLRD 907.
64. National Flag and National Emblem Ordinance (Instrument A401); Regional Flag and Regional Emblem Ordinance (Instrument A602).

Decision on electoral reform in Hong Kong.[65] In essence, the Decision allowed for the Election Committee that currently picks the Chief Executive to transition into a nominating committee, and all registered Hong Kong voters would then vote on candidates who have been pre-screened by the pro-Beijing delegates on this nominating committee. Consequently, the Hong Kong government published various proposals on how the HKSAR could introduce electoral reform in accordance with this NPCSC Decision.[66] A pro-democracy activist was dissatisfied with the democratic reforms sanctioned by the NPCSC Decision and the constitutional proposals introduced, and she took the Hong Kong government to court. Nonetheless, the Court of First Instance (CFI) in *Leung Lai Kwok Yvonne v Chief Secretary for Administration*[67] swiftly refused to grant her leave to seek judicial review. The CFI held emphatically that "a decision of the NPCSC, is not subject to review by the court in Hong Kong, as the court simply has no jurisdiction to do so".[68] Since the NPCSC had the "ultimate authority to disapprove"[69] any constitutional proposals endorsed by the Hong Kong legislature, the CFI also ruled that the local government was under no legal duty to consult the people on "non-viable options"[70] that would contradict NPCSC's stipulated framework for electoral reform.

Similar judicial deference was accorded to NPCSC legislative acts in *Leung Chung Hang Sixtus v President of the Legislative Council*.[71] In that case, the CFI had to address the constitutionality of a Co-location Arrangement within West Kowloon Station. In furtherance of a seamless high-speed rail link connecting Hong Kong to the Mainland, this Co-location Arrangement carved out a "Mainland Port Area" (MPA) within the West Kowloon Station for mainland immigration personnel to conduct immigration procedures therein, and this MPA would also be placed under mainland jurisdiction. Notably, this Co-location Arrangement was formally approved by the NPCSC[72] before it was passed into law. While mainland laws would

65. Decision of the Standing Committee of the National People's Congress on Issues Relating to the Selection of the Chief Executive of the Hong Kong Special Administrative Region by Universal Suffrage and on the Method for Forming the Legislative Council of the Hong Kong Special Administrative Region in the Year 2016 (Adopted at the Tenth Session of the Standing Committee of the Twelfth National People's Congress on 31 August 2014).
66. *See* The Hong Kong Special Administrative Region Government, "Method for Selecting the Chief Executive by Universal Suffrage: Consultation Report and Proposals", April 2015, available at http://www.2017.gov.hk/filemanager/template/en/doc/report_2nd/consultation_report_2nd.pdf. The HKSAR government's eventual proposal for electoral reform was rejected by the Hong Kong Legislative Council on 18 June 2015; *see also* Albert H. Y. Chen, "Law and Politics of the Struggle for Universal Suffrage in Hong Kong, 2013–15" (2016) 3 *Asian Journal of Law and Society* 189, 197.
67. *Leung Lai Kwok Yvonne v Chief Secretary for Administration* [2015] HKEC 1034; [2015] HKCU 1238.
68. *Ibid.*, para 30.
69. *Ibid.*, para 33.
70. *Ibid.*
71. *Leung Chung Hang Sixtus v President of the Legislative Council* [2019] 1 HKLRD 292.
72. Decision of the Standing Committee of the National People's Congress on Approving the Co-operation Arrangement between the Mainland and the Hong Kong Special Administrative Region on the Establishment of the Guangzhou-Shenzhen-Hong Kong Express Rail Link for Implementing

be enforced within the MPA, ostensibly in violation of Article 18 BL,[73] the CFI once again reaffirmed that "Hong Kong courts have no power . . . to determine whether the NPCSC Decision is invalid under Hong Kong laws".[74]

In *HKSAR v Lai Chee Ying*,[75] the CFA handed down its first substantive decision on the NSL. That case concerned the legal threshold for judges granting bail under Article 42(2) of the NSL. In this decision, the CFA accepted the constitutionality of the NSL, but this was on the basis that counsel for the accused did *not* argue otherwise.[76] And the CFA also re-emphasised the relevance of *Ng Ka Ling (No 2)*:

> In our view, in the light of *Ng Ka Ling v Director of Immigration (No 2)*, the legislative acts of the NPC and NPCSC leading to the promulgation of the NSL as a law of the HKSAR, done in accordance with the provisions of the Basic Law and the procedure therein, are not subject to review on the basis of any alleged incompatibility as between the NSL and the Basic Law or the ICCPR as applied to Hong Kong.[77] [emphasis mine]

By doing so, the CFA coyly avoided addressing the outcome if the legislative acts leading to the promulgation of the NSL were *not* done in accordance with the BL.

If counsel in the future were to argue that specific provisions in the NSL are unconstitutional, how should the courts address this issue? Should Hong Kong judges exercise the power to invalidate individual NSL provisions that are deemed inconsistent with the BL? The short answer is no. Any such public declaration of invalidity would be a Pyrrhic victory as the NPCSC would simply rebuke the courts with an Interpretation. One may remember that *Ng Ka Ling* was reversed within six months. We can expect the NPCSC to be even more prompt vis-à-vis the NSL. Without the benefit of hindsight, we will not know how far the NPCSC will go as

---

Co-location Arrangement (English Translation), 27 December 2017, available at https://www.thb.gov.hk/eng/policy/transport/policy/colocation/EN%20Decision%20(2%20Jan).pdf.

73. *See* Po Jen Yap and Jiang Zixin, "Co-location Is Constitutional" (2018) 48 *Hong Kong Law Journal* 37, where we argue that Art 18 BL is not violated because the Hong Kong government has the *implied* power under Art 7 BL to relinquish legal control over land comprising the MPA in favour of the mainland authorities for immigration procedures. In Chan, Johannes, "Reconciliation of the NPCSC's Power of Interpretation of the Basic Law with the Common Law System in the HKSAR" (2020) 50 *Hong Kong Law Journal* 657, the author argues that the Hong Kong government has no such implied power: "[t]he same fallacy applies to a similar argument [that] has a power to dispose of land . . . In short, [the MPA] is outside the boundary and jurisdiction of the HKSAR and there is no power for the HKSAR to surrender jurisdiction." This is a non sequitur. The fact that the MPA is outside the jurisdictional control of the HKSAR, which we totally agree with, does *not* prove that the Hong Kong government has no such implied power in the first place to relinquish legal control over land. Ironically, it is Chan's argument that rests on a logical fallacy. Notably, as we have discussed in that article, the Hong Kong government regularly relies on other BL provisions to relinquish legal control over land established for foreign consulates.
74. *Leung Chung Hang Sixtus*, n 71 above, para 62.
75. [2021] 1 HKC 670.
76. *Ibid.*, para 33.
77. *Ibid.*, para 37.

they clip the judicial wings this time. At the very least, we know these judges will be ousted from hearing future national security cases.[78] There is no point winning a battle but losing the war.

IV. Remedial Interpretation of the NSL

The most viable path open to a Hong Kong judge is for the court to engage in a remedial interpretation of the NSL.[79] A remedial interpretation of an impugned law—whereby the courts read in words or read down the legal effect of statutory language, without resorting to an outright declaration of invalidation—has been defended by the CFA on the basis that the legislature would prefer "its legislative provision to have a valid, even if reduced, operation than to have no operation at all, so long as the valid operation is not fundamentally or essentially different from what it enacted".[80]

Common law courts enjoy "inherent and implied powers"[81] and the power to engage in remedial interpretation has been recognised as one of them.[82] The common law continues to apply vis-à-vis the NSL,[83] and the CFI in *Tong Ying Kit v HKSAR*[84] has even gone on to emphasise that *only* common law principles will be used to interpret the NSL.[85]

The Hong Kong courts have previously used remedial interpretation in three different ways, but the substantive effect on the impugned rule in all three circumstances is the same: additional words are judicially read into the text of the impugned law.

In the first way, the courts explicitly state that the law, as enacted, is unconstitutional and expressly adopts remedial interpretation to modify the text of the impugned legislation. For example, a "woman" in the Marriage Ordinance (Cap 181) has been judicially read by the CFA to include "*post-operative male-to-female transsexual persons*",[86] so that post-operative transsexuals can marry in their acquired gender. In the same vein, the CFA has read the phrase "husband and wife" in the Inland Revenue Ordinance (Cap 112) to mean "*a married person and his or her spouse*",[87] such that same-sex couples can now file taxes as a family unit. Vis-à-vis the NSL, for the reasons I have explained above, it would be prudent for the Hong

78. NSL, Art 44.
79. *See also* Johannes Chan, "National Security and Judicial Independence: A Clash of Fundamental Values" in this volume.
80. (2006) 9 HKCFAR 574, para 77.
81. *Ibid.*, para 69.
82. *Ibid.*
83. NSL, Art 41.
84. *Tong Ying Kit v HKSAR (No 1)* [2020] 4 HKLRD 382; [2020] 6 HKC 110.
85. *Ibid.*, para 49.
86. *W v Registrar of Marriages* (2013) 16 HKCFAR 112, para 123.
87. *Leung Chun Kwong v Secretary for the Civil Service* (2019) 22 HKCFAR 282, para 8.

Kong courts to avoid openly declaring any provision in the NSL unconstitutional. The CFA in *Lai Chee Ying* has also emphasised that if the NSL is *constitutional*, this *express* remedial interpretive method cannot be accepted.[88]

The second way that courts engage in remedial interpretation occurs when they construe legislation *consistently* with constitutional guarantees without *expressly* stating that the impugned law as enacted is unconstitutional. In *Yeung May Wan v HKSAR*,[89] the CFA held that police powers must be "construed consistently with our constitutional guarantees against arbitrary arrest".[90] Hence, the impugned statutory provision that permitted a police officer to apprehend a person "who he reasonably believes will be charged"[91] was "read to mean 'who he reasonably believes will be charged *on the basis of a reasonable suspicion that the arrested person is guilty of the offen[s]e to be charged*.'"[92] Similarly, in *HKSAR v Chow Nok Hang*,[93] a public order provision, which criminally sanctioned a person who acted "for the purpose of preventing the transaction of the business for [a] public gathering",[94] was interpreted such that it now only applies when the offender's "*purpose is to make it impossible in practical terms to hold or continue with the gathering; or, at least, to interrupt the gathering for such a duration or by using such means as substantially to impair the intended transaction of business*".[95] Herein, the remedial reading of the law was justified on the basis that restrictions on constitutional rights should be narrowly construed, and where the statutory provision can "properly be given a range of meanings, the Court inclines towards adopting a meaning which preserves a wider ambit for the relevant rights".[96]

The final and third way courts engage in remedial interpretation occurs when the impugned law is judicially modified under the guise of statutory interpretation and any recourse to the BL is deemed *unnecessary*. For example, the judiciary may exploit the textual ambiguity in the law to achieve a more rights-consistent outcome. For instance, when penal legislation is silent on *mens rea*, the CFA has determined that this mental requirement is not necessarily displaced. In fact, the "more serious the offense in terms of penalty and social obloquy, the less likely it is that the presumption of *mens rea* will be held to have been supplanted".[97] In

88. *Lai Chee Ying*, n 75 above, paras 33 and 36.
89. *Yeung May Wan v HKSAR* (2005) 8 HKCFAR 137.
90. *Ibid.*, para 66.
91. Police Force Ordinance (Cap 232), s 50(1).
92. (2005) 8 HKCFAR 137, para 66.
93. *HKSAR v Chow Nok Hang* (2013) 16 HKCFAR 837.
94. Section 17B(1) of the POO reads: "[a]ny person who at any public gathering acts in a disorderly manner for the purpose of preventing the transaction of the business for which the public gathering was called together or incites others so to act shall be guilty of an offense and shall be liable on conviction to a fine at level 2 and to imprisonment for 12 months."
95. *Chow Nok Hang*, n 93 above, para 58.
96. *Ibid.*, para 60.
97. *Kulemesin v HKSAR* (2013) 16 HKCFAR 195, para 59.

Kulemesin v HKSAR,[98] the CFA has recognised that there are five possible *mens rea* alternatives when penal legislation is ambiguous on this mental requirement:

(a) First, that the *mens rea* presumption persists and the prosecution must prove knowledge, intention, or recklessness as to every element of the offence (the First Alternative);
(b) Second, that the prosecution need not set out to prove *mens rea*, but if there is evidence capable of raising a reasonable doubt that the defendant may have acted or omitted to act in the honest and reasonable belief that the circumstances or likely consequences of his or her conduct were such that, if true, liability would not attach, he or she must be acquitted unless the prosecution proves beyond reasonable doubt the absence of such exculpatory belief or that there were no reasonable grounds for such belief (the Second Alternative);
(c) Third, that the presumption has been displaced so that the prosecution need not prove *mens rea* but that the accused has a good defence if he or she can prove on the balance of probabilities that he or she acted or omitted to act in the honest and reasonable belief that the circumstances or likely consequences of his or her conduct were such that, if true, he or she would not be guilty of the offence (the Third Alternative);
(d) Fourth, that the presumption has been displaced and that the accused is confined to relying on the statutory defences expressly provided for, the existence of such defences being inconsistent with the second and third alternatives mentioned above (the Fourth Alternative); and
(e) Fifth, that the presumption is displaced and the offence is one of absolute liability so that the prosecution succeeds if the prohibited act or omission is proved against the accused, regardless of his or her state of mind regarding the relevant elements of the offence in question (the Fifth Alternative).[99]

On the facts, the penal provision imposed sanctions on "any person who by any unlawful act . . . endangers . . . the safety of any person"[100] at sea. Even though "the legislature did not expressly address the mental element pertinent to the consequence of endangerment",[101] the CFA decided that the second *mens rea* alternative applied:

> If the defendant is able to rely on evidence which, if unrebutted, raises a reasonable doubt as to whether he acted or omitted to act in the honest belief on reasonable grounds that his conduct was not such as to cause danger to the safety of others . . . the prosecution [is required to establish] beyond reasonable doubt that the

98. (2013) 16 HKCFAR 195.
99. *Ibid.*, para 83.
100. Shipping and Port Control Ordinance (Cap 313), s 72.
101. *Kulemesin*, n 97 above, para 102.

defendant either did not have such belief or that his belief, although honestly held, was not based on reasonable grounds.[102]

In the same vein, the CFA in *HKSAR v Choi Wai Lun*[103] determined that a penal provision that criminalised indecent assault on a minor under the age of 16 did not impose absolute liability on the accused. Even though the law stated that "a person under the age of 16 cannot in law give any consent",[104] the Court decided that this only absolved the prosecution from proving "*mens rea* as to the girl's age, but the accused has a good defense if he can prove on a balance of probabilities that he honestly and reasonably believed that the girl was [sixteen] or over".[105] In short, the third *mens rea* alternative applied. But as the CFA explained:

> The inroad [this third alternative] makes into the presumption of innocence as the price of promoting necessary protection of a vulnerable class strikes a reasonable balance in the context of a fair trial for the accused.[106]

One must note what the CFA has been doing. In essence, the Court is construing ambiguous penal statutes in ways that advance substantive values of due process. But at the same time, these new principles are mere common law, clear-statement rules that allow the legislature to override the court's presumptions by *ordinary* legislation.[107] Until and unless the lawmakers overrule the courts, the CFA has imposed a new default rule that enhances criminal due process for the accused charged with serious crimes.

Sometimes the textual ambiguity arises from the English text of the penal law, and the Court reaches a more rights-friendly result by relying on the Chinese version instead. *T v Commissioner of Police*[108] is the most instructive example of this.[109] The central issue was whether a publicly accessible street can constitute a "place of public entertainment"[110] under the Places of Public Entertainment Ordinance (Cap 172) (PPEO), such that a licence is required for a performance therein. For the majority, the definition of the requirement that the public be *admitted* to the place is an

102. *Ibid.*, para 109(b).
103. *HKSAR v Choi Wai Lun* (2018) 21 HKCFAR 167.
104. Crimes Ordinance (Cap 200), s 122(2).
105. *Choi Wai Lun*, n 103 above, para 70.
106. *Ibid.*, para 69.
107. Po Jen Yap, *Constitutional Dialogue in Common Law Asia* (Oxford: Oxford University Press, 2015), pp 216–218.
108. *T v Commissioner of Police* (2014) 17 HKCFAR 593.
109. See Po Jen Yap, "Public Entertainment and the Interpretive Dilemma in *T v Commissioner of Police*" (2015) 45 *Hong Kong Law Journal* 1.
110. According to s 2 of the PPEO, "place of public entertainment" means (a) so much of any place, building, erection or structure, whether temporary or permanent, capable of accommodating the public; and (b) any vessel, in or on which a public entertainment is presented or carried on whether on one occasion or more. And "public entertainment" means any entertainment within the meaning of this ordinance to which the general public is admitted with or without payment.

integral part of the definition of a "place of public entertainment".[111] And the use of the term "admitted" suggests "an active sense of giving permission to enter or have access or letting a person in",[112] and this statutory reading would therefore exempt publicly accessible roads from the licensing requirement. On the other hand, the dissent argued that an entertainment becomes a public entertainment whenever the general public is "admitted" to the *entertainment*;[113] the definition of a "public entertainment" is concerned only with the nature of the entertainment in question and it is "not about the characteristics of the site where it is presented".[114] This ambiguity over the interpretive scope of the PPEO is resolved when one turns to the Chinese text of "admitted"—入場—which reinforces the view that PPEO is concerned with the admission into a locality and not merely to the entertainment itself.[115] One may note that since the statutory construction issue was resolved in favour of the applicant, the majority held that it was unnecessary to examine whether the PPEO licensing requirement was constitutional.

Vis-à-vis the NSL, the CFA in *Lai Chee Ying* rejected using the first type of remedial interpretation as the NSL's constitutionality was not challenged,[116] but the Court also implicitly endorsed the third remedial method:

> NSL [Article] 4 and NSL [Article] 5 expressly stipulate that those rights, freedoms and values are to be protected and adhered to in applying the NSL. They provide the context in which NSL [Article] 42(2) must be construed and applied. As far as possible, NSL [Article] 42(2) is to be given a meaning and effect compatible with those rights, freedoms and values.[117]

In view of these remedial techniques discussed above, I will now explain how Hong Kong judges can use them to shape the NSL's operative scope. My analysis herein is intended to be illustrative and not exhaustive.

Terrorism under the NSL has been defined to include the "sabotage of means of transport"[118] for political ends. Does "sabotage" herein include the intentional blocking of train doors or undue pressing of emergency buttons?[119] The short answer is no. While the English text is ambiguous as to whether mere obstruction of train operations would constitute "sabotage", one can turn to the Chinese text of the NSL for guidance. Specifically, the Chinese text uses the term 破壞 *pohuai*, which

111. *T*, n 108 above, para 228.
112. *Ibid.*, para 250.
113. *Ibid.*, para 51.
114. *Ibid.*, para 57.
115. *Ibid.*, para 166.
116. *Lai Chee Ying*, n 75 above, para 36.
117. *Lai Chee Ying*, n 75 above, para 42.
118. NSL, Art 24(3).
119. Rachel Yeo and Linda Lew, "Protesters Cause Rush Hour Chaos on Hong Kong Trains", *South China Morning Post*, 24 July 2019, available at https://www.scmp.com/news/hong-kong/politics/article/3019845/extradition-bill-protesters-cause-rush-hour-chaos-hong-kong.

reinforces the view that actual physical damage must be inflicted on the trains for terrorism to be established. As the CFA did in *T v Commissioner of Police*, Hong Kong courts can use the Chinese text of the impugned law to limit the legislation's operative scope, especially since the Chinese text—and not its English translation—is the only authoritative version of the NSL.[120]

Subversion of state power is defined to include any participation in any act that seriously disrupts or undermines the performance of duties and functions of the body of central power of the PRC or the body of power of the HKSAR by force or threat of force or other unlawful means.[121] Does this law prohibit the mere criticism of the PRC and HKSAR government if any of their laws and policies are undermined as a consequence? Again, the answer is no. Absent the use or threat of the use of force, the putative act that undermines the exercise of state power must be in itself *unlawful*.[122] Therefore, unless the putative act is *independently* illegal under any statutory or common law rule, the fact that the act seriously undermines or disrupts state functions does *not* in itself constitute a crime under the NSL. To give full measure to the freedom of expression, restrictions on constitutional rights should be narrowly construed, and where the NSL can "properly be given a range of meanings, the Court inclines towards adopting a meaning which preserves a wider ambit for the relevant rights".[123]

Collusion with foreign powers is defined to include the direct or indirect receipt of instructions, funding, or support from a foreign country, organisation, or person outside of the Mainland, Hong Kong, and Macao to commit a variety of prohibited acts.[124] Does the prosecution need to prove that the alleged offender knows that his or her sources of support are foreign entities? Or has the law displaced a *mens rea* requirement? The NSL is silent on this. Therefore, Hong Kong judges should apply *Kulemesin* and identify an appropriate *mens rea* alternative for this statutory provision so as to safeguard the presumption of innocence.[125]

120. Decision of the Standing Committee of the National People's Congress on the Addition to the List of National Laws in Annex III to the Basic Law of the Hong Kong Special Administrative Region of the People's Republic of China (Adopted at the Twentieth Session of the Standing Committee of the Thirteenth National People's Congress on 30 June 2020).
121. NSL, Art 22(3).
122. *See also* Albert Chen, "The National Security Law of the HKSAR: A Contextual and Legal Study" in this volume.
123. *Chow Nok Hang*, n 93 above, para 60.
124. NSL, Art 24(3).
125. *See also* Simon N. M. Young, "Old Law in New Bottles: Reintroducing National Security Legislation in Hong Kong", in Cora Chan and Fiona de Londras (eds), *China's National Security Law: Endangering Hong Kong's Rule of Law* (Oxford: Hart Publishing, 2020), p 214.

V. Conclusion

Beijing's muscular assertion of state power in Hong Kong has rightly raised alarm. But while the law is a done deal, its *interpretation* is not. In the coming months and years, as NSL cases snake their way through the appeals process, the Hong Kong judiciary would face an interpretive dilemma: how can the judiciary preserve its autonomy whilst quelling Beijing's concerns that Hong Kong courts, if left unleashed, would turn the city into another "renegade province" in the south?[126]

If the CFA unshackles the NSL from the BL, Beijing would simply circumvent this ruling with an NPCSC Interpretation that censures the Court and circumscribes its powers further. On the other hand, if the CFA capitulates on all national security controversies, the NSL will become the Trojan horse that turns Hong Kong into Shenzhen South.

The Hong Kong judiciary cannot hollow out the NSL, but it can read it down. If the courts do not challenge China's right to rule, Beijing in turn will tolerate the judges' choice to trim the NSL's operative scope. This is not some phantasm of hope. Hong Kong's continued viability as an international financial centre—undergirded by a respected independent judiciary—is indispensable to Beijing for linking the Mainland to the world economy so that China can generate capital in Hong Kong to fund its global political ambitions abroad. Socialism with Chinese characteristics just means capitalism *without* democracy. And neo-capitalist China cannot afford an exodus of multinational companies from Hong Kong to Singapore. So long as the Hong Kong judiciary accepts Beijing's plenary constitutional prerogatives, China will overlook occasional contretemps over the interpretive scope of the NSL. For Hong Kong judges, the rhetoric of transformation that *Ng Ka Ling* heralds must now give way to the realities of accommodation. Remedial interpretation is not mere palaver, for it is the arcana of judging.

126. Po Jen Yap, "Constitutional Review under the Basic Law: The Rise, Retreat and Resurgence of Judicial Power in Hong Kong" (2007) 37 *Hong Kong Law Journal* 449; Po Jen Yap, "Twenty Years of the Basic Law: Continuity and Changes in the Geoffrey Ma Court" (2019) 49 *Hong Kong Law Journal* 209.

8

Police Powers under the National Security Law

A Commentary

Simon N. M. Young

Introduction

The chapter is a commentary on the police powers provided for in the National Security Law (NSL).[1] It addresses three broad questions. First, how does the NSL extend the existing scope of duties and functions of police in Hong Kong? Second, how are existing police powers in Hong Kong extended? Third, how does the NSL alter the existing mechanisms of keeping police powers in check? The first two questions are related because the distinct duties and functions of national security police are related to the powers these officers need to discharge their duties and functions. The third question explores the methods and mechanisms of limiting these powers.

In many ways, these questions are novel. Before the promulgation of the NSL on 30 June 2020, police powers in Hong Kong were either found in the common law or created by Hong Kong legislation.[2] This is the first occasion for national law to be directly applied to confer powers on the Hong Kong police. How this affects the equilibrium of police and resident relations in the context of law enforcement is the focus of this chapter.

Extending the Duties and Functions of Police in Hong Kong

The NSL did not intend to create a new and separate Hong Kong law enforcement agency to enforce the NSL.[3] The new department for safeguarding national security (NS department) is part of the Hong Kong Police Force (HKPF). However, this

1. The Law of the People's Republic of China on Safeguarding National Security in the Hong Kong Special Administrative Region, GN (E) 72 of 2020; (2021) 60 ILM 1, entering into force on 30 June 2020 (NSL).
2. *See* generally *Archbold Hong Kong 2020* (Hong Kong: Sweet & Maxwell 2019) Ch 15; Law Reform Commission of Hong Kong, *Report on Arrest [Topic 25]*, August 1992.
3. Art 16(1) of the NSL provides: "The Police Force of the Hong Kong Special Administrative Region shall establish a department for safeguarding national security with law enforcement capacity."

special unit of the HKPF is distinct in several ways. The head of the NS department is appointed by the Chief Executive (CE), consistent with the CE's constitutional power to appoint all holders of public office.[4] But the CE must seek in writing the opinion of the Office for Safeguarding National Security of the Central People's Government in the Hong Kong Special Administrative Region (CPG Office) before making the appointment.[5] This procedure ensures the proposed appointee has the support of the Central People's Government (CPG) and, in substance, is similar to the appointment process for the Commissioner of Police and other heads of major law enforcement bodies, who are nominated by the CE for appointment by the CPG.[6]

The enumerated list of duties and functions of the NS department is also different in material ways from the statutory duties of the police force.[7] With the NS department, there are the added functions in intelligence gathering concerning national security, planning, and co-ordination of operations for safeguarding national security, and conducting counter-interference investigation and national security reviews.[8] The latter function would presumably involve counter-espionage operations directed at foreign governments and entities. These functions are more akin to those associated with spy agencies and intelligence services.[9] In both lists of functions, there is also a material difference in the catch-all clause. In the Police Force Ordinance, the police force is to execute "such other duties as may *by law be imposed* on a police officer", the emphasis being on lawful duties imposed on officers.[10] In the NSL, the NS department is to carry out "*tasks* of safeguarding national security *assigned* by the Committee for Safeguarding National Security of the Hong Kong Special Administrative Region" (Committee), there being no apparent limits to the scope of tasks that can be assigned.[11] The CPG's national security advisor, a member of the Committee, may provide advice on matters relating to the duties and functions of the Committee, whose work is secret and decisions are not amenable to

4. NSL, Art 16(2); The Basic Law of the Special Administrative Region of the People's Republic of China, adopted by the National People's Congress on 4 April 1990, (1990) 29 ILM 1511 (Basic Law), Art 48(7).
5. NSL, Art 16(2).
6. Basic Law, Art 48(5), referring also to the "Commissioner Against Corruption . . . Director of Immigration and Commissioner of Customs and Excise".
7. Police Force Ordinance (Cap 232), s 10 (Duties of police force).
8. NSL, Art 17.
9. Compare with the Canadian Security Intelligence Service described by Jez Littlewood, "The Canadian Security Intelligence Service (CSIS)" in Stephanie Carvin, Thomas Juneau, and Craig Forcese (eds), *Top Secret Canada: Understanding the Canadian Intelligence and National Security Community* (UTP 2020) 45–71.
10. Police Force Ordinance (Cap 232), s 10(r).
11. NSL, Art 17(5).

judicial review.[12] While the CPG Office must "perform its mandate in strict compliance with the law", no similar provision pertains to the Committee.[13]

While the HKPF is the only law enforcement agency given specific and new functions for safeguarding national security, the NSL expects other law enforcement agencies, e.g. customs, immigration, fire services, etc, to play their part in enforcing the laws to prevent and suppress acts endangering national security.[14] A page on the Security Bureau's website titled "Safeguarding national security—our collective responsibility" explains how law enforcement agencies, other than the HKPF, e.g. Immigration Department, Hong Kong Customs, etc, have organised efforts to safeguard national security.[15] The only agency not mentioned on the webpage is the Independent Commission Against Corruption (ICAC), as it reports directly to the CE and does not come under the policy purview of the Security Bureau.[16] The Commissioner of the ICAC is also not a member of the Committee, a stark omission given that the heads of immigration and customs are members. This might partially be explained by the special status of the ICAC under the Basic Law, which specifically guarantees its functional independence.[17]

The new CPG Office established in Hong Kong is also a law enforcement body in two senses. It has a general mandate of "collecting and analysing intelligence and information concerning national security".[18] This mirrors the intelligence gathering role of the NS department. The NSL contemplates there will be regular sharing of intelligence between the CPG Office and the NS department.[19] The CPG Office also has a more traditional law enforcement role, when the exceptional jurisdiction in Article 55 is activated to exercise jurisdiction over a case concerning an offence endangering national security under the NSL.[20] Presumably, the CPG Office will conduct investigations to determine if and when the Article 55 jurisdiction should

12. NSL, Arts 14 and 15.
13. NSL, Art 50. But, by Art 6, any "institution, organisation or individual in the Hong Kong Special Administrative Region shall abide" by the NSL and "the laws of the Region in relation to the safeguarding of national security". However, the juxtaposition in Art 14 suggests the Committee does not come within the category "institution, organisation or individual". Nonetheless, the "principle of the rule of law shall be adhered to in preventing, suppressing, and imposing punishment for offences endangering national security" (Art 5).
14. NSL, Art 8.
15. Hong Kong Security Bureau website, accessible at https://www.sb.gov.hk/eng/nsl/nsed.html (accessed 20 September 2021).
16. Although the website of the Independent Commission Against Corruption (ICAC) does not have a page on the NSL, it is referred to in "Anti-Corruption and the Rule of Law", ICAC Post, Issue 41, December 2020, accessible at https://www.icac.org.hk/icac/post/issue41/en/main_article_01.html (accessed 20 September 2021).
17. Basic Law, Art 57.
18. NSL, Art 49(3).
19. NSL, Art 53(2) ("establish mechanisms for collaboration . . . to enhance information sharing and operations coordination").
20. NSL, Art 55. Enforcement action can only be taken upon the approval of the CPG of a request by the Hong Kong Government or the CPG Office.

be invoked, and thus it has a general mandate of "handling cases concerning offence endangering national security in accordance with the law".[21]

Widening the Scope of Existing Police Powers

By Article 43, the NSL confers wide police powers on the new NS department. Article 43 is not an empowering provision which delegates authority to prescribe police powers in the Implementation Rules (IR).[22] It provides for the measures themselves. This is to be contrasted to the regulations made by the CE in implementing the resolutions of the United Nations (UN) Security Council made under Chapter VII of the UN Charter.[23] Such regulations provide for police powers directly. As the IR is not a set of rules "made under or by virtue of any Ordinance", it is not regarded as "subsidiary legislation" or "regulations" under Hong Kong law.[24]

Two categories of powers are conferred on the NS department: (a) the body of existing law enforcement powers; and (b) enumerated powers, listed in items (1) to (7). As to the first category, Article 43 states the NS department "may take measures that law enforcement authorities, including the Hong Kong Police Force, are allowed to apply under the laws in force in the Hong Kong Special Administrative Region in investigating serious crimes".[25] Three observations can be made about this clause. First, the intent is to vest the NS department with all the existing police powers which Hong Kong law enforcement agents have under the law. Second, it applies to the powers possessed by all law enforcement agencies, not only the Hong Kong Police Force. For example, any power which only the Hong Kong Customs enjoys under the present law is now vested in the NS department. Third, it only applies to powers to investigate "serious crimes". Hong Kong law does not recognise a general category of "serious crimes" unless the term is taken to refer to the broad category of indictable offences. Keeping with a restrictive interpretation, a more plausible category is that of "specified offence" in the Organized and Serious Crimes Ordinance.[26] As bribery offences are specified offences, this might suggest ICAC powers are vested in the NSL department, but, given the functional independence of ICAC under the Basic Law, the position is unclear.

---

21. NSL, Art 49(4).
22. Implementation Rules for Article 43 of the Law of the People's Republic of China on Safeguarding National Security in the Hong Kong Special Administrative Region, LN 139 of 2020, coming into operation on 7 July 2020 (IR).
23. *See* United Nations Sanctions Ordinance (Cap 537), s 3(1) and the regulations made thereunder by the CE. *See also* Cheng Yan Ki Bonnie, "Implementing Security Council Resolutions in Hong Kong: An Examination of the United Nations Sanctions Ordinance" (2008) 7 *Chinese J Int'l Law* 65.
24. Interpretation and General Clauses Ordinance (Cap 1), s 3 (definition of "subsidiary legislation", "regulations", "Ordinance") (IGCO).
25. And, by NSL Art 41, "the laws of the Hong Kong Special Administrative Region shall apply to procedural matters, including those relating to criminal investigation, prosecution . . . , in respect of cases concerning offence endangering national security over which the Region exercises jurisdiction".
26. *See* Organized and Serious Crimes Ordinance (Cap 455) (OSCO), s 2(1) and Schedules 1 and 2.

The enumerated powers, items (1) to (7), list out a wide range of powers that police already have in other contexts and new powers that they did not have before the NSL:

(1) search of premises, vehicles, vessels, aircraft, and other relevant places and electronic devices that may contain evidence of an offence;
(2) ordering any person suspected of having committed an offence endangering national security to surrender travel documents, or prohibiting the person concerned from leaving the Region;
(3) freezing of, applying for restraint order, charging order and confiscation order in respect of, and forfeiture of property used or intended to be used for the commission of the offence, proceeds of crime, or other property relating to the commission of the offence;
(4) requiring a person who published information or the relevant service provider to delete the information or provide assistance;
(5) requiring a political organisation of a foreign country or outside the Mainland, Hong Kong, and Macao of the People's Republic of China, or an agent of authorities or a political organisation of a foreign country or outside the Mainland, Hong Kong, and Macao of the People's Republic of China, to provide information;
(6) upon approval of the Chief Executive, carrying out interception of communications and conducting covert surveillance on a person who is suspected, on reasonable grounds, of having involved in the commission of an offence endangering national security; and
(7) requiring a person, who is suspected, on reasonable grounds, of having in possession information or material relevant to investigation, to answer questions and furnish such information or produce such material.

The intent was to give the NS department all the powers which the police already have, and to this extent there is an overlap in the two categories of powers conferred. The new powers in items (4) to (6) relate to the deletion of information published by service providers, requiring foreign political organisations and foreign agents to provide information, and enabling the CE to authorise interception of communications and covert surveillance operations. Such powers reflect the reality of national security policing in the digital age and cater to the intelligence gathering and proactive policing functions of the new NS department.

Important questions pertain to the relationship between Article 43 and the IR. The IR, which was made by the CE in conjunction with the Committee, came into operation seven days after the promulgation of the NSL.[27] The speed by which this detailed 116-page code of police powers appeared and came into operation suggests the rules were being drafted before the promulgation of the NSL. As the language

27. IR, Preamble and r 1.

of the IR closely models the wording and format used in existing statutory police powers, the drafters were evidently familiar with Hong Kong criminal procedures and case law.

The IR consists of a preamble, four rules, and seven schedules, each corresponding to the powers listed in items (1) to (7) of Article 43. Rule 2 identities who may exercise the enumerated powers, which ranges from a police officer, the Secretary for Justice, the Secretary for Security, the Commissioner of Police, and an officer of the Police Force.[28] It is unclear if "police officer" refers to only police officers assigned to the NS department or all police officers of the HKPF.[29] The former would be the more natural and reasonable meaning. In practice there might not be any complications since IR powers are specific to safeguarding national security and only police officers in the NS department would be carrying out such investigations. It is also unclear if the term "police officer" is the same as "officer of the Police Force", the latter of which are specifically conferred powers under Schedule 6 and arguably on its plain terms is a broader category than the former.[30] Rule 3 makes clear only magistrates and judges designated under Article 44 of the NSL can handle applications made under the IR.[31]

Article 43 states that "relevant implementation rules" are made "for the purpose of applying the measures under the first paragraph of this Article". It is unclear if "measures" refers to the two categories of conferred powers. It is unnecessary to resolve this question at the moment as the IR clearly only relates to the enumerated powers. It seems possible there could someday be other implementation rules under the NSL that relate to the application of measures in the existing body of law enforcement powers applicable to investigating serious crimes.

A critical question is whether the enumerated powers of Article 43 may be exercised in the absence of the IR. It is submitted the answer is no. Given the purpose statement in Article 43, implementation rules must exist for the Article 43 powers to be applied, otherwise they cannot be applied. This notion is captured in Rule 2 of the IR, which provides that each of the enumerated powers must be exercised "in accordance with" the relevant schedule.[32] Additionally, the Legislation Law of the People's Republic of China (Legislation Law) provides that laws "shall be clear, specific, targeted and enforceable".[33] In the absence of the IR, which pro-

28. IR, r 2.
29. Police Force Ordinance (Cap 232), s 3 defines "police officer" as including "any member of the police force".
30. IR, r 2(6) and Schedule 6. Some confirmation of this point is found in s 3 of Schedule 6, which limits the class of "officer of the Police Force", who are entitled to apply for a prescribed authorisation under the schedule to only those "responsible for the enforcement of the [NSL]".
31. IR, r 3.
32. IR, r 2(1)–(7).
33. Legislation Law of the People's Republic of China, adopted by the National People's Congress on 15 March 2000, revised according to the Decision of the National People's Congress adopted on 15 March 2015 (Legislation Law), Art 6.

vides the detailed procedural regime for the exercise of the powers, the enumerated powers in Article 43 are not sufficiently clear and specific to be relied upon directly as law. They are bare statements of the power without any safeguards or procedural limitations.

A related question is whether the authorities have acted unlawfully if they fail to follow or act in breach of the rules in the IR. As the IR is not itself a law that confers police powers, every breach of or non-compliance with the IR cannot be said to be an unlawful exercise of police power. What matters is whether the authorities in question have exceeded the scope of Article 43, i.e. acted *ultra vires* Article 43. For example, if the police officer purports to exercise a power not known to the existing body of law enforcement powers and not enumerated in Article 43, then the exercise of that power would be unlawful. Use of torture or other improper means to obtain a confession would be an example. Another example is requiring a person not suspected on reasonable grounds to have material information to answer questions when the power in item (7) explicitly imposes a reasonable suspicion standard.

Given the broad and unrestricted language of the enumerated powers in Article 43, many breaches of the IR, especially technical ones, are not likely to be in excess of the article. In such a case, the official conduct may be in breach of the IR but lawful in the sense of not being in breach of Article 43. Though the enumerated powers are broad, it is submitted they have express and implied minimum standards and do not authorise the officers to act carte blanche in their investigations. For example, as mentioned already, the powers in items (6) and (7) require the officers, as a minimum standard, to have suspicion based "on reasonable grounds". Given the importance of respecting human rights and adhering to the principle of the rule of law, recognised by Articles 4 and 5 of the NSL, it is submitted that some of the basic requirements in the IR, such as the prerequisite condition of having at least reasonable suspicion, should also be treated as minimum standards, the breach of which would amount to a breach of Article 43.

Finally, there is the question of whether the 17 offences prescribed in the IR are enforceable.[34] Some of the offences are severe, punishable up to seven years' imprisonment and an unlimited fine.[35] If the IR was subsidiary legislation, a good argument could be mounted that these offences are *ultra vires* the NSL because Article 43 does not specifically delegate a power to create offences, let alone offences that exceed the usual maximum for offences in subsidiary legislation, i.e. six months' imprisonment and a HK$5,000 fine.[36] However, the IR is not subsidiary legislation and thus this instance of *ultra vires* would not arise. Nonetheless, certain provisions

34. IR, Schedule 3, ss 3(8)–(9), 5(6)–(7), 6(6), and (8); Schedule 4, ss 10(1), 12(1); Schedule 5, ss 2(3)–(4), 3(2)–(4); Schedule 7, ss 2(13)–(14), 4(12), 5(3).
35. *See* e.g. Schedule 7, s 5(3), which is the penalty for the offence of making a disclosure intending to prejudice an investigation.
36. IGCO, s 28(1)(e).

of the Legislation Law embody the same principle, that regulations and rules should not reduce the rights of citizens unless the basis for doing so is prescribed by laws. For example, Article 80 of the Legislation Law provides:

> Without the bases prescribed by laws . . . , department rules shall not contain provisions that reduce the rights or increase the obligations of citizens, legal persons and other organizations, and shall not contain provisions that enhance the power or reduce the statutory duties of the department concerned.[37]

The question is whether Article 43 prescribes a basis for incorporating criminal offences in the IR, if not expressly, then by necessary implication. As the purpose of the IR is to enable the application of the enumerated powers, the question of necessary implication can be answered by asking, for each criminal offence, whether criminal liability is necessary for the effective application of the relevant power. As many of the offences serve the purpose of ensuring compliance with the relevant powers, their necessity is plain. Similarly, offences that protect the integrity of investigations will also be needed. The only questionable offence is the one that punishes anyone who fails to disclose suspicious transactions and property.[38] The basis is purportedly item (3) of Article 43, but this item makes no reference to disclosure of information by members of the public. However, this duty to disclose is well known and an integral feature of anti-money laundering laws that enable the restraint and confiscation of criminal property.[39] The duty, coupled with the "no consent" scheme of the police, provides another tool for freezing suspected criminal property, a purpose mentioned in Article 43(3).[40] The question is whether it is needed given the wide power in Schedule 3 of freezing property by notice in writing of the Secretary for Security, a power which was applied to the assets of media tycoon Jimmy Lai leading ultimately to the demise of the *Apple Daily* newspaper.[41] This question, however, may be moot because, even if the duty to disclose (and related offences) was omitted from Schedule 3, the duty and "no consent" scheme in the Organized and Serious Crimes Ordinance would still apply, as it applies to all indictable offences.[42]

---

37. *See also* Arts 9 and 82 of the Legislation Law.
38. IR, Schedule 3, s 5(6).
39. OSCO, s 25A; United Nations (Anti-Terrorism Measures) Ordinance (Cap 575) (UNATMO), s 12.
40. A person or body who has made a suspicious report to the authorities must await the consent of the authorities if they are to deal with the relevant property safely. *See* IR, Schedule 3, s 5(2)(a). The analogous regime in the OSCO was found to be constitutional by the Court of Appeal in *Interush Ltd v The Commissioner of Police* [2019] 1 HKLRD 892 but found to be *ultra vires* the OSCO in *Tam Sze Leung v Commissioner of Police* [2021] HKCFI 3118 (per Coleman J).
41. IR, Schedule 3, s 3. *See* HKSARG Press Release, "S for S Issues Notices to Freeze Property Pursuant to Schedule 3 to Implementation Rules", 14 May 2021, available at https://www.info.gov.hk/gia/general/202105/14/P2021051400829.htm (accessed 20 September 2021).
42. OSCO, ss 25 and 25A. By virtue of NSL Art 43(3), offences endangering national security are to be tried on indictment.

As mentioned, the CPG Office may play a more traditional law enforcement role when it exercises jurisdiction over a case pursuant to Article 55.[43] When this occurs, the CPG Office will apply police powers under Chinese national law, rather than under Hong Kong law. Article 57 provides that the "Criminal Procedure Law of the People's Republic of China and other related national laws shall apply to procedural matters including those related to criminal investigation, examination and prosecution". Law enforcement authorities must "exercise powers in accordance with the law".[44] Legal documents issued pursuant to mandatory and investigation measures or judicial decisions "shall have legal force" in Hong Kong.[45] Institutions, organisations, and individuals concerned must comply with measures taken by the CPG Office in accordance with the law.[46] This is a rare example of an enforcement jurisdiction of a mainland body applied extraterritorially to Hong Kong.[47]

Changes to the Mechanisms of Keeping Police Powers in Check

For most of the powers in the IR, courts have a role to ensure they are kept in check. The role is either one of *ex ante* authorisation or *ex post* review, or both (see Appendices 1 and 2 for a detailed breakdown of the various applications that may be made). In this sense, the powers are familiar to the Hong Kong legal system.[48]

The search warrant power in Schedule 1 is consistent with the constitutional law norm, which has developed in recent years, that warrants to enter premises to search and seize items should be authorised by a court if the warrant is reasonably practicable to obtain.[49] This is an important "judicial gatekeeping role".[50] The powers in Schedules 2, 3, and 7 are modelled on the powers in the Prevention of Bribery Ordinance, the Organized and Serious Crimes Ordinance, and the United Nations (Anti-Terrorism Measures) Ordinance, and have the same safeguards provided for

43. NSL, Art 56 goes on to provide that when exercising jurisdiction over a case pursuant to Art 55, the CPG Office "shall initiate investigation into the case".
44. NSL, Art 57.
45. *Ibid.*
46. *Ibid.*
47. In 2016, when the so-called case of the missing booksellers arose, the then Chief Executive, Mr Leung Chun-ying, reportedly stated that it was unacceptable and unconstitutional for mainland agencies to take law enforcement action in Hong Kong; *see* Phila Siu and Lai Ying-kit, "CY Leung on Hong Kong's Missing Booksellers: Mainland China Law Enforcement Actions 'Unacceptable'", *South China Morning Post*, 3 January 2016.
48. Some case law has already been generated: see *Lai Chee-Ying v Secretary for Security* [2021] 4 HKLRD 695 (CFI) (concerning construction of and licences under Schedule 3 powers); *J v Commissioner of Police* [2021] HKCFI 3586 (application to vary Schedule 7 production orders to have information redacted).
49. See *Keen Lloyd Holdings Ltd v Customs* [2016] 2 HKLRD 1372, [75] (CA); *Sham Wing Kan v Commissioner of Police* [2020] 3 HKC 254, [67] (CA).
50. *Keen Lloyd Holdings Ltd* (n 49) [39], [71]–[75]; *Sham Wing Kan* (n 49) [56], [105].

in those laws.[51] Where powers do not provide for judicial oversight, e.g. those in Schedules 4 to 6, persons affected may apply for judicial review to challenge the relevant executive decision on relevant public law grounds.[52] Judicial review is a less effective remedy against executive authorisations of interception and covert surveillance under Schedule 6, as persons affected will often be ignorant of having their privacy invaded.[53]

Two significant changes that reduce the ability of courts to keep the new police powers in check is the lack of constitutional review and the non-application of the special warrants regime for journalistic materials. Since 1991, there have been several cases in which courts have found certain warrantless search powers to engage privacy protections in the Basic Law and Hong Kong Bill of Rights.[54] Courts will no longer be able to conduct such constitutional review after the Court of Final Appeal's decision in *HKSAR v Lai Chee Ying*.[55] To review the IR for Basic Law compatibility is to question Article 43's compatibility with the Basic Law, being another national law, and only the National People's Congress or the Standing Committee of the National People's Congress is competent to conduct such a review.

Even if the courts had the power of constitutional review, the only arguable challenge, based on existing jurisprudence, would be against the new executive powers to authorise interception of communications and Type 1 surveillance. Under the Interception of Communications and Surveillance Ordinance (ICSO), executive authorisation of the less intrusive form of Type 2 surveillance is already possible and has been found to be a proportionate restriction on the right to privacy.[56] Interception of communications and Type 1 surveillance under the ICSO normally requires the prior authorisation of a panel judge, hence courts have not considered if executive authorisation of such powers would be constitutionally compliant. It is not certain at all that constitutional review of the new executive powers would lead to a finding of unconstitutionality, given the legitimate aim of national security. The courts in 2006 struck down the previous regime of executive authorisations

51. *See* Prevention of Bribery Ordinance (Cap 201), ss 14, 17A; OSCO, ss 3, 4, and Parts III to V; UNATMO, s 6 and Parts 4 and 5. *See also* HKSARG Press Release, "Implementing Rules for Article 43 of the Law of the People's Republic of China on Safeguarding National Security in the Hong Kong Special Administrative Region Gazetted", 6 July 2020. But note *Lai Chee-Ying* (n 48) [76]–[80] referring to the NSL and IR having a "wider purpose" than the UNATMO, rendering the latter less helpful on questions of interpretation.
52. The Rules of the High Court (Cap 4A), O. 53. For relevant authorities in the context of search warrants, see *Next Digital Limited v Commissioner of Police* [2021] 5 HKC 411, [9]–[22] (CFI). See also *P v Commissioner of Independent Commission Against Corruption* (2007) 10 HKCFAR 293.
53. As Bokhary PJ noted in *Koo Sze Yiu v Chief Executive* (2006) 9 HKCFAR 441, [37], "the actual matters involved in covert surveillance at any given time is not generally known".
54. *See* e.g. *Keen Lloyd Holdings Ltd* (n 49); *Sham Wing Kan* (n 49); *HKSAR v Yu Lik Wai William* [2019] 1 HKLRD 1149 (CA).
55. *HKSAR v Lai Chee Ying* (2021) 24 HKCFAR 33, [37].
56. Interception of Communications and Surveillance Ordinance (Cap 589) (ICSO), s 14; *Yu Lik Wai William* (n 54).

of interception under the Telecommunications Ordinance and covert surveillance pursuant to an executive order.[57] But that regime enabled the Governor, before 1997, and the CE to order interception in the "public interest" with no other constraints or judicial supervision.[58] The executive order on covert surveillance, not being a general law, lacked the necessary legal certainty to amount to legal procedures and qualify as a restriction on a fundamental right.[59]

In comparison, there is little doubt the NSL's Article 43 together with the IR has the status of law.[60] The NSL regime consists of a detailed set of procedures with evidential and other prerequisite conditions to limit the exercise of the powers. There is a set of written operating principles and guidelines that informs the application of the interception and surveillance powers in Schedule 6; officers of the Police Force have a duty to comply with these guidelines.[61] The guidelines state that applications likely to result in the acquisition of information subject to legal professional privilege (LPP) "should only be made in exceptional circumstances with full justifications".[62] While the NSL regime does not have the oversight mechanism of the Commissioner, who under the ICSO must be a former or serving High Court judge or former permanent judge of the Court of Final Appeal, the IR has provided for the role of an "independent person" who is appointed by the CE to assist the Committee "in fulfilling its supervising responsibility" stipulated in Article 43.[63] There is also the possibility of judicial review of executive authorisations, but as mentioned, this remedy may be illusory if affected persons do not know their privacy has been invaded. Ultimately, in a (hypothetical) constitutional review, the issue will be whether the NSL regime has sufficient safeguards to guard against abuse.[64] While on paper there appear to be plenty of safeguards, the question is whether in practice the authorisation process is rigorous, impartial, and independent and whether the oversight conducted by the Committee and independent person is adequate and fair. As with the annual reports by the ICSO Commissioner, periodic reports of the

57. *Leung Kwok Hung v Chief Executive* (CACV 87/2006, 10 May 2006), affirming (HCAL 107/2005, 9 February 2006, Hartmann J).
58. *See* previous Telecommunications Ordinance (Cap 106), s 33.
59. *Leung Kwok Hung* (n 57) (CA) [29]–[39]; *Leung Kwok Hung* (n 57) (CFI), [136]–[151].
60. *HKSAR v Lai Chee Ying* (n 55) [17]–[20]. NSL Art 43 specifically authorises the CE, in conjunction with the Committee, to make relevant implementation rules for the purpose of applying the measures enumerated under the first paragraph of the article.
61. Operating Principles and Guidelines for Application for Authorization to Conduct Interception and Covert Surveillance, issued pursuant to section 20 of Schedule 6 of the IR for Article 43 of the NSL, GN (E) 74 of 2020 (Operating Principles), [1].
62. Operating Principles, *ibid.* [5].
63. Compare ICSO, s 39 and Part 4 with IR, Schedule 6, s 19, and Operating Principles (n 61) [29].
64. See *Keen Lloyd Holdings Ltd* (n 49) [62], [69], [71], [75], [90], [108], [111] and [120]; *Sham Wing Kan* (n 49) [46], [69], [106], [107], [205], [206] and [210]; *Yu Lik Wai William* (n 54) [90], [247]–[249] and [275].

operation of the NSL regime will help to inform the public as to whether the system is working with integrity.[65]

In the litigation against Jimmy Lai and *Apple Daily*, there were concerns whether the special statutory regime of search warrants for journalistic materials should have applied when searches were conducted in the offices of *Apple Daily*.[66] However, the statutory regime only applies to search powers conferred by an Ordinance or subsidiary legislation under an Ordinance, not when conferred by a national law.[67] Nonetheless, given the importance of the freedoms of speech, the press, and publication in Hong Kong society, as recognised in Article 4, the prospect that journalistic materials (similar to LPP-protected information) would be interfered with must be weighed and taken into account in a balancing exercise preliminary to any authorisation.[68] This is explicitly mentioned for CE authorisations for interception and surveillance.[69] There is no good reason why LPP and journalistic materials should not be afforded the same degree of protection with the other powers in the IR given the constitutional significance of LPP and journalistic materials.

The antidote to these changes to the scope of judicial checks on police powers is the continued close scrutiny of applications and the imposition of reasonable conditions and requirements necessary for the lawful exercise of such powers. Courts have been doing this for centuries, whether it is the common law requirement of knocking on a residence before entering by warrant or the exception of oppressive compliance in response to ICAC production orders.[70] Similarly, to protect the constitutional right to LPP, Hong Kong courts have set out a special procedure for the execution and review of search warrants for law offices to ensure the optimal protection of LPP-protected material.[71]

---

65. ICSO, s 49. The annual reports of the Commissioner, available on the website of the Secretariat, Commissioner on Interception of Communications and Surveillance (https://www.sciocs.gov.hk/en/publication.htm (accessed 21 September 2021)), are normally tabled at the Legislative Council, where the Commissioner would brief members of the public, legislature, and media.
66. IGCO, Part XII (Search and Seizure of Journalistic Materials). *See also* Chris Lau and Natalie Wong, "Hong Kong National Security Law: Apple Daily Arrests Could Encourage Self-Censorship, Experts Warn, but Legal Scholars Insist Reporters Have Little to Fear", *South China Morning Post*, 18 June 2021.
67. IGCO, ss 3 and 83. In obiter, the court in *A v Commissioner of Police* [2021] 3 HKLRD 300, [35]–[38] (CFI), reached the same view that the IGCO, Part XII, does not apply to IR, Schedule 7, for the same reason and the additional reason that Schedule 7 provides for production powers and not powers of entry, search, and seizure.
68. In *A v Commissioner of Police* (n 67) [39]–[44], the court held that it was a relevant consideration to the exercise of the IR, Schedule 7 power to require production that the items to be produced may be journalistic materials, citing to NSL Art 4 and the Court of Final Appeal's decision in *P v ICAC* (n 52) [24] and [28].
69. Operating Principles (n 61) [12], [15] and [26].
70. *See* e.g. *Semayne's Case* (1604) 5 Co Rep 91a; *P v ICAC* (n 52) [29]–[30]. See also *"K" v Commissioner of Police* [2020] 1 HKLRD 606, [37] (CFI).
71. See *Philip KH Wong, Kennedy YH Wong & Co v Commissioner of Independent Commission Against Corruption (No 2)* [2009] 5 HKLRD 379 (CA). See also *A v Commissioner of Police* (n 68) [9]–[14], where the court inspected the sealed documents and upheld the claim of privilege.

An important issue is the power of the courts to exclude evidence obtained in breach of the IR. As mentioned above, a breach of the IR may or may not result in a breach of Article 43. Only if the breach contravenes a minimum standard of the enumerated power in Article 43 will the article be breached. It is submitted this distinction is important when it comes to the exclusion of evidence obtained. Evidence obtained in breach of the IR without breaching Article 43 should only be considered for exclusion pursuant to the common law discretion to exclude recognised in *Secretary for Justice v Lam Tat Ming*.[72] It would be akin to a breach of the Rules and Directions for Questioning of Suspects and the Taking of Statements, which are only guidelines for law enforcement issued by the Secretary for Security.[73] Where breach of the rules limits the suspect's right of silence or results in evidence more prejudicial than probative, the common law discretion to ensure a fair trial for the defendant is engaged.[74]

If, however, the evidence was obtained in breach of the IR and Article 43, then it is submitted the discretion recognised in *HKSAR v Muhammed Riaz Khan* can also be applied to have the evidence excluded.[75] This discretion is broader than the common law one by taking into account the implications of admitting the evidence for the repute and integrity of the justice system. It looks beyond the fairness of the trial as the criteria for exclusion and considers whether the admission of the evidence is reconcilable with individual rights and can lead to a repeat of the impugned police conduct.[76] The *Muhammed Riaz Khan* discretion applies when evidence is obtained in violation of a constitutional right.[77] This can occur where Article 43 is breached because such a breach amounts to an unlawful exercise of police powers and, consequently, Article 14 of the Hong Kong Bill of Rights, which prohibits "arbitrary or unlawful interference" with a person's privacy, is violated.[78] Note that such analysis does not contradict the holding in *HKSAR v Lai Chee Ying* because the Basic Law compatibility of Article 43 is not being questioned.[79] Article 43 is unquestionably valid, but the NSL officer has not complied with it and this has implications for the exclusion of evidence.

Another important judicial safeguard that will continue to apply is the jurisdiction of courts to stay a proceeding for abuse of process. Though the exercise of the jurisdiction is rare, it can be exercised to halt the prosecution's case if either a fair trial for the defendant is impossible or there has been such an affront to the public

72. *Secretary for Justice v Lam Tat Ming* (2000) 3 HKCFAR 168.
73. *Ibid.* 178E-I, 179G-I. Rules and Directions for the Questioning of Suspects and the Taking of Statements, Hong Kong Gazette No 40/1992, 2nd Supplement, No 5, E3, issued by the Secretary for Security on 2 October 1992.
74. *Ibid.* 178J–179J.
75. *HKSAR v Muhammed Riaz Khan* (2012) 15 HKCFAR 232.
76. *Ibid.* [20].
77. *Ibid.* [2].
78. Hong Kong Bill of Rights, Art 14, in s 8 of the Hong Kong Bill of Rights Ordinance (Cap 383).
79. *Lai Chee Ying* (n 55).

conscience to require the proceedings to be stayed. If the circumstances in *HKSAR v Wong Hung Ki* were repeated in an NSL case, there is nothing in either the NSL or IR to preclude the court from ordering the same stay of proceedings.[80] Indeed, Article 41 reassures that the stay power continues to apply because Hong Kong law "shall apply to procedural matters, including those related to criminal investigation, prosecution, trial, and execution of penalty".

Finally, there are also administrative accountability mechanisms in place for NS department officers. The complaints mechanisms for individual or systemic police misconduct will continue to apply, with complaints filed with the HKPF's Complaints Against Police Office and monitoring of the process by the Independent Police Complaints Council.[81] What is new is that the Committee will also serve a supervisory role. Article 43 provides that the Committee "shall be responsible for supervising the implementation of the measures . . . by law enforcement authorities including" the NS department. The broad language suggests the Committee also has oversight over other Hong Kong law enforcement agencies assisting with national security cases. The guidelines on interception and surveillance explain that "implementation of measures" means the operational tasks of carrying out interception and conducting surveillance.[82] The guidelines provide that if an officer fails to comply with Schedule 6, the terms of the authorisation or warrant or the provisions of the guidelines themselves, the Police Force "should report" the failure to the Committee.[83] The Commissioner of Police will also "keep under regular review" the compliance by officers with the regime.[84] If such reviews reveal non-compliance, there should be in place an arrangement to notify the non-compliance to the Committee as soon as practicable, followed by a full report.[85] The guidelines also state unequivocally that officers who fail to comply "would be subject to disciplinary action or, depending on the case, the common law offence of misconduct in public office, in addition to continuing to be subject to the full range of existing law".[86] Officers are to be "fully briefed" on the requirements of Schedule 6 and briefed on updates to the guidelines and other important recommendations or directives when made by the Committee.[87] While the guidelines only pertain to the powers in

80. *HKSAR v Wong Hung Ki* [2011] 1 HKLRD 183 (CA). Officers of the ICAC knowingly recorded and listened to privileged communication between clients and solicitors during a meeting at a restaurant. The Court stayed the proceedings on the ground of abuse of process.
81. *See* Independent Police Complaints Council Ordinance (Cap 604). *See* generally Graham Smith, "The Tripartite Police Complaints System of Hong Kong" (2014) 15 *Asia-Pacific Journal on Human Rights and the Law* 119.
82. Operating Principles (n 61) [29].
83. *Ibid.* [1].
84. *Ibid.* [30].
85. *Ibid.* [31].
86. *Ibid.* [39].
87. *Ibid.*

Schedule 6, they are commendable standards and should be adopted for all Article 43 powers.

A different picture emerges when it comes to accountability for CPG Office personnel who are exercising a law enforcement role.[88] The intent of the NSL is for such officers to be subject to their existing accountability mechanisms under Chinese national law and not to be subject to those under Hong Kong law. Thus, Article 60 provides that the "acts performed in the course of duty by the [CPG Office] and its staff in accordance with this Law shall not be subject to the jurisdiction" of Hong Kong. The qualified language in this clause still leaves limited room for Hong Kong courts to determine the jurisdictional questions of whether the CPG Office or staff in question were performing an act in the course of duty at the material time and whether they were acting in accordance with the NSL. Thus, if the CPG Office or a staff member was found to have acted not in the course of duty or otherwise not in accordance with the NSL, the Hong Kong court may have jurisdiction to consider the merits of the application. But the Hong Kong court has no jurisdiction to consider whether the CPG Office staff was acting in accordance with Chinese laws such as the Criminal Procedure Law. In practice, so long as the CPG Office and its staff are acting officially in good faith and in compliance with the NSL, they will be immune from scrutiny by Hong Kong courts. Any complaints should be taken up by the CE and Committee and handled as an administrative matter with the CPG and the relevant national supervisory authorities.[89]

Conclusion

The NSL has brought about a shift in the equilibrium of police and resident relations in the context of law enforcement in Hong Kong. The shift comes about for the first time by the direct application of national law. A new mainland law enforcement body (CPG Office) is given enforcement jurisdiction in Hong Kong, albeit on limited terms and with marginal oversight by Hong Kong courts. The HKPF has a new NS department of distinct status accountable to the new national security Committee chaired by the CE. The Committee is under the supervision of and accountable to the CPG.[90]

The NS department is both an intelligence agency with a strong preventive role and a regular police force investigating past and current offences. To ensure the effective operation of the NS department, the NSL invests the department with all existing police powers and then some. The new powers bring more persons within the radar of the police, whether they are suspected of a crime or not. Those who have control over online content may now be required to remove messages

88. NSL, Chapter V.
89. NSL, Arts 48 and 50.
90. NSL, Art 12.

endangering national security and provide information or assistance to the authorities. Those financially supported by a foreign government or foreign political organisation (including a Taiwan authority or Taiwan political organisation) and carry on activities for the benefit of that government or political organisation may be required to disclose information to the NS department. Those under investigation for offences endangering national security may find themselves effectively barred, by magistrate's notice, from leaving Hong Kong. Anyone with ties to those under investigation may find themselves subject to the IR powers on the ground that they are reasonably suspected to have information or items relevant to the investigation.

Perhaps of greatest concern in the new equilibrium is the extent to which private lives and conversations are at risk of coming under state surveillance. The role of the judiciary in checking these interception and surveillance powers is weaker under the NSL and IR than in other contexts. To ensure that human rights are protected and rule of law values are adhered to, all applicable accountability mechanisms under Hong Kong and mainland law must act robustly and transparently, keeping members of the public informed of matters vital to safeguarding their lawful rights and interests.

Appendix 1

Police Powers in the Implementation Rules by Authorising Authority

Nature of Power	Who Authorises?	Who Can Apply?	IR
1. Search warrant	Magistrate	Police officer	Sch 1, s 2(2)
2. Search without warrant	Police officer not below the rank of Assistant Commissioner of Police	Not applicable.	Sch 1, s 3(1)
3. Surrender of travel document by written notice	Magistrate	Police officer	Sch 2, s 2(1)
4. Freezing of offence-related property by notice in writing	Secretary for Security	Not applicable.	Sch 3, s 3(1)
5. Direct the seizure of property specified in notice	Secretary for Security	Not applicable.	Sch 3, s 3(7)
6. No consent to act in financing or assisting	Police officer	Not applicable.	Sch 3, s 5(2)
7. Restraint order	Court of First Instance	Secretary for Justice or authorised officer	Sch 3, s 7(1)
8. Charging order	Court of First Instance	Secretary for Justice or authorised officer	Sch 3, s 8(1)
9. Delivery of information to assist valuation of restrained or charged property	Police officer	Not applicable.	Sch 3, s 6(4)
10. Confiscation order	Court of First Instance or District Court	Secretary for Justice or authorised officer	Sch 3, s 9(6)
11. Variation of confiscation order	Court of First Instance	Authorised officer	Sch 3, s 10(2)
12. Appointment of receiver to enforce confiscation order	Court of First Instance	Not provided for.	Sch 3, s 11(1)
13. Forfeiture of offence-related property	Court of First Instance	Secretary for Justice (or on her behalf)	Sch 3, s 13(1)

Nature of Power	Who Authorises?	Who Can Apply?	IR
14. Require persons and providers to take disabling action on electronic message	Commissioner of Police, with approval of the Secretary for Security	Designated officer	Sch 4, s 6
15. Warrant to require provision of identification record or decryption assistance	Magistrate	Police officer	Sch 4, s 9(1)
16. Requiring provision of identification record or decryption assistance without warrant	Specified police officer (or police officer authorised by specified police officer)	Not applicable.	Sch 4, s 9(2)
17. Warrant to seize electronic device to remove message from platform	Magistrate	Police officer	Sch 4, s 11
18. Requiring by written notice foreign or Taiwanese political organisation to provide information	Commissioner of Police, with approval of Secretary for Security	Not applicable.	Sch 5, s 2(1)
19. Requiring by written notice foreign agent or Taiwanese agent to provide information	Commissioner of Police, with approval of Secretary for Security	Not applicable.	Sch 5, s 3(1)
20. Interception or covert surveillance (both Types 1 & 2)	Chief Executive	Officer of the Police Force, with approval of a directorate officer	Sch 6, s 4(2)
21. Type 2 surveillance	Authorising officer (designated by Chief Executive)	Officer of the Police Force	Sch 6, s 5(3)
22. Renewal of authorisation for interception or covert surveillance	Chief Executive	Officer of the Police Force, with approval of a directorate officer	Sch 6, s 6(2)
23. Renewal of authorisation for Type 2 surveillance	Authorising officer (designated by Chief Executive)	Officer of the Police Force	Sch 6, s 7(2)

Nature of Power	Who Authorises?	Who Can Apply?	IR
24. Emergency authorisation for interception or Type 1 surveillance	Commissioner of Police	Officer of the Police Force	Sch 6, s 9(2)
25. Confirmation of emergency authorisation	Chief Executive	Officer of the Police Force, as caused by Commissioner of Police	Sch 6, s 10(3)
26. Device retrieval warrant	Chief Executive	Officer of the Police Force	Sch 6, s 14(2)
27. Order to answer questions, furnish information, or produce material	Court of First Instance	Secretary for Justice	Sch 7, s 2(2)
28. Order to make material available	Court of First Instance	Secretary for Justice or authorised officer	Sch 7, s 3(2)

Appendix 2

Procedures for Relief under the Implementation Rules for Affected Persons

Nature of Power	Who Authorises?	Who Can Apply?	IR
1. Return of travel document	Commissioner of Police or Magistrate	Person who has surrendered a travel document	Sch 2, s 3(3)
2. Permission to leave Hong Kong	Commissioner of Police or Magistrate	Person on whom a notice is served	Sch 2, s 4(3)
3. Licence to deal with frozen property	Secretary for Security	Person affected by notice	Sch 3, s 3(1)
4. Revocation of freezing notice	Court of First Instance	Person affected by notice	Sch 3, s 4(1)
5. Grant or variation of licence to deal with frozen property	Court of First Instance	Person affected by notice	Sch 3, s 4(2)
6. Revocation or variation of direction to seize property specified in notice	Court of First Instance	Person affected by notice	Sch 3, s 4(2)
7. Discharge or variation of restraint order or charging order	Court of First Instance	Person affected by order	Sch 3, s 6(3)
8. Variation of confiscation order	Court of First Instance	Defendant (or personal representative if deceased)	Sch 3, s 10(1)
9. Compensation	Court of First Instance	Person with interest in relevant property	Sch 3, s 14(1), (4) & (6)

9

The Return of High Policing in Hong Kong

Hualing Fu and Xiaobo Zhai

Introduction

"What a disgrace!" lamented Xia Baolong, Director of the Office for Hong Kong and Macau Affairs, the highest-ranking official in the Central People's Government (CPG) in charge of Hong Kong affairs in a particularly condescending outburst to condemn the 2019 protests in Hong Kong.[1] That's how Beijing, Hong Kong's sovereign, perceived what happened in Hong Kong in 2019. For the CPG, what was presented as democratic protest by the international media was nothing short of systematic disorder and organised violence bordering on insurrection. What was shocking and extremely displeasing for the CPG was not only the level of violence and vandalism that some Hong Kong people proved to be capable of, but also the degree of sympathy and support they received from the larger communities in Hong Kong and internationally, and the incompetence and indifference of the Hong Kong government. In the CPG's eyes, Hong Kong has turned from an economic asset into a political liability. More importantly, the CPG believed that the unrest in Hong Kong exposed China to hostile international forces and put China's national security at grave risk.

The mass unrest creates the need—it also offers an opportunity—for the CPG to react forcefully and strongly to put violence to an end and to restore law and order. Its sharp and drastic action has taken the form of legislative suppression—the passing of the Law of the People's Republic of China for Safeguarding National Security in the Hong Kong Special Administrative Region (NSL). The law aims both at the immediate goals of "preventing, stopping and punishing" activities endangering national security and the long-term goal of changing the constitutional

1. "田北辰引述夏寶龍指反修例示威 '成何體統': 形容丟臉", *Radio Television Hong Kong*, 28 May 2020, available at https://today.line.me/hk/v2/article/kNvRDk.

structure of Hong Kong.[2] The law creates a range of new criminal offences, often broadly defined to cast a wide net against offences potentially endangering national security, exceeding China's own criminal law for some of the offences in its breadth.[3] It establishes a web of national security agencies with interlocking jurisdictions and duties with Beijing sitting at a comfortable, commanding height. The NSL expands police power and correspondingly either ousts or limits judicial authorities at multiple entry points, ranging from restricting bail, excluding juries, and enhancing secrecy in judicial proceedings. Beyond the immediate impact, the NSL attempts to tackle the root cause of the national security risks as China perceives them in Hong Kong—a vibrant and politically charged civil society comprising non-governmental sectors, such as education, the media, the internet, religion, or NGOs that were against the government. Through the NSL, high policing has returned to Hong Kong.

This chapter offers a preliminary study of the role and functions of the high policing, also called political or national security policing, which the NSL has introduced in Hong Kong, and its initial and long-term impact on the rule of law and rights and freedoms in Hong Kong.[4] The role that the political policing plays in Hong Kong largely depends upon the ultimate political end of the NSL. Beyond the immediate goal of ending violence, nipping the pro-independence movement in the bud, and stopping foreign political meddling in Hong Kong, to what degree does the CPG intend to reorient Hong Kong and to bring it into the Chinese orbit? Clearly, China continues to insist on the One Country Two Systems doctrine (OCTS), although to be enforced in a "correct way" that privileges its one country element. China, however, does not intend to turn it into just another Chinese city. In one of his speeches in 2017, President Xi Jinping highlighted Hong Kong's "distinctive strengths", including its pluralist and cosmopolitan society and its status as a major international financial centre.[5] China clearly stopped far short from imposing its own National Security Law (2015) upon Hong Kong, nor did it transplant its own national security practice in its entirety to Hong Kong. In enacting the NSL, China sent a clear signal that, while the excess in 2019 should not happen again, Hong Kong will remain a distinct Special Administrative Region (SAR) in the foreseeable

2. For the aims of the NSL, *see* Decision of the National People's Congress on Establishing and Improving the Legal System and Enforcement Mechanisms for the Hong Kong Special Administrative Region to Safeguard National Security, and also Art 1 of the NSL.
3. Chen in this volume.
4. For high policing, *see* Jean-Paul Brodeur, *The Policing Web* (Oxford: Oxford University Press, 2010), pp 223–254, and "High Policing and Low Policing: Remarks about the Policing of Political Activities" (1983) *Social Problems* 30, 507 and 514. For a useful survey of literature, *see* Gary T. Marx, "High Policing", *Encyclopedia of Criminology and Criminal Justice*, available at https://web.mit.edu/gtmarx/www/highpolicing.html.
5. "Xi Jinping Attended the HKSAR's Welcome Dinner and Delivered an Important Speech" (習近平出席香港特別行政區政府歡迎晚宴並發表重要講話), *Xinhua*, 30 June 2017, available at http://www.xinhuanet.com/politics/2017-07/01/c_1121244549.htm.

future. There is a long spectrum between the unrest in 2019 and the Chinese regime of national security: where would Hong Kong find itself in the post-NSL era?

This chapter explores three connected issues: 1) the political circumstances for the creation of the national security policing in Hong Kong; 2) the major features of the high policing that the NSL has created in Hong Kong, which are demonstrated by means of an analysis of the NSL and the immediate impact that the NSL may have on the rule of law and rights and freedoms in Hong Kong; and 3) a possible new equilibrium between the national security policing and Hong Kong's liberal rule of law under the OCTS doctrine.

I. The Prehistory of the NSL

The establishment of a network of national security apparatus, with a CPG-controlled enforcement mechanism, came as a shock to most, if not all, Hong Kong watchers. The CPG's demand for a national security law in Hong Kong and the latter's reluctance to deliver it had a long and tortured history which has been well documented.[6] But all along, the debates on Article 23 had focused exclusively on offences—that is whether Hong Kong should legislate new offences to satisfy the Article 23 requirement—with the unchallenged presumption that the new law, if ever passed, would be enforced in Hong Kong and by Hong Kong police. In the 2003 controversy,[7] how the offences were to be defined and how much power the Hong Kong police should have in enforcing the law were the only major concerns. Before the enactment of the NSL in 2020, it had been taken for granted that criminal law power lay exclusively within Hong Kong's autonomy and that Article 23 offences were criminal law matters pure and simple. It was settled that the operative words in Article 23 were "on its own", which indicated that national security legislation and enforcement were exclusively in Hong Kong's control: the National People's Congress (NPC) had delegated criminal law power, in its entirety, to the SAR, and it was unimaginable that the CPG could have any direct involvement in defining the offences and enforcing the law. While the CPG had urged Hong Kong to enact the Article 23 law whenever opportunities arose, it agreed that it was for the SAR to make the call.

That foundational position of the CPG started to shift after the Occupy Central Movement (OCM) in 2014—the mass civil disobedience demanding "genuine" universal suffrage according to the prevailing international human rights standard. The aftermath of the OCM witnessed the sudden emergence of secessionist forces, the abandonment of peaceful advocacy, and the rise of extremist confrontations

6. Fu Hualing, Carole J. Petersen, and Simon N. M. Young (eds), *National Security and Fundamental Freedoms: Hong Kong's Article 23 under Scrutiny* (Hong Kong: Hong Kong University Press, 2005); Cora Chan and Fiona de Londras (eds), *China's National Security: Endangering Hong Kong's Rule of Law?* (Oxford: Hart Publishing, 2020).
7. Fu, Petersen, and Young, n 6 above.

and violence. These new and serious challenges shifted the ground of the Article 23 debate. The Mong Kok riot, also dubbed the Fishball Revolution, in February 2016, was the first major mass unrest in Hong Kong since 1968.[8] One month later, in an unprecedented move, an obscure Andy Chan created the Hong Kong National Party, announcing the goal to build an independent and free republic of Hong Kong.[9] These two landmark events foreshadowed what was forthcoming in Hong Kong's large-scale street violence in 2019.

Over the years, the warnings given to Hong Kong not to encroach on China's security interest had become more and more frequent, coming from higher-ranking officials in more forceful and stern terms. As early as March 2013, in his capacity as a member of the Politburo Standing Committee, Yu Zhengsheng met with Hong Kong and Macau members of the Chinese People's Political Consultative Conference and gave a 20-minute speech, covering matters such as the contradictions between Hong Kong and the CPG, and the election of the Chief Executive (CE) by universal suffrage in 2017. Yu condemned protesters raising the "lion-dragon" flag of the colonial era as committing acts of subversion. He vowed that Hong Kong would not become a bridgehead for overthrowing China's socialist system and that protesters would not be allowed "to make irresponsible remarks" regarding the Mainland. Yu criticised the pro-Beijing camp's ambivalence and called for patriotic voices to turn up the volume, hinting that if Hong Kong were to be governed by people opposing the Central Government, this would be bad for Hong Kong and China. In short, "the consequences would be unimaginable".[10]

The Director of the Liaison Office, Zhang Xiaoming, made a speech on the Chinese New Year of 2015,[11] which represented Zhang's first public remark on the

---

8. Stuart Lau, Jennifer Ngo, Chris Lau, Ernest Kao, and Nikki Sun, "Mong Kok Riot: How Hong Kong's First Night in the Year of the Monkey Descended into Mayhem", *South China Morning Post*, 10 February 2016, available at https://www.scmp.com/news/hong-kong/article/1911341/mong-kok-riot-how-hong-kongs-first-night-year-monkey-descended-mayhem; Rachel Blundy and Laura Ma, "Fishball Revolution: Hong Kong's Social Media Users React to Violent Mong Kok Hawker Protest", *South China Morning Post*, 9 February 2016, available at https://www.scmp.com/news/hong-kong/law-crime/article/1910894/fishballrevolution-hong-kongs-social-media-users-react.
9. "Declaration of Establishment by the Hong Kong National Party" (香港民族黨宣布建黨), 28 March 2016, available at https://www.facebook.com/hknationalparty/posts/478117092387250; for a legal analysis of the government ban of the Party, *see* Carole Petersen, "Prohibiting the Hong Kong National Party: Has Hong Kong Violated the International Covenant on Civil and Political Rights" (2018) 48 *Hong Kong Law Journal* 789.
10. "Yu Zheng Sheng Indicates That Universal Suffrage Could Be Used for Subversion and the Chief Executive Must Love China and Love Hong Kong" (俞正聲指香港有人搞顛覆，普選特首須愛國愛港), *Radio France International*, 7 March 2013, available at https://www.rfi.fr; *see also* "Hong Kong Media Questioning Yu Zhengsheng's Accusation of Hongkongers' Subversion" (港媒質疑俞正聲有港人搞顛覆指責), *BBC News Chinese*, 7 March 2013, available at https://www.bbc.com/zhongwen/simp/china/2013/03/130306_hk_pressreview_npc.
11. "The Decision of the Standing Committee of the National People's Congress on Issues Relating to the Selection of the Chief Executive of the Hong Kong Special Administrative Region by Universal Suffrage and on the Method for Forming the Legislative Council of the Hong Kong Special Administrative Region in the Year 2016" (全國人民代表大會常務委員會關於香港特別行政區行政長官普選問題和

OCM. Zhang noted that a high degree of autonomy under OCTS does not mean that Hong Kong was not subject to the jurisdiction of the CPG and that the arrangement of universal suffrage, as a major issue of the political regime, was the preserve of Beijing. Moreover, he said that this issue should not become an excuse for the propagation of "Hong Kong independence" and called for strengthening national security awareness.[12] Later, in relation to the discussion of "Hong Kong independence" in high schools, the Liaison Office's legal chief, Wang Zhenmin, made an emotional appeal to the seven million people of Hong Kong not to allow "the poisoning of our children", reiterating two principles: first, not to allow "Hong Kong independence" forces to enter the government, courts or legislature, and secondly, not to allow them to gain an inch in schools.[13]

One year after the OCM, China enacted its own National Security Law, which includes Hong Kong and Macau in its national security consideration. Article 40 of the law provides that "Hong Kong and Macau SARs shall fulfil the responsibility of safeguarding national security" (Article 40(3)), and Article 11 stipulates that "safeguarding national sovereignty, unity, and territorial integrity is the common duty of all Chinese people, including compatriots of Hong Kong, Macau, and Taiwan" (Article 11(2)). While this law is not applicable in Hong Kong, Hong Kong appeared for the first time on China's national security horizon.

In the wake of the oath-taking controversy in 2016, the result of which was that elected Legislative Council (LegCo) members were not allowed to take office due to their inappropriate protests that betrayed independence leanings, the National People's Congress Standing Committee (NPCSC) gave an interpretation of Article 104 of the Basic Law, which effectively disqualified these legislators.[14] Li Fei, Chairman of the NPCSC's Basic Law Committee, explained that the legislators had publicly insulted the Chinese nation and that the foul language, deeds, and ugly performance of the "Hong Kong independence" elements had aroused the ire of the people and were denounced by all Chinese at home and abroad. Li said that the "Hong Kong independence" movement amounted to separatism and, as such, gravely breached the People's Republic of China (PRC) Constitution, Hong Kong's

2016年立法會產生辦法的決定), 31 August 2014, commonly known as the 31 August Decision (八三一決定), available at http://www.2017.gov.hk/filemanager/template/en/doc/20140831b.pdf.

12. Zhang Xiaoming, "Speech at the Spring Reception of 2015 Held by the CPG's Liaison Office in Hong Kong" (在中央政府駐港聯絡辦2015年新春酒會上的致辭), Liaison Office of the Central People's Government in the Hong Kong SAR, 4 February 2015, available at http://www.locpg.hk/jsdt/2015-02/04/c_127458640.htm.

13. Wang Zhenmin, "Advocates of Hong Kong Independence Are Not Allowed to Enter the Judiciary, Legislature, Administration, and Schools" (中聯辦王振民：主張港獨者不可進入司法、立法、行政機關 不可進中小學), *Standnews*, 16 August 2016.

14. Shirley Zhao, "Oath-Taking Antics: The Acts That Got Six Hong Kong Lawmakers Disqualified", *South China Morning Post*, 14 July 2017, available at https://www.scmp.com/news/hong-kong/law-crime/article/2102731/oath-taking-antics-acts-got-six-hong-kong-lawmakers; *see* Zhu Han and Albert Chen, "The Oath-Taking Cases and the NPCSC Interpretation of 2016: Interface of Common Law and Chinese Law" (2019) 49(1) *Hong Kong Law Journal* 381.

Basic Law, and relevant local laws, harming national sovereignty, security, and interests, and the prosperity of Hong Kong.[15] Shortly afterwards, Zhang Xiaoming proposed explicitly "three bottom lines", namely, threatening national sovereignty and security, challenging the authority of the Central Government and the Basic Law, and using Hong Kong to infiltrate and subvert the Mainland.[16] These three bottom lines were subsequently adopted almost verbatim by Xi Jinping in his speech on the twentieth anniversary of Hong Kong's handover, which formed a direct and serious warning from the highest authority.[17]

Zhang's replacement, Wang Zhimin, endorsed the "three bottom lines" on the first National Security Education Day in April 2018 when he said that the activities of "Hong Kong independence" extremist elements had violated the security of national sovereignty and exceeded the boundaries of academic freedom and the freedom of speech, calling upon the mass Hong Kong people to support the mission of national rejuvenation and the China Dream, and to show zero tolerance towards the independence movement.[18] These words were soon translated into action in July when the Hong Kong Police Force issued a notice under the *Societies Ordinance* to the convener of the *Hong Kong National Party*, Andrew Chan, stating that the party was banned on grounds of undermining national security.[19] The determination of the CPG to jealously guard the three bottom lines was reflected again in August when the *Foreign Correspondents Club* (FCC) hosted a lunchtime talk, providing a platform to Andrew Chan in spite of opposition from the CPG, the Hong Kong Special Administrative Region (HKSAR) government, and former Chief Executive C. Y. Leung. Vice-chair of the FCC Victor Mallet's work visa was revoked on his return from a trip to Thailand.[20]

The CPG continued to issue stern warnings to Hong Kong in the midst of the anti-extradition protests.[21] In August 2019, at a symposium jointly hosted by

15. "NPCSC Unanimously Passes Interpretation of the Basic Law, Li Fei Meets Journalists" (全國人大常委會全票通過釋法，李飛見記者), 8 November 2016, available at http://www.locpg.hk/jsdt/2016-11/08/c_129355715.htm.
16. "Director of the Liaison Office Zhang Xiaoming Says One Country Two Systems Must Observe Three Bottom Lines" (港中聯辦主任張曉明："一國兩制"須堅守三條底線), *United Morning News* (聯合早報), 3 January 2017, available at http://www.uzaobao.com/bolg/20170103/33027.html.
17. "Xi's Speech at Meeting Marking HK's 20th Return Anniversary, Inaugural Ceremony of 5th-Term HKSAR Gov't", 1 July 2017, available at http://www.fmcoprc.gov.hk/eng/Topics/pth/t1646265.htm.
18. Wang Zhimin, "Adhere to OCTS's Original Aspiration, and Safeguard Its Regime Safety" (王志民，"堅守'一國兩制'初心，維護'一國兩制'制度安全"), Liaison Office of the Central People's Government in the Hong Kong SAR, 15 April 2018, available at http://www.locpg.hk/jsdt/2018-04/15/c_129850781.htm.
19. Tony Cheung and Jeffie Lam, "Ban on Hong Kong National Party over 'armed revolution' call met with both cheers and fear", *South China Morning Post*, 24 September 2018, available at https://www.scmp.com/news/hong-kong/politics/article/2165439/hong-kong-issues-unprecedented-ban-separatist-party.
20. Jeffie Lam, Sum Lok-kei, and Kimmy Chung, "Journalist Victor Mallet Allowed Back into Hong Kong—for Seven Days Only", *South China Morning Post*, 8 October 2018, available at https://www.scmp.com/news/hong-kong/politics/article/2167429/financial-times-journalist-victor-mallet-re-enters-hong-kong.
21. For the anti-extradition protests in Hong Kong, *see* Heike Holbig, "Be Water, My Friend: Hong Kong's

the Hong Kong and Macau Affairs Office of the State Council and the Hong Kong Liaison Office, Zhang Xiaoming announced that "stopping violence and ending chaos" was the overwhelming priority, hinting that the Central Government had an abundance of methods to rapidly pacify Hong Kong. Citing the emergence of slogans, such as "Liberate Hong Kong" and "Revolution of Our Times", as well as protesters encircling the Liaison Office and defiling the national flag as evidence that a colour revolution was afoot in Hong Kong, Zhang called for a crackdown on the participants organising the protests through resolute legal actions.[22]

The CPG has in fact begun to rebuild its own national security capacity in Hong Kong after the collapse of the National Security Bill in 2003. The longer the delay in the enactment of a national security law in Hong Kong, the stronger the Chinese national security capacity in Hong Kong becomes, and the harder it will be for the national security matters to be left alone to Hong Kong. Gradually and decisively, the CPG's trust in the ability of the Hong Kong and the SAR government to sort out the national security problem slipped away. Confronted by the radicalisation of violent street politics and the mutation of localism into an independence movement, the patience of the CPG was fast running out. A sense of urgency has taken a strong hold: as time went by, in the large international environment in which China's rise encountered increasing challenges, Hong Kong, in the eyes of the CPG, was becoming a subversive basis to destabilise China on behalf of the Western powers.

A new doctrine emerged in 2014, stating that "the Central Government exercises overall jurisdiction (全面管治權) over the HKSAR".[23] The OCM offered a decisive impetus for the CPG to realise that it needed an institutional lever to exert hands-on control in Hong Kong. After the 2019 violent anti-extradition protests, the CPG did not entertain any hope that the HKSAR could be expected to pass an NSL. More significantly, the CPG found it necessary not only to create a range of new offences endangering national security but also to establish effective control over the enforcement from the police to the courts through changes in procedures and institutional design. The new narrative of creating a centralised enforcement mechanism in Hong Kong appeared all of a sudden and was made with force. That the CPG was contemplating an NSL-enforcement mechanism in Hong Kong was first made known in the *Communique of the Fourth Plenary Session of the 19th CCP Central Committee* announced on 31 October 2019, in which it is stated that the law and enforcement mechanism to safeguard national security in the SARs must

---

2019 Anti-Extradition Protests" (2020) 50(4) *International Journal of Sociology* 325–337, available at https://doi.org/10.1080/00207659.2020.1802556.

22. "Stopping Violence, Ending Chaos, and Restoring Order Are the Overriding Priorities for Hong Kong" (止暴制亂、恢復秩序 是香港當前壓倒一切的急迫任務), *Xinhua*, 7 August 2019, available at http://m.xinhuanet.com/2019-08/07/c_1124849007.htm.
23. "The Practice of the 'One Country, Two Systems' Policy in the Hong Kong Special Administrative Region", The State Council Information Office of the PRC, 10 June 2014, available at http://www.scio.gov.cn/zfbps/ndhf/2014/Document/1373163/1373163.htm.

be established and improved. In the same document, it was reiterated that the CPG will never tolerate any act that challenges the OCTS bottom lines, especially any secessionist act.[24]

The announcement seemed to have caused no alarm in Hong Kong about what was in store. On 31 October 2019, when the Chinese Communist Party (CCP) announced the creation of an enforcement mechanism for national security in Hong Kong, there was slight awareness of the gravity of the matter, and the violent confrontations continued on streets as they were planned and protests continued to escalate. It was only when an NSL bill was tabled for secret consultation in June 2020 that Hong Kong finally woke up to the fact that a ground-shaking law was being imposed on Hong Kong. Many may have scrambled to lobby the CPG to allow more participation from Hong Kong in the making of the NSL, but by then Hong Kong, as a whole, was no longer in a position to persuade the CPG to alter the course. On national security matters, Hong Kong had little support and few friends in Beijing. Whatever doubts and reservations there may have been on the part of the CPG against direct interference on national security matters in Hong Kong before 2019, they all vanished without a trace. For the first time, the CPG stated openly that the principle of two systems does not apply to the issue of national security, and the CPG is duty-bound to protect its security in Hong Kong. As the Foreign Minister stated directly: national security is under the jurisdiction of the Central Government, and a single national standard should apply under the CPG's leadership.[25] From the perspective of the CPG, the NSL and the built-in enforcement mechanism are simply a necessity to restore law and order in Hong Kong. With the NSL, for the first time since the handover of Hong Kong, the CPG has an effective institutional lever to enable it to exercise direct control in Hong Kong.

II. The National Security Policing under the NSL

The NSL has created a grid of institutions with multiple layers and nodes, setting up a watertight, ironclad national security system that is politically pre-eminent and legally powerful. Judicial and legislative supervision is intentionally constrained or

24. "The CCPCC's Decisions on Major Issues Regarding Upholding and Improving the Socialist System with Chinese Characteristics and Pushing Forward the Modernization of the System and Capacity of State Governance, Adopted at the Fourth Plenary Session of the 19th Central Committee of the Communist Party of China on 31 October 2019" (《中共中央關於堅持和完善中國特色社會主義制度、推進國家治理體系和治理能力現代化若干重大問題的決定》（2019年10月31日中國共產黨第十九屆中央委員會第四次全體會議通過）, available at http://www.gov.cn/zhengce/2019-11/05/content_5449023.htm.
25. "Wang Yi on CPG's Efforts on National Security Legislation for Hong Kong" (王毅谈中央政府推进香港国家安全立法), *Xinhua*, 24 May 2020, available at http://www.xinhuanet.com/politics/2020lh/2020-05/24/c_1210631733.htm; *see also* Wang Zhimin, "Adhere to OCTS's Original Aspiration, and Safeguard Its Regime Safety" (王志民：堅守"一國兩制"初心，維護"一國兩制"制度安全), Liaison Office of the Central People's Government in the Hong Kong SAR, 15 April 2018, available at http://www.locpg.hk/jsdt/2018-04/15/c_129850781.htm.

ousted, and the entire mechanism is allowed to operate on its own and in great secrecy.[26] The key national security apparatus in the grid is the Department for Safeguarding National Security (NSD) of the Hong Kong Police Force, which operates under the Committee for Safeguarding National Security (NSC) of the SAR government and the Office for Safeguarding National Security Office (NSO) dispatched by the CPG and permanently stationed in Hong Kong.

With these arrangements, the NSL has made national security in Hong Kong the heart of the CPG's governance of the SAR. The NSL may have been triggered by a quasi-emergency and a near insurrection, but by itself it is not an emergency law in the traditional sense that was enacted merely for managing a particular crisis. The NSL has institutionalised some emergency measures and translated some exceptional measures into permanent norms. In particular, it has authorised an organ of the CPG (i.e. NSO) to directly enforce certain laws upon Hong Kong residents even in normal times (Art 55 of the NSL, and Art 18(4) of the Basic Law) and has thereby revised the Basic Law regime.

In the following sections, we highlight three major features of the national security policing under the NSL. First, it is political policing, targeting political expressions and actions that may pose challenges to authorities. Second, it is pre-emptive and preventive policing in its operation, with the effect of the "policification" of the NSL: it locates the focal point of the NSL enforcement in the national security police. Third, it is centrally controlled. With these three features, the NSL creates a prerogative state in political policing in Hong Kong. As a consequence, a part of the Hong Kong criminal justice system has been effectively carved out and subjected to the control of a new set of institutions with a different logic and following different rules and procedures.

a. It Is Political

The NSD in part restores the old Special Branch of the police abolished in 1997 before reunification. The Special Branch was set up within the Hong Kong police to monitor and control political agitations, targeting principally Communist propaganda and mobilisation against colonial rule. The abolition of the Special Branch created a national security gap in the SAR until the arrival of the NSL.[27] While anti-terrorism policing was set up in Hong Kong in the newly established security wing in 2009,[28] political monitoring and control aiming at seditious libel and subversive activities were intentionally left out. As characteristic of the authoritarian practice

26. Jie Cheng and Johannes Chan in this volume.
27. Fu Hualing and Richard Cullen, "Political Policing in Hong Kong" (2003) 33(1) *Hong Kong Law Journal* 199–230.
28. "Taking the Weighty Responsibility of Security: How Much Do You Know about the Anti-Terrorism Elite of Hong Kong Police" (肩負安保重責：香港警隊"反恐精英"你知幾多？), *Think Hong Kong*, 14 December 2018, available at https://www.thinkhk.com/article/2018-12/14/31756.html.

in the Mainland and in Hong Kong's colonial past, such political monitoring was simply unacceptable in the new SAR practicing OCTS, which made Hong Kong a depoliticised administrative region. While the political offences in the Crimes Ordinance survived reunification, few in Hong Kong have thought to dust off them and put them to use prior to the radicalisation in the aftermath of the OCM. In any event, the prevailing view in the legal community was that they were very likely to be declared by courts to contravene the Basic Law and the international human rights regime it incorporates.

According to Beirne and Messerschmitt, political crimes are "threefold, entailing not only crimes against the state (violations of law for the purpose of modifying or changing social conditions) but also crimes by the state".[29] Crimes by the state can be called state crimes, including typically political corruption, illegal domestic surveillance, police use of excessive force, civil and human rights violations, and state corporate crimes. Crimes against the state can be called oppositional political crimes:[30] they are engaged not out of private greed or passion, or for personal gain; instead, they are committed out of political conviction or ideology, seeking to change or modify a particular social condition, including the integrity of its territory, the form of government or its constitutional system, and the organisation and function of the political powers. Very often, oppositional political crimes concern "matters of security and stability of the State in relation to conduct that negated and sought to obliterate the State or its government".[31] Challenging political authority and political order defines oppositional political offences and distinguishes them from ordinary offences.[32] Scholars argue that the core of oppositional political crime is that it affects "the power of the state, . . . leading ultimately to the effort to . . . overthrow the power". In simpler terms, a political crime "aims to obtain (redistribute), retain and further use . . . state power".[33]

National security crimes are typical oppositional political offences. Article 23 of the Basic Law requires the HKSAR to "enact laws on its own to prohibit any act of treason, secession, sedition, subversion against the Central People's Government, or theft of state secrets, to prohibit foreign political organizations or bodies from conducting political activities in the Region, and to prohibit political organizations

29. Piers Beirne and James Messerschmidt, *Criminology* (New York: Oxford University Press, 6th edn, 2015), 318.
30. Jeffrey Ian Ross, "Contemporary Political Crimes", and "Sociology of Political Crimes", in W. R. Miller (ed), *The Social History of Crime and Punishment in America: An Encyclopedia* (Thousand Oaks: Sage, 2012), 1376, 1386.
31. Andrea Mateus-Rugeles and Paula C. Arias, "Narcotraffic as Connected Political Crime in Colombia: The FARC Case" (2020) 51 *University of Miami Inter-American Law Review* 1, 25.
32. Ronald Christenson, "A Political Theory of Political Trials" (1983) 74 *Journal of Criminal Law and Criminology* 2, 73.
33. P. L. Fris, I. B. Medytskyi, Y. I. Mykytyn, and V. V. Shpiliarevych, "The Annexation of the Autonomous Republic of Crimea and the Armed Conflict in Eastern Ukraine as a Crime of Aggression by the Russian Federation against Ukraine" (2019) 10 *Journal of Advanced Research in Law and Economics* 165, 166.

or bodies of the Region from establishing ties with foreign political organizations or bodies". The NSL prohibits four major crimes, which are secession, subversion, terrorist activities, and collusion with a foreign country or with external forces to endanger national security. These national security offences are first and foremost political because they mostly challenge the political authorities and the political order they embody. "The specific political distinction," as Schmitt put succinctly, "is that between friend and enemy."[34] The essence of political crimes is to negate the existence of the established political order, and their perpetrators are therefore considered by the state as enemy.

Criminal law responds to enemies in a drastically different way. Jakobs has drawn a sharp contrast between enemy and citizen criminal law, and argued forcefully that they work under different logic, follow different rules, and impose different kinds of punishment for different reasons.[35] Citizen criminal law is communicative: "[i]t assumes that the offender remains a loyal citizen and that the offending behaviour was a lapse, which he or she now regards as a mistake, and so continues to address the offender as a 'person-in-law'."[36] On the other hand, "enemy criminal law is directed at individuals whose conduct manifests that they do not respect the validity of the legal system and no longer consider themselves bound by the law".[37] As such, enemy criminal law does not regard such individuals "as citizens or persons but rather as a source of danger", and it "is concerned not with communication or censure, but with management of risk".[38]

Enemy is an ill-defined concept. For Jakobs, enemies are those who cannot and do not act loyally to law and, as such, form a threat to security.[39] The idea of enemy criminal law can be supported by the idea of social contract: "when a criminal commits a crime he breaches a contract and, therefore, he cannot participate in its benefits (i.e., from that point on, he no longer has a legal connection with other people)."[40] Following Hobbes, who argues that in extreme cases, such as rebellion or treason denying sovereignty and renouncing subjection, offenders should "suffer not as subjects, but as enemies",[41] one may be tempted to opine that the NSL is

34. Carl Schmitt, *The Concept of the Political* (Chicago: University of Chicago Press, 2007), 25–26.
35. Günther Jakobs, "On the Theory of Enemy Criminal Law", in M. D. Dubber (ed), *Foundational Texts in Modern Criminal Law* (Oxford: Oxford University Press, 2014), 415–424; and Markus D. Dubber, *The Dual Penal State: The Crisis of Criminal Law in Comparative-Historical Perspective* (Oxford: Oxford University Press), 169–174. For elaborations on Jakobs' theory of enemy criminal law, *see* Stuart MacDonald, "Cyber Terrorism and Enemy Criminal Law", in *Cyberwar: Law and Ethics for Virtual Conflicts* (Oxford: Oxford University Press, 2015), and Carlos Gomez-Jara Diez, "Enemy Combatants vs. Enemy Criminal Law" (2008) 11 *New Criminal Law Review* 529.
36. Stuart MacDonald, n 35 above, 60.
37. Stuart MacDonald, n 35 above, 60–61.
38. Stuart MacDonald, n 35 above, 61.
39. Jakobs, n 35 above, 421–422; Dubber, n 35 above, 70.
40. Carlos Gomez-Jara Diez, n 35 above, 539.
41. Thomas Hobbes, *Leviathan*, Richard Tuck (ed), Ch 28 ([1651] 1982) (Cambridge: Cambridge University Press, 1996), 219; *see also* Carlos Gomez-Jara Diez, n 35 above, 540–541.

exactly an "enemy criminal law" targeting the enemy who aims at a regime change, or "threatens us constantly and does not wish to join us in a citizen-estate as a person".[42]

The gravitas of the concepts of political crime and enemy criminal law lies in the "policification" of criminal law in Jakobs' terms, by which he means the shift of a court-centred system to a police-centred system in dealing with national security offences—the police take actions and make decisions, combining the functions of legislator, adjudicator, and the traditional law enforcement officer without meaningful judicial and democratic control.[43] The NSL has shown early signs of the policification. The police now determine what constitutes subversion or secession through making arrests and laying charges, according to its own interpretation of the law, then denying bail leading to lengthy pretrial detention, and eventually making the police process the punishment. Courts in Hong Kong, in holding that the bail clause in the NSL has imposed substantive change to the pre-existing bail-friendly regime in Hong Kong, have effectively imposed a presumption against bail in all cases relating to national security laws, broadly defined. In doing so it endorses the policification of the NSL and makes the legal process the punishment.

b. It Is Preventive

"High policing", as developed by Brodeur, brings the matter to a sharp focus. For Brodeur, high policing concerns the protection of national security, political regime, and state apparatus,[44] whereas low police concerns the protection of individual victims and order maintenance and "refers to routine patrol and investigative work based on professionalism and reasonable and probable grounds".[45] The high policing is principally "absorbent policing" aimed at intelligence gathering (as illustrated by Articles 17, 43, 49 of the NSL)[46] and then using the information to "maximize state coercion of any group or individual perceived as threatening the established order".[47] The goal is decisively preventive of risks,[48] and the method is

42. Carlos Gomez-Jara Diez, n 35 above, 541.
43. *See* Jakobs, n 35 above, 415–424.
44. Jean-Paul Brodeur, *The Policing Web* (New York: Oxford University Press, 2010), 224; Gary T. Marx, "High Policing", *Encyclopedia of Criminology and Criminal Justice* (Springer, forthcoming), available at https://web.mit.edu/gtmarx/www/highpolicing.html, para 34.
45. Alex Luscombe and Kevin Walby, "High Policing and Access to Information" (2015) 16 *Police Practice and Research* 485.
46. Jean-Paul Brodeur, "High Policing and Low Policing: Remarks about the Policing of Political Activities" (1982) 30 *Social Problems* 507, 513–514. *See also* Brodeur, n 44 above, 224.
47. Greg Martin and Rebecca Scott Bray, "Discolouring Democracy? Policing, Sensitive Evidence, and Contentious Deaths in the United Kingdom" (2013) 40 *Journal of Law and Society* 624, 632.
48. Clifford Shearing, "Re-considering the Field of Policing: A Review of the Policing Web" (2011) 53 *Canadian Journal of Criminology and Criminal Justice* 325, 335.

covert involving secrecy and deceit.[49] The result is the effective NSL compliance as the police or the CPG in control of the NSD sees it.

With the prevalence of high policing in many societies, an important question is "whether in protecting the sovereign, police are also protecting the broader (civil) society".[50] And an important problem is that high policing "cannot accept either the spirit or the letter of the law", and it instead often turns into a repressive, intrusive arm of the state.[51] The answer to the above question may partly depend on whether the state is democratic and liberal. "In a democratic setting when police protect the leader, they ideally are also protecting the society's democratic constitution and institutions", whereas "[i]n an authoritarian or totalitarian setting high police act as a private police insuring the power of the rulers, (whether a king or political party) apart from the broader society."[52] We will return to this challenge in Hong Kong in the final section.

Aiming at removing any risks that may threaten regime survival, high policing is not geared to criminal law enforcement: its operations indeed are not bound by the criminal law logic of punishing past wrongs. It aims at pre-empting future risks by suspecting communities and members of those communities. The NSL repeats again and again that "effectively preventing national security offences" is its primary aim, prioritised over stopping and punishing them (Articles 1, 3, 5, 8, 9, 42 of the NSL). As such, the net is necessarily cast wide.

All high policing is preventive. If the goal is to prevent terrorist violence in Northern Ireland, the issue is not only whose finger is on the trigger of an AK-47 but also who speaks seditiously or even passionately in politics;[53] to gather information on the core members of radical Islamic groups, police may have to start with the youths in the Islamic community who posted online hate comments.[54] To fend off a colour revolution, an authoritarian regime is ready to suffocate advocacy NGOs and sever ties between domestic NGOs and their foreign supporters. Often, the target is not individuals, or a group of individuals, but an entire community which is regarded as politically troublesome—Catholics in Northern Ireland before and after the peace agreement,[55] or Islamic communities in the West.[56] In Hong Kong, the target is pan-democrats and even the whole civil society in Hong Kong,

49. Brodeur, n 44 above, 229–231; Brodeur, n 46 above, 514.
50. Gary T. Marx, n 44 above, para 34.
51. Jean-Paul Brodeur, "Trotsky in Blue: Permanent Policing Reform" (2005) 38 *Australian and New Zealand Journal of Criminology* 254, 263.
52. Gary T. Marx, n 44 above, para 34.
53. Kelvin Hearty, "Discourses of Political Policing in Post-patten Northern Ireland" (2018) 26 *Critical Criminology* 1.
54. David Lowe, "The Lack of Discretion in High Policing" (2011) 21 *Policing and Society* 233, 242.
55. Hearty, n 53 above, 1.
56. Henri Decaur, "The Criminalization of Armed Jihad under French Law: Guilt by Association in the Age of Enemy Criminal Law" (2017) 25 *European Journal of Crime, Criminal Law and Criminal Justice* 299.

which is clearly shown by Articles 9 and 10 of the NSL: "The Government of the HKSAR shall take necessary measures to strengthen public communication, guidance, supervision and regulation over matters concerning national security, including those relating to *schools, universities, social organisations, the media, and the internet*"; "The HKSAR shall promote national security education *in schools and universities and through social organisations, the media, the internet and other means*, to raise Hong Kong residents' awareness of national security and of the obligation to abide by the law."

To be effective in the preventive work, proactive and aggressive intervention is the principal modus operandi of high policing, which is more political (protecting regime safety) than legal (law enforcement). They often operate in great secrecy and enjoy exceptional—often extralegal—powers. To the degree that they are made politically and legally accountable, the architecture of their accountability differs significantly from that of the regular police. For example, according to the NSL, the work of the NSC—the bearer of the primary responsibility for safeguarding national security in Hong Kong (Art 12)—shall be interfered with by no institution, organisation, or individual; information relating to its work shall not be subject to disclosure; its decisions shall not be amenable to judicial review (Art 14(2)).

High policing poses two fundamental concerns for the rule of law. The first is with its boundary and the degree to which political monitoring is allowed in the legitimate sphere of political dissent or criticism. Brodeur made the influential argument that, because of its distinctive purpose, high policing would be wilfully blind to the differentiation between lawful dissent and unlawful or violent overthrow of the government.[57] This is the common pattern of high policing in a divided society with intense political contentions. In contemporary Northern Ireland, for instance, the police intentionally conflated legitimate opposition with support for political violence. The police identified groups that participated in political contentions and opposition politics, labelled them variously as dissident and anti-peace, and through a process of marginalisation and stigmatisation, subjected them to political monitoring of the police.[58] In Hong Kong, initial evidence tends to show that the so-called pro-democracy camp has become the main target of the NSD's attention and received discriminating, and selective treatment.[59]

---

57. Brodeur, 1982 and 2010.
58. Hearty, n 53 above. *See also* Kevin Hearty, "How the 'Suspect Community' Became 'Critical Engagers': The (Re)Framing of the Irish Republican Narrative on Policing in Northern Ireland" (2018) 33(1) *Irish Political Studies* 21–42.
59. Natalie Wong, "National Security Law: 47 Hong Kong Opposition Figures Charged with Conspiring to Subvert State Power, after Arrests over Roles in Bloc's Primary", *South China Morning Post*, 28 February 2021, available at https://www.scmp.com/news/hong-kong/politics/article/3123475/national-security-law-47-hong-kong-opposition-figures; Tai Hingshing, "The Effect of the NSL beyond the Imagination, Leading Pan-Democrats May Emigrate" (《港國安法》影響範圍超出想像，泛民政治人物未來或更多移居海外), *United Morning News* (聯合早報), 3 February 2021, available at https://www.zaobao.com/znews/greater-china/story20210203-1121309; Lo Mantuen, "The Implementation of the NSL Is Not

The second concern is the fusion of intelligence gathering through surveillance and criminal investigation for prosecution, leading to the contamination of the latter by the former in particular cases, thereby compromising the integrity of the system at large. The NSD of the Hong Kong police and the NSO of the CPG both have the power of intelligence gathering and criminal investigation (Art 17, and Art 49), which triggers the traditional rule of law concerns. The rule of law necessitates certain differentiation at two different levels to maintain the integrity of the legal system. At the level of individual cases, the institutionalised separation between intelligence and criminal investigation is often imperative to maintain the secrecy of the former and the integrity of the latter, given the political nature of the high policing and its propensity to violate normal criminal law rules. At an institutional level, mutual contamination may occur between enemy criminal law and citizen criminal law on the one hand, and between the investigation of political offences and that of ordinary offences on the other hand. As mentioned earlier, political dissent has a broad spectrum, and it is difficult to draw precisely a clear demarcation between legitimate dissent and the advocacy for subversion or secession.

To avoid an excessive concentration of power, there was often a clear institutional demarcation between high policing focused on intelligence gathering and pre-emption on the one hand, and regular law enforcement on the other. In the aftermath of the so-called "War on Terror", the fusion of these two functions was created in order to enhance anti-terrorism capacity and efficiency by means of information sharing, institutional interpenetration, interconnection, and co-operation. This kind of fusion has caused grave concerns, because it diminishes the rule of law value and the protection of human rights at large, which Hong Kong is likely to encounter in the near future.

c. It Is Controlled by the Central People's Government

The original OCTS design sought to maintain a high degree of autonomy with a relatively clear jurisdictional demarcation of matters within the autonomy of the SAR and those belonging to the CPG. While there were constant contestations and compromises across the frontier in relation to the exact position of the borderline, both sides were confident in their ability to maintain a boundary.

Prior to the enactment of the NSL, policing and criminal law power were clearly the responsibility of the SAR, which had a monopoly over the full spectrum of the criminal justice system, from the initiation of criminal investigation to the administration of penal institutions. There were no exceptions even for crimes endangering state security. Policing and criminal law power belonged exclusively to

---

Soft, and Pan-Democrats Should Not Pin Their Hopes on Chance" (國安法實施不手軟，泛民不可心存僥), *Mingpao*, 11 January 2021, available at https://news.mingpao.com/ins/文摘/article/20210111/s00022/1610267779663.

the SAR according to the original allocation of power under the Basic Law. There was significant institutional separation and autonomy for policing in general and political policing in particular on the SAR side, to the effect that central ministries, either the Ministry of Public Security (MPS) or the Ministry of National Security (MNS), were regarded as peer institutions and equal partners to co-operate with. Under Article 95 of the Basic Law, Hong Kong's police had co-operated with their mainland counterparts as they worked with foreign partners. The principle of equality between judicial organs of Hong Kong and the Mainland under the OCTS explained many of the failures in cross-border mutual legal assistance in criminal law matters.

The NSL has caused a structural modification to this institutional boundary in two significant ways. First, former partners, the MPS and MNS, to co-operate on equal footing have become supervisors of Hong Kong police, *de facto* or *de jure*, on national security matters (Art 48). Horizontal relations have turned vertical. Second, the central agencies have officially crossed the border and stationed permanently in Hong Kong, to exercise hands-on control. Hong Kong protested forcefully against the arrival of a few dozen mainland immigration officers under the co-location scheme in 2018 and fought fiercely against the extradition of serious fugitive offenders back to the Mainland in 2019. In 2020, it had to embrace a gigantic national security office of the CPG in Hong Kong. National security policing is now shared in form between the Central Government and the SAR, to be carried out in fact under the watchful eyes and direct guidance and supervision of the CPG. The organs of national security in Hong Kong enjoy far less autonomy or discretion than regular police officers normally exercise, mainly forming cogs in the rigid, well-structured political hierarchy controlled by the Central Government. The question is no longer whether Hong Kong still has exclusive control over the field but whether it has surrendered the entire field effectively to the CPG. The NSC is a powerhouse constituting the decision-making body of the highest order in Hong Kong. As part of the government of the HKSAR, the NSC assumes the primary responsibility for national security in Hong Kong (Art 12). The NSC is chaired by the Chief Executive, and other members include key officials in the Hong Kong government. Under Article 17 of the NSL, the NSC has the power to assign tasks to the NSD of the police for implementation, creating a statutory design to turn the NSD into an executive arm. To enable the executive's control over the high policing, the NSL (especially Art 14(2)) effectively shields national security apparatuses from meaningful legislative, judicial, and social control in Hong Kong.[60]

The NSC is also under the supervision of the CPG due to two arrangements in the NSL, which ensure the CPG's effective and direct central control over the national security matters. First, the NSC has a secretariat and its secretary-general is to be directly appointed by the CPG upon nomination by the CE (Art 13(2)).

60. *See* Chan in this volume.

Second, under Article 15, a National Security Adviser is appointed by the CPG to give advice to the NSC and, significantly, to attend meetings of the NSC. This key provision creates a legal mechanism whereby the CPG, for the first time since the handover, has direct access to the internal policy-making process of the HKSAR government. The first National Security Adviser is the director of the CPG's Liaison Office in Hong Kong, in theory the highest-ranking CCP official in Hong Kong.

Furthermore, the powerful NSC is also highly susceptible to central control. Article 12 provides that it "is supervised and can be held to account by the CPG". Article 53 expressly authorises the NSO to "oversee and provide guidance to" national security matters in Hong Kong. As a result, the institutional autonomy and the high degree of professionalism and political neutrality that had characterised Hong Kong police since the 1970s[61] has become vulnerable under the new regime of political policing.

The new special branch, that is, the NSD, is a specialised, highly independent unit within the police: its head is appointed by the Chief Executive and its budget is allocated by the Financial Secretary without legislative approval (Art 16(2), and Art 19). Indeed, the unit is so special that, despite nominally being a unit within the police force, the police do not seem to have any substantive control over it. In contrast, direct central control or influence is readily apparent as it is enshrined in the NSL: the CE is required to consult the NSO before appointing the Head, and the NSD is duty-bound to follow instructions of the NSC and carry out tasks assigned by it (Art 17). Given the special role of the NSO in Hong Kong, it is well positioned to influence the NSD directly or through the NSC (Art 49(2)). There is a real possibility of hands-on control of the NSD by the CPG just as Britain's control over the Special Branch during the colonial era. Besides, Article 16(3) creates a possibility that the NSD of the Hong Kong police could be staffed by "professionals and technicians" from "outside of Hong Kong", opening a door to mainland officers to occupy important posts in it.

In summary, as the implementation of the NSL continues, it is possible to envisage a scenario whereby the NSD becomes a powerful force in Hong Kong for handling national security-related matters, whereas the Hong Kong police and the SAR government exercise little if any control over the NSD's key personnel and operational decisions. In such a scenario, it is the CPG, towered high above, through the numerous institutional designs, that assumes substantive control over the investigation of all national security-related offences, intelligence gathering, and surveillance. The institutional design of the NSL on high policing is such that it has torn down the legal and institutional barriers there had been between Hong Kong and the rest of China, creating an open national security corridor between the two

61. Peter Wang, Paul Joosse, and Lok Lee Cho, "The Evolution of Protest Policing in a Hybrid Regime" (2020) *British Journal of Criminology* 1–24; Carol Jones (with Jon Vagg), *Criminal Justice in Hong Kong* (London: Routledge-Cavendish, 2007), Ch 20.

systems, through which the CPG has decisive control over the national security operations in Hong Kong.

To doubly ensure that China's national interest and security be safeguarded in Hong Kong, a nuclear option providing for the operation of a national jurisdiction is outlined in Article 55. Once triggered, the national procedures and laws kick in, and a case will be taken out of Hong Kong's jurisdiction and be placed within the mainland's jurisdiction. Thus, the Two Systems end and One Country takes over: such cases will be prosecuted in the PRC courts on the Mainland under Chinese procedural and substantive laws. Article 55 creates a central jurisdiction over certain national security offences and brings the mainland national security regime to Hong Kong in specified cases, creating a striking exception to Hong Kong's normal national security regime as the CPG sees fit. The irony is that there was a clear political offence exception in the aborted Extradition Bill to limit the extradition arrangement to ordinary offences, but this bill had triggered the violent protests in 2019 and the enacting of the NSL in 2020. Article 55 reverses the aborted bill by creating an entirely free corridor for some political offences to be transferred to the mainland's jurisdiction while leaving ordinary crimes intact.

III. Riding the Tiger of the NSL

This section tries to answer whether the NSL, with the new institutional design, will bring Hong Kong's high policing into a converging course with the high policing in China. Before that question can be answered, one has to first identify the key features of China's high policing and the political and social context in which it operates, and then to assess the degree to which high policing in Hong Kong can be absorbed nearer or into the national system.

How should Chinese high policing be characterised? China has developed two concepts of high policing and corresponding institutional designs: a narrow one that focuses on pre-emption, including surveillance and preventive interventions, backed by coercive powers, legal or otherwise; and a broad one that embeds national security deep in the political structure and social milieu. China's high policing needs to be understood in its political context and social milieu. To a large degree, the effectiveness of the authoritarian high policing in its narrow sense depends on the political support it receives and the participation in it of the masses, willingly or not.

The national security agents in China are able to monitor the academic, media, and religious institutions not only because of their broadly framed legal powers, but also because of their ability to embed themselves pervasively in those institutions and their ability to act through them in achieving their goals. China has been able to build a truly national security state. There is a well-built national security infrastructure on which high policing operates, and which often appears to be bottom-up and inside-out. Open political surveillance, monitoring of activists, or prosecution of dissidents cannot, on their own, produce national security. More importantly, the political order is maintained through typical authoritarian designs such as censorship of the press, restrictions on NGOs, development of informants, other measures of early, proactive interventions, and above all, pervasive self-censorship.

Can there still be "two systems" for national security in Hong Kong? In making the NSL, the CPG has reiterated that, when it comes to national security, the two systems concept ceases to apply, and one country and one national security regime prevails. To assess the validity and feasibility of that claim, we need to return to the question of whether the NSD retains some autonomy under the national guidance in ways that are special to the constitutional design of the SAR. This inquiry necessarily raises a *constitutional* question about the national security systems in China and Hong Kong.

The NSL and the enabling NPC decision that authorised the NPCSC to enact the NSL have certainly brought Hong Kong nearer the national constitutional order. Whatever confidence one may have had to expect that the Basic Law could provide a shield to maintain the self-contained nature of the Basic Law in the past has been confronted with a different reality now. Since the NPCSC's Decision on a joint checkpoint for the high-speed rail link from Hong Kong to Guangzhou,[62] it has become established that the NPC or its Standing Committee is constitutionally capable of legislating on Hong Kong matters as long as the legislation does not contravene the Basic Law, confirming the political doctrine that the Constitution and the Basic Law jointly form the constitutional foundation for Hong Kong's governance. Article 31 of the Constitution that has created the SAR did not create a self-contained system independent of the constitution after all.

The enactment of the NSL involves a significant constitutional ground shifting. If Article 23 was a delegation of power from the NPC to Hong Kong to legislate on national security law, the NPC, through enacting the NSL, has effectively revoked the delegation within the scope that the NSL covers.[63] What remains in Article 23 of the Basic Law, after being stripped of the key offices of secession and subversion in particular, has become a less significant concern. In this way, the gravitas of national security in Hong Kong has shifted from Hong Kong to Beijing and from the Basic Law to the NSL. As the CPG reiterates, national security is a matter outside the HKSAR's autonomy and within the purview of the CPG, which "has an overarching responsibility for national security affairs relating to the HKSAR" (Art 3(1)). The NSL shall prevail where provisions of Hong Kong's local laws are inconsistent with it (Art 62). Established by and with powers to be interpreted by the NPCSC (Art 65), the NSL is a creature of Chinese legal system: it will be anchored to the Constitution

62. "The NPCSC Has Approved 'the Co-operation Agreement between the Mainland and the HKSAR on the Establishment of the Port at the West Kowloon Station of the Guangzhou-Shenzhen-Hong Kong Express Rail Link for Implementing Co-location Arrangement" (全國人大常委會批准《內地與香港特別行政區關於在廣深港高鐵西九龍站設立口岸實施"一地兩檢"的合作安排》), *Xinhua*, 27 December 2017, available at http://www.xinhuanet.com/politics/2017-12/27/c_1122175282.htm.
63. Fu Hualing, "National Security Law", in Chan and Lim (eds).

in China and given meaning according to the Chinese interpretation. Courts would need to treat the NSL as a Chinese law and defer to Chinese legal doctrines and principles, as the government has submitted to the court in *Tong Ying Kit* and *Lai Chee Ying*.[64] The court in Hong Kong has grown more deferent to the NSL. For example, in *HKSAR v Lai Chee Ying*, the CFA states, "the legislative acts of the NPC and NPCSC leading to the promulgation of the NSL as a law of the HKSAR, done in accordance with the provisions of the Basic Law and the procedure therein, are not subject to review on the basis of any alleged incompatibility as between the NSL and the Basic Law or the ICCPR [International Covenant on Civil and Political Rights] as applied to Hong Kong."[65]

There are also signs that the NSL is expanding and developing a life of its own. The Chinese concept of national security is an expansive and inclusive one, touching on the totality of the political, economic, and social spheres.[66] A persistent problem of enemy criminal law, as discussed above, is the risk of contamination: "the existence of radical measures that govern a discrete area of criminal law ends up contaminating many other areas of criminal law."[67] This is because we may not be able or willing to draw a clear distinction between enemy criminal law and citizen criminal law in the real world, given the vagueness of the definition and the preventive nature of high policing.[68] The NSD proves to be the pioneer in the boundary-spanning and boundary-pushing endeavours. Article 17(3) of the NSL provides that the NSD has the power of "investigating offences endangering national security". The investigative jurisdiction of the NSD is not limited to the offences contained in the NSL and has become open-ended and expanded to other offences that may, in substance, endanger national security broadly defined. One controversy in the past related to the legality of the NSD's investigation of seditious libel, an offence provided not in the NSL but in the Crimes Ordinance, which was enacted during the colonial era to clamp down anti-government expressions.

On 6 September 2020, Hong Kong opposition activist Tam Tak-chi, vice president of People Power, was arrested for "uttering seditious words", a crime under section 10 of the Crimes Ordinance (Cap 200).[69] Prosecutors alleged that Tam used anti-police slogans and phrases like "liberate Hong Kong" and "five demands, not

64. *Tong Ying Kit v HKSAR*, HCAL 1601/2020 [2020] HKCFI 2133, paras 26, 49; *HKSAR v Lai Chee Ying*, FACC1/2021 Appellant's Case: 4 (a), (b), and (c); *HKSAR v Lai Chee Ying*, FACC1/2021 [2021] HKCFA 3, para 32.
65. *HKSAR v Lai Chee Ying*, FACC1/2021 [2021] HKCFA 3, para 37.
66. See *Xi Jinping on China's Holistic Approach to National Security* (《習近平關於總體國家安全觀論述摘編》) (Beijing: Zhongyang Wenxian Chubanshe, 2018).
67. Manuel Cancio Melia, "Terrorism and Criminal Law: The Dream of Prevention, the Nightmare of the Rule of Law" (2011) 14 *New Criminal Law Review* 108, 121.
68. Manuel Cancio Melia, n 68 above, 121.
69. AFP, "Hong Kong Activist Tam Tak-chi Arrested for 'Uttering Seditious Words'", *Hong Kong Free Press*, 6 September 2020, available at https://hongkongfp.com/2020/09/06/hong-kong-activist-tam-tak-chi-arrested-for-uttering-seditious-words/.

one less" in January, and between March and July on several occasions.[70] Tam was arrested by the NSD, although he was not arrested under the NSL.[71] As to why the NSD was leading the arrest, senior superintendent Li Kwai-wah explained that Tam was suspected of committing "incitement to secession" under Article 21 of the NSL at the initial stage of investigation, "[b]ut after collecting evidence and consulting the Department of Justice, we [Li Kwai-wah speaking on behalf of the police and the department of justice] decided that it is more suitable to use the Crimes Ordinance."[72] This is because "[t]he slogans Tam is accused of using are illegal under the NSL", but "authorities have said the law shall not be retrospectively applied to acts committed before 30 June this year".[73]

As the case clearly shows, Article 17(3) of the NSL will be a hole through which the NSD's investigative powers can seep into other areas, including education, journalism, NGOs, religion, legal professions, and others which may be regarded as the potential soft spots of the NSL. It would not be surprising to find one day the influence of the NSD in the cases of the registration of teachers and punishment of journalists. This seepage would be constitutionally confusing and problematic if the powerful NSD used the special powers granted by the NSL to investigate cases where the police are not explicitly given these powers. One can imagine a dangerous scenario where the NSD crosses the boundary between the normal and exceptional zones without being properly monitored and held to account. The CFA in recent decisions has recognised and endorsed that expansive version of the high policing power in bail decisions under the NSL.[74] According to the latest plan to reform Hong Kong's electoral system, the NSD and the NSC will give advice to the vetting committee, which will be set up to screen out candidates deemed "unpatriotic".[75]

An alternative reading, however, is still possible. By being added to Annex III of the Basic Law and promulgated by the CE of the HKSAR, the NSL is in fact localised in that is has to be enforced in the SAR legal context. From the perspective of Hong Kong courts, the NSL embedded in Hong Kong's legal system could be isolated from the mainland interpretative context and treated as part of Hong Kong law in the same way as the Basic Law has been.[76] That is allegedly the legislative intention of the NSL, that is, to create a short-term impact without endangering the core of

70. Helen Davidson, "Hong Kong Activist Denied Bail after Being Charged with Sedition", *The Guardian*, 17 September 2020, available at https://www.theguardian.com/world/2020/sep/17/hong-kong-activist-denied-bail-after-being-charge-with-sedition-tam-tak-chi.
71. AFP, n 70 above.
72. AFP, n 70 above.
73. Helen Davidson, n 71 above.
74. Johannes Chan, "Judicial Responses to the National Security Law: *HKSAR v Lai Chee Ying*" (2021) 51(1) *Hong Kong Law Journal* 1.
75. Lilian Cheng, "Past Actions, Words by Candidates Will Be Considered by Vetting Committee Set up under Hong Kong's Electoral Overhaul: City's Justice Chief", 3 April 2021, available at https://www.scmp.com/news/hong-kong/politics/article/3128210/past-actions-words-candidates-will-be-considered-vetting.
76. Fu, n 64 above.

Hong Kong's liberal legal design and its cultural make-up that treasures rights and freedom. In spite of the overwhelming changes it brings to Hong Kong, the NSL as a whole and Article 4 enshrining human rights protection and Article 5 enshrining the internationally practised principles of the rule of law in particular[77] set Hong Kong's national security regime decisively apart from that in the Mainland.

Article 4 of the NSL mentions specifically that rights and freedoms shall be protected, especially those enshrined in the ICCPR, which does not apply in the Mainland. In his *Explanation of the Draft Decision of NPC on Establishing and Improving the Legal System and Enforcement Mechanisms for Safeguarding National Security in the HKSAR*, Wang Chen stressed, the NSL "aims to better protect the lives, property, fundamental rights and freedoms of the vast majority of Hong Kong residents . . . Any work and law enforcement to safeguard national security shall not infringe upon the legitimate rights and interests of any Hong Kong resident".[78] All this shows that the NSL clearly intends to subject the operation of high policing to the control of the ICCPR jurisprudence, signifying the uniqueness of Hong Kong in the national security context: the NSD and other national security apparatuses have to be held accountable to the human rights and rule of law standards promised by the NSL.

Besides, and more significantly, high policing here operates in a different legal system, political context, and social milieu. According to the NPCSC, a working principle of drafting the NSL is "accommodating the differences between the mainland and the HKSAR, and striving to address the convergence, compatibility and complementarity between this law, and . . . local laws of the HKSAR";[79] the NPCSC emphasised that the NSL "has full regard to the differences between the two systems as well as the actual circumstances in Hong Kong. It . . . is compatible with Hong Kong's existing legal system".[80] Consequently, when applying the NSL, one of the principles ought to be giving it a meaning which is compatible and coherent with Hong Kong's local laws.[81] In addition, Hong Kong's local laws "apply to procedural

77. "Li Zhanshu Delivered a Speech at the Twentieth Session of the 13th National People's Congress Standing Committee" (栗戰書在第十三屆全國人大常委會第二十次會議上的講話), 30 June 2020, available at http://www.nxrd.gov.cn/zlzx/ldjh/202007/t20200708_189977.html.

78. "Wang Chen: Explanation on the Draft Decision of the National People's Congress on Establishing and Improving the Legal System and Enforcement Mechanisms for the Hong Kong Special Administrative Region to Safeguard National Security" (王晨作關於《全國人民代表大會關於建立健全香港特別行政區維護國家安全的法律制度和執行機制的決定（草案）》的說明), The National People's Congress of the PRC, 22 May 2020, available at http://www.npc.gov.cn/npc/c30834/202005/e235c7a3e-bea43ca98aa80032590e924.shtml.

79. "Explanation on the Law of the People's Republic of China on Safeguarding National Security in the Hong Kong Special Administrative Region" (關於《中華人民共和國香港特別行政區維護國家安全法（草案）》的說明), The National People's Congress of the PRC, 21 June 2020, available at http://npc.people.com.cn/n1/2020/0621/c14576-31754045.html.

80. "Li Zhanshu Delivered a Speech at the Twentieth Session of the 13th National People's Congress Standing Committee" (栗戰書在第十三屆全國人大常委會第二十次會議上的講話), 30 June 2020, available at http://www.nxrd.gov.cn/zlzx/ldjh/202007/t20200708_189977.html.

81. This position in fact is adopted by the CFA, *HKSAR v Lai Chee Ying*, FACC1/2021 [2021] HKCFA 3,

matters" in respect of offences of endangering national security (Art 41(1), and Art 42(1)). Lazar, among other scholars on constitutional crises, has argued forcefully that legislative and executive measures that have been enacted in liberal societies to manage emergencies are often subjected to rigorous and effective scrutiny of pre-established liberal institutions, and that executive powers are often made accountable thanks to the pre-existing constitutional design.[82] The NSD, therefore, despite its extensive power and discounted accountability, has to operate in an overall liberal-minded legal system and society that take rights and freedoms seriously. Academic freedom is vulnerable but remains robust; courts are under a stress test but remain confident in maintaining their independence; and after the first shock waves, media, religions, and civil society in general have survived, while looking warily forward to an uncertain future. The NSL may appear to present a Schmittan moment in which decisionalism may have prevailed and the prerogative state can trump the rule of law at a single stroke of the pen. But in reality, the pre-existing liberal order in Hong Kong can still impose a degree of discipline over the sovereign power. Besides, the success of the Chinese practice of national security relies on a powerful and pervasive support infrastructure of censorship and compliance. Absent this infrastructure, the effectiveness of the national security apparatuses would be substantially discounted. In any event, the history of the OCTS in the age of NSL remains to be written.

Conclusion

Beijing's displeasure over Hong Kong's lack of attention to its national security concerns and the CPG's deep distrust towards Hong Kong across the entire political spectrum led to the NPCSC's making of the NSL and the CPG's tight control over national security affairs in Hong Kong through direct or subtle enforcement mechanisms. The NSL is indubitably here to stay, the Special Branch has returned, and the Chinese high policing has a foothold in Hong Kong. It is now part of the OCTS design. What then is the future prospect?

The NSL has carved out a national security space from the Basic Law regime, and, in Jakobs's terms, introduced the concept of enemy criminal law into Hong Kong. It assigns national security offences for exceptional and special treatment, thereby distinguishing this area from the pre-existing normal system of citizen criminal justice. That exceptional regime is endowed with a special identity: it is subject to a distinctive system of laws and constituted by a new set of institutions with extraordinary political functions and powers. It follows a different logic. Putting it together, the NSL has created an apparently seamless, cohesive, and

---

paras 42, 43, 44.

82. Nomi Claire Lazar, *States of Emergency in Liberal Democracies* (Cambridge: Cambridge University Press, 2013); "Decision and Decisionalism", in Nicolas Guilhot and Daniel Bessner (eds), *The Decisionist Imagination* (New York: Berghahn, 2018), 109–134.

powerful regime of political policing in Hong Kong that is beyond the traditional legislative and judicial control.

This is a dynamic system put in place to manage a volatile domestic and international circumstance. Once established, the system grows, reaches out, and develops a life of its own. It is clear that the jurisdiction of the high policing is not limited to the NSL offences and would reach out to other national security-related offences. Given its broad functions in education, policy making, and surveillance, it has the potential to penetrate every fabric of the Hong Kong society to create a total national security community. It has created a national security corridor between Hong Kong and the CPG, removing any barriers to cross-border co-operation that were in place under the original Basic Law design.

Nevertheless, the NSL does not intend to fully integrate Hong Kong into the Chinese national security regime, and a complete convergence does not seem to be on the CPG's political agenda. There may be one, and only one, national security interest throughout China. However, national security has unique meanings and takes different shades in the OCTS context. As the NSL itself has made clear, the national security policing in Hong Kong is subject to the control of the ICCPR jurisprudence and internationally practised principles of the rule of law. Hong Kong's pre-existing institutions, such as an independent judiciary and legal profession, media and academic freedom, its vibrant religious sector and civil society, and its cosmopolitanism and the overall liberal mindset will also prevent any easy transplanting to Hong Kong of the Chinese regime of national security. Chinese high policing is determined and effective in removing any immediate real or perceived national security risks, but may have to moderate itself when it comes face to face with Hong Kong's liberal propensities.

10

State Secrets in the Hong Kong National Security Law

Zheng Tang and Xu Huang

Introduction

States have an interest in preventing unauthorised disclosure of state secrets or intelligence which may jeopardise state security and other essential concerns. Nearly all countries have enacted specific domestic legislation regulating obtaining, retaining, and disclosure of state secrets.[1] The impact of these laws on the freedom of information and governmental accountability must be assessed.[2] The conflicting interests of national security and freedom of information mean that national security legislation has to strike an appropriate balance to provide adequate protection of national security and to prevent the potential abuse of governmental power designed to deal with the handling of state secrets. International principles and standards, such as those contained in the Johannesburg Principles on National Security, Freedom of Expression and Access to Information 1997 and the Global Principles of National Security and the Rights to information 2013, have been adopted. They typically treat the freedom of information as the primary principle, with the need to regulate state secrets as an exception. They also provide detailed guidance on how such legislation should be designed.[3]

Would those principles have any bearing on Hong Kong's (HK) National Security Law (NSL)? Article 29 of the NSL provides:

1. Specific domestic statutes on state secrets can be found in Canada, India, New Zealand, Singapore, and the UK, among others.
2. Hitoshi Nasu, "State Secrets Law and National Security" (2015) 64 *International & Comparative Law Quarterly* 365, 366.
3. J. Chan, "National Security and the Unauthorized and Damaging Disclosure of Protected Information", in Hualing Fu, C. J. Petersen, and S. N. M. Young (eds), *National Security and Fundamental Freedoms: Hong Kong's Article 23 under Scrutiny* (Hong Kong: Hong Kong University Press, 2005), p 251.

> [a] person who steals, spies, obtains with payment, or unlawfully provides State secrets or intelligence concerning national security for a foreign country or an institution, organisation or individual outside the mainland, Hong Kong and Macao of the People's Republic of China shall be guilty of an offence.

This provision in the NSL generates uncertainty and controversy which stem from three potential problems: the ambiguity of the concepts used, the low threshold of criminal liability, and the lack of procedural due process. This risks an unnecessarily negative impact on press freedom, government transparency, and business security.

I. State Secrets Legislation in Hong Kong and the NSL

The United Kingdom (UK), reputedly "one of the most secretive democracies in the world today",[4] enacted the Official Secrets Act in 1889. This Act was repealed by the Act 1911, which was amended in 1920, 1939, 1972 and 1989.[5] They were used as models for Hong Kong and other Commonwealth countries. The UK Official Secrets Act 1989 was implemented in Hong Kong by the Official Secrets Act (Hong Kong) Order 1992. After handover in 1997, the Official Secrets Act was repealed and replaced by the Official Secrets Ordinance (Cap 521) (OSO).[6]

The OSO, following its British example, has a relatively narrow application. It applies to espionage,[7] unlawful disclosure of classified information by members of the security and intelligence services,[8] and unlawful disclosure of such information by a public servant or a government contract.[9] It applies to the general public only when an individual possesses protected information through an unlawful disclosure and knowingly or negligently makes harmful disclosure.[10] The protected information is also narrowly defined to include information in relation to security or intelligence, defence, international relations, and offences and criminal investigation.[11]

The narrow scope of the OSO is inadequate to protect state secrets in compliance with the requirements of Article 23 of the Basic Law. The OSO does not criminalise activities such as illegally obtaining protected information, including stealing, spying, or illegally obtaining with payment, but Article 23 of the Basic

4. Debra L. Silverman, "Freedom of Information: Will Blair Be Able to Break the Walls of Secrecy in Britain?" (1997) 13 *American University International Law Review* 471, 471.
5. For the history of the UK Official Secrets Act, see Gail Bartlett and Michael Everett, 'The Official Secrets Acts and Official Secrecy', House of Commons, Briefing Paper, No. CBP07422, 2 May 2017, 6–20.
6. L.N. 369 of 1997, commenced on 27 June 1997 (an ordinance to control the unauthorised obtaining or disclosure of official information).
7. OSO, ss 3–6.
8. *Ibid.*, s 13.
9. *Ibid.*, ss 14–17.
10. *Ibid.*, s 18.
11. *Ibid.*, ss 14–17.

Law expressly requires the Hong Kong Special Administrative Region (HKSAR) to enact laws to prohibit "theft of state secrets". Furthermore, it is not proper to classify secrets of China as information relating to "international relations".[12]

The National Security (Legislative Provisions) Bill 2003 aimed to amend the OSO by addressing some existing problems. This Bill would have extended the protection to information on the relations between the HKSAR and China Central Authority, and information acquired by illegal means by a member of the public.[13] However, the changes were criticised for being uncertain and ambiguous,[14] having the potential to be abused, and for unduly hampering freedom of information.[15] Due to the strong protest against the Bill in general, it was later abandoned.

Article 29 of the NSL is a provision substantively different from the OSO in definition, scope, objectives, purposes, elements, criteria, and penalties. Article 62 provides that the NSL has precedence if it conflicts with Hong Kong local law. Article 29 of the NSL tackles only unlawful acquisition and disclosure of state secrets for foreign entities. "Foreign entities" is defined in Article 29 to include "a foreign country or institution, organisation or individual outside China". "Outside China" (境外) is not defined, and it is unclear whether it refers to geographical location or personal status, such as nationality or residence. Since both the Mainland and HK adopt the concept of incorporation, it is likely that companies outside China refers to companies incorporated according to foreign law, even if they operate in China or have a branch or representative in China. As the NSL does not repeal the OSO, the coexistence of two sets of laws adds complexity and uncertainty in practice.

The first question is one of interpretation. Article 29 of the NSL is ambiguously drafted. A number of concepts require interpretation, such as "state secrets", "intelligence", "national security", "stealth", "spying", and "unlawful disclosure". It is also unclear whether there are other implicit requirements necessary to constitute this crime, such as *mens rea*. Should these concepts be interpreted as Hong Kong law should, perhaps taking on board the OSO, or pursuant to the standards applied in the Mainland? Pursuant to Article 65, the power to interpret the NSL is vested in the Standing Committee of the National People's Congress (NPCSC). It is likely that the NPCSC will interpret these terms consistently with similar concepts in mainland law—both are enacted by the NPCSC for the same purpose, namely, to protect national security and essential national interests of China. The purpose of enacting the NSL is to fill the "loophole" of the existing HK law, and it is obvious that the

12. Section 16. "International relations" include relations between HK and the UK and other external relations (sec 2). After reunification, the UK will be replaced by China, but the relationship is still framed as "international" under the OSO.
13. Sections 16 A and 18.
14. J. Chan, n 3, 275.
15. J. Chan, "Unauthorized and Damaging Disclosure of Protected Information", Submission No. 155, available at https://www.legco.gov.hk/yr02-03/english/bc/bc55/papers/bc55-s155-e.pdf (accessed 28 January 2021).

NPCSC deems the OSO inadequate. Nonetheless, when the NPCSC interprets the NSL, it is likely also to take account of international principles and existing Hong Kong law, albeit in a non-binding or persuasive manner.

However, it is unclear whether the HK courts have the power to interpret the NSL. The NSL does not include any provision similar to Article 158 of the Basic Law that authorises HK courts to interpret relevant provisions of the law in adjudicating cases in HK and provides procedural rules for referring questions to the NPCSC. However, it should not be concluded that HK courts have no power to interpret the NSL. The NSL does not explicitly exclude HK courts from interpreting the NSL. Neither the NPCSC nor the Hong Kong courts have raised any objection to the Hong Kong courts interpreting the NSL. The NPCSC has not yet issued any legislative interpretation, and even if some are issued in the future, they cannot possibly cover all matters that may arise in individual cases. It is impractical and unrealistic to deprive HK courts of the power of interpretation. It is likely that the HK courts will exercise the power of interpretation when adjudicating cases under the NSL, subject to the supervision of the NPCSC. It is possible that the NSL is listed in Annex III of the Basic Law and the Article 158 procedure should apply. This matter requires clarification.

II. State Secrets or Intelligence: Risk of Over-classification

(a) Ambiguous Definition

Three approaches are adopted to classify state secrets in international legislative practice: source-based, class-based, and prejudice-based.[16] The source-based approach relies on the designated authorities to classify the information. The class-based approach lists different categories of protected information in legislation. The prejudice-based approach is based on the prejudicial effects of unauthorised disclosure.[17] The OSO adopts a combination of the class-based and prejudice-based approach, listing four categories of official secrets that relate to the work of the security or intelligence services and requiring a showing of harmful effects on unauthorised disclosure for most individuals.[18] It is important to note that the OSO does not adopt a source-based approach, the approach which is adopted in China. Chinese law does not use any prejudice-based criterion. Instead, it uses a combination of source-based and class-based criteria with the result that Chinese law has a rather

16. Nasu, n 2 above, p 377. Cf C. Pourgourides, "Fair Trial Issues in Criminal Cases concerning Espionage or Divulging State Secrets", Report to the Committee on Legal Affairs and Human Rights, Parliamentary Assembly of the Council of Europe Doc 11031 (2006), paras 56–68, available at https://assembly.coe.int/Documents/WorkingDocs/2006/EDOC11031.pdf.
17. Nasu, n 2 above, p 378.
18. Members of the security or intelligent services are liable without proof of harmful consequences (sec 13).

low definitional threshold for state secrets. Hong Kong's OSO, which in most cases requires proof of prejudice, is a much narrower definition.[19]

The NSL does not provide a definition of "[s]tate secrets or intelligence concerning national security". Given the different origins of the NSL and the OSO, this concept in the NSL is likely to be strongly influenced by its definition in the mainland legal system. China's legal regime for the protection of state secrets consists mainly of the provisions of the State Secrets Law (SSL)[20] and the 2014 Implementation Rules.[21] Two other statutes, the People's Republic of China (PRC) Criminal Law[22] and the PRC National Security Law[23] also contain provisions which deal with offences relating to state secrets. Unfortunately, none provide a clear definition of state secrets. The Interim Provisions on the Administration of Classification of State Secrets[24] repeats the content of the 2014 Implementation Rules on classification and declassification and provides no clue to the definition of state secrets. The Supreme People's Court (SPC) held in its judicial interpretation that the term "state secrets" in Article 111 of the Criminal Law refers to the concept used in the SSL and 2014 Implementation Rules.[25] Therefore, administrative rules and judicial interpretation do not provide any further clarification.

The SSL defines state secrets as "matters which relate to the national security and interests as determined under statutory procedures and access to which is vested in a limited scope of persons during a given period of time".[26] This definition can barely help as it is ambiguous and tautological. Article 9 of SSL stipulates the basic scope of state secrets by way of enumeration.[27] It lists seven categories covering politics, economy, national defence and military affairs, foreign affairs, science and technology, social development, and criminal offences. However, this enumeration cannot provide much help. Firstly, the scope of some listed matters is too broad. For example, national security explicitly includes classified matters involved in the

19. OSO, s 12(7).
20. "*Zhonghua Renmin Gongheguo Baoshou Guojia Mimi Fa Shishi Tiaoli*" [Implementing Regulations for the People's Republic of China Law on Protection of State Secrets], State Council of the People's Republic of China Decree, 2014, No 646, available at http://www.gov.cn/zwgk/2014-02/03/content_2579949.htm.
21. "Implementing Regulations for the People's Republic of China Law on Protection of State Secrets", State Council of the People's Republic of China Decree, 2014, No 646.
22. PRC Criminal Law, Art 111.
23. PRC National Security Law, Art 4(3).
24. "Guojia Mimi Ding mi Guanli Zhanxing Guiding" [Interim Provisions on the Administration of Classification of State Secrets], Order of the National Administration for the Protection of State Secrets, 2014, No 1.
25. Article 1, "Zuigao Renmin Fayuan Guanyu Shenli Wei Jingwai Qiequ, Citan, Shoumai, Feifa Tigong Guojia Mimi, Qingbao Anjian Juti Yingyong Falv Ruogan Wenti de Jieshi" [Interpretations of the Supreme People's Court on several issues concerning application of law to the hearing of cases of stealing, spying, obtaining with payment or unlawfully providing state secrets or intelligence for overseas parties], Fa Shi [2001] No 4.
26. SSL, Art 2.
27. *Ibid.*, Art 9.

"national economic and social development"[28] or "science and technology".[29] These fields are not covered in the traditional national security in relation to state sovereignty, territorial integrity, and social stability. They are extensive in scope and include a wide range of potentially confidential issues. This large scope leaves classification authorities a broad discretion to classify such items as anything from state secrets or trade secrets to examination questions.[30] It is also noted that the source of information alone may render information a state secret, regardless of the quality or nature of the information.[31] There is a risk that scientific research funded by the state government, technology in relation to environmental protection, and commercial secrets of a state-owned company may all have the potential to be treated as state secrets.

More importantly, Article 9(7) is a "catch-all" provision that stipulates as a state secret "other classified matters as determined by the state secrecy administrative department". This provision potentially leads to an unrestricted designation of state secrets in any circumstances an authority may feel fit, and this may lead to abuse of power.[32]

In addition, Article 29 of the NSL also uses the term "intelligence", which is a concept adopted in Article 111 of the PRC Criminal Law.[33] The SPC held in its judicial interpretation that the intelligence as prescribed in Article 111 refers to the matters that concern national security and interests which have not been publicised, or shall not be publicised, in accordance with the relevant provisions.[34] The legislative documents suggest that, firstly, intelligence is a matter other than state secrets. Secondly, intelligence should have the same essential characteristics of national security and national interests as state secrets. Thirdly, the determination of "intelligence" is results-oriented. Its nature of influencing national security and interests is

28. *Ibid.*, Art 9(4).
29. *Ibid.*, Art 9(5).
30. *Gao Xinmao v Beijing Yidege Ink Ltd. and Beijing Chuanren Culture Ltd.* [2011] Minjianzi No 414 (申請再審人高辛茂與被申請人北京一得閣墨業有限責任公司、原審被告北京傳人文化藝術有限公司侵犯商業秘密糾紛案[2011] 民監字第414號) (classify trade secrets as state secrets); *China v Li Baoan and Others*, Hubei Province Xiaogan IPC, available at www.pkulaw.cn, CLI.C.240421 (李寶安、普旺木、李興安故意泄露國家秘密案，湖北省孝感市中級人民法院，2002.9.6, 北大法寶引證碼CLI.C.240421)；*China v Song Fulai and Others*, Beijing Dongcheng DPC [2008] Dongxingchuzi No 390 (宋福來等故意泄漏國家秘密案，北京市東城區人民法院 [2008] 東刑初字第390號) (classify exam questions as state secrets).
31. Richard Wigley, "China's State Secrets Law and Compliance Issues for Foreign Companies", *China Law Insight*, 25 September 2014, available at https://www.chinalawinsight.com/2014/09/articles/intellectual-property/chinas-state-secrets-law-and-compliance-issues-for-foreign-companies/.
32. The 2014 Implementation Rules do little to help discern the meaning of state secrets. Art 8, which aims to define the specific scope of classified information, should have provided the relevant basis for the specific scope of state secrets. However, Art 8 simply repeats the SSL provision, which does not provide substantive assistance in defining the scope of classified information.
33. Art 111 of PRC Criminal Law covers "steals, spies into, buys or unlawfully supplies state secrets or intelligence for an organ, organization or individual outside China".
34. n 24 above, Article 1.

not determined by legal procedures but by whether foreign institutions or individuals use it to harm China's national security and interests. Nevertheless, it does not require actual harm caused as a consequence of disclosure. There are many matters in some institutions which are known to a relatively large number of people because the information does not fall within the scope of state secrets.[35] These matters, such as economic data, prison facilities,[36] training and equipment of the army,[37] and newspaper or magazines sponsored by the Chinese People's Liberation Army,[38] while known to a large number of people and not classified, may nevertheless be related to the national security and interests to a certain extent, even if they are only related to a small degree and the relationship may not be obvious. Once they are used by foreign entities to endanger the national security and interests of China, these matters will fall within the definition of "intelligence" and become subject to the relevant criminal provisions.[39] As with the concept of state secrets, intelligence is another ambiguous term which risks abuse of power by the authorities.

(b) Classification Authority

Since China adopts a source-based approach,[40] state secrets are classified by an authority specified by law. The ultimate authority for determination of state secrets is the National Administration for the Protection of State Secrets,[41] which formulates nation-wide binding norms on the scope of secrets and the basis for classification. It

35. *China v Tan Weiqiang and Li Yunxiu* [2019] Xiang 0111 Xingchu No 130 (譚偉強、李運秀行賄案 [2019] 湘0111刑初130號). The State Secrecy Bureau identifies all the financial data of enterprises from 2013 to 2016 of Hunan Province and Shenzhen Municipality as the intelligence specified in Art 111 of the Criminal Law.
36. *China v Peter H. Wu*, Hubei Province Wuhan IPC, available at www.pkulaw.cn, CLI.C.67540 (美國籍案犯彼德吳為境外機構、組織竊取、刺探、收買、非法提供國家秘密和冒充國家工作人員招搖撞騙案，湖北省武漢市中級人民法院，1995.08.24).
37. *China v Zhang Hao*, Guizhou Province Guiyang City Intermediate People's Court, (2016) Qian 01 Xin Chu 41 (張豪為境外非法提供國家秘密、情報案，貴州省貴陽市中級人民法院，（2016）黔01刑初41號) (photos of army training are not state secrets but intelligence because it "should not be disclosed").
38. *China v Lin*, Fujian High Court, (2000) Min Xin Zhong Zi 24 (林某為境外竊取、收買、非法提供國家秘密、情報案，福建省高級人民法院，（2000）閩刑終字第24號).
39. Li Min, "A Brief Discussion on 'Information' in Article 111 of the Criminal Law" (2000) 3 *Zhongyang Zhengfa Guanli Ganbu Xueyuan Xuebao* [Journal of the Central Academy of Political Science and Law] 20.
40. Article 11, SSL: "The specific scope of state secrets and scope of each classification level shall be determined by the state secrecy administrative department respectively with the foreign affairs department, the public security department, the national security department and other relevant central organs. The scope of state secrets in the military field and the scope of each classification level shall be determined by the Central Military Commission."
41. According to the Notice of the State Council on the Establishment of National Bureaus under the Administration of Ministries and Commissions, the State Secrecy Bureau and the Office of the Central Secrecy Commission are one organisation with two brands. The Communist Party of China as the ruling party handles all administrative work about protecting state secrets.

exercises a centralised macro-control.[42] However, the detailed classification remains with government organs at or above the level of districted cities and autonomous prefectures, and organs or entities authorised by them.[43] A small number of specific individuals have the responsibility for classification, and they are accountable for wrong classifications through disciplinary measures.[44]

Nonetheless, the classification system in China is decentralised in practice because of the absence of tangible standards or guidance. Classification of sensitive information closely relates to a particular industry and department, and this makes uniform guidance at the national level unrealistic. The nature of the state secrets makes the classification decision confidential and subject to a high level of discretion exercised by individual authorities. This renders centralised supervision impractical. This decentralised classification system leads to difficulty in knowing what information is a state secret, inconsistency between different departments and government organs, and the risk of over-classification.[45] In cases where the state secrets of China are involved, the classification by the relevant authorities in China has to be followed, and the courts in HK, as with the mainland courts, have no power to review the classification.[46] In contrast, the classification of protected official information in Hong Kong is not source-based under the OSO, and there was no designated classification authority under HK law before the NSL came into effect.

The NSL does not specify how state secrets in HK should be classified and by which authority. It is unclear, under the NSL, whether the classification of state secrets in HK will be left to the court, or whether the relevant authorities will be designated as classification authorities. If the latter approach is adopted, would the HK courts have the power to review the decision? Considering Article 47, it is likely the HK courts will have no power to review the classification decision of the classification authority if the source-based system is introduced in HK. It may be argued that judges do not have professional competence in identifying state secrets and have to rely on the reasoning and decision of classification authorities.[47] Judges in United States (US) courts are also reluctant to review the finding of state secrets by a state agency and will do so only when the administrative agency's decision is

42. Hualing Fu, "The Secrets about State Secrets: The Burden of Over-Classification" (2019) 14 *Journal of Comparative Law* 259.
43. SSL, Arts 12 and 13.
44. *Ibid.*, Art 49.
45. Fu, n 42 above, pp 256–257.
46. "*Zuigao Renmin Fayuan, Guojia Baomi Ju Guanyu Yinfa 'Renmin Fayuan, Baomi Xingzheng Guanli Bumen Banli Qinfan Guojia Mimi Anjian Ruogan Wenti de Guiding' de Tongzhi, Baofa [2020] 2 Hao*" [Notice by the Supreme People's Court and the National Administration of State Secrets Protection of issuing the provisions on several issues concerning the handling of cases of encroachment on State secrets by people's courts and secrecy administrative departments, No 2 [2020] of the National Administration of State Secrets Protection] , Art 3.
47. Xu Lianli, "The Secret Review System in Government Information Disclosure Litigation: American Practice" (2011) 3 *Huanqiu Falu Pinglun* [Global Law Review] 96.

flawed, or there are reasons to believe it is so.[48] However, it is fundamentally different between judges without reviewing power and judges denying exercising such power for convenient or technical reasons.

The NSL gives no indication as to whether HK courts have the power to classify or to review the classification of state secrets by governmental authorities.

III. The Offence: Low Threshold

(a) Offender

Article 29 does not stipulate any special identity of persons punishable under this provision. Instead, it applies in a broad and indiscriminate manner, and equally to security and intelligence officials, other public officials and contractors, and members of the public.

State secrets offences are closely connected with the identity of the offender. Different categories of potential offenders have different levels of access to state secrets or intelligence, different duties to guard the protected information, and different degrees of comprehension and knowledge of the nature of the information and consequence of its release. Members of security or intelligence services should bear a strict duty of confidentiality as they are likely to have long-term access to state secrets and intelligence. This follows from their professional duty under their employment contracts. In contrast, public servants and government contractors are less frequently exposed to state secrets and intelligence. They, typically, have lower levels of professional training and special knowledge. Members of the public may also encounter state secrets, but they usually have no contractual duty, special expertise, or proper training in safeguarding state secrets.

OSO provides a clear distinction between different categories of people and imposes stricter obligations on members of the security and intelligence services.[49] Public servants and government contractors are subject to the offence if the unauthorised disclosure is "damaging".[50] Members of the public may only be liable if they make damaging disclosures of information received through the unlawful disclosure of public servants or government contractors.[51] State secret crimes in China's PRC Criminal Law, though generally applicable to all, prescribe

48. Harry A. Hammitt, Ginger MaCall, Marc Rotenberg, John A. Verdi, and Mark S. Zaid, *Litigation under the Federal Open Government Laws 2010* (EPIC Publications: Access Reports; The James Madison Project, 25th ed, 2010), p 400, quoted in Zheng Chunyan, "Open Government Information and the Protection of State Secrets" (2014) 1 *Zhongguo Faxue* [China Legal Science] 155.
49. OSO, Sec 13.
50. OSO, Secs 14, 15, and 16.
51. OSO, Sec 18.

different charges and penalties for public officials on the one hand and members of the public on the other.[52]

Notably, foreign entities, such as states, organisations, or institutes, that acquire state secrets or intelligence are punishable as the co-offenders.[53] Foreign institutes are defined broadly to include a wide range of institutes, political or non-political, military or non-military, including news media, educational and research institutes, and commercial enterprises. They are all subject to the same liability. This is highly inappropriate as these "institutes" may need to acquire all kinds of information in the course of their legitimate work. For example, "institutes" set up for cross-border academic collaboration in research on contemporary Chinese affairs, internal politics and fundamental policy, sensitive social issues, and political scandals may easily come to possess classified information or intelligence. Foreign research funders that provide research grants for these issues stand in danger of being treated as purchasing state secrets. The foreign press will be vulnerable when they report on governmental scandals or political affairs. Article 29 may, therefore, have a significant impact on research co-operation, academic exchange and communication, how the media is to operate, and how investments can be safely made.

(b) *Actus Reus*, *Mens Rea*, and Effects

Article 29 criminalises four activities: stealing, spying, obtaining with payment, and unlawfully providing state secrets to foreign entities. There are potentially many forms of stealing, including stealing state secrets and intelligence through the use of technical means such as eavesdropping, photographing, screen shooting, or infiltrating relevant computer systems.[54] The term "spying" refers to the act of secretly obtaining the state secrets or intelligence through information provided by others by means of secret inquiry.[55] In *China v Peter H. Wu*, the defendant went to some prisons in Xinjiang Uygur Autonomous Region with camouflaged camera equipment interviewing and recording prison management and facilities in the name of investigating the Silk Road.[56] He was charged with "spying". The term "obtaining with payment" refers to the act of obtaining the state secrets or intelligence materials from someone possessing or having access to the state secrets or intelligence by means of money or other material benefits or by providing services.

52. Art 109 only applies to public officials. Art 398 stipulates the separation of public officials from ordinary people.
53. NSL, Art 29.
54. n 24 above, Art 6.
55. *China v Lin Xuliang*, Fujian Xiamen IPC, [2014] Xia Xing Chu Zi No 134 (林旭亮為境外刺探國家秘密案，[2014]廈刑初字第134號); *China v Peter H. Wu*, Hubei Province Wuhan IPC, available at www.pkulaw.cn, CLI.C.67540 (美國籍案犯彼德吳為境外機構、組織竊取、刺探、收買、非法提供國家秘密和冒充國家工作人員招搖撞騙案，湖北省武漢市中級人民法院，1995.08.24，北大法寶引證碼CLI.C.67540).
56. *China v Peter H. Wu*, n 35.

"Unlawful providing" refers to the holder of state secrets illegally selling, delivering, or informing another person who is not entitled to have access to them.[57] Unlawful providing of state secrets and intelligence may take the form of delivery of state secrets and intelligence to foreign institutions. State secrets or intelligence may also be conveyed to foreign institutions through wireless telecommunications, computer networks, or other means.

Article 29 does not specify whether the unlawful acquisition and provision of state secrets is punishable only when it causes damage, or is likely to cause damage. It is worded in a way that suggests that proof of damage or risk of damage is unnecessary. This source-based, as opposed to a consequence- or effect-based, approach imposes a high obligation on individuals and makes state secrets crimes easy to establish. The seriousness of damage or risk of damage are only relevant to the penalty. China's Criminal Law is similar.[58] In contrast, under the OSO, an offence is committed only if the disclosure is damaging, unless the offender is a member of the security or intelligence services.[59] The sentence is relatively milder under the OSO.[60]

Article 29 does not explicitly define the *mens rea*. It does not mean Art 29 does not require *mens rea*. Some assistance may be sought from Chinese law and cases. Pursuant to the interpretation of Article 111 of the PRC Criminal Law, the perpetrator needs to know or ought to have known that the information is classified, or relates to national security and interests.[61] There can be no conviction if the defendant has no reason to believe the information is protected or classified.[62] Whether knowledge or negligence exists can be inferred from circumstantial evidence, such as the offender's position, expertise, and the beliefs and attitudes of reasonable

57. *China v Fu Jian*, Liaoning Province Jinzhou IPC, available at www.pkulaw.cn, CLI.C.67690 (付健為境外竊取、非法提供國家秘密、情報案，遼寧省錦州市中級人民法院，2003.02.28，北大法寶引證碼CLI.C.67690).
58. Article 111, Criminal Law. State secrets crimes usually warrant a sentence of between 5 to 10 years of fixed-term imprisonment; when the circumstances are particularly serious, the perpetrator may be sentenced to not less than 10 years of fixed-term imprisonment; and relatively minor damage may result in less than 5 years of fixed-term imprisonment.
59. OSO, Sec 13–16, and sec 18.
60. OSO, Secs 10 and 25. Penalties include a fine or a much shorter prison sentence (three or six months or two years) for unlawful disclosure.
61. *See* n 43 above, Art 5.
62. *Qinyang People's Procuratorate of Henan Province v Yu Ping*, Heibei Province Jiaozuo IPC, available at www.pkulaw.cn, CLI.C.67617 (河南省沁陽市人民檢察院訴於萍故意泄露國家秘密案，河南省焦作市中級人民法院，2002.05.23，北大法寶引證碼CLI.C.67326) (case of divulging state secrets on purpose); *China v Zhao Jinrong and Others*, Hebei HPC, available at www.pkulaw.cn, CLI.C.67617 (趙金榮、徐志國、趙永強、劉淑紅玩忽職守、泄露國家秘密案，河北省高級人民法院，1994.05.13，北大法寶引證碼CLI.C.67617).

people.[63] However, it does not require the accurate knowledge of the classification of the information, but a perception of its importance and relevance to the national interests is enough. Given the broad scope of national security and state secrets, and the very flexible terminology of "national interests", it is not practically difficult to prove that the perpetrator "ought to have known" the information relates to national interests. There is also no requirement that such information is difficult to obtain.[64]

This differs from the OSO, under which it is a defence that a person charged for unlawful disclosure did not know nor had no reasonable cause to believe, at the time of the alleged offence, that the information related to security or intelligence.[65] For defendants other than members of the security and intelligence services, the prosecution must also prove knowledge of the damaging consequence of disclosure, or negligence thereof.[66]

The above discussion reveals that the threshold to convict state secrets crime under the NSL is very low. In particular, the lack of a requirement for damaging consequences and the flexible *mens rea* element make it possible to convict any ordinary individuals who, or "institutes" which, acquire and disclose information without realising the information is classified, if the mainland standard applies. When interpreting the law, the NPCSC needs to specify whether the unlawful acquisition and provision of state secrets is punishable only when it causes damage, or is likely to cause damage, and it ought to explicitly define the *mens rea*.

IV. Due Process Protection

The third difficulty is the potential lack of due process protection. Under Article 41 of the NSL, when a trial may involve state secrets or public order, the defendant may be, fully or partially, deprived of a public hearing. By Article 46, upon a certificate issued by the Secretary for Justice, the defendant may also be deprived of a jury trial. These procedural provisions are similar to those of mainland China.[67] PRC

63. *China v SUN Zheng and Others*, Beijing Xicheng DPC, available at www.pkulaw.cn, CLI.C.860279 (孫振、伍超明故意泄露國家秘密案，北京市西城區人民法院，2011.09.08，北大法寶引證碼CLI.C.860279) (repeatedly commit a crime or serve as a functionary of a state organ); *China v HUANG*, available at www.pkulaw.cn, CLI.C.74261023 (黃某某為境外刺探、非法提供國家秘密案，北大法寶引證碼CLI.C.860279) (collate the collected information); *China v WANG Xuejun and Others*, Jiangsu Rudong DPC, available at www.pkulaw.cn, CLI.C.86967332 (王學軍、翁其能等非法獲取國家秘密、非法出售、提供試題、答案案，江蘇省如東縣人民法院，北大法寶引證碼CLI.C.86967332) (integrate important information of fragments with expertise); *China v WU Zhiwen*, Beijing No 1 IPC [2012] Yi Zhong Xing Zhong Zi No 577 (伍誌文非法獲取國家秘密案，[2012]一中刑終字第577號) (require others to take care of information to be confidential).
64. *China v Lin Xuliang*, Fujian Xiamen IPC [2014] Xia Xing Chu Zi No 134 (林旭亮為境外刺探國家秘密案，[2014] 廈刑初字第134號).
65. OSO, secs 13(3), 14(3)(a), 15(3)(a), 16(4)(a).
66. OSO, secs 14(3)(b), 15(3)(b), 16(4)(b), 17(3).
67. Sigrid Ursula Jernudd, "China, State Secrets, and the Case of Xue Feng: The Implication for International Trade" (2011) 12 *Chicago Journal of International Law* 309, 330.

Criminal Procedure Law stipulates that cases involving state secrets shall not be heard in public.[68] The purpose of "secret trials" is to protect state secrets from being leaked out. However, it also enables the government or state agency to be free from public scrutiny. It is particularly worrying in the event of an oppressive prosecution for political reasons. A balance between national security and procedural justice is required. The similar balance can be found in other countries. For example, a fair and public hearing is a fundamental right recognised by the European Convention of Human Rights[69] and EU Charter of Fundamental Rights,[70] but an exemption is allowed for cases involving national security and state secrets. Procedural justice is particularly important in the absence of a public hearing: an independent and impartial tribunal, a rigorous and adversarial process, and publicly available judgments. Arguably, some of these elements remain for an NSL trial. Art 41 of the NSL specifies that even where a public hearing is denied, the judgment should be publicly announced. However, it would not be enough to build public confidence and trust by just announcing the conviction and penalties. The judgment should include sufficient details of the grounds on which the judgment is based to the extent that no harm is caused to the national interests.

However, procedural protection also faces two challenges. Firstly, due to the relatively low threshold of conviction, and the lack of an explicit requirement to prove a "damaging" result, the classification of the information as a state secret is crucial. But Hong Kong courts may not be able to review the classification by the relevant authorities in China.[71] The level of judicial review of the classification of "state secrets" in HK is also uncertain. The potential lack of judicial scrutiny on this crucial element weakens procedural fairness. Secondly, national security judges are selected by the Chief Executive (CE) of the HKSAR with the restriction that the selected judge shall have not "made any statement or behaved in a manner endangering national security".[72] A judge who has made such statements or behaved in that manner, if already chosen, may be removed. This Executive-led selection of judges raises questions concerning the independence and impartiality of the tribunal and may generate public concern, especially in a trial which is not held in public.

Another matter that needs to be clarified is the effect of Article 47, which states that whether a trial involves state secrets or not is to be decided by the Chief Executive, not the court. This article does not mean to give the Chief Executive the power to classify state secrets for the purpose of establishing an element of the

68. PRC Criminal Procedure Law, Art 188.

69. Convention for the Protection of Human Rights and Fundamental Freedoms, Art 6(1).

70. Art 47(2).

71. *SFC v Ernst & Young (a firm)* [2015] 5 HKLRD 293; [2014] 3 HKC 406. For more details, *see* Peter So and Karen Menon, "Ernst & Young Ordered to Produce Accounting Records and Audit Papers to the SFC", *Deacons*, 16 September 2014, available at https://www.deacons.com/news-and-insights/publications/ernst-and-young-ordered-to-produce-accounting-records-and-audit-papers-to-the-sfc.html.

72. Art 44.

charge. It is to deal with trials of offences for which "state secrets" is not an element of the charge, but where the question of whether or not state secrets are involved arises evidentially or procedurally. An example is where it has to be decided whether the trial or any part of it needs to be closed to the public. The NSL is unclear as to the basis upon which the Chief Executive is to make the classification. It is likely that if the information originated in the Mainland, the Chief Executive may need to follow the classification by the mainland authority; if the information originated in HK, the classification authority and standard is uncertain. Nevertheless, Article 47 clearly excludes the power of the HK courts to review this matter. The certificate by the Chief Executive binds the courts. Due to the importance of public hearing and due process protection, placing the power of the CE beyond the reach of judicial review risks unreasonably extending executive power and may undermine public confidence in the criminal proceedings.

V. Impact of Art 29

(a) Press Freedom

Freedom of the press is mentioned in the NSL and China's Constitution Law.[73] Article 4 of the NSL provides:

> [t]he rights and freedoms, including the freedoms of speech, of the press, of publication, of association, of assembly, of procession and of demonstration . . . shall be protected in accordance with the law.

However, no detailed measures are provided to protect the exercise of the freedom of expression and of the press, or to reconcile the potential conflict between the exercise of these freedoms and the safeguarding of state secrets. Will Article 4 have a significant impact in empowering judges to prevent the introduction of the mainland-style control of foreign media and journalists to Hong Kong through Article 29? There is a lively set of cases in which HK courts review legislation on the basis of Basic Law protection of rights and freedom,[74] but the question is whether HK courts are compelled to treat the NSL differently and immune from review. If judicial review of the NSL itself is not allowed, can the courts use Articles 4 and 5 in interpreting ambiguous provisions in the NSL?

In mainland China, the tension between press freedom and state secrets has always been resolved by repressing press freedom. China has a long tradition of guarding secrets, imposing strict regulations, and penalty for any breach of secrecy

73. PRC Constitution Law, Art 35.
74. Dinusha Panditaratine and Rehan Abeyratine, "Basic Law, Hong Kong Bill of Rights and the ICCPR"; Po Jen Yap, "Freedom of Expression", in J. Chan and C. L. Lim (eds), *Law of The Hong Kong Constitution* (Hong Kong: Sweet & Maxwell, 3rd edn, 2021).

laws.[75] The biggest media agencies in China are state-run, affiliated to the Chinese Communist Party (CCP) and the Central Government, having the privilege to access confidential or classified information. The Chinese media were deemed the "throat and tongue" of the CCP and the Government. Three approaches are adopted to prevent media from leaking confidential information. The first is to directly control the media. The 1992 Regulations on Confidentiality in Publishing and the Media (CPM Regulations) are still in effect.[76] China's press and publishers are to implement a census system combining self-censorship and official approval.[77] The second is to rely on the media to control their employees. Journalists shall not disclose or release information on their occupational behaviour through channels in violation of any stipulations in the confidentiality agreement.[78] The third is to impose responsibility on the online platform to control the self-media led by the general public through identifying the owner of the account, strengthening control, strictly implementing a real-name registration system, including the incorporation of self-media into the unified registration management, and the regular inspection system.[79]

Since Article 29 only criminalises unlawfully acquiring and releasing state secrets for foreign entities, this level of regulation may not need to be transplanted to Hong Kong to regulate HK media. However, the approaches in the Mainland to regulate foreign media and domestic journalists or citizens engaging with foreign media will be relevant to the future operation of mass media in Hong Kong and the likely enhancement of censorship and self-censorship in the media sector.

Firstly, journalists employed by the mainland state-owned media are prohibited from providing information to foreign media and websites, or acting as "special reporters", "special correspondents", "special writers", or columnists for overseas media.[80] The Administrative Regulation imposes obligations on local media to control their employees.[81] The local media must enter into confidentiality agreements with their employees and adopt internal codes of practice to require training

75. Zhang Qun, "Confidentiality Ideology and Legal System in Ancient China: Secrecy Makes Things Succeed, and Betrayal Makes Things Fail" (2013) 1 *Nanjing Daxue Falu Pinglun* [Legal Review of Nanjing University] 103.
76. "Xinwen Chuban Baomi Guiding" [1992 Regulations on confidentiality in publishing and the media], *Guo Bao* [1992] 34.
77. The press or publishing houses should carry out self-censorship in accordance with the relevant confidentiality provisions. Where it is unclear whether information should be classified and protected, the matter shall be submitted to the relevant competent authorities or their superior authorities or units for assessment. CPM Regulations, Art 6.
78. "*Xinwen Congye Renyuan Zhiwu Xingwei Xinxi Guanli Banfa*" [Measures for the administration of information on the occupational conduct of journalists], State Administration of Press, Publication, Radio, Film and Television, Xin Guang Chu Fa [2014] No 75, Art 7.
79. Li Nianfeng, "Self-Media Should Not Be 'Self-Absorbed'" (2019) 10 *Baomi Gongzuo* [Secrets Protection Work].
80. n 78 above, Art 5.
81. *Ibid.*

and exercise control. For example, the *Guangming Daily* has revised and improved a series of working rules and codes of conduct, including the Code of Practice for Journalists, the Code of Confidentiality of State Secrets, the Confidentiality Agreement for On-the-Job Staff, the Confidentiality Agreement for Service Conduct, and the Letter of Confidentiality for On-Post Staff.[82]

Secondly, there is government supervision and control of Chinese citizens employed by foreign media and journals. Employment of Chinese citizens by foreign media or journals must be done through organisations providing services to foreign nationals designated by the Foreign Ministry or the foreign affairs office of the local government commissioned by the Foreign Ministry.[83] Chinese citizens can only conduct auxiliary work. Controlling employment of local citizens is another way to control the foreign media's sources of information. Thirdly, foreign journalists interviewing entities in China must receive the interviewee's permission.[84] Notably, PRC law does not prevent Chinese citizens or entities from giving interviews with foreign media, and there are no regulations to this effect. However, the implementation of the SSL and PRC NSL, and the potential over-classification of state secrets, causes many Chinese citizens to be reluctant to co-operate with foreign media in practice. It is worrying that a similar chilling effect may result from the NSL.

Art 54 of the NSL expressly requires the Chinese and HK authorities to collaborate and "take necessary measures to strengthen . . . the management of . . . news agencies of foreign countries". A similar kind of control, either by governmental authorities or private institutes and self-censorship in Hong Kong in the post-NSL era, would be a foreseeable consequence.

(b) Open Government Information

The right of the public to obtain information about any act or potentially improper act of the government, and the dissemination and exchange of public opinion, is the best way to curb government corruption.[85] Article 29 may also affect the citizen's right to know. The relationship between open government information (OGI) and state secrets is dynamic.[86] State secrets are known to a limited number of people for a given period of time, indicating that the existence of the secret is relative and temporary. With changes in science and technology, the economy, society, and the international situation, the classification of state secrets is also constantly adjusting

82. Zhou Hua, "Establishing Rules and Regulations, Strictly Management" (2014) 21 *Chuanmei* [Media].
83. "Waiguo Changzhu Xinwen Jigou he Waiguo Jizhe Caifang Tiaoli" [Regulation of the People's Republic of China on news coverage by resident offices of foreign news agencies and foreign correspondents], PRC State Council [2008] No 537, Art 18.
84. *Ibid.*, Art 17.
85. *Grosjean v American Press Co.* 297 US 233 (1936).
86. Wang Fei, "Definition of 'State Secrets' in Open Government Information System" (2012) 35 *Xueli Lun* [Theory Research] 89.

to them. Classified information may be subject to OGI disclosure after the protective period expires or if it is declassified.

China has adopted the OGI Regulation to improve government transparency.[87] Foreign citizens, entities, and organisations can rely on this Regulation to apply for disclosure of OGI.[88] However, the "Regulation" ranks below "Law" in the hierarchy of the Chinese legislative system.[89] The disclosure of information is under the control of the SSL. The interpretation of state secrets restricts the information that may be disclosed under the OGI Regulation.[90] Government departments usually need to go through a censorship to determine whether the information to be made public falls within the scope of state secrets. The classification exercise may occur in two circumstances—at the formation of the information, and at the disclosure of government information upon application. Once the information is classified, it is difficult to make it public. Information not classified as a state secret at the time of formation is examined again for secrecy before it is released by the administrative organ, on its own initiative or upon application. Information classified as a state secret at the time of its formation may not be declassified through this procedure. So, the result of the secrecy review process is an increase of the scope of classified information.[91]

In addition, this Regulation is ineffectively implemented in practice. Article 23 of the OGI Regulation stipulates that administrative agencies shall take the initiative to disclose government information by means of publication in the government gazette, government websites, press conferences, newspapers and periodicals, radio, television, and other means that make it convenient for the public to access. However, the public has very little access to the government information in reality. With the popularisation of the internet, the most convenient means for the public to access the government information is through the government official website. However, these official websites are usually not updated promptly and often include old, irrelevant, or overly general information that lacks sufficient details.

HK has no statute dealing directly with the disclosure of government information. Instead, this matter is managed by a non-statutory, self-regulatory Code on Access to Information.[92] This Code covers voluntary disclosure of information and disclosure upon requests. Any entity, irrespective of nationality, is entitled to apply

---

87. Open Government Information Regulation of the PRC (2019 Revision), State Council [2019], No 711.
88. *Ibid.*, Art 1.
89. Hu Yuhong, "Standards for Division of the Ranking of Law" (2004) 3 *Zhongguo Faxue* [China Legal Science] 24.
90. Zhang Jiansheng, "'State Secrets' in Open Government Information" (2012) 6 *Jaingsu Daxue Xuebao (Shehui Kexue Ban)* [Journal of Jiangsu University (Social Science)] 11.
91. Wang Xixin, "Discussion on 'State Secrets' in the Context of Open Government Information" (2009) 3 *Zhengzhi yu Falu* [Politics and Law] 9.
92. Some commentators argue that HK government information has a high degree of transparency. Chen Xuezhen and Li Mengqi, "Legislative Analysis on the Crime of 'Illegal Disclosure of Protected Information' in Hong Kong" (2018) 2 *Gangao Yanjiu* [Hong Kong and Macau Studies] 61.

for disclosure, and disclosure may expose the relevant government agencies or civil servants to the state secrets offence under Article 29. Under the NSL, the disclosure of information by the HK government may face the same problems as experienced in mainland China. The broad and vaguely defined concept of state secrets unnecessarily limits information disclosure. Furthermore, it inevitably introduces a climate of secrecy and censorship of disclosable government information in government departments and administrative agencies.

(c) Detriment to Business and the Economy

Article 29 creates additional risks for foreign companies engaging in transactions with state-owned enterprises (SOE) and their HK business establishments. SOEs usually possess a large number of trade secrets which have commercial significance.[93] Most trade secrets do not affect the national economic interests and should not be classified as state secrets. However, some trade secrets may be protected as such, like those relating to China's regional economic development strategy, the competitive advantages of China in the international market, and the protection of state-owned intangible assets.[94] It is for this reason that economic spies will target them for information theft.[95] Trade secrets and state secrets may overlap,[96] but a clear distinction must be made to avoid arbitrarily defining crimes related to trade secrets which are also state secrets as this may jeopardise the legitimate commercial activities of foreign institutions.

Trade secrets concern technical and operational information held by persons in competition in the market,[97] while state secrets protect national security. Three approaches are proposed to distinguish between trade secrets which should be state secrets and those which should not. The first is a harm-based approach, centred on the consequence of, and the interests harmed by, unauthorised disclosure of the information.[98] Disclosure of state secrets endangers national security and interests, while disclosure of trade secrets (which are not also state secrets) endangers only the interests of the holder of the secret information. If disclosure of operational and technical information risks damage to national security and interests, or seriously

93. PRC Anti-Unfair Competition Law 2019, Art 9.
94. Xu Mingxun, "The Difference between the Crime of Infringing State Secrets and the Crime of Infringing Commercial Secrets" (2012) 1 *Bijiaofa Yanjiu* [Comparative Law Research] 70. For example, the technology for manufacturing cold isostatic pressing fine ceramic rollers was listed as a state secret. See *Ceramic Research Institute of Guangdong Fotao Group v Nanhai Shishan Special Ceramics Industrial Company*, Guangdong Foshan IPC [1994] *Fuo Zhong Fa Jing Chu Zi* No 112 (廣東佛陶集團股份有限公司陶瓷研究所與南海市獅山特種陶瓷實業公司案，[1994] 佛中法經初字第112號).
95. Xu, n 94 above, p 72.
96. Fu Ying and Yu Guohong, "Discussion on the Relationship between State Secrets and Trade Secrets" (2010) 3 *Xueli Lun* [Theory Research] 33.
97. PRC Unfair Competition Law 2019, Art 10.
98. Reng Shijie, "The Difference between State Secrets, Trade Secrets and Work secrets" (2001) 1 *Daqing Shehui Kexue* [Daqing Social Sciences] 57.

endangers market order, such information and technical information should be classified as state secrets.[99]

The second approach is an identity-based approach. Market-operating enterprises hold technological and operational information generated by market activities. Enterprises that produce military products may acquire information involving both state secrets and trade secrets.[100] However, many SOEs are also market oriented, and military enterprises also have ordinary market-operating activities. Therefore, it is not beneficial to distinguish state secrets from trade secrets based on a literal or semantic approach.

The third approach is based on the importance and sensitivity of the information involved. The criterion between state secrets and trade secrets from the importance of information itself may give people the illusion that state secrets must have a certain degree of importance or sensitivity. However, some information which does not qualify under this criterion, such as certain types of maps of the Chinese border, the weather forecast, and publicly available newspaper archives have been, in the past, classified as state secrets.[101]

The classification of what is a state secret may change with time and this further blurs the distinction between information which is a state secret and that which is only a trade secret. If a trade secret implicates national security and interests, it can become a state secret if it is classified as such by a qualified authority.[102] If a state secret has economic value, it can be declassified and used in the market, and even transferred to gain commercial benefits. With the progress of science and technology, the impact of information on national security and interests may be weakened. The information thus loses the characteristics of a state secret and may be declassified. However, the information may still be of great value to the enterprise and remains a trade secret after declassification.

In China's judicial practice, the distinction between state secrets and trade secrets has been vague. For example, in the *Rio Tinto* case, an executive officer, Stern Hu, was detained for allegedly leaking state secrets, including key information about the iron and steel enterprise's production arrangements, steelmaking ratio, procurement plans, gross profit margins, inventories, and even the policy and bottom line of iron ore negotiations to iron ore suppliers. The negotiation policies and bottom line of iron ore had commercial value in the steel industry and should be trade

99. *Ibid.*, p 57.

100. Chen Qingan, "The Difference between Commercial Secrets and State Secrets in Domestic Criminal Law" (2017) 3 *Zhengzhou Daxue Xuebao (Zhexue Shehuike Ban)* [Journal of Zhengzhou University (Social Science Page)] 37.

101. *Gu Ximing v Shanghai Government*, [2019] *Zui Gao Fa Xing Shen* No 12702 (顧錫明、上海市人民政府再審審查與審判監督糾紛案，[2019] 最高法行申12702號). The Supreme People's Court considered that Gu Ximing had obtained the information through books in the Shanghai Library and could not deny the basic fact that the information involved in the case belonged to state secrets.

102. Zhao Xiangru, "The Demarcation between Commercial Secrets and State Secrets and Crimes" (2017) 3 *Xingfa Luncong* [Criminal Law Review] 234.

secrets.[103] Eventually, Hu was prosecuted for leaking trade secrets. Commentators argue the downgrading may have been caused by a change of policy rather than a change of the legal criterion for a state secret

China has been trying to disentangle the relationship between SOEs and the government after accession to the World Trade Organization and to preserve the Chinese SOE image in the international market.[104] It does not mean that China has taken a softer stand on state secrets in general. Since the delineation between state secrets and trade secrets is vague and the threshold for committing a crime is low, it causes uncertainty and creates a legal risk for foreign companies investing or trading in Hong Kong.

VI. Conclusion

This discussion suggests that Article 29 of the NSL, as vaguely drafted, is likely to create unpredictable results to the detriment of the freedom of information. The three deficiencies (an ambiguous concept, a low threshold, and a lack of sufficient procedural due process) combine to disproportionately safeguard government information. The law fails to strike a fair balance between the freedom of information and the protection of legitimate state secrets, and this may have a negative impact on the interests protected by the freedom of information and eventually on the economy. The NPCSC should publish a legislative interpretation to clarify the meaning of Article 29.

---

103. "Lituo An Dingxing Da Jiangge, Bushi Guojia Jimi Zhishi Shangye Mimi" [The Rio Tinto case is not a state secret but a secret], *China News*, 14 August 2009, available at http://www.chinanews.com/cj/cj-gncj/news/2009/08-14/1817897.shtml.

104. *Ibid.*

11

Extraterritorial Application of the Hong Kong National Security Law

A Legal Appraisal

Bing Ling

Amongst the many controversial aspects of Hong Kong's National Security Law (NSL) are its provisions on the extraterritorial effect of the Law. Part 6 of Chapter III of the NSL sets forth three articles[1] that make it possible for the NSL to apply to acts and omissions that occur outside the Hong Kong Special Administrative Region (HKSAR). Given the serious concerns over the compatibility of the NSL with the internationally recognised human rights,[2] the application of the NSL outside Hong Kong would potentially put the Law in direct conflict with the rights and freedoms guaranteed by the national laws of other countries, and place the nationals and residents of other states in legal peril. Not surprisingly, international concerns were voiced shortly after the NSL was adopted over the extraterritorial reach of the Law.[3]

Legislating criminal law is part of the sovereign power of every state. But the legislation becomes a matter of international concern when it claims to apply

1. NSL, Arts 36–38. The four types of crimes under the NSL can all potentially be committed outside Hong Kong, although the crime of Collusion with a Foreign Country or with External Elements seems particularly susceptible to extraterritorial jurisdiction. *See*, in particular, Art 29(3) (applicable to "[t]he institution, organisation and individual outside the mainland, Hong Kong and Macao of the People's Republic of China").
2. *See*, in addition to the relevant chapters of this book, letter of 1 September 2020 by the UN human rights experts on Hong Kong's National Security Law, available at https://spcommreports.ohchr.org/TMResultsBase/DownLoadPublicCommunicationFile?gId=25487; L. Wong and T. Kellogg, *Hong Kong's National Security Law: A Human Rights and Rule of Law Analysis*, February 2021, available at https://www.law.georgetown.edu/law-asia/wp-content/uploads/sites/31/2021/02/GT-HK-Report-Accessible.pdf.
3. *See*, e.g., Council of the European Union, "Council Conclusions on Hong Kong", 24 July 2020, available at https://www.consilium.europa.eu/media/45222/council-conclusions-on-hong-kong.pdf (indicating that EU would "[m]onitor . . . the extraterritorial effect of the national security legislation"); Congressional Research Service, *China's National Security Law for Hong Kong: Issues for Congress*, 3 August 2020, available at https://crsreports.congress.gov/product/pdf/download/R/R46473/R46473.pdf/, p 42 (noting that the US President is required to report on "a strategy for protecting United States citizens and businesses in Hong Kong" in light of the extraterritorial effect of the NSL).

beyond the border in the territories of foreign states, and thus encroaches upon the rights and interests of another state. Although the NSL lays down the final word in Hong Kong law on Hong Kong's extraterritorial jurisdiction in respect of the national security offences, the mere enactment by China of the Law does not imply an international legal entitlement to do the same; it is international law that defines the permissible scope of the legislative jurisdiction of China on the basis of which the NSL was enacted.[4] The formulation and exercise of the extraterritorial jurisdiction must conform to the applicable principles of international law. Where the legislation is unclear, the court must take into account the international legal limits in construing and applying the NSL.[5]

This chapter will appraise the legality of the three extraterritorial provisions of the NSL and discuss international legal limits on the exercise of the extraterritorial power. The analysis in this chapter will focus on the relevant principles of international law, on the basis of which possible solutions to the jurisdictional conflicts between Hong Kong and other states will be explored. The chapter will start with an overview of the legality of extraterritorial criminal jurisdiction in international law. The three extraterritorial provisions of the NSL will be examined next, each in relation to an applicable principle of international law. They are followed by an examination of the legal limits on extraterritoriality arising from international human rights obligations. The chapter concludes by discussing legal strategies for the management and resolution of jurisdictional conflicts that may arise from the extraterritorial effect of the NSL.

I. International Legality of Extraterritorial Criminal Jurisdiction

International law on state jurisdiction defines the limits of a state's power to regulate human relations and activities, and the law on criminal jurisdiction delimits the boundary of the state's monopoly of violence and dispensation of criminal justice. In that sense, the territoriality of criminal law is fundamental as it ensures that every state establishes and sustains the distinctive public order of its own and fulfils the mandates of self-determination and sovereign equality.[6] Territoriality is taken by most states as the primary basis of criminal jurisdiction.[7] Territorial jurisdiction

4. See *Oppenheim's International Law*, 9th edn, vol 1, 1996, pp 456–457; W. Beckett, "The Exercise of Criminal Jurisdiction over Foreigners", 6 *Brit. Y.B. In'l L.* 44 (1925).
5. See *US v Bowman*, 260 U.S. 94, 98 (1922), where Chief Justice Taft stated that statutory construction on the scope of jurisdiction depends "upon the territorial limitations upon the power and jurisdiction of a government to punish crime under the law of nations".
6. As stated in *Somchai Liangsiriprasert v Government of USA* [1991] 1 AC 225, at 244, "the criminal law is developed to protect English society and not that of other nations which must be left to make and enforce such laws as they see fit to protect their own societies". *See* C. Staker, "Jurisdiction", in M. Evans (ed), *International Law* (Oxford: Oxford University Press, 5th edn, 2018), p 290.
7. League of Nations Committee of Experts for the Progressive Codification of International Law, "Criminal Competence of States in Respect of Offences Committed Outside Their Territory", 20 *Am. J. Int'l L. Spec. Sup.* 17 (1926).

manifests, as an English judge put it, "an essential attribute of the sovereignty of this realm, as of all sovereign independent States, that it should possess jurisdiction over all persons and things within its territorial limits and in all causes civil and criminal arising within these limits".[8] The centrality of territorial jurisdiction is underscored by strong functional considerations in terms of investigation of the crime, reparation for the victim, and rehabilitation of the offender and the community.[9]

Extraterritorial criminal jurisdiction[10] is, however, not forbidden by international law. The Permanent Court of International Justice settled the matter in 1927 in its controversial judgment in the *Lotus* case. In an oft-quoted passage, the Court stated:[11]

> Though it is true that in all systems of law the principle of the territorial character of criminal law is fundamental, it is equally true that all or nearly all these systems of law extend their action to offences committed outside the territory of the State which adopts them, and they do so in ways which vary from State to State. The territoriality of criminal law, therefore, is not an absolute principle of international law and by no means coincides with territorial sovereignty.

Justifications have been offered in practical terms for extraterritorial jurisdiction,[12] given that national boundaries become less relevant in light of the

8. *Compania Naviera Vascongado v SS Cristina* [1938] AC 485, at 496–497 (per Lord Mcmillan).
9. See *Arrest Warrant of 11 April 2000 (Democratic Republic of the Congo v Belgium)*, I.C.J. Reports, 2002, p 3, at 37 (Separate Opinion of President Guillaume); "Codification of International Law: Part II—Jurisdiction with Respect to Crime" (Research in International Law under the Auspices of the Faculty of the Harvard Law School) (hereinafter "*Harvard Research*"), 29 *Am. J. Int'l L. Supp.* 435, 483 (1935). *Brownlie's Principles of Public International Law* (Oxford: Oxford University Press, 9th edn, 2019), p 442. Territorial jurisdiction over aliens is also justified on the basis of a temporary allegiance that a resident alien is said to owe to the territorial state in return for the protection that the local sovereign affords. See *Amsterdam v Minister of Finance*, Israel Supreme Court, ILR, 1952, p 240; *Ex parte Blain* (1879) 12 ChD 522, at 526; Beckett, supra, n 4, pp 51–52.
10. As the *Lotus* judgment made clear, extraterritorial jurisdiction discussed here does not refer to the power to enforce one's criminal law in a foreign state, a power that is strictly territorial, but the power to exercise jurisdiction in one's own territory in respect of a crime that has taken place abroad. "*The Case of the S.S. Lotus (France v Turkey)*, Publications of PCIJ, Series A, No 10, p 4, at 18–19.
11. *Id.*, at 20.
12. The Secretariat of the UN International Law Commission (ILC) listed the following motivating factors: (a) the increase in the movement of persons beyond national borders; (b) the growing number of multinational corporations; (c) the globalisation of the world economy, including international banking and international stock exchanges; (d) the increase in transnational criminal activities, including drug trafficking, money laundering, securities fraud and international terrorism; (e) the increase in illegal migration; and (f) the increasing use of the internet across national borders for legal or illegal purposes, such as electronic contracts, e-commerce and cybercrimes. ILC Secretariat. "Extraterritorial Jurisdiction (Annex V to the Report of the International Law Commission on the work of its fifty-eighth session)." *U.N. Yb. Int'l L. Comm.*, vol II (2), 2006, p 229. See also *Starke's Introduction to International Law* (London: Butterworths, 11th edn, 1994), p 183; F. Mann, "The Doctrine of Jurisdiction in International Law", (1964-I) 111 *Recueil des Cours* 36–37. However, given the small number of prosecutions based on extraterritorial principles, whether there is real need for extraterritoriality may be open to question. *See* European Committee on Crime Problems (Council of Europe), "Extraterritorial Criminal Jurisdiction" (1992) 3 *Crim. L. Forum*, 447–448.

increasing facility in transnational movement and communication and the increasingly cross-border nature of civil and commercial transactions and criminal activities.[13] The development of international law since the *Lotus* case has witnessed a trend of expanding claims of extraterritorial jurisdiction.[14] This is so despite the fact that extraterritorial jurisdiction often gives rise to frictions and controversies between states as well as hardship and inconvenience to individuals subject to the jurisdiction, not to mention the practical difficulties in the investigation of the crime and arrest, prosecution, and trial of the accused.[15] Several principles are now commonly invoked as the accepted bases for applying criminal legislation to crimes committed abroad. They include:[16]

(a) the territorial principle, including the so-called objective territorial principle and the effects doctrine;
(b) the active personality (or nationality) principle;
(c) the protective principle;
(d) the passive personality principle;[17]
(e) the universality principle.

Many international legal authorities now consider these seemingly independent principles as manifestations of a single unifying principle in international law which requires a sufficiently close connection between the object of jurisdiction (the offence) and the legislating state.[18] The sufficient connection required must

13. See *Somchai Liangsiriprasert*, supra, n 6, at 251, where Lord Griffiths observed: "Unfortunately in this century crime has ceased to be largely local in origin and effect. Crime is now established on an international scale and the common law must face this new reality."
14. *See* ILC Secretariat, supra, n 12, p 232 (referring in particular to crimes having an international scope and effect, such as terrorism, cybercrimes, and drug offences). The individual judges in the *Arrest Warrant* case were divided in their assessment of the trend of international law towards extraterritoriality. See *Arrest Warrant*, supra, n 9, at 43 (Separate Opinion of President Guillaume), 57–58 (Declaration of Judge Ranjeva) and 76–78 (Joint Separate Opinion of Judges Higgins, Kooijmans, and Buergenthal).
15. *See* M. Krizek, "The Protective Principle of Extraterritorial Jurisdiction: A Brief History and an Application of the Principle to Espionage as an Illustration of Current United States Practice" (1988) 6 *B.U. Int'l L.J.* 337, 358.
16. ILC Secretariat, supra, n 12, p 231; *Restatement (Fourth) of The Foreign Relations Law of the United States*, 2018, § 402(1). Other generally accepted bases of jurisdiction include the principle of flag state jurisdiction and the "representation" principle. *See* Council of Europe Committee, supra, n 12, p 447.
17. The Hong Kong Government invoked, as one of the international law principles justifying extraterritorial effect of the NSL, "the passive personality principle—jurisdiction is prescribed for acts abroad which are harmful to the nationals of the forum state". *Replies of the Hong Kong Special Administrative Region of the People's Republic of China to the List of Issues in relation to the Fourth Periodic Report*, UN Doc CCPR/C/CHN-HKG/RQ/4, available at https://www.cmab.gov.hk/doc/en/documents/policy_responsibilities/response_to_loi-iccpr-en.pdf. This is inapposite as none of the provisions of the NSL appear to base their specified extraterritorial effect on the nationality of the victim of the offense.
18. ILC Secretariat, supra, n 12, p 231; *Restatement (Fourth)*, supra, n 16, § 407; *Oppenheim's International Law*, supra, n 4, pp 457–458; *Brownlie's Principles*, supra, n 9, pp 441 and 461; *Amsterdam v Minister of Finance*, supra, n 9, p 239.

embody genuine and valid interest of the state in regulating the subject matter that is capable of overriding any competing interests of other states.[19]

A long-standing question that stemmed from the *Lotus* judgment is whether, for an assertion of extraterritorial jurisdiction to be valid, the legislating state must demonstrate that its claim conforms with one of the accepted bases of extraterritorial jurisdiction in international law or, more generally, with the requirement for a sufficiently close connection with the crime. The Permanent Court in *Lotus* made the following statement:[20]

> Far from laying down a general prohibition to the effect that States may not extend the application of their laws and the jurisdiction of their courts to persons, property and acts outside their territory, it leaves them in this respect a wide measure of discretion which is only limited in certain cases by prohibitive rules; as regards other cases, every State remains free to adopt the principles which it regards as best and most suitable.

The statement has sometimes been construed to mean that a claim of extraterritorial jurisdiction is presumed to be valid unless a prohibitive rule can be established in international law which the extraterritorial claim has contravened.[21] In the *Arrest Warrant* case, Belgium relied on the *Lotus* statement in support of its claim of universal jurisdiction.[22] The International Court did not rule on the issue in that case, and individual judges expressed mixed views on Belgium's reliance on the *Lotus* judgment.[23] The correctness of the reading of *Lotus* as establishing the presumed validity of extraterritorial jurisdiction has been disputed,[24] and the interpretation was opposed by eminent authorities even at the time when *Lotus* was decided.[25] State practice and recent authorities have clearly taken a contrary

19. See *Oppenheim's International Law*, supra, n 4, pp 457–458. Mann suggested in his influential work on the subject that the "legally relevant point of contact" in determining the existence of jurisdiction is not a "merely political, economic, commercial or social interest" but a "contact with a given set of facts [that] is so close, so substantial, so direct, so weighty, that legislation in respect of them is in harmony with international law and its various aspects". Mann, supra, n 12, p 49.
20. *Lotus*, supra, n 10, p 19. The Court appears to have premised the statement on the classical positivist view that international law emanates only from the consent of states and "[r]estrictions upon the independence of States cannot therefore be presumed". *Id.*, p 18.
21. *See*, e.g., C. Blakesley, "Extraterritorial Jurisdiction", in M. Bassiouni (ed), *International Criminal Law* (Leiden: Brill, 2008), vol 2, p 112.
22. *Arrest Warrant of 11 April 2000* (*Democratic Republic of the Congo v Belgium*), Counter Memorial of the Kingdom of Belgium, 28 September 2001, available at https://www.icj-cij.org/public/files/case-related/121/8304.pdf, p 95. Belgium accepted, though, that extraterritorial legislation "must be reasonable and not infringe on the principle of non-intervention". *Id.*, at 96.
23. President Guillaume stressed that, under classical international law, extraterritorial jurisdiction exists "only if" the offender or the victim has the nationality of the legislating state or if the crime threatens its internal or external security. *Arrest Warrant*, supra, n 9, pp 38, 41, and 43–44. In contrast, Judges Higgins, Kooijmans, and Buergenthal considered the *Lotus* statement "represents a continuing potential in the context of jurisdiction over international crimes". *Id.*, at 78.
24. *See* Staker, supra, n 6, p 295.
25. Beckett, supra, n 4, p 50.

position so that a claim of extraterritorial jurisdiction is valid only if it is permitted by international law when it is shown to be based on one of the accepted principles of jurisdiction or to have a sufficiently close connection between the crime and the forum state.[26] Failing such a showing, exercise of extraterritorial jurisdiction would be treated as a breach of international law (presumably the principle of sovereignty and the obligation not to interfere with the domestic legal order of another state).[27] Other states would be entitled to refuse to recognise the effect of an illegal claim of jurisdiction and the injured state may claim reparation.[28]

In the case of the NSL, the onus would be on China to demonstrate that its extraterritorial provisions conform to accepted bases of jurisdiction under international law. This chapter will examine below whether such international legal bases exist and, if so, the limits to which the exercise of extraterritorial jurisdiction is subject.

II. Extraterritoriality under the Territorial Principle

The first extraterritorial provision of the NSL is also the most clearly justifiable under international law. The first paragraph of Article 36 states:

> This Law shall apply to offences under this Law which are committed in the Hong Kong Special Administrative Region by any person. An offence shall be deemed to have been committed in the Region if an act constituting the offence or the consequence of the offence occurs in the Region.

The formulation follows closely the corresponding provisions in the People's Republic of China (PRC) Criminal Law.[29] It is based on the territoriality of criminal jurisdiction, which is as well established as any principle in international law could be.[30] The territorial principle specifies the jurisdiction on the basis of the locus situ of the crime, which is determined in many states according to the so-called principle of ubiquity, whereby an offence as a whole may be considered to have been committed in the place where a part of it has taken place.[31] In this way, the territorial

---

26. ILC Secretariat, supra, n 12, p 234; *Restatement (Fourth)*, supra, n 16, § 407 Reporters' Note 1; *US v James-Robinson*, 515 F. Supp. 1340, 1344 (S.D. Fla., 1981); Council of Europe Committee, supra, n 12, p 459; Staker, supra, n 6, p 295; Bing Ling, "A Case for Extraterritoriality", in Fu Hualing et al. (eds), *National Security and Fundamental Freedoms: Hong Kong's Article 23 under Scrutiny* (Hong Kong: Hong Kong University Press, 2005), pp 422–423.
27. *Compagnie Europeenne des Petroles S.A. v Sensor Nederland B.V.*, The Hauge District Court, 1982, 22 ILM 66, 72–73 (1983); *US v Campbell*, 798 F. Supp. 2d 293, 308 (D.C., 2011).
28. *See* text accompanying notes 135–137, infra.
29. PRC Criminal Law (as amended in 2020), Art 6(1, 2).
30. *See* text accompanying notes 6 to 9, supra.
31. Council of Europe Committee, supra, n 12, p 446. Following the same approach, in cases involving participation, procuring the commission of an offence, attempted offences, planning an offence, offences of omission, continuous offences, a series of offences violating several legal interests, and connected offences, the acts associated with the principal act would form a unity with that act, which then leads to a unity of jurisdiction. *Id.*, at 447.

principle enables a criminal law to be applied extraterritorially to an offence that occurs in part in a foreign state. The most familiar instance of the ubiquity principle is to localise an offence based on the locus of its effects or consequences, an approach that is commonly known as the objective territorial principle.[32] As formulated by the Permanent Court in *Lotus*, the rule states that "offences, the authors of which at the moment of commission are in the territory of another State, are nevertheless to be regarded as having been committed in the national territory, if one of the constituent elements of the offence, and more especially its effects, have taken place there".[33] The apparent incongruence with the territoriality of criminal law has been explained on a variety of grounds, including the right of the forum state to self-defence,[34] the indistinguishable nature of the effect from the crime,[35] and the "constructive presence" of the offender within the territory.[36] The better justification seems to be the close connection between the crime and the state in which the crime produces the consequences, which, in an appropriate case, is sufficient to justify the jurisdiction.[37]

The objective territorial principle is generally accepted by states.[38] Extraterritorial application of the NSL founded on the situation of the consequences of a crime in the territory of Hong Kong, even though the crime may have been committed in a foreign state, would seem to afford little ground for complaint by foreign states in international law.[39] The human rights limitations on extraterritorial jurisdiction, to be discussed later, would qualify the objective territorial principle as well. For the purpose of establishing jurisdiction on the objective territorial basis, the effects or consequences must be an essential element of the crime in question.[40] As the *Lotus* judgment observed, the kind of offences covered by the objective territorial theory

32. *Id.*, at 446; *Harvard Research*, supra, n 9, pp 503–504, 506–507. In contrast, jurisdiction based on the locus of the author of an offence is usually referred to as the subjective territorial principle. *Id.*, pp 484–487; *Oppenheim's International Law*, supra, n 4, pp 459–460.
33. *Lotus*, supra, n 10, p 23.
34. Beckett, supra, n 4, p 55; *Harvard Research*, supra, n 9, p 494.
35. *Lotus*, supra, n 10, p 37 (Dissenting Opinion by M. Loder).
36. *Simpson v State*, 17 SE 984, 985 (Ga., 1893) ("The well-established theory of the law is that where one puts in force an agency for the commission of crime, he, in legal contemplation, accompanies the same to the point where it becomes effectual.").
37. *Oppenheim's International Law*, supra, n 4, p 458; Ling, supra, n 26, p 413.
38. ILC Secretariat, supra, n 12, p 231; League of Nations Committee of Experts, supra, n 7, p 255.
39. *Treacy v Director of Public Prosecutions* [1971] AC 537, 562 (the foreign state "may be under no obligation in comity to punish those acts itself, but it has no ground for complaint in international law if the state in which the harmful consequences had their effect punishes, when they do enter its territories, persons who did such acts").
40. *Restatement (Fourth)*, supra, n 16, § 408, Comment c; ILC Secretariat, supra, n 12, p 231; *Treacy v DPP*, supra, n 39, p 560. This distinguishes the objective territorial principle from the more controversial effects doctrine which does not require effects to be a constituent element of the act. *Restatement (Fourth)*, supra, n 16, § 409, Comment a; *Oppenheim's International Law*, supra, n 4, pp 474–475. The NSL does not appear to engage the effects doctrine, whose field of application is, at any rate, covered by the objective territorial principle and the protective jurisdiction. *See* Ling, supra, n 26, pp 414–415.

(such as homicide) are those for which the elements of commission and effect "are, legally, entirely inseparable, so much so that their separation renders the offence non-existent".[41] Also, the harmful consequences under the objective territorial principle must have actually occurred in the territory of the forum state, as opposed to merely producing potentially adverse effects in the forum state.[42] The latter situation is covered by the protective principle, which furnishes a broader basis for extraterritorial jurisdiction.

The second paragraph of Article 36 of the NSL is equally well founded in international law. It provides:

> This Law shall also apply to offences under this Law committed on board a vessel or aircraft registered in the Region.

The jurisdiction of a state over crimes committed on board a ship or aircraft that flies its flag or is registered in the state is universally recognised, either by virtue of extension of the territorial or nationality principles or as an independent basis of jurisdiction.[43] Flag state jurisdiction is not only a competence, but is also required under the Law of the Sea Convention.[44] Conflicting jurisdiction may arise when a crime takes place on board a ship situated in the territorial or internal waters of a foreign state, or on board an aircraft in the territory of a foreign state. The issue of jurisdictional conflicts is discussed later in the chapter.

III. The Active Personality Principle

That a state may apply its laws, including criminal statutes, to its nationals even whilst they are abroad is hardly disputable.[45] The active personality or nationality principle, as it is commonly known, is justified on a variety of grounds, notably the bond of allegiance and protection between individuals and their national states.[46] It is sometimes said that a state's subjection of its nationals to its own laws pertains to that state's domestic domain and is not a matter for international law at all.[47] This position is hardly tenable today, not only in light of the pervasive development of human rights law governing the relations between a state and its nationals, but also in respect of the possible impact of the extraterritorial application of a state's

41. *Lotus*, supra, n 10, p 30.
42. See *US v Pizzarusso*, 388 F.2d 8, 11 (2nd Cir., 1968); *US v Keller*, 451 F. Supp. 631, 635 (D.P.R., 1978); *US v Columba-Colella*, 604 F.2d 356, 358 (5th Cir., 1979); *Restatement (Second) of the Foreign Relations Law of the United States*, 1965, § 33 Comment c.
43. *Harvard Research*, supra, n 9, pp 508–519; ILC Secretariat, supra, n 12, p 231; Council of Europe Committee, supra, n 12, pp 449–450.
44. United Nations Convention on the Law of the Sea, Art 94(1).
45. *Lotus*, supra, n 10, pp 92–93 (Dissenting Opinion by Mr Moore); League of Nations Committee of Experts, supra, n 7, p 253; ILC Secretariat, supra, n 12, p 231.
46. *See* Council of Europe Committee, supra, n 12, p 448; *Harvard Research*, supra, n 9, pp 519–520.
47. *Lotus*, supra, n 10, pp 92–93 (Dissenting Opinion by Mr. Moore); Staker, supra, n 6, p 300.

criminal law. Extraterritorial jurisdiction on the active personality principle should not be exercised in a way that infringes upon the territorial sovereignty or other legal rights of a foreign state.[48] Criminalising a national's conduct that is done in a foreign state which permits or even requires it raises questions of jurisdictional conflicts, which will be examined later.

Article 37 of the NSL follows a modified and less well-settled version of the active personality principle. It provides:

> This Law shall apply to a person who is a permanent resident of the Hong Kong Special Administrative Region or an incorporated or unincorporated body such as a company or an organisation which is set up in the Region if the person or the body commits an offence under this Law outside the Region.

Whilst the active personality principle allows extraterritorial jurisdiction over a state's nationals, international law does not limit the connecting factor to nationality alone.[49] Whether the domicile or residence of an alien could be such a connecting factor is not entirely without dispute,[50] but the growing trend in state practice in terms of national legislation[51] and case law[52] seems clearly to favour accepting domicile or residence as a legitimate basis for extraterritorial jurisdiction. The position taken in the NSL appears, therefore, to be supported by prevailing authorities in international law.[53] Extraterritorial jurisdiction over resident aliens is sometimes explained in terms of the protection provided to the alien while they are in the resident state and to their family and effects that are left behind while they are

48. See *Skiriotes v Florida*, 313 U.S. 69, 73–74 (1941).
49. So, for instance, an alien who is engaged to perform a public function of the forum state is subject to the jurisdiction of the state and may be prosecuted and punished for a crime they have committed abroad in connection with the discharge of the public function. *Harvard Research*, supra, n 9, p 539; M. Akehurst, "Jurisdiction in International Law" (1972–1973) 46 *Brit. Y.B. Int'l L.* 156–157; M. Sorensen, *Manual of Public International Law* (New York: St. Martin's Press, 1968), p 361.
50. See *Harvard Research*, supra, n 9, pp 533–534 (rejecting extraterritorial jurisdiction over domiciled aliens in view of other legal bases upon which extraterritorial jurisdiction may be imposed on aliens); Sorensen, supra, n 49, p 361 (noting, however, that a few states, including Denmark, Liberia, and Norway, have asserted such jurisdiction without evoking objection from the national states of the domiciled aliens).
51. *See*, e.g., UK Terrorism Act 2000, sections 63A and 63B (as amended by section 52 of Crime (International Co-operation) Act 2003); UK Bribery Act 2010, section 12; UK Sexual Offences Act 2003, section 72; US Foreign Corrupt Practices Act, § 78dd-2; Israel Penal Law 5737-1977, section 15(a).
52. See *Public Prosecutor v Drechsler*, 13 ILR 73 (1946) (Norwegian Supreme Court); *Re Bittner*, 16 AD 95 (1949) (Belgian Court of Cassation); *Giles v Tumminello*, 38 ILR 120, 122–123 (1963) (Supreme Court of South Australia); *In re P (GE) (An Infant)*, (1964) 3 All ER 977, 981–982 (England, Court of Appeal); *XYZ v Commonwealth* (2006) 227 CLR 532, 535–536 (High Court of Australia).
53. Council of Europe Committee, supra, n 12, p 449; *Restatement (Fourth)*, supra, n 16, § 410, Comment c and Reporters' Note 3; *Brownlie's Principles*, supra, n 9, p 443; Akehurst, supra, n 49, pp 156–157; Staker, supra, n 6, p 301.

abroad.[54] But the better justification may lie in the sufficiently close connection to be found between the offence and the state where the offender is usually or habitually resident.[55]

In the case of permanent residents of Hong Kong, there seems to be a strong case for establishing a sufficiently close connection on which to base jurisdiction.[56] Hong Kong permanent residents, even of non-Chinese nationality, enjoy a wide range of legal rights under the laws of Hong Kong, including the right of abode, the right to vote, and the right to stand for election, many of which are usually reserved to nationals in other states. Whilst there appear to be solid grounds on which to assimilate Hong Kong's permanent residents to the position of nationals for jurisdictional purposes, it should be noted that Hong Kong's permanent residents of a non-Chinese nationality remain subject to the personal jurisdiction of their national states, which may give rise to competing claims of jurisdiction.[57]

Article 37 of the NSL applies also to "an incorporated or unincorporated body such as a company or an organisation which is set up in the Region". Whilst the application of the active personality principle to corporations based either on the place of incorporation or the place of its seat or centre of control is generally accepted,[58] it is unclear whether the same principle extends to unincorporated bodies or other organisations. It may be that extraterritorial jurisdiction over these entities is better founded on other bases of jurisdiction, including the protective principle.

IV. Protective Jurisdiction

The extraterritorial jurisdiction under Article 38 of the NSL is possibly the most likely to give rise to international controversies. It states:

> This Law shall apply to offences under this Law committed against the Hong Kong Special Administrative Region from outside the Region by a person who is not a permanent resident of the Region.

The primary international legal basis for the provision is the principle of protection.[59] Although there were divided views on the validity of the principle

54. See *Joyce v Director of Public Prosecution* [1946] AC 347, 366–368. See also *In re P (GE)*, supra, n 52, at 981, where Lord Denning MR said that a resident alien "cannot throw off his allegiance simply by departing from the country".
55. See *Oppenheim's International Law*, supra, n 4, p 469.
56. Ling, supra, n 26, p 421.
57. See *Oppenheim's International Law*, supra, n 4, p 461; Ling, supra, n 26, p 421.
58. *Restatement (Fourth)*, supra, n 16, § 410, Comments a and b, Reporters Note 2; ILC Secretariat, supra, n 12, p 231.
59. Article 38 applies to "a person who is not a permanent resident of the Region", who may or may not be a Chinese national. A Chinese national who is not a Hong Kong permanent resident is bound by the national Criminal Law if they commit a crime outside China. PRC Criminal Law, Art 7. The jurisdiction in such a case would be based on the nationality principle rather than the protective principle.

amongst individual judges in the *Lotus* case,[60] it is now well settled that a state may apply its criminal law to the conduct of a foreigner committed outside its territory that endangers the security or a limited class of other vital interests of the state.[61] National security has always been the primary state interest covered by the protective principle. Although early cases of protective jurisdiction over national security crimes tended to focus on offences connected with wars in which the forum state was engaged,[62] the principle clearly applies to cases arising outside of wars.[63]

A wide range of arguments have been made in support of protective jurisdiction. The principle is often justified on the basis of a state's inherent right to self-defence.[64] In the field of national security, protective jurisdiction is regarded as an essential attribute of sovereignty.[65] A state is the judge of what endangers and how to protect its own security, and must not surrender to other states the protective competence that is necessary to maintain its public order.[66] Although international law obligates a state not to allow knowingly its territory to be used for acts contrary to the rights of another state,[67] the duty is ill-defined and does not generally go beyond prohibiting the launch of armed or terrorist attacks on another state.[68] The national laws of some states provide for protection of the security of other states,[69] but by and large such protection is considered far from adequate and dependable.[70] As security offences covered by the protective principle are often political in nature, extradition

60. See *Lotus*, supra, n 10, at 35–36 (Dissenting Opinion by M. Loder), 56–57 (Dissenting Opinion by Lord Finlay) and 91–92 (Dissenting Opinion by Mr Moore).
61. *Arrest Warrant*, supra, n 9, at 38, 43–44 (Separate Opinion of President Guillaume); ILC Secretariat, supra, n 12, p 231; *Harvard Research*, supra, n 9, pp 543 and 561 *Restatement (Fourth)*, supra, n 16, §§ 402 and 412; Beckett, supra, n 4, p 56; *Oppenheim's International Law*, supra, n 4, pp 470–471; *Brownlie's Principles*, supra, n 9, p 446.
62. See *In re Urios*, ILR, vol 1, 1920, p 107 (French Court of Cassation); *In re Bayot*, ILR, vol 2, 1923, p 109 (French Court of Cassation); *Nusselein v Belgian State*, ILR, 1950, p 136 (Belgian Court of Cassation); *Joyce v DPP*, supra, n 54, at 93.
63. *See*, e.g., *US v Yousef*, 327 F.3d 56, 110 (2nd Cir., 2003) (terrorism); *US v Zehe*, 601 F. Supp. 196, 198 (D. Mass., 1985) (espionage); *US v Egan*, 501 F. Supp. 1252, 1257 (S.D.N.Y., 1980) (drug offence); *US v Sihai Cheng*, 392 F. Supp. 3d 141, 152 (D. Mass., 2019) (export control violation).
64. D. Bowett, *Self-Defence in International Law*, 1958, p 62; *In re Bayot*, supra, n 62, at 109; *Harvard Research*, supra, n 9, p 556. But *see* I. Cameron, *The Protective Principle of International Criminal Jurisdiction* (Dartmouth 1994), p 46 (arguing that protective principle now covers more than matters of self-defence).
65. *US v Rodriguez*, 182 F. Supp. 479, 491 (S.D. Cal., 1980) ("the concept of essential sovereignty of a free nation clearly requires the existence and recognition of an inherent power in the state to protect itself from destruction"); *Rocha v US*, 288 F.2d 545, 549 (9th Cir., 1961); *Harvard Research*, supra, n 9, p 554.
66. League of Nations Committee of Experts, supra, n 7, pp 255–256; *Harvard Research*, supra, n 9, pp 554–555; Council of Europe Committee, supra, n 12, p 451.
67. *Corfu Channel Case* (Merits) (*United Kingdom v Albania*), (1949) I.C.J. Reports 4 at 22.
68. See *Harvard Research*, supra, n 9, p 552; Bowett, supra, n 64, p 64.
69. See *Re van den Plas*, ILR, 1955, p 207 (French Court of Cassation); Cameron, supra, n 64, p 48; *Harvard Research*, supra, n 9, p 552.
70. Bowett, supra, n 64, p 64; *Italian South Tyrol Terrorism Case (No 2)*, 71 ILR 242, 245 (1970) (Austrian Supreme Court); *Harvard Research*, supra, n 9, p 552.

of the offender to the state adversely affected may be legally impossible.[71] When an alien acts in a foreign state against the security of the forum state, that state, it is argued, simply cannot rely for its protection on the criminal laws of the foreign state who may in some cases sympathise with the offender, but must assert its own jurisdiction.[72]

A perennial issue with the protective principle is the lack of clarity and consensus over the range of state interests to be protected and the types of crimes to be made punishable under the protective jurisdiction.[73] There is little dispute that the protective principle should cover interests that are essential or vital to the legislating state,[74] and there is general agreement over a shortlist of crimes that are subject to protective jurisdiction.[75] But state practice in recent decades has steadily broadened the scope of application of the protective principle.[76] The inherently vague and self-judging nature of the concept of "national security" has contributed to the expansion of jurisdiction into new areas of national concern. For instance, the United States has declared drug trafficking and human trafficking to be a threat to the US national security, taking into account the severity of drug and sex trafficking problems in the country, which enabled the US courts to establish extraterritorial jurisdiction on protective grounds.[77]

In the case of the crimes specified in the NSL, the crimes of secession, subversion, and terrorist activities would fit easily under the protective principle as applied to national security interests. The crime of "collusion with a foreign country or with external elements" follows loosely the protective cases involving espionage or collusion with wartime enemies. Given its essential connection with foreign or external elements, the offence is not dependant on its locality and could be as easily committed by foreigners abroad as by Hong Kong residents at home;[78] extraterritorial jurisdiction could presumably be asserted under the protective principle if the crime, in China's determination, endangers national security.

71. *See* Bowett, supra, n 64, p 65; *Re van den Plas*, supra, n 69, p 207.
72. League of Nations Committee of Experts, supra, n 7, pp 255 and 258; Cameron, supra, n 64, p 31.
73. Beckett, supra, n 4, p 56; Council of Europe Committee, supra, n 12, p 451; *Brownlie's Principles*, supra, n 9, p 446.
74. *See* Council of Europe Committee, supra, n 12, pp 457–458 (arguing that the principle should protect only those interests that are "vital for the existence of the state, its institutions and its constitutional and social order").
75. The list commonly includes espionage, acts of terrorism, murder of government officials, counterfeiting of the state's seal or currency, falsification of official documents, perjury before consular officials, and conspiracy to violate immigration, customs or public health laws. *Restatement (Fourth)*, supra, n 16, § 412; *Oppenheim's International Law*, supra, n 4, pp 470–471.
76. *See* ILC Secretariat, supra, n 12, p 232 (referring to expanded jurisdiction over crimes of terrorism, cybercrimes, and drug offences).
77. *See*, e.g., *US v Egan*, supra, n 63, at 1258; *US v Lawrence*, 727 F.3d 386, 395 (5th Cir., 2013); *US v Aybar-Ulloa*, 913 F.3d 47, 56 (1st Cir., 2019); *US v Baston*, 818 F.3d 651, 670–671 (11th Cir., 2016). *See also* E. Meyer, "Drug Smuggling and the Protective Principle: A Journey into Uncharted Waters", 39 *La. L. Rev.* 1189, 1200 (1978).
78. See *US v Bowman*, supra, n 5, at 98.

By imposing criminal liability on foreigners for their conduct in a foreign state, the protective principle runs the risk of infringing upon the sovereignty and internal affairs of foreign states. Its ill-defined scope as well as the political nature of the offences involved give rise to grave concerns over the potential abuse of criminal jurisdiction to illegitimate ends.[79] Would a state be allowed to punish a foreign national for writing an essay critical of its government in the foreign press in the guise of protective jurisdiction?[80] A number of limits and conditions have been suggested on the claim of protective jurisdiction, and they deserve a careful examination.

First, it is said that protective jurisdiction is only tenable in a case if the act of the accused is demonstrated to have a specific effect on the national security (or another vital interest) of the state.[81] The test does not require the effect to be actual; a potential effect would also do. Nor does it require the adverse effect to be recognised by other states. What it does require is that the effect be specific rather than generalised or fancied. So, even though the US claims protective jurisdiction over drug trafficking as a threat to US security, it has no jurisdiction over a stateless ship carrying marijuana with foreign crewmen on the high seas 400 miles from the US territory.[82] The test seems to be unexceptionable as it aligns with the *raison d'être* of protective jurisdiction and the general requirement of a sufficiently close connection for extraterritorial jurisdiction. In the case of the NSL, Article 38 applies only if a foreigner's offence is "committed against [Hong Kong]". In a particular case, whether the defendant's act, such as writing a critical essay or chanting a protest slogan, has a specific effect on Hong Kong's national security will need to be examined in order to establish extraterritorial jurisdiction.

Second, an early proposal by the Institute of International Law suggested that protective jurisdiction apply over crimes "if they are not provided for by the criminal law of the country in whose territory they took place".[83] The proposal treats protective jurisdiction as subsidiary to *lex loci delicti commissi* and presumes that the crimes will be punished under that law.[84] Given the general recognition of the inadequacy of the local law, the position was untenable and reversed in a later resolution of the Institute.[85]

---

79. See *Harvard Research*, supra, n 9, p 553; Staker, supra, n 6, pp 391–392; N. Bialostozky, "Extraterritoriality and National Security: Protective Jurisdiction as a Circumstance Precluding Wrongfulness" (2013) 52 *Colum J. Trans. L.* 631–635 (criticising US protective jurisdiction under the material support of terrorism laws).
80. League of Nations Committee of Experts, supra, n 7, pp 255–256.
81. See *US v James-Robinson*, supra, n 26, at 1344–1345; *US v Aybar-Ulloa*, 913 F.3d 47, 58–59 (1st Cir., 2019) (dissenting opinion by Judge Torruella).
82. *US v James-Robinson*, supra, n 26, at 1346.
83. "Resolution Relative to Conflicts of Penal Laws with Respect to Competences", adopted by the Institute of International Law, 7 September 1883, Art 8, in *Harvard Research*, supra, n 9, p 637.
84. *See* Cameron, supra, n 64, p 40.
85. "Resolution on the Conflict of Penal Laws with Respect to Competence", adopted by the Institute of International Law, 31 July 1931, Art 4, in *Harvard Research*, supra, n 9, p 644.

Third, the PRC Criminal Law has adopted the dual criminality requirement for its protective jurisdiction.[86] By criminalising a foreigner's act done in a foreign state only if it is also criminalised by the state in whose territory it is committed, the requirement is based on international comity and has the virtue of accommodating the civil liberties and penal policy of the territorial state, and thus reducing potential disputes with foreign states.[87] Outside cases of political offences, the requirement also facilitates extradition of the offender to the forum state. But from early on the position was rejected by most national statutes and widely opposed by international lawyers.[88] The dual criminality requirement is seen as contradicting the very purpose of protective jurisdiction since matters of national security should not be left to the legislative choices of a foreign state, and the protection afforded by foreign states is inadequate. However, as discussed in the next section, the dual criminality requirement may very well be necessary and desirable when one considers the effect of human rights law on the exercise of extraterritorial jurisdiction. Its role as a limit to protective jurisdiction deserves to be re-examined.

Fourth, the Draft Convention on Jurisdiction with Respect to Crimes, published as part of the Harvard codification project in 1935, suggested that protective jurisdiction in the national security area should apply if "the act or omission which constitutes the crime was not committed in exercise of a liberty guaranteed the alien by the law of the place where it was committed".[89] Examples of such liberties include free speech, freedom of the press, and free assembly.[90] The proposed exception is seen to provide protection for individuals exercising civil liberties against unreasonable intrusions of foreign regimes.[91] However, it is not clear how this rule differs substantively from the dual criminality requirement; the arguments against the latter may apply equally to the former. In a case such as *Joyce v DPP*,[92] could not the American citizen broadcasting anti-British propaganda in Germany during the Second World War have been considered as exercising a "liberty" (albeit in the most vexed sense) protected by the law of Germany? Yet, the British Court saw no legal barrier in trying and punishing the accused for treason. Also, with the development of international human rights since the publication of the Draft Convention, the formulation of the rule seems obsolete. The core concerns underlying the rule may now be better addressed on the basis of international human rights obligations (to be discussed in the next section).

86. PRC Criminal Law, Art 8.
87. *See* Ling, supra, n 26, pp 417–418.
88. Resolution by the Institute of International Law, supra, n 85, Art 4; *Harvard Research*, supra, n 9, pp 553 and 557; Council of Europe Committee, supra, n 12, p 451.
89. *Harvard Research*, supra, n 9, at 543. *See* Cameron, supra, n 64, pp 339–340.
90. *Harvard Research*, supra, n 9, at 557.
91. Bowett, supra, n 64, p 63; Cameron, supra, n 64, p 34.
92. *Joyce v DPP*, supra, n 54.

Fifth, the American Law Institute, in the second Restatement of the US Foreign Relations Law published in 1965, proposed to permit protective jurisdiction if the charged act "is generally recognized as a crime under the law of states that have reasonably developed legal systems".[93] The provision, like the two previous requirements, attempted to address the concerns over possible abuse of protective jurisdiction at the expense of civil liberties of foreign nationals. Its core weakness lies in the fact that the standard of "the law of states that have reasonably developed legal systems" is not only borderline colonial, but unduly vague. As a result, it could not limit protective jurisdiction save in the plainest cases. The authors of the Second Restatement gave the illustration of a national of State A criticising in State A the president of State B and suggested that State B should not apply its criminal law to the criticism.[94] But would the conclusion be different if the accused (a) criticises the president of State B in libellous terms, (b) calls for regime change in State B "by all necessary means", or (c) discloses classified documents of State B (noting that most states do not criminalise disclosure of foreign state secrets)? In those alternative scenarios, the identification and application of "the law of states that have reasonably developed legal systems" would be highly problematic. Although the Second Restatement provision is followed in some American Court decisions,[95] there is little acceptance outside the US and the provision was dropped in later Restatements.[96] It is submitted that it would be more principled and workable if protective jurisdiction is controlled by the standards of international law (such as those on human rights and criminal justice) rather than by an ambiguous set of laws of developed states.

Sixth, another possible limitation that has been suggested in literature is to require exercise of protective jurisdiction to "be in conformity with the state practice of a substantial part of the community of states".[97] It is of course unobjectionable that the exercise of extraterritorial jurisdiction must ultimately conform to international law as evidenced in state practice, including the requirement of a sufficiently close connection. Yet, to try to stifle the growth of protective jurisdiction to the level of present-day practice is neither desirable nor realistic. The emergence of new threats to states, such as cybercrimes and terrorism, often justify new claims of jurisdiction. As discussed earlier, state practice in recent decades has indeed moved beyond past bounds on protective jurisdiction.

To sum up, although limitations on the protective principle have been considered desirable and necessary for many years, state practice so far has not come up with a generally agreed and uniform set of standards. It does not mean that states

93. *Restatement (Second) of the Foreign Relations Law of the United States*, 1965, § 33(1).
94. *Id.*, § 33, Comment d, Illustration 2.
95. See *US v Baston*, supra, n 77, at 670; *US v Pizzarusso*, supra, n 42, at 10. See also *Oppenheim's International Law*, supra, n 4, p 470, n 28.
96. The rule was mentioned in a comment in the third Restatement, *Restatement (Third) of the Foreign Relations Law of the United States*, 1987, § 402, Comment f, and disappeared in the fourth Restatement.
97. Council of Europe Committee, supra, n 12, p 468; Cameron, supra, n 64, pp 330–331.

have at present unfettered power to impose criminal liability all over the world. The modern-day development of international law on human rights imposes binding obligations on states to which claims of protective and other types of extraterritorial jurisdiction are subject.

V. Human Rights Obligations and Extraterritorial Criminal Jurisdiction

The development of international human rights since the end of the Second World War has provided significant guarantees on a wide range of rights and freedoms of individuals and has in turn reshaped the criminal laws and criminal justice systems of states all over the world. So, it may come as a surprise that the new human rights law has hardly impacted on the competence of states to apply their criminal laws abroad, except in the area of universal jurisdiction where human rights treaties have allowed states to expand extraterritorial jurisdiction over certain serious violations of human rights. As the scope of application of international human rights requires the determination of state jurisdiction,[98] the question of jurisdiction would be logically prior to the application of human rights;[99] yet it does not follow that the exercise of jurisdiction by a state is not governed by its human rights obligations. Having discussed the international legal bases of the extraterritorial provisions of the NSL, we need now to examine the ways in which Hong Kong's human rights obligations may regulate the exercise of extraterritorial jurisdiction under the NSL.

To begin with, it is evident that to the extent an act is protected by international human rights norms, that act must not be criminalised and punished by the state. So if, for instance, an anti-government speech is covered by the free expression guarantee under Article 19(2) of the International Covenant on Civil and Political Rights (ICCPR), a state party would be legally obligated not to impose criminal penalty on the author of the speech, whether the speech has been uttered in or out of the state's territory, and whether or not the author is a national (or resident) of the state. In this sense, human rights law forms a general limitation on the exercise of all forms of criminal jurisdiction, territorial or otherwise; it serves to control any abuse of criminal jurisdiction at source.[100] In the case of protective jurisdiction, it follows that a state may not apply its criminal law to the acts of a foreigner committed in a foreign country if those acts are protected by the law on international human rights. Such a limitation does not detract from the importance of national security or other vital state interests;[101] it merely requires the state to carry out the protection of its national security or other interests in a manner that is consistent with international

98. *See*, e.g., International Covenant on Civil and Political Rights (ICCPR), Art 2(1); European Convention on Human Rights (ECHR), Art 1.
99. See *Ould Dah v France*, 2009, European Court of Human Rights, available at http://hudoc.echr.coe.int/eng?i=001-113014, p 14; Cameron, supra, n 64, pp 340–341.
100. *Id.*
101. See *US v Rodriguez*, supra, n 65, at 491.

legal obligations that the state has assumed. In the case of the NSL, Article 4 makes clear that "[h]uman rights shall be respected and protected in safeguarding national security in the Hong Kong Special Administrative Region".[102] The extraterritorial jurisdiction under the NSL must, therefore, be interpreted and applied consistently with international human rights instruments binding on Hong Kong, including the ICCPR and the International Covenant on Economic, Social, and Cultural Rights.

Whilst the making and enforcement of criminal law (including the NSL) is generally governed by human rights law, the question remains as to what specific human rights norms may restrict the exercise of extraterritorial criminal jurisdiction. Although major human rights instruments contain no provision that specifically addresses the matter, several rules of human rights law impose specific requirements of accessibility and foreseeability on state laws which are directly relevant to the exercise of extraterritorial legislative jurisdiction.

It may be noted that one of the major concerns relating to the extraterritorial application of criminal law, even when the law is otherwise compliant with human rights guarantees, is the absence of "recognisability" or "fair warning" to the individuals subject to the jurisdiction.[103] The requirement of notice is crucially important in the area of criminal law,[104] and is enshrined in the fundamental principle of *nullum crimen, nulla poena sine praevia lege poenali*. As provided in Article 15(1) of the ICCPR:

> No one shall be held guilty of any criminal offence on account of any act or omission which did not constitute a criminal offence, under national or international law, at the time when it was committed. Nor shall a heavier penalty be imposed than the one that was applicable at the time when the criminal offence was committed. If, subsequent to the commission of the offence, provision is made by law for the imposition of the lighter penalty, the offender shall benefit thereby.

Widely adopted in international human rights instruments,[105] the *nullum crimen* principle is considered an "essential element of the rule of law",[106] and adopted expressly in the NSL.[107] In the jurisprudence of the European Court of Human Rights, the principle is construed to require that "criminal law must clearly define the offences and the sanctions by which they are punished, such as to be

102. *See* Shen Chunyao, "Explanations of the Draft Law of the People's Republic of China on Safeguarding National Security in the Hong Kong Special Administrative Region", *Gazette of the Standing Committee of the National People's Congress*, 2020, no 3, p 603.
103. Council of Europe Committee, supra, n 12, p 460; Cameron, supra, n 64, p 34.
104. See *Board of Trade v Owen* [1957] AC 602, 633 ("the criminal law requires the maximum degree of definition").
105. Universal Declaration of Human Rights, Art 11(2); ICCPR, Art 15; ECHR, Art 7; American Convention on Human Rights, Art 9.
106. *Korbeley v Hungary* (2010) 50 E.H.R.R. 48, § 69, p 1229.
107. NSL, Arts 5(1) and 39.

accessible and foreseeable in its effects".[108] The criminal law on the basis of which a person is to be convicted and punished must satisfy the qualitative requirements of "accessibility" and "foreseeability".[109] Where a person is charged with an act in violation of the criminal law of a state other than that where the act is committed, how would the two requirements be satisfied? How would a person be expected to know the content of, and the consequences for violating, a foreign law? In other words, if a person is alleged to have violated the NSL outside Hong Kong, under what conditions could that person be held to have had access to the NSL and to have been able to foresee the consequences of their act?

Of the two requirements, the question of foreseeability depends on the content of the legal text and whether it enables a person to assess the consequences of their act under the law (even if it may be necessary for them to take appropriate legal advice).[110] Whether the NSL has defined the crimes in sufficient detail and precision is treated in other chapters of the book. In regard to extraterritorial jurisdiction, the requirement of accessibility presents the most pressing challenges.

On the issue of accessibility, it may be noted that the question was raised even in a case applying the NSL in Hong Kong. In *Tong Ying Kit v HKSAR*,[111] the defence argued that the NSL is an "inaccessible" law because it is promulgated in the Chinese language and the English version as gazetted is not verified or authentic but issued for "information" only. Rejecting that argument, the Court of First Instance answered that there is no requirement under Hong Kong law that a national law (such as the NSL) promulgated in the Chinese language should have an authentic English text, and that the defendant in the case was a Chinese individual who presumably could read and understand the Chinese language.[112] Could that answer apply if the accused had committed the alleged offence outside Hong Kong? Would the *nullum crimen* principle bar the prosecution because the NSL was inaccessible to a person outside Hong Kong, especially if that person is not a Hong Kong permanent resident and does not read Chinese?

In the European case law, the European Court reviewed the question in a number of cases involving using international law as the basis of criminal convictions. In *Korbeley v Hungary*, a case involving crimes against humanity in Hungary under Article 3(1) of the Geneva Conventions, the Court noted that the text and a synopsis of the Conventions were published in official publications in Hungary at the time the offence took place and found that the Conventions were sufficiently

108. *G.I.E.M. S.r.l. and Others v Italy*, European Court of Human Rights, 2018, available at http://hudoc.echr.coe.int/eng?i=001-184525, § 242, p 50.
109. *Cantoni v France*, European Court of Human Rights, 1996, available at http://hudoc.echr.coe.int/eng?i=001-58068, pp 14–15.
110. See *Van Anraat v The Netherlands*, European Court of Human Rights, 2010, available at http://hudoc.echr.coe.int/eng?i=001-99990, p 36.
111. [2020] 4 HKLRD 382.
112. *Id.*, at 413–414.

accessible to the accused.[113] In *Vasiliauskas v Lithuania*, a case involving genocide in Lithuania under the Genocide Convention, the Court observed that genocide was codified in the 1948 Genocide Convention and also acknowledged and condemned by the United Nations in 1946. On that basis, the Court found that the international legal instruments prohibiting genocide were sufficiently accessible to the defendant.[114] In these cases, international law was found accessible either through official publications of the state or by virtue of the acts of the United Nations.

The question of accessibility of a foreign law was addressed by the European Court in *Ould Dah v France*.[115] In that case, the French courts asserted universal jurisdiction over a Mauritanian national for the acts of torture committed in Mauritania. The French courts based the conviction on the provisions of the French Criminal Code and the UN Convention against Torture. Reviewing the case under Article 7 of the European Convention on Human Rights (the provisions embodying the *nullum crimen* principle), the European Court observed that the question of the jurisdiction of the French courts "does not fall within the scope of Article 7".[116] On the questions of accessibility and foreseeability, the Court noted that "at the time of the offence of which the applicant was accused, . . . both torture and acts of barbarity were expressly referred to in Article 303 of the Criminal Code".[117] The Court then concluded that the offences in the case "were defined with sufficient accessibility and foreseeability under French law and international law, and that the applicant could reasonably, if need be with the help of informed legal advice, have foreseen the risk of being prosecuted and convicted for acts of torture committed by him between 1990 and 1991".[118] Notably, the Court did not examine whether the French Criminal Code was published or otherwise available in the Arabic-speaking Mauritania, a former French colony that gained independence in 1960, at the time the offences were committed. The fact that the Convention against Torture[119] was cited as one of the grounds of the conviction may perhaps suggest that French law became accessible through the medium of international law in the case. If the Convention against Torture is considered accessible, it would be right to conclude that the defendant must have had notice at the time of the alleged acts that the acts of torture were criminal.

113. *Korbeley v Hungary*, supra, n 106, at § 75, p 1230.
114. *Vasiliauskas v Lithuania* (2016) 62 *E.H.R.R.* 31, at § 168, p 1011.
115. *Ould Dah v France*, 2009, European Court of Human Rights, available at http://hudoc.echr.coe.int/eng?i=001-113014.
116. *Id.*, p 14.
117. *Id.*, p 18.
118. *Id.*, p 19.
119. The Court failed to mention that the Convention against Torture was not acceded to by Mauritania until 2004. But that may not be a decisive barrier against the accessibility of the Convention given that the UN-sponsored Convention entered into effect in 1987, and its prohibitions of torture have attained the status of *jus cogens* as the Court underscored. *Id.*, p 16.

In light of the fact that the NSL was promulgated in the Chinese language in China and Hong Kong, how would the Law be shown to be accessible to a person acting outside Hong Kong? For permanent residents of Hong Kong, their close connection with Hong Kong could make it very arguable that the Law is accessible to them through the gazetted Chinese text and the unofficial English translation published by the SAR Government, even though the individuals may reside outside Hong Kong. The argument is less tenable in regard to a person who is not a permanent resident of Hong Kong but may be subject to the NSL based on the objective territorial principle or protective principle. Some of the terrorist offences under the NSL may also be criminalised under international treaties, and the relevant provisions of the NSL could be considered accessible on that basis. In regard to those crimes not prohibited by international law, current international law and practice are unclear on how a foreign law may be considered accessible if it is not officially published in the state where the alleged offence occurs (not to mention the problem of how one could be properly advised on a question of foreign law).[120] It would not seem right to suggest that a person plotting an armed rebellion against a foreign state could be allowed to argue that they do not have notice of the criminality of their act, given that their act is almost universally prohibited. The better approach would seem to be to apply the dual criminality requirement, so that a foreign law rule criminalising a particular act would be deemed accessible if a similar rule exists in the local law that also criminalises the act. Here, the dual criminality test is not based on comity between states, but on the need to protect an individual's right to fair notice in respect of their criminal responsibility. In a case where an individual may not be reasonably expected to have access to a foreign law, dual criminality ensures that the individual is forewarned of the criminality of their conduct based on a similar prohibitive rule in the law of the place where the conduct occurs so that the fundamental requirement of the *nullum crimen* principle may be satisfied.[121] In line with that analysis, the dual criminality rule does not apply in all cases of extraterritorial jurisdiction but only in cases involving defendants who are not permanent residents of Hong Kong.

The requirements of accessibility and foreseeability stem not only from the *nullum crimen* principle, but also from other rules on particular human rights. Where the ICCPR allows restriction on a particular right, it is often required that the restriction be "provided by law".[122] The requirements of accessibility and foresee-

120. *See* Council of Europe Committee, supra, n 12, p 461.

121. The test of dual criminality is to be applied *in abstracto* rather than *in concreto*. *See* Council of Europe Committee, supra, n 12, pp 48–49. National security crimes are often nationally linked, so that a particular act (for instance, obtaining or disclosing state secrets) is a crime only if it is directed against the forum state, but not so if it is against a foreign state. In that light, the proper test to be applied is to ask, not whether spying against State A is a crime under the law of State B, but whether spying in abstract is prohibited by State B.

122. *See* ICCPR, Arts 12(3) and 19(3).

ability apply to such "law" as well.[123] So, for instance, if State A restricts freedom of expression by criminalising hate speech on national security grounds, whether or not the law of State A may be applied extraterritorially in State B would depend on whether it meets the accessibility and foreseeability test in State B in order that the extraterritorial application should constitute a permissible restriction on free speech in State B under the ICCPR. By the foregoing analysis, the dual criminality requirement should also apply where the case involves foreign nationals (or, in the case of NSL, persons who are not Hong Kong permanent residents) so that they may only be punished under the law of State A if State B has a similar law prohibiting hate speech.

VI. Regulating Jurisdictional Conflicts

Extraterritorial criminal jurisdiction is now more or less claimed by states all over the world. As a result, criminal cases are increasingly subject to overlapping jurisdiction of two or more states. In practice, concurrence of jurisdiction in most cases is tolerable and does not give rise to disputes.[124] Considerations of comity, good sense, and reasonableness would lead to forbearance by one state from exercising jurisdiction in favour of the other if no substantial state interest is involved.[125] Conflict is less avoidable if both states are strongly interested in prosecuting the case (as in *Lotus*), which could result in hardship and double jeopardy on the individuals concerned. Also, if two states have opposing interests in the matter, as in *Arrest Warrant*, with one intending on punishing a perceived offence and the other interested in shielding the accused from prosecution, there is potentially a full-blown international dispute. The problem is aggravated when geopolitical contention underlies the controversies in extraterritorial cases, as may very well happen in the case of the NSL. There are at present no coherent and clear principles of international law that regulate and resolve conflicts of criminal jurisdiction between states. A number of observations may be made, though, that may shed light on the current state of international law on the subject.

First, it is often said that there is no hierarchy of the various bases of jurisdiction in international law.[126] The three bases of extraterritoriality relied on in the NSL are not legally required to yield to the territorial jurisdiction of the state in which the offence occurs. Whilst this may be strictly correct, it should be underscored that territorial jurisdiction is an attribute and manifestation of territorial sovereignty whose protection lies at the heart of modern international law. As discussed

123. *See* ICCPR General Comment No. 34, U.N. Doc. CCPR/C/GC/34, § 25, which states that the "law" restricting freedom of expression "must be formulated with sufficient precision to enable an individual to regulate his or her conduct accordingly and it must be made accessible to the public".
124. *Oppenheim's International Law*, supra, n 4, p 457.
125. *Id.*, at 457, 463–464.
126. *Restatement (Fourth),* supra, n 16, s 407, Comment d; *Brownlie's Principles*, supra, n 9, p 469.

earlier,[127] territorial jurisdiction defines the scope of independent, self-governing communities in the world today; the existence and exercise of territorial jurisdiction enables and signifies the self-determination and the distinctive public order of a sovereign community. Every instance of extraterritorial jurisdiction is in a way an encroachment upon that order and must be justified. It is well established that the principles of sovereignty and non-interference limit the exercise of extraterritorial jurisdiction; excessive claims of criminal jurisdiction over what takes place in the territory of another state would be an international wrong if it is excessive and amounts to interference with the legal order of the foreign state.[128] Whilst the thresholds of these principles in regard to territorial jurisdiction is often elusive,[129] territorial jurisdiction is accorded primacy so that, for instance, a state should not compel its nationals to commit an act in a foreign state which prohibits it.[130]

Second, it is often suggested that, in managing jurisdictional conflicts, states should act in the spirit of accommodation, mutual respect, moderation, and proportionality.[131] Whilst the suggestion makes perfect sense, state practice in this regard is probably motivated by considerations of comity rather than law.[132] The third Restatement of the US Foreign Relations Law also proposed a requirement in international law for a state to weigh the competing interests of other states against its own and exercise jurisdiction only if it is reasonable.[133] The position was reversed in the more recent fourth Restatement which flatly denied the legal character of the requirement of reasonableness.[134] How to regulate conflicts of jurisdiction between states with competing interests remains one of the most vexing problems in international law.

Third, there are principles of international law that govern the claim and exercise of extraterritorial jurisdiction. Extraterritorial application of law must be shown to be based on one of the accepted principles of jurisdiction, or there must be a sufficiently close connection between the legislating state and the object of jurisdiction. Apart from the principles of sovereignty and non-interference, human rights law provides an important source of obligations on the exercise of criminal jurisdiction.

---

127. *See* text accompanying nn 6–9, supra.
128. *Oppenheim's International Law*, supra, n 4, p 477; *Brownlie's Principles*, supra, n 9, p 469.
129. *See* Cameron, supra, n 64, p 345.
130. *Oppenheim's International Law*, supra, n 4, pp 458 and 464; Staker, supra, n 6, p 309; *Restatement (Fourth)*, supra, n 16, § 442.
131. See *Brownlie's Principles*, supra, n 9, p 469; Council of Europe Committee, supra, n 12, p 459; Staker, supra, n 6, p 313.
132. *Restatement (Fourth)*, supra, n 16, § 402, Comment c.
133. *Restatement (Third)*, supra, n 96, § 403. See also *Oppenheim's International Law*, supra, n 4, pp 465–466.
134. *Restatement (Fourth)*, supra, n 16, § 407, Reporters' Note 3. The suggestion of a state weighing competing claims of jurisdiction by the standard of reasonableness has been criticised for being vague and unworkable and hardly followed outside the US. States scarcely have confidence in a foreign court weighing up competing national interests impartially, and most US courts in practice came down in favour of the US interest. *See* Cameron, supra, n 64, pp 335–336; Staker, supra, n 6, p 310.

A state which claims and exercises extraterritorial jurisdiction in excess of those legal limits would be guilty of an internationally wrongful act.

Fourth, exorbitant exercise of extraterritorial jurisdiction leads to responsibility of the forum state. States whose territorial sovereignty is infringed or whose nationals are subjected to jurisdiction are entitled to make international claims.[135] They may refuse to recognise the effect of the illegitimate jurisdiction and take "blocking" measures to deny co-operation with the legislating state.[136] In the case of the NSL, the suspension by several states of their extradition agreements with Hong Kong fell in that category. If the assertion of extraterritorial jurisdiction in a criminal statute contravenes international law, whether the mere enactment of the statute without actual enforcement constitutes an actionable wrongful act is somewhat unclear. To the extent that the making of the law activates a threat, or creates a risk of sanctions, that affects the behaviour of foreign states and nationals, the states that are affected would seem to have legitimate grounds for complaint in international law.[137]

Fifth, one of the legal principles that regulates cases of concurrent jurisdiction is that of *non bis in idem*, which prohibits exposing a person to double jeopardy for the same offence.[138] It should be noted that the Human Rights Committee has in its jurisprudence consistently denied the international effect of the principle as laid down in the ICCPR, so that the prohibition of double jeopardy is applicable with regard to an offence adjudicated in a given State only.[139] This is regrettable, given the acceptance of an international *non bis in idem* principle by many national and international jurisdictions.[140] Although the NSL does not include a provision on *non bis in idem*, it should be recognised and applied in future national security cases so as to avoid jurisdictional conflicts and prevent undue hardship to the individuals concerned.

Conclusion

Since the NSL came into effect in Hong Kong in July 2020, there has so far not been a single prosecution of extraterritorial offences. Any actual exercise of the power in the future will most likely trigger international controversies. Following

135. *Oppenheim's International Law*, supra, n 4, p 485; Beckett, supra, n 4, p 45.
136. ILC Secretariat, supra, n 12, pp 234–235; Council of Europe Committee, supra, n 12, pp 469–470.
137. See *Brownlie's Principles*, supra, n 9, p 461; Staker, supra, n 6, p 310.
138. ICCPR, Art 14(7).
139. ICCPR General Comment No. 32, U.N. Doc. CCPR/C/GC/32, § 57; *A. P. v Italy*, Communication No. 204/1986, U.N. Doc. CCPR/C/OP/2 at 67 (1990), § 7; *A. R. J. v Australia*, Communication No. 692/1996, U.N. Doc. CCPR/C/60/D/692/1996, § 6.4. *See also* Council of Europe Committee, supra, n 12, pp 471–472.
140. *Harvard Research*, supra, n 9, pp 602–603; Statute of the International Criminal Tribunal for the Former Yugoslavia, Art 10; Rome Statute of the International Criminal Court, Art 20. *See*, generally, C. Wyngaert and G. Stessens, "The International *Non Bis in Idem* Principle: Resolving Some of the Unanswered Questions" (1999) 48 *Int'l & Comp. L.Q.* 779.

the commitment to human rights protection and rule of law as enunciated in the NSL itself, the governments and courts in Hong Kong and China should exercise the extraterritorial power in the NSL cautiously and in strict compliance with the applicable principles of international law and ensure that the application of the NSL does not infringe the sovereignty and independence of other states and the individual rights and freedoms guaranteed under international law. As the European Committee on Crime Problems pointed out, "[i]nternational conflicts of criminal jurisdiction may frequently be only a manifestation of underlying international conflicts. . . . [C]riminal law is not omnipotent. It cannot be used to right every social wrong or to eliminate ideological or political frictions."[141] From the very beginning, the NSL has been embroiled in international geopolitical rivalries, and any future disputes over the extraterritorial effect of the NSL could very well carry broad political implications. One could only hope that the parties concerned will have the wisdom in properly managing and resolving the conflicts by taking seriously and applying judiciously the principles of international law and comity.

141. Council of Europe Committee, supra, n 12, p 477.

12

Academic Freedom in the Shadow of Hong Kong's National Security Law

Kelley Loper and Carole J. Petersen

Introduction

This chapter analyses the impact of the Law of the People's Republic of China on Safeguarding National Security in Hong Kong (NSL) on educational autonomy and academic freedom, two core values that the "One Country Two, Systems" (OCTS) model of autonomy is supposed to protect. Due to space constraints, this chapter primarily focuses on academic freedom in tertiary education. However, it will also address certain contentious issues which have arisen in primary and secondary schools.

Following this introduction, Part I reviews the concept of academic freedom, its value to society, and the ways in which it can be undermined. Part II then analyses the situation in the Hong Kong Special Administrative Region (SAR) prior to the enactment of the NSL. Although academic freedom and educational autonomy are expressly protected in the Hong Kong Basic Law (BL), changes to university governance in the past two decades have made universities and individual academics more vulnerable to political pressures.

Part III of the chapter analyses provisions in the NSL that could further inhibit academic freedom and educational autonomy. The NSL obligates the local government to "promote national security education in schools and universities" and creates several new criminal offences, which also apply extraterritorially. The NSL also created new security agencies and endowed them with extensive powers. On the other hand, Article 4 provides that human rights shall continue to be protected, including the rights stated in the BL, the International Covenant on Civil and Political Rights (ICCPR) and the International Covenant on Economic, Social and Cultural Rights (ICESCR). These two treaties have a special place in Hong Kong's legal framework due to Article 39 of the BL and the Bill of Rights Ordinance (Cap

383) (which duplicates most of the provisions of the ICCPR).[1] Thus, any policies adopted by Hong Kong's educational institutions should comply with both treaties. When cases are litigated the local courts should use the ICCPR as a guide to interpret vague language in the NSL. Thus, the views of the United Nations (UN) Human Rights Committee, the expert body tasked with monitoring states parties' implementation of the ICCPR, are particularly relevant. The UN Committee on Economic, Social and Cultural Rights, the monitoring body for the ICESCR, can also offer guidance, particularly in the context of the right to education. These international standards and their direct incorporation into Hong Kong law allow room for the courts and others to support academic freedom. At the same time, legal protection alone is unlikely to be sufficient. Other non-legal strategies, such as the drafting and enforcement of robust academic freedom policies by tertiary institutions themselves, are needed to strengthen academic freedom in Hong Kong going forward. Indeed, we conclude that the academic community has an obligation to adopt such policies and that the Hong Kong government has a constitutional obligation to respect them. Suggested language for a university policy on academic freedom is therefore included at the end of this chapter.

I. The Concept of Academic Freedom

The concept of academic freedom began as the right to pursue truth in research. Over time, it has expanded to include the right of academics to determine how they will teach, to criticise their own institutions, and to speak out on societal issues.[2] The United Nations Educational, Scientific and Cultural Organization (UNESCO) defines academic freedom as: "the right, without constriction by prescribed doctrine, to freedom of teaching and discussion, freedom in carrying out research and disseminating and publishing the results thereof, freedom to express freely their opinion about the institution or system in which they work, freedom from institutional censorship and freedom to participate in professional or representative academic bodies".[3] This definition recognises four key components: (1) freedom in teaching; (2) freedom to conduct research; (3) freedom of intramural expression,

---

1. Hong Kong Bill of Rights Ordinance (Cap 383). For analysis of its constitutional status, *see* Dinusha Panditaratne and Rehan Abeyratne, "Basic Law, Hong Kong Bill of Rights and the ICCPR", in Johannes Chan and C. L. Lim (eds), *Law of the Hong Kong Constitution* (Hong Kong: Sweet & Maxwell, 2021), Ch 16.
2. For further analysis of the concept of academic freedom, how it has changed over time, and the extent to which it has been embraced in different regions, *see* Jan Currie, Carole J. Petersen, and Kaho Mok, *Academic Freedom in Hong Kong* (Lanham: Lexington Books, 2006), Ch 1.
3. UNESCO, Recommendation Concerning the Status of Higher-Education Teaching Personnel, 11 November 1997, available at http://portal.unesco.org/en/ev.php-URL_ID=13144&URL_DO=DO_PRINTPAGE&URL_SECTION=201.html; *see also* UNESCO, Protecting Academic Freedom is as Relevant as Ever, 18 October 2017, available at https://en.unesco.org/news/protecting-academic-freedom-relevant-ever.

including the right to critique one's own university and to take part in its management; and (4) freedom of extramural expression, including the right to share one's research outcomes and disseminate the knowledge acquired.

Academic freedom is legally grounded in international human rights norms. Although not explicitly mentioned in the ICCPR, it is supported by several rights stated in the treaty, including the freedoms of opinion, expression, peaceful assembly, association, thought, conscience, religious belief, and movement, and the right to privacy.[4] Academic freedom is also crucial for several of the rights in the ICESCR, including the right to education[5] and the right to enjoy the benefits of scientific progress.[6] Indeed, the free exchange of ideas is essential to all aspects of a university's public mission, including the provision of quality education, research collaboration, the pursuit of truth, and the production and transmission of knowledge. At its core, academic freedom protects scholars when they are teaching, conducting research, and disseminating knowledge within their disciplinary field. However, more expansive interpretations of the concept include activities outside an academic's professional capacity. Thus, so long as they make it clear that they are not representing their institutions, scholars should be free to express their opinions on controversial issues in the broader community.[7] This is part of their general freedom of expression as protected by Article 19 of the ICCPR.

Legal protections for academic freedom are essential but not sufficient. This is because academics and university administrators are vulnerable to many subtle political and economic pressures, which can be applied without any recourse to law. Thus, any stated "right" to academic freedom needs to be backed up by institutional protections. These include: institutional autonomy (to protect the university from undue interference from the government or other powerful interests in society); tenure for individual academics (protecting an academic from dismissal unless there is compelling evidence of incompetence or unprofessional behaviour); and a system of shared governance (in which elected representatives of the faculty share governance rights with the administration). There should also be strong university policies proclaiming the right to academic freedom, which are backed up by effective complaints mechanisms.

---

4. David Kaye, Report of the UN Special Rapporteur on the promotion and protection of the right to freedom of opinion and expression, UN Doc. A/75/261, 28 July 2020, especially paras 5 and 19.
5. UN Committee on the Economic, Social and Cultural Rights, General Comment 13: The Right to Education, UN Doc. E/C.12/1999/10, 8 December 1999, paras 38–39 (defining academic freedom as including, inter alia, the right to "pursue, develop and transmit knowledge and ideas, through research, teaching, study, discussion, documentation, production, creation or writing" and the liberty to "express freely opinions about the institution or system in which they work").
6. UN Committee on the Economic, Social and Cultural Rights, General Comment 25: The Right to Science, UN Doc. E/C.12/GC/25, 30 April 2020, para 13.
7. *See*, for example, Currie, Petersen, and Mok, n 2 above, pp 18–25; Keith E. Whittington, "Academic Freedom and the Scope of Protections for Extramural Speech: Why Controversial Remarks by Faculty Must Be Protected", *AAUP*, Winter 2019, available at https://www.aaup.org/article/academic-freedom-and-scope-protections-extramural-speech#.X-Eem-lKjFw.

Academic freedom is, however, not an absolute concept. It is socially constructed, frequently contested, and can evolve over time. Even when there are no formal amendments to the law or university policies, the practice of academic freedom can change significantly in response to political and economic circumstances. For example, in the United States (US), the need to stretch academic budgets by hiring non-tenured "adjunct" faculty has been identified as one of the greatest threats to academic freedom.[8] Decreased funding for public education in many jurisdictions has also led universities to adopt more corporate-like strategies and to enter into partnerships with industry, which can affect the impartiality of research findings.[9] Similarly, government-sponsored "accountability" exercises (such as the British quality audits) can decrease academic freedom by steering academics to produce a certain type of research so as to generate the highest possible performance indicators for their institution.[10]

A government's desire to protect national security (or to protect its own political power) can pose special threats to academic freedom. Democratic nations are not immune to these phenomena, as evidenced by the enactment of the US Patriot Act following the terrorist attacks of September 2001. Among other things, the Act asked universities to track international students and restricted access to certain "unclassified but sensitive" information. In 2002, the American Association of University Professors (AAUP) created a special committee to study the impact of these developments on academic freedom.[11] More recently, the AAUP highlighted threats to academic freedom under the Trump administration, including its overt hostility to the field of climate science and the targeting of Chinese and Chinese-American scientists for espionage investigations.[12]

Academics in authoritarian regimes are, however, far more vulnerable to interference in the name of national security. In Turkey, for example, academics who signed a petition criticising human rights violations by the military were accused of treason, and thousands lost their jobs in the purge following the failed coup attempt

8. *See* Currie, Petersen, and Mok, n 2 above, pp 33–36; Johann Neem, "The Subtle Erosion of Academic Freedom", *Inside Higher Ed*, 16 April 2019, available at https://www.insidehighered.com/views/2019/04/16/three-subtle-forces-weakening-academic-freedom-opinion.
9. *See*, for example, Jasmine Banks, "Blueprints for Protecting Academic Freedom from Dark Money Donations" (2020) 69(3) *Communication Education* 383; and Currie, Petersen, and Mok, n 2 above, pp 38–42.
10. *See*, for example, Ann Martin-Sardesai, Helen Irvine, Stuart Tooley, and James Guthrie, "Government Research Evaluations and Academic Freedom: A UK and Australian Comparison" (2017) 366(2) *Higher Education Research & Development* 371; Carl Rhodes, "Academic Freedom in the Corporate University: Squandering Our Inheritance?" in Michał Izak, Monika Kostera, and Michał Zawadzki (eds), *The Future of University Education* (London: Palgrave, 2017), p 19.
11. AAUP, "Academic Freedom and National Security in a Time of Crisis", October 2003, available at https://www.aaup.org/report/academic-freedom-and-national-security-time-crisis.
12. AAUP, "National Security and the Assault on Science, and Academic Freedom", December 2017, available at https://www.aaup.org/report/national-security-assault-science-and-academic-freedom.

against President Erdogan in 2016.[13] Similarly, in mainland China, the government has regularly cited "national security" as a reason for strict controls on academic research, teaching, and conferences.[14] Surveillance of scholars in mainland China has become particularly intense in recent years. Some teachers report that their lectures are continuously recorded to ensure that they comply with party doctrine.[15] Finally, it should be noted that such repression does not necessarily stay within the borders of authoritarian regimes. The internationalisation of higher education, while beneficial in many respects, has enabled certain governments to export censorship and political repression to democratic countries. In some cases, this takes the form of direct surveillance and intimidation of students and faculty when they go abroad. There is also evidence of self-censorship by universities that have become financially dependent upon students and donations from repressive regimes.[16]

As demonstrated in the next section, the Hong Kong SAR does provide significant legal protection for academic freedom. However, even before the enactment of the NSL, the autonomy of universities was somewhat fragile, and academics were already vulnerable to political interference.

II. Academic Freedom in Hong Kong Prior to the Enactment of the NSL

Hong Kong's first university, the University of Hong Kong (HKU), was founded in 1911. The colonial government initially exercised significant control over the university as well as over primary and secondary education.[17] In the 1960s, the government established the Chinese University of Hong Kong and created the University Grants Committee (UGC), which supposedly serves as a buffer between the universities and the government. The colonial government also established several "polytechnics", which later became universities. In 1991, the government established the Research Grants Council and began encouraging universities to compete globally as research and teaching institutions. The University of Science and Technology was also established in 1991 and became a respected institution in a remarkably short period of time. Currently, Hong Kong has eight UGC-funded universities, each of

13. Muzaffer Kaya, "Turkey's Purge of Critical Academia", *MERIP*, Fall 2018, available at https://merip.org/2018/12/turkeys-purge-of-critical-academia/.
14. Scholars at Risk, "Obstacles to Excellence: Academic Excellence and China's Quest for World-Class Universities", 24 September 2019, available at https://www.scholarsatrisk.org/resources/obstacles-to-excellence-academic-freedom-chinas-quest-for-world-class-universities/.
15. Jennifer Ruth and Yu Xiao, "Academic Freedom and China: Every Scholar Walks on Thin Ice", *AAUP*, Fall 2019, available at https://www.aaup.org/article/academic-freedom-and-china#.X53R6pNKgUo.
16. For a recent study of this phenomena in British universities, *see* Saipira Furstenberg, Tena Prelec, and John Heathershaw, "The Internationalization of Universities and the Repression of Academic Freedom", *Freedom House*, 2020, available at https://freedomhouse.org/report/special-report/2020/internationalization-universities-and-repression-academic-freedom.
17. John P. Burns, "The State and Higher Education in Hong Kong" (2020) 244 *The China Quarterly* 1031.

which is established by its own ordinance.[18] Despite its tiny size, Hong Kong has developed into a regional hub for higher education with five universities ranked in the top one hundred in the world.[19] When analysing the factors underlying this success, experts have consistently pointed to the fact that Hong Kong universities have enjoyed greater educational autonomy and academic freedom than universities in mainland China.[20]

Indeed, on paper, Hong Kong has strong legal protections for academic freedom. The Sino-British Joint Declaration, which was ratified in 1985 and registered with the UN, promised that Hong Kong would maintain its separate common law legal system for at least 50 years after the resumption of Chinese sovereignty in 1997.[21] The treaty contains detailed provisions protecting civil liberties, including an express promise that the freedom to conduct academic research will be protected by law.[22] The Joint Declaration also promises that the ICCPR and ICESCR shall continue to be enforced in Hong Kong.[23] As noted earlier in this chapter, these two treaties contain numerous rights that support academic freedom. Finally, the Joint Declaration provides that the territory "shall maintain the educational system previously practiced in Hong Kong" and that educational institutions will maintain their autonomy.[24]

The BL, which was enacted in 1990 and went into force on 1 July 1997, largely repeats the promises made in the Joint Declaration. Article 27 protects the freedoms of speech, the press, and publication. Article 34 provides that all residents shall enjoy the freedom to engage in "academic research, literary and artistic creation and other cultural activities". Article 136 provides that the Hong Kong government will formulate education policies "on its own", and Article 137 provides that educational institutions will "retain their autonomy and enjoy academic freedom". These provisions have been considered by Hong Kong courts in several cases.[25] In

18. Hong Kong also has many privately funded, degree-awarding institutions, but the private sector plays a relatively small role in higher education in the territory. *Ibid.*
19. For example, *see* QS World University Rankings 2020, available at https://www.topuniversities.com/university-rankings/world-university-rankings/2020.
20. *See*, for example, Wai-wan Chan, "Social Capita—A Super Connector for Internationalization and Integration: The Role of Hong Kong Universities in the Development of the Greater Bay Area" (2018) 10 *International Higher Education* 14; and Philip Altbach and Gerald A. Postiglione, "Hong Kong's Academic Advantage" (2012) 66 *International Higher Education* 22.
21. Joint Declaration of the Government of the United Kingdom of Great Britain and Northern Ireland and the Government of the People's Republic of China on the Question of Hong Kong, Instrument A301, available at https://www.elegislation.gov.hk/hk/capA301, especially paras 3(4) and 3(12) (Joint Declaration).
22. *Ibid.*, para 3(5) and Annex I(XIII).
23. *Ibid.*, Annex I(XIII).
24. *Ibid.*, Annex I(X).
25. In addition to the cases discussed below, *see Loh Ming Yin v Hong Kong Examinations and Assessment Authority* [2020] 6 HKC 565 (a challenge to the Education Bureau's invalidation of a history question on the Hong Kong Diploma of Secondary Education Examination); and *Yu Hung Hsua Julie v Chinese University of Hong Kong* [2016] 5 HKLRD 393 (involving a decision by a university panel to change the grades a teacher had originally given her students).

addition, Article 39 of the BL provides that the ICCPR and ICESCR shall remain in force and be implemented through the laws of Hong Kong. As mentioned above, most of the ICCPR's substantive provisions have been directly incorporated in the Bill of Rights Ordinance, a statute that has achieved constitutional status.[26] Hong Kong courts have frequently cited the views of the UN Human Rights Committee (the treaty-monitoring body for the ICCPR) when applying these provisions. As the ICESCR has not been domesticated in the same way as the ICCPR, Hong Kong courts have tended to treat it as more of an "aspirational" treaty and accorded a wide margin of discretion to the government in cases involving socio-economic policy.[27] Nonetheless, the Court of First Instance has favourably cited a General Comment on the right to education issued by the Committee on Economic, Social and Cultural Rights in two cases concerning academic freedom.[28]

Under this legal framework, Hong Kong academics have, thus far, enjoyed far greater freedoms than their colleagues living in mainland China, including a legal right to publish research that is critical of both the local and Central governments. Many Hong Kong academics have also been active in politics and in the local democracy and human rights movements.[29] However, the universities have always had an uncomfortably close relationship with the local government. In the colonial period, the Governor served as the Chancellor of all of the publicly funded universities, and this position was inherited by the Chief Executive of the Hong Kong SAR in 1997. This means that the Chief Executive appoints the external members of university councils and the chairperson of each council, ensuring that both the government and the business community have significant influence over university governance.

The Central Government has also developed ways to influence universities in Hong Kong. This process began during the transition period leading to 1997 when Beijing appointed local university leaders to various bodies. For example, the

26. *See* n 1 above.
27. *See*, for example, *Chan To Foon v Director of Immigration* [2001] 3 HKLRD 109, *Lubiano Nancy Almorin v Director of Immigration* [2020] 5 HKLRD 107; and *GA v Director of Immigration* (2014) 17 HKCFA 60. *See also* Carole J. Petersen, "Embracing Universal Standards? The Role of International Human Rights Treaties in Hong Kong's Constitutional Jurisprudence", in Hualing Fu, Lison Harris, and Simon N. M. Young (eds), *Interpreting Hong Kong's Basic Law: The Struggle for Coherence* (New York: Palgrave Macmillan, 2007), p 33; and Kelley Loper, "Dignity as a Constitutional Value in Hong Kong: Toward a Contextual Approach?", in Chia-Shin Hsu (ed), *Human Dignity in Asia: Dialogue between Law and Culture* (Cambridge: Cambridge University Press, forthcoming).
28. *Secretary for Justice v Commission of Inquiry on Allegations Relating to the Hong Kong Institute of Education* [2009] 4 HKLRD 11, para 64; and *Loh Ming Yin v Hong Kong Examinations and Assessment Authority* [2020] 6 HKC 565, paras 277–279.
29. For examples during the transition leading to 1997, *see* Carole J. Petersen, "Preserving Institutions of Autonomy in Hong Kong: The Impact of 1997 on Academia and the Legal Profession" (1998) 22 *Southern Illinois University Law Journal* 337. For more recent examples, *see* Carole J. Petersen and Alvin Y. H. Cheung, "Academic Freedom and Critical Speech in Hong Kong: China's Response to Occupy Central and the Future of 'One Country, Two Systems'" (2017) 42 *North Carolina Journal of International Law* 665, 697–698.

heads of most of the universities in Hong Kong were appointed to the Preparatory Committee, a body established by the National People's Congress (NPC) in Beijing in 1996. This group was tasked with forming the Provisional Legislative Council and a Selection Committee responsible for choosing the first Chief Executive of Hong Kong, among other responsibilities. This type of "co-option" appeared to be designed to reduce resistance among the academic community.[30] The UGC has also actively encouraged local universities to collaborate with mainland China, without any explicit consideration of the potential threats to academic freedom.[31] The UGC views internationalisation as an indicator of institutional success and it treats "increased engagement with mainland China" as a form of internationalisation. On the surface this makes sense because there is an immigration border between the two jurisdictions. Students from mainland China also pay higher tuition than local Hong Kong students, helping to compensate for reductions in government funding for higher education.[32] However, there is a risk that this dependence on tuition from mainland China will encourage Hong Kong universities to practise self-censorship. Just like the water supply, which comes mainly from sources over the border in Dongjiang, Guangdong Province,[33] the Central Government can stop the flow of students to Hong Kong at any time.

The "Robert Chung affair" demonstrated the dangers of these links between universities and the local and Central governments. In 2000, Dr Chung alleged that HKU's Vice-Chancellor had sent him a message (through a Pro-Vice-Chancellor) urging him to stop a public opinion research project because it had displeased Tung Chee-hwa, the first Chief Executive of the Hong Kong SAR. The Vice-Chancellor denied the allegation, compelling HKU's Council to establish an Independent Investigation Panel. After conducting public hearings, the Panel produced a detailed report confirming that Andrew Lo, an assistant to Tung Chee-hwa, had visited HKU's Vice-Chancellor to complain about Chung's research project and that the Vice-Chancellor had subsequently sent a message to Dr Chung that was "calculated to inhibit" his right to academic freedom.[34] The report also found that the Vice-Chancellor and Andrew Lo were less than truthful in their testimony. Tung Chee-hwa responded by publicly defending his assistant. This placed the chairman

30. Wing-wah Law, "The Accommodation and Resistance to the Decolonisation, Neocolonisation and Recolonisation of Higher Education in Hong Kong" (1997) 33(2) *Comparative Education* 187.
31. Hong Kong University Grants Committee, "Internationalisation and Engagement with Mainland China", available at https://www.ugc.edu.hk/eng/ugc/faq/q6.html.
32. William Yat Wai Lo and Felix Sai Kit Ng, "A Critical Reflection on Internationalization of Higher Education in Hong Kong: The Search for a Cosmopolitan Alternative" (2013) 2(1) *Asia-Pacific Journal of Educational Development* 37.
33. Government of the Hong Kong SAR, "Hong Kong: The Facts: Water Supplies", available at https://www.wsd.gov.hk/en/publications-and-statistics/pr-publications/the-facts/index.html.
34. The University of Hong Kong Investigation Panel, "Report to the Council of the University of Hong Kong by the Independent Investigation Panel", 26 August 2000, available at https://archive.is/20130430085147/http://jmsc.hku.hk/HKUPanel/transcripts/Report/PollHearing_Report_01.htm.

of HKU's Council, Sir T. L. Yang, in an awkward position because he was simultaneously serving as a member of Tung Chee-hwa's Executive Council (Hong Kong's equivalent of a cabinet). Recognising that Sir T. L. Yang would be reluctant to take any action that would embarrass Tung Chee-hwa, more than half of the academics at HKU signed a petition asking the Council to accept the Investigation Panel's report. Eventually, the Vice-Chancellor resigned, saving the Council from having to take any formal action. Instead, the Council simply noted the Investigation Panel's conclusions regarding the HKU employees and carefully distanced itself from any findings relating to the Chief Executive or his assistant.

In some respects, the Robert Chung affair was a victory for academic freedom because an academic had the courage to complain about interference and was vindicated. However, the links between HKU's Council and the local government weakened the Council's response.[35] In the aftermath of the Robert Chung incident, HKU created the Senate Task Force on Academic Freedom, which received submissions from students and faculty. The Task Force reported that "a number of members of this university have felt that their academic freedoms have been infringed" and recommended reforms, including the adoption of a working definition of academic freedom and the establishment of a proper mechanism to deal with complaints of infringement.[36] Although HKU posted an academic freedom policy on its website, the university did not take up most of these proposals and took no steps to reduce the government's role in its governance.

Indeed, after the Robert Chung incident, HKU and other universities in Hong Kong became even more vulnerable to external pressures. This is partly due to the 2002 "Sutherland Report" which concluded that Hong Kong's traditional universities were distributing power among too many bodies and using outmoded systems of governance, including deans elected by members of their faculties.[37] Following publication of this report, universities were encouraged to conduct internal management reviews. In theory, each institution was allowed to make its own decisions. In practice, the UGC expected universities to embrace the Sutherland Report's recommendations. As a result, deans are now all appointed, power is more centralised, and university councils are more dominated by external members. In a previous study of academic freedom in Hong Kong, many interviewees predicted that these changes to university governance would undermine academic freedom.[38]

35. For further details, *see* Carole J. Petersen, "Preserving Academic Freedom: Lessons from the Robert Chung Affair" (2000) 30 *Hong Kong Law Journal* 165.
36. University of Hong Kong, "Academic Freedom Policy", available at https://www.hku.hk/about/policies_reports/acad_freedom.html.
37. Stewart R. Sutherland, "Report of the University Grants Committee Commissioned by the Secretary for Education and Manpower", March 2002, available at https://www.legco.gov.hk/yr01-02/english/panels/ed/papers/ed0326-ugc-report-e.pdf.
38. Currie, Petersen, and Mok, n 2 above, p 153.

Meanwhile, the incentives for the Hong Kong government to interfere have also increased. As a result of the delays in introducing democratic reforms, the appointed local government has little or no mandate from the Hong Kong people. This naturally makes government officials more sensitive to criticism and the academic community is often the source of that criticism. An early example was the Hong Kong government's first attempt to implement Article 23 of the BL in 2002–2003. Article 23 mandates that Hong Kong enact "on its own" laws prohibiting offences related to national security. Academics played a significant role in critiquing that legislation, and it was withdrawn after a huge protest march on 1 July 2003.[39] Academics have also clashed with the government regarding proposals for education reforms. In 2007, it was alleged that high-level officials tried to silence this criticism by putting improper pressure on the Hong Kong Institute of Education.[40] A Commission of Inquiry determined that Mrs Fanny Law (the Permanent Secretary for Education at the time) had contacted the Vice-Chancellor of the Institute on at least four occasions to seek his assistance in curbing criticisms made by members of his faculty. The Commission concluded that these complaints constituted improper interference with the academics' right to academic freedom.[41] The Commission also found that the Permanent Secretary acted improperly when she telephoned one of the academics directly to remonstrate him regarding his criticisms. This particular finding led to an application for judicial review by the government. The Court of First Instance agreed with the government that in the absence of a threat, mere discussions between a government official and an individual academic, even if heated, would not violate academic freedom. However, it also affirmed that Article 137 of the BL (which provides constitutional protection for academic freedom) extends to the faculty as well as to the educational institution.[42]

Conflicts also arose when Hong Kong's Education Bureau suggested that local students needed to develop greater national identity and "affection" for the country.[43] Many Hong Kong residents viewed the suggested introduction of a "Moral and National Education" curriculum as a form of brainwashing and large-scale protests were organised to oppose it. The movement attracted significant international

39. For details *see* Carole J. Petersen, "Hong Kong's Spring of Discontent: The Rise and Fall of the National Security Bill in 2003", in Hualing Fu, Carole J. Petersen, and Simon N. M. Young (eds), *National Security and Fundamental Freedoms: Hong Kong's Article 23 under Scrutiny* (Hong Kong: Hong Kong University Press, 2005), p 17.

40. The Institute has since been retitled as the Education University of Hong Kong.

41. Yeung Chun Kuen and Lee Jark Pui, "Report of the Commission of Inquiry on Allegations Relating to the Hong Kong Institute of Education", June 2007, at Summary of Findings and Conclusions, available at https://www.gov.hk/en/residents/government/policy/government_reports/reports/docs/HKIEd.pdf.

42. *Secretary for Justice v Commission of Inquiry on Allegations Relating to the Hong Kong Institute of Education* [2009] 4 HKLRD 11, para 156.

43. Curriculum Development Council, "Moral and National Education Teaching Guide, Primary 1 to Secondary 6, April 2012", April 2012, available at https://www.edb.gov.hk/attachment/en/curriculum-development/moral-national-edu/MNE%20Guide%20(ENG)%20Final_remark_09102012.pdf.

attention and generated a crisis for Hong Kong's third Chief Executive, C. Y. Leung.[44] The proposal was ultimately withdrawn, but the underlying assumption—that Hong Kong's education system has not been sufficiently patriotic—has persisted.

In 2014, Occupy Central (which later became known as the "Umbrella Movement") further heightened the conflicts between the government and the academic community. Although people from all walks of life participated in the movement, two of the three original proponents were academics (Benny Tai, an Associate Professor in HKU's Law Faculty, and Professor Chan Kin-man, a sociologist from the Chinese University of Hong Kong). Tai widely published his theory that the threat of a sustained campaign of "civil disobedience" would help to persuade Beijing to allow Hong Kong to elect its Chief Executive through universal suffrage.[45] However, the actual occupation of the streets not far from the central business district and government buildings was launched by university students who protested against the NPC's Decision of 31 August 2014 (which appeared to rule out any significant changes to the process of selecting Hong Kong's Chief Executive).[46] The occupation was entirely peaceful, but it blocked traffic in downtown Hong Kong for more than three months and was ultimately unsuccessful. Indeed, Hong Kong became even less democratic after Occupy Central, initially due to a campaign to disqualify prodemocracy legislators that began after Occupy Central.[47]

In the aftermath of Occupy Central, Beijing and its supporters also embarked on a campaign of retribution against its perceived political enemies in the academic community, including Benny Tai and other prominent academics.[48] One well-known example is the smear campaign against Professor Johannes Chan, who played no role in Occupy Central but was Benny Tai's Dean when Tai began promoting his ideas. When Chan was unanimously selected by the Search Committee for the position of Vice President at HKU, he was vilified in the pro-Beijing media for failing to stop Tai from participating in Occupy Central.[49] Ultimately, HKU's Council did

---

44. *See* Petersen and Cheung, n 29 above, pp 697–698.
45. Benny Tai, "Civil Disobedience as a Weapon of Mass Destruction" (in Chinese), *Hong Kong Economic Journal*, 16 January 2013, cited in Karen Kong, "Human Rights Activist Scholars and Social Change in Hong Kong: Reflections on the Umbrella Movement and Beyond" (2019) 23(6) *The International Journal of Human Rights Law* 899.
46. Petersen and Cheung, n 29 above, pp 702–704. For the text of the Decision, *see* Government of the Hong Kong SAR, "Decision and Explanations of the NPCSC", available at http://www.2017.gov.hk/en/decision/index.html.
47. "Explainer: How and Why Hong Kong's Legislative Opposition Ground to a Halt", *Hong Kong Free Press*, 12 November 2020, available at https://hongkongfp.com/2020/11/12/explainer-how-and-why-hong-kongs-legislative-opposition-ground-to-a-halt/. Subsequently, in 2021, Beijing announced an overhaul of the local political system to ensure that only "patriots" can serve in the Legislative Council. For a summary, *see* John Burns, "Hong Kong's Electoral Changes: The Communist Party Is Taking Over", *Hong Kong Free Press*, 10 April 2021.
48. Petersen and Cheung, n 29 above, pp 704–716. *See also* Burns, n 17 above.
49. For details, *see* Johannes M. M. Chan and Douglas Kerr, "Academic Freedom, Political Interference, and Public Accountability: The Hong Kong Experience" (2016) 7 *AAUP Journal of Academic Freedom*, available at https://www.aaup.org/sites/default/files/ChanKerr.pdf.

not confirm his appointment.[50] HKU also later fired Benny Tai as a direct result of his role in Occupy Central.[51] Numerous other academics reported that their email accounts were hacked or that they were subjected to politically motivated harassment after Occupy Central.[52]

The conflicts between the universities and the government reached a boiling point in 2019 during the protests against the government's proposal to allow "case by case" extradition, including to mainland China.[53] There is no formal rendition agreement between Hong Kong and mainland China and immigration matters fall within the scope of Hong Kong's autonomy.[54] The sheer number of protesters created a crisis for the government, with an estimated two million people taking to the streets on 16 June 2019. Initially the protests were peaceful and sought only the formal withdrawal of the Extradition Bill. However, by the time the government withdrew the Bill (in late October of 2019) the protesters were frustrated and making more demands, including an independent investigation into alleged police brutality, the resignation of the Chief Executive, and democratic reforms. The government did not try to negotiate but rather depended entirely on the local police to put down the movement. There were thousands of arrests and increasingly violent clashes between protesters and police. [55] Some of the worst battles occurred on university campuses.[56] Many Hong Kong students (not only university students but also high school students) were injured or arrested when the police finally regained control.

The turmoil of 2019 may explain why Hong Kong's university leaders did not object when Beijing announced, in May 2020, that it would impose a new national security law on Hong Kong.[57] In early June, all of the governing councils of the eight

50. A judicial review application challenging the decision (partly on the basis of Art 137 of the BL) failed because the position had been filled with another candidate by that time, rendering the issue moot. *See Li Fung Kei v Council of University of Hong* [2018] 4 HKC 231, paras 25–30, 36.

51. *See* Emma Graham-Harris and Patrick Wintour, "Prominent Hong Kong Professor and Pro-Democracy Activist Fired by University", 28 July 2020, *The Guardian*, available at https://www.theguardian.com/world/2020/jul/28/benny-tai-university-of-hong-kong-fired.

52. Petersen and Cheung, n 29 above, pp 714–716.

53. For a discussion of the 2019 protest movement, *see*, for example, Kong, n 45 above; and Cora Chan, "Demise of 'One Country, Two Systems'? Reflections on the Hong Kong Rendition Saga" (2019) 49 *Hong Kong Law Journal* 447.

54. BL, Art 154.

55. In light of the millions of people involved, proposals for a general amnesty were discussed but ultimately rejected. For details, *see* Anna Dziedzic and Julius Yam, "Amnesty for Street Protesters" (2020) 50 *Hong Kong Law Journal* 585 and other articles in that issue.

56. For videos of battles between police and students on campuses, *see* K. K. Rebecca Lai, "How Universities Became the New Battlegrounds in Hong Kong's Protests", *New York Times*, 19 November 2019, available at https://www.nytimes.com/interactive/2019/11/18/world/asia/hong-kong-protest-universities.html.

57. *See* Chan Ho-him, "Councils of Eight Universities in Hong Kong Back New Security Law", *South China Morning Post*, 1 June 2020, available at https://www.scmp.com/news/hong-kong/education/article/3086955/five-hong-kong-university-heads-cite-stability-supporting.

publicly funded universities and five university presidents expressed support for the introduction of a new law protecting national security.[58] However, like other residents of Hong Kong, these university leaders had no opportunity to read the NSL until the night of 30 June 2020, when it was brought into force. When the NSL was finally published, many lawyers were surprised at the broad definitions of the criminal offences, the far-reaching powers of the new security agencies, and the extraterritorial reach of the law.[59] As demonstrated in the next section, it will be challenging for universities to comply with the new law while also maintaining academic freedom and fulfilling Hong Kong's overriding obligations under the ICCPR and the ICESCR. However, we argue that Hong Kong academics and university leaders can rise to this challenge if (1) universities draft robust policies that protect academic freedom, drawing upon international jurisprudence; and (2) the local government fulfils its constitutional duties under BL Articles 34 and 137 and does not abuse its new powers under the NSL.

III. Interpreting the NSL to Preserve Academic Freedom

(a) General Principles

Before reviewing the new criminal offences in the NSL, a few preliminary points are needed. First, Article 9 obligates the Hong Kong government to strengthen its regulation of matters concerning national security, including in schools and universities. Article 10 further directs the local government to promote national security education in schools and universities. These provisions have already been used by various branches of the Hong Kong government to increase interference in educational institutions. Within days of the enactment of the NSL, the Education Bureau directed libraries to remove books that might violate the NSL.[60] Authorities have also disciplined more than 150 primary and secondary school teachers—and have even deregistered four teachers for life—for involvement in anti-government protests in 2019 and other activities deemed as "defaming the nation".[61] The Chief Executive

58. *Ibid.*
59. *See*, for example, Elson Tong, "'Worse than the Worst-Case Scenario': Lawyers Dismayed at Hong Kong National Security Law", *Hong Kong Free Press*, 2 July 2020; and Carole J. Petersen, "The Disappearing Firewall: International Consequences of Beijing's Decision to Impose a National Security Law and Operate National Security Institutions in Hong Kong" (2020) 50 *Hong Kong Law Journal* 633.
60. *See* Chan Ho-him, "National Security Law: Hong Kong Schools Told to Remove Books that Might Fall Foul of the Legislation", *South China Morning Post*, 6 July 2020, available at https://www.scmp.com/news/hong-kong/education/article/3092043/national-security-law-hong-kong-schools-told-remove-books.
61. *See* Chan Ho-him, "Hong Kong Visual Arts Teacher Facing Disciplinary Action over 'Inappropriate' Political Cartoons Shared Online", *South China Morning Post*, 30 April 2021, available at https://www.scmp.com/news/hong-kong/education/article/3131831/hong-kong-visual-arts-teacher-facing-disciplinary-action, and Chan Ho-him, "Two More Hong Kong Teachers Deregistered for Life, One for 'Defaming The Nation' and the Other for a Protest-Related Crime", *South China Morning Post*, 30 April 2021, available at https://www.scmp.com/news/hong-kong/education/article/3131821/two-more-hong-kong-teachers-deregistered-life-one-defaming.

made it clear, in her 2020 Policy Address, that the local government intends to implement "moral and national education" in the schools and to exert more control over curriculum and assessment in secondary schools.[62] In February 2021, the government issued "guidelines and curriculum arrangements for safeguarding national security and national security education", and it has since introduced further guidance for the integration of national security education across several secondary school subjects.[63] A controversial "liberal studies" subject, which some government supporters had blamed for radicalising students, has been revamped and renamed "citizenship and social development".[64] Other events include the introduction of a controversial National Security Education Day on 15 April 2021[65] and arrests of students who protested at a graduation ceremony at the Chinese University of Hong Kong in November 2020.[66] Two universities have recently cut support for their student unions due to "inflammatory and potentially unlawful public statements"[67] and recent reports suggest frustration among some academic staff in Hong Kong

62. *See* Chief Executive's 2020 Policy Address, paras 152–154, available at https://www.policyaddress.gov.hk/2020/eng/p152.html. The Chief Executive singled out the Hong Kong Examinations and Assessment Authority for criticism, citing the government's decision to disregard the answers to a controversial question on a public examination. China's Foreign Ministry had strongly criticised the question, arguing that it was biased and would injure the feelings of the Chinese people. *See* Karen Zhang, Chris Lau, and Kimmy Chung, "How a History Question Stirred up Controversy over China, Japan, and Hong Kong's Education System", *South China Morning Post*, 16 May 2020, available at https://www.scmp.com/news/hong-kong/education/article/3084674/how-history-exam-question-stirred-controversy-over-china.
63. *See* The Government of the Hong Kong Special Administrative Region, "EDB Announces Guidelines and Curriculum Arrangements for Safeguarding National Security and National Security Education", 4 February 2021, available at https://www.info.gov.hk/gia/general/202102/04/P2021020400806.htm; *see also* Chan Ho-him, "National Education to Be Stepped up on 'All Fronts' for Hong Kong's Youth, Carrie Lam Vows, after Admitting 'Deficiencies' in Current System", *South China Morning Post*, 28 April 2021, available at https://www.scmp.com/news/hong-kong/education/article/3131485/national-education-be-stepped-all-fronts-hong-kongs-youth.
64. *Ibid.* (Chan Ho-him).
65. Tony Cheung and Natalie Wong, "Hong Kong Marks National Security Education Day with Anti-Terrorism Drills, Weapons Displays for Students as Top Official Urges Resolve in Defending 'Bottom Line,'" *South China Morning Post*, 15 April 2021, available at https://www.scmp.com/news/hong-kong/politics/article/3129602/hong-kong-must-show-resolve-defending-bottom-line-national.
66. Clifford Lo and Phila Siu, "Hong Kong National Security Police Unit Puts University Campus in Cross Hairs with Arrest of Three Students over Rally", *South China Morning Post*, 7 December 2020, available at https://www.scmp.com/news/hong-kong/law-and-crime/article/3112821/hong-kong-graduate-arrested-over-chinese-university; and Rhoda Kwan, "Security Law: Hong Kong Police Arrest Another CUHK Student over Peaceful Pro-Democracy Campus Demo Last Nov", *Hong Kong Free Press*, 19 February 2021, available at https://hongkongfp.com/2021/02/19/security-law-hong-kong-police-arrest-another-cuhk-student-over-peaceful-pro-democracy-campus-demo-last-nov/.
67. Emily Tsang and Danny Mok, "Hong Kong National Security Law: Chinese University Cuts Ties with Student Union, Accuses Body of 'Exploiting' Campus, Bringing School into 'Disrepute,'" *South China Morning Post*, 25 February 2021, available at https://www.scmp.com/news/hong-kong/education/article/3123175/hong-kong-national-security-law-chinese-university-cuts; and Chan Ho-him, "University of Hong Kong Cuts off Services to Student Union over Accusations It Spread 'Propaganda' on Campus", *South China Morning Post*, 30 April 2021, available at https://www.scmp.com/news/hong-kong/politics/article/3131764/university-hong-kong-cuts-services-student-union-over.

regarding the lack of support from their universities since the introduction of the NSL.[68]

On the other hand, the Hong Kong government has also reaffirmed the right to academic freedom (at least in tertiary education), stating that the "specific safeguards of academic freedom and institutional autonomy enshrined in Articles 34 and 137 of the Basic Law remain in full force".[69] In our view, this interpretation of the relationship between the NSL and rights stated in the BL is correct. Indeed, Article 4 of the NSL expressly provides for the continued enforcement of the rights that Hong Kong residents have enjoyed under the BL, including freedom of expression and publication and, in particular, for the continued application of the ICCPR and ICESCR. Article 5 of the NSL further mandates adherence to the rule of law and the principle of legality "in preventing, suppressing, and imposing punishment for offenses endangering national security". It also provides that "[a] person is presumed innocent until convicted by a judicial body. The right to defend himself or herself and other rights in judicial proceedings that a criminal suspect, defendant, and other parties in judicial proceedings are entitled to under the law shall be protected. No one shall be liable to be tried or punished again for an offense for which he or she has already been finally convicted or acquitted in judicial proceedings."

The Court of Final Appeal (CFA) affirmed the significance of Articles 4 and 5 in its first NSL-related decision in February 2021. In *HKSAR v Lai Chee Ying*,[70] the government appealed a lower court decision[71] which had granted bail to Jimmy Lai, a prominent media mogul and pro-democracy activist in Hong Kong charged with national security offences, among other crimes.[72] The CFA was asked to interpret Article 42(2) of the NSL which provides: "No bail shall be granted to a criminal suspect or defendant unless the judge has sufficient grounds for believing that the criminal suspect or defendant will not continue to commit acts endangering national security." In doing so, the court held that Article 42(2) is a specific exception to the ordinary bail regime in Hong Kong, including the presumption of bail, and requires judges to adopt a more stringent standard when considering bail applications in national security cases. This decision departed from an earlier, more liberal interpretation of Article 42(2) by the Court of First Instance in *Tong Ying Kit*

68. Timothy McLaughlin, "How Academic Freedom Ends", *The Atlantic*, 6 June 2021.
69. *See* Government of the Hong Kong Special Administrative Region, "EDB's Clarifications Regarding Inaccurate Media Report on University Exchange", 22 December 2020, available at https://www.info.gov.hk/gia/general/202012/22/P2020122200792.htm?fontSize=1. The government issued this statement to correct what it claimed were inaccurate media reports that it might seek to curtail university exchange programmes between Hong Kong and Taiwan.
70. [2021] HKCFA 3.
71. *HKSAR v Lai Chee Ying* [2020] HKCFI 3161.
72. *See* the discussion below on Article 29 of the NSL which prohibits "collusion with foreign elements".

v HKSAR.[73] However, the CFA also explained that Articles 4 and 5 are "centrally important to the interpretation of the NSL" and stated:

> that is not at all to say that human rights and freedoms and rule of law values are inapplicable. On the contrary, NSL 4 and NSL 5 expressly stipulate that those rights, freedoms and values are to be protected and adhered to in applying the NSL. They provide the context in which NSL 42(2) must be construed and applied. As far as possible, NSL 42(2) is to be given a meaning and effect compatible with those rights, freedoms and values. Save insofar as NSL 42(2) constitutes a specific exception thereto, that corpus of law, comprising not only the human rights and rule of law principles but also the generally applicable HKSAR rules governing the grant or refusal of bail is intended to have continued effect in NSL cases.[74]

Therefore, although the Hong Kong courts must enforce the express provisions of the NSL, they should still try to interpret any vague clauses so as to comply with Articles 4 and 5.[75] In particular, ambiguous language in the definitions of the new criminal offences should be interpreted to comply with Article 19 of the ICCPR, which permits restrictions on freedom of expression in the name of national security but only to the extent that they are necessary and proportionate. As mentioned above, Article 19 has particular relevance for academic freedom, and it is replicated in Article 16 of the Hong Kong Bill of Rights. In a General Comment on the right to freedom of opinion and expression, the Human Rights Committee explained that the scope of expression protected by this provision is broad and includes "the expression and receipt of communications of every form of idea and opinion capable of transmission to others".[76] This might include "political discourse, commentary . . . on public affairs . . . discussion of human rights, journalism, cultural and artistic expression, teaching, and religious discourse" and "embraces even expression that may be regarded as deeply offensive".[77] The modes and means of expression include published writing and the internet, among others.[78] This breadth certainly encompasses the educational and research activities that universities and scholars pursue.

Although, as mentioned, the ICCPR allows freedom of expression to be restricted for certain legitimate purposes, including national security,[79] a govern-

73. [2020] HKCFI 2133. The CFI had rejected the argument that Article 42(2) departed from the usual criteria to apply when determining whether to grant bail. Tong Ying Kit was ultimately convicted by the Court of First Instance which failed to use the ICCPR as a guide to interpreting the NSL. *See* Carole J. Petersen, "Hong Kong's First Conviction for Incitement to Secession: What Role for the International Covenant on Civil and Political Rights?", (2021) 25 *ASIL Insights* (American Society of International Law), available at: https://www.asil.org/insights/volume/25/issue/22.
74. *See* n 70 above, para 41.
75. *See also* Po Jen Yap, "Judging Hong Kong's National Security Law", Chapter 7 of this volume.
76. UN Human Rights Committee, General Comment 34, Article 19, Freedoms of Opinion and Expression, 12 September 2011, CCPR/C/GC/34, para 11.
77. *Ibid.*
78. *Ibid.*
79. ICCPR, Art 19(3).

ment bound by the treaty cannot simply invoke "national security" as a justification for suppressing information of legitimate public interest. Because there is a presumption of freedom, governments must demonstrate specifically the precise nature of the threat posed to national security.[80] Any restrictions adopted in the name of national security "must be appropriate to achieving" the "protective function", the least intrusive option, and "proportionate to the interest to be protected".[81] Hong Kong courts have developed a similar proportionality test, based on these standards, in cases involving freedom of expression.[82]

The Hong Kong courts' past use of these materials in human rights cases provides a foundation for their future application, not only in court but also in the drafting of university policies on academic freedom.[83] As demonstrated below, it is important that the vaguely defined offences in the NSL be interpreted in a manner that fully complies with both the ICCPR and the ICESCR.

(b) Secession: Articles 20 and 21 of the NSL

An example of vague language in the NSL is the offence of "secession" and the related inchoate offences. Article 20 provides:

> A person who organizes, plans, commits or participates in any of the following acts, whether or not by force or threat of force, with a view to committing secession or undermining national unification shall be guilty of an offence:
>
> (1) separating the Hong Kong Special Administrative Region or any other part of the People's Republic of China from the People's Republic of China;
> (2) altering by unlawful means the legal status of the Hong Kong Special Administrative Region or of any other part of the People's Republic of China; or
> (3) surrendering Hong Kong or any part of China to a foreign country.

This definition is broader than the definition of secession proposed in 2003, when the government first attempted to implement Article 23 of the BL, because it does not require force or threat of force.[84] The phrase "with a view to . . . undermining national unification" is also extremely vague. One can understand why

80. *See Tae-Hoon Park v Republic of Korea*, Communication No. 628/1995 (UN Human Rights Committee, 1998), para 10.3, available at https://www.refworld.org/cases,HRC,3f588effe.html.
81. General Comment 34, n 76 above, para 34, citing Human Rights Committee, General Comment 27.
82. *See*, for example, *HKSAR v Ng Kung Siu* (1999) 2 HKCFAR 442 (concerning flag desecration); and *HKSAR v Fong Kwok Shan Christine* (2017) 20 HKCFAR 425.
83. The Court of Final Appeal has indicated, however, that certain treaty body materials, such as Concluding Observations on states parties' reports, are not "binding" and General Comments may not provide sufficient reasoning for determining the issue at hand. *See ZN v Secretary for Justice & Ors* (2020) 23 HKCFAR 15.
84. For analysis of the definition of secession proposed in 2003 and its relationship to other offences in that bill, *see* Kelley Loper, "A Secession Offence in Hong Kong and the 'One Country, Two Systems' Dilemma", in Fu, Petersen, and Young, n 39 above, Ch 6.

academics might be nervous regarding publications or lectures that discuss controversial topics, such as the right to self-determination under international law, independence movements around the world, or China's many territorial disputes. However, under Article 20, the prosecution would need to prove that the defendant organised, planned, committed, or participated in one of the three specified acts (1) separating territory; (2) altering by unlawful means the legal status of territory; or (3) surrendering territory to a foreign country. In our view, delivering a lecture, publishing an academic article, or leading a class on one of these topics would not contravene Article 20, unless the prosecution could prove that the academic's activities were part of some plan to actually deprive the People's Republic of China (PRC) of its territory. We believe that a Hong Kong court would agree, because the new criminal offences should be interpreted (pursuant to Article 4 of the NSL) in a manner that complies with the ICCPR and the ICESCR. However, the local courts may never have the opportunity to try a case with these facts. Thus, it is important for university leadership (and the local and Central governments) to make it clear that they will also interpret Article 20 in a manner that fully complies with the ICCPR and the ICESCR, so as to reassure academics that there is no need to practise self-censorship in the course of normal academic activities.

Of course, one can imagine an extreme situation in which an academic publication might lead to a prosecution under Article 20. For example, if a group of academics drafted, published, and distributed a proposed constitution for the "independent state of Hong Kong", then that might provide evidence of a plan to separate Hong Kong from the PRC. Alternatively, such a publication might fall within the scope of Article 21, which provides that a person who "incites, assists in, abets or provides pecuniary or other financial assistance or property for the commission by other persons of the offence under Article 20" shall also be guilty of an offence. But there is a clear difference between this kind of publication and a typical academic publication, which would be well outside the scope of Articles 20 and 21.

Lectures and classroom discussions of controversial topics should be protected in a similar manner. For example, courses on international human rights law generally include analysis of the right to self-determination under international law (as it was central to the decolonisation project of the United Nations and is provided in Article 1 of both the ICCPR and the ICESCR). Human rights courses also commonly include the concept of "remedial secession" as a remedy for extreme violations of human rights. Discussion of such topics should not be treated as a violation of Articles 20 or 21 of the NSL unless the prosecution could prove that a teacher was deliberately teaching these topics to recruit students to help her or him deprive the PRC of its territory, through one of the three acts specified in Article 20. Once again, it is important to reassure academics that they can continue to teach such topics; otherwise, there is a real danger that academics will practise self-censorship in the classroom, which would effectively deprive students of their right to education under Article 13 of the ICESCR.

Unfortunately, there are signs that the Hong Kong government is doing the opposite and attempting to shut down discussions of controversial issues. The Education Bureau recently cancelled the registration of a schoolteacher on the ground that he designed lesson plans on the subject of independence. The Secretary for Education maintained that independence for Hong Kong is not open for discussion; if students raise the issue, then teachers should simply "help them to understand that the HKSAR is an inalienable part" of the PRC and "promote students' sense of national identity".[85] When asked whether such a policy infringes on academic freedom, the Secretary claimed that it had "nothing to do with academic freedom" because teachers "should never spread incorrect values or law-breaking concepts to students on the pretext" of academic freedom. Of course, the Secretary was speaking about public primary and secondary schools, and he has no power to set curriculum at the university level. Nonetheless, his comments regarding the scope of academic freedom are worrying.

(c) Subversion: Articles 22 and 23 of the NSL

The new offence of "subversion" also needs to be interpreted in a manner that complies with the ICCPR and the ICESCR. The list of prohibited acts in Article 22 is rather vague (including not only "overthrowing" the government but also "undermining the basic system" of the PRC and "seriously interfering in, disrupting, or undermining the performance of duties and functions" of the local and Central governments). This is worrying because academics regularly produce research that is critical of government policies and proposals, and government officials often resent this criticism. One can imagine a scenario in which the local or Central Government might allege that vigorous academic criticism of its actions or policies has seriously "disrupted" the performance of the government's duties and functions. For example, in September 2020, academics specialising in epidemiology and microbiology issued statements critiquing the local government's testing scheme for COVID-19. The Chief Executive, Carrie Lam, reacted strongly to these criticisms, perhaps because the testing programme was being conducted with significant assistance from mainland China. It is important to note that Lam did not just disagree with the scientists' analysis of the scheme. Rather she attacked their motivations, claiming that the "so-called experts" were deliberately "smearing" the Central Government and trying to "sever Hong Kong's relations" with it.[86] Lam's

85. *See* Government of the Hong Kong SAR, "Reply of the Secretary for Education to Question by Dr Helena Wong, LCQS", 28 October 2020, available at https://www.info.gov.hk/gia/general/202010/28/P2020102800515.htm.
86. Rachel Wong, "Covid-19: Carrie Lam Says Critics of City-Wide Testing Projects Are 'Smearing' and Trying to Damage Hong Kong-China Relations", *Hong Kong Free Press*, 25 August 2020, available at https://hongkongfp.com/2020/08/25/covid-19-carrie-lam-says-critics-of-city-wide-testing-project-are-smearing-and-trying-to-damage-hong-kong-china-relations/.

strong statements could easily have a chilling effect on academic commentary, particularly as she made her comments only two months after the enactment of the NSL. It is important to realise that it is not only the individual academics who suffer if such commentary is stifled; rather, society at large could suffer injury. The UN Committee on Economic, Social and Cultural Rights has recognised this important connection between academic freedom and society's right to enjoy the benefits of academic research.[87]

Fortunately, Article 22 also requires the prosecution to prove that the defendant organised, planned, committed, or participated in one of the prohibited acts "by force or threat of force or other unlawful means with a view to subverting the State power". In this respect, Article 22 is significantly narrower than the definition of secession in Article 20. It is therefore important that universities resist any suggestion that Article 22 restricts academic research and commentary, even when it makes it more challenging for the Hong Kong government to implement one or more of its proposed policies. Similarly, Article 23 (which prohibits a person from providing assistance for acts that are prohibited under Article 22) should not be interpreted as criminalising individuals who fund or otherwise assist research that is critical of the local or Central governments.

(d) Collusion with Foreign Elements: Article 29 of the NSL

In our view, Article 29, which defines "collusion with a foreign country or with external elements to endanger national security", has the greatest potential to chill academic research, particularly where it involves researchers or research funding from overseas. Article 29 provides, in relevant part, that a person shall be guilty of an offence if s/he "directly or indirectly receives instructions, control, funding or other kinds of support from a foreign country or an institution, organization or individual outside mainland China, Hong Kong, and Macao of the People's Republic of China, to commit any one of" a long list of prohibited acts.

Granted, the list of prohibited acts includes some typical national security offences (such as waging war against the PRC, which was already prohibited in Hong Kong as a form of treason). However, Article 29 also includes a number of vaguely defined acts, such as foreign sanctions or "other hostile activities" and "seriously disrupting the formulation and implementation of laws or policies by the Government of the Hong Kong Special Administrative Region or by the Central People's Government, which is likely to cause serious consequences". It is important that provisions like this be interpreted narrowly. Otherwise, there is a risk of criminalising transnational academic research that is critical of either the Hong Kong or Central governments.

87. *See* Committee on Economic, Social and Cultural Rights, n 6 above.

The ongoing prosecution of Jimmy Lai, as discussed above, is an example of how critical commentary might expose a person to prosecution. Lai has been charged, pursuant to Article 29(4) of the NSL, with requesting a foreign government to impose sanctions or other "hostile activities" against Hong Kong or mainland China. When considering Lai's application for bail, Judge Lee noted that Lai did not appear to have made any explicit requests for sanctions after the NSL came into force. Rather, the two statements relied upon by the prosecution "on their face appear to be comments and criticisms rather than requests".[88] The prosecution argued that the Court could infer that Lai's critical statements were "requests in disguise".[89] However, the Court concluded that Lai's position (that he had made no actual request for sanctions) was "on its face arguable" and initially granted bail, albeit with strict conditions.[90] Although Lai is not an academic, the ultimate outcome of this case (and charges that have been filed against journalists who worked at *Apple Daily*)[91] could have significant implications for academic freedom because it will provide insight into how the Hong Kong courts are likely to interpret Article 29.

The vague language used in Article 29 is particularly worrying in light of the extraterritorial provisions of the NSL (contained in Articles 35–38).[92] In short, anyone, regardless of nationality or residency, can be prosecuted for acts that are committed in Hong Kong. Moreover, the NSL deems an act to have been committed in Hong Kong as long as the consequences are felt in the territory.[93] When these provisions are combined with the language in Article 29, one can understand why foreign academics may be reluctant to participate in certain conferences and research projects based at Hong Kong universities—or even to publish an article that is critical of the Hong Kong or Central governments.[94] This demonstrates why it is so important for Hong Kong universities to develop policy documents and procedures that fully comply with the BL, the ICCPR, and the ICESCR.

---

88. *HKSAR v Lai Chee Ying* [2021] 1 HKC 331, para 19.
89. *Ibid.*
90. *Ibid.*, paras 19 and 35. Jimmy Lai was, however, returned to jail after the prosecution sought leave from the CFA to appeal the decision to grant bail. *HKSAR v Lai Chee Ying* [2021] HKCFA 45, paras 20 and 33. As discussed above, the CFA eventually determined that Judge Lee misapplied NSL Article 42(2) and erred in his approach to bail.
91. *See* Candace Chau, "Security Law: Ex-Apple Daily Editorial Writer Arrested at Hong Kong Airport amid Reported Ultimatum to Defunct Paper", *Hong Kong Free Press*, 28 June 2021.
92. The extraterritorial application of the NSL is analysed in greater depth in Bing Ling, "Extraterritorial Application of the Hong Kong National Security Law: A Legal Appraisal", Chapter 11 of this volume.
93. NSL, Art 36.
94. *See*, for example, Association for Asian Studies, "Statement on the 2020 Hong Kong National Security Law", 10 July 2020, available at https://www.asianstudies.org/aas-statement-on-the-2020-hong-kong-national-security-law/; and Nikkei Asia, "Hong Kong Security Law Spurs Fears over Academic Freedom: Overseas Scholars and Students Shun Territory's Universities", 10 September 2020, available at https://asia.nikkei.com/Business/Education/Hong-Kong-security-law-spurs-fears-over-academic-freedom.

IV. Conclusions and Suggested Language for University Policies

Interviews and surveys conducted in the early years following the handover revealed that most Hong Kong academics cherish academic freedom and educational autonomy. Many interviewees were also acutely aware of how challenging it would be to maintain those freedoms as Hong Kong became more integrated with mainland China.[95] However, for the most part, the UGC and university leaders have never fully acknowledged that reunification with China poses special threats to academic freedom. Even when clear breaches have occurred, they have tended to treat them as unfortunate exceptions to the rule rather than as evidence of a systemic threat. As a result, the institutional protections for academic freedom have not been sufficiently strengthened. Indeed, by promoting more centralised and less democratic systems of university governance, the UGC has arguably increased the opportunities for interference by both the local and Central governments.

With the enactment of the NSL, however, the threats to academic freedom are now even more evident and must not be ignored by university leaders. Indeed, the impact of the NSL extends beyond the potential application of the criminal offences. The law has already created a chilling effect, and the implications for universities of other provisions in the law, such as Articles 9 and 10, are still uncertain. Some have suggested that the law aims to reverse the development of Hong Kong's distinct cultural and political identity defined in contrast to mainland China. However, if that occurs and Hong Kong's unique identity is diminished, then the "comparative advantage" that its universities have been able to offer students and faculty may also disappear. Indeed, there are already many negative reports on the future of education in the territory,[96] and some commentators have gone so far as to accuse university administrators of actively assisting the government to stifle free speech.[97] Unless Hong Kong's universities make it crystal clear that they will protect academic freedom to the fullest extent allowed by the law, their global rankings will likely decline over time.[98]

Fortunately, the Hong Kong government's December 2020 statement, which reaffirmed that the NSL should not curtail academic freedom (at least not in tertiary

95. *See*, for example, Currie, Petersen, and Mok, n 2 above, especially Ch 6.
96. *See*, for example, Patrick Wintour, "Academics Warn of 'Chilling Effect' of Hong Kong Security Law", *The Guardian*, 12 October 2020, available at https://www.theguardian.com/education/2020/oct/12/academics-warn-of-chilling-effect-of-hong-kong-security-law; and "China Is Killing Academic Freedom in Hong Kong", *The Economist*, 23 August 2020, available at https://www.economist.com/china/2020/08/23/china-is-killing-academic-freedom-in-hong-kong.
97. *See*, for example, Jeffrey Wasserstrom and Shui-Yin Sharon Yam, "Beijing's Hong Kong Fables Have Unhappy Endings", *Foreign Policy*, 30 December 2020, available at https://foreignpolicy.com/2020/12/30/beijing-hong-kong-fables-unhappy-endings/.
98. For evidence of the relationship between academic freedom and the global rankings of UK universities, *see* Terence Karran and Lucy Mallinson, "Academic Freedom and World-Class Universities: A Virtuous Circle?" (2019) 32 *Higher Education Policy* 397.

institutions), has created an opening.[99] It is essentially an invitation for universities to draft strong policies and procedures protecting academic freedom and university autonomy, even in the shadow of the NSL. While university leaders can draw upon international policies, we suggest that they also expressly cite the special protections in the BL and Article 4 of the NSL, as well as the Hong Kong government's assurance that it will continue to respect and enforce academic freedom. Some suggested language appears below, in the final section of this chapter, although such a policy may take many forms, and the drafting process should allow input from all members of a university community. If a university's leaders fail to take the initiative, then individual academic units might consider taking a "bottom-up" approach and drafting their own policies.

Suggested Language for a Policy on Academic Freedom in Hong Kong

Academic freedom is the freedom to engage in research, scholarship, or other creative work, to publish research findings, and to teach and to learn in an atmosphere of unfettered free inquiry and exposition. Academic freedom is essential to the university's public mission and advances the common good, including students' right to obtain a quality education and the community's right to benefit from academic research and from cultural and scientific progress.

This university is committed to protecting academic freedom and university autonomy to the fullest extent permitted by law. The Basic Law of the Hong Kong Special Administrative Region (SAR) protects academic freedom and university autonomy, not only in Articles 34 and 137, but also in Article 39, which provides for the implementation of the International Covenant on Civil and Political Rights (ICCPR) and the International Covenant on Economic, Social and Cultural Rights (ICESCR). In addition, the university, as a public body, is bound by the Hong Kong Bill of Rights Ordinance. Articles 4 and 5 of the Law of the People's Republic of China on Safeguarding National Security in Hong Kong (the NSL), enacted in 2020, also confirm the continued application of these important treaties and the human rights provisions of the Hong Kong Basic Law.

The Education Bureau of the Government of the Hong Kong SAR has frequently affirmed the importance of academic freedom, noting that it is "an important social value treasured by Hong Kong and the cornerstone of our higher education sector's success and renown in the world". The Education Bureau has also confirmed that Hong Kong's higher education institutions are "independent and autonomous bodies that enjoy autonomy in managing their own affairs". (See: Hong Kong Government Press Release of 22 December 2020, available at https://www.info.gov.hk/gia/general/202012/22/P2020122200792.htm?fontSize=1.)

99. *See* n 69 above.

Members of the faculty and students are, therefore, entitled to full freedom to engage in research, scholarship, and creative work and to publish or produce the results, subject to responsible performance of these and other academic duties. A faculty member is likewise entitled to freedom in teaching and discussing the subject matter, which is essential to our students' right to obtain a quality education. A concomitant of these freedoms is a commitment to accuracy and integrity. Controversy is a normal aspect of free academic inquiry and teaching, and it is proper to incorporate both the knowledge and the beliefs of the faculty member into that which is taught; however, the freedom to teach must be joined by a constant effort to distinguish between knowledge and belief.

Every university faculty member is a citizen, a member of a learned profession, and an officer of an educational institution. When the faculty member speaks or writes as a citizen, he or she should be free from institutional censorship or discipline. However, the faculty member's special position in the community imposes certain obligations. As a person of learning and an educator, a faculty member should remember that the public may judge the profession and institution by the faculty member's utterances. Hence, the faculty member should be at all times accurate, should exercise appropriate restraint, should show respect for the opinions of others, and should make every effort to indicate that the faculty member is not speaking for the institution.

13

The Business of National Security in Hong Kong

Do Human Rights Matter?

Surya Deva

Introduction

Facing imminent promulgation of the then proposed National Security Law (NSL),[1] 50 of the 68 independent United Nations (UN) thematic experts[2] issued a joint statement on 26 June 2020 raising serious concerns about the NSL specifically and the human rights situation in China generally.[3] The statement included the following observation: "[t]he national security law would also undermine the ability of businesses operating in Hong Kong to discharge their responsibility to respect human rights in line with the UN Guiding Principles on Business and Human Rights."[4]

This chapter will assess this prediction by the UN experts about the NSL's impact on the ability of business enterprises to meet their human rights obligations or responsibilities under all relevant national or international norms. It will especially focus on challenges posed by the NSL for businesses incorporated in, or having operations in, Hong Kong (Hong Kong businesses) in the following three types of situations:

1. The Law of the People's Republic of China on Safeguarding National Security in the Hong Kong Special Administrative Region, GN (E) 72 of 2020, available at https://www.gld.gov.hk/egazette/pdf/20202448e/egn2020244872.pdf.
2. Independent human rights experts, who are appointed by the UN Human Rights Council, have thematic or country-specific mandates. They may have the title of a Special Rapporteur, Independent Expert, or Working Group. *See* Office of the United Nations High Commissioner for Human Rights (OHCHR), "Special Procedures of the Human Rights Council", available at https://www.ohchr.org/EN/HRBodies/SP/Pages/Welcomepage.aspx. The author was one of the experts who signed this statement. The views expressed in this chapter are personal opinions of the author.
3. OHCHR, "UN Experts Call for Decisive Measures to Protect Fundamental Freedoms in China", 26 June 2020, available at https://www.ohchr.org/EN/NewsEvents/Pages/DisplayNews.aspx?NewsID=26006.
4. *Ibid.*

(1) *Type 1 dilemma*: a conflict between the NSL and extraterritorial legislation or executive regulations of other countries such as the United States (US);
(2) *Type 2 dilemma*: a conflict between complying with the NSL and other Hong Kong laws including the Basic Law and the Bill of Rights Ordinance (Cap 383) (BORO); and
(3) *Type 3 dilemma*: a conflict between the NSL and soft international human rights law standards such as the UN Guiding Principles on Business and Human Rights (UNGPs)[5] and the Organisation for Economic Co-operation and Development Guidelines for Multinational Enterprises (OECD Guidelines)[6] that expect businesses to respect internationally recognised human rights throughout their operations.

While the NSL raises complex questions for businesses, the interface of the private sector with national security issues is nothing new. For centuries, business enterprises have been involved in managing national security or fighting wars for sovereign states. The operations of the British East India Company[7] are a case in point.[8] In addition, private military and security companies all over the world have become prominent players in national security operations and fighting wars, including in conflict zones.[9] More recently, businesses are getting embroiled in international politics around "national security". For example, the Indian government banned hundreds of Chinese apps[10] and several Western countries have decided to exclude Huawei from 5G contracts[11] on the ground of national security

5. Human Rights Council, "Report of the Special Representative of the Secretary-General on the Issue of Human Rights and Transnational Corporations and Other Business Enterprises, John Ruggie—Guiding Principles on Business and Human Rights: Implementing the United Nations 'Protect, Respect and Remedy' Framework", A/HRC/17/31, *OHCHR*, 21 March 2011, available at https://ap.ohchr.org/documents/dpage_e.aspx?si=A/HRC/17/31. For an analysis, *see* John G. Ruggie, *Just Business: Multinational Corporations and Human Rights* (New York: WW Norton & Company, 2013). For critique, *see* Surya Deva and David Bilchitz (eds), *Human Rights Obligations of Business: Beyond the Corporate Responsibility to Respect?* (Cambridge: Cambridge University Press, 2013).
6. Trade Union Advisory Committee to the OECD, "OECD Guidelines for Multinational Enterprises: Recommendations for Responsible Business Conduct in a Global Context", 25 May 2011, available at https://members.tuac.org/en/public/e-docs/00/00/10/2F/document_doc.phtml.
7. The official name of the Company was "The Company of Merchants of London Trading into the East Indies". *See* John Keay, *The Honourable Company: A History of the English East India Company* (London: HarperCollins Publishers, 1991), p 9.
8. *See* William Dalrymple, *The Anarchy: The East India Company, Corporate Violence and the Pillage of an Empire* (London: Bloomsbury Publishing, 2019).
9. Evgeni Moyakine, *The Privatized Art of War: Private Military and Security Companies and State Responsibility for Their Unlawful Conduct in Conflict Areas* (Antwerp: Intersentia, 2015).
10. "India Bans PUBG, Baidu and More Than 100 Apps Linked to China", *BBC*, 2 September 2020, available at https://www.bbc.com/news/technology-53998205.
11. Tim Bowler, "Huawei: Why Is It Being Banned from the UK's 5G Network?", *BBC*, 14 July 2020, available at https://www.bbc.com/news/newsbeat-47041341; Stuart Lau, "In Banning Huawei and ZTE, Sweden Calls China a National Security Threat", *South China Morning Post*, 21 October 2020, available at https://www.scmp.com/news/china/article/3106358/banning-huawei-and-zte-sweden-calls-china-national-security-threat.

concerns. It seems that the NSL adds a unique dimension to the interface between businesses and national security: companies are expected to not only comply with the law but also show publicly their support for the NSL.[12]

In this chapter, I will argue that although Hong Kong businesses are bound by the NSL, they are also expected to follow applicable laws of other countries and / or soft international human rights standards. Therefore, compliance with the NSL should be done not in isolation but in a holistic manner. By adopting various strategies, businesses may be better placed to act in conformity with not only the NSL but also their independent responsibility to respect internationally recognised human rights.

Part I of the chapter will develop an analytical context to examine the NSL's impact on human rights obligations or responsibilities of businesses. It will do so by reviewing two key underlying causes of dilemmas faced by Hong Kong businesses: conflicting or competing regulatory norms at national and international levels, and the changing socio-legal expectation from business. Part II will then review business dilemmas related to three types of situations concerning conflict of norms. It will use selected real or hypothetical case studies to analyse the nature and extent of such dilemmas. Part III will discuss several strategies that Hong Kong businesses might employ to navigate through these dilemmas and, in turn, earn "profit with principles". A reference will again be made to analogical examples derived from business practice. Part IV will offer some concluding thoughts.

I. Underlying Causes of Business Dilemmas

This part analyses two key underlying causes of dilemmas faced by Hong Kong businesses: conflicting or competing regulatory norms at national and international levels, and the changing socio-legal expectations from businesses. For instance, in addition to complying with the NSL, businesses in Hong Kong need to follow not only Hong Kong laws (including those concerning human rights) but also laws of other relevant jurisdictions due to the transnational nature of business operations in a globalised market economy and increasing use of extraterritorial regulations by states.[13]

Moreover, all businesses—including those incorporated in or operating from Hong Kong—are expected to follow "soft" international human rights norms. Although these norms are soft, businesses—especially those with a global presence or market visibility—cannot afford to ignore them in practice. In fact, the binary

---

12. "Hong Kong Businesses Back New Security Law Despite Fears of Curtailed Freedoms", *Hong Kong Free Press*, 4 July 2020, available at https://hongkongfp.com/2020/07/04/hong-kong-businesses-back-new-security-law-despite-fears-of-curtailed-freedoms/.
13. Both the NSL and the HRA Act are extraterritorial in nature.

distinction between hard and soft norms may not always be very illuminating: hard norms may be soft in practice (because of weak implementation), while soft norms may become hard in practice (because of social or market sanctions). Hence, lawyers advising businesses are increasingly expected to look beyond hard law.[14] In other words, a Type 3 dilemma for Hong Kong businesses is no less potent than the Type 1 or Type 2 dilemmas noted above.

Resolving regulatory conflicts would have been much easier for businesses had they been expected to follow Milton Friedman's oft quoted assertion that the only social responsibility of business is to maximise its profits.[15] However, Friedman is no longer the guiding mantra for many businesses. Due to a range of "push and pull" factors, winds of stakeholder governance—rather than shareholder primacy—are blowing.[16] For instance, the US government's ban on import of cotton and tomatoes from Xinjiang in China because of serious allegations of forced labour[17] will force the involved businesses to think beyond maximising profits.[18] The US government's June 2021 business advisory cautioning its businesses about "emerging risks to their operations and activities in Hong Kong" is another such factor.[19] Businesses are also facing pressure from investors, employees, consumers, and the media to not be part of the evil in their quest to make profits. Google was forced to terminate its "dragonfly" project proposing a censored search engine in China because of social pressure from various stakeholders.[20]

14. *See*, for example, International Bar Association, *IBA Practical Guide on Business and Human Rights for Business Lawyers* (London: IBA, 2016); Law Society of England and Wales, *Business and Human Rights: A Practical Guide* (London: The Law Society, 2019).
15. Milton Friedman, "The Social Responsibility of Business Is to Increase Its Profits", *New York Times Magazine*, 13 September 1970, p 33; Milton Friedman, *Capitalism and Freedom* (Chicago: Chicago University Press, 1962), pp 133–136.
16. John Gerald Ruggie, Caroline Rees, and Rachel Davis, "Ten Years After: From UN Guiding Principles to Multi-Fiduciary Obligations" (2021) 6 *Business and Human Rights Journal* 179.
17. Jeanne Whalen and Eva Dou, "Trump Administration Bans Imports of Cotton and Tomatoes from China's Xinjiang Region, Citing Forced Labor", *Washington Post*, 14 January 2021, available at https://www.washingtonpost.com/us-policy/2021/01/13/us-ban-xinjiang-cotton-tomatoes/.
18. The governments of UK and Canada are also introducing a ban on imports from Xinjiang-linked products. *See* "Canada, Joining UK, Clamps Down on Imports Made by Chinese Forced Labor", *Reuters*, 12 January 2021, available at https://www.reuters.com/article/canada-china/update-1-canada-joining-uk-clamps-down-on-imports-made-by-chinese-forced-labor-idUSL4N2JN3BI. Moreover, the Australian Senate passed a law banning import of goods made with forced labour. *SBS News*, "Proposal for Australia to Ban the Import of Goods Made with Forced Labour Passes the Senate", 23 August 2021, available at https://www.sbs.com.au/news/proposal-for-australia-to-ban-the-import-of-goods-made-with-forced-labour-passes-the-senate.
19. US Department of State, "Issuance of a Hong Kong Business Advisory", 16 June 2021, available at https://www.state.gov/issuance-of-a-hong-kong-business-advisory/.
20. "Google's Project Dragonfly 'Terminated' in China", *BBC*, 17 July 2019, available at https://www.bbc.com/news/technology-49015516.

(a) Conflicting or Competing Regulatory Norms

i. National Security Law

The NSL creates four national security-related offences—namely secession, subversion, terrorist activities, and collusion with a foreign country or with external elements to endanger national security—and prescribes punishment for them.[21] It also modifies or creates special criminal procedures. For example, Article 42 reverses an ordinary rule regarding granting of bail and provides that no bail "shall be granted to a criminal suspect or defendant unless the judge has sufficient grounds for believing that the criminal suspect or defendant will not continue to commit acts endangering national security". The open trial rule may also be dispensed with in certain situations: "all or part of the trial shall be closed to the media and the public" if the trial involves state secrets or public order.[22] Moreover, in case of any inconsistency between the NSL and local laws, the former shall prevail.[23]

Since the NSL has wide extraterritorial effect,[24] its potential reach is global. It applies to a company which "is set up in the Region if the person or the body commits an offense under this Law outside the Region".[25] The NSL also applies "to offenses under this Law committed on board a vessel or aircraft registered in the Region".[26]

Under the NSL, companies may face liability for aiding, abetting, assisting in, or supporting the commission of the four offences. For example, a company which "incites, assists in, abets or provides pecuniary or other financial assistance or property" for committing secession or subversion will be guilty of these offences.[27] Similarly, a company which "provides support, assistance or facility such as training, weapons, information, funds, supplies, labour, transport, technologies or venues to a terrorist organisation or a terrorist, or for the commission of a terrorist activity" will be caught.[28] Inciting the commission of a terrorist activity is also an offence.[29] Moreover, a company which "directly or indirectly receives instructions, control, funding or other kinds of support from a foreign country or an institution, organisation or individual outside the mainland, Hong Kong, and Macao of the People's Republic of China" may be accused of collusion with a foreign country or with external elements.[30]

21. NSL, Arts 20–30.
22. *Ibid.*, Art 41.
23. *Ibid.*, Art 62.
24. *Ibid.*, Arts 36–38.
25. *Ibid.*, Art 37.
26. *Ibid.*, Art 36.
27. *Ibid.*, Arts 21 and 23.
28. *Ibid.*, Art 26.
29. *Ibid.*, Art 27.
30. *Ibid.*, Art 29. *See* analysis by Chen and Young about the scope of Article 29(4): Albert H. Y. Chen and Simon N. M. Young, "Liability for Imposing Sanctions under Hong Kong's National Security Law" (2020) 50 *Hong Kong Law Journal* 353.

For many Hong Kong companies, a "financial nexus" with the four NSL crimes will be an obvious connection to look for and avoid. However, assistance or incitement could take various non-financial forms too, such as social media companies allowing use of their platforms to post politically inflammatory messages (or not removing messages promptly despite the police request), or gig workers of companies knowingly providing a ride or food to suspected offenders which may trigger liability. Similarly, a company not complying with freezing, confiscation, or forfeiture of "property used or intended to be used for the commission" of the four offences may face criminal liability.[31] To comply with the NSL, businesses "should therefore conduct appropriate levels of due diligence and monitoring on their business counterparties with whom they have or will have dealings".[32]

Companies breaching the NSL face significant penalties: in addition to the imposition of fines on a company punished for committing an offence, its operation "shall be suspended or its licence or business permit shall be revoked".[33] Moreover, proceeds "obtained from the commission of an offense under this Law including financial aid, gains and rewards, and funds and tools used or intended to be used in the commission of the offense shall be seized and confiscated".[34]

ii. Reactive Regulatory Responses

The NSL has triggered reactive or retaliatory regulatory measures, especially from the US government, to impose sanctions on individuals and entities accused of undermining Hong Kong's autonomy.[35] A few countries have also suspended or terminated their extradition treaties with Hong Kong in response to the enactment of the NSL.[36] Moreover, in 2020, the United Kingdom (UK)[37] and the European Union (EU)[38] adopted new "Magnitsky"-style regulations to impose sanctions on

31. NSL, Art 43(3).
32. Keith Brandt and Henry Li, "Hong Kong's National Security Law—Things That Businesses Should Know About", *Dentons*, 4 August 2020, available at https://hongkong.dentons.com/en/insights/articles/2020/august/4/hong-kongs-national-security-law-things-that-businesses-should-know-about.
33. NSL, Art 31.
34. NSL, Art 32.
35. Toru suggests that these sanctions have escalated the "new cold war" between the US and China. *See* Toru Kurata, "Development of the Hong Kong Pro-Democracy Protest into a 'New Cold War': Shift from Opposing the Fugitive Offenders (Amendment) Bill to Opposing the Hong Kong National Security Law" (2020) 27(2) *Asia Pacific Law Review* 94, 104–106.
36. Shannon Tiezzi, "US Becomes Latest Country to Suspend Extradition Treaty with Hong Kong", *Diplomat*, 20 August 2020, available at https://thediplomat.com/2020/08/us-becomes-latest-country-to-suspend-extradition-treaty-with-hong-kong/.
37. Global Human Rights Sanctions Regulations 2020, available at https://www.legislation.gov.uk/uksi/2020/680/made.
38. EU, "Council Regulation (EU) 2020/1998 of 7 December 2020 Concerning Restrictive Measures against Serious Human Rights Violations and Abuses" (2020) 63 *Official Journal of the European Union* 1, available at https://eur-lex.europa.eu/legal-content/EN/TXT/PDF/?uri=OJ:L:2020:410I:FULL&from=EN.

individuals and entities for indulging in serious human rights abuses. As discussed below, some of these regulatory measures might create a compliance dilemma for businesses in Hong Kong.

On 14 July 2020, the Hong Kong Autonomy Act (HKA Act) came into force.[39] Section 5(a) of the HKA Act requires the US Secretary of State to submit a report to Congress identifying any foreign person who "is materially contributing to, has materially contributed to, or attempts to materially contribute to the failure of the Government of China to meet its obligations under the Joint Declaration or the Basic Law" as well as providing for "a clear explanation for why the foreign person was identified and a description of the activity that resulted in the identification". Section 5(b) then requires the Secretary of Treasury to submit a report identifying any foreign financial institution that "knowingly conducts a significant transaction" with a foreign person identified above. Based on these time-bound identifications, sections 6 and 7 allow for imposition of sanctions against the designated foreign persons and foreign financial institutions. While sanctions against foreign persons may include a travel ban to the US and prohibiting or restricting transactions concerning any property subject to US jurisdiction, a range of sanctions are possible against foreign financial institutions (e.g. a prohibition on lending by US financial institutions; restrictions on banking transactions; and travel ban against corporate officers, principals, or significant shareholders).[40]

In its exercise of powers under the HKA Act, the US government has imposed sanctions against several officials of the governments of China and Hong Kong.[41] Although no similar sanction has yet been imposed on Hong Kong businesses, the HKA Act is already impacting how businesses—especially Hong Kong–based banks (including Chinese banks with operations in the US)—have changed their operating practices.[42] The situation is likely to become more difficult to navigate once China's anti-sanction law is applied in Hong Kong.[43]

---

39. Hong Kong Autonomy Act, available at https://www.congress.gov/116/plaws/publ149/PLAW-116publ149.pdf.
40. For an analysis, *see* Duncan A. W. Abate, and Tamer A. Soliman, "The Hong Kong Autonomy Act", *Mayer Brown*, 17 July 2020, available at https://www.mayerbrown.com/en/perspectives-events/publications/2020/07/the-hong-kong-autonomy-act; Wendy Wysong, Susan Munro, Ali Burney, and Nick Turner, "U.S. Sanctions and Hong Kong: Summary of the Hong Kong Autonomy Act", *Hong Kong Lawyer*, 10 July 2020, available at http://www.hk-lawyer.org/content/us-sanctions-and-hong-kong-summary-hong-kong-autonomy-act.
41. *See*, for example, US Department of Treasury, "Treasury Sanctions Individuals for Undermining Hong Kong's Autonomy", *US Consulate General Hong Kong & Macau*, 7 August 2020, available at https://hk.usconsulate.gov/n-2020080702/; US Department of State, "Designating PRC and Hong Kong Officials after Widespread Pro-Democracy Arrests in Hong Kong", *US Consulate General Hong Kong & Macau*, 15 January 2021, available at https://hk.usconsulate.gov/n-2021011501/.
42. Amy Gunia, "How U.S. Sanctions on Hong Kong Could Leave Banks Caught in the Middle", *Time*, 13 August 2020, available at https://time.com/5878037/us-sanctions-hong-kong-banks/.
43. Yan Zhao and Jerome Taylor, "China's Anti-Sanctions Law a New Headache for Banks in Hong Kong", *Hong Kong Free Press*, 12 August 2021, available at https://hongkongfp.com/2021/08/12/chinas-anti-sanctions-law-a-new-headache-for-banks-in-hong-kong/.

In July 2020, the UK government issued the Global Human Rights Sanctions Regulations (UK Regulations) to deter, and provide accountability for, serious human rights violations by individuals and entities.[44] An activity will be captured by the UK Regulations if carried out by, or on behalf of, a state within the territory of that state, which would amount to "a serious violation by that State of an individual's (a) right to life; (b) right not to be subjected to torture or cruel, inhuman or degrading treatment or punishment; or (c) right to be free from slavery, not to be held in servitude or required to perform forced or compulsory labour".[45] The UK Regulations provide for asset-freeze, travel ban, and prohibition on making funds and economic resources available to the designated persons or entities.[46] The UK government has already used these regulations to impose sanctions against 49 nationals or organisations of Russia, Saudi Arabia, Myanmar, and North Korea.[47] Although not yet used against Hong Kong businesses, they may fall foul of the UK Regulations if involved in the listed serious human rights abuses.

On 7 December 2020, the Council of the European Union adopted its "Magnitsky"-style regulation (EU Regulation) to establish "a global human rights sanctions regime . . . that will allow it to target individuals, entities and bodies—including state and non-state actors—responsible for, involved in or associated with serious human rights violations and abuses worldwide, no matter where they occurred."[48] The EU Regulation will apply to genocide, crimes against humanity, and other serious human rights violations or abuses (i.e. torture and other cruel, inhuman, or degrading treatment or punishment; slavery; extrajudicial, summary, or arbitrary executions and killings; enforced disappearance of persons; and arbitrary arrests or detentions).[49] More importantly, the Regulation will also apply to other human rights violations or abuses of "widespread, systematic or . . . otherwise of serious concern as regards the objectives of the common foreign and security policy" set out in Article 21 of the Treaty of the European Union.[50] Two illustrative examples of such serious violations directly relevant in the current Hong Kong context are "violations or abuses of freedom of peaceful assembly and of association" and "violations or abuses of freedom of opinion and expression".[51] In ascertaining the meaning of these serious violations or abuses, "regard should be had to

44. The UK Regulations were issued under the Sanctions and Anti-Money Laundering Act 2018.
45. UK Regulations, para 4(2).
46. *Ibid.*, paras 11–15 and 17.
47. "UK Announces First Sanctions under New Global Human Rights Regime", *UK Government*, 6 July 2020, available at https://www.gov.uk/government/news/uk-announces-first-sanctions-under-new-global-human-rights-regime.
48. "EU Adopts a Global Human Rights Sanctions Regime", *Council of the EU*, 7 December 2020, available at https://www.consilium.europa.eu/en/press/press-releases/2020/12/07/eu-adopts-a-global-human-rights-sanctions-regime/.
49. EU Regulation, Art 1(1).
50. *Ibid.*, Art 1(1)(d).
51. *Ibid.*, Art 1(1)(d).

customary international law and widely accepted instruments of international law", such as the core international human rights conventions, the Rome Statute, and the European Convention for the Protection of Human Rights and Fundamental Freedoms.[52]

Any natural or legal person, entity, or body will fall foul of the EU Regulation if it (1) is "responsible for" above acts; (2) provides "financial, technical, or material support for or are otherwise involved" in above acts, including "by planning, directing, ordering, assisting, preparing, facilitating, or encouraging such acts"; or (3) is "associated with the natural or legal persons, entities or bodies covered" by (1) and (2).[53] It is thus clear that Hong Kong businesses could fall within the purview of the EU Regulation in a variety of ways. In terms of consequences, apart from travel or transit bans against the involved natural persons,[54] all "funds and economic resources belonging to, owned, held or controlled by any natural or legal person, entity or body" accused of breaching the regulation shall be frozen.[55] Moreover, the EU will not make available directly or indirectly any "funds or economic resources . . . to or for the benefit" of the covered natural or legal persons, entities, or bodies.[56]

The Council, on request from a member state or from the High Representative of the EU for Foreign Affairs and Security Policy, will "establish, review and amend the sanctions list".[57] The EU "has already listed more than 200 individuals and entities" for human rights violations or abuses.[58] In March 2021, the EU imposed sanctions against four individuals and one business entity, Xinjiang Production and Construction Corps Public Security Bureau, in relation to labour rights abuses in Xinjiang.[59]

iii. International Human Rights Standards

Out of several international human rights standards directly applicable to businesses, the relevant provisions of two standards deserve attention: the UNGPs and the OECD Guidelines.

---

52. *Ibid.*, Art 1(2).
53. *Ibid.*, Art 3(3).
54. *Ibid.*, Art 2(1).
55. *Ibid.*, Art 3(1).
56. *Ibid.*, Art 3(2).
57. *Ibid.*
58. European External Action Service, "Questions and Answers: EU Global Human Rights Sanctions Regime", 7 December 2021, available at https://eeas.europa.eu/headquarters/headquarters-homepage/90013/questions-and-answers-eu-global-human-rights-sanctions-regime_en.
59. Jacob Fromer and Finbarr Bermingham, "US, EU, UK, Canada Launch Sanctions Blitz against Chinese Officials; Beijing Hits Back", *South China Morning Post*, 22 March 2021, available at https://www.scmp.com/news/china/diplomacy/article/3126487/xinjiang-eu-hits-china-first-sanctions-tiananmen-square.

On 16 June 2011, the UN Human Rights Council unanimously endorsed the UNGPs.[60] The UNGPs comprise thirty-one principles divided into three pillars: Pillar I on the state duty to protect human rights (Principles 1–10); Pillar II on the business responsibility to respect human rights (Principles 11–24); and Pillar III on access to remedy (Principles 25–31). Each principle is accompanied by a commentary. Although the UNGPs—which apply to all states and to all business enterprises, regardless of their size, sector, location, ownership, and structure—are not binding of themselves, they are based on binding international human rights norms and are supported by a "thick stakeholder consensus".[61] For the purpose of this chapter, Pillar II and certain provisions of Pillar III will be especially relevant.

The UNGPs establish a "differentiated but complementary responsibility" of all business enterprises to respect all "internationally recognised human rights". This is an "independent" responsibility of businesses: irrespective of what states do or do not do, they should respect human rights. Moreover, the responsibility is over and above following local laws. In other words, merely complying with national laws will not be good enough if these laws fall short of international human rights standards.

Respecting human rights means that businesses "should avoid infringing on the human rights of others and should address adverse human rights impacts with which they are involved" (Principle 11). "Internationally recognised human rights" are "understood, at a minimum, as those expressed in the International Bill of Human Rights and the principles concerning fundamental rights set out in the International Labour Organization's Declaration on Fundamental Principles and Rights at Work" (Principle 12).

In terms of causation, Principle 13 provides for a tripartite typology: business enterprises may cause, contribute to, or be directly linked to adverse impacts through their operations, products, or services by their business relationships. Businesses have a responsibility, though of a varying degree, in all three situations. Although this responsibility applies to all enterprises "regardless of their size, sector, operational context, ownership and structure", the "scale and complexity of the means through which enterprises meet that responsibility may vary according to these factors and with the severity of the enterprise's adverse human rights impacts" (Principle 14).

Principle 15 outlines three steps that every business should take to discharge its responsibility to respect human rights: (1) adopt a policy commitment to respect human rights; (2) conduct human rights due diligence (HRDD) to identify, prevent, mitigate, and account for how they address their impacts on human rights; and (3)

60. Human Rights Council, "Guiding Principles on Business and Human Rights Endorsed by the UN Human Rights Council", *OHCHR*, 16 June 2011, available at https://www.ohchr.org/Documents/Publications/GuidingPrinciplesBusinessHR_EN.pdf.

61. John Ruggie, "The Social Construction of the UN Guiding Principles on Business and Human Rights", in Surya Deva and David Birchall (eds), *Research Handbook on Human Rights and Business* (Cheltenham, UK: Edward Elgar Publishing, 2020), 63 at 77–79.

have processes in place to enable remediation of any adverse impact they cause or contribute to. A human rights policy should be "approved at the most senior level of the business enterprise", "publicly available and communicated internally and externally" to all relevant stakeholders, and "reflected in operational policies and procedures" to embed it throughout the business enterprise (Principle 16).

HRDD is the central tool to enable businesses "to identify, prevent, mitigate and account for how they address their adverse human rights impacts" (Principle 17).[62] It is an ongoing process entailing four steps: identify and assess any actual or potential adverse human rights impacts; take appropriate action by integrating the findings from impact assessments; track the effectiveness of their response; and communicate externally how adverse impacts are being addressed (Principles 18–21). Pillar II also introduces the notion of "leverage": if a business enterprise has leverage (or can acquire it) to prevent or mitigate adverse human rights impacts, it should exercise it.[63] As it may not be possible to prevent or mitigate all adverse impacts, Principle 22 provides that where "business enterprises identify that they have caused or contributed to adverse impacts, they should provide for or cooperate in their remediation through legitimate processes".

Principle 23 of the UNGPs is directly relevant to the issue of conflict among competing norms explored in this chapter. It provides that business enterprises should:

> (a) Comply with all applicable laws and respect internationally recognized human rights, wherever they operate;
> (b) Seek ways to honour the principles of internationally recognized human rights when faced with conflicting requirements;
> (c) Treat the risk of causing or contributing to gross human rights abuses as a legal compliance issue wherever they operate.[64]

The commentary to Principle 23 further elaborates: "Where the domestic context renders it impossible to meet this responsibility fully, business enterprises are expected to respect the principles of internationally recognized human rights to the greatest extent possible in the circumstances, and to be able to demonstrate their efforts in this regard." Moreover, it is pointed out that some "operating environments . . . may increase the risks of enterprises being complicit in gross human rights abuses committed by other actors" and that "business enterprises should treat this risk as a legal compliance issue, given the expanding web of potential corporate legal liability arising from extraterritorial civil claims".[65]

62. HRDD "is the practice of a company looking for risks to people which are connected to what the company does, including who it relates to, and taking appropriate action to ensure that those risks do not turn into an adverse impact on people's rights", *see* Mark B. Taylor, "Human Rights Due Diligence in Theory and Practice", in Deva and Birchall, *ibid.*, 88 at 92.
63. Commentary to Principle 19.
64. UNGPs, Principle 23.
65. UNGPs, commentary to Principle 23.

If it is necessary to prioritise actions to address actual and potential adverse human rights impacts, business enterprises "should first seek to prevent and mitigate those that are most severe or where delayed response would make them irremediable" (Principle 24). In terms of access to remedy, "business enterprises should establish or participate in effective operational-level grievance mechanisms for individuals and communities who may be adversely impacted" (Principle 29). However, such mechanisms "should not be used to undermine the role of legitimate trade unions in addressing labour-related disputes, nor to preclude access to judicial or other non-judicial grievance mechanisms".[66]

The OECD Guidelines, which were originally adopted in 1976, were updated in May 2011 to align with the UNGPs. The Guidelines are voluntary "recommendations jointly addressed by governments to multinational enterprises"[67] operating in or from OECD countries. They may apply to many Hong Kong businesses in one of the following two ways: if they are subsidiaries, or part of the supply chains, of companies incorporated in any of the OECD countries, or other countries adhering to the OECD Guidelines.

Like the UNGPs, the OECD Guidelines expect businesses to respect internationally recognised human rights by conducting regular HRDD throughout their operations.[68] In May 2018, OECD issued detailed generic guidance on how to conduct HRDD.[69] For example, HRDD "should be commensurate to the severity and likelihood of the adverse impact. When the likelihood and severity of an adverse impact is high, then due diligence should be more extensive. Due diligence should also be adapted to the nature of the adverse impact."[70] Tailored guidance on HRDD is also provided for specific sectors such as the financial sector.[71]

There are two key differences between the OECD Guidelines and the UNGPs. First, apart from focusing on human rights, labour rights, and environmental rights, the OECD Guidelines also set out norms on issues such as bribery, consumer interests, science and technology, competition, and taxation. Second, a complaint could be made to the National Contact Points (NCPs) for an alleged breach of the OECD Guidelines by covered businesses. At this point in time, 50 states (38 OECD states and 12 other states) have established the NCPs,[72] which operate as non-judicial

66. Commentary to Principle 29. *See also* General Assembly, "Report of the Working Group on the Issue of Human Rights and Transnational Corporations and Other Business Enterprises: 'Access to Effective Remedies under the Guiding Principles on Business and Human Rights: Implementing the United Nations Protect, Respect and Remedy Framework'", A/72/162, *OHCHR*, 18 July 2017, para 71, available at https://ap.ohchr.org/documents/dpage_e.aspx?si=A/72/162.
67. *See* n 6 above, Ch I Concepts and Principles, para 1.
68. *See* n 6 above, Ch II General Principles, para 2; Ch IV Human Rights.
69. OECD, *OECD Due Diligence Guidance for Responsible Business Conduct* (Paris: OECD, 2018).
70. *Ibid.*, p 17 (emphasis in original).
71. OECD, "Responsible Business Conduct in the Financial Sector", available at https://mneguidelines.oecd.org/rbc-financial-sector.htm.
72. OECD, "National Contact Points", available at http://mneguidelines.oecd.org/ncps/.

grievance mechanisms under the OECD Guidelines.[73] The NCPs have dealt with over 500 complaints in over 100 countries and territories.[74] Although the NCPs only offer their "good offices" (i.e. dialogue, mediation, conciliation services) to resolve grievances and lack any power to enforce their recommendations, they have been able to provide remedies in some cases, especially in recent years.[75] Considering the alignment between the UNGPs and the OECD Guidelines, Hong Kong businesses may face complaints before the NCPs for breaching these international human rights standards.

iv. Hong Kong's Human Rights Laws

A full range of human rights are guaranteed under the Basic Law, the BORO, and other laws, such as the four anti-discrimination ordinances.[76] The NSL does not override the Basic Law.[77] Nor does it override all human rights. In fact, Article 4 of the NSL expressly declares that "[h]uman rights shall be respected and protected in safeguarding national security in the Hong Kong Special Administrative Region". Moreover, Article 5 provides that the "principle of the rule of law shall be adhered to in preventing, suppressing, and imposing punishment for offenses endangering national security".

At the same time, it is clear that various provisions of the NSL try to change the state of human rights in Hong Kong in the name of national security.[78] This conflict in norms may create a dilemma for businesses in Hong Kong in certain situations discussed in Part II. However, this conflict and consequent dilemmas would become potent mostly if the human rights provisions of the Basic Law and the BORO are applicable to businesses. Although constitutional rights are increasingly applied horizontally (either expressly or through a judicial interpretation) in

73. OECD, *National Contact Points for Responsible Business Conduct—Providing Access to Remedy: 20 Years and the Road Ahead* (OECD 2020), p 5.
74. *Ibid.*
75. *Ibid.*, pp 47–60.
76. The four ordinances are: Sex Discrimination Ordinance (Cap 480), Disability Discrimination Ordinance (Cap 487), Family Status Discrimination Ordinance (Cap 527), and Race Discrimination Ordinance (Cap 602).
77. Chen notes that there "is nothing in the NSL or in the NPC Decision that suggests that the NSL may override the Basic Law" and that the "better view is therefore that the NSL was intended to be consistent with the Basic Law"; *see* Albert Chen, "Constitutional Controversies in the Aftermath of the Anti-Extradition Movement of 2019" (2020) 50 *Hong Kong Law Journal* 609, 630. But *see* Brendan Clift, "Hong Kong's Made-in-China National Security Law: Upending the Legal Order for the Sake of Law and Order" (2020) 21 *Australian Journal of Asian Law* 1.
78. Petersen argues that the NSL weakens the "legal firewall" between mainland China and Hong Kong: Carole J. Petersen, "The Disappearing Firewall: International Consequences of Beijing's Decision to Impose a National Security Law and Operate National Security Institutions in Hong Kong" (2020) 50 *Hong Kong Law Journal* 633.

modern times,[79] it is unclear whether the Basic Law rights could be invoked directly against private companies.[80] It is, though, arguable that if the protection of these rights is not expressly tied to the government, courts should apply them at the horizontal level as well, especially if the nature of a right and the context so requires.

On the other hand, the BORO binds not only the government but also "public authorities" and "any person acting on behalf of the Government or a public authority".[81] Such a person could be a company as well. Since government nowadays operates through a variety of statutory bodies and organisations, the term "public authority" should be interpreted broadly,[82] as done by courts in other common law jurisdictions.[83] It is worth noting that a provision in the BORO to limit its scope to the government and public authorities was inserted only at the last stage,[84] and later an amendment was introduced to apply the BORO horizontally, though this amendment was repealed after the handover on 1 July 1997.[85]

Justice Keith in *Hong Kong Polytechnic University v Next Magazine Ltd* observed that a body will be a public authority for the purpose of the BORO if it is brought into the "public domain" by certain variables, such as public funding, governmental control or monitoring of performance, or some form of public accountability.[86] In *A Solicitor v The Law Society of Hong Kong*,[87] the court listed several factors determinative of whether a body is a public authority or not: the nature and constitution of the body, the way in which it was run, its functions, the measure of governmental control or monitoring of its performance, its public accountability, and its powers and the effect of their exercise on the public.[88]

---

79. For example, s 8(2) of the South African Constitution provides: "[a] provision of the Bill of Rights binds a natural or a juristic person if, and to the extent that, it is applicable, taking into account the nature of the right and the nature of any duty imposed by the right." For a judicial application of constitutional rights horizontally, *see* the Indian Supreme Court's decision in *Vishaka v State of Rajasthan* (1997) 6 *SCC* 241. For an analysis of horizontality, *see* Mahendra P. Singh, "Fundamental Rights, State Action and Cricket in India" (2006) 13 *Asia Pacific Law Review* 203; Dawn Oliver and Jörg Fedtke (eds), *Human Rights and the Private Sphere: A Comparative Study* (Abingdon: Routledge-Cavendish, 2007).
80. Dinusha Panditaratne, "Basic Law, Hong Kong Bill of Rights and the ICCPR", in Johannes Chan and C. L. Lim (eds), *Law of the Hong Kong Constitution* (Hong Kong: Sweet & Maxwell, 2nd edn, 2015), 521 at 538.
81. Section 7(1) reads: "This Ordinance binds only—(a) the Government and all public authorities; and (b) any person acting on behalf of the Government or a public authority."
82. *See* Johannes Chan and C. L. Lim, "Interpreting Constitutional Rights and Permissible Restrictions", in Chan and Lim, n 80 above, 565 at 583–585.
83. India is one such example. *See* Mahendra P. Singh, *VN Shukla's Constitution of India* (Lucknow: Eastern Book Company, 12th edn, 2013), pp 27–37.
84. Danny Gittings, *Introduction to the Hong Kong Basic Law* (Hong Kong: Hong Kong University Press, 1st edn, 2013), p 275.
85. Chan and Lim, n 82 above, p 584.
86. *Hong Kong Polytechnic University v Next Magazine Ltd* [1997] HKRLD 102 at 106.
87. [2006] 2 HKC 40.
88. Regarding who is amenable to judicial review, Gordon and Mok note that bodies in Hong Kong that derive their authority from an Ordinance will be generally amenable to judicial review provided that

By applying these criteria, companies like the Mass Transit Railway (MTR)[89]—which enjoys a government-conferred monopoly over rail transport in Hong Kong and in which the government owns more than 75 per cent shares—should be treated as a public authority for the purpose of the BORO. The same could be said about publicly funded educational institutions,[90] banks which are authorised to issue notes in Hong Kong, companies engaged to perform typical government functions such as managing security at the airport, and companies contracted by the government to provide essential public services such as water, electricity, and health facilities. Consequently, they would be expected not to ignore human rights provisions in the Basic Law and the BORO while complying with the NSL.

As far as the four anti-discrimination ordinances are concerned, they apply to businesses directly and may become relevant in indirect discrimination situations, for example, if a company discriminates against a political activist and one of the reasons for such discrimination is sexual orientation, race, or disability. Similarly, a surveillance order which (mostly) targets non-Chinese employees of an organisation will smell of racial discrimination. In other words, businesses should comply with the NSL in a non-discriminatory fashion and be conscious of not indulging in indirect discrimination or perpetuating discriminatory social norms.

(b) Changing Socio-legal Expectations

In the early 1930s, two leading legal scholars, Adolph Berle and Merrick Dodd, debated whether businesses should merely act for the benefit of their shareholders or also consider the interest of the community.[91] Berle's views that corporations should exercise their power only for the benefit of their shareholders were taken forward forcefully by Milton Friedman and more recently by Elaine Sternberg. For Sternberg, the "defining purpose of business is maximising owner value over the long term by selling goods or services"[92] and using "business resources for non-business purposes [social responsibility] is tantamount to theft".[93] These views are reflective of the "shareholder primacy" model.

they act in a public capacity. Richard Gordon and Johnny Mok, *Judicial Review in Hong Kong* (Hong Kong: LexisNexis, 2009), 9.

89. *MTR Corporation Ltd v Tsang Kin Shing* [2019] 3 HKLRD 285.
90. See *Leung Chak Sang v Lingnan University* [2001] 2 HKC 435.
91. Adolph A. Berle, "Corporate Powers as Powers in Trust" (1931) 44 *Harvard Law Review* 1049; E. Merrick Dodd, "For Whom Are Corporate Managers Trustees?" (1932) 45 *Harvard Law Review* 1145; Adolph A. Berle, "For Whom Are Corporate Managers Trustees: A Note" (1932) 45 *Harvard Law Review* 1365.
92. Elaine Sternberg, *Just Business: Business Ethics in Action* (Oxford: Oxford University Press, 2nd edn, 2000), p 32 (emphasis in original).
93. *Ibid.*, p 41 (emphasis in original).

However, the validity of the shareholder primacy model has been challenged by scholars on legal, normative, and practical grounds,[94] so much so that not many companies would now claim—at least publicly—that their sole objective is to maximise profits irrespective of any adverse impact on society. In fact, in August 2019, the Business Roundtable—an association of chief executive officers of America's leading companies—issued a statement on the purpose of a corporation, which "overturned a 22-year-old policy statement that defined a corporation's principal purpose as maximizing shareholder return".[95] This statement, which has been signed by over 200 chief executive officers, declares that "companies should serve not only their shareholders, but also deliver value to their customers, invest in employees, deal fairly with suppliers and support the communities in which they operate".[96] Commenting on the fiftieth anniversary of Friedman's 1970 *New York Times* article, Rajan argued that time has come to broaden the investors of a firm to include those who make "non-financial investment" in its success.[97]

Progressive institutional investors have also started taking a public position on the need for responsible business conduct. For example, the Investor Alliance for Human Rights—comprising "over 160 institutional investors, including asset management firms, trade union funds, public pension funds, foundations, endowments, faith-based organizations, and family funds" and representing "a total of over US$5 trillion in assets under management and 18 countries"[98]—is a case in point. The Norwegian Government Pension Fund Global offers another example of ethical investment.[99] On recommendations of the Council on Ethics, the Norges Bank can exclude companies from the Fund's investment universe or place them on an observation list if "there is an unacceptable risk that the company contributes to or is responsible for: a) serious or systematic human rights violations, such as murder, torture, deprivation of liberty, forced labour and the worst forms of child labour".[100]

---

94. Paddy Ireland, "Company Law and the Myth of Shareholder Ownership" (1999) 62 *Modern Law Review* 32; Jennifer Hill, "Visions and Revisions of the Shareholder" (2000) 48 *American Journal of Comparative Law* 39; Beate Sjåfjell, "How Company Law Has Failed Human Rights—and What to Do About It" (2020) 5 *Business and Human Rights Journal* 179.
95. Business Roundtable, "One Year Later: Purpose of a Corporation", available at https://purpose.businessroundtable.org/.
96. *Ibid.*
97. Raghuram Rajan, "'50 Years Later, It's Time to Reassess': Raghuram Rajan on Milton Friedman and Maximizing Shareholder Value", *Promarket*, 18 September 2020, available at https://promarket.org/2020/09/18/50-years-later-its-time-to-reassess-raghuram-rajan-on-milton-friedman-and-maximizing-shareholder-value/.
98. Investor Alliance for Human Rights, "About the Investor Alliance for Human Rights", available at https://investorsforhumanrights.org/about.
99. Government of Norway, "Responsible Investments: Government Pension Fund", available at https://www.regjeringen.no/en/topics/the-economy/the-government-pension-fund/responsible-investments/id446948/.
100. Guidelines for observation and exclusion from the Government Pension Fund Global, s 3, available at https://www.regjeringen.no/globalassets/upload/fin/statens-pensjonsfond/formelt-grunnlag/guidelines-for-observation-and-exclusion-from-the-gpfg---17.2.2017.pdf. *See also* Norges Bank

This major turnaround in social expectations from businesses can be labelled as a shift from the "business or human rights" era to the era of "business and human rights".[101] A "thick stakeholder consensus" around the UNGPs[102] played a key role in this transition. A number of other developments are also turning this social expectation into legal expectation, such as the enactment of corporate transparency laws,[103] judicial evolution of the principle of direct duty of care of parent companies,[104] push for mandatory human rights legislation in Europe,[105] and the emergence of specialised civil society campaigns.[106] Considering all these "push and pull" factors, businesses—including those based in, or operating from, Hong Kong—might have to reorient their business models so as not to ignore or externalise the adverse human rights impacts of doing business.

II. Businesses Dilemmas

As illustrated in this part, a combination of conflict between competing norms and the growing socio-legal expectation from businesses to respect human rights creates operational dilemmas for businesses in Hong Kong. It should be noted at the outset these dilemmas are not unique to the NSL or Hong Kong. For instance, when the US government requested Apple to unlock an iPhone of a suspected offender, Apple resisted to do so because "civil liberties" are at stake.[107] Apple has also refused to create a "backdoor" for law enforcement agencies to its encryption, as this tool

Investment Management, "Observation and Exclusion of Companies", available at https://www.nbim.no/en/the-fund/responsible-investment/exclusion-of-companies/.

101. Surya Deva, "From 'Business or Human Rights' to 'Business and Human Rights': What Next?", in Deva and Birchall (eds), n 61 above, p 1.
102. John Gerard Ruggie, "Global Governance and 'New Governance Theory': Lessons from Business and Human Rights" (2014) 20 *Global Governance* 5, 10.
103. Radu Mares, "Corporate Transparency Laws: A Hollow Victory?" (2018) 36(3) *Netherlands Quarterly of Human Rights* 189; Jena Martin, "The Use of Disclosure-Based Regulation to Advance the State's Duty to Protect", in Deva and Birchall, n 61 above, p 176.
104. *Chandler v Cape* [2012] EWCA Civ 525; *Choc v Hudbay Minerals Inc* 2013 ONSC 1414; *Vedanta Resources PLC v Lungowe* [2019] UKSC 20; *Nevsun Resources Ltd v Araya* 2020 SCC 5. *See also* Marilyn Croser et al., "Vedanta v Lungowe and Kiobel v Shell: The Implications for Parent Company Accountability" (2020) 5 *Business and Human Rights Journal* 130; and Tara Van Ho, "Vedanta Resources Plc and Another v. Lungowe and Others" (2020) 114(1) *American Journal of International Law* 110.
105. Business and Human Rights Resource Centre, "Towards EU Mandatory Due Diligence Legislation: Perspectives from Business, Public Sector, Academia and Civil Society", available at https://www.business-humanrights.org/en/from-us/briefings/towards-eu-mandatory-due-diligence-legislation/.
106. *See*, for example, Cotton Campaign, "Cotton Campaign to End Forced and Child Labor in the Cotton Fields of Uzbekistan and Turkmenistan", available at http://www.cottoncampaign.org/.
107. Amanda Holpuch, "Tim Cook Says Apple's Refusal to Unlock iPhone for FBI Is a 'Civil Liberties' Issue", *The Guardian*, 22 February 2016, available at https://www.theguardian.com/technology/2016/feb/22/tim-cook-apple-refusal-unlock-iphone-fbi-civil-liberties.

could compromise the privacy and security of all its users.[108] One may also recall here the dilemma faced by businesses operating in South Africa during the apartheid regime consequent to multiple calls for them to follow the Sullivan Principles and divest from South Africa,[109] even if their operations were in line with the then discriminatory laws of South Africa.

The Hong Kong General Chamber of Commerce welcomed the NSL as it will be "instrumental in helping to restore stability and certainty to Hong Kong".[110] On the other hand, surveys conducted by various foreign chambers of commerce such as of America,[111] Japan,[112] and Switzerland[113] revealed their member companies have concerns about the NSL. Foreign companies in Hong Kong are also "concerned about the city's judicial independence and political stability" due to the NSL.[114]

Interestingly, some institutional investors too have raised concerns about the NSL. For example, the Chief Investment Officer of Aviva Investors, a major shareholder of both HSBC and Standard Chartered, observed:

> We are uneasy at the decisions of HSBC and Standard Chartered to publicly support the proposed new national security law in Hong Kong without knowing the details of the law or how it will operate in practice. . . . If companies make political statements, they must accept the corporate responsibilities that follow. Consequently, we expect both companies to confirm that they will also speak out publicly if there are any future abuses of democratic freedoms connected to this law.[115]

While the NSL has not—and might not—affect all Hong Kong businesses, it is likely to create a "normative" dilemma for many of them. The dilemma will also be "real", in particular, for two categories of businesses: local businesses who have

108. Lauren Feiner, "Apple Refuses Government's Request to Unlock Pensacola Shooting Suspect's iPhones", *CNBC*, 14 January 2021, available at https://www.cnbc.com/2020/01/14/apple-refuses-barr-request-to-unlock-pensacola-shooters-iphones.html.
109. *See* Paul Lansing, "The Divestment of United States Companies in South Africa and Apartheid" (1981) 60 *Nebraska Law Review* 304; Teoh Siew Hong, Ivo Welch, and C. Paul Wazzan, "The Effect of Socially Activist Investment Policies on the Financial Markets: Evidence from the South African Boycott" (1999) 72(1) *Journal of Business* 35.
110. HK General Chamber of Commerce, "Law to Help Restore Stability and Certainty", 30 June 2020, available at https://www.chamber.org.hk/en/media/press-releases_detail.aspx?ID=3662.
111. American Chamber of Commerce, "AmCham Temperature Survey Findings: OFAC's Sanction on Hong Kong & National Security Law", 13 August 2020, available at https://www.amcham.org.hk/news/amcham-temperature-survey-findings-ofacs-sanction-hong-kong-national-security-law.
112. Takeshi Kihara, "Hong Kong Downsizing Considered by One-Third of Japanese Companies", *Nikkei Asia*, 20 October 2020, available at https://asia.nikkei.com/Business/Business-trends/Hong-Kong-downsizing-considered-by-one-third-of-Japanese-companies.
113. Swiss Chamber of Commerce, "National Security Law Survey", available at https://www.swisscham.org/hongkong/survey-national-security-law/.
114. Mark O'Neill, "HK: Foreign Firms' Concern about Judicial Independence, Stability", *Ejinsight*, 14 December 2020, available at https://www.ejinsight.com/eji/article/id/2660267/20201214-HK:Foreign%20firms%E2%80%99-concern-about-judicial-independence,-stability.
115. Christopher Copper-Ind, "Aviva lambasts UK banks' stance over Hong Kong", 9 June 2020, available https://www.internationalinvestment.net/news/4016291/aviva-lambasts-uk-banks-stance-hong-kong.

been or are supportive of the pro-democracy movement; and global businesses with operations in Hong Kong, especially if they enjoy a social visibility. They may face Type 1 (a conflict between the NSL and extraterritorial laws of other countries), Type 2 (a conflict between the NSL and other human rights–related Hong Kong laws), or Type 3 (a conflict between the NSL and soft international standards applicable to businesses) dilemmas noted in the introduction. Table 13.1 provides some illustrative examples of these real or hypothetical dilemmas.

Table 13.1: A mapping of NSL-related business dilemmas

Factual scenario	Category of business (local v global)	Nature of dilemma (real v hypothetical)	Typology of dilemma (Type 1, 2, or 3)
1. Social media companies (Google, Twitter, and Facebook) deciding to suspend sharing of data with government authorities	Global	Real	2 and 3
2. Government authorities asking an internet service provider (HK Broadband Network) to block a particular website	Local	Real	2 and 3
3. Government authorities asking a telephone company to share call details of certain users	Local; global	Hypothetical	2 and 3
4. Government authorities asking banks to report suspicious transactions regularly	Local; global	Real	2 and 3
5. Banks deciding not to do transactions with sanctioned government officials due to extraterritorial regulations of other states	Global	Real	1 and 3
6. Banks deciding not to do transactions with pro-democracy activists	Local; global	Real; hypothetical	1, 2, and 3
7. Companies asking their employees not to comment publicly, or on social media, about the NSL-related issues	Local; global	Real; hypothetical	2 and 3
8. Schools or universities asked to monitor emails or classes of certain teachers	Local	Hypothetical	2 and 3

Factual scenario	Category of business (local v global)	Nature of dilemma (real v hypothetical)	Typology of dilemma (Type 1, 2, or 3)
9. Police asking the MTR to stop services on certain stations during a given day and time	Local	Real; hypothetical	2 and 3
10. Government authorities asking hotels and travel agents to share details of their guests	Local; global	Hypothetical	2 and 3
11. Police asking a bus company (KMB) to provide details of Octopus payment transactions	Local	Real	2 and 3
12. Companies supplying security-related technology and crowd-control weapons to Hong Kong police	Global	Real	3
13. Companies deciding not to produce publicity or campaign materials for pro-democracy activists	Local	Hypothetical	2 and 3
14. A company asking another company (Chickeeduck) to remove a protest symbol (e.g., "lady liberty") from its shop	Local	Real	2 and 3
15. A public broadcasting company (RTHK) targeting journalists who challenged the government's narratives on social unrest or the NSL	Local	Real	2 and 3

Based on the above mapping of selected scenarios, several preliminary conclusions could be drawn. First, it is likely that businesses in certain sectors such as education, banking, social media, information technology, security, and communication will face the NSL-related dilemmas more (scenarios 1–6, 8, 12, and 15).

Second, some Hong Kong businesses which are owned or controlled by the government or are not aware of their human rights responsibilities under soft internal standards might not see any dilemma, because they will comply with the NSL-related directions without any hesitation (scenarios 2, 9, 11, 14, and 15). In such cases, the business dilemma will be merely normative, rather than real.

Third, although most of the dilemmas will arise in a vertical setting involving government authorities pitted against businesses, some dilemmas may also arise at the horizontal level, i.e. involving two companies or a company and its employees (scenarios 7, 14, and 15).

Fourth, while only a few businesses will face the Type 1 dilemma (conflict between the NSL and extraterritorial regulations of other states), many Hong Kong businesses will face a Type 2 dilemma (conflict between the NSL and other human rights–related Hong Kong laws). On the other hand, the Type 3 dilemma (conflict between the NSL and soft international human rights standards) is likely to arise in all scenarios. This dilemma will become more complicated in situations where soft standards are turning hard in countries such as France with the enactment of the Duty of Vigilance Law in 2017.[116] Somewhat similar laws have been enacted in Germany, Norway, Switzerland, and the Netherlands, while the European Commission is set to release the draft of a mandatory human rights and environmental due diligence law.[117]

Fifth, it is foreseeable that individuals or companies may rely on their constitutional / human rights to challenge the legality of NSL-related actions. It is difficult to predict yet how Hong Kong courts will strike a balance between national security and human rights in such cases.[118] However, irrespective of that outcome, businesses should start developing balancing policies and strategies, as they have an independent responsibility to respect human rights. How businesses can do this is discussed below in Part III.

III. Strategies to Navigate Business Dilemmas

Considering that businesses have an "independent responsibility" to respect human rights to complement states' tripartite human rights obligations, they should on their own take steps to overcome dilemmas which might undermine their ability to discharge their responsibility. Businesses may employ several strategies to navigate through regulatory dilemmas posed by conflicting regulatory norms or due to increasing socio-legal expectations of not ignoring human rights while earning profits.

116. The Duty of Vigilance Law requires French companies above a certain size to establish, publish, and implement a vigilance plan to identify and prevent risks of serious infringements of human rights and fundamental freedoms. The relevant companies may be sued for failing to establish a plan or implement it effectively. Sandra Cossart et al., "The French Law on Duty of Care: A Historic Step Towards Making Globalization Work for All" (2017) 2 *Business and Human Rights Journal* 317.

117. Business & Human Rights Resource Centre, "National & Regional Developments on mHRDD", available at https://www.business-humanrights.org/en/big-issues/mandatory-due-diligence/national-regional-developments-on-mhrdd/.

118. The early indications are not very promising: *HKSAR v Lai Chee Ying* [2021] HKCFA 3; *Tong Ying Kit v Secretary for Justice* [2021] HKCA 912; *HKSAR v Tong Ying Kit* [2021] HKCFI 2200. *See also* Surya Deva, "Putting Byrnes and Hong Kong in a Time Machine: Human Rights in 2021 under the Shadow of Beijing's National Security Law" (2021) 27 *Australian Journal of Human Rights* 467–486.

(a) Conducting Regular HRDD

The first step for all Hong Kong businesses who may be affected by the NSL should be to conduct an initial light human rights impact assessment. If this assessment brings some yellow or red flags, businesses should put in place a robust and regular HRDD process. This exercise should prevent or minimise—if not totally avoid—the adverse impact on the human rights of various stakeholders. It should also assist the relevant companies in managing risks to them, though one should not assume that HRDD can provide companies an automatic defence in litigation concerning alleged human rights abuses. The commentary to Principle 17 of the UNGPs makes both these points clear:

> Conducting appropriate HRDD should help business enterprises address the risk of legal claims against them by showing that they took every reasonable step to avoid involvement with an alleged human rights abuse. However, business enterprises conducting such due diligence should not assume that, by itself, this will automatically and fully absolve them from liability for causing or contributing to human rights abuses.

There is some evidence of a few companies already conducting HRDD about the impact of the NSL on their operations. For example, shortly after the NSL's enactment, several companies such as Facebook, Twitter, and Google suspended "processing requests for user data from Hong Kong law enforcement agencies".[119] WhatsApp's spokeswoman explicitly made a reference to HRDD: it said that reviews would be paused "pending further assessment of the impact of the National Security Law, including formal human rights due diligence and consultations with human rights experts."[120]

Conducting HRDD would mean that companies should not put unreasonable restrictions on their employees' freedom of speech and expression or start discriminating on the ground of holding certain political opinions. Similarly, banks should do a "political risks" screening of their clients for linkages to the pro-establishment or pro-democracy camp in a balanced and proportional manner. The proportionality principle should be adopted by social media companies too when faced with requests to provide personal data about their users to government authorities.

As noted in the introduction, HRDD must be conducted in a transparent manner and in meaningful consultation with external stakeholders, such as regulators, service users, human rights experts, civil society organisations, trade unions, human rights defenders, and national human rights institutions. However, where no meaningful HRDD is feasible in certain extreme cases, businesses may need to

119. Newley Purnell, "Google, Facebook and Twitter Suspend Review of Hong Kong Requests for User Data", *The Wall Street Journal*, 7 July 2020, available at https://www.wsj.com/articles/whatsapp-to-suspend-processing-law-enforcement-requests-for-user-data-in-hong-kong-11594034580.
120. *Ibid.*

withdraw from such markets. Companies sourcing cotton from Xinjiang or operating in Myanmar subsequent to the 2021 coup offer examples of this scenario. Due to the NSL, selected companies in Hong Kong may find themselves in a similar situation of being unable to conduct meaningful HRDD. In such extreme cases, the relevant companies would need to consider whether to continue operating in Hong Kong or move elsewhere.[121]

(b) Establishing Internal Policies and Mechanisms

Businesses in Hong Kong should develop internal policies and procedures to deal with compliance with the NSL as well as on how to respond to requests made by government agencies established under the NSL. These policies and procedures should be informed by HRDD conducted by businesses. Adopting such policies will not only assist business employees in handling better day-to-day dilemmas (e.g. what conduct of fellow employees to report to the police hotline) but also clarify expectations to public about their modus operandi.

Businesses should also establish internal independent mechanisms to deal with any grievances related to their decisions.[122] For example, Facebook has established an independent Oversight Board of external experts to review its decisions (e.g. taking down or keeping certain materials) which may abridge the freedom of speech and expression.[123] The Board's decisions will be binding on Facebook unless implementing them could violate the law. On a referral from Facebook, the Board accepted a case to examine its decision "to indefinitely suspend former US President Donald Trump's access to post content on Facebook and Instagram".[124] Facebook has also "requested policy recommendations from the Board on suspensions when the user is a political leader".[125]

121. Zimmerman, a former corporate lawyer who has resided in Hong Kong since 1997, observed: "Think of the national security law as a sorting mechanism: companies that will not comply with China's political bottom lines are encouraged to stay away, while companies willing to abide by China's rules have a leg up on the nation's massive economy. Businesses must decide for themselves whether to accept this bargain." Joshua M. Zimmerman, "What Hong Kong's National Security Law Makes Clear: Politics Trumps Business", *South China Morning Post*, 9 July 2020, available at https://www.scmp.com/comment/opinion/article/3092156/what-hong-kongs-national-security-law-makes-clear-politics-trumps.
122. Such mechanisms should meet the "effectiveness criteria" of Principle 31 of the UNGPs.
123. Oversight Board, "Ensuring respect for free expression, through independent judgement", available at https://oversightboard.com/.
124. Oversight Board, "Oversight Board Accepts Case on Former US President Trump's Indefinite Suspension from Facebook and Instagram", 21 January 2021, available at https://oversightboard.com/news/236821561313092-oversight-board-accepts-case-on-former-us-president-trump-s-indefinite-suspension-from-facebook-and-instagram/.
125. *Ibid.*

(c) Exploiting Vagueness

It is widely accepted that the NSL provisions are intentionally vague[126] to allow a liberal use to suppress any kind of dissent from the pro-democracy camp.[127] This is generally regarded problematic from the perspective of businesses who generally prefer clarity and certainty. However, businesses can also use such an ambiguity in the NSL provisions to their advantage. If two or more reasonable interpretations of a provision are possible, they may adopt an interpretation that allows them to comply with other competing hard or soft human rights norms. Doing so will also be consistent with Articles 4 and 5 of the NSL.[128] Businesses should stipulate such positions in their internal policies and procedures mentioned above.

For example, if a Hong Kong subsidiary of a US bank stops doing any transaction with people sanctioned by the US government under the HKA Act, this conduct may seem in breach of the NSL (e.g. subversion or collusion with a foreign country). In such situations of conflicts between competing norms, vague provisions could be interpreted narrowly to comply with both the NSL and the HKA Act. Chen and Young, for example, argue that a financial institution in Hong Kong which is required by the law of a foreign country to perform an act in the course of its business to implement a sanction imposed by the said country against the Chinese or Hong Kong government will not breach Article 29(4) of the NSL.[129] Their argument is that Article 29(4) "must be interpreted contextually as part of an offense concerned with collusion with outsiders in endangering national security" and that this offence comprises "acts that are only capable of being performed by a state, head of state or international organisation, and thus a financial institution, giving effect to sanctions against Hong Kong, cannot be regarded as 'receiving instructions' to 'impose sanctions,' which have already been imposed by a foreign state".[130]

In other words, Hong Kong businesses should adopt, based on legal advice, more human rights–friendly interpretations of the NSL wherever ambiguous provisions make this feasible.

---

126. "The law is so uncertain that everybody is afraid of speaking up and that is clearly the intention of the law"; *see* Stephen Mulrenan, "Business Navigates Hong Kong's New National Security Law", *International Bar Association*, 25 September 2020, available at https://www.ibanet.org/Article/NewDetail.aspx?ArticleUid=ACD909C3-15D4-4817-8D2A-0EE0D39D3028.
127. Toru, n 35 above, 102–104.
128. For example, the Court of First Instance observed that the provision of Art 42 (the right to bail) should "be construed and applied, so far as reasonably possible, in a manner which is consistent with the protection of fundamental rights, including the right to liberty of the person under [A]rt 28 of the Basic Law and [A]rt 5 of the Hong Kong Bill of Rights"; see *Tong Ying Kit v HKSAR (NO 1)* [2020] 6 HKC 110 at 127.
129. Chen and Young, n 30 above. Art 29(4) criminalises the act of receiving "instructions, control, funding or other kinds of support from a foreign country" for "imposing sanctions or blockade, or engaging in other hostile activities against the Hong Kong Special Administrative Region or the People's Republic of China".
130. Chen and Young, n 30 above, 354 (emphasis in original).

(d) Complying Creatively

Principle 23(b) of the UNGPs expects business enterprises to seek "ways to honour the principles of internationally recognized human rights when faced with conflicting requirements" such as compliance with the NSL. In a non–human rights context, businesses regularly comply with taxation or anti-competition regulations in a way to minimise the burden on them. In other words, they comply with the letter of the law but perhaps not its spirit. Businesses may achieve this goal, for instance, by employing complex group structures or exploiting loopholes in the drafting of laws.

Hong Kong businesses should use similar creative compliance strategies in relation to the NSL. A good example of creative compliance with the NSL is provided by Google. Instead of flatly declining to comply with data requests from Hong Kong police under the NSL, it requested the police to use "diplomatic procedures" to access data if needed.[131] Adopting such a policy strikes a balance in complying with legitimate requests for users' data and safeguarding the privacy and other human rights of Google users.

We can take another example where creative compliance may be useful. Hong Kong banks are required to report any suspicious transactions to the Hong Kong Monetary Authority as part of anti-money laundering and counter-financing of terrorism measures, and this includes the NSL-related reporting.[132] Instead of complying with this regulation in an "over-inclusive" manner and, in turn, ignoring completely their human rights responsibilities towards customers, banks may first conduct an internal assessment and report only those activities which pass an objective threshold endangering national security. In this process, they may also consult customers and give them a soft warning about any suspicious activity before making any formal reporting. Such pre-screening might also be more efficient from the perspective of the Monetary Authority and national security agencies.

(e) Inserting Human Rights Clauses in Contracts

Companies which supply dual-use goods or services are increasingly inserting human rights clauses in their contracts with users. This is partly due to certain states introducing more stringent control over export of dual-use goods.[133] Companies

131. Danny Lee and Chris Lau, "National Security Law: Google Urges Hong Kong Police to Use 'Diplomatic Procedures' for Data Requests", *South China Morning Post*, 14 August 2020, available at https://www.scmp.com/news/hong-kong/law-and-crime/article/3097478/national-security-law-google-urges-hong-kong-police.
132. The Hong Kong Association of Banks, "Frequently Asked Questions in Relation to Anti-Money Laundering and Counter-Financing of Terrorism", 30 September 2020, available at https://www.hkma.gov.hk/media/eng/doc/key-functions/banking-stability/aml-cft/FAQ_amlcft_sep_2020.pdf.
133. *See*, for example, European Parliament, "Dual Use Goods: Parliament and EU Ministers Agree on New EU Export Rules", 9 November 2020, available at https://www.europarl.europa.eu/news/en/press-room/20201105IPR90915/dual-use-goods-parliament-and-eu-ministers-agree-on-new-eu-export-rules.

are also using the same technique of inserting human rights clauses or a code of conduct in their supply chain contracts to encourage their business partners to respect human rights.[134]

This strategy may be especially useful for businesses supplying security-related technologies or crowd-control weapons to government agencies in Hong Kong. Bringing up human rights issues upfront during contract negotiations and then inserting them in legal contracts will set clear expectations for buyers of products and services. Consequences attached to breach of contracts may also discourage buyers of products or services to think carefully before ignoring human rights issues.

(f) Speaking Up Privately, Publicly, and Collectively

Contrary to a suggestion that businesses do not have a mandate or responsibility to speak up against problematic laws such as the NSL or human rights,[135] there are good legal, economic, and moral reasons for businesses to stand up for human rights. Zeid Ra'ad Al Hussein, the former UN High Commissioner for Human Rights, observed: "Business actors can be powerful advocates for the human rights which build resilient, peaceful and stable societies, able to overcome conflict and look to the future. Already, some corporate leaders realise it is in their interest to combat discrimination, inequalities, xenophobia, violence, and hate—including by lobbying authorities to take action, and by empowering their staff to stand up for rights."[136] Another former UN High Commissioner for Human Rights, Mary Robinson, reminded companies that "threats to human rights are also a threat to business".[137]

In recent times, some progressive businesses have started taking a public stand against government policies or decisions that breach internationally recognised human rights norms. For example, many companies spoke against Trump's travel

134. British Institute for International Comparative Law and Norton Rose Fulbright, *Making Sense of Managing Human Rights Issues in Supply Chains* (London: British Institute for International Comparative Law, 2018); Sarah Dadush, "Contracting for Human Rights: Looking to Version 2.0 of the ABA Model Contract Clauses" (2019) 68 *American University Law Review* 1519.

135. The former Chairman of the Hong Kong Bar Association, Philip Dykes, observed: "[c]ompanies will have to be very careful about with whom they speak; they will not want to stand out and make their position known about the law . . . As the local bar association, we have an obligation under our constitution to speak up on matters affecting basic law and the protection of human rights . . . But private firms don't have that mandate so they will keep their heads down," *see* Mulrenan, n 126 above.

136. Zeid Ra'ad Al Hussein, "Dollars and Sense: How—and Why—the Private Sector Needs to Stand Up for Human Rights", *UN—Office of the Secretary-General's Envoy on Youth*, available at https://www.un.org/youthenvoy/2017/01/dollars-sense-private-sector-needs-stand-human-rights/.

137. Mary Robinson, "It's Time for Business to Stand Up for Human Rights", *The B Team*, 10 December 2018, available at https://bteam.org/our-thinking/thought-leadership/time-business-stand-human-rights.

ban against selected Muslim countries.[138] Hong Kong businesses should draw inspiration from these instances and be willing to speak truth to power publicly in suitable cases involving misuse of the NSL. Moreover, as businesses regularly meet government officials in private settings, they may also use these private bilateral meetings to stress concerns flowing from the NSL for the private sector.

Businesses can also enhance their leverage by acting as well as speaking collectively on certain human rights issues impacted by the NSL. For example, all businesses should speak together against attempts to undermine autonomy, independence, and freedom of media companies as well as journalists. Sector-specific industry associations or chambers of commerce could also take a collective stand against various efforts aimed at interfering with the independence of the judiciary, because lack of judicial independence will harm business interests too.

IV. Conclusion

National security is an important goal for states. China (including Hong Kong) is no exception. However, the protection of human rights is an equally important goal, something that is no longer dismissed by the Chinese Government[139] though their understanding of human rights may not always match with how human rights are understood at the international level or in liberal democracies. As businesses are part of society, they have a key role to play in contributing to the realisation of both national security and human rights.

As analysed in this chapter, the enactment of the NSL has trigged a conflict of norms, thus creating dilemmas for Hong Kong businesses. In other words, the UN experts were correct in assessing in late June 2020 that the NSL would undermine the ability of—at least some—Hong Kong businesses to discharge their responsibility to respect internationally recognised human rights. Nevertheless, it is still possible for Hong Kong businesses to navigate through these dilemmas. Gone are the days when businesses were facing pressure only from regulators and / or profit-maximising investors. Rather, they are now facing pressures from multiple sources pulling them in different directions. In such a situation, they need to act in a principled manner and make independent decisions that would strike a reasonable balance between competing socio-legal expectations. In this chapter, I have highlighted not only real or hypothetical NSL-related dilemmas faced by Hong Kong businesses but also suggested several strategies that businesses may employ to earn "profit with principles".

---

138. Salil Tripathi, "The World Is Watching—Corporate Action on Trump Travel Ban", *Open Global Rights*, 3 February 2017, available at https://www.openglobalrights.org/world-is-watching-corporate-action-on-trump-travel-ban/.

139. *See*, for example, The State Council of the People's Republic of China, "National Human Rights Action Plan of China (2016–2020)", 29 September 2016, available at http://english.www.gov.cn/archive/publications/2016/09/29/content_281475454482622.htm.

14

Echoes Enhanced to a Cacophony

Hong Kong's Security Law Compared to Illiberal Elements of the Security Laws of Liberal Democracies

Kent Roach*

Introduction

The 2020 Law of the People's Republic of China on Safeguarding National Security in the Hong Kong Special Administrative Region[1] (NSL) drew strong criticism from liberal democracies despite its professed commitment in Articles 4 and 5 to human rights and the rule of law. The United States (US) enacted the Hong Kong Autonomy Act[2] that condemns the NSL. During the forty-fourth session of the United Human Rights Council, the United Kingdom (UK) spoke on behalf of 26 other countries who raised concerns about the NSL and urged China "to engage Hong Kong's people, institutions and judiciary"[3] to prevent further erosion of rights and freedoms long enjoyed in Hong Kong. The critics included 15 members of the European Union. Notably, however, it did not include Italy, Hungary, Poland, and Spain, countries noted for backsliding on liberal democratic principles or, in the case of Spain, for opposition to secession.

At the same time, Cuba spoke on behalf of 52 other states who supported the NSL. They included China, Egypt, Iran, Iraq, Myanmar, Sri Lanka, Saudi Arabia,

---

* I thank Michael Hor, Hualing Fu, and Simon N. M. Young for their valuable comments on an earlier draft while taking responsibility for all views expressed in this chapter and all mistakes.

1. Available at https://www.gld.gov.hk/egazette/english/gazette/volume.php?year=2020&vol=24&no=48&extra=1&type=0. The English language translation is not official despite English being one of Hong Kong's official languages under Art 9 of the Basic Law.
2. Public Law 116–149, 134 Stat 663. *See also* Hong Kong Rights and Democracy Act 22 USC ss 5721–5726 (2019). *See* Jason Buhi, "America's New Covenant with Hong Kong: The Hong Kong Human Rights and Democracy Act of 2019" (2020) 55(2) *Texas International Law Journal* 269.
3. Government of the UK, "UN Human Rights Council 44: Cross-Regional Statement on Hong Kong and Xinjiang", 30 June 2020, available at https://www.gov.uk/government/speeches/un-human-rights-council-44-cross-regional-statement-on-hong-kong-and-xinjiang.

Syria, and Venezuela.[4] The support for the law, especially in Africa, is related to China's increased economic and political power.[5] As Carole Petersen has noted, all the countries that opposed the law are regarded as free while those who supported the law are generally seen as authoritarian and / or rely on aid from China.[6] The law has been politically defined as part of a skirmish in a new Cold War pitting liberal democracies against China.

Such a new Cold War narrative holds some truths. Nevertheless, it ignores arguments that western liberal democracies and especially the UK and the US are being hypocritical given their own post 9/11 expansion of security laws. Hong Kong Chief Executive Carrie Lam argued shortly after the law had been drafted and enacted by China that "compared with the national security laws of other countries, it is a very mild law. Its scope is not as great as that in other countries and even China".[7] A spokesperson for China's foreign ministry responded to British criticism by urging "Britain to abandon their colonialist ideals and stop other hypocritical acts and double standards".[8] Wuhan University law scholars Jie Zhu and Xiaoshan Zhang argued that the "UK, Spain, Russia and Canada are also haunted by separatism. And these countries spare no effort to crack down separatism forces".[9]

This chapter will proceed on the basis that claims made by supporters of the NSL of hypocrisy and double standards should be taken seriously as a prelude to any meaningful scholarly, political, and judicial engagement with the new law. Hong Kong authorities have pushed the hypocrisy of the west thesis by charging a protester Tam Takchi ("Fast Beat") not under the new law but with a sedition offence from the British colonial era.[10] The US's response to the 6 January 2021

---

4. Eleanor Albert, "What Countries Support the New Hong Kong Security Law?", *The Diplomat*, 6 July 2020, available at https://thediplomat.com/2020/07/which-countries-support-the-new-hong-kong-national-security-law/.
5. Yash Ghai and Jill Cottrell Ghai, "Security, Politics and the Chinese Agenda", in Cora Chan and Fiona de Londras (eds), *China's National Security: Endangering Hong Kong's Rule of Law* (London: Bloomsbury, 2020), p 290.
6. Carole Petersen, "The Disappearing Firewall: International Consequences of Beijing's Decision to Impose a National Security Law and Operate National Security Institutions in Hong Kong" (2020) 50 *Hong Kong Law Journal* 633, 635.
7. "National Security Law Not 'Doom and Gloom', Carrie Lam Says", *Global News*, 6 July 2020, available at https://globalnews.ca/news/7146211/hong-kong-security-law-carrie-lam/. *See also* Regina Ip, "Hong Kong Is China, Like It or Not", *New York Times*, 1 October 2020, available at https://www.nytimes.com/2020/10/01/opinion/hong-kong-china-security-law.html.
8. Victor Ting and Cheryl Heng, "Britain Rebuked by Beijing and Hong Kong Government", *South China Morning Post*, 23 November 2020, available at https://www.scmp.com/news/hong-kong/politics/article/3111069/britain-review-arrangements-judges-sitting-hong-kongs-top.
9. Zhu Jie and Zhang Xiaoshan, *Critique of Hong Kong Nativism from a Legal Perspective* (Singapore: Springer, 2019), p 5. They bemoan that "it is right and proper for the Western civilized countries to legislate to protect national security, but in the 'autocratic and backward' China, national security acts could be 'distorted' and 'abused' any minute", *ibid.*, pp 173–174.
10. This was the first sedition charge under the 1938 offence used since the 1997 handover. For my previous arguments that sedition is a widely criticised offence and rarely used in liberal democracies and is associated with "old" and archaic forms of security, *see* Kent Roach, "Old and New Versions of Security: Article

assault on the Capitol including seditious conspiracy charges has also been taken as a sign of hypocrisy given American praise for the 1 July 2019 assault and occupation of Hong Kong's legislature.

Even if partially valid, claims about liberal democracies engaging in double standards provide warnings to liberal democracies and the United Nations (UN) Security Council about the uses of expanded security laws and practices.[11] Slides towards authoritarianism in countries such as Hungary and Poland have been facilitated by borrowing and combining some of the worst practices from other countries including those from liberal democracies.[12]

A comparison of Hong Kong's new law with those from other liberal democracies can also illuminate some of the implicit practices and institutions tied to the rule of law which temper the effects of overbroad security laws in liberal democracies and which may not mitigate some of the effects of the NSL. It also supports an approach to comparative law that focuses less on comparing the text of laws and more on broader institutional, cultural, and political factors.[13]

---

23 Compared to Post-September 11 Security Laws", in Fu Hualing, Carole Petersen, and Simon Young (eds), *National Security and Fundamental Freedoms: Hong Kong's Article 23 under Scrutiny* (Hong Kong: Hong Kong University Press, 2005), pp 125–129. The national security branch of the Hong Kong police created by the NSL has also charged five union members under the colonial-era sedition offence, which has a maximum penalty of two years' imprisonment, for publishing a children's book about a village of sheep holding wolves at bay on the basis that the book was trying to incite children's hatred of the Hong Kong government and judiciary and to incite violence and illegal acts. "Five arrested in Hong Kong for sedition over children's book about sheep" The Guardian 22 July 2021 at https://www.theguardian.com/world/2021/jul/22/five-arrested-in-hong-kong-for-sedition-over-childrens-book-about-sheep

11. For accounts and critiques of the influence that the UN Security Council has had over post 9/11 security laws, *see* Kim Lane Scheppele, "The International Standarization of National Security Law" (2010) 4 *Journal of National Security Law* 437; Kent Roach, *The 9/11 Effect: Comparative Counter-Terrorism* (Cambridge: Cambridge University Press, 2011), Ch 2. For a recognition that China has seen 9/11 drawn on the increased emphasis of the UN and western countries as "rhetorical fodder" or "benchmarks" for its own security law and has argued that western critics are throwing rocks at China from a "glass house", *see* Jacques DeLisle, "Security First?: Patterns and Lessons from China's Use of Law to Address National Security Threats" (2010) 4 *Journal of National Security Law* 397 at 431, 435. Various special rapporteurs for the UN have criticised the NSL in particular for its broad definition of security offences and its adverse effects on freedoms and civil society. *See* Fionnuala Ní Aoláin et al., Letter of Special Rapporteurs, 1 September 2020, available at https://spcommreports.ohchr.org/TMResultsBase/DownLoadPublicCommunicationFile?gId=25487. But for arguments that both the General Assembly and the Human Rights Council have been marginalised in the UN's security initiatives, *see* Roach, *The 9/11 Effect*, supra at pp 63–76.
12. Kim Lane Scheppele, "Autocratic Legalism" (2018) 85 *University of Chicago Law Review* 545; Kim Lane Scheppele, "The Opportunism of Populists and the Defence of Constitutionalism Liberalism" (2019) 20 *German Law Journal* 314.
13. For my attempts to move away from the traditional questionnaire approach to comparative law in this area, *see* Kent Roach (ed), *Comparative Counter-Terrorism Law* (Cambridge: Cambridge University Press, 2015), pp 4–13, 779–788.

The first part of this chapter will suggest that the NSL has many echoes of illiberal elements of security laws and anti-secession rulings in liberal democracies and counter-terrorism strategies promoted by the UN Security Council. These include broad definitions of terrorism, a focus on speech associated with terrorism, Central Government pre-emption of regional and local governance with respect to security threats, a willingness to use education to counter opinions that it is feared may lead to security crimes, and the creation of new police powers and institutions to deal with "homeland security".

The second part will argue that the echoes of security laws in liberal democracies have been enhanced and distorted in the NSL to form a cumulative cacophony that threatens the "Two Systems" part of the Hong Kong "One Country Two Systems" (OCTS) compromise. Considered as a whole, the NSL undermines the rule of law[14] in Hong Kong including a broader "rule of law culture"[15] that values freedoms, dissent, and rights. It threatens to replace a rule of law with its attention to the separation of powers with rule by law which fuses powers or provides a credible threat of such fused power. This is symbolized by the fact that the NSL was neither debated nor enacted in Hong Kong. Its text was kept secret before it was unanimously approved by the Standing Committee of the National People's Congress (NPCSC) in Beijing. This was done despite the provision in Article 23 of the Basic Law that provides that Hong Kong "shall enact laws *on its own* to prohibit any act of treason, secession, sedition and subversion against the Central People's Government".[16]

The Hong Kong executive will be able to decide what judges cannot sit on national security cases and whether such cases will be transferred to be heard on the Mainland. Beijing will be the ultimate interpreter of the NSL. The real mischief of the NSL is not the breadth of its new offences or the fact that it is much less restrained than the withdrawn 2003 Article 23 Security Bill, though it is all of that. The real mischief is how the law attempts to undermine the independence of the courts, the legislature, the bar, the press, pro-democracy movements, the academy, and civil society—all institutions that are vital for mitigating the most illiberal features of the security laws and practices of liberal democracies.

---

14. Yash Ghai has succinctly described the essence of rule by law approaches as follows: "In China, the power to interpret belongs to the same organ as makes the law. Law is seen as the will of the ruling class, and the principles of checks and balance and the separation of powers are not applicable." Yash Ghai, "Introduction", in Simon Young and Yash Ghai (eds), *Hong Kong's Final Court of Appeal* (Cambridge: Cambridge University Press, 2013), p 10. He elaborates that China's ability to interpret the Basic Law means that "the power about interpretation . . . is not simply about the meaning of laws, but about power relationships". Yash Ghai, "Autonomy and the Final Court of Appeal", in Ghai and Young, *ibid.*, p 61.
15. Benny Tai, "Challenges to the Rule of Law in Semi-Authoritarian Hong Kong" (2020) 29(1) *Social and Legal Studies* 110, 120.
16. Basic Law, Art 23.

I. Echoes of Illiberal Laws Enacted by Liberal Democracies

Those of us fortunate enough to live in liberal democracies who study comparative security laws should be candid, humble, and self-critical about the many excesses and flaws in our own security laws and in the processes used to enact, administer, and interpret them.[17]

(a) Making Secession Illegal

Article 20 of the NSL criminalises even peaceful attempts for Hong Kong to separate from China. The Chinese government takes the threat of secession seriously with mainland scholars warning that "what has happened in Taiwan could happen in Hong Kong".[18]

Liberal democracies including Canada,[19] Spain, and the US do not recognise a right of secession. In the wake of a civil war that left over 600,000 dead, the US Supreme Court invalidated Texas's secession. It ruled that the United States was "indissoluble" and a "perpetual union".[20] In 2010, an Alaskan court upheld a denial of an attempt to place the secession of that state on the ballot on the basis that secession is not constitutional.[21] In 2014, the Spanish Constitutional Court also held that Spain was "indissoluble" in the face of a declaration of Catalonian sovereignty. It will be suggested in the second part, however, that the NSL goes far beyond how liberal democracies respond to separatist movements and does so in a way that infringes expressive and associational freedoms that are vital to a broader rule of law culture.

(b) Broad Security Offences

Article 24 creates a very broad terrorism offence that includes not only violence but "sabotage", serious interference with essential public services, arson, and "other

17. For collections of work from a range of democratic and non-democratic countries stressing excesses in a variety of security laws, *see* Kent Roach (ed), *Comparative Counter-Terrorism* (Cambridge: Cambridge University Press, 2015); Victor V. Ramraj et al. (eds), *Global Counter-Terrorism Law and Policy* (Cambridge: Cambridge University Press, 2nd edn, 2012). For my own critical take on Canadian security laws, *see* Kent Roach, *September 11: Consequences for Canada* (Montreal: McGill Queens, 2003); Craig Forcese and Kent Roach, *False Security: The Radicalization of Canadian Anti-Terrorism Law* (Toronto: Irwin Law, 2015).
18. Zhu and Zhang, n 9 above, p 55. They argue for a "grand unification ethics, established in the great history of China" that "restricts not only separatist trends in Hong Kong, Taiwan, Xinjiang, and Tibet, but also the policy discretion and choices of Chinese leaders and decision-makers", *ibid.*, p 87.
19. *Reference re Quebec Secession* [1998] 2 SCR 217 recognising no unilateral right to secession but that the rest of Canada would have to respond if the people of Quebec clearly voted for secession. *See also* Clarity Act S.C. 2000, c 26 providing that Canada would not negotiate with Quebec unless there was a clear majority on a clear question in favour of secession.
20. *Texas v White* 74 US 700 (1868), at 726.
21. *Kohlaas v Officer of the Lieutenant Governor* 223 P 3d 105 (2010).

dangerous activities which seriously jeopardise public health, safety or security". In some respects, this is not as broad as some British and existing Hong Kong definitions of terrorism that include property damage. Article 24 follows templates found in international covenants and British terrorism laws by restricting the above harms to attempts to coerce governments (limited to China's and Hong Kong's) or international organisations "or intimidating the public in order to pursue a political agenda".

Article 26 provides a broad offence targeting financing, training, and other forms of support for terrorist organisations. Article 25 follows Commonwealth anti-terrorism laws in criminalising the leadership and active participation in a terrorist organisation. Similar provisions are found in the laws of liberal democracies.

The continued inability of the international community to agree on a definition of terrorism has allowed both liberal democracies and authoritarian states to enact broad terrorism offences. The NSL responds to criticisms that an undefined reference to "serious criminal means" in the withdrawn 2003 Security Bill was vague.[22] Zhu and Zhang argued in 2019 that because the 2003 Bill was criticised as "being unclear, ambiguous, and unspecific, so the new national security act should be clear, explicit, and specific". The new terrorism offence may be clearer, but it remains very broad. As such, it has not fulfilled Zhu and Zhang's prediction that a clearer law will "ease the public's concerns".[23] The rule of law is more about restraint in the substance of the law than clarity with respect to the text of the law.

Article 22 creates a broad subversion offence that was used to arrest in early January 2021 over 50 people who organised or ran in primaries in July 2020 in an attempt to co-ordinate pro-democracy movements. It is broader than the 2003 Security Bill because it applies to undermining either the Beijing or Hong Kong governments or their performance of their duties "by force or threat of force or by unlawful means". In the 2003 Bill, subversion was limited to "force or serious criminal means".

All of the security offences are greatly expanded by the inclusion of separate provisions that apply to those who incite, advocate, assist, conspire, abet, or provide financial assistance or property for the commission of the offence.[24] This follows trends in liberal democracies in relying on inchoate and speech-based forms of liability and attempts to punish all forms of assistance including financing.[25]

22. Roach, n 10 above, pp 138–139.
23. Zhu and Zhang, n 9 above, p 106.
24. NSL, Art 23. *See also* Art 21 for similar expansion of secession offence, Arts 26–27 in relation to terrorism and Art 30 in relation to foreign collusion.
25. *Holder v Humanitarian Law Project* 561 US 1 (2010).

(c) Terrorism Speech Offences

Article 27 makes it a crime punishable by up to 10 years' imprisonment to advocate terrorism or incite the commission of a terrorist activity. Ever since the UK-led Security Council Resolution 1624 enacted in response to the 2005 London bombings, terrorism laws have increasingly focused on speech. Speech can also be targeted by the new subversion offence that extends to sanctions, blockades, or "hostile acts" and unlawfully "provoking hatred" against the Chinese or Hong Kong governments.[26] Hate offences in liberal democracies protect vulnerable minorities as opposed to the state.

(d) Asserting Universal Jurisdiction

Article 38 of the NSL provides that the law applies to offences outside Hong Kong "by a person who is not a permanent resident of the region". When combined with Article 55, it allows serious national security cases to be transferred to China. This possibility set off a storm of controversy. Noted Chinese law expert Jerome Cohen warned those outside Hong Kong that "you can be locked up for as long as six months incommunicado, subject to torture, coerced confessions, no access to counsel or family and friends".[27] Article 38 played an important role in a number of western democracies suspending their extradition treaties with Hong Kong.[28]

It is hypocritical to oppose the assertion of universal jurisdiction because many liberal democracies assert even broader forms of universal jurisdiction in their terrorism laws than Article 38 which still requires offences outside Hong Kong to be aimed at Hong Kong. For example, the UK has prosecuted as terrorists those who fought against the Gaddafi regime in Libya. Moreover, the UK Supreme Court has recognised the potential injustice of applying broad terrorism offences to events committed in other countries[29] but no parliamentary reform has been forthcoming.

(e) Enhanced Punishments

The four new security offences (secession, subversion, terrorism, and collusion with a foreign country) provide for minimum punishment that depends on vague

26. NSL, Arts 22(3), 22(4), 29(4), and 29(5).
27. Javier Hernandez, "Harsh Penalties, Vaguely Defined Crimes: Hong Kong Security Law Explained", *New York Times*, 30 June 2020. Note that the withdrawn Article 23 bill also had extraterritorial effects, available at https://www.nytimes.com/2020/06/30/world/asia/hong-kong-security-law-explain.html. Bing Ling, "A Case for Extraterritoriality", in Fu, Peterson, and Young, n 10 above.
28. "Canada Suspends Extradition Treaty with Hong Kong over Security Law", *CBC News*, 3 July 2020, available at https://www.cbc.ca/news/politics/canada-suspending-extradition-treaty-hong-kong-over-security-law-1.5636479; Shannon Tiezza, "US Becomes Latest Country to Suspend Its Extradition Treaty with Hong Kong", *The Diplomat*, 20 August 2020, available at https://thediplomat.com/2020/08/us-becomes-latest-country-to-suspend-extradition-treaty-with-hong-kong/.
29. *R v Gul* [2013] UKSC 64.

classifications of the seriousness of the consequences of the particular crime. They do not provide for capital punishment, as do some American terrorism offences. The maximum punishment is life imprisonment. The Hong Kong courts pointedly noted in the first case that sentenced a person under the NSL that some terrorism offences in Australia, Canada, and the United Kingdom have maximum life sentences.[30]

There is also a recognition in the NSL that those who accept guilt or inform on others can receive more lenient treatment, something that has been used extensively in Italy. Disqualifications from running or holding office are also included, but these are not completely unprecedented as Article 3 of the Fourteenth Amendment provides for similar disqualification for those who have taken an oath to uphold the American Constitution but have engaged in "insurrection or rebellion" or "given aid or comfort to the enemies thereof". This archaic old security provision has not yet successfully been used in relation to the 6 January 2021 attack on the Capitol. Trump may be banned from Twitter, but he can still run again for office.

(f) Echoes of Countering Violent Extremism

Articles 9 and 10 of the NSL provide that the Hong Kong government "shall take necessary measures to strengthen public communication, guidance, supervision and regulation over matters concerning national security, including those relating to schools, universities, social organisations, the media, and the internet" and that it "shall promote national security education in schools and universities and through social organi[z]ations, the media, the internet and other means to raise the awareness of Hong Kong residents of national security and of the obligation to abide by the law."

In some respects, these provisions echo British programmes designed to counter extremism that have even been extended to universities.[31] Trump's 1776 Report similarly called for "patriotic education".[32] Articles 9 and 10 echo how since the Paris attacks, the UN Security Council has promoted programmes to counter

30. *HKSAR v Tong Ying Kit* [2001] HKCFI 2239 at para 26. The accused received a sentence of nine years' imprisonment in total for inciting secession and committing terrorism. The accused had previously been denied habeas corpus and unsuccessfully challenged bail and punishment provisions of the NSL and the failure to enact an official English version. *Tong Ying Kit v HKSAR* [2020] HKCFI 2133.

31. Counter-Terrorism and Security Act 2015 c 6 s 26. *See* generally Lucia Zedner, "Counterterrorism on Campus" (2018) 68 *University of Toronto Law Journal* 545.

32. President's Advisory 1776 Commission, "The 1776 Report", January 2021, p 16. The report claims that American universities "are often hotbeds of anti-Americanism, libel and censorship that combine to generate in students and the larger community at the very least outright disdain and at worst outright hatred for this country", *ibid.*, p 18.

violent extremism and "terrorist narratives".[33] The Security Council has used Chapter VII powers since 9/11 without sufficient attention to human rights, accountability, and the very different contexts in which the counter-terrorism instruments that it has promoted are used.[34]

(g) Use of Immigration for National Security Purposes

Article 34 of the NSL provides: "A person who is not a permanent resident of the Region may be subject to deportation if he or she contravenes the provisions of this Law but is not prosecuted for any reason." This provision employs immigration law with its lower standards of proof and wider acceptance of evidence for national security purposes. Immigration law is now being applied to activists who are attempting to leave Hong Kong. It had previously been used in Hong Kong to keep Falun Gong supporters out. The courts upheld the government's decision despite concerns that the underlying intelligence from China about security threats had been destroyed.[35]

Liberal democracies use immigration law for security purposes. They also use intelligence as evidence, albeit increasingly with special advocates and unclassified summaries designed to allow some adversarial challenge. In the US, there was a pre-textual use of immigration law to detain and deport Muslim males immediately after 9/11. Travel bans targeting people mainly from Muslim majority countries was the centrepiece of the Trump's administration security policies. Even more disturbingly, the US Supreme Court upheld both policies by deferring to the executive, though they have been repealed since the election of Biden as president.[36] The UK authorised indeterminate detention of suspected terrorists after 9/11 who could not be deported because of a risk of torture in their home country. The courts found this to be discriminatory, and the UK subsequently unsuccessfully tried to convince the European Court of Human Rights to alter its absolute ban on deportation to torture. Canada also relied on immigration detention of terrorist suspects in the immediate wake of 9/11, and its Supreme Court refused to rule out deportation to torture in "exceptional circumstances".[37]

---

33. UN Security Council Resolution 2178 (2014), para 15–19. *See also* UN Security Council Resolution 2535 (2020) enacted a few weeks after the NSL which at para 7 "stresses the importance of providing opportunities for young people to strengthen resilience against radicalization to violence and terrorist recruitment".
34. Kent Roach, "The Migration and Evolution of Programs to Counter Violent Extremism" (2018) 68 *University of Toronto Law Journal* 588.
35. *Chu Woan Chyi v Director of Immigration* [2009] 6 HKC 77. For a similar decision in Canada, but one that declared the destruction of intelligence about individuals subject to legal proceedings to be unlawful, see *Charkaoui v Canada* 2008 SCC 38.
36. *Ashcroft v Iqbal* 556 US 662 (2009) (qualified immunity prevents damage awards); *Trump v Hawaii* 138 SCt 2398 (2018) (deference to presidential power to protect national security).
37. *Suresh v Canada* [2002] 1 SCR 3, para 78. The West does not have clean hands when it comes to security excesses.

(h) Special National Security Courts and Limits on Trial by Jury

Article 46 of the NSL allows the Secretary of Justice, an executive official, to require that a trial should be in the High Court without a jury "on the grounds of, among others, the protection of State secrets, involvement of foreign factors in the case, and the protection of personal safety of jurors and their family members". A jury trial could be most useful for the accused and most dangerous for the state in the trial of protesters who have peacefully exercised expressive or associational freedoms. The reference in Article 46 to the executive taking away jury trials because of "the involvement of foreign factors in the case" re-enforces the idea of a nationalist approach and distrust of the Hong Kong citizenry.[38]

Liberal democracies have accepted limits on trial by jury in national security cases. Laura Donohue has noted: "Jurors' presence at terrorist trials risks juror intimidation, politicalisation of the jury, and the erection of obstacles to the state's use of classified information."[39] India abolished jury trials, non-jury Diplock courts can be used in terrorism cases in Northern Ireland, and the "jury" used by military commissions by the US at Guantanamo Bay is composed of officers serving in the US military. At the same time, trial by jury has figured prominently in national security trials in Australia, Canada, New Zealand, and the US.

Part of the move towards special courts in national security cases is a fear that regular courts may leak state secrets. Article 41 provides that when state secrets are involved "all or part of the trial shall be closed to the media and the public but the judgment shall be delivered in open court". Article 63 imposes confidentiality requirements on defence counsel who have access to "confidential [s]tate secrets, trade secrets or personal information". Liberal democracies have used publication bans, though they are generally temporary. They have also placed restrictions on the ability of lawyers to share secret information with those they represent.

(i) New Whole of Government National Security Institutions

The NSL creates new institutions to intensify and co-ordinate security activities. Many commentators see these as even more troubling than the new offences.[40] Articles 12 and 13 create a new national security committee chaired by the Chief Executive and containing senior financial, immigration, justice, and policing

38. Zhu and Zhang write about a form of Hong Kong "chauvinism" which is more cosmopolitan and looks down on those from mainland China. *See* Zhu and Zhang, n 9 above, Ch 3. Conversely this leads to suspicions that some Hongkongers are not sufficiently loyal to China.
39. Laura Donohue, "Terrorism and Trial by Jury: The Vices and Virtue of American and British Criminal Law" (2007) 59 *Stanford Law Review* 1321, 1324.
40. Petersen, n 6 above, p 646; Fu Hualing, "National Security", in Johannes Chan and C. L. Lim (eds), *Law of Hong Kong Constitution* (Hong Kong: Sweet & Maxwell, 3rd edn, 2021). As will be discussed in the second part of this chapter, these new security institutions will also take on the task of vetting candidates for office for loyalty.

officials. This committee follows a whole of government approach to security matters that most liberal democracies have taken since 9/11.

The new law also creates a national security "special branch" within the Hong Kong police. This follows colonial practices including in Hong Kong where the Special Branch under colonial rule traditionally targeted communists. Over 1000 of Hong Kong's colonial Special Branch members were pensioned and many returned to the UK before the handover.[41] The new institutions have dual, blurred, and potentially dangerous roles in collecting both intelligence and evidence, but this has also occurred in liberal democracies especially after 9/11.[42]

(j) Central Government Pre-emption and Extradition

The Basic Law recognised that China had interests in national defence and foreign policy matters in Hong Kong. The NSL adds national security to this list. That said, liberal democracies such as Australia, Canada, and the US allow their Central Governments to pre-empt local and regional institutions with respect to national security matters.

The new Beijing funded and appointed "Office for Safeguarding National Security of the Central People's Government in the Hong Kong Special Administrative Region" has wide-ranging policy, co-ordination, intelligence, investigative, and prosecutorial functions. It has symbolically taken up residence opposite the main rallying point for public protests in Hong Kong.

Article 55 provides that security cases that are "complex due to the involvement of a foreign country or external elements" or otherwise deemed serious can be transferred to the Mainland. As with the pre-emption of jury trials, the theme of mistrust and fear of the foreign is evident.

At the same time, extradition has frequently been used in post 9/11 security cases. The US courts, unlike many other common law countries, accept jurisdiction even when the accused has been subject to unlawful forms of extradition.[43] Even in cases where judicial review is exercised with respect to extradition, it is often deferential.[44]

---

41. Hualing Fu and Richard Cullen, "Political Policing in Hong Kong" (2003) *Hong Kong Law Journal* 199, 211.
42. In Canada, the Royal Canadian Mounted Police collected and distributed sometimes faulty intelligence after 9/11 that led the US to subject Maher Arar to extraordinary rendition to Syria. Canadian intelligence agencies have also been given powers to take physical steps to reduce threats to the security of Canada but with important restrictions that such powers could not be used to detain or physically harm people.
43. *US v Alavarez-Machain* 504 US 655 (1992).
44. *Diab v France* 2014 ONCA 374. But see *US v Khadr* 2011 ONCA 358 asserting common law powers to prevent abuse of process and preventing extradition from Canada to the United States because of American abuses in the capture of the fugitive.

(k) Increased Police Powers

Article 43 expands policing powers in national security cases with respect to searches, freezing and confiscation orders; take-down orders; requiring persons and foreign organisations to provide information to assist investigations; and enhancing electronic and covert surveillance. At the same time, many liberal democracies have expanded police powers in security cases since 9/11. The Patriot Act expanded powers to collect foreign intelligence. Both Australia and Canada enacted new powers that allowed for a person to be detained and questioned to provide information, though Canada has repealed the latter power. Liberal democracies have also provided for preventive arrests in security cases. In North America, elaborate undercover stings are allowed with no prior *ex ante* regulation and very rare *ex post* judicial invalidation.[45] New policing powers have generally not been matched with increased accountability mechanisms, especially when the police act in concert with domestic and foreign intelligence agencies.[46]

(l) Co-ordinate Construction of the Law by the Legislature

Article 65 of the NSL provides: "The power of interpretation of this Law shall be vested in the Standing Committee of the National People's Congress." This follows the ability of the NPCSC to give definitive interpretations under Article 158 of the Basic Law.

American presidents, most notably Thomas Jefferson, Andrew Jackson, and George H. W. Bush, have asserted their power to interpret the Constitution for themselves. Despite the danger that the executive and the legislature will engage in self-interested interpretations of the laws that are meant to restrain themselves, this practice has been defended by American scholars such as Mark Tushnet.[47]

Many liberal democracies do not embrace co-ordinate construction to the same degree, but many allow for legislative derogation from rights as they have been interpreted by the independent courts or do not allow unelected courts to invalidate democratically enacted laws. Nevertheless, it will be suggested in the second part of this paper that these practices differ significantly from the powers that the NPCSC have both under the NSL and the Basic law.

45. The only stay of proceedings related to entrapment techniques in terrorism cases in North America that I am aware of came in *R v Nuttall* 2018 BCCA 479.
46. But *see* National Security Act, 2017 SC c 13 expanding the jurisdiction of a review committee to apply to the national security activities of both the Royal Canadian Mounted Police and intelligence agencies.
47. Mark Tushnet, *Taking the Constitution Away from the Courts* (Princeton: Princeton University Press, 1999). My own views on co-ordinate construction are that it should only be used to depart from judicial interpretations when an explicit derogation is made from rights. Kent Roach, *The Supreme Court on Trial* (Toronto: Irwin Law, 2nd edn, 2016).

II. The Cacophony of Illiberal Elements in the NSL

In this part, I will argue that while the NSL picks up echoes and illiberal strands from the laws of liberal democracies, it is far from the "mild law" that Chief Executive Carrie Lam has claimed. More fundamentally, I will argue that by attacking the independence of the judiciary, the free press, free political parties, the academy, and civil society that engages in protests and critique, the NSL threatens to replace the OCTS compromise that preserved the rule of law with China's authoritarian rule by law culture.[48] The NSL embraces an extremely broad understanding of national security that has totalitarian dimensions.

The critique in this section also attempts to reveal the limits of a parsing or questionnaire approach to comparative law. It is especially important in the study of comparative security law to "be attentive not just to the law in the books, but the broader legal, social and political structures in which the law is put into action".[49] Even the text of the law cannot be understood apart from the process and context of its enactment.

Liberal democracies have often rushed their enactment of security laws,[50] but they have not enacted them in complete secrecy designed to stifle debate and criticism. They have sometimes created special security courts, but they have not given the executive the power on a yearly basis to exclude members at all levels of the judiciary from sitting on national security cases. They have not proposed "national security education" from primary school to university. They have not restricted office to those who meet loyalty tests of patriotism. Any one of these powers could threaten the rule of law. Their cumulative effect may well undermine the rule of law and replace it with rule by law determined by raw power.

(a) Meta-political Crimes of Secession and Subversion

Even if one concludes, following cases in the US, Spain, and Canada, that Hong Kong does not have a unilateral right of secession,[51] that hardly justifies the broad crimes of peaceful organisation and advocacy of separation found in Articles 20 and 21 of the NSL. These offences go far beyond those contemplated in the withdrawn

48. As Owen Fiss has written, "democracy not only requires a free press and free speech but a multitude of political parties . . . In China there is in reality only one party. In Hong Kong, there are four or five major parties, including some that openly oppose Beijing and its policies." Owen Fiss, "Hong Kong Democracy" (1998) 36 *Columbia Journal of Transnational Law* 493, 495.

49. Kent Roach, "Comparative Counter-Terrorism Comes of Age", in Kent Roach (ed), *Comparative Counter-Terrorism Law* (Cambridge: Cambridge University Press, 2015), p 44.

50. Andrew Lynch, "Legislating Anti-Terrorism: Observations on Forms and Process", in Victor Ramraj et al. (eds), *Global Anti-Terrorism Law and Policy* (Cambridge: Cambridge University Press, 2nd edn, 2012).

51. Lin Feng, "Is it Constitutional to Demand Hong Kong Independence? A Comparative Study" (2019) 49 *Hong Kong Law Journal* 507.

2003 Security Bill that would have required the use of force or serious criminal means. Rather, the new Article 20 offence follows Article 103 of the PRC Criminal Code in making it an offence subject to up to life imprisonment "to split the country and undermine national unification". It ignores Simon Young's argument that advocacy of secession should not be made criminal.[52] It could override the Court of Final Appeal's interpretations of regulations against wearing messages on clothing that was made in order to protect freedom of expression.[53] It runs counter to the 2001 Shanghai Convention[54] signed by China which limits its prohibition of separatism to violent attempts to achieve such ends.

Both the new meta-political crimes of secession and subversion are influenced by mainland criminal offences.[55] They are both featured on the Hong Kong police's purple warning banners to protesters that: "You are displaying flags, or banners/chanting slogans or conducting yourselves with an intent such as secession or subversion, which may constitute offences under the HKSAR's National Security Law. You may be arrested and prosecuted." Inciting secession has already emerged as the police's favourite charge when arresting people at protests. Having banners with slogans that have "a secessionist meaning" such as "Liberate Hong Kong: Revolution of Our Times" can lead to arrest and severe punishment.[56] Draconian offences do not have to be applied often to chill expressive and associational activities.

Independence movements in Catalonia, Hawaii, Scotland, and Quebec remain vibrant and represented by political parties and civil society because of liberal democratic institutions and respect for free speech and association and executive restraint in applying laws to peaceful and expressive activity. In a democracy, independence movements do not need to succeed to nourish national and democratic spirits. In Quebec, they provided a democratic alternative that won out at the polls over the use of political violence and terrorism. Even when advocacy of independence or association with terrorist groups is illegal in democracies, it is often tolerated. A 2017 ruling by the Spanish Constitutional Court that an independence referendum by Catalonia was illegal did not prevent the referendum from being held. The

52. Simon N. M. Young, "Old Wine in New Bottles: Reintroducing National Security in Legislation in Hong Kong", in Chan and de Londras, n 5 above, pp 214–215, who also note that there is nothing in China's 2005 Anti-Secession Law aimed at Taiwan that would require "that the advocacy of peaceful secession be criminalized".

53. *HKSAR v Fong Kwak Shan Christine* (2017) 20 HKCFAR 425.

54. Shanghai Convention on Combatting Terrorism, Separatism, and Extremism, Art 1. On the dualism behind current Chinese constitutional thinking, see Ryan Mitchell, "Theories of Sovereignty in the Origins and Implementation of Hong Kong's National Security Law", Chapter 4 of this volume.

55. *See* Albert Chen, "The National Security Law of the HKSAR: A Contextual and Legal Study", Chapter 2 of this volume.

56. *HKSAR v Tong Ying Kit* [2021] HKCFI 2200 at 178 convicting a man of inciting secession and *HKSAR v Tong Ying Kit* [2001] HKCFI 2239 at para 26 assessing six and a half years' imprisonment for an act of inciting secession classified by the court as serious.

convictions of Catalonia secessionist leaders have been followed by pardons.[57] In liberal democracies, rule of law traditions of freedom will often prevail over the letter of the law. It was in the deeper spirit of the rule of law that the Supreme Court of Canada recognised that a clear vote in favour of secession would require some negotiating response from the Central Government. The response would not be based on criminal offences of inciting secession, trials outside of Quebec, trials without juries, or the use of military force.[58]

To be sure, the separatist Hong Kong National Party was not approved under the Societies Ordinance (Cap 151) in 2014.[59] But the broad new offence of advocacy of even peaceful forms of secession combined with a broad subversion offence targeting the undermining of, disrupting, or promoting hatred against the Beijing or Hong Kong governments are meant to draw a red line to restrain speech and association and perhaps thought.

The secession offences combined with those aimed at subversion and foreign collusion provide a potent mix against a broad array of associational and expressive freedoms that are supposed to be protected under Chapter III of the Basic Law. Warnings by the Chief Executive that primaries held in July 2020 could constitute subversion, followed by the arrest of 53 people involved in them, underlines how secession and subversion offences go well beyond the post 9/11 expansion of terror laws by targeting and essentially forbidding democratic movements.[60] These charges follow from disqualification of pro-democracy candidates from office and the exit of the remaining pro-democracy legislators from the Legislative Council. The power of meta-crimes of unacceptable politics extends far beyond those who are charged or convicted of them.

Attempts to argue that the new secession and subversion offences are necessary to nip violence in the bud are not persuasive. Jie Zhu and Xiaoshan Zhang provided some of the intellectual underpinning for the NSL by their arguments that Hong Kong protests against the 2003 Bill, patriotic national education, and the Umbrella movement were evolving towards separatism and terrorism and their utter refusal to

57. Feng, n 51 above, p 530. It should be noted, however, that secessionist leaders in Spain were subsequently convicted in 2019 of sedition but acquitted of rebellion. They were sentenced to 9 to 14 years' imprisonment with appeals pending but were pardoned and released in mid-2021. Nicholas Casey, "Spain Pardons Jailed Catalan Separatist Leaders", *New York Times*, 22 June 2021.

58. *Re Quebec Secession* [1998] 2 SCR 217. A critic might reasonably cite the October 1970 declaration of martial law in response to two kidnappings by Quebec separatists in response. For arguments that both the Quebecois and Canada came to view this as a mistake and took steps, including the election of a separatist provincial government, two referenda, the creation of a constitutional bill of rights and new restraints on police and intelligence agencies in the years to come, *see* Forcese and Roach, n 17 above, pp 25–45.

59. Petersen, n 6 above.

60. Natasha Kham, "Hong Kong Police Arrest 53 Opposition Figures over Alleged Subversion", *Wall Street Journal*, 6 January 2021, available at https://www.wsj.com/articles/hong-kong-police-arrest-dozens-of-opposition-politicians-over-alleged-subversion-11609895177.

imagine that China could exercise colonial-type powers over Hong Kong.[61] Existing offences, however, are being applied to those who rioted and stormed the legislature in 2019. Some of the pre-existing offences such as sedition are problematic and have a long colonial legacy.[62] Nevertheless, the new offences of undermining and subverting state power and advocating peaceful secession extend even farther in limiting speech. It threatens to place Hong Kong in the same position that Tibet[63] and Xinjiang[64] find themselves in as they are ruled from Beijing in a nationalistic, authoritarian, and colonial manner.[65]

(b) Offences Targeting Speech, the Foreign Media, and Civil Society

Although the NSL creates broad terrorism offences similar to those found in liberal democracies, it contains none of the exemptions that some laws, including Hong Kong's United Nations (Anti-Terrorism Measures) Ordinance,[66] provide for "advocacy, dissent or industrial action". The Article 27 "advocating terrorism" offence contains no definition of either term. On the one hand, this may chill freedom of expression by allowing the executive to broadly interpret the speech crime. On the other hand, this creates space for the judiciary to employ what Po Jen Yap and Michael Hor defend in this volume as interpretative remedies that effectively read down the broad offence.[67] For example, the Supreme Court of Canada did this when it interpreted an undefined reference to "terrorism" in Canadian immigration law to refer only to intentional deaths or serious bodily harm and when it read down broad post 9/11 terrorism offences not to apply to peaceful protests.[68] One of the likely reasons why the Supreme Court of Canada took this course was sustained criticism from the independent academy, bar, and civil society about the dangers of overbroad definitions of terrorism. This again underlines the importance of

61. Zhu and Zhang, n 9 above, p 161 (arguing "all around the world, separatists have less and less influence and channels of expression" and suggesting that because of this "separatists resorted to street violence" and other crimes).
62. Fatemah Alzubairi, *Colonialism, Neo-Colonialism and Anti-Terrorism Law in the Arab World* (Cambridge: Cambridge University Press, 2019), pp 68–71.
63. Human Rights Watch, *Relentless: Detention and Prosecution of Tibetans under China's "Stability Maintenance Campaign"* (New York: Human Rights Watch, 2016), Ch 2, detailing detentions for peaceful protests including wearing a "Middle Way" t-shirt in reference to the Dalai Lama's proposal for a negotiated solution with China or photographs of him.
64. Human Rights Watch, "Devastating Blows: Religious Repression of the Uighurs in Xinjiang", April 2005, pp 71–75; Human Rights Watch, "Eradicating Ideological Viruses", September 2018.
65. The treatment of Hong Kong, Tibet, and Xinjiang are more directly colonial than the economic colonialism of the Belt and Road Initiative. David Brewster, "Colonialism with Chinese Characteristics", *Asia and Pacific Policy Forum*, 27 September 2018, available at https://www.policyforum.net/colonialism-chinese-characteristics/.
66. Cap 575.
67. Po Jen Yap, "Judging Hong Kong's National Security Law", Chapter 7 in this volume; Michael Hor, "The New National Security Law: Exploring a Meaningful Comparison with Singapore", Chapter 16 in this volume.
68. *Suresh v Canada* [2002] 1 SCR 1, para 94; *R v Khawaja* [2012] 3 SCR 555 at paras 49–53.

understanding how civil society will or will not support attempts by judges to restrain broadly worded laws.[69]

The first case convicting a person of terrorism under the NSL demonstrates little judicial appetite for interpreting statutory requirements as a means to restrain overbreadth. The Court of First Instance held that Tong Ying Kit's avoiding of police barriers and his crash into the police the day after the NSL was enacted constituted "serious violence against persons" causing "grave harm to the society" and "intimidating the public in order to pursue a political agenda".[70] The Court focused on the accused's political motives, concluding that the accused "targeted against those in the community who did not support the said political agenda, thereby seeking to contain or suppress counter voices". [71] The Court relied on the subjective "shock"[72] of some citizens at the accused's "deliberate challenge" of the police as a "symbol of Hong Kong's law and order". It rejected arguments that the acts constituted dangerous driving but not terrorism.[73] If sustained on appeal, this interpretation by a three-judge panel (the accused was denied trial by jury by the executive) would suggest that much politically motivated defiance of the police could constitute an act of terrorism under the NSL. The conviction is particularly ominous because it comes under the most restrictive part of the broad definition of terrorism which requires serious violence against persons.[74]

The record in the first year of the NSL does not support the hopes that the Hong Kong judiciary will restrain the breadth of the NSL. Judicial decisions to restrain the law and protect liberal values of freedom of expression—should they be made in the future—will not likely be supported by protests featuring a half million Hongkongers or more.

The maximum penalty for terrorist speech offences is relatively high at 10 years. At the same time, some of the more lenient penalties for such speech are also troubling because they provide for property confiscation, fines, and "short-term detention or restriction". Financial penalties could be used effectively to dismantle newspapers, websites, and bookshops. "Short-term detention or restriction" could be used to impose effective controls on vocal protesters. The Singaporean

69. Charles Epp, *The Rights Revolution* (Chicago: University of Chicago Press, 1998).
70. NSL Art 24.
71. *HKSAR v Tong Ying Kit* [2021] HKCFI 2200 at para 168.
72. *Ibid.* at 163.
73. *Ibid.* at para 171.
74. The court also ruled that the actions were "dangerous activities which seriously jeopardized public safety or security", *ibid.* at para 166. Other broader parts of Article 24 define the harms of terrorism as including arson, sabotage, serious interference with public services, or "other dangerous activities which seriously jeopardize public health, safety or security." For criticisms of the conviction, *see* Eric Lai and Thomas Kellogg, "Judgment in Tong Ying Kit's Case Sets Dangerous Precedent", *Hong Kong Free Press*, 31 July 2021, available at https://hongkongfp.com/2021/07/31/judgement-in-tong-ying-kits-case-sets-dangerous-precedent-ignores-human-rights-law/. For a defence of the verdict with reference to the laws of liberal democracies, *see* "Vitality of National Security Law Lies in Its Implementation", *Global Times*, 30 July 2021, available at https://www.globaltimes.cn/page/202107/1230135.shtml.

experience with the Internal Security Act demonstrates how the executive can effectively manage dissent through a combination of severe and less severe penalties. The law has already deterred printers and bookstores in Hong Kong from publishing books on recent Hong Kong history.[75] The chilling effects of the law on expressive and associational freedoms is much greater than the sum of its individual parts.

The broad speech offences in the new law should not be viewed in isolation. Article 54 contemplates that the new Beijing office will "take necessary measures to strengthen the management of and services for organs of foreign countries and international organisations in the Region, as well as non-governmental organisations and news agencies of foreign countries". There is a danger that foreign media and civil society will be less able to publicise national security abuses. To be sure, there are many post 9/11 stains on the liberal democratic record. They are, however, visible stains because of the courageous work of leakers, civil society groups, and investigative reporters.[76]

Article 29 of the NSL exposes people in and outside of Hong Kong to a new foreign collusion offence with respect to disruption, sanction, and unlawfully promoting hatred towards either the Hong Kong or Beijing governments. To be sure, there is some wiggle room for judicial interpretation, but much damage can be done by even failed prosecutions and pretrial detention. Article 29 is one of many provisions that demonstrate a form of legal nationalism[77] that is hostile to international civil society. This is significant because various international advocacy groups have played a very important role since 9/11 in protecting a broader rule of law and human rights culture.[78] The Chinese nationalism in the NSL and fear of the foreign

75. Kent Ewing, "My Ill-Fated Book Deal Reveals Self-Censorship under Hong Kong's Security Law", *Hong Kong Free Press*, 15 December 2020, available at https://hongkongfp.com/2020/12/15/kent-ewing-my-ill-fated-book-deal-reveals-hong-kong-self-censorship-under-the-security-law/.

76. Kent Roach, "Accountability Mechanisms for Transnational Counter-Terrorism", in Benjamin Goold and Liora Lazarus (eds), *Security and Human Rights* (Oxford: Bloomsbury, 2nd edn, 2020).

77. The fact that the NSL is only official in its Chinese version despite references in the Basic Law to English being an official language is also a sign of a new nationalism that could make it more difficult for the law to be subject to international criticism.

78. Civil society groups, such as Human Rights Watch, Amnesty International, and the International Commission of Jurists, have played a key role in publicising and criticising national security excess in countries throughout the globe. In July 2020, the International Commission of Jurists strongly criticised the NSL and called on China to repeal the law. It raised particular concerns about judicial independence. It noted, "according to Article 44 of the Law, the Chief Executive shall designate a number of judges to handle cases concerning national security-related offences. Before making such a designation, the Chief Executive may consult the Committee for Safeguarding National Security of the Hong Kong Special Administrative Region and the Chief Justice of the Court of Final Appeal. This further weakens an already flawed appointment process for judges adjudicating cases involving national security interests, by potentially removing them from the Hong Kong judicial structure entirely." International Commission of Jurists, "The Law of the People's Republic of China on Safeguarding National Security in the Hong Kong Administrative Region, Legal Briefing, July 2020, available at p 11 at https://www.icj.org/wp-content/uploads/2020/07/Hong-Kong-National-Security-Law-Briefing-Paper-ENG-2020pdf.pdf. On the importance of civil society groups in publicising and

has more in common with Saudi terrorism offences than British ones.[79] It will be recalled that Saudi Arabia was one of the supporters of the NSL in the UN Human Rights Council.

(c) Loyalty Oaths and Office Disqualifications

Under Article 6, all those who stand for office or hold public office must pledge allegiance through an oath. This needs to be understood in the context of China's demands in a 2014 White Paper that local officials must be "patriots" and that "loving the country is a basic political requirement" for such positions and a 2016 ruling by the NPCSC that one must be sincere in pledging loyalty to China.[80] Loyalty oaths are an example of what I criticised as an older vision of national security seen in the 2003 Article 23 Bill that focused on crimes such as treason as the betrayal of the state. I argued that such older forms of security were becoming anomalous and anachronistic in liberal democracies.[81]

Loyalty oaths were first used as a means of keeping Catholics from serving under Henry VIII. They played a role in the Irish Civil War because of a refusal of some republicans to swear an oath to the Queen.[82] They were also used during the McCarthy era in the United States.[83] American courts were reluctant to invalidate them as a requirement for public employment,[84] though some were invalidated on

---

campaigning against national security excess in the US, *see* David Cole, *Engines of Liberty: The Power of Citizen Activists to Make Constitutional Law* (New York: Basic Books, 2016).

79. For example, a woman's rights activist Loujain al-Hathloul was convicted by a special terrorist court of "communicating with international bodies and organisations . . . [and] terrorists individuals and entities hostile to the Kingdom and a series of foreign journalists", *see* "Loujain's Arrest", *Loujain al-Hathloul,* available at https://www.loujainalhathloul.org/arrest-torture-charges#charges. The 2017 Saudi counter-terrorism law is similar to the Hong Kong NSL in prohibiting exposure of national unity to danger and focusing on foreign interference. It subjects those who "sympathize or incite" terrorism with up to 8 years' punishment and subjects those to 15 years' imprisonment who misuse "academic or social status or media influence to promote terrorism". Human Rights Watch, "Saudi Arabia: New Counterterrorism Law Enables Abuse", 23 November 2017, available at https://www.hrw.org/news/2017/11/23/saudi-arabia-new-counterterrorism-law-enables-abuse.
80. Petersen, n 6 above, p 641.
81. Roach, n 10 above. For a different approach, *see* Giorgio Agamben, *The Sacrament of Language* (Cambridge: Polity Press, 2011).
82. Philip J. Dykes, "The Allegiance Element in Official Oaths: A Historical Overview" (2017–2019) 6 *City University of Hong Kong Law Review* 29.
83. J. Edgar Hoover defended loyalty oaths and the FBI's role in them by arguing that his agents did not "investigate political activities, unless the authors hold to the view that organisations such as the German-American Bund and the Communist Party are political activities rather than have themselves viewed in their true light of 'Fifth Columnists.' The FBI does not, has not, and never will so long as I am Director investigate political views." J. Edgar Hoover, "A Comment on the Article 'Loyalty among Government Employees'" (1949) 52 *Yale Law Journal* 401, 406.
84. *Adler v Board of Education* 342 US 485 (1952); *Cole v Richardson* 405 US 676 (1972). In Canada a citizenship oath that requires allegiance to the Queen has been upheld from Charter challenge: *Roach v Canada (Minister of State for Multiculturalism and Citizenship* 1994 CanLII 3453 (FCA); [1994] 2 FC 406.

the basis of overbreadth or vagueness.[85] Some judges such as Justice Black took a bolder approach concluding that loyalty oaths "are notorious tools of tyranny".[86] He also warned that loyalty oaths were an attempt to produce "a stultifying conformity" and that true loyalty "can never be secured by the endless proliferation of 'loyalty' oaths; loyalty must arise spontaneously from the hearts of people who love their country and respect their government".[87] More recently, Cass Sunstein has argued that loyalty oaths are a product of fear and that "no loyalty oath is required when loyalty is not in question".[88]

The NSL provides for disqualification of people convicted of security offences from holding elected or appointed office or even running for office.[89] As discussed above, there are more limited office disqualifications in the American Constitution for those who have engaged in "insurrection or rebellion", but even those can be abrogated by a two-thirds vote of Congress. In any event, they are rarely used. Liberal democracies do not vet candidates for office for loyalty as will the new security branch of the Hong Kong police and its new national security committee.[90]

Irish nationalists have a long history of being elected to the UK Parliament. They often refused to take their seats, but more as a protest than a legal disqualification. The official opposition in Canada's Parliament has at times been a party committed to the peaceful separation of Quebec from Canada, something that would literally split the country in two. Although it has not been perfectly consistent, the US Supreme Court has held that some office disqualifications should be prohibited as a bill of attainder in which the legislature exercises judicial functions.[91] In contrast, the NPCSC had no hesitation on 11 November 2020 in specifying that four legislators were ineligible to take office in the Legislative Council.[92] The naming of specific individuals in legislation is offensive to the role of courts under the rule of law.

---

85. *Cramp v Board of Public Instruction* 368 US 278 (1961).
86. *Wieman v Updegraff* 344 US 183 (1952) at 193.
87. *Speiser v Randall* US 513 (1952) at 532.
88. Cass Sunstein, "Unity and Plurality: The Case of Loyalty Oaths" (1990) 2 *Yale Journal of Law and Humanities* 101, 102–103.
89. Art 35.
90. Austin Ramzi and Tiffany May, "How China Plans to Control Hong Kong's Elections", *New York Times*, 31 March 2021, available at https://www.nytimes.com/2021/03/30/world/asia/china-hong-kong-elections.html.
91. *United States v Brown* 381 US 437 (1965) holding that disqualifications constitute a bill of attainder contrary to the separation of powers.
92. The Decision of the NPCSC on Issues Relating to the Qualification of the Members of the Legislative Council of the HKSAR, 11 November 2020, available at https://www.info.gov.hk/gia/general/202011/11/P2020111100779.htm.

(d) Patriotic National Security Education

As mentioned in Part I, there are echoes in the references in Article 10 to "national security education" to the countering of violent extremism programmes promoted by the UN. Such programmes are used in the UK and also contemplated in Article 29 of China's 2015 Counter-Terrorism Law which provides for re-education for those "who participated in terrorist or extremist activities". That said, the whole of society scope of Articles 9 and 10 is breathtaking. They go beyond the more narrowly tailored re-education provisions in mainland China that can apply to those that have been convicted of security offences.

National security education can extend to all aspects of social life. It is reminiscent of what Hualing Fu has noted is a tendency of China under Xi to define almost all matters of governance as matters of national security.[93] The shadow of massive internment and "re-education" programmes in Xianjing hangs over these provisions.

Articles 9 and 10 should also be understood in the context of prior battles over patriotic education that were successfully resisted in 2012.[94] Plans to drop references to the separation of powers in school texts to reflect what Carrie Lam has defended as the "executive-led" nature of Hong Kong[95] as well as the Education Secretary's announced ban on the song "Glory to Hong Kong"[96] are telling. They have led to concerns that the new law is part of a process that will make "Hong Kong China".[97] This again serves as a reminder of the importance of understanding security laws in their broader historical, social, and political context.

(e) Beijing-Led Security Institutions That May Be Immune from the Rule of Law

Although the new Hong Kong National Security Committee on its face seems unexceptional as a whole of government means of co-ordination, the role of the Beijing appointed national security advisor in providing "advice" to it raises concerns. This is a non-transparent yet potentially potent source of power especially given that the national security advisor is also currently the head of Beijing's Liaison Office

93. Fu Hualing, "China's Imperatives for National Security Legislation", in Chan and de Londras, n 5 above.
94. Even before the law, some educational materials that taught students about the Basic Law cast protesting in a negative light. Peace Chiu, "Is Chinese National Education Set to Make a Comeback in Hong Kong? It's Not If, but How, Experts Say", *South China Morning Post*, 4 August 2017, available at https://www.scmp.com/news/hong-kong/politics/article/2105343/chinese-national-education-set-make-comeback-hong-kong-its.
95. "Hong Kong's New Security Law Is Being Applied Sparingly, So Far", *The Economist*, 10 October 2020, available at https://www.economist.com/china/2020/10/08/hong-kongs-new-security-law-is-being-applied-sparingly-so-far.
96. Government of HKSAR, "Restricting Students' Freedom of Expression", 8 July 2020, available at https://www.info.gov.hk/gia/general/202007/08/P2020070800306.htm.
97. Michael C. Davies, *Making Hong Kong China* (New York: Columbia University Press, 2020), pp 50, 91.

in Hong Kong. Article 14 provides no check on the Committee's power by providing that no institution including the courts "shall interfere" with its work. Greater Chinese influence over Hong Kong security institutions creates a threat to self-government especially because national security is a far broader and elastic concept than foreign affairs and national defence.

Beijing's new National Security Office created by the new law is especially troubling. Although Article 50 proclaims that it "shall not infringe upon the lawful rights and interests of any organisation", Article 60 provides that the new Office and its staff "shall not be subject to the jurisdiction of the Hong Kong Special Administrative Region". These two provisions are contradictory, something that suggests that they threaten the rule of law.[98] Articles 60 and 61 expand the contradictory nature of the new law by providing, on the one hand, that Hong Kong authorities must co-operate with the new Beijing-appointed National Security Office, including prosecuting those who are "obstructing" the performance of its mandate. On the other hand, they provide that anyone who shows identification or certification documents issued by the new Office "shall not be subject to inspection, search or detention by law enforcement officers of the Region". In short, the law requires Hong Kong officials to assist the Beijing office, but it does not allow them to apply the law to its officials. Taken to the extreme, the rule of law carve out for the Beijing office could amount to a rule by law version of James Bond's fictional "license to kill".[99] Lest this be dismissed as hyperbole, Article 71 of China's 2015 Anti-Terrorism Law allows the military or police to leave the country on undefined "counter-terrorism missions".

Hong Kong courts could and should in the best common law tradition hold that Article 60 does not clearly oust their jurisdiction to review the activities of the new Beijing National Security Office. Writing in early 2020 before the enactment of the NSL, Cora Chan and Fiona de Londras have suggested that, while "China's conceptions of national security are inherently incompatible with Hong Kong's conception of the rule of law",[100] creative and wise actions by the Hong Kong judiciary are still possible. I fear that this approach may now be overly optimistic. Article 60 seems to be a legalised version of Oren Gross's extralegal powers model without even the restraint provided by possible review or prosecution.[101]

If Hong Kong courts are able to resist the idea that the Beijing Office is effectively a lawless office immune from rule of law, such last gasps of the rule of law

98. Lon Fuller, *The Morality of Law* (New Haven: Yale University Press, 1969).

99. But see s 7 of the UK's Intelligence Services Act, 1994 c 13 allowing for Executive authorisation of acts outside the UK that make members of the Security Service immune from prosecution. For a more restrained version that prohibits Canadian intelligence agents inside and outside of Canada from intentionally or negligently causing death, bodily harm, detention, torture, or participating in cruel or degrading treatment or property damage endangering the safety of an individual, *see* Canadian Security Intelligence Service Act s 12.2.

100. Cora Chan and Fiona de Londras, "Introduction", in Chan and Londras, n 5 above, p 22.

101. Oren Gross, "Chaos and Rules" (2003) 112 *Yale Law Journal* 1011.

could be smothered by an unreasoned rule by law decision of the NPCSC to interpret the new law to give the new Beijing Office immunity from the rule of law. Hong Kong courts that make liberal decisions in an attempt to preserve the rule of law risk a permanent and authoritarian rule by law backlash. This may help explain how deferential the Hong Kong courts have been in the first year of the NSL, though some may argue that the courts will become more active when the emergency or crisis has passed.

Both the new National Security Office and a new special branch in the Hong Kong police now have overlapping mandates to collect national security intelligence. If the Hong Kong police adhere to common law notions of police independence from executive direction of their law enforcement activities, this may provide justification for the new Beijing office to assert its jurisdiction. Only the Hong Kong police are subject to the jurisdiction of the Independent Police Complaints Council which had to go to court to conduct an audit of the Hong Kong's public order policing and has no power to compel co-operation in its reviews. National security investigation and intelligence gathering may be even more resistant to review and the application of the rule of law.

(f) Special National Security Courts That Imperil Judicial Independence

Although some liberal democracies (and many more authoritarian ones) employ special national security courts, they tend to be limited to a special trial level court. Article 44 of the NSL is extraordinarily troubling because it requires the Chief Executive to designate judges at all levels from trial to the Court of Final Appeal on a yearly basis to "handle cases concerning offence regarding national security". To make sure that the message for using only "safe hands" in the judiciary is not lost on the Chief Executive, Article 44 bluntly and inelegantly declares:

> A person shall not be designated as a judge to adjudicate a case concerning offence endangering national security if he or she has made any statement or behaved in any manner endangering national security. A designated judge shall be removed from the designation list if he or she makes any statement or behaves in any manner endangering national security during the term of office.

The text of Article 44 requires something akin to a yearly security clearance and loyalty oath for judges as determined by the Chief Executive. It could result in judges—perhaps especially foreign judges on the Court of Final Appeal—being precluded by the executive from sitting on national security cases. As with other loyalty oaths, this suggests that China fears both threats to its national security in Hong Kong[102] and the Hong Kong judiciary. As with the 2016 Interpretation from

102. For an account that stresses China's fears about Xinjiang and Tibet, see Fu Hualing, "China's Imperatives for National Security Legislation", in Chan and de Londras, n 5 above.

the NPCSC, this speaks to a desire to shut down judicial opinions that Beijing views as dangerous before they are spoken.

In my view, the Chief Executive's powers under Article 44 should be a critical issue as foreign judges decide whether to remain on or accept appointments on the Court of Final Appeal. Some legislators in 2018 expressed concerns about Lady Hale or Chief Justice McLachlin sitting on cases involving China's "national interest".[103] Justice Spigelman of Australia resigned because of the content of the NSL.[104] This is a difficult issue given that the exit of esteemed foreign judges could hasten a move to rule by law.

Canada's former Chief Justice McLachlin agreed in August 2021 to stay on the Court of Final Appeal. She apparently did so on the understanding that Hong Kong's Chief Justice and not its Chief Executive would assign judges to sit on national security cases and that she would not be disqualified from sitting on such cases. She added that if judicial independence is "challenged in any way that is inconsistent with my principles, then I'm gone. I'm sorry, I won't be part of it."[105] This raises concerns about the lack of transparency about how the executive's power under Article 44 is exercised and how it interacts with the judiciary's own power to assign judges to sit on particular cases. Unless Article 44 is being disregarded, it is difficult to see how the yearly executive designation of national security judges will not affect the power of the judiciary to assign judges to preside in specific national security cases.

The High Court of Hong Kong has tried to put a rule of law face on Article 44 by stressing that the judiciary still assigns judges to hear the particular case, and judges remain duty bound to decide cases free from government "interference

103. Lo Puiyin, "Twilight of the Idolized: Backsliding in Hong Kong and China's Legal Culture", in Chan and de Londras, n 5 above, p 137.

104. "Australian Judge James Spigelman Says He Resigned over Hong Kong's National Security Law", *The Standard*, 18 September 2020, available at https://www.thestandard.com.hk/breaking-news/section/4/155773/Australian-judge-James-Spigelman-says-he-resigned-over-HK's--national-security-law. Lord Hodge, President of the UK Supreme Court, however, has accepted an appointment as a part-time foreign judge. Lady Hale has subsequently not sought an additional term on the Court of Final Appeal. She noted that, while the rule of law is protected in Hong Kong in commercial cases, "the jury is out" on how courts "will be able to operate" under the NSL with "all sorts of question marks up in the air". Ben Rigby, "UK Judge Steps Down from Hong Kong's Final Court of Appeal", *The Global Legal Post*, 2 June 2021, available at https://www.globallegalpost.com/big-stories/uk-judge-steps-down-from-hong-kongs-court-of-final-appeal-2702789/. *See* Johannes Chan, "National Security and Judicial Independence: A Clash of Fundamental Values", Chapter 6 in this volume.

105. Chief Justice McLachlin added, "I don't think we're providing cover for anything. I am a judge on the court. I am not a participant in the government in Hong Kong in any way. That court is independent . . . and I believe for the benefit of the citizens of Hong Kong who seek justice, it should remain that way." She added that departure of foreign judges would be "a negative development for Hong Kong". Tom Blackwell, "Former Canadian Chief Justice Says She's Staying on Hong Kong Court to Help Preserve City's 'Last Bastion of Democracy'", *National Post*, 6 August 2021, available at https://nationalpost.com/news/world/former-canadian-chief-justice-says-shes-staying-on-hong-kong-court-to-help-preserve-citys-last-bastion-of-democracy.

or influence".[106] This, however, avoids the question of executive interference with judicial independence by yearly designations by the Chief Executive of what judges are eligible or ineligible to sit on national security cases. If the executive's yearly master list of designations is restrictive, then the judiciary's power to select who will sit on a particular national security case will be constrained. The judicial power to pick among judges that the executive approves on a yearly basis as trustworthy enough to sit on national security cases is not in my view a sufficient protection for judicial independence. Indeed, it may simply provide a false façade of judicial independence.

Under Article 47, the Chief Executive also has the power to issue a "binding" certificate of secrecy. To be sure, executives in liberal democracies have extensive first mover powers to assert secrecy, but they are subject to judicial review which seems more clearly to be ousted in Article 47 than in other parts of the new law.[107] What makes the NSL different from the national security laws of liberal democracies is the frequency in which it enshrines raw and unchecked executive power, whether it be on what judges are eligible to preside over national security cases, whether the accused can have trial by jury, or over what information can, because of secrecy claims, be disclosed to the accused or the court.

Given the exclusion and exit of pro-democracy legislators and increased control and security oaths for the executive, the judiciary remains the only state institution in Hong Kong likely to defend freedom and the rule of law. Hong Kong judges must walk a fine line between doing their jobs in a traditional rule of law manner, but also consider resigning when that is no longer possible. The first year of the NSL has not seen a major judicial pushback against its extraordinarily broad terms and powers.

(g) Rule by Law and Command from the Executive in Hong Kong and Beijing

Article 7 of the NSL signals that more security legislation is to come. Within a few days of its enactment, the Hong Kong executive issued over a hundred pages of Implementation Rules establishing new police powers and offences, including one punishable by up to seven years' imprisonment for prejudicing a national security

---

106. *Tong Ying Kit v HKSAR* [2020] HKCFI 2133; [2020] 4 HKLRD 382; [2020] 6 HKC 110, paras 51–64. The Court downplayed the power of the executive to exclude judges at all levels from sitting on national security cases under Article 44 by stressing that, despite the yearly executive designations, the judges for particular national security cases are still selected by the judiciary and still hold security of tenure. Although this approach has the good news of affirming continuing judicial independence, it downplays the plain words of Article 44. The Court in the same case rejected challenges to the presumptions against bail, mandatory penalties, and the lack of an official English version of the NSL.

107. For persuasive arguments that Art 47 goes well beyond executive powers under the Basic Law with respect to foreign powers and national state and common law act of state doctrine, *see* Johannes Chan, "National Security and Judicial Independence: A Clash of Fundamental Values", Chapter 6 in this volume.

investigation. This will adversely affect the media.[108] New provisions for elections are also driven by security-based concerns to limit democratic opposition and ensure loyalty to China. The top-down process of imposing first a security law and then an election law from Beijing seems designed to avoid debate and dissent which is an essential part of a broader rule of law culture. It is too blinkered a view of comparative law simply to compare the NSL with broad security laws in liberal democracies and to find some similarities.

The differences between rule of law and rule by law are critical in understanding why Hong Kong's security law present a greater threat to rights and freedoms than even the most illiberal of security laws in liberal democracies.[109] Article 65 of the NSL vests final interpretative authority to the NPCSC, which under Article 158 of the Basic Law also can interpret the Basic Law. The latter power has not produced interpretations of the Basic Law but rather terse and unreasoned commands that are added as appendices to the Basic Law and are not questioned by Hong Kong courts. As Johannes Chan writes in this volume: "[i]n the mainland legal system, the power of interpretation is a legislative process that can be invoked [at any time] to fill a gap in existing legislation."[110]

As Mark Daly has argued, the power of the NPCSC to declare "the law as it always has been and at a stroke (and without open debate)" makes its role less about co-ordinate construction and more about asserting authoritarian and neocolonial forms of rule by law.[111] This view is supported by Benny Tai who has argued that the NPCSC can "give any meaning to the Basic Law whatever and whenever it desires even if the meaning is something which the language of the constitution cannot bear. Such additional meanings can even apply retroactively".[112] As Tai notes, such interpretations can pre-empt judicial rulings as they did in the 2016 Oath Taking case and again with respect to the disqualification of four legislators in November 2020.

The Chinese approach to definitive interpretations goes well beyond the powers of co-ordinate construction that in the US arguably resulted in the torture memos. The torture memos at least attempted to interpret the relevant law. They were leaked, published by a free press, and their reasoning of what constituted torture was widely

108. LN 139 of 2000, Sch 7 s 5.
109. Another helpful example to distinguish rule of law from rule by law is the contrast of the rule of law idea that the Basic Law provides a division of powers between Hong Kong and China with the latter having powers over national defence and foreign relations and the idea defended by Zhu and Zhang that the entire Basic Law is simply "an authorization of power" from China's People Congress. Zhu and Zhang, n 9 above, p 101.
110. Johannes Chan, "National Security and Judicial Independence: A Clash of Fundamental Values", Chapter 6 in this volume. See also *Director of Immigration v Chong Fong Yuen* (2001) 4 HKCFAR 211 at 222–223, stressing that the Standing Committee's power to interpret the Basic Law is derived from the mainland Chinese system.
111. Mark Daly, "A Human Rights Lawyer's Perspective", in Young and Ghai, n 14 above, p 217.
112. Tai, n 15 above, p 117.

demolished. They were eventually withdrawn and would not have bound American courts. Guantanamo has resulted in an avalanche of litigation that was not stopped by the original executive decrees that declared that no court in the world could review them. Co-ordinate construction in liberal democracies at least allows courts, legislatures, and the executive to compete over the meaning of basic laws. In contrast, the Chinese approach seems based on unreasoned and unitary command.

The Hong Kong courts assisted by an independent bar could still attempt to interpret at least the more ambiguous parts of the NSL in a manner consistent with rights. I am a fan of common law constitutionalism including interpretative remedies that reconcile legislative objectives with rights.[113] At the same time, judicial warnings and nudges presume that legislatures, the executive, and ultimately the public will be attentive and able to respond to their nuanced signals. Moreover, it assumes that there is a high political price for overriding judicial signals in favour of rights and liberty that may no longer be true in Hong Kong.

There is a danger, already seen in the High Court's insistence that executive designation of judges in national security cases does not violate judicial independence, [114] of using the rule of law reputation of Hong Kong courts to legitimate rule by law and unreasoned executive command that would not be accepted in liberal democracies. This danger is acute because it may suggest that the rule of law is still alive when perhaps it is not.

Some might argue that the 2019 protests and riots, including the occupation of the legislature, produced a state of emergency, and it is hypocritical not to allow China, like liberal democracies, to take strong actions in response. An important restraint on emergency derogations from rights in liberal democracies, however, is that they are time-limited and must be renewed by open legislative debate.[115] Even if, as now appears unlikely, Hong Kong courts were to find the new security to be a disproportionate violation of rights,[116] Beijing retains the ability permanently to overrule such interpretations through edicts and bald commands.

113. See Kent Roach, "Common Law and Constitutional Dialogues between the Supreme Court of Canada and Canadian Legislatures" (2000) 80 *Can Bar Rev* 481.

114. *Tong Ying Kit*, n 106 above, para 3.

115. Kent Roach, "Ordinary Laws for Emergencies and Democratic Derogations from Rights", in Victor Ramraj (ed), *Emergencies and the Limits of Legality* (Cambridge: Cambridge University Press, 2008), p 244.

116. Compare *A v Home Secretary* [2004] UKHL 56 where the British courts subjected even derogations to judicial review with *HKSAR v Lai Ching Yee* [2021] HKCFA 3 at 37 disclaiming the ability of Hong Kong courts to review the NSL under the Basic Law or the International Covenant on Civil and Political Rights. See also *Tong Ying Kit v Secretary of Justice* [2021] HJCFI 1397 at 7 noting, "There is and can be no challenge to the constitutionality of NSL s.46(1)" allowing the executive to designate non-jury trials under the new law.

Conclusions

China's defence of the NSL as one that builds on elements of post 9/11 security laws and practices in the UK and US and promoted by the UN Security Council has a grain of truth. Liberal democracies should recognise this in their critique of the new law. Moreover, they should pay attention to how their own laws provide some semblance of legitimacy to repressive laws adopted by authoritarian states and by democracies that are moving to authoritarianism.

Although liberal democracies and the UN deserve some of the blame for Hong Kong's security law, the law takes illiberal elements in the security laws of liberal democracies and turns the volume up to maximum. When the Basic Law was created, national security was not specifically enumerated in Beijing's powers. It now has become a defining feature of Beijing's regulation of many elements of Hong Kong society including education, elections, and holding office. The exhaustive and exhausting legalism of the act builds to a cacophony of illiberal ideas that may spell the end of the OCTS approach and the rule of law in Hong Kong.

The August 2021 conviction and nine-year sentence of Ton Ying Kit for inciting secession and terrorism for using a political slogan and dangerous driving takes what in liberal democracies are strained hypotheticals about the reach of broad post 9/11 security laws and transforms them into a grim reality of convictions and long prison sentences under the NSL.[117] The NSL takes its meaning not only from clauses influenced by illiberal elements of the security laws of liberal democracies but also from how it is administered by the executive and the judiciary and the threat that, if courts take a more liberal approach, they may quickly be overruled by Beijing.

An appreciation of the significance of the NSL requires more than a careful parsing of its words and a comparison to the security laws of liberal democracies. It must also be understood in its historical, social, and political context. Although the NSL was defended as a response to protests and riots in 2019, it also can be seen as an aggressive "in your face" response to successful opposition that forced the withdrawal of the 2003 Article 23 Bill and the 2019 Extradition Bill. As Johannes Chan has observed, "[OCTS] was always a highly asymmetrical model, the success of which rests entirely on the restraint of the sovereign power."[118] With the exception of the refusal to use the death penalty, such restraint is not evident in the NSL. Some

117. Chief Justice McLachlin dismissed the idea that a broad terrorism offence enacted in Canada after 9/11 could ever be applied to peaceful protest or to lawyers or others who provided professional services to terrorists. See *R v Khawaja* [2012] 3 SCR 555 at paras 49–53 concluding that a terrorism offence would not apply to "a person who marches in a non-violent rally" because such conduct would be "essentially harmless" and does not constitute "a real risk to Canadian society". She dismissed hypotheticals presented by academics as based on "an incorrect interpretation" of the law. *Ibid.* The author unsuccessfully argued for the British Columbia Civil Liberties Association that the broad Canadian terrorism offence was unconstitutionally overbroad.

118. Johannes Chan, "Maintaining Institutional Strength: The Court, Act of State and the Rule of Law", in Chan and de Londras, n 5 above, p 257.

may have believed that OCTS only had to be maintained for 50 years, because by 2047 reforms would have moved China in the direction of Hong Kong. Alas, the 2020 NSL suggests that this optimistic "end of history"[119] vision is unlikely to occur. It is Hong Kong that is becoming "more like the Mainland".[120]

If this triumph of authoritarian rule by law comes to pass, it will not be because liberal democracies aided and abetted by the UN Security Council engaged in post 9/11 security excess. It will be because of Beijing's rule by law attack on Hong Kong's distinctive system of law and politics and its commitment to the rule of law. It remains to be seen whether the Hong Kong courts, the press, the bar, the academy, and civil society will be able to use their voices to resist. The alternatives for the more advantaged will be to take the exit option and to migrate to liberal democracies.[121] For the rest, I fear that the only option will be to succumb to Beijing's exercise of power through rule by law that is demanding unconditional loyalty to China and that sadly has Hong Kong "going in the direction of authoritarianism".[122]

---

119. Francis Fukuyama, *The End of History and the Last Man* (New York: Free Press, 1992).
120. A conclusion reached by commentators regardless of whether they think such movement is desirable. Zhu and Zhang, n 9 above, pp 102–103; Davies, n 97 above.
121. A. O. Hirschman, *Exit, Voice and Loyalty* (Cambridge: Harvard University Press, 1970).
122. Tai, n 15 above, p 116.

15

Media Freedom and Censorship under Post-Orwellian Authoritarianism

Cherian George

Introduction

In the weeks following the imposition of the National Security Law (NSL) on Hong Kong, there were conflicting prognoses about how the legislation would affect press freedom. Some commentators opined that the media would have nothing to fear if they behaved responsibly—an international euphemism for toeing the line, wherever authorities choose to draw it. But setting aside apologists for illiberal media control, even those with a vested interest in maintaining the territory's freedoms offered contrasting verdicts. "[T]his is not the rule of law. This is not even rule by law. This is rule by decree," said pro-democracy lawmaker and former journalist Claudia Mo. "Free press could just be announced dead in Hong Kong," she added.[1] The director of a leading journalism school in the city obliged: "Press is dead as far as I'm concerned." On the other hand, editors at *Apple Daily* and *South China Morning Post* summarised their newspapers' responses in the same three words: "business as usual".[2]

Both sides, whether expressing fatalist or hopeful views, were probably sloganeering: one side to sound the alarm, the other to express fortitude. In *Apple Daily*'s case, the bravado lasted less than a year. Under intense pressure from the authorities, the territory's most popular newspaper closed down in June 2021. Its founder, Jimmy Lai, and senior *Apple Daily* staff were charged under the NSL for calling for international sanctions against the Beijing and Hong Kong governments, a crime

1. Rachel Wong, "'A calculated weapon of repression': Democrats, activists, NGOs raise alarm over Hong Kong security law as gov't hails enactment", *Hong Kong Free Press*, 1 July 2020, available at https://hongkongfp.com/2020/07/01/a-calculated-weapon-of-repression-democrats-activists-ngos-raise-alarm-over-hong-kong-security-law-as-govt-hails-enactment/.
2. Greg Torode and James Pomfret, "HK Tycoon Jimmy Lai Arrested under Security Law, Bearing Out 'Worst Fears'", *Reuters*, 10 August 2020, available at https://cn.reuters.com/article/hongkong-security-idCNL4N2FC027.

under Article 29, which prohibits collusion with foreign individuals or groups. The new law has several other features that alarm media. The ban on secessionist activity, for example, is drafted broadly. Article 20 criminalises "organising, planning, committing or participating" in either separating Hong Kong or any other part of the country from China, or "altering by unlawful means" their "legal status". Inciting or assisting in such actions is also punishable under Article 21. Journalists hope that merely reporting such activity would not be an offence, but they cannot be sure. Article 10 requires the Hong Kong government to carry out national security education through the media—this could mean something as innocent as advertising campaigns, or as intrusive as Mainland-style propaganda directives.

The crackdown on *Apple Daily* certainly removed all doubts about China's determination to rid Hong Kong of the anti-Beijing elements it held responsible for the traitorous and tumultuous protests of 2019. It signalled that Beijing does not feel bound by the principles of necessity or proportionality when restricting free speech, as required by the International Covenant on Civil and Political Rights (ICCPR). What remained unclear, at the time of writing, was how far upstream it would go to reform Hong Kong's political culture, including its tradition of press freedom. The Hong Kong government stated repeatedly that its actions against Jimmy Lai and *Apple Daily* should not be construed as part of a broader attack on media freedom.[3] Many media professionals were understandably sceptical. "Journalists who witnessed the final days of Apple Daily will be frightened by the turn of events," the Hong Kong Journalists Association said.[4]

Hong Kong is in uncharted territory. Its legal and political precedents are of limited predictive value. To make out what may lie ahead, there is an obvious need to decipher the NSL—an exercise to which this volume is dedicated. This chapter, however, proceeds from the premise that deep dives into the text of the NSL can only reveal so much about Hong Kong's shrinking media freedom. This is partly because authorities intent on taming Hong Kong's media can use other legal and non-legal weapons, several of which have already been deployed with decisive effect. For example, the government has been able to rely on pre-existing administrative levers to rein in the public service broadcaster, RTHK (Radio Television Hong Kong). One of the last remaining independent news sites, Stand News, closed down after authorities arrested seven individuals linked to the outlet under a colonial-era anti-sedition law.[5] Therefore, the NSL may be just the tip of the iceberg.

3. "S for S Speaks on Arrest Operation by Hong Kong Police's National Security Department", Hong Kong SAR Government Press Release, 17 June 2021, available at https://www.info.gov.hk/gia/general/202106/17/P2021061700449.htm.
4. "HKJA Response of Apple Daily Closure", Hong Kong Journalists Association, 23 June 2021, available at https://www.hkja.org.hk/en/statements/hkja-response-of-apple-daily-closure/.
5. Christy Leung, Emily Tsang and William Yiu, "Hong Kong's Stand News shuts down after national security police arrest 7, freeze HK$61 million in assets", *South China Morning Post*, 29 December 2021, available at https://www.scmp.com/news/hong-kong/law-and-crime/article/3161360/hong-kong-national-security-police-arrest-6-ties-stand.

Furthermore, although the NSL is a law of frightening reach, it is not necessarily the case that it will be applied to its full extent. Here is where legal studies alone can be misleading. Legal scholars, like media organisations' counsel, have an occupational tendency—indeed, a professional responsibility—to spell out worst case scenarios based on a maximal reading of legislation. But that is not necessarily how states use their repressive laws. Experienced editors and publishers understand this and tend to treat their legal counsel's advice as just one point of reference. They surveil the environment, weigh contextual factors, and take calculated risks. Especially in jurisdictions with weak rule of law (or strong "rule by law"), justice is not blind: law is applied inconsistently, such that political judgment becomes an essential survival skill for journalists.

Hong Kong's media professionals generally lack such experience, handicapping them as the city enters unfamiliar terrain. But in a world where most journalists work in environments that are at best semi-free, there is no shortage of relevant precedents to learn from. This chapter argues that while the NSL is a formidable weapon, comparative censorship studies suggest that the authorities will eventually refrain from using it routinely. They may gradually shift toward means of media manipulation that are less coercive but more insidious—including economic carrots and sticks. At their most effective, strategies of calibrated and selective censorship contribute to authoritarian rule that is resilient and hegemonic. Singapore offers one case study, which this chapter analyses in some detail. The comparison with Singapore is especially compelling to Hong Kong. The two cities have a shared legal tradition and are both wealthy cosmopolitan hub cities with ethnic Chinese majorities. The Southeast Asian republic is often mentioned as a potential model for a reformed Hong Kong. Compared with Hong Kong, Singapore is more prosperous and stable, despite—or, as political conservatives argue, due to—its tightly constrained civil liberties, including a more controlled press. Like Singapore's ruling party, Hong Kong's political masters may indeed succeed in having their cake and eating it too, presiding over a flourishing but illiberal society. However, the kind of hegemonic domination that the Singapore regime achieved over mainstream media—where resistance is conspicuous in its absence—may be harder to replicate. This chapter explains why a Singapore-style equilibrium will elude Hong Kong's grasp.

I. Global Trends in Censorship

The scholarship on how China and other authoritarian states restrict media freedom is fairly substantial but quite recent, which explains why lay perceptions lag behind, tending to underestimate the sophistication with which such regimes operate. The long delay in close study of these societies is partly because, during the Cold War and beyond, there was little demand for nuance in analysing freedom of expression on either side of the ideological divide. Western commentators assumed that non-democracies were totalitarian regimes in the mould of George Orwell's *1984*—where censorship was like an all-consuming black hole, and where even "thoughtcrime" was banned. Such caricatures were ideologically useful in the Cold War battle against communism.[6] Then, in the decade after the collapse of the Soviet Union, it was widely assumed that remaining authoritarian states did not deserve close empirical study since they would inevitably converge towards liberal democracy.[7] Modernisation theory—the idea that capitalist development, education levels, and a rising middle class would democratise societies[8]—continued to be influential, adding to the expectation that emerging economies would free up their politics along with their markets. The arrival of the world wide web in the mid-1990s heightened hopes that despots would have to bow to new "liberation technologies".[9]

In the 2000s, though, it became clear that authoritarian states were more resilient than previously believed. Strong states such as Singapore and China could generate impressive economic growth and performance-based legitimacy without conceding much to liberal democratic values. Such regimes, it transpired, could even coexist with a vibrant internet.[10] Since then, in-depth research on the media and politics of such societies has burgeoned. Social scientists today have a much clearer idea of, for example, how authoritarian regimes maintain their grip on political discourse while at the same time satiating their publics' desire for more media choice and avoiding the backfire effects that often accompany censorship. The overwhelming evidence from a number of disciplines is that these states know better than to try to replicate the absolutist ideology or totalitarian methods of the likes of Adolf Hitler and Josef Stalin, or Mao Zedong's Cultural Revolution—the kind of worldview that Orwell crystallised in the 1940s. The evidence also tells us that censorship practices cannot be straightforwardly predicted from their written laws and regulations. University of Chicago law professor Eric Posner has observed that almost all legal scholarship on human rights analyses the law without studying its effects on the ground.[11] If so, this underlines the importance of drawing from social science and historical research on media and politics, not just the field of law.

While censorship studies have made a decisively post-Orwellian turn, popular discourse continues to be gripped by totalitarian nightmares. Much of the discussion

---

6. John C. Nerone (ed), *Last Rights: Revisiting Four Theories of the Press* (Urbana: University of Illinois Press, 1995).
7. Francis Fukuyama, *The End of History and the Last Man* (New York: Simon and Schuster, 1992).
8. Seymour M. Lipset, "Some Social Requisites of Democracy" (1959) 53(1) *American Political Science Review* 69.
9. Larry Diamond and Marc F. Plattner, *Liberation Technology: Social Media and the Struggle for Democracy* (Baltimore: Johns Hopkins University Press, 2012).
10. Gary King, Jennifer Pan, and Margaret E. Roberts, "How Censorship in China Allows Government Criticism but Silences Collective Expression" (2013) 107(2) *American Political Science Review* 326; Cherian George, "Neoliberal 'Good Governance' in Lieu of Rights: Lee Kuan Yew's Singapore Experiment", in Monroe Price and Nicole Stremlau (eds), *Speech and Society: Comparative Perspectives* (Cambridge: Cambridge University Press, 2018), p 114.
11. Eric Posner, *The Twilight of Human Rights Law* (Oxford; New York: Oxford University Press, 2014).

about the NSL has taken place within the old paradigm. This is a problem not only because it may exaggerate the sharp threats contained in the NSL (which could indeed materialise), but because it underestimates subtler dangers (which are not only more likely but may also be more impactful in the long run). This chapter tries to bridge the knowledge gap by taking a step back from Hong Kong and the NSL to survey the global landscape of media freedom and censorship. Conveniently for those interested in Hong Kong's future, many recent studies focus on China. In addition to this secondary literature, I draw on my own research on Singapore, which is of special relevance given how regularly Singapore's model is invoked as a possible end point for post-NSL Hong Kong.

II. Strategic Self-Restraint in the Use of Law

Regimes that are termed authoritarian, autocratic, or despotic form a diverse group. They include one-party communist states, military juntas, absolute monarchies, and electoral authoritarian systems (the latter forms the largest category, comprising countries with periodic elections that are monopolised by a ruling elite, aided by weak rule of law). In such societies, states are more or less able to suppress media freedom with impunity. They usually have at their disposal sweeping security and other laws that they are able to apply with wide discretion and little or no pushback from independent courts. Many are also able to muster extralegal violence against media, using paramilitaries, security agencies, and hired goons. For individual journalists and other media workers, the price of challenging authority can amount to assassinations, forced disappearances, long jail terms, and torture. Media outlets may be banned or suspended.

Such incidents are all too common. The most extreme cases—such as Saudi agents' murder and dismemberment of journalist Jamal Khashoggi in 2018—make global headlines. These marquee events, though, tend to overshadow a separate trend in media repression: while autocratic states hoard coercive powers just in case, they usually choose not to use them to the full extent possible. This self-restraint is not driven by any guilt arising from some closeted respect for human rights. It is strategic and self-interested, based on their recognition that maximal coercion is rarely optimal. Authoritarian states that take a long view know that it is not smart to overplay their hands.

By the 2010s, this pattern had registered on media freedom watchdogs' radars. In 2015, a cover story in the *Columbia Journalism Review* on "21st Century Censorship" documented how governments around the world were using "stealthy strategies" to manipulate the media.[12] The same year, Joel Simon of the Committee to Protect Journalists released his book *The New Censorship*, the thrust of which was

12. Philip Bennett and Moises Naim, "21st-Century Censorship", *Columbia Journalism Review*, February 2015, available at https://www.cjr.org/cover_story/21st_century_censorship.php.

to warn that enemies of press freedom were not solely relying on "brute force and direct control" but also using "stealth, manipulations, and subterfuge".[13] Freedom House, in a 2017 report on "modern authoritarians", including China, observed that force was being "used more selectively, so that most of the population rarely experienced state brutality".[14]

Miklós Haraszti in Hungary had noted this trend as far back as the 1980s. His book *The Velvet Prison* distinguished the prevailing system of state socialism from the "primitive totalitarianism" of the Stalinist period. "Partnership displaces dictatorship," he wrote. "Sticks are exchanged for carrots."[15] A similar shift was evident by the 1990s in Singapore—where the ruling People's Action Party (PAP) government has always tended to be ahead of the curve, not only in its economic development policies but also in the finer points of resilient authoritarian rule. The PAP mastered the art of "calibrated coercion", which I define as the technique of using just enough force to secure the regime's political objectives, but not so much as to backfire.[16]

The idea that regimes consolidate power by dialling down violence is at least a century old. It is central to Antonio Gramsci's theory of hegemony in which coercion underwrites domination without routinely manifesting itself.[17] There are several practical reasons why states confronted with speech they do not like may refrain from the most repressive responses available to them, or indeed not act at all. None of the following factors is embraced by authoritarian regimes as clinching arguments against censorship. The point, rather, is that it is simplistic to expect states to react automatically with maximum force. Smart authoritarian regimes know that censorship entails trade-offs. While there may be situations where they come down on the side of a shock-and-awe show of force to scare the public into submission, they may also find good reasons to moderate their response, even if it means looking the other way.

First, flagrant censorship can play into opponents' hands. It can heighten the appeal and impact of the very ideas that the censors find objectionable. This has come to be known as the Streisand Effect named after the singer Barbra Streisand's ill-advised legal bid to suppress aerial photographs of the California coastline that happened to show her seaside mansion.[18] Her lawsuit increased the audience of those photos from dozens to millions. A disproportionately severe response can

13. Joel Simon, *New Censorship: Inside the Global Battle for Media Freedom* (Wheaton: Columbia University Press, 2014), p 32.
14. Arch Puddington, *Breaking down Democracy: Goals, Strategies, and Methods of Modern Authoritarians* (Washington: Freedom House, 2017).
15. Miklós Haraszti, *The Velvet Prison: Artists under State Socialism* (London: Tauris, 1988), p 74.
16. Cherian George, "Consolidating Authoritarian Rule: Calibrated Coercion in Singapore" (2007) 20(2) *The Pacific Review* 127.
17. Thomas R. Bates, "Gramsci and the Theory of Hegemony" (1975) 36(2) *Journal of the History of Ideas* 351.
18. T. C., "What Is the Streisand Effect?", *The Economist*, 15 April 2013, available at https://www.economist.com/the-economist-explains/2013/04/15/what-is-the-streisand-effect.

also backfire by generating public outrage around which opponents can mobilise. The Soviet Union's treatment of Alexandr Solzenitzyn, for example, made him a celebrity. He became a potent symbol of not only the tyranny of the censorship bureaucracy but also the repressiveness of the entire Soviet system.[19]

Second, violent reprisals can isolate rulers by undermining their own power base. Hannah Arendt, contemplating fascist regimes, noted that rulers cannot govern single-handedly. They require the co-operation of lieutenants and fellow elites. Dictators, therefore, face a dilemma: they can seize control through violence, but violence alone cannot sustain their hold on power.[20] The dictator's dilemma applies to media and communication. Rulers of any large nation state require reliable information from the ground. They cannot afford to be the last to know that a harvest has failed, that workers are restive, or that their lieutenants' corruption is getting out of hand. A political system in which officials and media are afraid to be bearers of bad news will leave rulers in the dark, along with their subjects, and thus vulnerable to revolutionary tendencies.[21]

Third, individuals and firms in market economies require a reasonably free flow of information to guide their decisions. As even communist countries such as China and Vietnam transitioned away from their centrally planned economies and placed greater faith in market mechanisms from the 1980s, they felt compelled to cede some control over news and information as well. While certainly not surrendering to the liberal model of press freedom, neither have they wished to maintain the kind of absolute control over news media that they exercised prior to their pro-market reforms. The dilemma of balancing open commerce with closed politics was accentuated by the arrival of the internet, a platform that became indispensable for business but could also double up as a medium for political dissent.

Fourth, most citizens in most countries desire choice in media. Authoritarian regimes seeking mass support hope that their lack of procedural legitimacy (the kind that emerges from free and fair elections and the rule of law) can be compensated for through performance legitimacy (by delivering socio-economic progress). The problem for control-minded governments, though, is that access to abundant media—particularly in entertainment and, more recently, social networking platforms—is widely regarded as part and parcel of social mobility and a desirable lifestyle. Even where states have successfully pushed back against the import of Western-style democratic values, they have found it difficult to resist demands for media choice, especially on television and online. In a middle-income country, a

19. Sue Curry Jansen and Brian Martin, "Making Censorship Backfire" (2003) 7(3) *Counterpoise* 5, available at http://ro.uow.edu.au/artspapers/54.
20. Hannah Arendt, *On Violence* (Orlando: Harcourt Brace Jovanovich, 1970), p 54.
21. Greg Chih-Hsin Sheen, Hans H. Tung, and Wenchin Wu, "Tell Me the Truth: (Un)committable Media Freedom in Dictatorships" (2018) In Annual American Political Science Conference, Chicago, IL.; Peter Lorentzen, "China's Strategic Censorship" (2014) 58(2) *American Journal of Political Science* 402, available at https://doi.org/10.1111/ajps.12065.

government that denies high-speed internet, multi-channel television and online social networks to its people risks undermining its performance legitimacy.

Fifth, the goals of 21st-century authoritarians are much more modest than the utopian visions of Stalin, Mao, or Pol Pot in the mid-20th century. The old-style totalitarians were ideologues who demanded complete consensus and conspicuous loyalty. Depoliticising one's work and refraining from challenging authority was not an option for journalists, artists, and intellectuals. "Neutrality is treason; ambiguity is betrayal," Haraszti said of the Stalinist period. Compared with Stalin, or the ideologues behind China's Cultural Revolution or Cambodia's Year Zero, modern autocrats are "not animated by an overarching ideology or the messianic notion of an ideal future society"; nor do they demand total control over "people's everyday lives, movements, or thoughts", a Freedom House report notes.[22] Even if their legal weapons allow such control, their political missions do not demand it.

Rather than issue a stream of detailed orders, today's authoritarians are more likely to provide general guidelines and allow editors and publishers to use their own judgment most of the time. They rely on self-censorship, which can be defined as a set of practices that speakers engage in without being explicitly told to, to preempt punishment or in anticipation of reward from external actors that have power over them.[23] A government's reluctance to micro-manage every eventuality should not be mistaken for an act of charity. There are self-interested reasons why it would prefer to delegate authority to editors and publishers. Most obviously, in a large and complex country, it is simply not possible to anticipate every situation. Nor is it necessarily smart for leaders to demand that underlings inform and consult them about everything that is out of the ordinary. The caricature of the Big Brother state is contradicted by studies of organisational behaviour showing that it is not always in leaders' interests to know and control everything. To avoid informational overload, leaders may be better off defining their core business narrowly and delegating authority for non-core decisions to their agents.[24] The advantages of a self-censorship regime are so considerable that some theorists argue that it should not be regarded as a category secondary to direct censorship. Instead, it is better to think of censorship as failed self-censorship—a second-best option.[25]

When authoritarian states deal with media, then, their practical challenge is how to balance their desire, on the one hand, to restrict expression that may weaken their grip on power and, on the other, to minimise the risk of backfire and serve

22. Puddington, n 14 above, p 1.
23. Chinchuan Lee, "Press Self-Censorship and Political Transition in Hong Kong" (1998) 3(2) *The Harvard International Journal of Press/Politics* 55; Francis L. F. Lee, "Self-Censorship", in Tim P. Vos and Folker Hanusch (eds), *The International Encyclopedia of Journalism Studies* (Hoboken: John Wiley & Sons, 2019), available at https://doi.org/10.1002/9781118841570.iejs0096.
24. Philippe Aghion and Jean Tirole, "Formal and Real Authority in Organizations" (1997) 105(1) *Journal of Political Economy* 1, available at https://www.jstor.org/stable/2138869.
25. Matthew Bunn, "Reimagining Repression: New Censorship Theory and After" (2015) 54(1) *History and Theory* 25, available at https://doi.org/10.1111/hith.10739.

various interests—consumers, businesses, and the state itself—that demand a reasonably well-functioning media system. Although there is no guarantee that they can easily reconcile these competing interests, they try to do so through two broad strategies: calibrated coercion and selective censorship.[26]

(a) Calibrated Coercion

States have a wide range of means to control media. They vary in the level of violence, from extreme (murder) to none (bribes and other inducements for co-operation). They also vary in visibility, from the spectacular (police raids and arrests in daylight) to stealthy (algorithmic interventions to make problematic online content harder to find). Violent and highly visible censorship is prone to backfire. In contrast, there is negligible political cost to interventions that are harder to detect and even seem victimless. This is precisely the broad direction in which many authoritarian regimes have preferred to go.

The media policies of Singapore's PAP government epitomise calibrated coercion. In the decade following the city state's attainment of independence in 1965, the government used sweeping security laws to ban publications and detain journalists. Then, despite the absence of any parliamentary opposition to question those powers (which remain in the statute books), the government switched to new legislation that enabled it to exercise behind-the-scenes supervision. It thus managed to institutionalise a robust system of self-censorship that worked with, rather than against, the prevailing market orientation of media. The republic is currently the only country that ranks among the very top in economic competitiveness,[27] transparency perception,[28] and human development,[29] while maintaining a "not free" media system that is consistently ranked among the bottom 20 per cent.[30] Singapore is thus the glaring exception to the general rule associating advanced economies with press freedom. This section takes a closer look at how Singapore's approach to media regulation evolved.

Post-colonial Singapore, like Malaysia, inherited a suite of sweeping security laws from the British. Originally intended to counter communist insurgency and communal violence, these powers were retained by Lee Kuan Yew's PAP government

26. Cherian George, "Journalism and Authoritarian Resilience", in Karin Wahl-Jorgensen and Thomas Hanitzsch (eds), *The Handbook of Journalism Studies* (New York: Routledge, 2nd edn, 2020), p 538.
27. "IMD World Competitiveness Ranking 2020: Showing Strength of Small Economies", *IMD*, June 2020, available at https://www.imd.org/news/updates/IMD-2020-World-Competitiveness-Ranking-revealed/.
28. "Corruption Perceptions Index 2019", *Transparency International*, 2020, available at https://images.transparencycdn.org/images/2019_CPI_Report_EN_200331_141425.pdf.
29. United Nations Development Programme, "Human Development Reports 2020: Singapore", 2020, available at http://hdr.undp.org/en/countries/profiles/SGP.
30. Michael J. Abramovitz, "Freedom of the Press 2017", *Freedom House*, 2017, available at https://freedomhouse.org/report/freedom-press/freedom-press-2017; "2020 World Press Freedom Index", *Reporters Without Borders*, available at https://rsf.org/en/ranking.

to cripple opposition and clear the way for its pro-business economic policies and its pragmatic promotion of English-language education. Up to the 1970s, it detained journalists without trial under the Internal Security Act (ISA), which, as Michael Hor points out in Chapter 16, is a piece of legislation that in some respects is more fearsome than the NSL. Singapore authorities also deployed the Printing Presses Ordinance—under which periodicals had to obtain annual publishing permits that could be granted or revoked at any time, entirely at ministers' discretion—to suppress newspapers that challenged the government's authority. In May 1971, six years after independence, Lee was uninhibited in his use of these powers. His government revoked the licence of one English-language newspaper, *Singapore Herald*, and accused another, *Eastern Sun*, of being a vehicle for black operations, upon which its staff exited, precipitating its collapse before any government action was needed. The biggest scalp, though, was the leading Chinese-language newspaper, *Nanyang Siang Pau*, four of whose top executives, including one of its family owners, was detained without trial under the ISA. Its publisher was arrested two years later, spending five years in detention.[31]

Just as events in 2021 in Hong Kong established that the authorities would brook no dissent from the media, the crackdown in Singapore 50 years earlier dispelled all doubts about the PAP's political will to strip the press of any Fourth Estate pretensions. Having demonstrated his resolve, though, Lee changed tack. He did not wish to repeat the cycle of arrests and bans. Nor did he choose to take over ownership of the press, either by law (communist governments' final solution) or through businesses owned by the ruling party or its cronies (like in neighbouring Malaysia). Instead, he devised a system to ensure that newsrooms would be controlled by pro-establishment editors, while keeping ownership in the hands of the private sector.

His custom-built mechanism was the Newspaper and Printing Presses Act (NPPA) of 1974. The NPPA retained the 50-year-old system of annual permits. But it contained a novel feature: it required newspaper owners to be publicly listed companies. This was remarkably counter-intuitive at a time when conventional wisdom held that capitalism was a gateway drug to democracy. The new law also prohibited any investor from controlling a majority of shares (the cap is currently 12 per cent). The legislation thus spread newspaper ownership thinly across the stock market. Lee understood that commercial media as such were not a threat to a pro-business government. More problematic were individual and family owners—like *Nanyang Siang Pau*'s—willing to use their newspapers to champion non-pecuniary causes. By spreading ownership, newspapers' orientation would be reduced to shareholders' lowest common denominator: their profit motive.

31. Francis T. Seow, *The Media Enthralled: Singapore Revisited* (Boulder: Lynne Rienner Publishers, 1998).

To allow the government to guide newspapers' editorial direction, the NPPA also gave it a say in appointments of company directors and top editors. Lee again sought inspiration from the commercial world, borrowing the concept of super-voting shares. Newspaper companies such as the *New York Times* and the *Wall Street Journal* used this mechanism to keep key decisions in the hands of families that saw themselves as custodians of the papers' values, even when they held minority stakes. Under the NPPA, newspaper companies must designate certain shares as "management shares". Management shares have 200 times the voting power as ordinary shares on resolutions relating to the appointment or dismissal of a director or any member of the staff. The government decides whose shares count as management shares. In practice, management shareholders of the national newspapers are mostly financial institutions deeply invested in Singapore's political stability. Some of these corporations, such as Singapore Telecom, are government-linked.[32]

As the annual permit system remained in place, the government was even able to direct industry restructuring. Its interventions culminated in the consolidation of all Singapore dailies under a single corporation, Singapore Press Holdings (SPH). Although journalists were not happy, SPH's monopoly served both shareholders as well as the government's agenda: having a solitary newspaper company made political co-ordination easier and diminished the competitive pressures that often drive news outlets to take political risks.

With the domestic media dealt with, Lee turned his attention to influential foreign newsweeklies and dailies, such as the Hongkong-based *Far Eastern Economic Review* and *Asiaweek*, and global brands *Time*, *Asian Wall Street Journal*, and the *Economist*. Two Singaporean correspondents for the *Far Eastern Economic Review* were detained under the Internal Security Act for around two months each in 1977. The government also had the power to ban these publications under existing laws. But Lee wanted to deny foreign media the moral high horse he knew they would mount were the Singapore government to react in such an extreme fashion. Again, he sought more calibrated tools. In 1986, NPPA amendments allowed the government to set circulation caps on foreign publications that it deemed were trying to interfere in Singapore's domestic politics. The test, not written into the legislation but clarified in its application, was whether these publications would give the government the unedited right of reply. Those that refused would have their access to one of Asia's most lucrative markets limited, though not completely blocked. Lee's goal was to make the publications' corporate owners feel the financial pain when their editors took on his government in the name of press freedom. Lee's battle with major western media titles was hardly low profile, but it was more calibrated than banning them. Furthermore, his use of the NPPA—together with defamation suits and contempt of court prosecutions—did have some success in

32. Cherian George, *Freedom from the Press: Journalism and State Power in Singapore* (Singapore: National University of Singapore Press, 2012).

getting publishers and their lawyers to advise editors to exercise more care in their Singapore coverage.[33]

With the NPPA and other measures in place, the government had no need to activate its more draconian laws. The last time the ISA was used against working journalists was 1977; the last time a daily newspaper was banned was 1971. In the day-to-day work of media organisations, Singapore's security laws have a mostly symbolic function, reminding journalists that the government will always prevail in any contest with the press. Extreme measures do not need to be used because the media would never challenge either Singapore's national security or the PAP's rule, thanks to the NPPA's institutionalisation of self-censorship in privately owned news organisations.

The openness of the internet has complicated the PAP's media management system. The government has not attempted to reproduce online its system of discretionary licensing of news organisations: individuals and firms do not need prior permission to set up a news outlet on the internet. Furthermore, individuals can use the internet to address a mass audience directly, bypassing the editors running newspapers and broadcast media. Ironically, the freedom to bypass censorship has resulted in a greater incidence of post-publication punishment. The government, unwilling to give up its illiberal philosophy, has had to roll out its older, more punitive laws to discipline online speech. For example, the sweeping Sedition Act—a colonial power that had fallen into disuse soon after independence—was applied periodically against online expression post-2000.[34]

Just like in the 1970s, though, the government was keen to develop more calibrated legislation tailor-made for the internet. These efforts resulted in the Protection from Online Falsehoods and Manipulation Act 2019 (POFMA). In keeping with the government's drift-net approach to speech regulation, POFMA allowed government ministers wide discretion to initiate action against online content that they believed contained false statements contrary to the public interest, without needing to go through an independent regulator or the courts.[35] What was novel about the law, though, was that aside from providing for jail terms and large fines, it gave the government the less coercive option of issuing correction or take-down orders. Defending POFMA against critics, the government pointed out that it already had sweeping powers under existing legislation, such as the Broadcasting Act and the

33. Garry Rodan, "Asian Crisis, Transparency and the International Media in Singapore" (2000) 13(2) *The Pacific Review* 217.

34. Jaclyn Lingchien Neo, "Seditious in Singapore! Free Speech and the Offence of Promoting Ill-Will and Hostility between Different Racial Groups" (2011) *Singapore Journal of Legal Studies* 351.

35. International Commission of Jurists, "Legal Briefing: Protection from Online Falsehoods and Manipulation Bill No. 10/2019", 12 April 2019, available at https://www.icj.org/wp-content/uploads/2019/04/Singapore-online-regulation-bill-briefing-advocacy-open-letter-2019-ENG.pdf.

Telecommunications Act. POFMA would provide a narrower set of powers "with remedies that are calibrated", it said.[36]

As the eventual targets of the correction orders included opposition politicians and activists who complained loudly about the measures, POFMA did not succeed in rendering censorship invisible, the way NPPA did. Whether POFMA is less coercive than earlier laws is also arguable. The earlier take-down powers were so manifestly disproportionate that the government did not try to use them against the opposition. In contrast, the fit-for-purpose POFMA was applied immediately and frequently. Ironically, therefore, the more calibrated tool resulted in more censorship. As theory would predict, the backfire effects of these highly visible interventions were considerable: each correction order generated controversy, multiplying the audience of the offending post, as well as scorn for the government. Even for the PAP, calibrated coercion does not always hit the sweet spot of cost-free censorship.

The trend in the PAP's methods of speech regulation away from bans and arrests towards less coercive, less visible interventions—which is consistent with how its management of trade unions, civil society, professions, and religious groups has evolved over the past 50 years[37]—has helped it consolidate its hegemonic authoritarian rule. Whether other governments can use these strategies as successfully as Singapore's PAP is doubtful. (I will return to the question of replicability later, when discussing what these trends mean for Hong Kong.) But global evidence from media freedom monitors, cited earlier, does suggest that many other authoritarian regimes appreciate the need to diversify their repertoires of control and moderate their repression, in order to consolidate their power.

Even when governments decide to use law, they need not reach for their most extreme measures. They can instead selectively enforce tax or labour regulations, for example, to wear down independent news organisations. The *Philippine Daily Inquirer*, the country's largest newspaper, succumbed to tax probes against its family owners in 2017. Under intense pressure, the owners sold the newspaper group to Ramon Ang, a tycoon friendly to President Rodrigo Duterte. In Turkey, a similar tactic tamed the newspapers *Milliyet* and *Hürriyet* in 2018. The government of Recep Tayyip Erdoğan levelled criminal charges on the newspapers' owner, media magnate Aydin Doğan, for evading taxes associated with another of his businesses,

36. Singapore Ministry of Law, "Second Reading Speech by Minister for Law, K Shanmugam on The Protection from Online Falsehoods and Manipulation Bill", 7 May 2019, available at https://www.mlaw.gov.sg/news/parliamentary-speeches/Second-Reading-Speech-by-Minister-for-Law-K-Shanmugam-on-The-Protection-from-Online-Falsehoods-and-Manipulation-Bill.
37. Cherian George, "The Art of Calibrated Coercion", in Cherian George, *Air-Conditioned Nation Revisited: Essays on Singapore Politics* (Singapore: Ethos Books, 2020), p 37.

fuel distributor Petrol Ofisi. Doğan got the message and sold his media business to a corporation friendlier to the president.[38]

Aside from legal strategies, governments can flex their economic muscle. In many countries, the state is the single biggest advertiser. When a government chooses to withhold its advertising and publicity budget from a troublesome news outlet, this can amount to a crippling attack on media independence. Although an abuse of the government's fiscal powers, an advertising boycott tends not to excite public indignation the way arrests or bans do.[39] Economic weapons work by exploiting the news industry's internal contradictions. Mass media have risen over the past two centuries on the back of capitalism and consumerism.[40] Revenues from advertisers as well as audiences turned news into big business, attracting investments in technology and manpower. From the early 20th century, many large news organisations possessed the economic power and political influence to defend themselves against governments. But the high-cost, commercial model of news production also accentuated a conflict of interest within media organisations, between journalists' professional norms of public service and their employers' often more self-serving orientations.[41] Compared with regulated professions such as law and medicine, journalism is relatively defenceless when employers place corporate interests ahead of professional norms and ethics.

Authoritarian leaders who understand the tensions within news media's business models have—like Duterte and Erdoğan—been able to complement their visible and violent interventions with more calibrated, but highly effective, economic strikes against news organisations. They have been greatly aided by the news industry's chronic financial crisis. In better times, publishers were more able to afford respecting corporate firewalls between their newsrooms and other departments: they protected their editors from financial blackmail by governments and businesses. Operating with much thinner—or negative—margins, the internal balance of power within most news organisations has shifted away from their news operations (seen as a cost centre) and towards departments dealing with advertising sales, business development, and other revenue-generating activities. This near-universal shift has made journalism much more vulnerable to economic carrots and sticks. In China, the erosion of investigative journalism since 2012, usually attributed solely

38. "IPI Troubled by Tax Case Targeting Turkey Media Owner", *International Press Institute*, 8 July 2016, available at https://ipi.media/ipi-troubled-by-tax-case-targeting-turkey-media-owner/; "Turkish Media Group Bought by Pro-Government Conglomerate", *New York Times*, 21 March 2018, available at https://www.nytimes.com/2018/03/21/world/europe/turkey-media-erdogan-dogan.html.
39. Don Podesta, *Soft Censorship: How Governments around the Globe Use Money to Manipulate the Media* (Washington: Center for International Media Assistance, National Endowment for Democracy, 2009), available at https://www.cima.ned.org/wp-content/uploads/2015/01/CIMA-Soft_Censorship-Report.pdf.
40. Victor Pickard, "The Violence of the Market" (2019) 20(1) *Journalism* 154.
41. Wolfgang Donsbach, "Journalists and Their Professional Identities", in Stuart Allan (ed), *The Routledge Companion to News and Journalism* (London and New York: Routledge, 2009), p 38.

to Xi Jinping's crackdown on dissent, is partly due to the waning financial fortunes of commercially oriented news media.[42]

(b) Satiating Public Demand through Selective Pluralisation

If calibrated coercion has to do with the *intensity* of repression, selective pluralisation—or the other side of the coin, targeted censorship—is about its *breadth*. One of the dilemmas facing dictators is that the ambition of total information control turns out to be unachievable and unwise: it drives individuals and firms to resist or exit, and deprives the state itself of the intelligence it needs for planning and co-ordination. Therefore, resilient authoritarian regimes do not attempt to saturate the media environment with their own propaganda and outlaw everything else. Instead, they pick their battles. They allow most media sectors to become "pluralistic, with high production values and entertaining content" while maintaining "state or oligarchic control over information on certain political subjects and key sectors of the media".[43] Much of what we know about this strategy comes from research on China.

States place media content on a continuum from harmless to intolerable. In a small set of circumstances, the authorities can practise case-by-case prior censorship. This is often the approach taken with films slated for cinematic release. The number of movies to vet is relatively small, and lead times are long enough for censors to scrutinise every scene and to order cuts before clearing a film for exhibition. Serials produced for free-to-air broadcast can also be manageably subject to prior censorship by an external body. However, this is not practical for the vast majority of media content, including most news. Instead, governments usually group media into different categories, subjecting each to different levels of censorship based on how likely they are to pose problems.

Thus, even if news remains tightly supervised, entertainment media have been allowed to proliferate as a concession to consumers demanding more choice, as well as to corporations eager to profit from this market. The neoliberal wave of the 1990s saw many states give up their monopolies over broadcasting, resulting in a boom in commercial free-to-air and cable and satellite channels. In many cases, including Malaysia and Singapore, the resulting pluralisation was largely limited to entertainment programming, with domestic television news continuing to be monopolised by the government and its allies. Similarly, after the Arab Spring of 2010–2011, regimes tended to protect their state television outlets.[44] In China, CCTV's evening news bulletin out of Beijing is sacrosanct, carried throughout the country including on channels owned by provincial governments. But provincial channels have been

42. Haiyan Wang and Colin Sparks, "Chinese Newspaper Groups in the Digital Era: The Resurgence of the Party Press" (2019) 69(1) *Journal of Communication* 94.
43. Puddington, n 14 above, p 6.
44. Marc Lynch, "After the Arab Spring: How the Media Trashed the Transitions" (2015) 26(4) *Journal of Democracy* 90.

allowed to innovate in entertainment and often succeed in producing massively popular shows. Entertainment values have also been permitted to seep into news organisations, just as they have in the democratic world. Concerned about losing the attention of younger Chinese, the staid party mouthpiece *People's Daily* fills its social media platforms with apolitical posts designed for mass appeal, more than party dogma.

Another common strategy is to segment the news and information audience, granting more choice to urban elites while closely supervising what the masses consume. Such differentiation is not difficult to implement, since different segments of the public have their own media consumption habits. In most countries, free-to-air radio and television in the local language are the most widely accessed news sources and are therefore the most tightly controlled. At the other extreme, the upmarket business press and alternative websites—particularly if they are in English—are consumed only by a small minority of local elites and the expatriate community. Governments can often afford to give these media more latitude, in order to satisfy their more highly educated and cosmopolitan publics as well as the business community. China's *Caixin* is a prominent example. It has built a reputation for investigative journalism and analysis that is relatively hard-hitting.

When regulating news and information about the state, authoritarian governments do not operate with the binary categories of banned versus approved. Between these extremes lies a continuum, from the grudgingly excused and barely tolerated, to the quietly welcomed. This range of responses reflects the ambivalence referred to earlier. Competent authoritarian states recognise that some reliable feedback mechanism is needed to keep the system running smoothly. They have also had to acknowledge that they do not have unlimited power to suppress people's demand for news and information about major events that impact them directly.

Therefore, although the Chinese authorities treat a vast range of topics as sensitive—from ghost stories to Tibet—they are not all treated the same. Some are seen as meriting total bans, while others are subject to managed coverage. One study of more than 1,400 secret directives issued by the Chinese propaganda apparatus found that officials were banning fewer reports and moving to a strategy of "conditional public opinion guidance".[45] Stories about religion, protest, and human rights abuses were the most likely to be banned outright. However, news about disasters and accidents was harder to suppress due to the affected publics' irrepressible demand for information in a fast-moving context. Propaganda directives required media to report these events according to narrative supplied by *Xinhua* and other official sources, instead of pretending they never happened.

45. Tai Qiuqing, "China's Media Censorship: A Dynamic and Diversified Regime" (2014) 14(2) *Journal of East Asian Studies* 186.

China also practises hierarchical differentiation in its censorship: there is more room to report lower-level misdeeds than to investigate top leaders.[46] Although even that space has shrunk in the Xi Jinping era, the authorities continue to apply significantly different censorship standards depending how high up the hierarchy watchdog journalists are trying to bite. Exposing misconduct or incompetence among local subordinates need not threaten regime stability. It could even help the regime sustain itself, including by neutralising opponents within the establishment.[47] The state also needs media to educate workers about their rights under labour and employment laws so that they are not too easily abused by local officials. Emotive human-interest content about ordinary citizens mistreated by their employers and local officials (and eventually being saved by the legal system) are not just good for commercial media but also "promotes the state's goals of enhanced legitimacy through rule of law".[48] The strategic value of hierarchically differentiated media control has been corroborated by game theory models showing that a central authority can benefit from allowing the media to report protests against local officials, as this can release revolutionary pressure against the regime and force local governments to be less corrupt.[49]

Even behind its Great Firewall, there are limits to the Chinese Communist Party's ability to manage the sheer volume of internet activity. In her study of China's internet censorship, Margaret Roberts shows that the authorities are not attempting the futile exercise of total control, nor do they need to. As long as they add enough friction to the experience—by requiring virtual private networks or VPNs, for example—most people will be deterred from trying to access the discouraged material. Only highly motivated users, such as journalists and activists, would bother to invest the necessary time and money. Segmenting the public in this way makes it hard for better-informed elites to influence the masses. But the strategy only works if the approved internet services can satisfy most people's informational, entertainment, and social needs most of the time. Otherwise, frustration with censorship would result in mass disobedience. Censors therefore try to strike a balance between central control and consumer choice. One trivial but highly illustrative example is social media users' freedom to change their profile photos. Some users have exploited this feature to replace their headshots with political symbols, such as a lighted candle to commemorate the 1989 Tiananmen Square crackdown. To

46. Peter Lorentzen, "China's Strategic Censorship" (2014) 58(2) *American Journal of Political Science* 402.
47. Georgy Egorov, Sergei M. Guriev, and Konstantin Sonin, "Why Resource-Poor Dictators Allow Freer Media: A Theory and Evidence from Panel Data" (2009) 103(4) *American Political Science Review* 645, available at https://papers.ssrn.com/sol3/papers.cfm?abstract_id=898888; Tai Qiuqing, "China's Media Censorship: A Dynamic and Diversified Regime" (2014) 14(2) *Journal of East Asian Studies* 185.
48. Daniela Stockmann and Mary E. Gallagher, "Remote Control: How the Media Sustain Authoritarian Rule in China" (2011) 44(4) *Comparative Political Studies* 436.
49. Haifeng Huang, Serra Boranbay-Akan, and Huang Ling, "Media, Protest Diffusion, and Authoritarian Resilience", *Political Science Research and Methods* (forthcoming), available at https://papers.ssrn.com/sol3/papers.cfm?abstract_id=2770149.

remove this functionality entirely would probably anger millions of users who enjoy changing their profile photos for totally apolitical reasons. So, social media companies have taken to disabling profile photo changes only during sensitive periods, such as in the days before and after major events.

The consistent picture that emerges from censorship research in China and other authoritarian regimes is of governments with no moral compunctions about trampling on human rights or liberal democratic values, but that are also cognisant that attempts to control too much would strain their capacities and exact a political cost. Political scientists have tried constructing elaborate models to specify the relationship between the likelihood of repression and various other factors such as the levels of dissent, regime stability, foreign scrutiny, and so on. War and civil unrest, not surprisingly, tend to lower states' inhibitions. Overall, though, it is easier for historians to look back and explain why an authoritarian regime acted or didn't act in the way it did than for political scientists to predict their behaviour. What comparative research does make clear is that control-minded regimes have a wide array of methods to choose from. For reasons articulated earlier, states try to shift as soon as possible to less coercive and more targeted tools to discipline media.

III. What This Means for Hong Kong

As pointed out in the introduction, regardless of legal opinion, it is political judgment that holds sway on the ground. At the time of writing, professional media in Hong Kong appear to be operating with a rule of thumb that distinguishes among factual reporting, commentary, and campaigning. Quoting independence slogans within a news story, for example, is deemed as safe practice—unlike on the Mainland where certain topics are unmentionable and subject to total blackouts. Commentary and analysis are a grey area. The press seems to be able to describe and explain the perspectives of individuals and groups who have been accused of NSL violations but is taking care not to be perceived as allowing them a free platform or advocating on their behalf. Advocacy—actively campaigning for a cause identified as non-compliant with the NSL—is off-limits, as has become abundantly clear from the treatment meted out to Jimmy Lai and *Apple Daily*.

The Hong Kong government's assertions that its actions against the newspaper and its founder were not a press freedom issue[50] seem to be based on a limited understanding of "the press" as comprising only balanced, factual reporting; *Apple*

50. Candice Chau, "Hong Kong Leader Places National Security Law Onus on Journalists; Says Media Must Not Subvert Gov't", *Hong Kong Free Press*, 22 June 2021, available at https://hongkongfp.com/2021/06/22/hong-kong-leader-places-national-security-law-onus-on-journalists-says-media-must-not-subvert-govt/; Chris Law and Jaffie Lam, "Spotlight on Hong Kong's Apple Daily Columns, as Legal Experts Debate Alleged National Security Law Breach", *South China Morning Post*, 18 June 2021, available at https://www.scmp.com/news/hong-kong/politics/article/3137967/spotlight-hong-kongs-apple-daily-columns-legal-experts.

Daily's activist orientation thus disqualified it from the protections promised to the media in the Basic Law and reiterated in the preamble to the NSL. Although many news organisations around the world voluntarily subscribe to a professional ethos of detachment and reject explicit partisanship, such distinctions are not germane to the history or philosophy of press freedom as a democratic right. Indeed, the professional norm of objectivity is a relatively recent development, having been embraced by the press from the late 19th century.[51] Press freedom was written into liberal constitutions long before, mainly to protect publishers who used their pamphlets and tracts to pursue their adopted causes and personal political ambitions. Across the globe today, the tradition of the journalist as interventionist change agent coexists with the objectivism of the "detached watchdog".[52] A diversity of approaches to journalism is, indeed, a requirement for a democratic media system.[53] A mismatch of expectations between officials and the media profession (and its public) over what the "press" in "press freedom" is remains one reason why Hong Kong's media system may stay in a state of fractious disequilibrium.

In the NSL's shadow, reporters have been finding it much harder to get sources to talk to them on sensitive topics. In many respects, though, things may indeed be business as usual. Journalists would continue to probe the finances and private lives of Hong Kong politicians. Columnists would still be free to express contempt for the Chief Executive and other officials. The space for critical coverage of Mainland affairs, including topics that are blacked out there, may still exist, even if it is reduced. Even *Epoch Times*, the newspaper of the banned Falun Gong movement, may continue to be distributed openly in busy Causeway Bay. On many matters authorities may choose to look the other way—again, not out of magnanimity, but because organisations often prefer not to know, rather than take on the capacity-sapping management burden that comes with acknowledging a problem.

To get a sense of what Hong Kong's post-NSL era portends for media, it is important to think of the NSL not only in legalistic terms but as a political statement. On the bright side, this could mean that a maximal and literal reading of its text is uncalled for. As the preceding discussion suggests, smart authoritarian regimes—including the Chinese Communist Party—know the follies of overreach, even if they frequently err on the side of coercion. One of the unprecedented NSL-enabled acts of censorship was taken against a protest website, HKChronicles. The site had operated as a doxxing platform, revealing personal information about both

51. Michael Schudson, *Discovering the News: A Social History of American Newspapers* (New York: Basic Books, 1978).
52. Thomas Hanitzsch, "Populist Disseminators, Detached Watchdogs, Critical Change Agents and Opportunist Facilitators: Professional Milieus, the Journalistic Field and Autonomy in 18 Countries" (2011) 73(6) *The International Communication Gazette* 477–494, available at https://doi.org/10.1177/1748048511412279.
53. Cherian George, *Contentious Journalism and the Internet: Towards Democratic Discourse in Malaysia and Singapore* (Singapore and Seattle: National University of Singapore Press and University of Washington Press, 2006).

the police and pro-Beijing supporters. In January 2021, police instructed Hong Kong internet providers to block the website, citing Article 43 of NSL and its implementation rule 4, which allows for blocking access to electronic content deemed likely to constitute or cause an offence endangering national security.[54] While the move raised the spectre of Hong Kong being moved behind the Great Firewall, there has been no indication so far that mass internet censorship is on the way.

On the flip side, there are several threats to media freedom beyond the legal provisions contained in the NSL. As a symbolic declaration of Beijing's indomitable will, the NSL seems to be emboldening local authorities and non-state actors to sweep aside Hong Kong's liberal norms and obstruct what used to be considered standard journalistic practices. One prominent example was the use of the Road Traffic Ordinance to punish an RTHK producer. She was fined HK$6,000 for violating the ordinance when she accessed vehicle information from a public database, as many investigative reporters before her had. The new online interface did not allow her to pick "other" as a reason for needing the information, so she selected "traffic and transport-related matters", which the court deemed to be a false statement. As the producer had used the information for a segment critical of police conduct in the notorious 2019 Yuen Long mob attack, most journalists regarded her prosecution as vindictive and intended to discourage investigative reporting on the police.[55]

The government has not needed to invoke the NSL to restrain RTHK, which runs three TV stations and seven radio channels. RTHK is a very Hong Kong institution in that its freedom is as much a product of habit and culture as of legal guarantees. It has, by convention, acted like an independent public service broadcaster. Formally, though, it is a government department. Officials have therefore been able, by administrative fiat, to modify RTHK's internal governance structures and reallocate funding away from hard-hitting political coverage and towards national education. In February 2021, the government released an 85-page report criticising RTHK of weak editorial accountability and failing to fulfil its charter as a government department. It announced veteran journalist Leung Ka-wing would end his term as Director of Broadcasting earlier than planned.[56] Patrick Li Pak-chuen, a senior civil servant with no media experience, took over in May 2021. Li, who

54. Cannix Yau and Christy Leung, "Hong Kong Police Use National Security Law for First Time to Block Access to Website Recording Anti-Government Protests, Officers' Details", *South China Morning Post*, 9 January 2021, available at https://www.scmp.com/news/hong-kong/law-and-crime/article/3117072/hong-kong-police-use-national-security-law-block.

55. Brian Wong, "Hong Kong Protests: RTHK Freelance Producer Bao Choy Convicted and Fined HK$6,000 over Charges Relating to Yuen Long Mob Attack Documentary", *South China Morning Post*, 22 April 2021, available at https://www.scmp.com/news/hong-kong/law-and-crime/article/3130624/hong-kong-protests-rthk-freelance-producer-bao-choy.

56. Denise Tsang and Nadia Lam, "Government Report Slams Hong Kong Public Broadcaster RTHK, Accuses It of Lack of Editorial Accountability; Director to Step Down Early", *South China Morning Post*, 19 February 2021. available at https://www.scmp.com/news/hong-kong/society/article/3122292/embattled-director-hong-kong-public-broadcaster-rthk-step.

promised to lead more "visibly", blocked several episodes of shows on the grounds of failing to meet required standards of balance, objectivity, and impartiality.[57]

As for non-state actors, extreme pro-Beijing elements have always been a vocal—and sometimes violent—part of Hong Kong's plural political scene, but the difference now is that they face less pushback. The targets of their ire cannot be sure whether any particular attack is entirely entrepreneurial, or part of a loosely co-ordinated campaign, or at the direct behest of some arm of the state. Such assessments mattered less when Hongkongers could rely on the rule of law. But in a post-NSL context, they have to take seriously the possibility that any harassment—including wild charges by pro-Beijing Hong Kong media such as *Wen Wei Po* and *Ta Kung Pao* about allegedly unpatriotic activities[58]—will escalate into non-state violence or unchecked state action. Journalism educators are among the groups being targeted. Thus, my own university blocked the prestigious World Press Photo Exhibition that my department was scheduled to host in March 2021.[59] Pro-Beijing propaganda outlets complained that the exhibition included a handful of images from Hong Kong's 2019 protests. The university cancelled the event four days before it was due to open, citing "campus safety and security" concerns.[60] In its symbolic effect, the NSL can be compared to various vague and sweeping statutes around the world that punish insult of monarchical authority or religious belief, such as *lèse-majesté* in Thailand or blasphemy laws in Pakistan. Various groups treat such laws as providing moral justification for extralegal attacks on their opponents.

Comparative studies also tell us that an authoritarian regime can capture media organisations via their owners and other financial backers.[61] For Hong Kong, this would not be a new development. Freedom House had downgraded Hong Kong's press freedom status from "free" to "partly free" as far back as 2008, mainly due to growing doubts about journalists' independence from their employers. Ten Hong Kong media owners had been appointed to a Mainland political advisory body, and there were also reports that media platforms were shutting out critics of Beijing.[62] Surveys by the Hong Kong Journalists Association in the early 2010s also high-

57. Chris Lau and Emily Tsang, "Hong Kong Public Broadcaster RTHK Takes Current Affairs Documentary Off Air, While Popular Talk Show Has Also Been Suspended, Sources Say", *South China Morning Post*, 29 March 2021, available at https://www.scmp.com/news/hong-kong/politics/article/3127528/hong-kong-public-broadcaster-rthk-takes-current-affairs.
58. Rachel Wong, "Scholar Who Said 'Hong Kong Belongs to the World' Refutes Pro-Beijing Press Claim She May Have Violated Security Law", *Hong Kong Free Press*, 19 November 2020, available at https://hongkongfp.com/2020/11/19/scholar-who-said-hong-kong-belongs-to-the-world-refutes-pro-beijing-press-claim-she-may-have-violated-security-law/.
59. Phila Siu, "Hong Kong Baptist University Calls Off Exhibition Featuring Photos of 2019 Protests over Fears of Clashes, Source Says", *South China Morning Post*, 26 February 2021.
60. Organisers found an alternative venue. Learning from experience, they did not publicise its opening in advance, and the exhibition ran without incident.
61. Marius Dragomir, *Media Capture in Europe* (New York: Media Development Investment Fund, 2019).
62. Freedom House, "Freedom of the Press 2009", 2009, available at https://freedomhouse.org/sites/default/files/FOTP%202009%20Final%20Full%20Report.pdf.

lighted journalists' concerns about self-censorship; they considered media owners a key threat to press freedom.[63]

The strategy of gradual co-optation of media, working in concert with market forces, has been employed with exceptional success in Singapore. The equatorial city state has shown that it is possible to marry tight control of the press with high approval ratings for the government, social stability, and economic dynamism. The lack of open resistance means coercion is rarely necessary. However, Hong Kong is unlikely to be able to hit this authoritarian sweet spot. Their contexts are very different. First, Singapore's substitution of direct and coercive censorship with self-censorship was achieved over decades. It required a scorched earth strategy to remove once and for all any oppositional media in the 1960s and 1970s. To achieve this, the PAP government could count on discretionary powers—including detention without trial and newspaper licensing—inherited from the British. Hong Kong still does not possess equivalent legislation. Having absolute control over access to the news industry through the permit system, the Singapore government could keep the number of news organisations manageably small. This made it easier to cultivate a self-censorship regime. The omnipresent Sword of Damocles turned government requests into offers that publishers and editors could not refuse.

If coercion is one side of the hegemonic coin, the other is consent. On that score, too, Hong Kong is unlikely to reach Singapore's levels. The main reason is the obvious one: Singapore's leaders are directly elected and enjoy far more legitimacy. The republic's elections, though certainly not fair, are free enough to result in the occasional ouster of cabinet ministers. Hence, the PAP's increasingly sophisticated practice of targeting only a small number of dissidents for visible coercion, while using economic and ideological means to encourage the vast majority of citizens—including most working journalists—to accept that it rules with the consent of the governed. The PAP consolidated its rule during the "tiger economy" decades of relatively easy growth and rapid social mobility in East Asia. Singaporeans were probably more easily persuaded in the 1970s and 1980s to exchange their civil liberties for economic rewards than Hongkongers would be today.

Singapore's small size means that wherever he or she is on the island, a minister would never be more than 50 kilometres away from any other part of the country. Unlike Hong Kong's distant rulers, Singapore's executives are never removed from the effects of its crisis mismanagement, making leaders less likely to respond in a clumsy and uncalibrated manner. Singapore's compact size has also enabled the PAP to operate a relatively simple top-down state structure, which allows for a cohesive and less fractured ruling elite than found in larger countries. This has enabled the state to execute interventions with fine-tuned levels of force and visibility. For all

63. The Hong Kong Journalists Association, "Public Evaluation of Hong Kong Press Freedom Drops to New Low Central Government Becomes the Major Source of Stress", 11 April 2018, available at https://www.hkja.org.hk/en/press-freedom-index/public-evaluation-of-hong-kong-press-freedom-drops-to-new-low-central-government-becomes-the-major-source-of-stress/.

of Xi Jinping's efforts, it is not certain that he has completely neutralised all potential sources of competition within the party. Beijing has not been able to achieve its desired law-based governance and continues to resort to coercive measures such as extralegal detentions.[64]

Another key unknown is Beijing's strategic objective for Hong Kong. Does it want Hong Kong's media system to resemble the Mainland's as soon as possible? Or will the authorities be content once they exact retribution for the crimes of 2019 and extract total renunciation of Hong Kong as a pressure point for Western meddling? If it is the latter, it is conceivable that an equilibrium will be reached that is distinctly freer than other Chinese cities, even if it is a far cry from pre-2019 Hong Kong. For reasons highlighted earlier, any such equilibrium will also be different from the exceptional oasis of calm that Singapore is. Hong Kong authorities may wish for a media scene as placid as Singapore's but are likely to get something much messier—like the majority of semi-free, semi-closed societies. There will be periodic arrests and other direct and coercive attacks on media freedom. Other journalists will find their employers pressuring their newsrooms to avoid annoying the authorities. The profession will also have to protect itself from vigilante violence and harassment by pro-government, non-state actors who are incited by signals from the top that independent media are enemies of the people. Police officers may take similar cues.

Faced with this proliferation of legal, economic, and mob threats, it is no wonder some are prepared to declare the death of Hong Kong's press freedom. Media freedom is essential for upholding freedom of expression as a fundamental human right and is required for democratic and sustainable development. The ICCPR standard recognises that media freedom should only be restricted to the extent required to achieve legitimate aims specified in the treaty. Yet, the jury is out on whether meaningful journalism is only possible in a liberal democratic context that guarantees press freedom.[65] Outstanding public interest journalism is practised in a wide range of political environments. Till now, Hong Kong media's main reference points have been liberal democracies where journalists' protection from government censorship and repression is largely guaranteed by law. In the coming years, the territory's journalists will need to learn from peers in the much wider world where there is no assurance of safe passage. Hong Kong journalists may discover that a mental map of their unfree political landscape need not be a no-man's land where they will be shot on sight, but a navigable, though certainly dangerous, minefield.

---

64. Wang Xiangwei, "China's Extralegal Detentions Undermine Xi's Rule of Law Ambitions", *South China Morning Post*, 21 November 2020, available at https://www.scmp.com/week-asia/opinion/article/3110710/chinas-extralegal-detentions-undermine-xis-rule-law-ambitions.
65. Beate Josephi, "How Much Democracy Does Journalism Need?" (2013) 14(4) *Journalism* 474.

16

The New National Security Law

Exploring a Meaningful Comparison with Singapore

Michael Hor

This chapter compares the National Security Law in Hong Kong and the Internal Security Act in Singapore from the angle of their capacity to cause persons or entities dealing with or observing these jurisdictions to fear unacceptable abridgement of human rights and liberties. A technical analysis of the letter of the law reveals a potentially far more authoritarian executive detention without trial in Singapore, compared with even the modified criminal law embodied in the National Security Law of Hong Kong. Yet, the contrasting rights trajectory of Singapore and Hong Kong, and the more ominous current political context of the National Security Law, more than makes up for the initial favourable comparison. The chapter ends with a brief thought, gleaned from the Singapore experience, of how those who still care about human rights in Hong Kong should respond.

I. Moving to Singapore?

The coming into force of the Law of the People's Republic of China on Safeguarding National Security in the Hong Kong Special Administrative Region (NSL)[1] at 11 pm on 30 June 2020 sent shock waves which reverberated across the globe to wherever the future of Hong Kong's legal system mattered, and to whomever it mattered. Talk had already been brewing of looking for a substitute to Hong Kong since the 2019–2020 anti-extradition unrest which stunned Hong Kong, China, and its

1. GN (E) 72 of 2020, available at https://www.gld.gov.hk/egazette/pdf/20202448e/egn2020244872.pdf. This English version is published only "for information", the official text being in Chinese. This does have the potential of adding to the apprehensions of those who are not literate in Chinese or conversant with the way Chinese statutes are interpreted.

observers.[2] The NSL, meant by the Chinese Central Government to be the solution to the discontent, or at least a part of it, was regarded by many others as possibly the proverbial last straw on the little dragon's back.[3] On not a few occasions has Singapore—that other dragon—been raised as the front-running alternative for those in Hong Kong who are disconcerted by these series of events.[4] Too much goes into the stew of "Is Singapore any better?" than can be tackled comprehensively in this chapter. The ambition is more modest—it is to compare and evaluate the essential features of the legal regimes which have been put in place in Hong Kong, and in Singapore, to deal with activities which the authorities deem to be prejudicial to national security, and then to explore how the differences might be expected to affect the degree of confidence one might repose in either Hong Kong or Singapore.

II. NSL vs ISA: The Infant and the Septuagenarian

The Singapore counterpart of Hong Kong's NSL is the Internal Security Act,[5] known and feared more by its acronym, the ISA. While the NSL is barely a year old, The ISA, in some form or other, has been in force in Singapore since shortly after the Second World War.[6] Meant to deal with what has come to be known as the "Communist Insurgency", it has proved so valuable to successive generations of governments that there is absolutely no indication, more than seven decades on, that its key provisions will be changed significantly or done away with anytime soon.[7] Neither the passage of time nor the recession and disappearance of the original reason for the ISA has dampened its vitality—this is a sprightly septuagenarian. So, the first potential

2. E.g., Alexander Gorlach, "Will Singapore or Taiwan Replace Hong Kong as Asia's Financial Hub?", *Deutsch Welles*, 26 November 2020, available at https://www.dw.com/en/g%C3%B6rlach-global-will-singapore-or-taiwan-replace-hong-kong-as-asias-financial-hub/a-55740513; Nir Sadeh, "Looking beyond Hong Kong: What Are the Alternatives", *International Banker*, 3 September 2020, available at https://internationalbanker.com/brokerage/looking-beyond-hong-kong-what-are-the-alternatives/.
3. "Will companies flee Hong Kong? New law could imperil business in one of the world's biggest financial hubs: Loss of autonomy could be 'last straw' for some companies", 28 May 2020, Associated Press, available at https://www.marketwatch.com/story/will-companies-flee-hong-kong-new-law-could-imperil-business-in-one-of-worlds-biggest-financial-hubs-2020-05-28.
4. E.g., Laura He, "Hong Kong Has Only One Real Rival for Businesses Thinking about Leaving", *CNN*, 10 June 2020, available at https://edition.cnn.com/2020/06/10/investing/singapore-hong-kong-american-companies-intl-hnk/index.html.
5. Internal Security Act (Cap 143), available at https://sso.agc.gov.sg/Act/ISA1960.
6. Terence Foo, "Internal Security Act", *Singapore Infopedia*, available at https://eresources.nlb.gov.sg/infopedia/articles/SIP_2014-10-13_105937.html; and Michael Hor, "Law and Terror: Singapore Stories and Malaysian Dilemmas", in Victor V. Ramraj, Michael Hor, and Kent Roach (eds), *Global Anti-Terrorism Law and Policy* (Cambridge: Cambridge University Press, 2005), Ch 13.
7. The official attitude is very much that which is expressed by Minister of Home Affairs, K. Shanmugam, reported in Neo Chai Chin, "Substantial Support for ISA in Singapore, Says Shanmugam", *Today*, 14 November 2016, available at https://www.todayonline.com/singapore/substantial-support-isa-spore-says-shanmugam.

source of difference—their vintage—turns out not to be of much consequence. We turn from history to substance.

III. Criminal Law vs Preventive Detention

In a nutshell, the primary difference between the NSL and the ISA is that, while the NSL hews to the traditional strategy of using the criminal law, the ISA sets out an alternative extra criminal regime for detention and restriction of freedoms.[8] Indeed, the NSL contains a ringing declaration of respect for and protection of human rights and compliance with the Basic Law, and with the International Covenants of Civil and Political Rights and of Economic, Social and Cultural Rights.[9] The ISA, on the other hand, needs a special constitutional dispensation from a host of fundamental rights and liberties in order to legalise the power of detention and restriction without trial. Article 149 of the Singapore Constitution[10] expressly exempts the ISA from compliance with due process, retrospectivity and double jeopardy, equality, and freedoms of movement, speech, assembly, and association. As if to bring the point home, judicial review of ISA decisions is to be only on grounds of procedural irregularity, whatever the constitutional vesting of judicial power in the judiciary may mean in other contexts.[11]

Yet the ISA does set up a body apart from the enforcers of the act—the Advisory Board—to receive representations from those who have been subjected to the ISA's powers of detention without trial, and to make recommendations as to the need to detain them any further.[12] It is clear that this Advisory Board procedure is meant to be a verisimilitude of a criminal trial. Yet, a brief look at the details will show that it does not have certain key features of a criminal trial, or at least one which purports to follow due process. Although the Board is believed to be, in practice, chaired by

8. Essentially s 8(1)(a) of the ISA, n 5 above, confers the power of detention, and s 8(1)(b) allows the Minister to impose a list of restrictions of movement, speech, and association which do not amount to detention.
9. NSL, Art 4.
10. Constitution of the Republic of Singapore, available at https://sso.agc.gov.sg/Act/CONS1963.
11. Article 149(3), read with s 8B of ISA. These provisions were put in place in response to a Court of Appeal decision which declared, on the basis of the constitutionally enshrined separation of powers and vesting of judicial power in the judiciary, that ISA decisions were reviewable on the usual common law grounds. A brief account is found in Michael Hor, "Constitutionalism and Subversion", in Li-ann Thio and Kevin Y. L. Tan (eds), *Evolution of a Revolution: Forty Years of the Singapore Constitution* (London: Routledge, 2009), Ch 18 at p 277. Although there have been potentially pro-review developments in recent ouster clause jurisprudence (Swati Jhaveri, "Administrative Law in Singapore: Recent Developments and Looking Ahead", *Law Gazette*, May 2019, available at https://lawgazette.com.sg/feature/administrative-law-in-singapore-recent-developments-and-looking-ahead/), the ISA ouster clause appears to be not just regular legislation but constitutionally entrenched.
12. ISA, ss 12–16. For what it's worth, the Advisory Board procedure is constitutionally mandated by Art 151.

a sitting Supreme Court Judge,[13] that is not a legal requirement. Its members are chosen by the government and do not enjoy judicial security of tenure. The proceedings are in secret, as is the advice of the Board.[14] Critically, the recommendation of the Board does not bind the government unless the president agrees with it.[15] It is clear that, were it not for the express exemptions, the Advisory Board process will not survive, for example, a constitutional due process challenge. In short, while under the NSL the locus of ultimate authority remains with the judiciary,[16] under the ISA it rests with the executive government, essentially unsupervised by judicial review.[17]

The NSL, on the other hand, appears to adopt the essential features of the regular criminal process and to be in conformity with constitutional due process.[18] Yet, there are aspects of NSL criminal law and procedure which are out of the ordinary.[19] While it may not be particularly fruitful to inquire if these provisions of the NSL are or are not constitutional,[20] and the Court of Final Appeal has indeed ruled that it does not have the jurisdiction to embark on such an exercise,[21] it is interesting to compare the NSL with Singapore's ISA regime.

13. Although there is no consistent publicity regarding the membership of the Advisory Board, its composition is revealed from time to time. For example, *see* "Government Statement on the Recommendation of the Advisory Board on the Jemaah Islamiyah Case", 30 May 2002, available at https://www.nas.gov.sg/archivesonline/data/pdfdoc/20020530-MHA.pdf, p 1.
14. ISA, s 16, gives the Minister and members of the advisory board and related public servants the discretion to refuse to disclose anything which they consider to be against the national interest to do so. They can, of course, do so voluntarily, as has happened on occasion in the past, *see* n 13.
15. ISA, Art 13A and Constitution, Art 151(4).
16. Subject, of course, to the NPCSC's power to interpret the NSL, and therefore the substantive and procedural criminal law therein, with finality. Although Art 65 of the NSL vests the power of interpretation only in the NPCSC, a political body, it does seem that practically, the courts of Hong Kong must perform some sort of initial interpretation when they hear NSL prosecutions. The degree to which the Hong Kong courts are "in charge" will depend on how hands-on the NPCSC is about its power of interpretation of the NSL, especially when it is unbidden by the courts of Hong Kong.
17. The executive government in Singapore is, of course, broadly accountable for its use of the ISA through the electoral process, as the government has been at pains to point out: *see* n 7 above. But elections are obviously a very blunt measure of public approval of specific policies.
18. As if to anticipate criticism on this score, the NSL expressly pays homage to human rights (Art 4) and the rule of law (Art 5). Specific rights like the presumption of innocence and double jeopardy are specifically mentioned, as is the principle against retrospectivity (Art 39).
19. While Hong Kong law is presumptively applicable to NSL prosecutions (Art 5), where there is inconsistency, the NSL prevails (Art 62). In effect, the NSL has constitutional status at the level of the Basic Law, rather like Art 149 of the Singapore Constitution which legitimises the ISA.
20. Technically, if I am right in that the NSL is at the same constitutional level as the Basic Law, where there is an inconsistency, the NSL will operate as a constitutional exception to the Basic Law. Notably, the NSL itself declares that none of its provisions are contrary to the Basic Law (Art 4). As the ultimate authority of interpretation of the Basic Law and the NSL is the NPCSC, and the source of the NSL is the NPCSC, it must be taken that the NPCSC, in settling on the words for the NSL, has impliedly issued a ruling that none of its provisions are contrary to the Basic Law.
21. *HKSAR v Lai Chee Ying* [2021] 1 HKC 670, paras 30–37, available at https://www.hklii.hk/en/cases/hkcfa/2021/3. Compare the Court of Final Appeal's earlier and more general position that it does indeed have the power and indeed the obligation to review "legislative acts of the National People's

First, the NSL does create a handful of offences which have caused observers to be apprehensive about how they may impact adversely on the freedoms enjoyed in Hong Kong.[22] Events since the coming into force of the NSL have given cause for concern about the breadth and clarity of the offence of "secession".[23] While it is clear that activity in the nature of "separating Hong Kong" from the People's Republic of China, with a view to undermining national unification, will fall foul of this provision, it is unclear if incitement thereof might include, for example, expressing a view that Hong Kong will be better off with greater and not less autonomy, or that the Central Government ought to "leave Hong Kong alone". If so, there is a danger that meaningful discussion about the precise relationship between the Central Government and the Hong Kong government might be "chilled".[24] Another offence which has become prominent is the offence of subversion in the form of seriously interfering in, disrupting, or undermining the functions of the Hong Kong

Congress or its Standing Committee": *Ng Ka Ling v The Director of Immigration* [1999] HKCFA 72, paras 62–72, available at https://www.hklii.hk/en/cases/hkcfa/1999/72. Practically, in the current political climate and especially in the context of the NSL, it is difficult to imagine that, even if the Court of Final Appeal were to declare a provision in the NSL to be contrary to the Basic Law, the NPCSC would not immediately overrule that decision via its ultimate authority to interpret the Basic Law. In calmer times, it is conceivable that the NPCSC would consider such a ruling by the Court of Final Appeal more favourably and perhaps think of amending the legislation to be compliant to the Court of Final Appeal's interpretation of the Basic Law. For an accessible discussion of the relationship between the Court and the NPCSC, *see* Cora Chan, "The Legal Limits on Beijing's Powers to Interpret Hong Kong's Basic Law", *Hong Kong Free Press*, 5 November 2016, available at https://hongkongfp.com/2016/11/05/legal-limits-beijings-powers-interpret-hong-kongs-basic-law/.

22. For example, "Hong Kong Security Law: What Is It and Is It Worrying?", *BBC*, 30 June 2020, available at https://www.bbc.com/news/world-asia-china-52765838.
23. Arts 20–21. Secession prosecutions have been launched against Adam Ma, former food delivery worker, for chanting slogans promoting Hong Kong independence at 10 locations: Brian Wong, "Hong Kong's First National Security Law Prosecution for Pro-Independence Chanting Launches at Kowloon Court", 24 November 2020, *Yahoo!News*, available at https://sg.news.yahoo.com/hong-kong-first-national-security-105448319.html?guccounter=1&guce_referrer=aHR0cHM6Ly93d3cuZ29vZ2xlLmNvbS8&guce_referrer_sig=AQAAAMd8esi6FOBXasr0J4JQu07O2UxBmb3i_lyXsh-wSqPRb8-bhQ2SzVyKmcapVbV6quazA_a3VZ-nvPb9MeGo2Fi3P--djCF8Ypt1c5ZD6OEwBqgVC-DAPj_TKyV1eLWmleTwQKwNE5fXjomt-l7O7XUi2rMCg7MMozJtaEGztHJ_0g. Tong Ying Kit, 23-years-old, for riding a motorcycle into a gathering of policemen, bearing a flag with the slogan "Liberate Hong Kong, Revolution of Our Times": *Tong Ying Kit v HKSAR* [2020] 4 HKLRD 382; [2020] 6 HKC 110, para 6; Tony Chung, "localism" convenor for being responsible for social media content calling for a Hong Kong nation: *see* Kelly Ho, "Hong Kong Court Denies Bail to Activist Tony Chung, Charged with Secession under Security Law", *Hong Kong Free Press*, 29 October 2020, available at https://hongkongfp.com/2020/10/29/breaking-hong-kong-court-denies-bail-to-activist-tony-chung-charged-with-secession-under-security-law/. While not enough is known about the prosecution of Tony Chung, Adam Ma's alleged misdeeds hardly seem to be the stuff that would rattle national security, and Tong Ying Kit should, if the allegations are proven, be held accountable for injuring the police officers, and not so much than for the national security implications of the banner he was holding.
24. Briefly, the phenomenon of "chilling" lawful speech occurs when a potential speaker wants to say something but is unsure if it will subsequently be considered to be an offence, and so refrains from saying it, although that speech might turn out to be entirely lawful. It is the penumbral damage done to free expression which attends broad or vaguely defined offences. The terminology was developed in the United States Supreme Court in its constitutional jurisprudence.

government.[25] A band of opposition-related people has been charged thereunder for activities which in some other jurisdictions would have been the perfectly legitimate exercise of "primaries" preceding an election—on the basis that it was all meant to seriously undermine the workings of the Hong Kong government.[26] If the prosecutions succeed, difficult questions will arise with respect to what exactly a political "opposition" can or cannot do, and even if there can be such a thing as lawful opposition anymore. A third offence which has been in the limelight is that of "collusion with external elements" in the form of requesting a foreign entity to impose sanctions or engaging in "hostile activities" against Hong Kong or China.[27] Capable of being interpreted to prohibit a host of lobbying activity human rights proponents routinely do, this could well spell the end of human rights advocacy with respect to Hong Kong or China.

The ISA counterpart of an offence is the precondition for the exercise of executive powers of detention and restriction—the satisfaction of the executive government that it is necessary to prevent anyone acting "in any manner prejudicial to the security of Singapore" or to "the maintenance of public order or essential services".[28] It is difficult to imagine a broader, or less specific, formulation of the triggering conduct than this. The government of Singapore has always sought to defend the breadth of this power by saying that it has been very judicious and circumspect in the actual exercise of that power.[29] We shall have occasion to look at that aspect of the ISA, but there is no denying that, on the face of it, and in terms of legal formulation, there is far greater uncertainty in the interpretation of "prejudicial to

25. NSL, Art 22(3).
26. Eric Cheung, Jadyn Sham, Helen Regan, Ally Barnard, and James Griffith, "47 Hong Kong Opposition Figures Charged under National Security Law", *CNN*, 1 March 2021, available at https://edition.cnn.com/2021/02/28/asia/hong-kong-lawmakers-charged-nsl-intl-hnk/index.html.
27. Article 29(4). Prominent government critic, Jimmy Lai, has been famously charged for this offence: Theodora Yu, Shibani Mahtani, and Eva Dou, "Hong Kong Media Publisher Jimmy Lai Is Charged under National Security Law", *Washington Post*, 12 December 2020, available at https://www.washingtonpost.com/world/asia_pacific/hong-kong-national-security-law-jimmy-lai/2020/12/11/58e7cc5c-3b69-11eb-aad9-8959227280c4_story.html. Activity amounting to the offence of collusion with foreign powers figured prominently in the removal of opposition Legislative Council (Legco) members which prompted the resignation of all opposition LegCo members. No question of criminal prosecutions arose as the activities concerned predated the NSL. There can be no doubt that similar activity now would potentially be prosecuted under the NSL. *See* the contrasting "spin" in Stephen McDonell, "Hong Kong Pro-Democracy Lawmakers Resign after China Ruling", *BBC*, 12 November 2020, available at https://www.bbc.com/news/world-asia-china-54899171; *see also* "The Four Disqualified Legislators Broke Rules on Foreign Collusion", *CGTN*, 12 November 2020, available at https://news.cgtn.com/news/2020-11-12/The-four-HK-legislators-disqualified-for-foreign-collusion-VlUjbSU7wA/index.html.
28. ISA, s 8.
29. Minister of Home Affairs was reported as saying that "our population is highly educated and very aware of what's happening and know that any abuse of the Act would immediately lead to consequences by the population", *see* Neo, n 7 above.

the security of Singapore" than in the task of working out what the NSL offences potentially cover.[30]

Second, the NSL creates a specialised or parallel track for the processing of national security offences, from a new Department of National Security of the Police Force,[31] to a National Security Division in the Department of Justice to handle prosecutions,[32] to specially designated judges at all levels to hear national security prosecutions.[33] While specialised enforcement agencies are certainly not unknown,[34] and specialised divisions in the Justice Department are uncontroversial,[35] specially appointed national security judges raise concerns about judicial independence.[36] This is especially so when it is the chief executive who holds the power of appointment, which is to be renewed, or not, on a yearly basis.[37] The fear and danger, of course, is that judges who are perceived by the chief executive not to be pro-prosecution enough will not be appointed, or reappointed, with the result that the national security bench will become unfairly tilted towards the prosecution.[38] This innovation clearly raises questions about whether the chosen judges, as a whole, are seen to be independent enough to adjudicate national security prosecutions.

---

30. I explored this question in Hor, n 11 above.
31. NSL, Art 16.
32. *Ibid.*, Art 18.
33. *Ibid.*, Art 44.
34. Notably, the Independent Commission Against Corruption set up by the eponymous Independent Commission Against Corruption Ordinance (Cap 204).
35. There are six other divisions, apart from the National Security Prosecutions Division; *see* the organisation chart of the Department of Justice on its website, available at https://www.doj.gov.hk/en/about/organisation.html.
36. In the regular, non-national security context, while there is executive input in the appointment of superior judges (Art 88 of the Basic Law), the designation of judges to particular cases is, presumably, at the discretion of the head of that particular level of the Judiciary: *see* Hong Kong Bar Association, "Statement of the Hong Kong Bar Association on the Proposed Designation of Judges by the Chief Executive in National Security Cases", 23 June 2020, available at https://www.hkba.org/sites/default/files/20200623%20-%20HKBA%20Statement%20on%20%20the%20Proposed%20Designation%20of%20Judges%20by%20the%20Chief%20Executive%20in%20National%20Secu%-3Brity%20Cases%20%28E%29.pdf. The usually circumspect former Chief Justice Andrew Li was sufficiently moved to express his concern: *see* "National security law: chief executive picking judges to hear cases undermines judiciary, warns former Hong Kong chief justice", 23 June 2020, South China Morning Post, available at https://www.scmp.com/news/hong-kong/politics/article/3090156/national-security-law-chief-executive-picking-judges-hear.
37. NSL, Art 44.
38. This is certainly not to say any appointed judge would be likely to act in bad faith. They are, after all, appointed as judges in general in the regular fashion. The reality is, however, that judges are human and they too will have particular "political" inclinations. Overall balance is achieved, in the normal course, by a bench with a spectrum of different inclinations. The power of the chief executive to select judges from this pool raises fears that only judges of particular inclinations will be chosen. Even if this does not happen in practice, it is enough that justice would not have been seen to be done.

The functional equivalent of the police, the prosecutor, and the court under the ISA is a specialised Internal Security Department[39] with the supervising Minister of Home Affairs. We are already acquainted with the very limited role played by the Advisory Board, and no more need be said of it. Whatever the apprehensions are about the, essentially, chief executive-appointed national security police, prosecutors, and judges, they are at least individuals who are members of the regular police force, regular prosecutors in the Department of Justice, and regular judges.[40] Again, on the face of it, the apprehensions of independence under the NSL pale in comparison to fears that might be expected to attend the Internal Security Department (and the supervising minister), which merges the powers of all three institutions into what is essentially one entity.

Third, concern has been expressed over certain defence-unfriendly modifications imposed by the NSL on aspects of the criminal process for national security prosecutions. The NSL says, and the Court of Final Appeal has declared, that the usual presumption in favour of bail is to be turned on its head for national security prosecutions—it is now a presumption against bail and the accused must persuade the court that, exceptionally, bail ought to be given.[41] The NSL also gives discretion to the Secretary for Justice to avoid trial by jury in favour of trial by a bench of three judges.[42] Both bail and trial by jury are seen as bellwethers of respect for due process values, and a shift against them as moving the balance in favour of the prosecutor and against the defence.

Under the ISA, the question of bail is moot. If detention is thought necessary, it follows that no question of being released on bail arises. There is no trial, as such, to wait for.[43] As for trial by jury, it is doubly moot. As for ISA detention, no trials are envisaged. More generally, jury trials were abolished in Singapore many years ago, so even if trials were involved, it would not have been trial by jury and

39. Although the Internal Security Department functions very much like a specialised police force, it is not placed under the police force and reports directly to the Minister of Home Affairs. The Central Narcotics Bureau has a similar position. *See* the website of Ministry of Home Affairs, available at https://www.mha.gov.sg/about-us/how-mha-works#HowMhaTabs2.

40. It is conceivable that officials of the Internal Security Department may concurrently hold posts in the regular police force, but that is not a requirement. They do not, of course, concurrently hold positions in the prosecutorate or judiciary.

41. NSL, Art 42, interpreted in *Lai Chee Ying*, n 21 above. The "marathon four-day" bail hearing for the 47 pro-democracy accused captured international attention: Helen Davidson, "All 47 Hong Kong Activists Kept in Custody after Bail Hearing", *Guardian*, 4 March 2021, available at https://www.theguardian.com/world/2021/mar/04/hong-kong-court-denies-bail-to-32-detainees-under-security-law.

42. NSL, Art 46. Jury trial has been compulsorily waived for the trial of Tong Ying Kit on grounds of "personal safety" of jurors and their family: "'No Jury' for First National Security Prosecution", *RTHK*, 9 February 2021, available at https://news.rthk.hk/rthk/en/component/k2/1574857-20210209.htm.

43. The authorities do, from time to time, impose restrictions (s 8(1)(b)) instead of detaining the person concerned, especially those who are considered to be less dangerous. Occasionally, those who are under detention are released conditionally, subject to certain restrictions of movement, speech, and association (s 10). But these measures are, of course, entirely at the discretion of the Internal Security Department and its supervising Minister.

would not have been so for many years.[44] Yet again, on its face, as far as bail and juries are concerned, Singapore's position would seem to be considerably more defence-unfriendly.

IV. The Devil You Know

Yet it is undeniable that the sentiment does not match the technical comparison[45] we have just engaged in. Developments in Hong Kong have been met with international reactions which dwarf contemporaneous expressions of unhappiness with Singapore's human rights situation.[46] No doubt there is a certain "novelty effect". Whatever is going on in Singapore has been going on for decades—more than enough time for the expected desensitisation. That Singapore is "like that" is no longer news. Hong Kong's changes are fresh, barely a year old. Hong Kong is not supposed to be "like this".

V. Is the Best Yet to Be or behind Us?

But there is something more—and this is the matter of trajectory. Sentiment is affected not so much by the letter of the law than by the way in which it is used. Observers of how Singapore's ISA has been employed in practice now recognise that, following the "high watermark" of the arrest and detention of the "Marxist Conspirators" and related events in the late 1980s, the use of the ISA has since been used with greater circumspection.[47] Briefly, the alleged "Marxist Conspirators" were a group of Catholics who took their social mission as Christians rather more

44. Jury trial was abolished in 1969. Founding Prime Minister Lee Kuan Yew was famously unimpressed by the jury system, having undeservedly (in his view) won acquittals for clients whom he felt were clearly guilty while he was defence counsel. *See* Andrew Phang Boon Leong, "Jury Trial in Singapore and Malaysia: The Unmaking of a Legal Institution" (1983) 25 *Malaya Law Review* 50.
45. This kind of "technical" analysis was used in Phil C. W. Chan, "Singapore Is No Alternative for Hongkongers Angered by Loss of Freedoms—The Lion City's Restraints Go Far beyond Hong Kong's", *South China Morning Post*, 25 October 2019, available at https://www.scmp.com/comment/opinion/article/3034336/singapore-no-alternative-hongkongers-angered-loss-freedoms-lion.
46. This is not to say that the current context of what many believe to be superpower rivalry between China and the Liberal West does not also play a significant role in the adverse publicity. Hong Kong has notably been enlisted as evidence of China's lack of respect for human rights: Justin McCurry, "US and China Publicly Rebuke Each Other in First Major Talks of Biden Era", *Guardian*, 19 March 2021, available at https://www.theguardian.com/world/2021/mar/19/us-china-talks-alaska-biden-blinken-sullivan-wang. Another extralegal consideration associated with the emerging superpower status of China is that it is probably easier to step on the toes of the government of China—and thus provide a reason for powers under the NSL to be used (or abused, if one does not agree with its use)—than it is to annoy the government of Singapore, whose sensitivities are likely be within a smaller compass. These matters are probably analysed by those with the necessary expertise.
47. I discuss this in greater detail in Michael Hor, "Singapore's Anti-Terrorism Laws: Reality and Rhetoric", in Victor V Ramraj, Michael Hor, Kent Roach, and George Williams (eds), *Global Anti-Terrorism Law and Policy* (Cambridge: Cambridge University Press, 2nd edn, 2012), Ch 11.

seriously than usual. They saw their commitment to "justice and peace" as extending to the "conscientisation" of workers, students, and the general public to social and economic injustices in Singapore society. The government's case was that this may all lead, somewhere down the road, to mass demonstrations, riots, and the breakdown of public order. Thus, it was argued, "national security" was sufficiently implicated for detention under the ISA.[48] Critics pointed out that educating people on the realities of inequality is far removed from significant social disorder—for just about anything critical of the government, somehow, somewhere down the road might contribute to dissatisfaction leading to protests and riots.[49] That this was controversial even then is attested to by the resignation of a prominent government minister who felt so strongly that the ISA ought not to have been used that he could no longer in good conscience work in the same Cabinet as his colleagues who supported the move.[50] As far as it is publicly known, this was unprecedented as it was never to be repeated.

Recent employment of the ISA has been almost exclusively to prevent religiously motivated terrorism, save for the odd case of espionage. While it may still be questioned why the usual processes of the criminal law are insufficient to deal with such activity,[51] the strongest argument in favour of a less transparent treatment of alleged religiously motivated terrorists is not so easily dismissed. This is the fear that a regular, public, criminal trial might adversely affect religious and racial harmony by inflaming passions even more. With the seemingly contemporary rise of "tribalism", even in the liberal West, this has become something which is not far-fetched. One might disagree with the use of the ISA in these situations, but the motivation behind its use in this context is not unreasonable. In short, the overwhelming perception, both within and without, towards the use of the ISA in Singapore is that, yes, it probably was used under questionable circumstances against the Marxist Conspirators in the 1980s, but that was in the past and unimaginable today, and its contemporary use against religiously motivated terrorists or would-be terrorists is, if not justified, not unreasonable.[52]

---

48. The official account is succinctly captured in "16 Are Arrested for Marxist Conspiracy—21 May 1987", *HistorySg*, available at https://eresources.nlb.gov.sg/history/events/78426a95-7114-4a12-be92-5d4d7ce40cca.
49. *See*, for example, my own articulation in Hor, "Constitutionalism and Subversion", n 11 above.
50. S. Dhanabalan, "Remembering Lee Kuan Yew: A Leader Who Was Ruthless in Demanding Honesty", *The Straits Times*, 24 March 2015, available at https://www.straitstimes.com/singapore/remembering-lee-kuan-yew-a-leader-who-was-ruthless-in-demanding-honesty.
51. I discuss this in Michael Hor, "Terrorism and the Criminal Law; Singapore's Solution" [2002] *Singapore Journal of Legal Studies* 30, 45–46. Even if it is felt that the existing reach of the criminal law is insufficient for this purpose, new offences can easily be created, as Hong Kong's experience shows.
52. To be sure, abhorrence to the very idea of detention without trial persists, and there is certainly advocacy towards its abolition: *see* website of Function 8, available at https://fn8org.wordpress.com/about/, a group of essentially ex-detainees from, tellingly, the pre-religious terrorist era.

It is also important to see the change in the use of the ISA in the context of a general trend towards the tempering and moderation of what has been criticised as "authoritarianism" in the governance of Singapore.[53] In the legal sphere, we see changes which were probably unthinkable before. Legislatively, exceptions have been created in the mandatory death penalty regime for murder and serious drug trafficking, conferring on judges sentencing discretion within those exceptions.[54] Again, one might say that the changes do not go far enough, but this development is nonetheless significant given the prominence the mandatory death penalty has played in the government's efforts to project a "zero tolerance" towards certain criminal activity. Judicially, quiet reforms have been and are being conducted to improve the fairness of the criminal law and its processes. In a stunning decision, the Court of Appeal essentially abolished constructive liability under the doctrine of common intention, a move which predated a similar United Kingdom Supreme Court decision to the same effect.[55] As this chapter is being written, a string of decisions has revolutionised the right of the accused to have pretrial access to material in the possession of the prosecution.[56] Both developments could not have been foreseen just over a decade ago.

This thawing of the authoritarian ice extends beyond the legal realm. The General Election of 2020 saw the opposition Worker's Party capturing the four-seat Group Representation Constituency of Sengkang, unseating a Cabinet Minister in the process.[57] This was a feat which the Worker's Party had done only once before.[58] For our purposes, what was significant was the reaction of the ruling

53. Stephen Ortmann, "Singapore: Authoritarian but Newly Competitive" (2011) 22(4) *Journal of Democracy* 153; Stephen Ortmann and Mark R. Thompson, "China and the 'Singapore Model'" (2016) 27(1) *Journal of Democracy* 39.
54. Misuse of Drugs (Amendment) Act 2012, which introduced s 33B, available at https://sso.agc.gov.sg/Acts-Supp/30-2012/Published/20121227?DocDate=20121227; and Penal Code (Amendment) Act 2012, which introduced s 202(2), available at https://sso.agc.gov.sg/Acts-Supp/32-2012/Published/20121227?DocDate=20121227.
55. *Daniel Vijay v PP* [2010] SGCA 33, predating *R v Jogee* [2016] UKSC 8; [2017] AC 387, by about five years.
56. From a position of practically no right to pretrial disclosure, a string of decisions following *Muhammad bin Kadar v PP* [2011] 3 SLR 1205 has dramatically altered the landscape. See Jumabhoy and Chia, "Levelling the playing field in criminal proceedings", [2021] SAL Prac 3, available at https://journalsonline.academypublishing.org.sg/Journals/SAL-Practitioner/Crime/ctl/eFirstSALPDFJournalView/mid/593/ArticleId/1561/Citation/JournalsOnlinePDF.
57. Natasha Meah, "GE2020: Sengkang GRC a 'Major Loss' to 4G Team, Says PM Lee", *Today*, 11 July 2020, available at https://www.todayonline.com/singapore/sengkang-grc-major-loss-4g-team-says-pm-lee.
58. Kenneth Paul Tan, *Governing Global-City Singapore: Legacies and Futures after Lee Kuan Yew* (London: Routledge, 2017), pp 1–3 (charts the significantly declining dominance of the ruling People's Action Party in the electoral figures). The aberrant results of the General Election of 2015 are widely believed to have been caused by "sympathy" votes following the death of founding Prime Minister Lee Kuan Yew just before the Elections in 2015. This appears to have been corroborated by the ruling Party's lowest share of the votes since Independence in the General Elections of 2020: Vernon Lee and Chia Han Keong, "GE2020: PAP Loses Most Seats to Opposition Since Independence, Vote Share Falls to 61.24%", *Yahoo!news*, 11 July 2020, available at https://sg.news.yahoo.com/

People's Action Party. Far from declarations to the effect of crushing the opposition "like a cockroach",[59] the government, in recognising the "strong desire among Singaporeans for a greater diversity of views" established the office of "Leader of the Opposition" and provided this office with staff and other resources and privileges.[60] This is in stark contrast to the late founding Prime Minister Lee Kuan Yew's proposal to change the one-man one-vote system in response to the dwindling share of votes the People's Action Party was getting from one General Election to the next.[61]

In short, the use of the ISA and the context of the general relaxation in the authoritarian strands of government both in the legal and political spheres significantly reduce whatever discomfort one might feel about the letter of the law.

When we turn to Hong Kong, we see the opposite trajectory. While the letter of the law does not seem all that ominous (at least when compared with the ISA), the way it is used and the context of other changes that have been effected or proposed accentuate apprehensions about the NSL. The sociopolitical space has been narrowed, or at least perceived to be so, by the creation of offences where there were none, or at least not clearly known to be in existence, before.[62] Not only do they now exist, but they are actively investigated and prosecuted. As previously mentioned, the new offences of collusion with foreign powers, incitement to secession, and of subversion by seriously interfering with the functions of government have been used against protesters and opposition figures for activity which was not forbidden before and which is not usually forbidden in liberal-democratic jurisdictions. And, as the Court of Final Appeal has recently ruled,[63] it has no jurisdiction to review the provisions of the NSL for breach of the human rights protections in the Basic Law or the ICCPR.

Nor does it have jurisdiction to review the NSL modification of significant aspects of the criminal process such as the reversal of the presumption in favour of

---

ge-2020-pap-suffers-worst-electoral-performance-since-independence-by-seat-loss-vote-share-falls-to-6124-211505852.html.

59. Taken from the script of Singapore's first English Television drama series, *Masters of the Sea*, in 1994.
60. Prime Minister's office Singapore, "Ministerial Statement on Duties and Privileges of the Leader of the Opposition, Delivered by Ms Indranee Rajah, Leader of the House of Parliament on 31 August 2020", 31 August 2020, available at https://www.pmo.gov.sg/Newsroom/Ministerial-Statement-on-Duties-and-Privileges-of-the-Leader-of-the-Opposition-Aug-2020.
61. Kenneth L. Whiting, "Married with Kids? Lee Kuan Yew Says Take Two Votes", *AP News*, 27 July 1994, available at https://apnews.com/article/a5a4e7dcaf8aa2ceeae5d0f7e6345ee4. Sitting Prime Minister, Lee Hsien Loong, famously said in 2006 that the more opposition members of Parliament there are, the more time he will need to "fix" them, and the less time he will have to focus on real government, available at https://www.youtube.com/watch?v=a1WhJKsYb50.
62. Chris Lau, "What Is Hong Kong's Colonial-Era Sedition Law, and How Does It Fit into the Landscape of National Security Legislation", *South China Morning Post*, 9 September 2020, available at https://www.scmp.com/news/hong-kong/politics/article/3100740/what-hong-kongs-colonial-era-sedition-law-and-how-does-it. It has not been clear how the prosecution decides to use the law of sedition or the NSL where both are potentially applicable.
63. *Lai Chee Ying*, n 21 above.

bail and the discretion of the Secretary of Justice to mandatorily direct juryless trials. Nor are these provisions dead letter—they are being actively employed to refuse bail and to deny trial by jury.[64] Needless to say, both bail and trial by jury are seen as important features of criminal process which ensure the fairness of the criminal process in Hong Kong: bail as an expression of the presumption of innocence,[65] and trial by jury as a bulwark against prosecutions which offend public sensibilities.[66]

Perhaps the most worrisome NSL innovation to the criminal process to many is the power of the chief executive to, effectively, determine who in the judiciary are "loyal" enough to hear national security prosecutions.[67] Even approved judges are kept on a short leash—appointments are to be for a period of one year at a time.[68] This potentially raises serious questions about judicial independence, but once again, the NSL cannot be reviewed by Hong Kong courts for unconstitutionality.[69] Similar concerns attend the creation of a National Security Division of the Department of Justice to handle national security prosecutions. The then sitting Director of Public Prosecutions resigned over not being nominated to be an "approved" national security prosecutor, raising suspicions that he was deemed to have not been "loyal" enough.[70]

---

64. Famously, bail has been denied to prominent dissident, Jimmy Lai, charged for collusion with foreign powers and many of the group of 47, charged with seriously interfering with government processes by conducting unofficial election primaries: Jerome Cohen, "The Long-Term Implications of the Jimmy Lai Bail Decision", *The Diplomat*, 11 February 2021, available at https://thediplomat.com/2021/02/the-long-term-implications-of-the-jimmy-lai-bail-decision/; Brian Wong, "National Security Law: Bail Denied Again for 11 of the 47 Hong Kong Opposition Figures Charged with Subversion", *South China Morning Post*, 12 March 2021, available at https://www.scmp.com/news/hong-kong/law-and-crime/article/3125152/national-security-law-bail-denied-again-11-47-hong. Tong Ying-kit, reputedly the first person to be charged under the NSL, will not be getting a jury trial: Tony Cheung, Chris Lau, and Jasmine Siu, "National Security Law: What You Need to Know about the Decision to Hold a Trial without a Jury", *South China Morning Post*, 11 February 2021, available at https://www.scmp.com/news/hong-kong/law-and-crime/article/3121493/national-security-law-what-you-need-know-about.
65. *See* the statement on the importance of bail in Hong Kong in Law Reform Commission of Hong Kong, "Bail in Criminal Proceedings (Topic No 16)", 1989, available at https://www.hkreform.gov.hk/en/docs/rbail-e.pdf, para 3.2.1.
66. *See* Peter Duff, Mark Findlay, Carla Howarth, and Chan Tsang-Fai, *Juries: A Hong Kong Perspective* (Hong Kong: Hong Kong University Press, 1992). The authors note at p 114 that "what was most striking was the massive support for the retention of the jury after 1997 [the Handover]" although "support for the jury tended to run ahead of actual knowledge about what it does", and concludes that "it is perhaps what the jury represents or symbolizes that is important".
67. *See* n 36 above.
68. *See* n 37 above.
69. At the risk of dwelling on what might have been, a constitutional attack might have succeeded as it did in the analogous case of *Liyanage v The Queen* [1967] AC 259 where Ceylonese legislation which gave power to a minister to nominate justices for a particular criminal prosecution was struck down as contrary to the separation of powers.
70. James Pomfret, "Hong Kong's Top Public Prosecutor Quits, Says He Was Cut Out of New National Security Cases", *Reuters*, 31 July 2020, available at https://www.reuters.com/article/us-hongkong-security-prosecutions-resign-idUSKCN24W1U0.

When we broaden the focus to the changes and expected changes to society at large, a consistent picture of decreasing sociopolitical space, or increasing authoritarianism, clearly emerges. The use, or the expected use, of the criterion of "loyalty" as a prerequisite of official positions, and even of the political opposition in the Legislative and District Councils, has the potential to reduce significantly the quality and quantity of criticism of what the government does.[71] Talk of reform of the judiciary can be expected to result in similar changes to an institution which most see as the canary in the coal mine of the Rule of Law in Hong Kong.[72] Attention was drawn to that unique institution of foreign judges sitting in the Court of Final Appeal by the resignation of one of them in response to the NSL.[73] Significantly, the only NSL appeal that has reached the Court of Final Appeal had a bench which did not include any foreign judge.[74] It is unclear how foreign judges would fit into the current "loyalty" imperative, and suspicions naturally arise as to the fate of that arrangement.

The "loyalty" initiative extends beyond high political institutions to, most prominently, the education system. From imminent changes in the school curriculum to inculcate love for Hong Kong and the country,[75] to the dismissal of an Occupy Central figure from the academic staff of Hong Kong's oldest university, against the advice of its own senate,[76] such developments have raised suspicions

71. Helen Davidson, "Hong Kong Plans to Make Politicians Swear Oath of Loyalty to Beijing", *Guardian*, 23 February 2021, available at https://www.theguardian.com/world/2021/feb/23/hong-kong-plans-to-make-politicians-swear-oath-of-loyalty-to-beijing; Greg Torode and Marius Zaharia, "What Is Love? Beijing Desires Unconditional Loyalty from Hong Kong", *Reuters*, 27 February 2021, available at https://www.reuters.com/article/us-hongkong-security-politics-explainer-idUSKBN2AR05L.
72. Jerome Cohen, "The Intensifying Pressures to Further 'Reform' Hong Kong's Courts", *The Diplomat*, 23 November 2020, available at https://thediplomat.com/2020/11/the-intensifying-pressures-to-further-reform-hong-kongs-courts/; Matthew Brooker, "The Twilight of Hong Kong's Independent Judiciary", *Bloomberg*, 6 March 2021, available at https://www.bloomberg.com/opinion/articles/2021-03-06/hong-kong-s-trusted-independent-judiciary-approaches-its-twilight. *See also* the spirited defence of the existing judiciary, and by implication opposition to calls for "reform", by immediate past Chief Justice Geoffrey Ma: Zen Soo, "Hong Kong's Top Judge Cautious on Calls for Judicial Reform", *Yahoo!news*, 5 January 2021, available at https://news.yahoo.com/hong-kongs-top-judge-cautious-090051168.html.
73. Gary Cheung, Jeffie Lam, and Jack Lau, "Veteran Australian Judge James Spigelman Resigns from Hong Kong's Top Court, Citing National Security Law", *South China Morning Post*, 18 September 2020, available at https://www.scmp.com/news/hong-kong/law-and-crime/article/3102051/veteran-australian-judge-james-spigelman-resigns-hong. *See also* the "pro-Beijing" account in Grenville Cross, "Judicial Independence: CFA Show Their Mettle and Reject Political Pressure", *China Daily*, 23 March 2021, available at https://www.chinadailyhk.com/article/a/161153.
74. *Lai Chee Ying*, n 21 above.
75. NSL, Art 10, specifically imposes a duty on the Hong Kong government to "promote national security education in schools and universities". Vivian Wang, "Hong Kong's Lesson to Schoolchildren: Love China, No Questions Asked", *New York Times*, 24 February 2021, available at https://www.nytimes.com/2021/02/24/world/asia/hong-kong-national-security-law-education.html.
76. "Benny Tai: Hong Kong University Fires Professor who Led Protests" 28 July 2020, BBC, available at https://www.bbc.com/news/world-asia-china-53567333.

that the essentially liberal educational policies of the past are at risk of adverse reform.[77]

It is not the intent of this chapter to sit in judgment of whether the NSL and these other moves were justified. There is no reason to doubt the motivations of those who were behind the NSL, which was clearly to deal with the unprecedented unrest following the ill-fated Extradition Bill. Whether it was right or wrong headed is an important question, but my purpose is only to explain the reason for the negative perceptions these events have generated both within and outside Hong Kong.

VI. One System vs Two Systems

The NSL contains one particular element which the ISA does not have to contend with—that of the presence of another legal system in the equation.[78] The Singapore legal system is what it is, like it or lump it. The NSL's "One Country Two Systems" context immediately gives rise to the question of how much the Chinese legal system should be made to bear on the Hong Kong legal system. There is no doubt that at the highest level, the Chinese system has the final word in that the Standing Committee of the National People's Congress (NPCSC) has the ultimate power of interpreting the Basic Law, the foundational law of the Hong Kong legal system.[79] But it spoke rarely, and even more so when it was not asked to, or at least that was the situation in the past.[80]

It is no secret that the attraction of Hong Kong to many is the very high degree of insulation of Hong Kong from the Chinese legal system, undergirded by the

77. These are just a handful of examples of initiatives which are generally perceived to be pushing Hong Kong rapidly towards authoritarianism. The appointment of a government bureaucrat to replace a journalist as head of RTHK, the premier broadcast medium of Hong Kong, is seen as another such development: Danny Mok, Tony Cheung, and Rachel Yeo, "New Boss Takes Helm at Under-Fire Hong Kong Public Broadcaster—and Is Greeted with Union Protest, Word of Resignations", *South China Morning Post*, 1 March 2021, available at https://www.scmp.com/news/hong-kong/society/article/3123661/new-boss-takes-helm-under-fire-hong-kong-public-broadcaster.

78. Former chief executive CY Leung reportedly said as much: Tony Cheung, "Hong Kong Is Not Independent Like Singapore and Those Who Challenge Beijing's Authority Are Separatists, Says CY Leung", *South China Morning Post*, 2 March 2021, available at https://www.scmp.com/news/hong-kong/politics/article/3123809/hong-kong-not-singapore-and-those-who-challenge-beijings.

79. Basic Law, Art 158.

80. For an accessible account, *see* Zheping Huang and Echo Huang, "A Brief History: Beijing's Interpretations of Hong Kong's Basic Law, from 1999 to the Present Day", *Quartz*, 7 November 2016, available at https://qz.com/828713/a-brief-history-beijings-interpretations-of-hong-kongs-basic-law-from-1999-to-the-present-day/. Some see the 2016 intervention of the NPCSC in the "oath taking cases", which essentially pre-empted Hong Kong courts from ruling on the matter, to be a sign that its reticence is a thing of the past: Suzanne Sataline, "The People of Hong Kong vs the People's Republic of China", *Foreign Policy*, 11 November 2016, available at https://foreignpolicy.com/2016/11/11/the-people-of-hong-kong-vs-the-peoples-republic-of-china/.

principle of "One Country Two Systems".[81] Indeed, this was the primary motivation for the eruption of protests following moves to put in place an extradition arrangement.[82] To put it bluntly, this constituency chose to be in Hong Kong because it did not wish to be subject to Chinese law. And the reason must be that it distrusts the Chinese legal system, either in terms of the letter of the law, or because of the way in which the law is enforced there. Again, it is beyond the purpose of the chapter and the expertise of the author to assess whether or not this fear or suspicion is justified—it is sufficient for our purpose if it is in fact held.[83]

For this constituency to see in the NSL the heavy involvement of Chinese institutions is enough to create all kinds of apprehensions. Right off the bat, the NSL was drafted and promulgated, it appears, with minimal Hong Kong input, if any.[84] It appeared that a "handful of Hong Kong delegates" to the NPCSC saw a draft of the law before it was passed.[85] The same body—the NPCSC—has also reserved for itself the ultimate power of interpretation of the NSL.[86] While the body directly responsible for implementing the NSL—the Committee for Safeguarding National Security—is essentially a Hong Kong one, one of its members is a nominee of the Central Government—the National Security Advisor.[87] This centrally appointed advisor is likely to play a key role. In addition, the NSL also established an Office for Safeguarding National Security of the Central Government—a body of the Central Government which, although charged to obey Hong Kong law, is not subject to

81. Provisions such as Art 18 (Chinese law not to apply in Hong Kong unless specified in Annex III) and Art 19 (vesting of independent judicial power in courts of Hong Kong) of the Basic Law, afforded a degree of comfort, but perhaps on the implicit assumption that the exceptions therein were to be truly exceptional. The NSL is, of course, enacted under the "Annex III exception".
82. Mike Ives, "What Is Hong Kong's Extradition Bill", *New York Times*, 10 June 2019, available at https://www.nytimes.com/2019/06/10/world/asia/hong-kong-extradition-bill.html, articulated the fear that the bill would have allowed "virtually anyone in the city to be picked up and detained in mainland China, a country in which judges must follow the orders of the Communist Party".
83. *See* e.g., Wang Xiangwei, "China's Legal System Has a Long Way to Go Before It Can Be Trusted", *South China Morning Post*, 13 July 2019, available at https://www.scmp.com/week-asia/opinion/article/3018421/chinas-legal-system-has-long-way-go-it-can-be-trusted.
84. By Art 18 of the Basic Law, the NPCSC has the power to introduce national legislation on Hong Kong. While it is not entirely clear who was consulted in the drafting process, it is widely believed that consultation with Hong Kong was minimal. Andrew Powner, "An Overview of Hong Kong's Security Law", *Hong Kong Lawyer*, 10 July 2020, available at http://hk-lawyer.org/content/overview-hong-kong's-national-security-law, described the NSL as having been passed "after much publicity but virtually no local consultation". The chief executive has, however, indicated that some sort of consultation took place: Tony Cheung and Jun Mai, "Beijing Has Heard Opinion of Hong Kong People and Remains 'Very Firm' on National Security Law for City, Carrie Lam Says after Visit", *South China Morning Post*, 3 June 2020, available at https://www.scmp.com/news/hong-kong/politics/article/3087426/beijing-has-heard-opinion-hong-kong-people-and-remains-very.
85. "National Security Law: Hong Kong Leader Carrie Lam Demands International Respect for the Legislation It Has Added to City's Basic Law", *South China Morning Post*, 30 June 2019, available at https://www.scmp.com/news/hong-kong/politics/article/3091119/hong-kong-national-security-law-passed-beijing-expected.
86. NSL, Art 65.
87. *Ibid.*, Arts 13 and 15.

Hong Kong jurisdiction.[88] This body is to monitor and advise its Hong Kong counterpart.[89] But it is its other function which is perhaps the most chilling feature of the NSL—the power to take over jurisdiction of particular prosecutions, either at the request of Hong Kong, or by its own motion.[90] The prosecution is then transferred to a court within China's judicial system to be processed in accordance with Chinese criminal process.[91] The degree of insulation from the Chinese legal process is even worse than the originally proposed extradition arrangement under which it was feared that Hong Kong courts would still have been under considerable pressure to grant the extradition order.[92] It is still too early to know if this extraordinary process of jurisdiction transfer will be used, and if so, how often and under what circumstances, but its very existence must be more than a little troubling to those who see the separation of the two legal systems as a good thing.

VII. Days of Future Past

It is time to draw the threads together and attempt that notoriously risky pastime of gazing into the future. We have seen that a surface comparison of the language of the ISA and the NSL yields a clear "winner" in the ISA in terms of the potential to scare the international community. From the viewpoint of human rights, even the modified criminal justice process of the NSL looks better than the plenary executive powers of detention and restriction under the ISA. We have also seen how Hong Kong's very different rights trajectory in the recent past, and struggle with the introduction of elements from a non–Hong Kong legal and political system, might explain the greater international apprehension with respect to Hong Kong under the NSL.

In the near future, the fear that Hong Kong will die, or become "just one of" the many cities of China, is unlikely to subside. The "loyalty" and "patriotic" campaign now underway is likely to run its course, with its expected increase in authoritarianism in governance. But Singapore's experience gives a glimmer of hope. There is life after "death". The "loyalty" imperative too will pass. While Singapore is not normally held out as a paragon of human rights and liberty, it is undeniable that things have improved significantly. One may not be particularly happy with the pace of change, but change it has. As for Hong Kong, apart from cultivating patience, an ability which is not to be downplayed, what exactly does one, who is concerned about

88. *Ibid.*, Art 50.
89. *Ibid.*, Art 49.
90. *Ibid.*, Art 55.
91. *Ibid.*, Arts 56 and 57.
92. Even the theoretical or residual discretion of the Hong Kong judiciary which it would have probably possessed under an extradition system does not exist under Art 55.

democracy, rights, and liberty do? The pro-democracy forces' "all or nothing" or "give me liberty or give me death" strategy has succeeded remarkably in galvanising international attention. But perhaps it is time to think of alternative, longer term, and more sophisticated strategies of avoiding the precipitation of large conflagrations in favour of keeping the smaller flames burning while the storm passes.

Take the example of what is perhaps the most prized possession of pro–human rights Hong Kong—the judiciary. I know that many still cling to the myth that judges decide according to law and not politics,[93] but the truth is that, in the difficult cases, adjudication is both law and politics. The methodology of the law, in controversial cases, leads not to one but to several possible conclusions. In deciding between these alternatives, judges would be foolish not to be cognizant of the political implications of the choice they have to make. In such a situation, for the court to stick to its common law guns and push human rights and liberty regardless of the political consequences would be to invite institutional homicide[94]—the forces of authoritarianism have the power to eviscerate the institution itself, and if suitably threatened, that is exactly what will happen. Yet, to be indiscriminately "subservient" would be akin to committing institutional suicide. A judiciary which always agrees with the government is hardly worth having at all. The judiciary has to walk this tightrope, but walk it it must if it is to retain any meaningful existence at all.[95]

It is a task which has long ago become second nature to those who were and are committed to the cause of human rights and liberty in Singapore—only in that way have the flames been kept alive to burn more brightly another day when the storm has passed.[96]

93. Although political pressure in the sense of direct intimations to the judiciary of how the governments of Hong Kong or China would like certain cases to be decided—via the proverbial "call in the middle of the night"—is probably unknown, indirect pressure in various forms have surfaced sufficiently for two successive chief justices to respond to it: Austin Ramzy, "Hong Kong's Courts Are Still Independent. Some Want to Reign Them In", *New York Times*, 30 November 2020, available at https://www.nytimes.com/2020/11/30/world/asia/hong-kong-china-courts.html; Hong Kong Court of Final Appeal, "Statement by the Honourable Chief Justice Geoffrey Ma", 23 September 2020, available at https://www.hkcfa.hk/filemanager/common/pdf/Statement%20by%20CJ%20of%20CFA%20(23%20Sep%202020)%20Eng.pdf; Government of Hong Kong Special Administrative Region, "Chief Justice Andrew Cheung's Speech at Ceremonial Opening of the Legal Year 2021", 11 January 2021, available at https://www.info.gov.hk/gia/general/202101/11/P2021011100559.htm.

94. An "all or nothing" strategy risks ending up with nothing.

95. A similar point could be made of all other sectors of the legal community—lawyers, academics, law students, and, for that matter, all who continue to cherish human rights and dignity.

96. Former Justice of the Court of Final Appeal Kemal Bokhary famously employed that weather phenomenon ("storm of unprecedented ferocity") to describe what the legal system in Hong Kong is beginning to face: Greg Torode and James Pomfret, "Hong Kong Judge Warns of 'Full Force Storm' over Protest-Hit City", *Yahoo!news*, 19 February 2020, available at https://ph.news.yahoo.com/hong-kong-judge-warns-full-105800791.html.

Abbreviations

AAUP	American Association of University Professors
BL	The Basic Law of the HKSAR of the PRC
BLDC	Basic Law Drafting Committee
BORO	The Bill of Rights Ordinance
CAPO	Complaints Against Police Office
CCC	Criminal Law of the PRC
CCP	The Chinese Communist Party
CE	The Chief Executive
CFA	Court of Final Appeal
CFI	Court of First Instance
CPG	Central People's Government
HKA Act	Hong Kong Autonomy Act
HKMAO	Hong Kong and Macau Affairs Office
HKPF	Hong Kong Police Force
HKSAR	Hong Kong Special Administrative Region
HKU	The University of Hong Kong
HRDD	Human Rights Due Diligence
ICCPR	International Covenant on Civil and Political Rights
ICESCR	International Covenant on Economic, Social and Cultural Rights
ICSO	Interception of Communications and Surveillance Ordinance
ISA	Internal Security Act
LegCo	The Legislative Council
LPP	Legal Professional Privilege

NPC	National People's Congress
NPCSC	National People's Congress Standing Committee
NPPA	Newspaper and Printing Presses Act
NSC	National Security Committee
NSD	National Security Department
NSL	National Security Law in the HKSAR
NSO	National Security Office
OCM	Occupy Central Movement
OCTS	One Country Two Systems
OECD Guidelines	The Organization for Economic Co-operation and Development Guidelines for Multinational Enterprises
OSO	Official Secrets Ordinance
PAP	People's Action Party
POFMA	Protection from Online Falsehoods and Manipulation Act
SOE	State-Owned Enterprises
SPH	Singapore Press Holding
UGC	University Grants Committee
UNESCO	The United Nations Educational, Scientific and Cultural Organization
UNGPs	UN Guiding Principles on Business and Human Rights

Contributors

[In alphabetical order by surnames]

Johannes Chan
Former Chair of Public Law, the University of Hong Kong; Visiting Professor, UCL

Albert H. Y. Chen
Cheng Chan Lan Yue Professor in Constitutional Law, Faculty of Law, the University of Hong Kong

Jie Cheng
Associate Professor of Law, the University of British Columbia

Surya Deva
Professor, Macquarie Law School, Macquarie University, Sydney; Adjunct Professor, School of Law, City University of Hong Kong

Hualing Fu
Professor of Law and Dean, Faculty of Law, the University of Hong Kong; holder of the Warren Chan Professorship in Human Rights and Responsibilities

Cherian George
Professor and Associate Dean (Research and Development), School of Communication, Hong Kong Baptist University

Michael Hor
Professor and Dean (2014–2019), Faculty of Law, the University of Hong Kong

Xu Huang
PhD candidate, Wuhan University Institute of International Law

Bing Ling
Professor of Chinese Law, the University of Sydney Law School

Kelley Loper
Associate Professor, Faculty of Law, the University of Hong Kong

Ryan Mitchell
Assistant Professor, Faculty of Law, the Chinese University of Hong Kong

Carole J. Petersen
Professor of Law, William S. Richardson School of Law, University of Hawai'i at Mānoa

Kent Roach
Professor, Faculty of Law, University of Toronto

Zheng Tang
Professor, Wuhan University Institute of International Law; Associate Dean, Wuhan University, Academy of International Law and Global Governance

Po Jen Yap
Professor of Law, the University of Hong Kong

Simon N. M. Young
Professor and Associate Dean (Research), Faculty of Law, the University of Hong Kong; Barrister-at-Law, Parkside Chambers

Xiaobo Zhai
Associate Professor, Faculty of Law, University of Macau

Han Zhu
Research Assistant Professor, Faculty of Law, the University of Hong Kong

Index

academic freedom
  concept, 256–259
  prior to National Security Law (NSL), 259–267
  post-NSL, 267–277
active personality, 238–240
anti-extradition
  background, 24–25, 126, 192–193
  comparison of Extradition Bill with extradition measures under NSL, 134, 150
  contradiction between socialist *Grundnom* and a self-contained legal system, 70
  NSL offences, 27, 33, 37
  institutional vacuum, 63
  One Country, Two Systems, 5
Apple Daily, 11, 46–47, 174, 178
  crackdown, 336
Article 23, Basic Law
  constitutional duty, 23, 25, 52 n 10
  duty under the NSL, 43 n 58
  legislative history, 21–23
  tension with Article 45, 2–5
Article 45, Basic Law
  tension with Article 23, 2–5

bail
  human rights, 370 n 65
  lengthy pre-trial detention, 129, 131 n 45, 132 n 47, 138
  presumption of/against bail, 135–139, 330 n 106, 365
  Singapore, 365
  under NSL, 8, 44 n 62, 58, 62, 100–101, 207, 269–270
Basic Law
  asymmetric structure, 111–112
  declaration to uphold, 110
  interpretation of, 4, 6 n 15, 14, 15 n 35, 56, 75,77, 89, 101, 102 n 34, 103, 157, 110, 121–122, 125, 130, 134, 145, 156–160, 191, 192 n 15, 331, 361 n 20, 372 n 80
  legislative history, 21–22
  National People's Congress Standing Committee (NPCSC) Interpretation, 23, 102 n 34, 103–104
  NSL is the second, 5
  NSL's compatibility with, 6–7, 13–14, 100, 151–159, 269, 361 n 20
  relationship with NSL, 27, 45
  two incompatible systems in, 2–3
Benny Tai
  Occupy Central, 75, 265–266
Bill of Rights
  NSL
    construction of NSL, 135
    subject to the NSL, 143
    Type 2 dilemma, 280
  university, 277

Canada
  constitutionality of citizenship oath, 324 n 84

extradition treaty with Hong Kong, 312 n 28
immigration detention, 314
imports from Xinjiang-linked products, 282 n 18
National Defence Act, 53
police powers, 317
pre-empt national security matters, 316
right of secession, 310
Quebec, 325
Security Intelligence Service, 168 n 9
separatism, 307
terrorism, 321
Carrie Lam
COVID-19, 273
election as Chief Executive, 23
enact Art 23 Legislations, 24–25
executive-led, 326
Catalonia, 310, 319–320
Chief Executive
appoint judges, 147
appoint National Security judges, 100, 106, 130–133, 223, 328–329, 364, 370
contempt, 353
election, 4, 18, 107, 122, 158
emergency power, 126
judicial independence, 101
mainland, 273
national security certificates, 59, 105, 130
National Security Committee, 202
National Security Department, 168, 203
resignation, 23, 266
Schmitt, Carl, 91
state secrets, 224
universal suffrage, 107, 190, 265
university councils, 261
Chief Executive in Council
emergency powers, 126
plenary power to legislate, 127
unlimited legislative powers, 145
China. *See* People's Republic of China
Chinese University of Hong Kong, 259, 265, 268
civil servants, 88, 228
collusion with foreign forces
academic freedom, 274–275
comparison with Chinese laws, 37–42, 59
extraterritorial application, 242
meaning, 59, 139 n 75, 165, 302
removal of LegCo members, 363 n 27
co-location arrangement
Annex III, Basic Law, 54
Basic Law, 56
demarcation between two systems, 122
judicial deference, 158
mainland laws, 57
NPCSC decision, 145
Constitution of the People's Republic of China
applied in Hong Kong, 54, 84
gap between Hong Kong legal system, 49–50
legality of National Security Law, 50–51, 55
legislative sovereignty, 83
legitimacy, 76
mother law, 51
Special Administrative Region, 26
ultimate supremacy, 93
Court of Final Appeal
reference to mainland laws, 59
resignation of Non-Permanent Judges, 329
Criminal Code of the People's Republic of China, 26

democracy
backsliding, 3
capitalism, 166, 344
concern over, 79
development. *See* pursuit
governance, 2, 276
liberal, 16, 111, 305–334, 357
pursuit, 5, 122, 139, 357
reform, 6, 18, 125, 264, 266
secretive, 212
universal suffrage, 107
democratic
accountability, 73
centralism, 83

constitution, 199
control, 198
deficit, 123
dictatorship, 82
media, 353
movement, 136, 261
pedigree, 76
democratisation
by peaceful means, 31–32
implement Art 23 of Basic Law, 23
incremental, 2

educational autonomy, 255, 258, 260
executive detention without trial
human rights, 109 n 61, 321 n 63
mainland, 68 n 90, 321 n 63, 357
Singapore, 16, 344, 360, 363, 365, 367, 374
United Kingdom, 314
extradition under Art 55 NSL
comparison with Extradition Bill, 134, 150
comparison with US, 316
extraterritorial jurisdiction
international legality, 232–236
under the NSL, 67, 240

fair trial, 179, 214
Freedom of Expression and Access to Information 1997, 211
freedom of speech, 321–324
anti-government speech, 246, 251, 319
hate speech, 251
Human Rights Due Diligence (HRDD), 300
search warrant, 178
secession, 141

Global Principles of National Security, 211
grundnorm
joint enterprise of Chinese Constitution and the Basic Law, 6
NSL, 50

hate speech, 251, 312
Hong Kong and Macau Affairs Office, 72, 112
attack judges, 127
Hong Kong Autonomy Act (HKA Act), 96 n 9, 285
Hong Kong General Chamber of Commerce, 296
Hong Kong University. *See* University of Hong Kong, the

Implementation Rules, Art 43, NSL
breach, 173
Implementation Rules for Art 43 NSL, 62
contravenes local ordinance, 62
criticisms, 62
in order for powers under Art 43 to be applied, 172
prescribe police powers, 172

Johannesburg Principles on National Security, 211
journalist
Apple Daily, 336–337
potential soft spots under NSL, 207
press freedom, 224–226, 357
search warrant, 176
Singapore, 344–348
judicial deference, 143–147
judicial discretion, 129–132
judicial independence, 91
ideology, 120–128
media pressure, 146
NSL judges, 100–101, 318, 328–329, 370
public confidence, 119
rule of law, 119, 318
special national security courts, 328–330
Supreme People's Court, 112
judiciary
independent. *See* judicial independence
interpretation, 103–104
autonomy, 166
deferential, 118
manoeuvre, 135
NSL, 80
right-consistent outcome, 161

Supreme Court of Canada, 321
jurisdictions
Annex III Basic Law, 157
National Security Committee, 62
National Security Office, 60
power to review NPCSC's legislative act, 103–106
Singapore, 360–361

Legal Professional Privilege (LPP), 178
Legislative Council (LegCo)
Anti-Extradition Movement damage, 33
coalition government, 108
composition, 122
election
NPCSC interpretation 2016, 4, 89, 125, 191
universal suffrage, 23, 151
NPCSC decision 2020, 55–56, 110, 144, 325
primary election, 41, 139, 320
provisional, 102, 262
Liberate Hong Kong; Revolution of Our Times, 140–141, 193, 206, 362 n 23
localism
movement, 5, 193
oath-taking, 23
organization, 99, 111

national identity, 264, 273
national laws, 116, 153, 159 n 73
application, 10, 53, 57–59, 153–154
co-location arrangement, 54
jurisdiction of Hong Kong courts, 106, 117
NSL, 15
national security
freedom of information, 211
human rights, 99, 136, 145, 208
legitimate aim, 176
managing, 280
British East India Company, 280
Huawei, 280
offences, 138, 143
offences endangering, 182
PRC, 154
protect, 21, 25
civil society, 199
constitutional duty, 25, 27
CPG's duty, 194
democratic, 199
interception communication, 45
police-centred, 198
preventive, 198–201
proactive, 200
rule of law, 182
two systems, 194
National Security Advisor
connecting point, 64, 114
non-transparent, 326
National Security Committee
executive-led government, 65
government approach, 315–316
Hong Kong's election, 66
National Security Advisor, 326
Special Prosecution Division, 65
National Security Department
designation of terrorist organisation, 35
Special Branch under the British Colonial government, 115 n 79
unified intelligence, security, and police power, 65
National Security Education, 23, 192, 200, 267–268, 313, 326
National Security (Legislative Provisions) Bill 2003
impossible to introduce, 25
Central People Government's beginning to rebuild, 193
in your face, 333
separatism, 320
reintroduce, 23
secession, 318–319
state secrets, 213
vague, 311
National Security Office, 133
court's jurisdiction, 327
deepen central authorities' reach into Hong Kong bureaucracy, 64, 66

executive privilege, 109
Hong Kong's election, 66
interventionism, 85
jurisdiction over NSL case, 133–134
law which it is subject to, 59–60, 66–67, 327
legal status, 59–60
national security policing, 202
NPC (National People's Congress), 25–26
Basic Law
Article 18, 22
Article 23 enactment, 189
authorisation of power, 51
Chinese Constitution
supervise, 7
electoral reform, 47
governance, 83
legislative acts, 155–160, 206
supreme organ, 25, 51, 82
NPC decision
on universal suffrage (2014), 18, 190 n 11
to safeguard National Security in HKSAR (2020), 24, 52, 54, 208
constitutional basis for NSL, 59
one-off power, 54
NPCSC decision, 115, 157–159
on Chinese version prevailing English version (1990), 70
on qualification of LegCo members (2020), 56, 110, 325
to approve co-location arrangement (2017), 54, 205
NSL
"two-step approach" enactment, 20, 24–25
background, 24–25
constitutionality, 100
interpretation, 14, 60–63, 104, 151, 160–165, 302, 361 n 20
power to make, 25
product of mainland legal system, 26
protection of human rights, 99, 255, 269, 277, 291

Occupy Central Movement, 23
academic freedom, 265
call to legislate NSL shifted to CPG, 189, 193, 261 n 29
gives rise to a group of political leaders adopting more aggressive means, 70, 125, 189
One Country, Two Systems, 2–3, 192 n 18
asymmetric structure, 112
enforcement difficulties, 70–71, 202
interpretations, 55
local autonomy, 111, 113, 115, 191, 201
NSL, 96, 115–116, 194, 209, 318, 333
resilience of, 12–15
shifting to "One Country", 47
subversion under, 31
White Paper, 75
open justice, 132
Organisation for Economic Co-operation and Development Guidelines for Multinational Enterprises (OECD), 280
conflict with NSL, 280

passive personality principle, 234
People's Republic of China
accountability, 70
arbitrary arrest, 129
authority, 109
civil society, 199
democratic constitution, 199
diplomatic procedures, 303
established basic policies, 55
mainland, 65
political monitoring, 200
protestors, 126
public law, 72
serious challenge to, 142
show identification, 146
state system, 76
state will, 77
police power
Bills of Rights, 161
Chinese law, 175
constitutional review, 176
control, 193
expanded by NSL, 61, 188

Implementation Rules under Art 43, 173
in check, 175–176
increased, 317
of foreign countries regarding national security cases, 317
United Security Council, 170
unlawful exercise of, 179
political agenda, 142, 322
polity
application of central legislations, 83
beyond constitution text, 7, 73
national, 77, 89
overrule lesser norms, 73
Party leadership, 86
political sovereign decisions, 84
pro-democracy camp
all or nothing, 375
legislators, 320, 330
mobilise social movements, 108, 111
movements, 297, 309, 311
National Security Department, 200
primary election, 41, 89
suppress, 302
tension with pro-establishment, 108
protected information, 212, 214
protection of privacy, 176
protective principle, 234
extraterritorial jurisdiction, 238
jurisdiction, 240–246
protest
abuse of power, 32
institutionalised, 108
Legislative Council, 33
policing, 203 n 61
political order, 117
violent, 8, 19, 24
public hearing, 222–224

Radio Television Hong Kong (RTHK), 298, 336, 354, 355 n 57, 372 n 77
rights to information 2013, 211
riots
1967, 24
2019, 332
NSL, Art 29
Robert Chung, 262
Royal Canadian Mounted Police, 316 n 42, 317 n 46
rule of law
administration of justice, 126
challenges, 57, 209
culture, 309–310, 318, 331
high policing, 188, 200–201
independent judiciary, 119–120
international confidence, 91
legitimacy, 351
monarchical Executive, 86
nullum crimen principle, 247
secession, 320
socialist, 73
substance of the law, 311
Xi Jinping, 81

secession
academic freedom, 271–273
comparison between the Hong Kong National Security Law and Chinese Criminal Code, 28–30
comparison with NSL subversion, 32
foreign laws, 310, 319–320
freedom of speech, 141, 362
incitement, 207, 270 n 73
Liberate Hong Kong; Revolution of Our Times, 141–142
movement, 5, 19, 189
peaceful advocacy of secessionist idea, 136
politically centred, 318–320
sedition
colonial-era, 307 n 10, 321
designated judges, 44 n 63
National Security Department, 206
politically centred, 195
Singapore, 346
self-defence, right, 6, 237
separation of powers
design of Basic Law, 126
dominance on executive government, 124

judicial independence, 120–121
oath, 88
rule of law culture, 309
school texts, 326
self-limitations, 91
Staatsrechtslehre, 86
state unity, 86
structure between Central People's Government and Hong Kong, 112
Singapore Press Holding, 345
Sino-British Joint Declaration
applying Chinese laws, 21
autonomy, 75, 84
basic policies, 156
China's obligations, 285
dualism, 79
legal validity, 75
NSL, 74
political decisions, 78
practical significance, 74
subordinate, 78
transfer of sovereignty, 75
United Kingdom, 74–75
sovereignty
exclusive, 73, 92
Hegel, 77
Hobbes, 197
legislative, 82–83
NSL
endanger, 40, 144 n 87
parliamentary, 102, 104
PRC's sovereignty on HKSAR
autonomy, 49, 84
CFA, 155–156
plenary jurisdictional authority, 75
protect, 52
resumption, 122, 155
Schmitt, Carl, 88
territory, 222–223, 239, 253
transfer, 75
Spain
secession, 310, 318, 320 n 57
separatism, 307
Special National Security Courts, 328
Specialised National Security Crimes Prosecution Division of the Department of Justice, 64
state secrets, 37–42, 59, 105, 211–230
designation, 216
actual harm, 217
classification authority, 217–219
results-oriented, 216
trial in closed doors, 132, 150, 283, 315
tried without jury, 129–130, 315
State Secrets Law of PRC
designation
decentralised in practice, 218
National Administration for the Protection of State Secrets, 217
source-based, 217
scope of state secrets, 215–216
subversion, 165, 190
academic freedom, 273–274
comparison with Chinese law, 30–34
evidence, 143
Hong Kong as a subversive base, 2–3, 193
inciting subversion, 68
politically centred, 198, 318–319
primary election, 41 n 53, 65 n 78, 139, 311, 320
Supreme People's Court
judicial interpretations
state secrets, 215

terrorism
advocating terrorism, 46, 142
business companies, 303
comparative, 308 n 11, 313 n 31, 315, 317 n 45, 318 n 49, 319, 321–322, 366 n 47
comparison with Chinese law, 35–37, 42–43
extraterritorial, 242
Hong Kong pre-NSL existing law, 42–43
human rights, 62 n 61, 109 n 61
international scope, 233 n 12, 234 n 14
Northern Ireland, 199, 315
prevention, 199, 206 n 67

prosecution of HKU Students' Union members, 46
protective jurisdiction, 240–241
Singapore, 17, 366–367
United Kingdom, 239 n 51, 314
United States 911 Attack, 258
terrorist organisation
Commonwealth, 311
definition, 37
designation by the National Security Department, 35
treason
Chinese Criminal Code, 28, 40
Hobbes, Thomas, 197
Turkey, 258
United Kingdom, 244

United Nations Security Council
expanded security laws and practice, 308
illiberal elements, 309
police powers, 170
prevention of terrorist acts, 42, 313–314
without sufficient attention to human rights, accountability, 314
universal suffrage, 23, 84, 107–108, 151, 153, 158 n 65–66, 189, 190–191, 265
University of Hong Kong, the
advocating terrorism, 46
Benny Tai, 265–266
politically sensitive topics, 99
Robert Chung, 262–263

White Paper on One Country, Two Systems
grundnorm, 6
judges, 124
loyalty, 124, 324
plenary jurisdictional authority, 75

Xi Jinping
concept of national security, 26
concept of rule of law, 79–80
independent judiciary, 124
strengths of Hong Kong, 188

www.ingramcontent.com/pod-product-compliance
Ingram Content Group UK Ltd.
Pitfield, Milton Keynes, MK11 3LW, UK
UKHW021835100926
8556IPUK00004B/363

9 789888 754199